# HOW
# TO PAY
# ZERO
# TAXES

# HOW TO PAY ZERO TAXES

**Hundreds of Ways
to Reduce Your Taxes
Legally—to Nothing!**

## THE 1989 EDITION

Jeff A. Schnepper

**Addison-Wesley Publishing Company, Inc.**

Reading, Massachusetts · Menlo Park, California · New York

Don Mills, Ontario · Wokingham, England · Amsterdam · Bonn

Sydney · Singapore · Tokyo · Madrid · San Juan

*The author wishes to thank Pat Berenson, Pat Forcey,
Ronnie Smith, Anne McVay, and Jennifer Everwine,
without whom this book could not have been written, and
the U.S. Congress and the IRS, without whom it need
not have been written.*

*I also want to thank Sayes B. Block for his
encouragement; Christopher Carduff, Doe Coover,
Brian Crokett, Si Goodwin, Perry McIntosh, Robin
Manna, Anne Rigney, Genoa Shepley, and Beverly
Thomas for their typing and editorial assistance;
and Robert Doyle, Steve Leimberg, and Thomas H. Peck,
CLU, MSFS, for their professional assistance.*

**Library of Congress Cataloging in Publication Data**

**How to pay zero taxes.—**
  —Reading, Mass.: Addison-Wesley Pub. Co.,
    v.; 24 cm.
  Annual.
  Began in 1982.
  Description based on: 2nd ed., published 1983.
  Editor: 1981–      Jeff A. Schnepper.
  Other title: How to pay 0 taxes

    1. Tax planning—United States.  I. Schnepper, Jeff A. ed.  II. Title: How
to pay 0 taxes.
KF6297.Z9H66            85-648763
343.7305′23′05—dc19
[347.30352305]  AACR 2  MARC-S
ISBN 0-201-07778-7

Cover design by Marshall Henrichs
Set in 11-point Baskerville by Ampersand Inc., Rutland, VT

Eighth Edition
ABCDEFGHIJ-DO-898

# Contents

*This book is dedicated to my mogul,*
*Barbara, who taught me how to love, and to*
*my children, Brandy, Joshua, and Allison,*
*who gave me three more reasons why.*

*If I had the choice of doing it all over*
*again, I would begin by loving you again.*

# Preface

*"Our income tax system is overly complex. It distorts investment decisions and encourages people to put money into schemes to reduce their tax bills instead of into enterprises to create jobs and help our economy grow."*

SENATOR BILL BRADLEY of New Jersey (1984)

*Question:* Who said, "The hardest thing in the world to understand is the income tax"?

*Answer:* Albert Einstein, who also said, when confronted with a Form 1040 Personal Income Tax Return, "I am a mathematician, not a philosopher."

"The words of such an act as the Income Tax . . . merely dance before my eyes in a meaningless procession: cross-reference, exception upon exception—couched in abstract terms that offer no handle to seize hold of—leave in my mind only a confused sense of some vitally important, but successfully concealed, purport, which it is my duty to extract, but which is within my power, if at all, only after the most inordinate expenditure of time. I know that these monsters are the result of fabulous industry and ingenuity, plugging up this hole and casting out the net, against all possible evasion; yet at times I cannot help recalling a saying of William James about certain passages of Hegel: that they were, no doubt, written with a passion of rationality; but that one cannot help wondering whether to the reader they have any significance save that the words are strung together with syntactical correctness. . . . " (Judge Learned Hand, *The Thomas Walter Swan,* 57 Yale L.J. 167, 169 (1947).)

On October 22, 1986, President Reagan signed a sweeping revision of the tax code that touched the lives of all American taxpayers. The text of the Tax Reform Act of 1986 bulks ten inches and weighs more than thirty-three pounds; it details changes in 2,704,000 subsections of the tax code that will cost the Internal Revenue Service an estimated $106,485,000 in fiscal year 1988 to implement. The act dramatically cut tax rates and pays for this decline by eliminating or reducing a vast array of tax breaks. Some changes in the tax law took effect in 1987; others apply in 1988. The American tax structure for 1988 is vastly different from that in 1987. For this reason, this 1989 edition of *How to Pay* Zero *Taxes* must and will serve a dual function. First, it will detail the law for your 1988 returns, to be filed on or before April 15, 1989. It will also offer you a summary of the Tax Reform Act of 1986 and explain not only its new provisions for tax year 1988 but how to use the new law and the strategies inherent in it for potential tax planning in order to reduce your taxes for 1989. Moreover, the fiscal 1988 budget, signed into law on December 22, 1987, included the Revenue Act of 1987, which effects a two-year $23 billion tax hike—a fact unknown to perhaps most Americans. The applicable provisions of this Revenue Act will also be covered here.

It has been claimed that the only difference between death and taxes is that death, on occasion, is allegedly painless. That claim is not completely accurate. Another difference is that death doesn't get worse every time Congress meets. If the average middle-income taxpayer's 1988 salary, starting from January 1, went to pay taxes, it would have taken until May 5 to meet all the federal, state, and local payments due. By comparison, this "Tax Freedom Day" in 1940 was March 8; and in 1930, it was February 13. It will take more than one-third of the year and two hours and forty-five minutes of each eight hours' earnings by the average middle-income taxpayer to produce one person's share of the 1988 tax bill.[1]

The combination of taxes and inflation has been likened to a plague of locusts on a field of wheat. A family earning $5,000 in 1970 needed $9,660 in 1980 to have the same after-tax purchasing power it had ten years before. A family earning $10,000 needed $20,187, and a family then earning $25,000 required $52,495 in 1980 just to stay even. Yet there are several individuals earning millions of dollars who pay little or no taxes and many more who earn hundreds of thousands of dollars each year whose tax bill is just as small. In 1982, there were 117 individuals who earned over $1 million and owed the IRS nothing. In 1983, 29,800 taxpayers with incomes

---

1. In 1930 it was 57 seconds!

Tax Freedom Day, Selected Years, 1930–1987

| Year | Tax Freedom Day |
| --- | --- |
| 1930 | February 13 |
| 1940 | March 8 |
| 1950 | April 3 |
| 1960 | April 17 |
| 1970 | April 28 |
| 1975 | April 28 |
| 1980 | May 1 |
| 1981 | May 4 |
| 1982 | May 3 |
| 1983 | April 30 |
| 1984 | April 28 |
| 1985 | April 30 |
| 1986[a] | April 30 |
| 1987 | May 4 |
| 1988 | May 5 |

SOURCE: Tax Foundation Incorporated
a) Revised.

of more than $250,000 paid less than 5 percent in income taxes, including 3,170 people who earned more than $1 million. And in 1986, 612 couples and individuals with incomes exceeding $200,000 paid zero taxes on their 1985 incomes. These people are able to avoid paying taxes by the use of sophisticated tax strategies devised by high-priced and very professional tax planners, who guide their clients along the cracks in the federal tax code.

Many of those cracks have been put there intentionally by Congress as economic and social incentives. For example, in order to encourage capital spending and to support the U.S. auto industry, a combination of provisions in the tax code allows a knowledgeable average taxpayer to buy a $6,000 car at a net cash cost of only $5,155 (see page 215). If that car is run only 60,000 miles in its first three years, the net cash outlay for the car can be reduced to less than *zero!* In effect, the taxpayer gets a free car; more important, his costless acquisition is completely legal. Exactly how to do this will be explained later in the book.

As the above examples indicate, what Congress has created is a financial mechanism whereby certain actions substitute for tax payments. Rather than taking the taxpayers' money in taxes and then paying it out in direct support for certain activities, Congress has indirectly accomplished the same goal by granting the taxpayers some credits and deductions if they make expenditures in certain defined areas. *How to Pay* Zero *Taxes* will expose these areas and detail how you, a now enlightened reader, can structure your transactions to benefit optimally from these completely legal strategies and techniques.

You first will learn how our tax system works and how the structure of the system provides opportunities to save money on your income tax. The crucial difference between tax deductions and tax credits will be explained, and the internal IRS chart detailing the average amount deducted for each tax bracket for each category of itemized deductions will be revealed.

You then will be transported into the nether world of tax shelters, both pre- and post-1988, and shown what to look for and what to avoid. The section on tax shelter strategies is followed by the fun part of the book—how to take tax deductions for your personal expenses and hobbies. Here you will be shown how to turn your normal living expenses into tax deductions. We all must pay housing and food costs, but *How to Pay* Zero *Taxes* will show you how to structure these costs to reduce your taxes. We all enjoy vacations—*How to Pay* Zero *Taxes* will show you how the federal government could pay part of their costs. If you have a hobby—stamp collecting, auto racing, etc.—*How to Pay* Zero *Taxes* will demonstrate how you can get the Internal Revenue Service to help finance it by converting it into a legitimate business.

Finally, *How to Pay* Zero *Taxes* will detail and explain those more sophisticated legal 1988 and 1989 tax techniques and instruments that have been developed for shifting income, deferring taxes, and avoiding payment completely. These techniques all have been court tested and approved. Most important, *How to Pay* Zero *Taxes* will not simply explain and document these tax savings strategies but will show you examples, provide you with guidelines and tax cases to support your deductions, and take you step by step through the creation of these money-saving instruments for your own use. Its objective is not merely to reveal and educate but to demonstrate and guide as well.

Taxpayers who can afford expensive professional tax planning don't pay high taxes. The goal of *How to Pay* Zero *Taxes* is to provide that planning and those techniques to those middle-income taxpayers who are unknowingly overpaying. Supreme Court Justice Sutherland once remarked, "The legal right of a taxpayer to decrease his taxes or to altogether avoid them by means which the law permits cannot be doubted."[2] *How to Pay* Zero *Taxes* is dedicated to that ideal.

---

2. *Gregory* v. *Helvering,* 35–1, USTC Par. 9043, 293 U.S. 463, 469 (1935).

# CHAPTER 1

# Is It Legal?

*"Taxation must not take from individuals
what rightfully belongs to individuals."*

HENRY GEORGE

"The purpose of the IRS is to collect the proper amount of
tax revenue at the least cost to the public, and in a manner
that warrants the highest degree of public confidence in
our integrity, efficiency, and fairness. To achieve that
purpose, we will: Encourage and achieve the highest
degree of voluntary compliance in accordance with the tax
laws and regulations; Advise the public of their rights and
responsibilities; Determine the extent of compliance and
the causes of noncompliance; Do all things needed for the
proper administration and enforcement of the tax laws;
Continually search and implement new, more efficient and
effective ways of accomplishing our Mission" (IRS
statement of organization and functions, 39 Fed. Reg.
11,572, 1974).

It has been said that "the Internal Revenue Code is a
remarkable essay in sustained obscurity . . . a conspiracy
and restraint of understanding" (*All State Fire Insurance
Company* [Ct. Cl.], 80-1 USTC-, 45 AFTR 2d, 80-1096).

When the modern income tax law was introduced in 1913, only one American in 271 was affected; the taxable incomes of the great majority did not exceed the exempt amount of $3,000 for individuals, $4,000 for couples. Those who were affected paid at the rate of 1 percent on taxable income up to $20,000 and, at most, 6 percent on income over that amount. More than 101 million individual income tax returns were filed in 1986 for 1985, the largest number ever filed and a 2.2 percent increase over 1984 returns filed in 1985.

You pay too much in taxes, and it costs too much for you to do your tax returns. Here are a few "for instances."

- According to the Tax Foundation, a moderate-income family—one worker earning $29,000 solely from wages, with a spouse and two dependent children—faced a tax bill of $7,551 for fiscal 1987.

- Add to this their $1,596 share of the federal deficit, and that family paid $9,147 to support our government's over $1 trillion in spending.

- According to University of Michigan economist Joel B. Slemrod, it takes a household an average of 21.7 hours to do federal and state tax returns, at an average cost of $231 in personal time plus $44 in fees for professional aid.

These dollars come out of your pocket and drain your ability to save and invest, while inflation compounds your financial concerns by draining your ability just to keep even.

Even if your earnings can keep even with inflation, you still lose. For example, assume you have a taxable income for 1988 of $43,150 and pay $9,761 in taxes. You have $33,389 left to spend. With both inflation and a raise of 8 percent, you will now earn $46,602 and pay $10,900 in taxes, leaving you $35,702 to spend. But due to inflation, this $35,702 is worth only $32,846. In real dollars, the progressive nature of your tax structure and the purchasing power decay caused by inflation have together reduced your real buying power by $33,389 minus $32,846 = $543! The impact of state and social security taxes further magnifies your financial dilemma.

In order to stay even with inflation, you needed to double your income between 1969 and 1979. But after paying the higher taxes expected from the considerably higher bracket that doubled income would place you in, you ended up way behind. A study by a major accounting firm found that between 1972 and 1979, executives whose compensation rose by as much as 104 percent suffered zero after-tax increases in income.

Federal Income Taxes Paid by High- and Low-Income Taxpayers, 1979 and 1984

| Adjusted Gross Income Class | Income Level | | Percentage of Tax Paid | | Average Tax | |
|---|---|---|---|---|---|---|
| | 1979 | 1984 (a) | 1979 | 1984 | 1979 | 1984 |
| Highest 5% | $39,901 or more | $59,460 or more | 37.6 | 38.2 | $17,407 | $23,313 |
| Highest 10% | 32,711 or more | 44,656 or more | 49.5 | 51.0 | 11,456 | 15,549 |
| Highest 25% | 21,759 or more | 29,316 or more | 73.1 | 74.0 | 6,769 | 9,035 |
| Highest 50% | 11,870 or more | 15,837 or more | 93.2 | 92.9 | 4,315 | 5,669 |
| Lowest 50% | 11,869 or less | 15,836 or less | 6.8 | 7.1 | 313 | 434 |
| Lowest 25% | 5,565 or less | 7,337 or less | .5 | .8 | 46 | 92 |
| Lowest 10% | 2,212 or less | 2,939 or less | (b) | .1 | 9 | 31 |

[a]Data for 1984 are preliminary.
[b]Less than .05 percent.
SOURCE: Tax Foundation computations based on Treasury Department data.

According to the Tax Foundation, the average family—one earner, employed full time, married, with two dependent children—had $2,010 less purchasing power in 1987 than 10 years before. Measured in constant 1987 dollars, that family's real income after direct federal taxes had gone up $1,242, or 5.6 percent, since 1981. But during the previous 4 years, the family's purchasing power actually declined by $3,252 in 1987 dollars.

What can you do? One simple answer is to try to reduce your taxes, and the rest of this book will tell you how to do so. Some of the techniques found in this book are the result of mixing complicated and convoluted tax code sections, but all of them are completely legal. Some are legal not because Congress intended them to be there but because both Congress and the Internal Revenue Service were lax in their homework and the tax code language allowing them is there. While Congress writes the tax law, that law is read and interpreted by the courts. Quite often the Internal Revenue Service and the courts differ in their interpretations of various code sections and their applications—the courts *always* win. Even if a tax effect is contrary to original congressional intent, the courts must and do support the language of the code. Such effects are the law and can be changed or eliminated only by congressional action. Until such action is taken, it is fully within the legal rights of the American taxpayer to use such code combinations to reduce, minimize, or even completely eliminate taxes. Each individual must pay taxes, but not one penny more than the law requires. If you want to make voluntary contributions to our federal treasury, you have bought the wrong book.

On the other hand, most of the techniques detailed here have been intended by Congress. In many cases, legally reducing your income tax liability is both good for you and good for America. Certain kinds of receipts are intentionally excluded from gross income for tax purposes in order to achieve some economic or social objective. These provisions are frequently referred to as "tax incentives" and are specifically designed to encourage certain types of activity. Tax incentives have the same impact on the federal budget as direct expenditures because they represent revenues not collected by the federal government. These special tax provisions, therefore, have been labeled "tax expenditures" or "tax aids" by the Treasury Department.

These expenditures are revenue losses arising from provisions of the tax code that give special or selective tax relief to certain groups of taxpayers. These provisions either encourage some desired activity or provide special aid to certain taxpayers. For example, the federal government seeks to encourage certain forms of investment. Thus business investment is encouraged by the accelerated rather than straight line depreciation. This tax advantage has been legislated so that business will have additional capital to be able to expand. Tax advantaged investment helps create new businesses and new jobs. These new jobs produce more paychecks and these additional paychecks produce more taxes. In the long run, if everything works as it should, everyone wins.

Alternatively, other tax expenditure provisions have been adopted as "relief provisions" to ease "tax hardships" or to "simplify tax computations." For example, the elderly and the blind receive special financial benefits through a deduction called the "additional amount." The other tax benefits for the aged—the retirement income credit and the potential exclusion of social security annuity payments from taxable income—also fall into this "personal or tax hardship" category.

These revenue losses are called tax "expenditures" because they are payments or expenditures by the federal government made through a reduction of taxes rather than a direct grant. Just as a forgiveness of debt is equivalent to a payment, so a remission of tax liability is equivalent to an expenditure.

According to the Congressional Budget Office, in 1980 a total of 92 provisions were considered tax expenditures. These were estimated to cost $206 billion in fiscal year 1981, based on laws in effect at the start of 1980. As of 1987, tax expenditures had grown to a list of more than 100 provisions, projected to reach a total of over $321 billion in the 1988 fiscal year. Tax subsidies for 1992 are forecast to equal almost $378 billion!

The financial benefits offered by tax expenditure provisions resemble those available through entitlement programs on the spending side of the budget. A tax expenditure provision can provide special tax relief in any of the following ways:

- *Special exclusions, exemptions, and deductions,* which reduce taxable income and thus result in a smaller tax liability. For example, tax-exempt municipal bond interest or the exclusion from taxable income of employee discounts or dependent care assistance programs.

- *Preferential rates,* which reduce liabilities by applying lower rates to all or part of the taxpayer's income. For example, the special 1987 28 percent maximum tax rate on long-term capital gain income.

- *Special credits*, which are subtracted from the tax liability rather than from the income on which the taxes are figured. For example, the earned income tax credit.

- *Deferrals of tax,* which generally result from allowing deductions that (according to standard accounting principles) are properly attributable to a future year. For example, accelerated depreciation allowances: The taxpayer, paying later rather than now, in effect receives an interest-free loan of the deferred liability.

Tax spending and direct spending are alternative methods of providing federal subsidies. Nearly any tax expenditure could be recast as a spending program, just as most spending programs could be replaced by tax expenditures. Thus, the choice between tax spending and direct spending is essentially a choice between alternative administrative mechanisms. Once it has been decided that a particular subsidy is worth providing, the question of the best method of providing that subsidy arises. In designing or evaluating any subsidy program, however, the following criteria have been applied:

- *Cost and efficiency.* How much does the program cost? How well targeted is the program—that is, does it reach those and only those it is intended to reach? Does it provide the incentive or benefit it was designed to offer? Does it achieve its goal at the least cost?

- *Fairness and equity.* Is the subsidy benefit fairly distributed?

- *Ease of administration.* How much does the program cost to administer? How quickly can the benefits be distributed? Can the benefits be distributed to those and only those for whom they are intended?

- *Budget visibility and control.* Is each program subject to periodic review by the Congress? Are its costs subject to control by the Congress?

In reality, though, many of these expenditures are the result of pressures applied by special interest groups seeking relief provisions for their own constituencies. For example, why is there an additional "standard deduction" amount for the blind and not for the deaf? The answer, I suggest, may have more to do with the political and lobbying power of the two groups than with any inherent difference between the hardships.

These special provisions also arise out of the political needs of our individual representatives in Congress. These are off-budget expenditures that show up as a reduction of revenues rather than as an increase in congressional spending. In effect they allow our representatives to increase our federal fiscal deficit, to spend more tax money, without appearing to do so. Arguments are made that these tax incentives are simple and involve far less government supervision and detail than direct expenditures. It has also been argued that these incentives encourage the private sector to participate in social programs and promote private decision making rather than government-centered decision making. One of the major objectives of the Tax Reform Act of 1986 was to reduce the availability of many of these off-budget tax expenditures for tax year 1987 and after. Still, some remain.

Whether these asserted virtues of tax incentives are in fact valid or whether their defects outweigh their claimed advantages is not the subject of this book. The fact that they do exist is critical. In order to minimize or to eliminate your taxes completely, you must first accept the fact that the techniques to be detailed in this book are both legal and, for the most part, specifically intended by Congress. That they have not been publicized or made widely known by the Internal Revenue Service is not surprising. Despite publicity releases and continuous claims to the contrary, the Internal Revenue Service is a revenue collector. While the professed goal is a fair administration of the tax law, the service's job is to collect your tax money. No Internal Revenue agent ever received or ever shall receive a raise or promotion by suggesting to a taxpayer how to arrange a financial situation to reduce or eliminate taxes. To discover those techniques, you either have to pay thousands of dollars to a professional tax practitioner, attorney, or accountant—or you can turn to the next chapter.

TABLE 1.  Tax Expenditure Estimates By Budget Function, Fiscal Years 1988–1992 (In billions of dollars)

| Function | Corporations | | | | | Individuals | | | | | Total 1988–92 |
|---|---|---|---|---|---|---|---|---|---|---|---|
| | 1988 | 1989 | 1990 | 1991 | 1992 | 1988 | 1989 | 1990 | 1991 | 1992 | |
| NATIONAL DEFENSE | | | | | | | | | | | |
| Exclusion of benefits and allowances to Armed Forces personnel | — | — | — | — | — | 1.8 | 1.7 | 1.8 | 1.8 | 1.9 | 8.9 |
| Exclusion of military disability pensions | — | — | — | — | — | 0.1 | 0.1 | 0.1 | 0.1 | 0.1 | 0.6 |
| INTERNATIONAL AFFAIRS | | | | | | | | | | | |
| Exclusion of income earned abroad by U.S. citizens | — | — | — | — | — | 1.2 | 1.3 | 1.3 | 1.4 | 1.5 | 6.7 |
| Exclusion of certain allowances for Federal employees abroad | — | — | — | — | — | 0.2 | 0.2 | 0.2 | 0.2 | 0.2 | 1.0 |
| Exclusion of income of foreign sales corporations (FSCs) | 0.9 | 1.0 | 1.0 | 1.1 | 1.3 | — | — | — | — | — | 5.3 |
| Deferral of income of controlled foreign corporations | 0.1 | 0.1 | 0.1 | 0.1 | 0.1 | — | — | — | — | — | 0.4 |
| Inventory property sales source rule exception | 0.5 | 0.5 | 0.5 | 0.5 | 0.5 | — | — | — | — | — | 2.6 |
| Interest allocation rules exception for certain nonfinancial institutions | (¹) | 0.1 | 0.1 | 0.1 | 0.1 | — | — | — | — | — | 0.4 |
| GENERAL SCIENCE, SPACE, AND TECHNOLOGY | | | | | | | | | | | |
| Expensing of research and development expenditures | 2.1 | 2.2 | 2.3 | 2.5 | 2.6 | 0.1 | 0.1 | 0.1 | 0.1 | 0.1 | 12.2 |
| Credit for increasing research activities | 1.8 | 0.9 | 0.5 | 0.2 | 0.1 | 0.1 | 0.1 | (¹) | (¹) | — | 3.7 |
| Modification in regulations providing for allocation of research and experimental expenditures | 0.1 | — | — | — | — | — | — | — | — | — | 0.1 |

**ENERGY**

| | | | | | | | | | | | |
|---|---|---|---|---|---|---|---|---|---|---|---|
| Expensing of exploration and development costs: | | | | | | | | | | | |
| Oil and gas | 1.0 | -0.8 | -0.5 | -0.1 | 0.2 | 0.1 | 0.1 | 0.5 | 0.5 | 0.6 | 0.2 |
| Other fuels | [1] | [1] | [1] | [1] | [1] | [1] | [1] | [1] | [1] | [1] | 0.1 |
| Excess of percentage over cost depletion: | | | | | | | | | | | |
| Oil and gas | 0.1 | 0.1 | 0.1 | 0.1 | 0.1 | 0.4 | 0.4 | 0.4 | 0.4 | 0.4 | 2.7 |
| Other fuels | 0.2 | 0.2 | 0.2 | 0.3 | 0.3 | [1] | [1] | [1] | [1] | [1] | 1.3 |
| Exception from passive loss limitation for working interests in oil and gas properties | — | — | — | — | — | 0.2 | 0.3 | 0.3 | 0.4 | 0.4 | 1.7 |
| Alternative fuel production credit | [1] | [1] | [1] | [1] | [1] | — | — | — | — | — | 0.1 |
| Business energy credits (solar, geothermal, ocean thermal and biomass) | 0.1 | [2] | [2] | [2] | [2] | — | — | — | — | — | [1] |
| Alcohol fuel credit[3] | [1] | 0.2 | 0.2 | 0.2 | 0.3 | [1] | [1] | [1] | [1] | [1] | 1.1 |
| Exclusion of interest on State and local government industrial development bonds for energy production facilities | [2] | [2] | [2] | [2] | [2] | 0.2 | 0.2 | 0.2 | 0.2 | 0.2 | 0.8 |
| Expensing of tertiary injectants | [1] | [1] | [1] | [1] | [1] | [1] | [1] | [1] | [1] | [1] | 0.1 |
| **NATURAL RESOURCES AND ENVIRONMENT** | | | | | | | | | | | |
| Expensing of exploration and development costs, nonfuel minerals | [1] | [1] | 0.1 | 0.1 | 0.1 | [1] | [1] | [1] | [1] | [1] | 0.3 |
| Excess of percentage over cost depletion, nonfuel materials | 0.3 | 0.3 | 0.4 | 0.4 | 0.4 | [1] | [1] | [1] | [1] | [1] | 1.9 |

Footnotes to appear at end of table.

(Continued)

TABLE 1.  (Continued)

| Function | Corporations | | | | | Individuals | | | | | Total |
|---|---|---|---|---|---|---|---|---|---|---|---|
| | 1988 | 1989 | 1990 | 1991 | 1992 | 1988 | 1989 | 1990 | 1991 | 1992 | 1988–92 |
| Investment credit and 7-year amortization reforestation expenditures | ([1]) | ([1]) | ([1]) | ([1]) | ([1]) | ([1]) | ([1]) | ([1]) | ([1]) | ([1]) | 0.3 |
| Expensing multiperiod timber growing costs | 0.3 | 0.3 | 0.3 | 0.3 | 0.4 | ([1]) | ([1]) | ([1]) | ([1]) | ([1]) | 1.7 |
| Exclusion of interest on State and local government sewage, water and hazardous waste facilities bonds | −0.3 | −0.3 | −0.4 | −0.4 | −0.4 | 1.8 | 1.8 | 1.9 | 2.1 | 2.2 | 8.1 |
| Investment tax credit and passive loss exception for rehabilitation of historic structures | 0.7 | 0.5 | 0.5 | 0.6 | 0.6 | 1.2 | 1.0 | 1.1 | 1.2 | 1.3 | 8.7 |
| Special rules for mining reclamation reserves | ([1]) | ([1]) | ([1]) | ([1]) | ([1]) | — | — | — | — | — | 0.1 |
| AGRICULTURE | | | | | | | | | | | |
| Expensing of certain capital outlays | ([1]) | ([1]) | ([1]) | ([1]) | ([1]) | ([1]) | ([1]) | 0.1 | 0.1 | 0.1 | 0.4 |
| Expensing certain multiperiod production costs | ([1]) | ([1]) | ([1]) | ([1]) | ([1]) | ([1]) | ([1]) | ([1]) | ([1]) | ([1]) | 0.1 |
| Deductibility of patronage dividends and certain other items of cooperatives | 0.6 | 0.6 | 0.6 | 0.7 | 0.7 | −0.1 | −0.1 | −0.2 | −0.2 | −0.2 | 2.4 |
| Exclusion of cost-sharing payments | — | — | — | — | — | ([1]) | ([1]) | ([1]) | ([1]) | ([1]) | 0.1 |
| Exclusion of cancellation of indebtedness income of farmers | — | — | — | — | — | ([1]) | ([1]) | ([1]) | ([1]) | ([1]) | 0.1 |
| Special investment tax credit carryback rules for farmers | — | — | — | — | — | 0.2 | ([2]) | ([2]) | ([2]) | ([2]) | 0.1 |

## COMMERCE AND HOUSING

*Financial institutions*

| | | | | | | | | | | | |
|---|---|---|---|---|---|---|---|---|---|---|---|
| Excess bad debt reserves of financial institutions | 0.2 | 0.2 | 0.2 | 0.2 | 0.2 | — | — | — | — | — | 1.0 |
| Merger rules for thrift institutions | 0.3 | 0.2 | 0.2 | 0.1 | 0.1 | — | — | — | — | — | 0.9 |
| Exemption of credit union income | 0.4 | 0.4 | 0.4 | 0.5 | 0.5 | — | — | — | — | — | 2.2 |

*Insurance companies*

| | | | | | | | | | | | |
|---|---|---|---|---|---|---|---|---|---|---|---|
| Exclusion of income on life insurance and annuity savings | 0.2 | 0.2 | 0.2 | 0.2 | 0.2 | 5.0 | 4.7 | 5.0 | 5.2 | 5.5 | 26.5 |
| Small life insurance company taxable income adjustment | 0.1 | 0.1 | 0.1 | 0.1 | 0.1 | — | — | — | — | — | 0.5 |
| Deduction of unpaid losses for property treatment of casualty insurance companies | 2.7 | 2.4 | 2.0 | 1.0 | 1.4 | — | — | — | — | — | 9.5 |
| Treatment of reserves of life insurance companies | 0.6 | 0.6 | 0.7 | 0.8 | 0.8 | — | — | — | — | — | 3.5 |
| Special alternative tax on small property and casualty insurance companies | 0.1 | 0.1 | 0.1 | [1] | [1] | — | — | — | — | — | 0.4 |
| Tax exemption for certain insurance companies | 0.1 | 0.1 | 0.2 | 0.2 | 0.2 | — | — | — | — | — | 0.9 |
| Special deduction for Blue Cross and Blue Shield companies | 0.1 | 0.1 | 0.2 | 0.2 | 0.2 | — | — | — | — | — | 0.9 |

*Housing*

| | | | | | | | | | | | |
|---|---|---|---|---|---|---|---|---|---|---|---|
| Deductibility of mortgage interest on owner-occupied principal and second residences | — | — | — | — | — | 28.9 | 28.4 | 29.6 | 30.8 | 32.1 | 149.8 |
| Deductibility of property tax on owner-occupied homes | — | — | — | — | — | 8.2 | 7.4 | 7.8 | 8.2 | 8.7 | 40.3 |
| Deferral of capital gains on home sales | — | — | — | — | — | 6.9 | 6.5 | 7.1 | 7.7 | 8.4 | 36.7 |

(Continued)

## TABLE 1. (Continued)

| Function | Corporations | | | | | Individuals | | | | | Total |
|---|---|---|---|---|---|---|---|---|---|---|---|
| | 1988 | 1989 | 1990 | 1991 | 1992 | 1988 | 1989 | 1990 | 1991 | 1992 | 1988–92 |
| Exclusion of capital gains on home sales for persons age 55 and over | — | — | — | — | — | 2.3 | 2.2 | 2.4 | 2.6 | 2.8 | 12.2 |
| Exclusion of interest on State and local government bonds for owner-occupied housing | 0.4 | 0.4 | 0.3 | 0.3 | 0.3 | 1.4 | 1.3 | 1.2 | 1.1 | 1.1 | 7.7 |
| Depreciation of rental housing in excess of alternative depreciation system | 0.2 | 0.2 | 0.3 | 0.4 | 0.4 | 0.9 | 0.9 | 1.0 | 1.1 | 1.1 | 6.4 |
| Credit and passive loss exception for low-income housing | (1) | 0.1 | 0.1 | 0.1 | 0.1 | 0.3 | 0.6 | 0.9 | 1.0 | 1.0 | 4.3 |
| Exclusion of interest on State and local government bonds for rental housing | 0.3 | 0.2 | 0.2 | 0.2 | 0.2 | 0.8 | 0.7 | 0.7 | 0.7 | 0.7 | 5.0 |
| *Other business and commerce* | | | | | | | | | | | |
| Depreciation on buildings other than rental housing in excess of alternative depreciation system | 3.5 | 3.6 | 3.9 | 4.0 | 4.1 | 2.8 | 2.9 | 3.1 | 3.1 | 3.3 | 34.3 |
| Depreciation on equipment in excess of alternative depreciation system | 22.4 | 25.6 | 29.2 | 31.3 | 33.2 | 6.4 | 7.3 | 8.4 | 9.1 | 9.7 | 182.2 |
| Investment credit other than ESOPs, rehabilitation of structures, reforestation, and energy property | 7.9 | 4.6 | 2.8 | 1.5 | 0.9 | 1.2 | 0.6 | 0.2 | 0.1 | 0.1 | 19.7 |
| Special investment credit carryback rules | 0.6 | (2) | −0.1 | −0.1 | −0.1 | — | — | — | — | — | 0.3 |

| | | | | | | | | | | | |
|---|---|---|---|---|---|---|---|---|---|---|---|
| Expensing up to $10,000 depreciable business property | 0.9 | 0.7 | 0.6 | 0.2 | 0.2 | 0.4 | 0.3 | 0.2 | 0.2 | 0.2 | 3.9 |
| Exclusion of capital gains at death | — | — | — | — | — | 4.4 | 4.9 | 5.3 | 5.6 | 6.0 | 26.2 |
| Amortization of business startup costs | [1] | [1] | [1] | [1] | [1] | 0.2 | 0.2 | 0.2 | 0.2 | 0.2 | 1.1 |
| Nonrecognition of gain on property distributions in pre-1989 liquidations | 3.9 | 4.1 | 4.3 | 4.4 | 4.5 | — | -0.3 | -0.3 | -0.4 | -0.4 | 19.6 |
| Reduced rates on first $75,000 of corporate taxable income | 5.6 | 5.0 | 5.2 | 5.5 | 5.7 | — | — | — | — | — | 27.0 |
| Deductibility of nonmortgage interest in excess of investment income | — | — | — | — | — | 5.7 | 3.0 | 1.6 | 0.4 | — | 10.7 |
| Permanent exemption from imputed interest rules | [1] | [1] | [1] | [1] | [1] | 0.1 | 0.1 | 0.2 | 0.2 | 0.2 | 1.0 |
| Expensing magazine circulation expenditures | [1] | [1] | [1] | 0.1 | 0.1 | [1] | [1] | [1] | [1] | [1] | 0.2 |
| Special rules for magazine, paperback, and record returns | [1] | [1] | [1] | [1] | [1] | — | — | — | — | — | [1] |
| Deferral of gain on installment sales | 0.1 | 0.1 | 0.1 | 0.1 | 0.2 | [1] | [1] | [1] | [1] | [1] | 0.7 |
| Completed contract rules | -1.1 | -2.1 | -0.9 | 0.2 | 0.4 | [2] | [2] | [2] | [1] | [1] | -3.6 |
| Cash accounting, other than agriculture | 0.1 | [1] | [1] | [1] | [1] | [1] | [1] | [1] | [1] | [1] | 0.4 |
| Exclusion of interest on State and local small issue bonds | -0.3 | -0.2 | -0.2 | -0.1 | -0.1 | 2.7 | 2.4 | 2.4 | 2.4 | 2.4 | 11.5 |
| Exception from passive loss rules for $25,000 of rental losses | — | — | — | — | — | 2.0 | 2.8 | 3.6 | 3.9 | 3.8 | 16.1 |
| TRANSPORTATION | | | | | | | | | | | |
| Deferral of tax on capital construction funds of shipping companies | [1] | 0.1 | 0.1 | 0.1 | 0.1 | — | — | — | — | — | 0.4 |

(Continued)

**TABLE 1.** (Continued)

| Function | Corporations | | | | | Individuals | | | | | Total |
|---|---|---|---|---|---|---|---|---|---|---|---|
| | 1988 | 1989 | 1990 | 1991 | 1992 | 1988 | 1989 | 1990 | 1991 | 1992 | 1988–92 |
| Exclusion of interest on State and local government bonds for mass transit commuting vehicles and facilities | (²) | (²) | (²) | (²) | (²) | 0.1 | (¹) | (¹) | (¹) | (¹) | 0.2 |
| COMMUNITY AND REGIONAL DEVELOPMENT | | | | | | | | | | | |
| Investment credit and passive loss exception for rehabilitation of structures, other than historic structures | 0.2 | 0.1 | 0.1 | 0.1 | 0.1 | 0.4 | 0.3 | 0.2 | 0.2 | 0.2 | 1.9 |
| Exclusion of interest on State and local government bonds for private airports and docks | −0.1 | −0.1 | −0.1 | −0.1 | −0.1 | 0.7 | 0.7 | 0.8 | 0.8 | 0.9 | 3.4 |
| Five-year amortization for housing rehabilitation | — | — | — | — | — | (¹) | (¹) | (¹) | (¹) | (¹) | 0.1 |
| EDUCATION, TRAINING, EMPLOYMENT, AND SOCIAL SERVICES | | | | | | | | | | | |
| *Education and training* | | | | | | | | | | | |
| Exclusion of scholarship and fellowship income | — | — | — | — | — | 0.7 | 0.6 | 0.6 | 0.7 | 0.7 | 3.3 |
| Parental personal exemption for students age 19 or over | — | — | — | — | — | 0.2 | 0.2 | 0.2 | 0.2 | 0.2 | 1.0 |
| Exclusion of interest on State and local government student loans | 0.1 | 0.1 | (¹) | (¹) | (¹) | 0.3 | 0.2 | 0.2 | 0.2 | 0.2 | 1.5 |
| Exclusion of interest on State and local government bonds for private educational facilities | 0.1 | 0.1 | 0.1 | 0.1 | 0.1 | 0.3 | 0.3 | 0.3 | 0.3 | 0.3 | 1.8 |

| Item | | | | | | | | | | | |
|---|---|---|---|---|---|---|---|---|---|---|---|
| Deductibility of charitable contributions for education | 0.4 | 0.5 | 0.5 | 0.5 | 0.6 | 1.2 | 1.1 | 1.1 | 1.2 | 1.2 | 8.3 |
| Exclusion of employer-provided educational assistance | — | — | — | — | — | ([1]) | — | — | — | — | ([1]) |
| *Employment* | | | | | | | | | | | |
| Targeted jobs credit | 0.3 | 0.2 | 0.1 | 0.1 | ([1]) | ([1]) | ([1]) | ([1]) | ([1]) | ([1]) | 0.9 |
| Exclusion of employee meals and lodging (other than military) | — | — | — | — | — | — | — | — | — | — | — |
| Employee stock ownership plans (ESOPs)[4] | 0.8 | 0.5 | 0.1 | 0.1 | ([1]) | — | — | — | — | — | 1.8 |
| Exclusion of cafeteria plans | — | — | — | — | — | 1.4 | 2.0 | 2.6 | 3.2 | 3.6 | 12.8 |
| Exclusion of rental allowances of minister's home | — | — | — | — | — | — | 0.2 | 0.2 | 0.2 | 0.2 | 0.9 |
| Exclusion of miscellaneous fringe benefits | — | — | — | — | — | 3.4 | 3.7 | 4.1 | 4.4 | 4.7 | 20.3 |
| Exclusion of income earned by benefit organizations: | | | | | | | | | | | |
|   Supplemental unemployment benefit trusts | — | — | — | — | — | ([1]) | ([1]) | ([1]) | ([1]) | ([1]) | 0.2 |
|   Voluntary employees' beneficiary associations | ([1]) | ([1]) | ([1]) | ([1]) | ([1]) | 0.4 | 0.4 | 0.5 | 0.5 | 0.5 | 2.2 |
| Reserves for vacation pay | 0.1 | ([1]) | ([1]) | ([1]) | ([1]) | ([1]) | — | — | — | — | 0.3 |
| Exclusion for employer contributions to prepaid legal services plans | — | — | — | — | ([1]) | ([1]) | — | — | — | — | ([1]) |
| Exclusion of employee awards | — | — | — | — | — | 0.1 | 0.1 | 0.1 | 0.1 | 0.1 | 0.4 |
| *Social services* | | | | | | | | | | | |
| Deductibility of charitable contributions, other than for education and health | 0.4 | 0.4 | 0.5 | 0.5 | 0.6 | 9.1 | 8.2 | 8.6 | 9.1 | 9.5 | 46.9 |

(Continued)

TABLE 1. (Continued)

| Function | Corporations | | | | | Individuals | | | | | Total |
|---|---|---|---|---|---|---|---|---|---|---|---|
| | 1988 | 1989 | 1990 | 1991 | 1992 | 1988 | 1989 | 1990 | 1991 | 1992 | 1988–92 |
| Credit for child and dependent care expenses | — | — | — | — | — | 3.3 | 3.5 | 3.8 | 4.2 | 4.6 | 19.5 |
| Exclusion for employer-provided child care | — | — | — | — | — | (¹) | 0.1 | 0.1 | 0.1 | 0.1 | 0.4 |
| Exclusion for certain foster care payments | — | — | — | — | — | (¹) | (¹) | (¹) | (¹) | (¹) | 0.1 |
| Expensing costs of removing architectural barriers | (¹) | (¹) | (¹) | (¹) | (¹) | (¹) | (¹) | (¹) | (¹) | (¹) | 0.1 |
| HEALTH | | | | | | | | | | | |
| Exclusion of contributions by employers and self-employed for medical insurance premiums and medical care | — | — | — | — | — | 24.2 | 26.5 | 27.8 | 29.6 | 31.1 | 139.2 |
| Deductibility of medical expenses | — | — | — | — | — | 2.3 | 2.3 | 2.6 | 3.0 | 3.3 | 13.6 |
| Exclusion of interest on State and local government bonds for hospital facilities | 0.1 | 0.1 | 0.1 | 0.1 | 0.1 | 2.4 | 2.3 | 2.5 | 2.6 | 2.7 | 12.9 |
| Deductibility of charitable contributions for health | 0.2 | 0.2 | 0.2 | 0.2 | 0.2 | 1.2 | 1.0 | 1.1 | 1.2 | 1.2 | 6.7 |
| Tax credit for orphan drug research | (¹) | (¹) | (¹) | (¹) | — | — | — | — | — | — | (¹) |
| MEDICARE | | | | | | | | | | | |
| Exclusion of untaxed medicare benefits: | | | | | | | | | | | |
| Hospital insurance | — | — | — | — | — | 3.8 | 4.2 | 4.7 | 5.1 | 5.6 | 23.4 |
| Supplementary medical insurance | — | — | — | — | — | 1.9 | 2.1 | 2.4 | 2.7 | 3.0 | 12.1 |
| INCOME SECURITY | | | | | | | | | | | |
| Exclusion of untaxed railroad retirement system benefits | — | — | — | — | — | 0.4 | 0.4 | 0.4 | 0.4 | 0.4 | 1.9 |

| | | | | | | |
|---|---|---|---|---|---|---|
| Exclusion of workmen's compensation benefits | — | 2.7 | 3.0 | 3.3 | 3.6 | 3.9 | 16.5 |
| Exclusion of special benefits for disabled coal miners | — | 0.2 | 0.2 | 0.2 | 0.2 | 0.2 | 0.9 |
| Exclusion of public assistance benefits | — | 0.3 | 0.3 | 0.3 | 0.3 | 0.3 | 1.5 |
| Net exclusion of pension contributions and earnings | — | 49.3 | 51.7 | 56.5 | 61.8 | 67.5 | 286.9 |
| Individual retirement plans | — | 8.5 | 8.4 | 8.9 | 9.3 | 10.2 | 45.3 |
| Exclusion of other employee benefits: | | | | | | | |
| Premiums on group term life insurance | — | 1.8 | 1.8 | 1.9 | 2.0 | 2.1 | 9.6 |
| Premiums on accident and disability insurance | — | 0.1 | 0.1 | 0.1 | 0.1 | 0.1 | 0.6 |
| Exclusion for employer-provided death benefits | — | (1) | (1) | (1) | (1) | (1) | 0.1 |
| Additional standard deduction for the blind and the elderly | — | 1.4 | 1.1 | 1.2 | 1.3 | 1.4 | 6.4 |
| Tax credit for the elderly and disabled | — | 0.2 | 0.2 | 0.2 | 0.2 | 0.2 | 0.8 |
| Deductibility of casualty and theft losses | — | 0.3 | 0.2 | 0.2 | 0.1 | 0.1 | 0.9 |
| Earned income credit[5] | — | 0.8 | 1.2 | 1.4 | 1.5 | 1.7 | 6.6 |
| SOCIAL SECURITY | | | | | | | |
| Exclusion of untaxed social security benefits: | | | | | | | |
| Disability insurance benefits | — | 1.5 | 1.4 | 1.5 | 1.6 | 1.7 | 7.7 |
| OASI benefits for retired workers | — | 12.5 | 11.7 | 12.5 | 13.2 | 14.1 | 64.0 |
| Benefits for dependents and survivors | — | 4.5 | 4.2 | 4.5 | 4.8 | 5.1 | 23.1 |
| VETERANS BENEFITS AND SERVICES | | | | | | | |
| Exclusion of veterans' disability compensation | — | 1.3 | 1.2 | 1.3 | 1.3 | 1.3 | 6.5 |

(Continued)

TABLE 1. (Continued)

| Function | Corporations | | | | | Individuals | | | | | Total |
|---|---|---|---|---|---|---|---|---|---|---|---|
| | 1988 | 1989 | 1990 | 1991 | 1992 | 1988 | 1989 | 1990 | 1991 | 1992 | 1988–92 |
| Exclusion of veterans' pensions | — | — | — | — | — | 0.1 | 0.1 | 0.1 | 0.1 | 0.1 | 0.7 |
| Exclusion of GI bill benefits | — | — | — | — | — | 0.1 | 0.1 | 0.1 | 0.1 | 0.1 | 0.3 |
| Exclusion of interest on State and local government veterans' housing bonds | 0.1 | 0.1 | 0.1 | (¹) | (¹) | 0.2 | 0.2 | 0.2 | 0.2 | 0.2 | 1.2 |
| GENERAL PURPOSE FISCAL ASSISTANCE | | | | | | | | | | | |
| Exclusion of interest on general purpose State and local government debt | 1.8 | 1.6 | 1.5 | 1.5 | 1.4 | 8.1 | 7.6 | 7.9 | 8.7 | 8.8 | 48.9 |
| Deductibility of nonbusiness State and local government income and personal property taxes | — | — | — | — | — | 18.3 | 16.7 | 18.0 | 19.5 | 21.2 | 93.5 |
| Exclusion and tax credit for corporations with possessions source income | 1.7 | 1.7 | 1.9 | 2.1 | 2.3 | — | — | — | — | — | 9.7 |
| INTEREST | | | | | | | | | | | |
| Deferral of interest on savings bonds | — | — | — | — | — | 0.8 | 0.8 | 0.8 | 0.8 | 0.8 | 4.0 |

Footnotes to Table 1:
[1] Positive tax expenditure of less than $50 million.
[2] Negative tax expenditure of less than $50 million.
[3] In addition, the 6-cents-per-gallon exemption from excise tax for alcohol fuels results in a reduction in excise tax receipts, net of income tax effect, of $0.2 billion in 1988, and less than $50 million in 1989.
[4] Includes effects of tax credit, dividend deduction, nonrecognition of gain on stock sales, and exclusion of interest on ESOP loans.
[5] The figures in the table show the effect of the earned income credit on receipts. The increases in outlays are: $3.3 billion in 1988, $4.8 billion in 1989, $5.2 billion in 1990, $5.6 billion in 1991, and $6.1 billion in 1992.
SOURCE: The Joint Committee on Taxation Staff, "Estimates of Federal Tax Expenditures for Fiscal Years 1988–1992," February 22, 1987.

ADDENDUM TO TABLE 1. Sum of Tax Expenditure Items by Type of Taxpayer, Fiscal Years 1988–1992 (Billions of dollars)

| Fiscal year | Corporations | Individuals | Total |
|---|---|---|---|
| 1988 | 62.0 | 259.1 | 321.1 |
| 1989 | 58.2 | 257.0 | 315.2 |
| 1990 | 61.3 | 274.4 | 335.7 |
| 1991 | 63.4 | 292.2 | 355.6 |
| 1992 | 66.6 | 311.2 | 377.8 |

Note: These totals represent merely the mathematical sum of the estimated fiscal year effect of each of the tax expenditure items included in table 1.

TABLE 2. Distribution by Income Class of All Returns, Taxable Returns, Itemized Returns, and Tax Liability, at 1988 Law and 1988 Income Levels[1] [Money amounts in millions of dollars, returns in thousands]

| Income class (thousands)[2] | All returns[3] | Taxable returns | Itemized returns Total | Itemized returns Taxable | Tax liability |
|---|---|---|---|---|---|
| Below $10 | 39,289 | 7,153 | 706 | 274 | 632 |
| $10 to $20 | 30,000 | 19,653 | 2,917 | 2,151 | 18,493 |
| $20 to $30 | 22,271 | 19,732 | 5,778 | 5,237 | 39,649 |
| $30 to $40 | 15,155 | 14,505 | 6,667 | 6,485 | 43,450 |
| $40 to $50 | 9,250 | 9,103 | 5,519 | 5,424 | 40,448 |
| $50 to $75 | 9,084 | 9,002 | 6,997 | 6,870 | 71,006 |
| $75 to $100 | 2,193 | 2,185 | 1,871 | 1,856 | 29,754 |
| $100 to $200 | 1,946 | 1,928 | 1,834 | 1,798 | 49,047 |
| $200 and over | 685 | 682 | 650 | 644 | 77,158 |
| Total | 129,873 | 83,943 | 32,939 | 30,738 | 369,636 |

[1]Tax law as in effect on January 1, 1988, is applied to the 1988 level and sources of income and their distribution among taxpayers. Excludes individuals under age 16.

[2]The income concept used to place tax returns into income classes is adjusted gross income plus (1) tax-exempt interest, (2) employer contributions for health plans and life insurance, (3) inside build-up on life insurance, (4) workers' compensation, (5) nontaxable social security benefits, (6) deductible contributions to individual retirement accounts, (7) the minimum tax preferences, and (8) net losses, in excess of minimum tax preferences, from passive business activities.

[3]Includes filing and nonfiling units. Filing units include all taxable and nontaxable returns. Examples of nonfiling units include dependents with earned or unearned income and individuals with income that is exempt from Federal income taxation (e.g., transfer payments, interest from tax-exempt bonds, etc.).

Note: Detail may not add to total due to rounding.

SOURCE: The Joint Committee on Taxation Staff, "Estimates of Federal Tax Expenditures for Fiscal Years 1988–1992," February 22, 1987.

**TABLE 3.** Distribution of Selected Individual Tax Expenditure Items by Income Class, at 1988 Rates and 1988 Income Levels[1] [Money amounts in millions of dollars, returns in thousands]

| Income class (thousands)[2] | Medical deduction | | Real estate tax deduction | |
|---|---|---|---|---|
| | Returns | Amount | Returns | Amount |
| Below $10 | 102 | 18 | 99 | 6 |
| $10 to $20 | 833 | 190 | 1,612 | 135 |
| $20 to $30 | 1,319 | 320 | 4,371 | 530 |
| $30 to $40 | 1,230 | 404 | 5,720 | 753 |
| $40 to $50 | 731 | 266 | 5,025 | 949 |
| $50 to $75 | 546 | 358 | 6,496 | 2,208 |
| $75 to $100 | 114 | 163 | 1,763 | 967 |
| $100 to $200 | 97 | 316 | 1,631 | 1,262 |
| $200 and over | 14 | 127 | 507 | 592 |
| Total | 5,036 | 2,161 | 27,225 | 7,401 |

| Income class (thousands)[2] | State and local income tax deduction | | Home mortgage interest deduction | |
|---|---|---|---|---|
| | Returns | Amounts | Returns | Amounts |
| Below $10 | 142 | 4 | 165 | 30 |
| $10 to $20 | 1,732 | 135 | 2,209 | 628 |
| $20 to $30 | 4,487 | 664 | 5,277 | 2,135 |
| $30 to $40 | 5,582 | 1,104 | 6,269 | 3,004 |
| $40 to $50 | 4,785 | 1,578 | 5,158 | 3,626 |
| $50 to $75 | 5,863 | 3,692 | 6,614 | 8,546 |
| $75 to $100 | 1,624 | 1,868 | 1,728 | 3,623 |
| $100 to $200 | 1,501 | 3,311 | 1,603 | 4,001 |
| $200 and over | 468 | 3,698 | 560 | 2,133 |
| Total | 26,185 | 16,053 | 29,583 | 27,726 |

| Income class (thousands)[2] | Deductibility of nonmortgage interest in excess of investment income | | Charitable contributions deduction | | Casualty loss deduction | |
|---|---|---|---|---|---|---|
| | Returns | Amount | Returns | Amount | Returns | Amount |
| Below $10 | 120 | 4 | 104 | 2 | 2 | 0 |
| $10 to $20 | 1,685 | 84 | 1,626 | 81 | 60 | 25 |
| $20 to $30 | 4,529 | 307 | 4,687 | 375 | 79 | 41 |
| $30 to $40 | 5,675 | 485 | 6,008 | 649 | 40 | 29 |
| $40 to $50 | 4,809 | 528 | 5,117 | 913 | 10 | 3 |
| $50 to $75 | 6,203 | 1,281 | 6,721 | 1,976 | 17 | 34 |
| $75 to $100 | 1,568 | 492 | 1,789 | 905 | 8 | 7 |
| $100 to $200 | 1,361 | 667 | 1,697 | 1,871 | 4 | 6 |
| $200 and over | 421 | 536 | 542 | 3,092 | 1 | 15 |
| Total | 26,371 | 4,385 | 28,291 | 9,865 | 221 | 161 |

(Continued)

**TABLE 3.** (Continued)

| Income class (thousands)[2] | Child care credit | | Earned income credit[3] | |
|---|---|---|---|---|
| | Returns | Amount | Returns | Amount |
| Below $10 | 80 | 20 | 2,925 | 2,040 |
| $10 to $20 | 1,040 | 426 | 7,101 | 3,533 |
| $20 to $30 | 1,978 | 841 | 1,109 | 389 |
| $30 to $40 | 2,043 | 870 | 155 | 66 |
| $40 to $50 | 1,537 | 623 | 34 | 15 |
| $50 to $75 | 1,383 | 541 | 12 | 8 |
| $75 to $100 | 218 | 78 | 0 | 0 |
| $100 to $200 | 137 | 51 | 0 | 0 |
| $200 and over | 20 | 8 | 0 | 0 |
| Total | 8,436 | 3,458 | 11,336 | 6,052 |

Footnotes to Table 3:

[1] Excludes individuals under age 16.

[2] The income concept used to place tax returns into income classes is adjusted gross income plus (1) tax-exempt interest, (2) employer contributions for health plans and life insurance, (3) inside build-up on life insurance, (4) workers' compensation, (5) nontaxable social security benefits, (6) deductible contributions to individual retirement accounts, (7) the minimum tax preferences, and (8) net losses, in excess of minimum tax preferences, from passive business activities.

[3] Includes the refundable portion of the earned income credit.

Note: Detail may not add to total due to rounding.

SOURCE: The Joint Committee on Taxation Staff, "Estimates of Federal Tax Expenditures for Fiscal Years 1988–1992," February 22, 1987.

# CHAPTER 2

# How Our Tax System Works

*"Kings ought to shear, not skin their sheep."*

English poet ROBERT HERRICK shortly after the
execution of Charles I, who had imposed numerous
burdensome taxes on his subjects

*"The greater the number of statutes, the greater the
number of thieves and brigands."*

LAO-TSE

Now that you understand the legal foundation for our tax sheltering and eliminating techniques, it remains necessary first to uncomplicate our federal income tax structure so that you can see where each shelter technique fits into the whole picture. You pay taxes on your taxable income. Your taxable income is your gross income less certain deductions. It is necessary, therefore, to define your "gross" income.

Gross income means *all* income, from whatever source derived, including (but not limited to) the following items:

Compensation for services, including fees, commissions, and similar items
Gross income derived from business
Gains derived from dealings in property
Interest
Rent
Royalties
Dividends
Alimony and separate maintenance payments
Annuities
Income from life insurance and endowment contracts
Pensions
Income from discharge of indebtedness
Distributive share of partnership gross income
Income in respect of a decedent
Income from an interest in an estate or trust
Unemployment compensation

*Income* has been defined by the Supreme Court as "all accession to wealth, clearly realized, over which you have dominion." Everything you receive for personal services must be included in your gross income. This includes many so-called "fringe benefits" as well as wages, salaries, commissions, tips, and fees. You must report income in any form other than cash at the fair market value of the goods or services received.

Amounts withheld from your pay for income and social security taxes or savings bonds are considered received by you and must be included in your income in the year they were withheld. The same generally is true of amounts withheld for pensions, insurance, and union dues.

If your employer uses your wages to pay your debt, or if wages are *attached* or *garnisheed,* the full amount is still considered received by you and must be included in your income. The same is true of fines or penalties withheld from your pay.

Vacation allowances paid to you from a vacation fund are wages and are also included in your income. Severance pay as well is taxable. A lump-sum payment for cancellation of your employment contract is income in the year you receive it.

Rewards and bonuses paid to you for outstanding work are income. These include such prizes as an all-expenses-paid vacation trip for meeting a sales goal and even prizes won on a TV quiz show. If a prize or award is in goods or services, you must include its fair market value in income. However, if your employer merely promises to pay you a bonus or award at some future time, it is not taxable until you receive it or it is made available to you.

If you buy property from your employer at a reduced price, you must normally include in your income as extra pay the excess of the property's fair market value over what you paid for it. If you receive a cash allowance from your employer for meals or lodging, you must include that cash allowance in your income. All tips you receive are also subject to federal income tax; they are not tax-free gifts. You must include in gross income the cash tips you receive directly from customers and the tips from charge customers that are paid to you by your employer.

Any interest that you receive or that is credited to your bank account is taxable income unless it is specifically exempt from tax. This is true even if that interest has not been entered in your bank book—it *has* been credited to you on the books of your bank. Certain distributions commonly referred to as dividends must be included in gross income as interest. You must report as interest the so-called "dividends" on deposits, withdrawals, or share accounts in:

Cooperative banks
Credit unions
Domestic building and loan associations
Federal savings and loan associations
Mutual savings banks

In addition, the fair market value of gifts or services received for making long-term deposits or opening accounts in savings institutions is interest and must be reported as income in the year received.

Amounts you receive as rental income must also be included in your gross income. Rental income includes not only the amount you receive for the occupancy of real estate or for the use of personal property but other amounts as well. For example, advance rent must be included in your rental income in the year you receive it regardless of the period covered or the accounting method used. Payments for the cancellation of a lease or the reduction in the principal of a mortgage (even on your home) if paid before due should also be included as income. So, too, are payments made directly by a tenant for any of *your* expenses. For example, if your tenant pays your heating bill in lieu of partial rent, that amount must be included as rental income.

You must also include in your gross income all fees for your services. Examples of these fees are payments you receive for services as:

A corporate director
An executor or administrator of an estate
A notary public
A member of a jury
An election precinct official
An accountant
An attorney
A medical practitioner

Income received in the form of property or services must be included in income at its fair market value on the dates received. If you receive the services of another in return for your services, and you both have definitely agreed ahead of time as to the value of the services, that value will be accepted as the fair market value unless the value can be shown to be otherwise. An exchange of property or services for your property or services is called bartering and should be included in your gross income.

Finally, dividends, capital gain distributions, and all gains on the sale of property also are included in your gross income. Dividends are distributions paid to you by a corporation. You also may receive dividends through a partnership, an estate, a trust, or an association that is taxable as a corporation.

When all of your gains, all of your "accessions to wealth, clearly realized, over which you have dominion," are added together, you arrive at your gross income amount. From this amount you next subtract your allowable deductions to arrive at your taxable income. Your tax is based on that taxable income. Therefore, in order to reduce or eliminate your tax, there are four possible avenues of attack:

1.  You can reduce or minimize your gross income figure by converting income that normally would be included in gross income into certain forms of income that can be excluded from the gross. This means that amount of income never will even enter into the tax computation picture.

2.  You can arrange your activities so that certain personal expenditures that you would normally make will be allowable as deductions, thus reducing both your gross income and your taxable income.

3.  You can take advantage of special credits that the tax code allows as dollar-for-dollar offsets to your final tax liability.

4.  You can reduce or eliminate your tax by attacking the progressivity of our tax rates structure through the allocation of family income to different family members and entities.

Chapter 8 discusses how this fourth very special and very sophisticated tax planning technique works.

The following chapters will take you through these tax sheltering and elimination approaches.

# CHAPTER 3

# Exclusions— Tax-Free Money

*"Thank God we don't get all the government we pay for."*

WILL ROGERS

In their infinite wisdom, Congress and the courts have decided that some income should not be taxed—that is, it should not even enter into the tax computation picture. The tax code and relevant case law therefore have provided that certain items received by you may be excluded from gross income for any one of the following four reasons:

1. The item may be excluded for constitutional reasons. For example, certain interest on state and municipal bonds is not subject to federal taxation because of the fear that "the power to tax is the power to destroy." Such interest, therefore, is constitutionally exempt from federal taxation.

2. The item received may not be true income but rather a return of cost. For example, when you lend money and then later collect it, the receipt of that money collected is merely a return of your original loan. Alternatively, when you sell property, part of the proceeds of the sale represents a return of your cost, and therefore only the excess of the proceeds over your original cost for that property represents true income.

3. Congress has from time to time seen fit to relieve certain items from taxation for equitable or other reasons. Each exclusion has its own legislative history and reason for enactment. Some exclusions are intended as a form of indirect welfare payments, as when certain injury or sickness payments are excluded from income. Other exclusions prevent double taxation of income or provide incentives for socially desirable activities. For example, scholarships for tuition may be excluded from the income of the recipient. Alternatively, other exclusions have been enacted by Congress to rectify the effects of judicially imposed decisions. For example, the value of improvements to property made by a leasee has been excluded from the leasor's income upon the termination of the lease in reaction to a Supreme Court decision that such value was taxable income.

4. Certain items have been excluded from gross income on the basis of administrative discretion and efficiency. For example, if you buy property from your employer at a reduced price, you normally must include in your income as extra pay the excess of the property's fair market value over what you paid for it. But if such employee discounts are generally available and are not part of negotiated compensation, the discounts are not generally included in your gross income. This is

because of the administrative difficulty the Internal Revenue Service would have in identifying and valuing such discounts. Other employee fringe benefits, such as free parking or nonbusiness use of your employer's facilities, would also be excluded from your gross income for the same reasons.

This chapter will detail those items that are not taxable and explain how you can use the availability of these items to reduce your income tax.

# A   Alternatives to "Earned Income"

The most important thing that you as a taxpayer can do to reduce your taxes to zero is to convert fully taxable income into excludable income. An *exclusion* is something that is not included in gross income. It is the best kind of revenue to receive. If you are in the 33 percent tax bracket (single, taxable income over $43,150), each dollar you convert to excludable income is the equivalent of getting a raise of 33 percent! Therefore, in negotiating compensation, you as an employee-taxpayer should examine the following forms of nontaxable remuneration for services rendered as alternatives to fully taxable cash income.

# 1

## Hospitalization Premiums (Sec. 106)

Hospitalization premiums, including premiums for supplementary medical insurance (Medicare) paid by your employer, or your former employer if you are retired, are excludable from your income. However, if you have the choice when you retire either to receive continued coverage under your employer's group medical insurance plan or to receive a lump-sum payment and you choose the lump-sum payment, you must include the amount of the payment in your gross income at the time you make the choice to receive it. If you choose continued coverage, or if you qualify for itemization of deductions, you may deduct the amount you include in your income as a medical insurance premium.

For example, if you normally would purchase hospitalization insurance costing $500 a year, and you are in the 33 percent tax bracket, you would require pretax earnings of $746 in order to make that purchase. Of that $746, 33 percent or $246 would go to paying your taxes. In other words, having your employer pay the hospitalization premiums ($500) for you is the equivalent of receiving compensation of $746 from your employer and then paying your own hospitalization premiums. The savings of $246 to your employer can come back to you in *additional* alternative compensation.

# 2

## Group Life Insurance Premiums (Sec. 79)

Group term life insurance coverage of $50,000 or less provided to you by your employer is excludable from your income. This rule applies even if you make an irrevocable assignment of your rights in the policy to another person who agrees to pay your part, if any, of the insurance premiums.

Group term life insurance is term life insurance protection (insurance for a fixed period of time) provided under a master policy or a group of individual policies. The policies must be life insurance contracts and form part of a plan of group insurance arranged for by an employer for all employees. The life insurance protection in a policy of permanent insurance (for example, a whole-life policy) is *not* term life insurance protection.

You are not taxed on the cost of group term life insurance protection of *more* than $50,000 if:

a) the coverage is provided after you have retired and are disabled;

b) your employer is the beneficiary of the policy for the entire period the insurance is in force during the tax year; *or*

c) the only beneficiary of the amount over $50,000 is a qualified charitable organization for the entire period the insurance is in force during the tax year. You do not make a deductible charitable contribution by naming a charitable organization as the beneficiary of your policy.

Where the policy provides only term insurance of $50,000 or less, the payment of premiums by your employer does not create *any* taxable income for you as an employee. The cost of insurance protection in excess of $50,000 paid by your employer is includable in your gross income according to the following table:

**Uniform premiums for $1,000 of group term life insurance protection**
(Annual cost per $1,000 of protection) [(Reg. 1.79–3)]

| Age | Amount Included in Income |
|---|---|
| Under 30 | $ .96 |
| 30-34 | $ 1.08 |
| 35-39 | $ 1.32 |
| 40-44 | $ 2.04 |
| 45-49 | $ 3.48 |
| 50-54 | $ 5.76 |
| 55-59 | $ 9.00 |
| 60-64 | $14.04 |

Those employees age 65 and over whose employment is not terminated will continue to have their insurance costs computed on the basis of the 60–64 category.

For example, assume you are 47 years old and your employer carries a group policy that provides you with $60,000 of term life insurance. You therefore must include only $34.80 ($3.48 × 10) in your income for your employer's payment of premiums. The rest of the premiums paid for you is tax-free income. Had you contributed $34.80 towards the purchase of the insurance, you would have had zero included in your income.

Furthermore, any amount contributed by you toward the purchase of such group term life insurance serves to reduce the amount of gross income that you realize.

If two or more employers provide you with group term life insurance coverage, you must figure the amount of income from this source. Moreover, the cost of group term life insurance provided to you is the cost of life insurance provided to you during the tax year, regardless of when your employers pay the premiums.

For example, assume you are 51 years old and work for two employers. Both employers provide group term life insurance coverage for you. Your coverage with the first employer is $35,000 and with the second is $45,000. You pay premiums of $50 a year under the second employer's group plan. The amount to be included in your gross income is figured as follows:

| | |
|---|---|
| First employer coverage | $35,000 |
| Second employer coverage | +45,000 |

| | |
|---|---:|
| Total coverage | 80,000 |
| Minus exclusion | −50,000 |
| | |
| Excess amount | 30,000 |
| Multiply cost per thousand, age 51 (from table) | × 5.76 |
| | |
| Cost of excess insurance for tax year | 172.80 |
| Minus premiums paid by you | − 50.00 |
| | |
| Amount included in income | $122.80 |

Clearly, if you need life insurance, the use of this technique provides that insurance at either a tax-reduced or completely tax-free cost.

## 3    Group Legal Services Plans (Sec. 120)

Amounts paid by your employer for a qualified group legal services plan and the value of the benefits you receive under such a plan can no longer be excluded from your income. This exclusion expired at the end of 1987 (Tax Reform Act of 1986).

## 4    Accident and Health Plans (Sec. 105)

Although you realize no taxable income from the benefits of an accident and health policy on which you pay your own premiums, it may be more tax advantageous to have these policies paid by your employer. The general rule is that any benefits received by you as an employee under such policies are includable in your gross income.

There are, however, certain exceptions permitting you to exclude specific benefits that would otherwise be taxable under the general rule:

1. You may exclude benefits received directly or indirectly as reimbursement for medical expenses incurred for yourself, your spouse, or your dependents. If you deducted such medical expenses in a prior year, however, the reimbursement for these expenses must be included in the current year's income.

2.  You may exclude benefits received for the permanent loss or the loss of the use of a member or function of the body, or a permanent disfiguration of yourself or your spouse, or dependents, so long as the benefits are not related to absence from work.

The value of the exclusion of accident and health benefits can be shown by the following example:

Assume you lost a leg in an automobile accident that was unrelated to your work and you collected $10,000 from an insurance policy carried by your employer. If the payments were computed with reference to the nature of the injury and were not related to the time period that you were absent from work, then the entire $10,000 would be excluded from your income. Furthermore, if you incurred $3,000 in medical expenses that were covered under an employer-sponsored hospitalization plan, those payments would also be excluded from your income.

# 5

## Employee Death Benefits (Sec. 101)

Amounts received as death benefits by your family or by your estate may be excluded up to an aggregate amount of $5,000 whether paid directly or indirectly by your employer.

This exclusion may not be claimed for accrued salary, unused leave, or compensation for past services. Furthermore, it may be claimed for a nonforfeitable amount you had the right to receive before your death *only* if it is received as a lump-sum distribution from a qualified plan or under an annuity contract purchased by an employer which is a tax-exempt organization.

# 6

## Merchandise Distributed to Employees on Holidays

Merchandise distributed to you as an employee on holidays, such as Christmas or New Year's Day, is excludable from your income if it is not of substantial value and is given for substantially noncompensatory reasons.

A turkey, for example, or similar merchandise given to you by your employer on a holiday therefore will not be includable in your taxable income. Unfortunately, this does not apply to cash distributions such as bonuses.

# 7

## "Expenses of Your Employer"

The law does not tax reimbursement expenses that are true reimbursements for expenses of your employer rather than income amounts truly compensatory in nature.

Under this category are such items as reimbursements for cab fares and the payment of supper money. Rather than being excludable on the basis of statutory or constitutional language, these items are truly nontaxable as the result of Internal Revenue Service recognition of the impossible administrative verification problems in auditing such expenses. For whatever reasons, therefore, they are nontaxable.

If you as an employee can arrange with your employer to work from 11:00 A.M. to 7:00 P.M. rather than from 9:00 A.M. to 5:00 P.M., and she agrees to provide you with supper money, these personal supper expenses therefore can be converted into nontaxable income. In effect, no matter what bracket you are in, you have arranged for the Internal Revenue Service to buy you dinner.

# 8

## Meals and Lodgings (Sec. 119)

The value of meals and lodgings provided to you, your spouse, and your dependents without charge by your employer is not taxable income if the following three criteria are met:

1. The meals or lodgings are provided at your employer's place of business.

2. The meals or lodgings are provided for the convenience of your employer.

3. In the case of lodging (but not meals), you must accept the lodging at your employer's place of business as a condition of your employment. This means that you must accept the lodging to carry out the duties of your job properly, for example, if you must be available for duty at all times.

Lodging includes the cost of heat, electricity, gas, water, sewerage service, and similar items that are necessary to make lodging habitable.

With reference to meals, you may exclude from income the value of meals provided to you during working hours so that you can be available for emergency calls, or because the nature of your employer's business restricts you to a short meal period. For example, if you are the only receptionist at your place of work, you must be available "at all times." If your employer provides you with lunch every day, that lunch is not includable in your income. Furthermore, the Supreme Court has ruled that such lunches do not constitute "wages" for social security taxes. They are truly *tax-free*.

However, if you receive a cash allowance from your employer for meals or lodging, you must include the cash allowance in your income. The solution, therefore, is to have your employer provide the food, not the dollars. The net effect is the same to you but the net cost is substantially less.

Situations in which meals and lodging are furnished for the convenience of the employer normally include the following:

- A waitress is required to eat her meals on the premises during the busy lunch and breakfast hours.

- A worker is employed at a construction site in a remote part of Alaska. The employer must furnish meals and lodging due to the inaccessibility of other facilities.

- A bank furnishes meals on the premises to limit the time tellers are away during the busy hours.

- A hospital provides a free cafeteria for its staff. The hospital's business purpose in providing the meals is to induce employees to stay on the premises in case an emergency arises. These meals are not includable in the income of the staff, even though staff members are *not* required to eat on the premises.

This technique should be used extensively when married couples run their own businesses or professions. For example, assume the situation where one spouse performs the services and the other runs the office. That second spouse needs to be available "at all times" to answer the phone, receive clients, etc., and therefore any meals provided to that spouse would be deductible by the business as an expense but not includable as income to the recipient. In effect, what we have done again is to convert a personal expense—a meal—into nontaxable compensation. Again, the Internal Revenue Service is put into the position of helping to pay for your dinner.

# 9

## Employee Discounts

You need not include as taxable income the discounts or privileges of relatively small value that you, as an employee, receive, where such discounts are given primarily to provide good employee relations and do not take on the character of additional compensation. This exclusion includes the usual courtesy discounts allowed to employees in many retail stores. But the value of discounts beyond a mere courtesy discount would be taxable income to you. Furthermore, if you buy property from your employer at less than a fair market value, the amount of that discount is income.

For example, if you pay $2,000 for one of your employer's company cars that has a fair market value of $6,000, you are considered to have earned $4,000 of income on the transaction.

# 10

## Workmen's Compensation (Sec. 104)

Workmen's compensation received for sickness or injury is fully exempt from tax. If you turn over your workmen's compensation payments to your employer, and all or part of your regular salary continues to be paid, the excess of the salary payments over the amount of workmen's compensation is taxable income.

For example, assume you are hurt on the job and are out of work for six weeks. Your employer continues to pay your salary of $200 a week, or $1,200 for the time you are absent. You also receive $75 a week, or a total of $450, in workmen's compensation. Under your employment contract, you turn over all your compensation to your employer. The $75 a week is fully excludable from your income and the balance of $125 a week is taxable income.

# 11

## "Cafeteria" Plans (Sec. 125)

Employee contributions under a written "cafeteria" plan, or "flexible benefit plan," permitting you as a participant to select between taxable and nontaxable benefits, are excludable from your income to the extent that you choose nontaxable benefits.

Nontaxable benefits include group life insurance (up to $50,000 coverage), disability benefits, accident and health benefits, and group legal services, to the extent that such benefits are excludable from gross income.
Such employer contributions may be excluded if the following conditions are satisfied:

- Participation in the cafeteria plan must be restricted to employees.

- The same service requirement must apply to all participants.

- The participant chooses nontaxable benefits.

- The plan's eligibility requirements do not discriminate in favor of "highly compensated individuals," defined as officers, shareholders owning more than 5 percent of the voting power or value of the sponsor's stock, highly compensated participants, employees earning more than $75,000, employees earning more than $50,000 and in the top 50 percent of employees ranked on the basis of compensation, and spouses and dependents of such individuals.

- Employer contributions and employee benefits do not favor "highly compensated participants," as defined above.

# 12

## Dependent Care Assistance Program (Sec. 129)

For tax years beginning after 1981, the value of the dependent care assistance that an employer provides to employees under a dependent care assistance program is not generally includable in the employee's gross income. However, if payments for child care expenses are made to someone who is a child under age 19 of the employee or who qualifies for a dependency exemption for the employee, the payments are not excludable.

The value of dependent care assistance that you may exclude from your pay is limited. If you are an employee who is not married at the end of the tax year, the limit is equivalent to your earned income for that year. For married employees the limit is the lesser of: (a) the employee's earned income for the tax year; or (b) the employee's spouse's earned income for the tax year. In addition, the Tax Reform Act of 1986 put a $5,000 cap on dependent care expenses.

A dependent care assistance program is a plan written by the employer for the exclusive benefit of the employees in that it meets the following requirements:

1. *Eligibility.* The program must benefit employees who qualify under a classification set up by the employer, and the Secretary of the Treasury must find it nondiscriminatory in favor of employees who are officers, owners, or highly compensated, or who are dependents of these employees. However, the employer does not have to include in this program employees who are covered by what the Secretary of Labor considers to be a collective bargaining agreement between employee representatives and one or more employers if there is evidence that the dependent care benefits were the subject of good faith bargaining between the representatives and the employer.

2. *Limitation on principal shareholders or owners.* Not more than 25 percent of the amounts paid or incurred by an employer for the dependent care assistance during the year may be for individuals who are shareholders or owners (or their spouses or dependents) each of whom—on any day of the year—owns more than 5 percent of the stock or of the capital or profit interest in the employer.

3. *Funding.* An employer is not required to fund a dependent care assistance program.

4. *Notification of availability.* An employer must provide all eligible employees with a reasonable notification of the availability and terms of the dependent care assistance program.

5. *Notification to participants.* The plan will give each employee, by January 31, a written statement showing the amounts paid for the expenses incurred by the employer in providing dependent care assistance to the employee during the calendar year.

# 13

## Employer Educational Assistance (Sec. 127)

This provision excluded from an employee's gross income employer-provided educational assistance, regardless of whether or not the education is job-related. The exclusion expired on December 31, 1987, under the Tax Reform Act of 1986. Employers were not required to withhold on educational assistance payments, but the exclusion was limited to $5,200 per individual per calendar year. Arguably, educational expenses that would be deductible by an employee as trade or business expenses if they had been paid by the employee are not subject to this $5,200 cap. Moreover, every employer who maintains an educational assistance program must file a return showing the number of employees eligible to participate in the program; the number participating; the total cost of the program; the employer's name, address, and taxpayer identification number; and the type of business in which the employer is engaged.

# 14

## Employee Awards (Sec. 274)

Under prior law, an employee award such as emblematic jewelry or an engraved plaque awarded an employee for job performance, which was not excludable as a scientific or other achievement award, was generally excludable from gross income if it qualified as a gift. If the employee award was includable in the employee's income, the employer was entitled to a deduction for the award as a business expense. If the award was excludable as a gift, the employer's deduction was limited to a maximum of $25 for the cost of gifts to any one employee in any one tax year.

If a gift of tangible personal property was awarded to an employee for length of service, safety achievement, or productivity, the deduction ceiling was raised from $25 to $400. If a length of service, safety, or productivity award was a *qualified plan award,* the ceiling on the employer's deduction was $1,600, provided that the average cost of all awards provided under the plan for qualified awards did not exceed $400. A qualified plan award was one awarded (a) under a permanent written program of the employer which (b) does not discriminate in favor of officers, shareholders, or highly compensated employees.

The Tax Reform Act of 1986 changed these rules. The new law states specifically that employee awards will *not* be excludable from the employee's income as gifts. Since such awards will no longer be treated as gifts (and are therefore fully includable as income to the employee), the limitations described above on employer deductions for business gifts will no longer apply. The entire amount of the award (assuming ordinary, necessary, and reasonable tests are met) will be deductible.

Employee awards generally will be includable in the income of the employee and will be deductible by the employer, subject to two limited exceptions. One exception applies to awards that are qualified plan awards.

The definition of a qualified plan award under new law is essentially the same as under prior law: one awarded (a) under a permanent written program of the employer which (b) does not discriminate in favor of officers, shareholders, or highly compensated employees. If an award is a qualified plan award, the award is excludable by the employee *and* deductible by the employer only to the extent that the cost to the employer of all such awards made to the employee during the taxable year (whether or not qualified plan awards) does not exceed $1,600. The $400 average cost limitation described above for qualified plan awards has been retained; that is, awards will not be considered qualified plan awards unless the average cost limitation is met.

The second exception applies to certain awards which are not qualified plan awards. If the award is not a qualified plan award (for example, if it is awarded under an informal plan or in a discriminatory fashion), the award will be excludable by the employee *and* deductible by the employer only to the extent that the cost of all such awards which are not qualified plan awards provided to the employee during the taxable year does not exceed $400.

Under new law if the cost to the employer of the qualified plan award exceeds the limits just described, then the employee must include in income the *greater* of (a) the excess of the cost of the award over the amount allowable as a deduction (but not more than the award's value), or (b) the excess of the value of the award over the amount allowable as a deduction. If the employer's cost is *not* over the applicable limit, the employee may exclude the award regardless of its value.

*Example:* If an employer gave an employee one qualified plan award that cost the employer $2,000 and had a value of $1,900, the employee would have to include $400 (cost minus $1,600 limitation) in income. If the award cost $2,000 and had a value of $2,200, the employee would have to include $600 in income (its value minus the $1,600 limitation).

Furthermore, to be excludable under *either* of the exceptions just described, an award must be an *employee achievement award.* Only awards that are length of service awards or safety achievement awards will qualify as employee achievement awards. Professional, administrative, managerial, and clerical employees do not qualify for safety achievement awards for tax purposes. A significant change in new law is that awards for productivity will no longer qualify for an exclusion. Awards for productivity will simply be treated as compensation.

Also, the new law specifically states that employee achievement awards must be tangible personal property (not cash, securities, or life insurance). To the extent employee awards are excludable from income, they are also exempt from social security and other employer withholding taxes.

Under new law there will no longer be any need to make the subjective determination as to whether the employee award is a gift. No employee awards will be treated as a gift for income tax purposes.

However, the new law creates a double whammy with respect to employee achievement awards that are in excess of the applicable limits. They are not deductible by the employer and must be included in the gross income of the employee. Because of this double whammy, beginning in 1987 employers should endeavor to keep employee achievement awards for length of service and safety achievement within the applicable dollar amount limitations.

*Example:* An insurance company has a program of employee achievement awards provided to employees for length of service achievement, but the arrangement discriminates in favor of highly compensated employees. In 1987 the company provides a top executive with a videocassette recorder that cost the company $600. The VCR has a value of $700. The cost of the video cassette recorder is deductible by the employer only to the extent of $400. Since the VCR's cost to the employer is more than $400, the executive must include the excess of its $700 value over the employer's $400 deductible portion in gross income. The reportable amount would be $300.

The new law does make it easier to plan employee achievement award programs since the interest of the employer corresponds with the interest of the employee; that is, the employer receives a deduction under the same circumstances that the employee receives an exclusion. The new law is less favorable with respect to employee awards in that the exclusion is not available for awards given for productivity of the employee.

The 1986 law does not change the rules for fringe benefits which are *de minimis* under Sec. 132(e). Under these rules employees may exclude from income employee awards that are of nominal value, such as holiday turkeys or employee picnics. However, the Senate Finance Committee's Report on the Tax Reform Act states that certain employee awards for length of service "such as a gold watch" may be treated under the *de minimis* provision! The rationale appears to be that such an award is the functional equivalent of several smaller gifts made over the course of many years of service. Or perhaps the committee has been too busy in recent years to follow the price of gold.

# B  Donative Items

## 15  Gifts, Bequests, and Inheritances (Sec. 102)

If you receive money or property by bequest, devise, or inheritance, that receipt does not constitute taxable income to you. (Any income produced by that money or property while in your hands, though, is taxable in the usual fashion.)

Only money and property received from a decedent or as a bona fide gift fall under this rule. For a transfer to constitute a gift, there must be a motive of "detached and disinterested generosity." The exclusion, though, applies only to the donee.

Here you must be careful. For purposes of taxation, a simple assignment of income is ineffective. For example, if you make a gift of salary receivable from your employer to your child, even though that check goes directly to your child, that income is still taxable to you. You were the one who earned it and therefore are the one who is taxed on that earning. Your child, however, will exclude the "gift" and not be taxed on its value.

But once property is conveyed, the impact of taxation does shift to the donee. Thus for example, if you are in the 33 percent bracket and own a bond yielding $500 in interest, you must pay taxes of $165, leaving you only $335 of after-tax disposable income. Alternatively, if you transfer that bond to your child and allow your child to receive the income, the first $500 of interest to that child will be completely tax-free. In terms of net family disposable income, the total amount available will be increased by $165.

The advantages of interfamily income allocation will be discussed extensively later in the book. The important thing to recognize under this section is that the transfer of the bond to your child is not at all a taxable transaction—that is, your child will not be taxed on the value of the bonds received. This exclusion of gifts from the gross income of the recipient constitutes the foundation of the income allocation strategies and techniques to be discussed later.

# 16

## Scholarships and Fellowships (Sec. 117)

Under prior law, if you received a scholarship or fellowship grant, you could exclude that amount from your gross income, subject to certain limits, depending upon whether you are a degree candidate. To qualify for this exclusion, the payment had to be made for your education and training. The payment did not qualify, however, if it was made to pay you either for past, present, or future services, or for studies or research conducted mostly for the grantor's benefit.

A scholarship generally means an amount paid for the benefit of a student at an educational organization, to aid in the student's pursuit of studies. An educational organization is any organization that normally maintains a regular faculty and curriculum and has a regularly organized body of students in attendance at the place where its educational activities are carried on. A fellowship is the same as a scholarship, but the individual receiving aid does not have to be enrolled at an educational institution, and research is usually the aim.

Under current law, the exclusion will be limited to scholarships or fellowship grants to individuals who are degree candidates at educational institutions that maintain a regular faculty and curriculum and have a regularly enrolled body of students. There will no longer be an exclusion available to nondegree candidates or for scholarships granted by organizations other than qualified educational institutions. In addition, the exclusion will be available only with respect to payments that are actually used for tuition, enrollment fees, books, supplies, and other equipment required for courses of instruction. Payments for teaching, research, or other services rendered to the institution by a degree candidate will no longer qualify for the exclusion.

The exclusion does apply to *qualified tuition reductions*. A qualified tuition reduction is a tuition reduction for the employees, spouses, and dependent children of employees of educational institutions for studies below the graduate level, under a plan that does not discriminate in favor of officers, owners, or highly compensated employees of the institution.

It is important to remember that this provision does not have a retroactive effect; that is, it does not apply to scholarships and fellowships granted before August 17, 1986.

For those awards, amounts received for expenses under a scholarship or fellowship grant, such as travel (including meals and lodging while traveling and an allowance for the travel expenses of your family), research, clerical help, or equipment, may continue to be excluded from your gross income. You may exclude these amounts without limit if you are a degree candidate. If you are not a degree candidate, you may exclude from your gross income the amount you receive as a scholarship or fellowship, including the value of services, room, and board provided to you, up to 300 times the number of months for which you receive amounts under the grant during the year. For example, if you receive $500 a month for six months, you will include $1,200 and receive 300 × 6 or $1,800 tax-free.

If you are *not* a degree candidate, such grants awarded prior to August 17, 1986, must be from one of the following to be excludable:

- The United States or one of its agencies; a U.S. state, territory, possession, or political subdivision, including the District of Columbia.

- A nonprofit organization exempt from federal income tax and operated exclusively for religious, charitable, scientific, literary, or educational purposes, testing for public safety, preventing cruelty to children or animals, or fostering national or international amateur sports competition.

- A foreign government.

- An international organization or an educational and cultural foundation or commission under the Mutual Educational and Cultural Exchange Act of 1961.

If you are not a degree candidate, the period for which you may exclude amounts you receive as scholarships or fellowship grants is limited to thirty-six months during your lifetime, which do not need to be consecutive. After they are over, you must include in your gross income all amounts you receive under your grant, including amounts for expenses, and the value of services, meals, and lodging given to you.

You are not a degree candidate if your studies merely allow you to practice a profession but do not lead to a degree. For example, if you are a registered nurse who receives a grant from a charity to take training leading to certification as a psychiatric nurse, these studies for certification do not make you a candidate for a degree.

Amounts paid to help you in pursuing your studies or research are not excludable if the studies or the research is mostly for the benefit of the grantor. However, if the main purpose is to further your education and training, and the amounts are not payment for services, they would be excludable. This is true even if you must give progress reports to the grantor, or if the results of your studies or research may slightly benefit the grantor.

Payments for your past, present, or future services are not excludable, *but* there is a very important exception that must be kept in mind: If you work for pay for a research project, you generally must include that pay in income. Your pay is not a scholarship or fellowship grant merely because the research can be used for credit toward a degree. However, if similar services are required of all candidates for the degree, as a reasonable condition for it, you may exclude the pay from your gross income.

Your pay for services over and above those specifically needed for the degree must be included in your gross income. Interns, resident physicians, and registered nurses in training in a hospital therefore must include their pay in gross income. But tuition and work payments given to you under a work study program are considered scholarships if your college, under its educational philosophy, requires all students to take part in a work program. These payments, therefore, are excludable from your income. Alternatively, payments you receive for service *not* required by the work program must be included in your income. Furthermore, amounts paid by your employer to you when you are on educational leave also are not excludable.

The following example will demonstrate the value of the potential exclusion of scholarships and fellowship grants from your income: In a contest sponsored by a business firm, you receive a scholarship award of $5,000 that you can use only for tuition, books, and supplies when enrolled as a candidate for a degree at a certain college. You do not include any of the $5,000 award in your gross income if:

a)  you are not employed by the firm at the time of the award;

b)  you are not being paid for services you provided for the firm in the past; *and*

c)  you are not required to provide future services for the firm.

If you are in the 33 percent bracket and desire to enroll as a candidate for a degree, you would have had to earn $7,463 before tax in order to have

$5,000 after tax to pay for the college tuition and fees. The enormous financial advantage of the exclusion of scholarships and fellowships from taxable income thus becomes very clear. Remember, however, that the same after-tax effect can be achieved if your employer establishes an employee education assistance plan as discussed earlier.

# 17

## Prizes and Awards (Sec. 74)

Prior to 1987, prizes and awards received in recognition of past accomplishments—in religious, charitable, scientific, artistic, educational, literary, or civic fields—were excludable income if the winners were chosen without action on their part and were not expected to perform any future services. For example, if you received a Pulitzer or Nobel Prize or any other award and were selected for your past work, this award was not includable in your income. Under the current law, the exclusion for scientific and other achievement awards is repealed. The only exception to the repeal is when the recipient assigns the award to a governmental unit or charitable organization.

The provision in the new law which permits you to exclude the value of the prize or award if you assign it to the government or a charity is of limited benefit. Under prior law an excludable award could be contributed to charity and the recipient contributor could take a deduction for the contribution. Under new law you may exclude the prize or award if you contribute it to a charitable organization, but your contribution is disallowed. The end result is that you have simply given away what you received and have no extra income and no deduction. In effect, this is no different from your having included the prize or award in gross income and then taken a charitable deduction for contributing it.

In addition, if you win a prize in a lucky number drawing, a televison or radio quiz program, a beauty contest, or some other event, that prize is taxable. So, too, are awards or bonuses given to you as an employee for your good work or for suggestions. These are not instances where the winners have been chosen without action on their part and are not expected to perform any future services.

Taxable prizes and awards in goods and services must be included in your income at their fair market value to you. This is very important. It is not the general fair market value but rather the fair market value of that prize *to you*. If you already have two attaché cases and win a third on a quiz show, the value of that third attaché case *to you* may be negligible. It clearly would not be its full retail selling price. However, when sold, the amount received for such prizes or awards is normally deemed to be equal to their fair market value. If, for example, you receive an award of a car that retails for $10,000 and immediately sell that car to a third party for $8,000, the amount to be included in your income would be the $8,000 figure rather than the $10,000 figure.

Be careful here. A bargain sale to a relative may be considered part sale, part gift. If you sold that $10,000 car to your brother for $5,000, the Internal Revenue Service might successfully argue that you received income of $10,000 and made a gift of the $5,000 difference to your brother. One technique that has been used to avoid this is to sell the car for $5,000 to an independent third party, who could turn around and resell the car to your brother for the same $5,000. Watch the structuring of such three-party transactions. There must be no prearranged agreement for the third party to resell to your brother, and that third party must be truly independent. Otherwise, if the Internal Revenue Service catches on, it will collapse the two transactions, deem the first sale to be a sham, and successfully establish the true nature of the gift to your brother.

## C Investors

# 18

### Interest on State and Municipal Obligations (Sec. 103)

You can exclude from gross income all interest earned on obligations of a state, territory, municipality, or any political subdivision, except in the case of arbitrage bonds issued after October 9, 1969.

An *arbitrage bond* is an obligation, the proceeds of which are reasonably expected to be used to acquire other securities or obligations that are expected over the term of the issue to yield a materially higher rate of return. This exception prohibits state and local governments from issuing bonds at a low interest rate because of their tax-exempt nature and using the proceeds to buy federal or industrial bonds returning a higher yield. Since the state or local government does not pay an income tax on the difference, this exception prevents the federal government from becoming an unintended source for financing state and local government operations.

If you are in a sufficiently high tax bracket, the advantages of purchasing a state or municipal bond can be substantial. If you are in the 33 percent bracket, a 6½ percent yield on a municipal obligation is the equivalent of a 9.7 percent yield on a nonexempt security. Moreover, the risk factor on a state or municipal obligation will normally be far lower than that on an industrial security.

The higher the tax bracket, the greater the attraction of a tax-exempt security. The following table shows the tax-exempt equivalent yield to a taxable investment at various marginal tax rates:

| If your 1988 marginal tax rate is: | And your tax-exempt investment yields | | | |
| | 6½% | 7% | 7½% | 8% |
| | it is the equivalent of a taxable investment yielding: | | | |
| --- | --- | --- | --- | --- |
| 15% | 7.64 | 8.23 | 8.82 | 9.41 |
| 28% | 9.02 | 9.72 | 10.41 | 11.11 |
| 33% | 9.70 | 10.45 | 11.19 | 11.94 |

# D    Benefits for the Elderly

# 19

## Public Assistance Payments

Benefit payments from a general welfare fund in the interest of the general public, such as payments to aid the indigent or the blind, or payments to crime victims, are excludable from your gross income. These welfare payments have been excluded by the Internal Revenue Service, because the IRS sees them in the nature of gifts.[1]

# 20

## Social Security and Other Retirement Benefits

Social security benefits under the federal social security programs are not taxable. Social security benefits received from foreign countries, however, are taxable unless they are specifically exempt by treaty.

Basic railroad retirement benefits are also not taxable. Railroad retirement lump-sum payments, commonly known as either the insurance

---

1.  Revenue Ruling 71–425, 1971–2 CB 76.

lump-sum payment or the residual payment, are excluded from your gross income as well.

The Internal Revenue Service tax code does not specifically exclude social security benefits, but these benefits have been declared not subject to tax by the Internal Revenue Commissioner.[2] According to the Internal Revenue Service, these payments are in part a return of the after-tax contributions made by the individual and in part a welfare or annuity payment from the government. These welfare payments have been viewed by the Internal Revenue Service as essentially in the nature of gifts.[3]

Moreover, basic Medicare benefits received under the Social Security Act are also excluded from gross income since they are considered social security payments. So also are supplementary benefits covering costs of doctors' services and other items not covered under basic Medicare, as they are in the nature of medical insurance payments.

Note, however, that beginning January 1, 1984, part of your Social Security benefits will be subject to tax if your income exceeds a specified level determined by formula. There are three factors used in determining how much of your Social Security benefits, if any, will be included in taxable income: (1) your *income*, defined as your Adjusted Gross Income for Federal income tax plus any tax-exempt interest, plus any foreign source income you receive during the year; (2) your *half-benefit*, defined as half the Social Security income you (and, if you're married and filing jointly, your spouse) receive during the year; and (3) your *base amount*, which is $25,000 for a single taxpayer, $32,000 for a married couple filing jointly, and zero for a married couple filing separately (unless they have lived apart for the entire tax year, in which case they qualify for the $25,000 base amount).

The amount of Social Security income to be reported, if any, will be 50% of the amount by which (1) your income plus (2) your half-benefit exceeds (3) your base amount. However, in no event will more than your half-benefit be reported as taxable income.

For example, assume a married couple filing jointly has an Adjusted Gross Income of $20,000 plus tax-exempt interest of $8,000. They therefore have *income* of $28,000. If they have Social Security income of $12,000 they will report $1,000 of that benefit as taxable income as follows:

2. Revenue Ruling 70–217, 1970–1 CB 12.
3. Revenue Ruling 71–425, 1971–1 CB 76.

| | |
|---|---:|
| Income | $28,000 |
| Half-benefit | +$ 6,000 |
| Total | $34,000 |
| Base Amount | −$32,000 |
| Difference | $ 2,000 |
| 50% of difference | $ 1,000 |
| Taxable S.S. benefit | $ 1,000 |

Now that social security payments may be taxable, recipients should find out whether their benefits are included as part of their adjusted gross income under the income tax laws of the states where they reside. Eleven states have exempted from their income taxes social security benefits now included in federal adjusted gross income: Delaware, Hawaii, Idaho, Indiana, Maine, New Mexico, New York, South Carolina, Virginia, West Virginia, and Wisconsin. Minnesota has provided an exclusion from federal adjusted gross income for social security benefits in a portion of the calculation of the maximum income exclusion for pensions and retirement benefits.

# 21

## Retirement Annuities (Sec. 72)

An annuity is a type of investment that requires you to pay a fixed amount in exchange for the right to receive periodic payments for your life or for some definite period. If the annuity payments are based on your life, or the life of another individual, the amounts of such payments are determined through the use of standard mortality tables.

When you receive the income from this annuity, part of what you are receiving represents a recovery of your initial investment. This recovery amount is fully excluded from income. The Internal Revenue Service provides tables with which you can compute your exclusion ratio. This exclusion ratio remains the same and continues to be applied to annuity payments even if you outlive your life expectancy.

For example, assume you have made principal payments into an annuity of $60,000 in return for payment of $500 per month for life. Also assume that the tables show that your life expectancy is 15 years from the annuity starting date. Your investment in the contract is $60,000 and your

## Life Expectancies

| Age | Years remaining | Age | Years remaining | Age | Years remaining |
|-----|-----------------|-----|-----------------|-----|-----------------|
| 5 | 76.6 | 42 | 40.6 | 79 | 10.0 |
| 6 | 75.6 | 43 | 39.6 | 80 | 9.5 |
| 7 | 74.7 | 44 | 38.7 | 81 | 8.9 |
| 8 | 73.7 | 45 | 37.7 | 82 | 8.4 |
| 9 | 72.7 | 46 | 36.8 | 83 | 7.9 |
| 10 | 71.7 | 47 | 35.9 | 84 | 7.4 |
| 11 | 70.7 | 48 | 34.0 | 85 | 6.9 |
| 12 | 69.7 | 49 | 34.0 | 86 | 6.5 |
| 13 | 68.8 | 50 | 33.1 | 87 | 6.1 |
| 14 | 67.8 | 51 | 32.2 | 88 | 5.7 |
| 15 | 66.8 | 52 | 31.3 | 89 | 5.3 |
| 16 | 65.8 | 53 | 30.4 | 90 | 5.0 |
| 17 | 64.8 | 54 | 29.5 | 91 | 4.7 |
| 18 | 63.9 | 55 | 28.6 | 92 | 4.4 |
| 19 | 62.9 | 56 | 27.7 | 93 | 4.1 |
| 20 | 61.9 | 57 | 26.8 | 94 | 3.9 |
| 21 | 60.9 | 58 | 25.9 | 95 | 3.7 |
| 22 | 59.9 | 59 | 25.0 | 96 | 3.4 |
| 23 | 59.0 | 60 | 24.2 | 97 | 3.2 |
| 24 | 58.0 | 61 | 23.3 | 98 | 3.0 |
| 25 | 57.0 | 62 | 22.5 | 99 | 2.8 |
| 26 | 56.0 | 63 | 21.6 | 100 | 2.7 |
| 27 | 55.1 | 64 | 20.8 | 101 | 2.5 |
| 28 | 54.1 | 65 | 20.0 | 102 | 2.3 |
| 29 | 53.1 | 66 | 19.2 | 103 | 2.1 |
| 30 | 52.2 | 67 | 18.4 | 104 | 1.9 |
| 31 | 51.2 | 68 | 17.6 | 105 | 1.8 |
| 32 | 50.2 | 69 | 16.6 | 106 | 1.6 |
| 33 | 49.3 | 70 | 16.0 | 107 | 1.4 |
| 34 | 48.3 | 71 | 15.3 | 108 | 1.3 |
| 35 | 47.3 | 72 | 14.6 | 109 | 1.1 |
| 36 | 46.4 | 73 | 13.9 | 110 | 1.0 |
| 37 | 45.4 | 74 | 13.2 | 111 | .9 |
| 38 | 44.4 | 75 | 12.5 | 112 | .8 |
| 39 | 43.5 | 76 | 11.9 | 113 | .7 |
| 40 | 42.5 | 77 | 11.2 | 114 | .6 |
| 41 | 41.5 | 78 | 10.6 | 115 | .5 |

expected return is $6,000 per year times 15 years, or $90,000. You would exclude two-thirds of each payment ($6,000 × ⅔) or a total of $4,000 yearly. That $4,000 is a nontaxable return of capital; the remaining $2,000 is taxable income.

If you die before the 15 years are up, you will have been taxed on some amounts that were actually a return of capital. But if you live for 20 years after the payments began, you could still exclude two-thirds of each payment from income, even though the entire investment was recovered after 15 years. Clearly, the secret here is to outlive your life expectancy. If it helps, use the promise of extra tax-free income as an incentive to live longer.

# 22

## Sale of Your Home (Sec. 121)

You may exclude from your gross income some or all of your gain from the sale or exchange of your main home, if you meet certain age, ownership, and use tests at the time of the sale or exchange. The timing of the exclusion is up to you, but you may exclude the gain only once.

You may choose to exclude from your gross income $125,000 (the maximum allowable) of gain on the sale or exchange of your main home *if:*

a)  you are age 55 or older before the date of the sale or exchange;

b)  you owned and lived in the property sold or exchanged as your main home for at least three years out of the five-year period ending on the date of the sale or exchange; *and*

c)  you or your spouse have never excluded gain on the sale or exchange of a home after July 20, 1981.

**THE AGE TEST**

You must reach age 55 before the date the home is sold to qualify for the $125,000 exclusion. You do not meet the age 55 test if you sell the property during the year in which you will be 55 but before you actually become 55.[4] The key tax saving technique here is that if you plan to sell or exchange your home, do not do so until your 55th birthday.

---

4.  Revenue Ruling 68-210, 1968–1 CB 61.

### THE THREE-YEAR TEST

The required three years of ownership and use during the five-year period ending on the date of the sale or exchange does not have to be continuous. You meet the test if you can show that you owned and lived in the property as your main home for either 36 full months or 1,095 days (365 times three) during the five-year period. Short temporary absences for vacations or other seasonal absences (even if you rent out the property during these absences) are counted as periods of use.

   If your previous home was destroyed or condemned, you may use the time that you owned and lived in that home to meet the ownership and use tests, but only if some part of any gain realized on your previous home was reinvested in the new home. Otherwise, you must have owned and lived in the same home.

### THE MAIN HOME TEST

Your main home is the place of your principal residence. It is the home in which you live for most of the year—your permanent address, as opposed to a vacation home.

### THE ONE-TIME EXCLUSION TEST

You can exclude gain for sales or exchanges made after July 20, 1981 only once in a lifetime. If you or your spouse choose to exclude gain from a sale or exchange, neither of you can do so again. If you each owned separate homes before your marriage, you may exclude the gain on the sale of one of them but not both. If you exclude once and then your spouse dies, or if you divorce and remarry, you are likewise prohibited from excluding in the future. However, you may revoke an earlier decision to exclude gain.

   You may make or revoke the choice to exclude gain for a particular sale or exchange at any time before the *latest* of the following dates:

- Three years from the due date of the tax return for the year of the sale.

- Three years from the date the return was filed.

- Two years from the date the tax was paid.

Once you are beyond these allotted periods, your decision is irrevocable. Furthermore, if you are married at the time you sell or exchange your main home, you may not choose to exclude the gain unless your spouse joins you in making the choice. Joint choices and revocations are needed even if:

a)  you and your spouse own separate homes;

b)  you and your spouse file separate returns; *or*

c)  your spouse does not own an interest in the home to be sold and has not lived in it for the required period before the sale or exchange.

If your spouse dies after the sale or exchange but before making the choice to exclude the gain, the deceased's personal representative (for example, an estate administrator or executor) must join with you in making the choice. You, as the surviving spouse, are considered the personal representative of the deceased only if no one else has been appointed.

This exclusion of the first $125,000 in gain provides substantial planning opportunities. For example, assume you want to give your $200,000 home to your two children but do not want to pay a gift tax on the transfer. One technique that is available to accomplish this is to sell them the home on an installment basis. If the gain you realize is not greater than $125,000 on the sale, no gain is taxable to you. You can then have your children pay you the $200,000 purchase price over ten years at $20,000 per year. But you and your spouse can *forgive* (make nontaxable gifts of) $20,000 per year to each child ($40,000 a year for the two children) without any income or gift tax consequences. (Note: Both of you must elect to file a split gift return.) Each year, therefore, you forgive the amount due on the sale of your house and you still have $20,000 of tax-free potential gifts available.

Furthermore, using the installment sales technique, any gain in excess of $125,000 is taxable ratably over the ten-year period. So, for example, if the net *gain* is $135,000, only $1,000 per year is included over the ten-year period.

In effect, what you accomplish is a gift of your appreciated house to your children with little if any income or gift tax consequences.

Alternatively, if the house is actually sold, you have $125,000 in tax-free gain without any requirements to reinvest that gain. In either case, smart tax planning and knowledge make you a winner.

# 23

## Buying Your Own Home—Twice!—The Schnepper Bootstrap

If you sell your principal home at a profit, that gain can be sheltered from tax if it is reinvested in a new home within two years. *Problem:* what if you have a new home but cannot find a buyer for your old home within the two-year period? In Letter Ruling 8350084, just before the two-year tax period was up, a taxpayer sold his old home to his own personal corporation. The IRS ruled that it was OK! So long as the sale was legitimate, there was no current tax.

This technique can be used to have your cake and eat it, too. Suppose that you want to move to a new home but do not want to give up the low interest rate mortgage on your old home. Furthermore, suppose that you want to rent your old home at a substantial positive cash flow because of a low mortgage debt service (monthly interest and principal). What you can do is set up an S corporation, sell the old home to that corporation at the high appreciated fair market value, then have that corporation rent the home to an outside tenant. Because you bought a new home within the two-year period, you will recognize no gain on the sale to your corporation. Even though Section 1239 will require that any recognized gain on the sale of the property to the S corporation (a related party) be treated as ordinary income, Section 1034 will generally postpone recognition of that gain so long as the cost of the new residence is equal to or greater than the old residence's adjusted sales price. Moreover, the S corporation will now be able to take *greater* depreciation deductions on the rental property because it bought that property at *appreciated* fair market value. Your tax benefit? Because this is an S corporation, all income and deductions—including the higher depreciation deductions—are now passed through to you and included on your own tax return.[5]

---

5.  See also Letter Ruling 8646036, wherein the Internal Revenue Service sanctioned a tax-free exchange of houses between shareholders (a married couple) and their 100-percent-owned S corporation. Moreover, the application of Section 1239 (treating gain on a sale or exchange of property that is depreciable by the transferee between shareholders and the controlled corporation as ordinary income) is deferred until the shareholders sell the newly acquired residence.

## E  Miscellaneous Individual Exclusions

# 24

### Carpool Receipts

If you form a carpool to carry passengers to and from work, the amounts received from these passengers are not included in your income. These amounts are considered reimbursement for transportation expenses incurred.

Although your cost of commuting back and forth to work has been subject to continually increasing costs as energy prices have risen, commuting costs are neither deductible nor normally excludable from income. But establishing a carpool can help you defray these expenses without incurring additional taxable income.

Therefore, what you should do is establish a carpool in which the passengers pay you amounts sufficient to cover the cost of your repairs, gasoline, and similar items used in connection with operating your car to and from work. In doing so, you convert personal nondeductible expenses into excludable income.

For example, if it has been costing you $100 a month to commute in the past, you have had to earn $149 (at the 33-percent tax bracket) in order to have the funds to pay for your commute. With a carpool arrangement in which your expenses are reimbursed, it costs you nothing. The establishment of a carpool, therefore, gives you an extra $149 in after-tax disposable income.

# 25

### Damages (Sec. 104)

Damages received in settlement of a lawsuit or awarded by a court are normally excluded from income under the return of capital doctrine. Theoretically, damages awarded for personal wrong committed against you (for instance, breach of promise to marry, invasion of privacy, libel, slander, alienation of affection) replace the personal capital destroyed by these wrongful acts.[6] Defamation awards are also excludable.[7] Amounts received as damages for personal injury are excludable under

---

6. Revenue Ruling 74–77, 1971–1 CB 33.
7. *Threlkeld,* 87 TC No. 76.

both this doctrine and specific congressional mandate.[8] However, damages received as a substitute for income are generally taxable, since they represent a restoration of lost wages or profits that would have been taxable upon receipt.

Amounts received to compensate for damages to property or to the good will of a business are also excludable up to the amount of the adjusted basis of the assets. Only receipts in excess of this basis will be taxable. For example, if your car, which cost you $500, is completely destroyed in an accident and you receive $600 as compensation for damages, the first $500 is nontaxable as a return of your capital; you include in your gross income only the $100 excess over your basis.

The difference between the taxable and excludable nature of alternative damages awarded provides an opportunity for sophisticated tax planning. For example, in arranging an out-of-court settlement of a suit involving personal injury and loss of income, you should be aware that damages from personal injury suits are excluded from income but the proportion representing loss of income is fully taxable. Therefore, negotiate for a maximum allocation to the personal injury portion of the settlement.

In fact, it may be more advantageous to take less, totally, if the tax-free portion is increased. Assume you are in the 33 percent bracket and are offered $10,000 for personal injury and $20,000 for loss of income. That leaves you with $23,400 after taxes. A settlement of $20,000 for personal injury and $7,500 for loss of income would give you $25,025, or $1,625 more after taxes. At the same time, it saves the payer $2,500. In such a case, everybody wins—except the Internal Revenue Service.

# 26

## Divorce and Separation Arrangements (Sec. 71)

Prior to July 18, 1984, alimony and support payments were taxable to the recipient spouse only if:

a)  the payments qualified as periodic payments *and*

b)  the payments were received under a decree of divorce or separate maintenance; *or*

---

8.  Internal Revenue Section 104(a) (2).

c) the payments were received under a written separation agreement (provided the husband and wife were not living together and did not file a joint return.)[9]

Alimony and support payments are termed periodic payments when no fixed total sum is established or when the cessation of payments is contingent upon the occurrence of some event, such as the death or remarriage of the divorced spouse or change in economic status of either spouse.

If you are the recipient spouse, you should be aware that lump-sum settlements are not taxed. Furthermore, where a fixed total sum is set and is payable in installments, the income is not taxable unless the sum is payable over a period of more than ten years.

For prior to 1984 arrangements, if a lump-sum settlement is payable in installments of more than ten years, payments in each year up to 10 percent of the principal sum will qualify as periodic payments and be taxable to you. Ordinary periodic payments are taxable when received, whether received in advance or arrears. Under this same rule, the 10 percent limitation applies to advance payments but not to delinquent installment payments. For example, if under decree of divorce you are to receive a total payment of $13,000 in thirteen annual installments, each payment regularly received will be taxable as a periodic alimony payment. But if your spouse becomes delinquent in one year and pays $2,000 in the following year, the $2,000 is taxable when received. However, if your spouse pays $1,000 as a regular annual payment and pays an additional $1,000 in advance, the taxable amount will be only $1,300 (10 percent of the principal sum).

The Tax Reform Act of 1984 made several significant changes in domestic relations taxation. Under prior law, gain generally was recognized on transfers of property in exchange for the release of marital claims. The Reform Act provides that transfers of property between spouses that are incident to divorce will generally be nontaxable, carryover basis transactions. This means that your spouse, who takes property from you incident to divorce, will have the same basis in that property that you had.

This provision of the Act applies to transfers after the date of the enactment (July 18, 1984), but not to transfers pursuant to instruments in

---

9. A married couple living in the same house are not separated and living apart as a *matter of law*. See *Hertsch*, T. C. Memo 1982–109 Par. 57,684; also see *Washington*, 77 T.C. No. 44; but for a contrary decision in the 8th Circuit, see *Sydnes* 78–2 U.S.T.C. Par. 9487, 42 AFTR 2d 78-5143.

effect on that date unless both parties elect to have the provisions apply. You and your spouse may, in addition, elect to have the provisions apply just to all transfers after December 31, 1983.

Moreover, the above rules for taxation of *alimony* have been changed significantly for agreements executed after 1984. The section on alimony starting on page 93 details these provisions.

If the alimony is taxable to the recipient under the above rules, that same amount can be used by the payer as a deduction for adjusted gross income, even if you do not itemize deductions. Child-support payments are never deductible nor are they ever included in the gross income of the recipient. The amount of child support included in the payments should be clearly designated as such by the decree or written separation agreement. Note, however, that a payment, even one clearly delineated as alimony, will not be considered or treated as alimony if the payment is reduced (a) on the happening of a contingency relating to a child of the payor or (b) at a time that can clearly be associated with such a contingency. For this purpose, a contingency relates to a child of the payor if it depends upon any event relating to that child, regardless of whether such event is certain or likely to occur. Events that relate to a child of the payor include the following: the child's attaining a specified age or income level, dying, marrying, leaving school, leaving the spouse's household, or gaining employment.

There are two situations, described below, in which payments that would otherwise qualify as alimony or separate maintenance payments will be treated as arising out of a contingency relating to a child of the payor. The first situation is when the payments are to be reduced not more than six months before or after the date that the child is to attain the age of 18, 21, or local age of majority. The second situation is when the payments are to be reduced on two or more occasions that occur not more than one year before or after a different child of the payor spouse attains a certain age between the ages of 18 and 24, inclusive. The certain age referred to in the preceding sentence must be the same for each child, but need not be a whole number of years.

The presumption in the two situations described above that payments are to be reduced at a time clearly associated with the happening of a contingency relating to a child of the payor may be rebutted by showing that the time at which the payments are to be reduced was determined independently of any contingencies relating to the children of the payor. The presumption in the first situation will be rebutted conclusively if the reduction is a complete cessation of alimony or separate maintenance payments during the sixth post-separation year or upon the expiration of a 72-month period. The presumption may also be rebutted in other circumstances, for example, by showing that alimony payments are to be made for a period customarily provided in the local jurisdiction, such as a period equal to one-half of the duration of the marriage.

For example, assume husband and wife are divorced on July 1, 1985, when their children—daughter (born July 15, 1970) and son (born September 23, 1972)—are 14 and 12, respectively. Under the divorce decree, husband is to make alimony payments to wife of $2,000 per month. Such payments are to be reduced to $1,500 per month on January 1, 1991, and to $1,000 per month on January 1, 1995. On January 1, 1991, the date of the first reduction in payments, daughter will be 20 years, 5 months, and 17 days old. On January 1, 1995, the date of the second reduction in payments, son will be 22 years, 3 months, and 9 days old. Each of the reductions in payments is to occur not more than one year before or after a different child of husband attains the age of 21 years and 4 months. Actually, the reductions are to occur not more than one year before or after daughter and son attain any of the ages of 21 years, 3 months, and 9 days through 21 years, 5 months, and 17 days. Accordingly, the reductions will be presumed to clearly be associated with the happening of the contingency relating to daughter and son. Unless this presumption is rebutted, payments under the divorce decree equal to the sum of the reductions ($1,000 per month) will be treated as fixed for the support of the children of husband and therefore will not qualify as alimony or separate maintenance payments.

Where payments constituting both alimony and child support are made but constitute less than the required amount each year, the payments are considered first to cover child support, with any excess deemed to be alimony.

The excludability of lump-sum alimony and child-support payments provides another avenue for sophisticated tax planning and negotiation. Remember, if the alimony payments are excludable, they are not deductible to the payer. The person making the alimony payments would clearly favor a divorce settlement that includes provisions for deductible alimony payments. On the other hand, the recipient would prefer that the payments do not qualify as includable income. If the payer is in a higher tax bracket than the recipient, both parties may benefit, after taxes, by increasing the payments and constructing them so that they qualify after taxes as "periodic."

For example, assume a husband and wife with no children are in the process of reaching a divorce agreement. If the wife is in a 15 percent tax bracket and the husband is in a 28 percent tax bracket, then $10,000 shifted from property settlement to alimony would produce a net savings of $1,300 [$10,000 × (28 percent minus 15 percent)]. Here again, the husband could pay the wife's taxes and share the $1,300 net savings, and both parties would still be ahead on an aftertax basis.

The same kind of planning can be used with child support. If the recipient is in a higher bracket than the payer, it is a good idea to negotiate for an increase in the amount designated as child support (excludable/ nondeductible) in exchange for a reduction in periodic alimony payments (includable/deductible). If the payer is in a higher bracket, increase the amount of includable/deductible alimony in exchange for a reduction in child support.

# 27

## Life Insurance (Sec. 101)

Life insurance proceeds paid to you because of the death of the insured are not taxable unless the policy was purchased by you or transferred to you for a price. This is true even if the proceeds are paid under an accident or health insurance policy or an endowment contract.

If the death benefits are paid to you in a lump sum rather than at regular intervals, they are included in your gross income only if they are more than the amount originally specified as payable at the time of the insured person's death. If the benefit payable at death was not specified, you include the benefit payments in income when they are more than the present value of the payments at the time of death.

If you receive life insurance proceeds in regular installments, you may exclude part of each installment from your income. To determine the excludable part, you must divide the amount held by the insurance company (generally, the total lump sum, the principal, payable at the death of the insured party) by the number of installments that are to be paid. Anything over this excludable part must be included as interest income.

There was one special exception: If insurance proceeds were payable to you after the death of your spouse, and you received the proceeds in installments, you could have excluded up to $1,000 a year of the interest included in the installments in addition to the part of each installment that was excludable as a recovery of the lump sum payable at death. Even if you remarried, you could have continued to take the exclusion. This provision, however, was repealed by the Tax Reform Act of 1986, effective for deaths occurring after the date of enactment (October 22, 1986).

Under current law, if you leave the proceeds from life insurance on deposit with an insurance company under an agreement to pay interest only, the interest paid to you is taxable.

There is an exception to the general rule that life insurance proceeds are excluded from income. This exception is applicable to a life insurance contract that has been transferred for a fee to another individual, who assumes ownership rights. Upon receipt of the proceeds, that individual must include as income the difference between the proceeds and the amount he or she paid for it, plus any premiums paid. For example, assume person A owns an insurance policy in the face amount of $10,000 upon the life of person B and subsequently sells the policy to you for $2,000. When B dies, you receive the proceeds of $10,000. The amount that you can exclude from gross income is limited to $2,000 plus any premiums you paid after the transfer.

There are, however, four exceptions to this rule. These are transfers to:

A partner of the insured
A partnership in which the insured is a partner
A corporation in which the insured is an officer or shareholder
A transferee whose basis in the policy is determined by reference to the transferror's basis

This last item translates into a basic exception for policies that are transferred as part of a tax-free exchange—for example, a transfer of insurance policies to a corporation by its controlling shareholders in exchange for the corporation's stock or securities.

## F  Schedule of Excludable Items

Accident and health insurance premiums paid by your employer
Accident and health proceeds (under insurance purchased by you or under an employee-supported plan) not attributable to a previous medical expense deduction
Annuities (cost excluded over life expectancies)

Awards for noncompetitive achievements (if contributed)

Bequests and devises

Carpool receipts for transportation of fellow employees

Child-support payments received

Contributions paid by your employer to accident and health plans and to sickness and disability funds under sick-benefit laws

Damages for alienation of affection, breach of promise, personal injuries or sickness, or slander or libel against personal reputation

Dependent care, employer-provided services

Disability payments other than for loss of wages

Disability payments under employer-financed accident and health plans

Employee death benefits up to $5,000 paid by or on behalf of employer

Endowment policy proceeds until cost is recovered

Fellowship and scholarship grants (limited)

Gain on sale of personal residence if you are age 55 or older

Gifts

Group term life insurance premiums—if coverage is $50,000 or less or if employees' contribution premiums exceed the cost of coverage over $50,000

Health insurance proceeds not attributable to medical expense deductions in prior years

Inheritances

Interest on bonds of the state, city, or other political subdivision

Life insurance proceeds paid on the death of the insured under the terms of the contract, unless paid to a transferee

Medical care payments under employer-financed accident and health plans

Merchandise distributed to employees on holidays

Nobel Prize, Pulitzer Prize, and similar awards (if contributed)

Railroad passes to employees and their families

Sickness and injury benefits equivalent to workmen's compensation

Social Security and disability benefits

Supper money paid by employer

Tuition paid by employer

Welfare payments

# CHAPTER 4

# Credits— Dollar-for-Dollar Tax Reductions

*"Taxing is an easy business."*

EDMUND BURKE
*Thoughts on the Cause of the Present Discontent*
1770

A *credit* is a dollar-for-dollar reduction in your tax; it is the best kind of expense to have. If you are in the 33 percent tax bracket, a deduction of $100 saves you $33 in tax, but a credit of $100 saves you $100 in tax. A credit, therefore, is a payment that counts in full as an offset to your tax liability. Because every dollar of credit is really an additional dollar in your pocket, it is imperative that you recognize those situations where credits are available and that you always claim them on your tax return. A lost or forgotten credit is money thrown away in tax dollars.

There are several areas in which potential credits are available. I shall examine each in turn and discuss the ways you can best take advantage of them. But first I want to detail two significant cash-saving techniques: estimating taxes and withholding exemptions.

## A  Estimated Tax and Withholding Exemptions

Significant savings can be realized by minimizing the amount of estimated tax payments or of taxes withheld from your income before they are actually due. You must pay estimated tax if your estimated total tax liability is more than $500 and you meet certain conditions (see below), but you still can minimize these payments. You should pay as little estimated tax as possible and therefore have the use and availability of these tax funds for as long as legally possible.

You need to pay estimated tax if your estimated tax liability is more than $500 and:

1. your expected gross income includes more than $500 in income not subject to withholding; *or*

2. your expected gross income is more than:

    a) $20,000 if you are single, a head of household, or surviving spouse; *or*

    b) $20,000 if you are married and might file a joint declaration, and your spouse has not received wages; *or*

    c) $10,000 if you are married and might file a joint declaration, and both you and your spouse have received wages; *or*

    d) $5,000 if you are married and might not file a joint declaration.

Estimated tax normally is paid in quarterly installments. You need *not file* a declaration of estimated tax after 1982 but payments must still be made. There is a penalty, which cannot be deducted as interest, of about 10 percent (this rate changes every 3 months) per year for underpaying the estimated tax—unless the total of all payments ("including withholding") made by the due date of each quarter is at least as much as the smallest of the following figures:

- The amount that you would have paid if the estimated tax were the same as the previous year's tax liability, provided the preceding taxable year was a year of 12 months and you filed a return.

- The amount you would have paid if the estimated tax were 90 percent of the tax on your income up to the month in which the installment date falls. For this purpose, the income is *annualized* (computed at an annual rate), based upon taxable income before exemptions, if deductions are itemized, and the alternative minimum tax if applicable.

The first exception is most advantageous when your current year's income is greater than that of the prior year. The last exception is most useful if the greater part of income is received in the later part of the year. In all cases the objective is to pay no more now than is required. Remember, while you may have to pay the tax on April 15, you will have had the use of the money and the interest earned on it during that interim period.

This same pay-as-you-go aspect of the federal income tax system requires your employers to withhold income tax on compensation (salaries, wages, tips) paid to you as their employee. The amount of tax withheld by your employer depends upon the amount of salary or wages paid to you and the information you furnish on the W–4 form (the Employee's Withholding Allowance Certificate) that you file with your employer. If you had no income tax liability for the past year and expect to have no tax liability for the current year, you may claim exemption from withholding of income tax. If you are exempt, your employer will not withhold federal income tax from your wages. To claim exemption from withholding, you still must give your employer a completed W–4 form. On it you need to write "exempt" and no withholding will be taken from your wages.

The money-saving technique recommended here is the same as that with the estimated tax. The objective is to minimize the amount of withholding taken out of each paycheck so that you will have the use and interest on the money until the final tax payment is due. There is no penalty on underwithholding as long as the total amount withheld for the year is equal to either 90 percent of your final tax liability or 100 percent of your last year's tax liability, whichever is smaller.

Unfortunately, most Americans do not underwithhold; they actually *overwithhold*. In 1981, 70 million Americans—fully 80 percent of the taxpayers affected by withholding—had too much money taken from their paychecks. While the Internal Revenue Service eventually returns all excess funds, the taxpayer loses the interest that the money would have generated during the time that it is in the hands of the government. In periods of high inflation, this is no insignificant loss, especially when one considers that the overwithholding averages approximately $700 per taxpayer. In 1982, over $75.2 billion were paid in refunds!

How then can you eliminate overwithholding—even better, how can you begin underwithholding? The first step is to get a W–4 form from your employer and see how many allowances you are currently claiming. Each allowance that you claim will reduce the amount that is withheld from your income.

Allowances are available for the following:

- You get an automatic allowance for each exemption you can claim on your tax—for yourself, your spouse, and your dependents.

- You get a special withholding allowance if you are single and have only one employer, or if you are married and have only one employer and your spouse is not employed.

- You get additional withholding allowances for the estimated tax credits you expect to take. If you expect to take the earned income credit, credit for child and dependent care expenses, or credit for the elderly, these credits may lower your tax and therefore make you eligible for additional allowances.

- You get additional withholding allowances for employee business expenses, moving expenses, and if you qualify for the additional standard deduction for the aged or the blind.

- You get additional withholding allowances for estimated net losses from your business or profession, from capital losses, from losses on rental property, and losses from farming expenses.

- You can get a special withholding allowance for potential contributions to an IRA.

- You can get additional withholding allowances if you expect to itemize your deductions and/or pay alimony during the year. (Section 3402 (F))

You can use creative accounting especially in these last areas. The key is expected, not actual, deductions, contributions, and losses. Additional allowances can always be claimed under the *expectation* of making charitable contributions, incurring higher medical expenses, or borrowing money and incurring an increase in interest expense. Additional withholding allowances are not permitted for anticipated tax credits as well. But be careful not to go overboard: If your total withholdings exceed last year's taxes or 90 percent of this year's taxes, you are immune from any penalties or interest. Under Reg. Sec. 31, 3420 (i)-2, employers must accede to an employee's request that withholdings be increased. Note that if you have more than ten withholding exemptions, your employer must notify the IRS of the fact.

The advantages of reducing your withholdings can be significant. For example, if you earn $20,000 a year and are single, one additional allowance that you claim reduces the withholding taken from your salary by about $30 per month. That adds up to $360 a year. With five additional allowances, you have the use and interest on $1,500 every year.

You may file a new W–4 form at any time if you wish to change your withholding allowances for any reason. This gives you yet another opportunity for tax savings. Some sophisticated, tax-knowledgeable individuals significantly underwithhold on their income for the first eleven months of the year, file amended W–4 forms and then significantly overwithhold in the final taxable month. A cooperative employer even may withhold your full final month's wages so that your total yearly withholding meets the 90 percent or 100 percent tests detailed above and you can avoid the penalty for underwithholding. In the meantime, you have had the use and interest on the underwithheld amount. Sadly, the Internal Revenue Service does not pay any interest on any amount overwithheld. In effect, overwithholding is nothing more than granting an interest-free loan to the Internal Revenue Service. Better that the interest is in your pocket.

# B  Credits

The remainder of this chapter discusses specific credits that can be taken to reduce your taxes due. Please take advantage of them.

# 28

## The Earned Income Credit (Sec. 32)

Under the Tax Reform Act of 1986, you may be entitled to a refundable credit of up to $800 if your earned income and your adjusted gross income are less than $17,000. This tax credit is 14 percent of the first $5,714 of earned income (maximum credit of $800). This credit will be phased down as income rises above $9,000, and no credit will be allowed if income is over $17,000. Furthermore, the credit will not be available to individuals subject to the alternative minimum tax.

A refundable credit is the best kind of credit to have. This credit may reduce your tax below zero and give you a refund even where no tax has been paid or withheld. Its purpose is to ease the tax burden on low-income taxpayers and to encourage individuals to find employment. Even if your income is so low that you are not required to file a return, you should always file if you can get a refund.

Earned income is mainly wages, salaries, and tips, but it also includes strike benefits and any other employee compensation (for services) you receive. It does not include pensions, annuities, or other kinds of income that are not essentially related to service compensation. For example, capital gains do not count as earned income. If you have your own business, your net earnings must be included in earned income. Losses from your business reduce your earned income.

There are five eligibility requirements for the earned income credit:

1. You must live in a home in the United States for the whole year. This home has to be the main home for you and at least one of your dependent children. If you file as head of household, your child must live with you; if your child is married, you must be able to claim the child as your dependent.

2. You must have a child—whether natural, adopted, or through marriage. A child placed with you by an authorized placement agency for legal adoption is your child.

3. You must not be entitled to exclude from your gross income any income that is earned from foreign countries or U.S. possessions.

4. You must have a full 12-month tax year.

5.  You must file a joint return if you are married.

If the placement or adoption of your child took place during the year, or if you gained a stepchild through marriage during the year, the whole-year home requirement will be satisfied also, as long as your home was this child's home from the date of adoption, placement, or marriage through the end of the year. In addition, a foster child who lived with you for the whole year also qualifies. However, if that child's natural or adoptive parents provided more than half of the child's support for that tax year, you may not claim the child as yours.

The earned income credit represents dollars in your pocket, but it must be claimed to be received. In effect, it is a form of negative income tax—that is, a refundable credit for taxpayers who do not even have a tax liability. If you are eligible, you may elect to receive advance payments of the earned income credit from your employer rather than from the Internal Revenue Service next year when you file your tax return. To make this election, you must file a certificate of eligibility with your employer and file a tax return for the year the income is earned. Again, the tax advantage here is the use of the money during the year and the potential interest that could be earned on it. If you think that you may be eligible for the earned income credit, immediately speak to your employer and file a certificate of eligibility. Not doing so would be another instance of making an interest-free loan to the Internal Revenue Service.

# 29

## Excess Social Security Tax

If you work for two or more employers during the tax year, too much social security tax may be withheld from your wages. You may claim this excess amount as a credit against your income tax.

Your social security tax obligation is computed each year by applying a fixed rate to your wages. There is, however, a maximum wage base (which is subject to change) to which this tax may be applied. For example, in 1987 all wages in excess of $45,000 will not be subject to social security tax. Therefore, if you work for two employers, earning $45,000 from each, both employers will take the maximum social security (7.51 percent $\times$ $45,000, or $3,379.50) from your wages. But because you are only liable for a maximum payment of $3,379.50, you can have a credit against your income tax for the additional $3,379.50 subtracted from your wages. This is money you should get back. Even if you owe no taxes, excess social security payments will be refunded to you.

# 30

## The Child and Dependent Care Credit

Congress has attempted to ease the tax burden of those citizens who must pay for dependent care while earning a living by allowing a child care credit. If, in order to work, you incur expenses in connection with the care of certain dependents, you are permitted a credit for those expenses. This credit, unlike the earned income credit or excess social security payments, cannot reduce your tax liability below zero—that is, it is not refundable.

To qualify for this credit:

1. Your child and dependent care expenses must be incurred to allow you to work, full-time or part-time, whether for others or in your own business or partnership. "Work" even includes actively looking for work. Furthermore, your spouse is considered to have worked if he or she:

   a) was a full-time student for five months during the tax year; *or*

   b) is physically or mentally unable to function without supervision or aid.

   This rule applies to only one spouse for any one month.

2. You must have income from work during the year. Unpaid volunteer work or work for a nominal salary does not qualify.

3. You must maintain a home in which you and one or more qualifying persons live. This means that you (and your spouse, if you are married) pay more than half the cost of maintaining your principal residence. If you are married, you and your spouse must live together.

Upkeep expenses normally include property taxes, mortgage interest, rent, utility charges, home repairs, insurance on the home, and food costs. Excluded from upkeep are payments for clothing, education, medical treatment, vacations, life insurance, transportation, mortgage principle, or the purchase, improvement, or replacement of property. For example, the cost of replacing a water heater is not considered upkeep, but the cost of repairing a water heater can be included.

A qualifying person is:

a) your dependent under age 15 for whom you may claim a personal exemption;

b) your dependent (or any person you could have claimed as a dependent if that person had not earned gross income of $1,000 or more) who is physically or mentally not able to care for himself or herself; *or*

c) your spouse, if physically or mentally unable to care for himself or herself.

The physical or mental incapacity must be disabling. People who are not able to dress, clean, or feed themselves because of physical or mental problems require constant attention to prevent them from injuring themselves or others.

Qualification is determined on a daily basis when the disability lasts for less than a calendar month. For example, if a dependent or spouse for whom you paid work-related expenses no longer qualifies on September 16, you may include in your computation all work-related expenses through September 15.

# 31

## Child Care Credits for Children of Divorced or Separated Parents

Expenses for the care of children of divorced or separated parents are also allowed for the above child care credit under certain conditions. If you are divorced, legally separated under a decree of divorce or separate maintenance, or separated under a written separation agreement, and you have custody of your child for a longer time during the calendar year than the other parent, your child qualifies if certain conditions are met.

To qualify, *all* these criteria must be met:

1. The child must be under age 15 and unable to care for himself or herself.

2.  The child must be in the custody of one or both of the parents for more than half the year.

3.  One or both of the parents must provide more than half of the child's support during the year.

4.  You must normally file a joint return if you are married. If you are legally separated from your spouse under a decree of divorce or separate maintenance, you are not considered married but can still file for child care credit. The credit may be claimed on a separate return. If you are married and file a separate return, you will not be considered married if:

    a)  your home is the home of a qualifying person for more than half the tax year; *and*

    b)  you pay more than half the cost of keeping up your home for the tax year; *and*

    c)  your spouse does not live in your home for the last six months of the year.

5.  You must pay someone other than your spouse or a person you can claim as a dependent for the child's care. You may count payments made to relatives who are not your dependents, even if they live in your home.

Only work-related expenses qualify for the child or dependent care credit, and your expenses must be for the well-being and protection of a qualifying person. Expenses are considered to be work-related if they allow you (and your spouse, if married) to work, not if you incur them while you are working. However, whether the purpose of the expenses is to allow you to work depends upon the facts. Work-related expenses may include the following:

## HOME EXPENSES

This covers the cost of ordinary services done in and around your home that are necessary to maintain the well-being and protection of a qualifying person. The services of a housekeeper, maid, or cook usually are considered necessary to run your home if performed at least partly for the benefit of the qualifying person. Payments for the services of a chauffeur or gardener are not included. The expense of food, clothing, education, or entertainment for the qualifying person is not included.

## CHILD CARE EXPENSES

These expenses are not limited to services performed in your home. You may include expenses for nursery school or day care for preschool children, or even summer camp (*ZOLTAN* 79 TC 1982) if these expenses allow you to work. The Revenue Act of 1987 excludes overnight camp expanses, but summer day camp expenses are still allowable. Amounts you pay for food, clothing, or schooling are not child care expenses. However, if a nursery school or day-care center provides these as part of its service, the entire cost is treated as child care. Schooling in the first grade or higher is not treated as part of child care. Neither is the cost of getting your child to and from the center, whether by bus, subway, taxi, or private care, unless the cost is included in the tuition and is not billed separately (IRS Letter Ruling 8303037).

## DISABLED SPOUSE OR DEPENDENT CARE EXPENSES

Expenditures for out-of-home, noninstitutional care of a disabled spouse or dependent who regularly spends at least eight hours a day in your home are eligible for the credit. Under prior law, services outside the home qualified only if they involved the care of a child under 15 years of age.

Meals and lodging provided for housekeepers may be added to your child care expenses, and also any added expenses for lodging your housekeeper. For example, if you have moved to an apartment with an extra bedroom for a housekeeper, you may include the added rent and utility expenses for this bedroom.

The *child care credit,* whether for married, divorced, or separated parents, provides a significant opportunity for effective tax planning. For example, if you have an elderly parent whom you wish to help support, money that you give for food may result in a gift tax liability for you. But if you have this parent baby-sit for your childen so that you can work, not only will you avoid a potential gift tax penalty on the money you pay that parent, but you will also receive an income tax credit. Furthermore, if that parent eats at your home while providing child care services, you will receive a tax credit for the value of the food eaten—and the value of that food will *not* be taxable income to your parent.

For example, assume you have your mother provide child care to your son so that you may work, and your mother eats $100 worth of food per week. Even if you pay her nothing in dollars, her income tax is unaffected, your gift tax is unaffected, but your income tax will be reduced by a $20–$30 credit for each week she qualifies.

There are limits on the amount of work-related expenses you may use to figure your credit. These are the earned income limit and the dollar limit.

1. **The earned income limit.**

   If you are single at the end of your tax year, the amount of work-related expenses that you may use to figure your credit may not be more than your earned income for the tax year. If you are married at the end of your tax year, the amount of work-related expenses may not be more than your earned income or the earned income of your spouse, whichever is *less*.

   If you are married and, for any month, your spouse is either a full-time student or not able to provide self-maintenance, your spouse is considered to have an earned income of $200 a month (if there is one qualifying person in your home) or $400 a month (if there are two or more qualifying persons in your home). That disabled spouse is counted as a qualifying person, along with a dependent child. This rule applies to only one spouse for any one month.

   Earned income is all wages, salaries, tips, other employee compensation, fees for professional services and net earnings from self-employment. It is reduced by any net loss in earnings from self-employment. It does not include pensions, annuities, or payments for your services that were distributions of earnings and profits, other than a reasonable amount for your work for a corportion. In addition, it does not include amounts received under accident or health plans that are not included in your gross income.

2. **The dollar limit.**

   The child and dependent care credit is computed on a three-tier basis. First, if you have an adjusted gross income of $10,000 or less, you are entitled to a credit equal to 30 percent of your work-related expenses. Then, the credit is reduced by 1 percentage point for each $2,000 of adjusted gross income (or fraction thereof) above $10,000. Finally, if you have an adjusted gross income of over $28,000, the credit is equal to 20 percent of the work-related expenses you paid during your tax year.

The maximum amount of work-related expenses to which you can apply the credit is $2,400 for one qualifying child or dependent, or $4,800 if more than one is involved. Thus, the maximum credit for one qualifying individual ranges from $720, if your income is below $10,000 ($2,400 × .30), to $480 if your income exceeds $28,000 ($2,400 × .20). Similarly, the maximum credit for two or more qualified individuals ranges from $1,440 to $960.

The following table outlines maximum credits available under the current rule:

| | | Maximum Credit | |
| Adjusted Gross Income | Applicable Percentage | One Qualifying Individual | Two or More Qualifying Individuals |
| --- | --- | --- | --- |
| Up to $10,000 | 30% | $720 | $1,440 |
| 10,001–12,000 | 29% | 696 | 1,392 |
| 12,001–14,000 | 28% | 672 | 1,344 |
| 14,001–16,000 | 27% | 648 | 1,296 |
| 16,001–18,000 | 26% | 624 | 1,248 |
| 18,001–20,000 | 25% | 600 | 1,200 |
| 20,001–22,000 | 24% | 576 | 1,152 |
| 22,001–24,000 | 23% | 552 | 1,104 |
| 24,001–26,000 | 22% | 528 | 1,056 |
| 26,001–28,000 | 21% | 504 | 1,008 |
| 28,001 and over | 20% | 480 | 960 |

This chart has been reproduced with permission from Economic Recovery Tax Act of 1981, published and copyrighted by Commerce Clearing House, Inc., 4025 W. Peterson Avenue, Chicago, Illinois 60646.

These figures are yearly limits. You use the $2,400 limit if you had one qualifying person at *any time* during the year. You use $4,800 if you had more than one at *any time* during the year. It is not based on the length of time during the year that your dependent qualified. However, include only the expenses you had for a qualifying person *during the time the person is qualified.* For example, if your child turned 15 in April, you are eligible for the entire

$2,400 limit, but only the expenses you had before your child's 15th birthday can be used. If you had expenses of less than $2,400 during that time, only the smaller amount can be used.

The following example shows you how the child care credit is computed. Assume you are a widow and that you maintain a home for yourself and your two preschool children, whom you claim as dependents. You had an earned income of $28,000 for the year and you incurred work-related expenses of $4,000 (for a housekeeper to care for your children in your home) and $1,200 (for child care at a nursery school).
Your credit is computed as follows:

| | | |
|---|---|---:|
| 1. | In-home child care expenses | $4,000 |
| 2. | Plus outside child care expenses | +1,200 |
| 3. | Total work-related expenses | $5,200 |
| 4. | Maximum allowable expenses for two qualifying children | 4,800 |
| 5. | Multiply by credit rate | ✕ .20 |
| 6. | Amount of credit | $960 |

Alternatively, assume you are married and have two children. You have an earned income of $28,000, and your spouse was a full-time student from January 2 through May 31 only. If you paid a housekeeper $450 a month from January 2 to May 31 (a total of $2,250) to look after your children, prepare meals, and do housework as time allowed, your credit is figured in this way:

| | | |
|---|---|---:|
| 1. | Total work-related expenses | $2,250 |
| 2. | Your earned income | 28,000 |
| 3. | Income considered earned by your spouse ($400/month for five months) | 2,000 |
| 4. | Multiply by credit rate | ✕ .20 |
| 5. | Allowable credit | $ 400 |

Remember: Work-related expenses cannot exceed either the $2,400 (for one child)/$4,800 (for two or more) limit *or* your own or your spouse's earned income, and you must use the smaller earned income in your computations.

# 32    Credit for the Elderly

To compensate for tax exclusions offered to recipients of social security benefits, this tax credit is offered to those taxpayers who are not covered by social security and spend their retirement years living off of past savings and investments. In this way, the credit attempts to help place all elderly taxpayers on a par.

Prior law provided that individuals aged 65 or over, or under 65 with income from a public retirement system, were eligible for a credit equal to 15 percent of the base amount. Beginning in 1984, the law increased the base amounts and limits the credit for those under age 65 to individuals with a permanent and total disability who received disability income from public or private employers on account of that disability. The change in base amounts is as follows:

| Description | Prior Law | New Law |
| --- | --- | --- |
| Married with one spouse eligible, or unmarried | $2,500 | $5,000 |
| Married, joint return, both spouses eligible | $3,750 | $7,500 |
| Married, filing separately | $1,875 | $3,750 |

These base amounts *are reduced*, however, by the following:

- Pensions or annuities received under Social Security, Railroad Retirement, and certain other pensions and annuities otherwise excluded from gross income; *and*

- One-half of adjusted gross income over:
  $ 7,500—single return
  $10,000—married, joint return
  $ 5,000—married, separate return

In the case of an individual under age 65, the base amount is limited in any event to the amount of his or her disability income. Note that under the Social Security Amendments in 1983, for a married disabled individual filing jointly, one spouse eligible, all disability income will be taxable and no tax credit will be available if adjusted gross income is $20,000 or more.

There are few tax planning strategies that can be employed with the retirement income credit except to note its existence and the fact that it must be claimed to be received. Any failure to recognize or to claim it represents little more than cutting a hole in your wallet and allowing your tax dollars to float freely in the wind.

# 33

## Credit for Interest Paid on Mortgage Credit Certificates

State and eligible local governments were authorized through 1987 to issue tax-exempt qualified mortgage bonds under Code Section 103A to provide financing for the purchase of a principal residence of a taxpayer. For calendar years 1984 through 1987, the governmental entity may elect to issue revocable mortgage credit certificates (MCCs) under a qualified mortgage credit certificate program to certain home buyers instead of issuing qualified mortgage bonds.

A qualifying home buyer who receives an MCC then arranges financing through conventional sources to acquire a personal residence without the use of tax-exempt obligations. Such indebtedness must be incurred before the close of the second calendar year following the calendar year for which the governmental entity makes the election, and only one MCC may be in effect for any residence at any given time.

An MCC entitles the home buyer–taxpayer to a nonrefundable personal credit for the applicable percentage of interest paid during any tax year during which the certificate is in effect. An MCC is in effect for interest attributable to the period beginning on the date the certificate is issued until either (a) it is revoked by the issuing authorities or (b) the taxpayer sells the residence or it ceases to be the taxpayer's personal residence.

No credit is allowed for any interest paid or accrued to a related person. The certificate credit rate specified in the MCC may range from 10 percent through 50 percent. *Certified indebtedness amount* means the amount of indebtedness specified in the MCC that (a) is incurred by the taxpayer in order to provide financing on the taxpayer's principal residence and (b) is issued to the taxpayer for the acquisition, qualified rehabilitation, or qualified home improvement of the taxpayer's principal residence. However, if the certificate rate exceeds 20 percent, the maximum credit is limited to $2,000. For example, if you receive a 50 percent MCC and pay $5,000 in mortgage interest, the amount of credit is limited to $2,000, and the remaining $3,000 ($5,000 interest paid less $2,000 credit) may be claimed as an itemized interest deduction.

The MCC program must be established by a state or eligible local government entity for a calendar year for which it is authorized to issue qualified mortgage bonds.

## C  Special Energy Conservation Credits

In the past, Congress has provided a number of tax incentives to encourage energy saving and the development of alternative energy sources. There are two residential energy credits in particular, each with its own conditions and limits. One credit is based on expenditures for home energy conservation, and the other on expenditures for property for renewable energy sources. If you did not take them when eligible, you can still file amended returns to take them now.

# 34

### Home Energy Conservation Costs (Sec. 23)

Credit for home energy conservation costs is available to you not only if you own a home but also if you rent and pay for the qualifying items. The home in which you install the qualified energy-saving items must be your main home, and it must be located in the United States. Furthermore, the home must have been substantially completed before April 20, 1977. For these purposes, a home is considered your main home for thirty days before you live in it.

The energy-saving items that you install must have been new, must be expected to last at least three years, and must meet performance and quality standards set by the Secretary of the Treasury. Qualifying energy-saving items are limited to the following:

- Insulation designed to reduce heat loss or heat gain in your home or your water heater.

- Storm or thermal windows or doors for the exterior of your home.

- Caulking or weather stripping of your exterior doors or windows.

- Clock thermostats or other automatic energy-reducing thermostats.

- Furnace modifications designed to increase fuel efficiency, including replacement burners, modified flue openings, and ignition systems that replace a gas pilot light.

- Meters that display the cost of energy use.

Items that do not qualify for the credit include heat pumps, fluorescent lights, wood- or peat-burning stoves, replacement boilers and furnaces, and hydrogen-fueled equipment.

The credit is equal to 15 percent of the first $2,000 you spend on qualified items to save energy in your home. The energy-saving items costing the first $2000 do not all have to be installed in a single year. Furthermore, a new $2,000 limit applies if you move to a second home. This is the case even if you spent $2,000 for energy conservation costs on your previous home. The $2,000 limit applies to each main home in which you live. This credit expired at the end of 1985, but can be claimed on amended returns through April 15, 1989, if you were entitled to such credits and did not claim them in prior years.

# 35

## Renewable Energy Source Costs (Sec. 23)

You may receive an *additional* energy credit for amounts you spent on solar, wind-powered, or geothermal property for your home. You figure this credit by taking 40 percent of the first $10,000 of these costs. An item qualifies when the original installation of the property is completed. As in the case of energy conservation costs, the full $10,000 limit on renewable energy source costs may be spread over several tax years, and a new $10,000 limit applies to each main home you live in during the period of the credit.

The renewable energy source equipment, such as solar collectors, windmills, or geothermal wells, must have been installed for use with your main home, which must be located in the United States. Unlike the credit for energy conservation costs, you could claim the credit for equipment installed for use with new as well as existing homes. It does not matter when your home was constructed, as long as the renewable energy source property was installed after April 19, 1977.

However, if renewable energy source property was installed during the construction or reconstruction of your home, the property qualifies for the credit from the time you start living in the new or reconstructed home. But if you reoccupy a reconstructed home that you have lived in as your main home before the reconstruction, the renewable energy source property is eligible for the credit when it was installed. "Reconstruction" is the replacement of most of the major structures of a home, such as floors, walls, and ceilings. For purposes of this credit, a home is considered your main home for 30 days before you live in it.

In order for renewable energy source property to qualify, it must have been new, be expected to last at least five years, and meet certain performance and quality standards set by the Secretary of the Treasury. The cost of the renewable energy source equipment includes labor properly allocatable to the on-site preparation, assembly, and installation of the equipment.

Renewable energy source property includes the following:

- Solar energy equipment for heating or cooling your home or for providing hot water for use within the home.

- Wind energy equipment for generating electricity or other forms of energy for personal home use.

- Geothermal energy equipment.

Your energy credit must be at least $10 in any one year before you can claim it. In addition, the credit may not be more than your tax. However, you may carry over an unused credit to the next tax year, and it may continue to be carried over to later tax years, through 1987.

These two residential energy tax credits provided you with an excellent opportunity to have the Internal Revenue Service subsidize a substantial part of your energy conservation expenditures. Potentially, up to $4,300 worth of such costs [($2,000 × .15) + ($10,000 × .40) + ($8,000 × .20)] could be paid for by the Internal Revenue Service in direct-credit tax reductions, if these energy tax credits are properly taken. What could be better than saving money on your heating or cooling bills and having the Internal Revenue Service partially finance the costs?

Unfortunately, this credit also expired at the end of 1985, but you can file an amended return through April 15, 1989, if you were entitled to such credits in prior years and did not claim them.

# CHAPTER 5

# General Deductions

*"Take it off. Take it all off...."*

GYPSY ROSE LEE

## INCOME TAX RATES

| Year | Maximum individual rate |
|------|--------------------------|
| 1914 | 7% |
| 1916 | 15 |
| 1917 | 67 |
| 1918 | 77 |
| 1920 | 65 |
| 1921 | 50 |
| 1924 | 40 |
| 1926 | 25 |
| 1934 | 63 |
| 1936 | 79 |
| 1941 | 81 |
| 1942 | 88 |
| 1944 | 94 |
| 1945 | 91 |
| 1951 | 92 |
| 1954 | 91 |
| 1964 | 77 |
| 1970 | 70 |
| 1981 | 50 |
| 1987 | 38.5 |
| 1988 | 28/33 |

Our tax system is founded on a multistep computation. You begin with gross income. This is *all* income, all accession to wealth, clearly realized, over which you have dominion, less those items defined earlier as tax exclusions. From gross income you then subtract a certain category of expenses called by tax practitioners adjustments or *"above the line" deductions.* A deduction is a reduction of your taxable income—the income base on which your tax is imposed. "Above the line" deductions include trade and business deductions, alimony, reimbursed expenses of employees, IRA, Keogh, and SEP deductions, and employee business expenses of performing artists.

Gross income less adjustments (*"above the line" deductions*) gives your adjusted gross income. From adjusted gross income, you then subtract the greater of your itemized deductions (*"below the line" deductions*) or your standard deduction. The standard deduction is basically similar to the old zero bracket amount. It is different from the zero bracket amount in that it is a deduction from adjusted gross income and not a tax bracket.

Unlike pre-1987 law, if you itemize your deductions you will not be required to reduce your itemized deductions by the amount of the standard deduction (zero bracket amount). Instead, you will deduct 100 percent of your itemized deductions and not take the standard deduction. Therefore, you will only itemize deductions if they exceed the amount of your standard deduction.

For 1987, the standard deduction amounts were as follows:

| | |
|---|---|
| Married taxpayers filing jointly | $3,760 |
| Heads of households | 2,540 |
| Single taxpayers | 2,540 |
| Married taxpayers filing separately | 1,880 |

For taxable years beginning in 1988, the standard deduction amounts are as follows:

| | |
|---|---|
| Married taxpayers filing jointly | $5,000 |
| Heads of households | 4,400 |
| Single taxpayers | 3,000 |
| Married taxpayers filing separately | 2,500 |

Prior to 1987, an additional personal exemption was available if you were 65 or older or blind. (For 1988 tax returns, a taxpayer is deemed to be 65 or older if his or her 65th birthday falls on January 1, 1989, or earlier; one is legally blind if one's central visual activity does not exceed 20/200 in the better eye with corrective lenses, or if the diameter of one's visual field subtends an angle of 20 degrees or less.) This additional personal exemption has been replaced by an increased standard deduction called "the additional amount." If you or your spouse qualified for the age or blindness exemptions under prior law, you will qualify for these additional amounts. The additional amounts are as follows:

1.  $750 for individuals who are not married and not filing as surviving spouses.

2.  $600 for all other taxpayers.

These additional amounts, if available, will be added to the regular standard deduction and treated in the same way as the standard deduction. However, any taxpayer who is the dependent of another taxpayer for purposes of the dependency exemption will have a limited standard deduction. Such a taxpayer's standard deduction will be the greater of either $500 or that individual's earned income up to the amount of the regular standard deduction.

For 1987, it was important to note that the above 1987 standard deduction amounts did *not* apply to taxpayers who were entitled to additional amounts either for age or for blindness. If, in 1987, you or your spouse qualified for the additional amounts for either age or blindness, you should have received such additional amounts plus the benefits of the *1988* standard deduction beginning in that year.

Your tax computation continues with a subtraction for your personal exemptions, leaving a figure called your taxable income. Your tax is based on your taxable income. For the taxable year 1987, the amount of the personal exemption was $1,900. For the taxable year 1988, the amount is $1,950. For taxable years beginning in 1989, the amount will be $2,000. For taxable years beginning in a calendar year after 1989, there will be an inflation adjustment to the exemption amount. This inflation adjustment will be based on the consumer price index for all urban consumers issued by the U.S. Department of Labor.

Table 1. Dollar Values of Deductions Claimed, 1988

| | Single | | | Married Filing Joint Returns and Qualifying Widows and Widowers | | | Married Filing Separate Returns | | | Head of Household | | |
|---|---|---|---|---|---|---|---|---|---|---|---|---|
| | Taxable Income | | Value of Each Dollar of Deductions | Taxable Income | | Value of Each Dollar of Deductions | Taxable Income | | Value of Each Dollar of Deductions | Taxable Income | | Value of Each Dollar of Deductions |
| | Over | But not Over | | Over | But not Over | | Over | But not Over | | Over | But not Over | |
| 1988 | $ 0 | $17,850 | 15¢ | $ 0 | $29,750 | 15¢ | $ 0 | $14,875 | 15¢ | $ 0 | $23,900 | 15¢ |
| | 17,850 | 43,150 | 28¢ | 29,750 | 71,900 | 28¢ | 14,875 | 35,950 | 28¢ | 23,900 | 61,650 | 28¢ |
| | 43,150 | 89,560 | 33¢ | 71,900 | 149,250 | 33¢ | 35,950 | 113,300 | 33¢ | 61,650 | 123,790 | 33¢ |
| | over 89,560 | | 28¢ | over 149,250 | | 28¢ | over 113,000 | | 28¢ | over 123,790 | | 28¢ |

In summary, the process appears as follows:

Gross Income
− Adjustments ("above the line" deductions)
_____
Adjusted Gross Income
− Itemized ("below the line") Deductions or Standard Deduction
_____
(Subtotal)
− Personal Exemptions
_____
Taxable Income

To reduce your tax you must reduce your taxable income. One of the most important things to do, therefore, is to recognize and claim all available deductions. The chart that follows shows the value of every dollar of deductions in terms of dollars saved for each taxpayer classification.

Note that the higher your taxable income, the more valuable the dollar of deductions. This is the result of our progressive tax structure. I will use this structure later to show you how you could reduce your taxes by shifting income from the 33 percent bracket (where you keep only 33¢ from each additional dollar you earn) to the 15 percent bracket (where you keep 85¢ from each additional dollar you earn). But first you must recognize and understand the concept of tax-deductible expenses. In order to do that, you must understand the basic difference between deductions *for* adjusted gross income ("above the line" deductions) and deductions *from* adjusted" gross income ("below the line" deductions).

## A  Deductions for Adjusted Gross Income

There are several categories of deductions for adjusted gross income that you must be aware of to minimize your taxes. We will take each in turn:

## 36  Trade and Business Deductions

All "ordinary and necessary expenses" paid or incurred by you during your taxable year in carrying on any trade or business are allowed as "above the line" deductions.

Here it is very important to understand that the words "ordinary and necessary" are words of art. In order for an expense to be deductible, it need not be absolutely necessary in the sense that you cannot conduct your trade without incurring such an expense. The courts have interpreted the words "ordinary and necessary" to mean "reasonable and customary," and this interpretation has been accepted by the Internal Revenue Service. Therefore, any expenses that you might incur in your business that are reasonable and customary for that business, even if not in any sense necessary, are deductible.

This provides you with an excellent opportunity to convert what would normally be nondeductible personal expenses into deductible business expenses. For example, assume that you have your own trade or business in New York and want to take a vacation in Miami. Alternatively, you could live in Miami and want to vacation in California. Almost all businesses have professional associations or trade groups who conduct seminars or hold meetings in resort areas. If you could schedule your vacation in these areas at the same time as the professional meeting and attend that professional meeting, your travel expenses, subject to the limits discussed in Chapter 8, would be converted from personal expenses into allowable, deductible business expenses. While attendance at these conventions or trade shows might not be necessary to your business, it would be reasonable and customary. Later in the book I will discuss more of these extensive tax advantages for those who own their own business.

# 37

## Employee Business Expenses of Actors and Other Performing Artists

Employee business expenses of actors and other performing artists are deductible in arriving at adjusted gross income. In order to qualify, the performing artist must have performed services in the performing arts as an employee for at least two employers during the year. For this purpose, a nominal employer, i.e., one from whom less than $200 was received for the performance of such services during the year, is excluded.

Moreover, the allowable expenses in connection with the performance of the services must be more than 10 percent of the taxpayer's gross income from the services, and the individual's adjusted gross income for the year, before deducting these expenses, cannot be more than $16,000.

A performing artist who is married at the end of the taxable year must file a joint return with his/her spouse to qualify for the above the line deduction unless both husband and wife live apart at all times during the year. In the case of a joint return, the two-employer requirement as well as the requirement that the expenses be more than 10 percent of gross income are applied separately with respect to each spouse. However, the $16,000 adjusted gross income test is applied to the combined adjusted gross income of both spouses. In effect, such performing artists are allowed the deductions as if they were independent contractors rather than employees.

Such deductions would be allowable "above the line" and would include all "ordinary and necessary" expenses incurred by you during your taxable year. These expenses are detailed in the section on Miscellaneous Itemized Deductions beginning on page 206.

# 38   Employee Reimbursements

An employee must generally include reimbursements for business expenses in gross income. To the extent that such reimbursements are included in gross income, the corresponding expense would be allowable as an "above the line" deduction in arriving at adjusted gross income.

If you are an employee who has an expense reimbursement arrangement with your employer under which you are not fully reimbursed for expenses, the unreimbursed portion can only be deducted as a miscellaneous itemized deduction.

# 39   Alimony

Certain payments that constitute "alimony" may be taken as above the line deductions by the payer. Such "alimony" payments may be made from husband to wife or from wife to husband. For illustration purposes, I will refer to payments coming from husband to wife.

The Internal Revenue Service tax code provides that periodic payments received by a wife in discharge of her husband's obligation of support arising out of the marital or family relationship are deductible if any one of the following situations is true:

1.  The payments are made in discharge of a legal obligation incurred under a court order, decree of divorce, or legal separation, where the spouses are either divorced or legally separated.

2.  The payments are made under a written separation agreement where the spouses are separated, living apart, *and* do not file a joint return.

3.  The payments are made under a court order or decree for the spouse's support or maintenance where the spouses are separated, living apart, *and* do not file a joint return.

PRE-TAX REFORM ACT OF 1984 LAW

Such payments are deductible by the husband and would therefore also be included in the wife's income. If any of the payments are fixed, in terms of a total amount of money or of payment for the support of minor children, they will not be deemed alimony and will neither be taxed to the wife nor deductible by the husband. Prior to the Tax Reform Act of 1984, to qualify as child support payments rather than periodic alimony, the amounts must been been designated specifically as child support and not left to determination by inference or conjecture. Any amounts paid will be applied first to child support if such amounts are less than the total required to be paid. To be child support, though, the payments must be used for the support of minor children of the payer, the age of majority to be determined by applicable state law.

Periodic alimony payments will be deductible by the payer as an above the line deduction for adjusted gross income. In order to be deductible, the payments must be periodic rather than installment payments of a principal sum. Whether the payments are made at regular intervals is irrelevant; the key is whether they are periodic or principal sum payments, and the distinction between these two is whether there is a total amount to be paid that can be computed with certainty. If this is the case, the payments are *not* periodic. If the payments are contingent on death, remarriage of the wife, or a change in the economic status of either spouse, they *are* deemed to be periodic. This contingency may be a result of the decree or the separation agreement, or may be imposed by local law.

There is an exception to this general rule: If the principal amount payable under the terms of the divorce or separation decree is to be paid over more than ten years from the date of the decree, then the payments *will* be considered periodic, but only the portion that equals 10 percent of the principal amount. For example, in a settlement of $300,000 to be paid over fifteen years, with a first payment of $40,000, the recipient must include as gross income $30,000; the remainder is excludable. This limitation does not apply to late payments, but it does apply to advance payments. Late payments are treated as if they were made on time, and since both parties are deemed to be cash-basis taxpayers, these payments will be deductible when paid.

A payer may establish a trust or use an existing trust to discharge an obligation created by the decree of separation or divorce. All periodic payment from this kind of trust will be taxable to the recipient. Payments made by the trust will not be deductible by the payer, but an amount of the trust income that is equal to what is paid to the recipient will be excludable from the payer's gross income. An equal inclusion and deduction therefore result.

Other payments may or may not be deductible as "periodic alimony." Payments for medical or dental insurance or direct medical or dental expenses for the spouse, even though made at irregular intervals, would be periodic. If the parties hold property jointly, any payments made that equal the recipient's interest in the property will be deductible by the payer— except where there is a right of survivorship. In that case, the payer will get a deduction only if the recipient is personally liable on the underlying debt or realizes an ascertainable increase in the value of the property that would be received as a survivor. No payments that are allocatable to the payer's interest in the property can be deducted by the payer or included in the recipient's income.

If the recipient resides in the home, utility expenses and repairs will be deductible regardless of ownership because the recipient is receiving a direct economic benefit. Capital expenditures must be capitalized rather than deducted. Periodic payments of life insurance premiums will also constitute deductible alimony payments if the recipient receives an economic benefit and is the absolute owner. Premium payments are not deductible if the policy is merely a security device, or if the recipient interest is contingent upon not remarrying or upon surviving the payer or the children who are the primary beneficiaries of the policy. In these cases, no present economic benefit to the recipient is ascertainable.

Property settlements, moreover, will not constitute periodic alimony. The intent of the parties, as determined by all of the facts and circumstances, will be the controlling factor here, rather than the label used. Property settlements *not* made out of the marital or family obligation of support will therefore be neither deductible nor includable. You should be aware, though, that if appreciated property is transferred in exchange for your spouse's inchoate marital rights, you will realize a gain equal to the full fair market value of the property less your costs or other basis. The character of the gain will be determined by the nature of the property you transfer. The spouse receiving the property will have a stepped-up basis and realize no gain. The amount realized there is deemed to be equal to what is exchanged.

If the property exchanged has depreciated in value, NEVER make the transfer until the marriage has been dissolved. Otherwise, the loss will not be recognized. An alternative route to avoid this tax trap would be to sell the property to a third party and give the proceeds to your spouse. Be aware, though, that the above rules do *not* apply in a community property state where all divisions are considered to be partitions of jointly owned property. There, taxable income, will be not be realized unless the division is clearly unequal in value.

POST-TAX REFORM ACT OF 1984 LAW

The Tax Reform Act of 1984 made significant changes both to the alimony rules and to property transfers incident to a divorce. With reference to property transfers incident to a divorce, the transfer will be treated in the same manner as a gift and therefore no capital gain or loss will be recognized for tax purposes. This rules applies to all transfers made after the date of enactment of the Act, or if both parties elect, to both transfers made between December 31, 1983 and the date of enactment as well as to transfers made after the date of enactment pursuant to instruments in effect before that date.

With reference to the rules governing alimony, the 1984 Act requires that alimony be paid in cash and terminate at the death of the payee spouse, that the parties may not be members of the same household at the time the payment is made, and that no amount will be deductible as alimony to the extent the payment is contingent on the status of a child (for example, if the payment terminates when a child marries, dies, or reaches maturity). Furthermore, under the 1984 Act, if payments in any year exceed $10,000, no part of such payments will be deductible unless the agreement provides that the payments be made for at least six years (unless the spouse dies or the payee spouse remarries), and a decline in excess of $10,000 in payments between any two successive years will cause a recapture of the excess amount. The effective date of the above rules was January 1, 1985 for divorce or separation agreements executed on or after that date. The provisions apply to divorce or separation agreements executed before January 1, 1985 but modified on or after such date if the modification expressly provides that these provisions will apply.

The Tax Reform Act of 1986, however, amended the above six-year rule. Under the new law, amounts that are considered "excess alimony payments" will be included in taxable income of the payer in the *third* post-separation year. This inclusion will eliminate the benefit of the previous deduction for such payments. The payee will also be permitted a deduction corresponding to the amount includable in the payer's income in that third year.

Excess alimony payments are determined as follows:

For the first postseparation year the excess alimony payment is that amount that exceeds the average of alimony payments in the second and third years plus $15,000. The excess alimony payment for the second year is that amount that exceeds the payment in the third year by more than $15,000. For example, a divorce agreement provides that husband will pay his former wife alimony over a three-year period as follows:

|          |          |
|----------|----------|
| 1st year | $35,000  |
| 2nd year | 10,000   |
| 3rd year | 20,000   |

To calculate the excess alimony payment for the first year, the average of the second- and third-year payments must be computed. This average is $15,000 ([$10,000 + $20,000] ÷ 2). The excess alimony payment for the first year is therefore $5,000 ($35,000 − [$15,000 + $15,000]). In the third year the husband will have to include the $5,000 excess alimony payment in income, and the ex-wife will receive a corresponding deduction of $5,000.

The formula is as follows:

$$\text{Excess payments} = \text{alimony paid in 1st year} - \left[\$15,000 + \frac{\text{alimony paid in 2nd year} - \text{excess payments in 2nd year} + \text{alimony paid in 3rd year}}{2}\right]$$

To complete the computation, the second-year excess amount must be determined first.

The excess payment for the second post-separation year is the excess of the second-year alimony paid over the sum of third-year alimony paid plus $15,000; i.e.,

$$\text{Excess payment} = \frac{\text{alimony paid}}{\text{in 2nd year}} - \left(\frac{\text{alimony paid}}{\text{in 3rd year}} + \$15,000\right)$$

If alimony consists of one payment of $30,000 in the first post-separation year, and no alimony is paid thereafter, the amount recaptured is $15,000:

$$\$30,000 - \left[\$15,000 + \frac{(0 - 0) + 0}{2}\right]$$

If alimony paid in the first post-separation year is $50,000, in the second is $25,000, and in the third is zero, the second-year excess payment is $10,000:

$$\$25,000 - (0 + \$15,000)$$

The first-year excess payment is $27,500:

$$\$50,000 - \left[\$15,000 + \frac{(\$25,000 - \$10,000) + 0}{2}\right]$$

The recapture amount is $37,500, the sum of the first- and second-year excess payments. If $25,000 had also been paid in the third year, the recapture amount would be $10,000, the amount of the first-year excess payment, as there is no second-year excess payment:

$$\$50,000 - \left[\$15,000 + \frac{(\$25,000 - 0) + \$25,000}{2}\right]$$

The objective is to allow alimony payments as deductible if they are made in as few as three years. However, if the first payment is made in December 1987, the second in January 1988, and the third in January 1989, the alimony will be deductible even though the payments are in fact spread over only 13 or 14 months.

Moreover, recapture is not required if alimony ceases when death or remarriage occurs before the end of the third post-separation year. Payments under temporary support agreements are also excluded from the recapture rules. In addition, the 1986 Act clarified that payments will not be disqualified from being treated as alimony simply because the divorce or separation agreement does not specifically state that the payments will terminate at the death of the recipient and, finally, that payments contingent on the fluctuating earnings of a business or property or from employment will also not result in recapture, if the obligation to pay extends for at least three years. These 1986 amendments apply to divorce or separation instruments executed after December 31, 1986, and divorce or separation instruments executed before that date if modified on or after such date to expressly state that the new provisions will apply.

The Tax Reform Act of 1984 also changed the rules with respect to which divorced parent receives the dependency exemption for a child. Beginning in 1985, the custodial parent is entitled to the exemption unless:

1. the custodial parent releases the exemption for the year, by written declaration on Form 8332, to the noncustodial parent. This form must be signed by the custodial parent and attached to the noncustodial parent's return.

2. a decree of divorce or separate maintenance or a written agreement was executed before 1985, under which the custodial parent released the exemption to the noncustodial parent. In this event, the noncustodial parent can claim the exemption if he or she provides at least $600 annually for the child's support. However, the parties can expressly modify the document to render this exception inapplicable.

3. A multiple support agreement is in effect.

Note also that under the 1984 Act, support by a remarried parent's new spouse is considered support furnished by that parent, and children of divorced parents are treated as *both* parents' dependents for medical deduction purposes. Hence, a parent can deduct medical expenses paid for a child even though the other parent gets the dependency exemption for that child.

Furthermore, a custodial parent who releases a dependency exemption will be considered as retaining that exemption when determining marital and head of household status, the earned income credit, and the child and dependent care credit. If otherwise eligible, such a parent could still qualify for unmarried and head of household status and those credits. For example, to claim head of household status, an individual must maintain a household as his or her home, which is also the principal place of abode for more than half a year for his or her unmarried children (or their unmarried descendants), married children (or their unmarried descendants) if they are dependents (including "would be dependents"), or other dependents. The status is also available, as before, if a household is maintained for a taxpayer's dependent parents for a full year.

Several additional tax planning strategies present themselves based upon the above rules. If a separation rather than a divorce is desired, you should be aware that while a *decree* of separate maintenance will prevent the filing of a joint return, mere physical separation will not. Physical separation, though, combined with a written separation agreement, will make any periodic payments "alimony," and deductible as such. Therefore, your first tax consideration must be to weigh the benefits of a joint return against an alimony deduction. Depending upon the marginal tax brackets of each party, a limited amount of shifting the tax burden may also occur here. Trade-offs, in terms of higher receipts in exchange for the filing of a joint return, may also be made by sophisticated and aware taxpayers.

You must carefully consider the character of any payments to be made—that is, whether they are for child support or alimony. Child support is neither includable nor deductible. Here again a certain amount of tax shifting is possible. If any payment for child support is not specifically designated as such, it potentially may be taxed or deducted as alimony. If the recipient is in a lower tax bracket than the payer, any increase in "alimony" from child support will be taxable at a lower marginal rate and deductible at the payer's higher marginal rate. Because of this tax savings, the payer can afford to pay a larger amount of "child support," enough to offset the recipient's increased tax burden, plus a little more.

For example, assume that in 1988, a husband-payer has a marginal tax bracket of 33 percent and his recipient-wife has a marginal tax bracket of 15 percent. The husband plans to pay periodic alimony of $10,000 and child support of $10,000 per year. The wife has agreed. This agreement would cost the husband $16,700 per year:

| | |
|---|---:|
| Child support (no deduction) | $10,000 |
| Alimony [$10,000 × (1 − .33)] | +6,700 |
| | $16,700 |

The wife would keep $18,500 per year:

| | |
|---|---:|
| Child support (no inclusion) | $10,000 |
| Alimony [$10,000 × (1 − .15)] | +8,500 |
| | $18,500 |

If the husband converted the whole $20,000 to alimony, it would cost him only $13,400:

Alimony [$20,000 × (1 − .33)] = $13,400

He therefore would save $3,300 over the original agreement. The wife would now have:

Alimony [$20,000 × (1 − .85)] = $17,000

which is a loss of $1,500. But this loss could be offset by the $3,300 saved by the husband. All he would have to do is increase the alimony payments to $22,500:

Cost to husband [$22,500 × (1 − .33)] = $15,075

Wife keeps [$22,500 × (1 − .15)] = $19,125

The result of this plan is that the husband would save $1,625 ($16,700 − $15,075) over the first plan. The wife's position would also be better—by $625 ($19,125 − $18,500)!

Another tax planning strategy involves post-1984 separations. If a husband transfers stock that has appreciated in value from $10,000 to $100,000, the 1984 law relieves him of the tax on the gain and gives it to his wife instead. This presents another alternative strategy for shifting income from a high bracket taxpayer (husband) to a lower bracketed taxpayer (wife). To offset this incidence of taxation, the recipient wife should again negotiate an increased payout to absorb, or reduce, the husband's net tax savings on the transfer of appreciated, rather than nonappreciated, property.

# 40

## Retirement Plan Payments

With any degree of inflation, it is important that you carefully provide for sufficient retirement funds. The same significant consideration must also be given to sheltering current income from the painful bite of our progressive tax system. The above the line deduction for retirement plan payments allows you to satisfy both of these needs.

If you are self-employed, which includes being an owner or a partner of an unincorporated business, you may provide for your retirement by setting up either a Keogh plan (H.R. 10 Plan) or an individual retirement plan, or both, as described below. Under the Self-Employed Individual's Tax Retirement Act of 1962 (also called the Keogh Act and H.R. 10), you are permitted to put a portion of your yearly earned income, on a tax-deferred basis, into a fund that can earn tax-free income until it starts paying out at retirement.

You are eligible for an individual retirement account (IRA) if you are employed, self-employed, or even covered by a corporate pension plan. You may even have an IRA in addition to a Keogh plan.

Under both an IRA and a Keogh plan, a portion of your income is sheltered from current taxation; there is no tax on the earnings of the fund until postretirement distribution; there is no tax on income contributed to the fund until postretirement distribution; and qualified contributions made by employers to provide employees with retirement benefits are deductible by the employers. Both Keogh plans and IRAs allow the self-employed owner of a business to shelter current earned income and allow that income to accumulate and earn currently nontaxable income until postretirement distribution.

The primary difference between a Keogh plan and an IRA is the amount of earnings that may be sheltered. Under an IRA, as much as 100 percent of compensation—up to a limit of $2,000 a year—may be put aside, and that amount, subject to the limits detailed below, is deductible. If you have a nonemployed spouse, the contribution maximum increases to $2,250. With a Keogh plan, the contribution limits are 25[1] percent of earned income or $30,000, whichever is less. (Defined benefit plans allow an amount computed to yield a maximum annual benefit of $94,023). A special type of IRA called a Simplified Pension Plan will also allow contributions— the lesser of $30,000 or 15 percent of earned income. The major constraint for both the Simplified Pension Plan and the Keogh plan is that in both cases the owner (considered an employee as well under certain plans) may be forced to make contributions for other employees as well; however, these contributions will be deductible. The ultimate decision as to whether to establish an IRA or Keogh plan or both should be made on the basis of which has the greatest cash savings after tax.

---

1.   For owner-employees only, this is 25 percent of income after the Keogh deduction. This really equals 20 percent of pre-Keogh earned income.

If you are an employer, you may set up an individual retirement account for yourself without setting up a similar one for your employees. With a Keogh plan you must cover your employees.

IRA PLAN

There are several advantages to an IRA. An IRA allows the owner of a business to shelter personal earned income for retirement *without* the requirement to make contributions for employees. As a taxpayer eligible for an IRA, you would be allowed to contribute for a nonemployed spouse and the contribution maximum would increase. The purpose of this is to provide retirement income for nonemployed homemakers. Contributions are deposited into separate accounts for you and your nonemployed spouse or into one account with subaccounts for each. No one account, however, may have attributed to it more than $2,000. In case of divorce, the home-maker keeps his or her share of the money. Of course, if both spouses are employed and are eligible, each can set aside 100 percent of earnings, up to $2,000 each year, in separate IRAs.

The tax deduction for the IRA contribution is available as an above the line deduction. Taxes on both contributions to and earnings of the account may be deferred until the funds are withdrawn as retirement benefits. At that time you may be in a lower tax bracket than previously and may qualify for retirement income credits. At age 65 you are entitled to the additional standard deduction. So during the period you receive your IRA funds, you will probably be paying a smaller percentage of your income for taxes than you did in earlier years. Benefits from IRA plans can be drawn without penalty anytime after reaching age 59½. Distribution must begin no later than age 70½.

Earnings eligible for IRA contributions include wages, salaries, or professional fees and other amounts received for personal services actually rendered, including (but not limited to) commissions paid to sales personnel, compensation for services on the basis of a percentage of profits, commissions on insurance premiums, tips, and bonuses. All contributions must be made in cash. No deductions are allowable for contributions of property.

If you receive payment from an IRA before you reach age 59½ or before you become disabled, the payment will be considered a premature distribution. That amount received is included in your gross income in the tax year of receipt. In addition, your income tax liability for that year will be increased by an amount equal to 10 percent of the premature distribution includable in gross income.

Taxable distributions from an individual retirement account are taxed as ordinary income regardless of their source. They are not eligible for capital gains treatment or the special averaging rules that apply to lump-sum distribution from qualified employer plans.

If you die before receiving the entire interest on your individual retirement account, the remaining interest must be distributed to your beneficiary within five years after death, or be applied to purchase an immediate annuity for the beneficiary payable over the life or for a period not exceeding the life expectancy of that beneficiary. Any annuity contracts so purchased must be distributed immediately to the beneficiary.

Tax deductible contributions to an IRA must be made through:

a) an individual retirement account at a bank, federally insured credit union, or savings and loan association, or with certain applicants, any of whom, under temporary regulations, may act as a trustee or custodian;

b) an individual retirement annuity of a life insurance company;

c) individual retirement bonds purchased from the U.S. government; *or*

d) a trust account established by employer or employee association.

The following transactions with IRA money are prohibited by law:

1. You cannot borrow money from your IRA.

2. You cannot use money in an IRA as collateral for a loan.

3. You cannot transfer property to an IRA in exchange for money.

4. You can put only cash into an IRA. For example, you cannot put stock that you currently own into an IRA account. You must sell the stock first, put the cash from that sale into your IRA, and then purchase the stock again if you want to have that stock in the IRA account.

Moreover, you should note that any stock in an IRA account that is sold loses the capital gains treatment. This means that when you withdraw your money from the IRA, gains cannot be offset by capital losses in excess of $3,000.

Starting with 1987, the Tax Reform Act of 1986 made substantial changes in IRA eligibility. The prior law IRA deduction is retained for returns of taxpayers who meet *either* of the following requirements:

1. The taxpayer is not an active participant in certain specified retirement arrangements for any part of the plan year ending with or within the taxpayer's tax year. Active participation status is determined without regard to whether a taxpayer has a vested right to any benefits under a plan and may depend upon the type of plan in which an individual participates or is eligible to participate. For example, for defined benefit plans, a person who is not excluded under the plan's eligibility provisions for any part of the plan year ending with or within the taxpayer's tax year is an active participant. Therefore, even if you elect not to participate in a plan or fail to make an employee contribution required to accrue a benefit attributable to employer contributions, you nevertheless are an active participant in the plan. For defined contribution plans, a taxpayer is an active participant if employer or employee contributions or forfeitures are required to be allocated to his account for a plan year ending with or within the taxpayer's tax year. According to the IRS, a taxpayer may be an active participant even if a required contribution for the plan year is not actually made. However, unlike defined benefit plans, an individual who does not meet the hours of service requirements of a defined contribution plan is not considered an active participant unless contributions or forfeitures have been allocated to his account. For a married individual filing a joint return, neither the individual taxpayer nor the taxpayer's spouse may be an active participant. Moreover, retirement arrangements not only include traditional qualified plans, annuity plans, and trusts, but also include simplified employee pensions and 401(k) plans.

2. The taxpayer has adjusted gross income that does not exceed the "applicable dollar amount." For a married couple filing jointly, combined income may not exceed the applicable dollar amount. The applicable dollar amount is (a) $25,000 for an individual, (b) $40,000 for a married couple filing a joint return, and (c) $0 for a married couple filing separately.

Active participants whose adjusted gross incomes exceed the applicable dollar amount by no more than $10,000 are still entitled to deduct IRA con-

## TABLE 2. Estimated IRA Deduction

If your Maximum Allowable Deduction is $2,000, use this table to estimate the amount of your contribution which will be deductible.

| Excess AGI | Deduction | Excess AGI | Deduction | Excess AGI |
|---|---|---|---|---|
| $ 0.00 | $2,000.00 | $2,000.00 | $1,600.00 | $4,000.00 |
| 50.00 | 1,990.00 | 2,050.00 | 1,590.00 | 4,050.00 |
| 100.00 | 1,980.00 | 2,100.00 | 1,580.00 | 4,100.00 |
| 150.00 | 1,970.00 | 2,150.00 | 1,570.00 | 4,150.00 |
| 200.00 | 1,960.00 | 2,200.00 | 1,560.00 | 4,200.00 |
| 250.00 | 1,950.00 | 2,250.00 | 1,550.00 | 4,250.00 |
| 300.00 | 1,940.00 | 2,300.00 | 1,540.00 | 4,300.00 |
| 350.00 | 1,930.00 | 2,350.00 | 1,530.00 | 4,350.00 |
| 400.00 | 1,920.00 | 2,400.00 | 1,520.00 | 4,400.00 |
| 450.00 | 1,910.00 | 2,450.00 | 1,510.00 | 4,450.00 |
| 500.00 | 1,900.00 | 2,500.00 | 1,500.00 | 4,500.00 |
| 550.00 | 1,890.00 | 2,550.00 | 1,490.00 | 4,550.00 |
| 600.00 | 1,880.00 | 2,600.00 | 1,480.00 | 4,600.00 |
| 650.00 | 1,870.00 | 2,650.00 | 1,470.00 | 4,650.00 |
| 700.00 | 1,860.00 | 2,700.00 | 1,460.00 | 4,700.00 |
| 750.00 | 1,850.00 | 2,750.00 | 1,450.00 | 4,750.00 |
| 800.00 | 1,840.00 | 2,800.00 | 1,440.00 | 4,800.00 |
| 850.00 | 1,830.00 | 2,850.00 | 1,430.00 | 4,850.00 |
| 900.00 | 1,820.00 | 2,900.00 | 1,420.00 | 4,900.00 |
| 950.00 | 1,810.00 | 2,950.00 | 1,410.00 | 4,950.00 |
| 1,000.00 | 1,800.00 | 3,000.00 | 1,400.00 | 5,000.00 |
| 1,050.00 | 1,790.00 | 3,050.00 | 1,390.00 | 5,050.00 |
| 1,100.00 | 1,780.00 | 3,100.00 | 1,380.00 | 5,100.00 |
| 1,150.00 | 1,770.00 | 3,150.00 | 1,370.00 | 5,150.00 |
| 1,200.00 | 1,760.00 | 3,200.00 | 1,360.00 | 5,200.00 |
| 1,250.00 | 1,750.00 | 3,250.00 | 1,350.00 | 5,250.00 |
| 1,300.00 | 1,740.00 | 3,300.00 | 1,340.00 | 5,300.00 |
| 1,350.00 | 1,730.00 | 3,350.00 | 1,330.00 | 5,350.00 |
| 1,400.00 | 1,720.00 | 3,400.00 | 1,320.00 | 5,400.00 |
| 1,450.00 | 1,710.00 | 3,450.00 | 1,310.00 | 5,450.00 |
| 1,500.00 | 1,700.00 | 3,500.00 | 1,300.00 | 5,500.00 |
| 1,550.00 | 1,690.00 | 3,550.00 | 1,290.00 | 5,550.00 |
| 1,600.00 | 1,680.00 | 3,600.00 | 1,280.00 | 5,600.00 |
| 1,650.00 | 1,670.00 | 3,650.00 | 1,270.00 | 5,650.00 |
| 1,700.00 | 1,660.00 | 3,700.00 | 1,260.00 | 5,700.00 |
| 1,750.00 | 1,650.00 | 3,750.00 | 1,250.00 | 5,750.00 |
| 1,800.00 | 1,640.00 | 3,800.00 | 1,240.00 | 5,800.00 |
| 1,850.00 | 1,630.00 | 3,850.00 | 1,230.00 | 5,850.00 |
| 1,900.00 | 1,620.00 | 3,900.00 | 1,220.00 | 5,900.00 |
| 1,950.00 | 1,610.00 | 3,950.00 | 1,210.00 | 5,950.00 |

| Deduction | Excess AGI | Deduction | Excess AGI | Deduction |
|---|---|---|---|---|
| $1,200.00 | $6,000.00 | $800.00 | $8,000.00 | $400.00 |
| 1,190.00 | 6,050.00 | 790.00 | 8,050.00 | 390.00 |
| 1,180.00 | 6,100.00 | 780.00 | 8,100.00 | 380.00 |
| 1,170.00 | 6,150.00 | 770.00 | 8,150.00 | 370.00 |
| 1,160.00 | 6,200.00 | 760.00 | 8,200.00 | 360.00 |
| 1,150.00 | 6,250.00 | 750.00 | 8,250.00 | 350.00 |
| 1,140.00 | 6,300.00 | 740.00 | 8,300.00 | 340.00 |
| 1,130.00 | 6,350.00 | 730.00 | 8,350.00 | 330.00 |
| 1,120.00 | 6,400.00 | 720.00 | 8,400.00 | 320.00 |
| 1,110.00 | 6,450.00 | 710.00 | 8,450.00 | 310.00 |
| 1,100.00 | 6,500.00 | 700.00 | 8,500.00 | 300.00 |
| 1,090.00 | 6,550.00 | 690.00 | 8,550.00 | 290.00 |
| 1,080.00 | 6,600.00 | 680.00 | 8,600.00 | 280.00 |
| 1,070.00 | 6,650.00 | 670.00 | 8,650.00 | 270.00 |
| 1,060.00 | 6,700.00 | 660.00 | 8,700.00 | 260.00 |
| 1,050.00 | 6,750.00 | 650.00 | 8,750.00 | 250.00 |
| 1,040.00 | 6,800.00 | 640.00 | 8,800.00 | 240.00 |
| 1,030.00 | 6,850.00 | 630.00 | 8,850.00 | 230.00 |
| 1,020.00 | 6,900.00 | 620.00 | 8,900.00 | 220.00 |
| 1,010.00 | 6,950.00 | 610.00 | 8,950.00 | 210.00 |
| 1,000.00 | 7,000.00 | 600.00 | 9,000.00 | 200.00 |
| 990.00 | 7,050.00 | 590.00 | 9,050.00 | 200.00 |
| 980.00 | 7,100.00 | 580.00 | 9,100.00 | 200.00 |
| 970.00 | 7,150.00 | 570.00 | 9,150.00 | 200.00 |
| 960.00 | 7,200.00 | 560.00 | 9,200.00 | 200.00 |
| 950.00 | 7,250.00 | 550.00 | 9,250.00 | 200.00 |
| 940.00 | 7,300.00 | 540.00 | 9,300.00 | 200.00 |
| 930.00 | 7,350.00 | 530.00 | 9,350.00 | 200.00 |
| 920.00 | 7,400.00 | 520.00 | 9,400.00 | 200.00 |
| 910.00 | 7,450.00 | 510.00 | 9,450.00 | 200.00 |
| 900.00 | 7,500.00 | 500.00 | 9,500.00 | 200.00 |
| 890.00 | 7,550.00 | 490.00 | 9,550.00 | 200.00 |
| 880.00 | 7,600.00 | 480.00 | 9,600.00 | 200.00 |
| 870.00 | 7,650.00 | 470.00 | 9,650.00 | 200.00 |
| 860.00 | 7,700.00 | 460.00 | 9,700.00 | 200.00 |
| 850.00 | 7,750.00 | 450.00 | 9,750.00 | 200.00 |
| 840.00 | 7,800.00 | 440.00 | 9,800.00 | 200.00 |
| 830.00 | 7,850.00 | 430.00 | 9,850.00 | 200.00 |
| 820.00 | 7,900.00 | 420.00 | 9,900.00 | 200.00 |
| 810.00 | 7,950.00 | 410.00 | 9,950.00 | 200.00 |
|  |  |  | 10,000.00 | 0.00 |

tributions, but only in a reduced amount calculated according to the following formula provided by the IRS:

$$\frac{\$10{,}000 - \text{excess adjusted gross income}}{\$10{,}000} \times \begin{array}{l} \text{the maximum permissible} \\ \text{dollar deduction defined} \\ \text{as the lesser of } 100 \\ \text{percent of compensation or} \\ \$2{,}000 \ (\$2{,}250 \text{ for spousal} \\ \text{IRAs}) \end{array} = \begin{array}{l} \text{adjusted} \\ \text{dollar} \\ \text{deduction} \\ \text{limit} \end{array}$$

Note that for this purpose, adjusted gross income includes social security benefits and passive income or losses, but not IRA contributions.

For example, assume that you and your spouse earn $25,000 and $20,000 in adjusted gross income (total $45,000) and that your spouse is a participant in a qualified pension plan. Your maximum permissible dollar deduction would be $4,000 ($2,000 for you and $2,000 for your spouse). Your maximum deductible IRA, however, would be computed as follows:

| | |
|---|---|
| Maximum IRA | $4,000 |
| Less: Phaseout over $40,000 | |
| $\dfrac{(\$45{,}000 - 40{,}000) \times \$4{,}000}{\$10{,}000} =$ | $2,000 |
| Tax-deductible IRA | $2,000 |

Your maximum tax-deductible IRA would therefore be only $2,000. Taxpayers not above the phaseout maximum ($50,000 for a joint return) are permitted a minimum IRA deduction of $200. Moreover, prior to the Tax Reform Act of 1986, a spousal IRA of $250 was allowed only if the spouse had no compensation. Under new law, an individual may elect to be treated as if he or she had no compensation for the taxable year. This means, for an otherwise qualifying couple, the annual deduction contribution is increased from $2,000 to $2,250.

The table on pages 106–107 details the estimated IRA deduction amount for a single person with a maximum allowable deduction of $2,000.

Starting in 1987, however, *nondeductible* contributions to an IRA may be made up to the maximum deduction, reduced by any deductible contributions. Therefore, even if your contribution deduction is reduced under the adjusted gross income limitation, you can contribute the difference without deducting it. The earnings on such contributions are not taxed until distribution. Any nondeductible contribution must be indicated on your tax return for the contribution year.

If nondeductible contributions are made, withdrawals from IRAs must be divided between taxable and nontaxable segments. The Tax Reform Act of 1986 uses an averaging approach to accomplish this task. For purposes of the computations, all of a taxpayer's IRAs are considered to be one single IRA and all withdrawals made during the year are added together and considered as one withdrawal. The percentage of an IRA withdrawal treated as a return of a nondeductible contribution, and therefore not taxable, is represented by a ratio whose numerator is the sum of all nondeductible contributions made to any of the taxpayer's IRAs and whose denominator is the sum of the balances in the taxpayer's IRAs at the end of the tax year plus withdrawals made during the year.

The tables on pages 109–10, developed by Jerrold J. Stern of the Graduate School of Business, Indiana University, show break-even points at various tax and interest rates for deductible IRA contributions and nondeductible IRA contributions. Note that the tables include a 10 percent penalty on withdrawals prior to age 59½. Where the taxable percentage of the principal is zero, the table assumes that tax and penalty are paid only on the interest earned, and that the principal contribution (for example, $2,000) withdrawn is received tax-free:

TABLE 3.  Years before Break-even: Deductible IRA Contributions

| Interest rates | Marginal tax rates | | |
|---|---|---|---|
|  | 15% | 28% | 33% |
| 4% | 22 | 14 | 13 |
| 6 | 15 | 10 | 9 |
| 8 | 12 | 8 | 7 |
| 10 | 10 | 6 | 6 |
| 12 | 8 | 5 | 5 |

**TABLE 4.** Years before Break-even: Nondeductible IRA Contributions Taxable Percentage of Principal = 0%

| Interest rates | Marginal tax rates | | |
|:---:|:---:|:---:|:---:|
| | 15% | 28% | 33% |
| 4% | 37 | 26 | 24 |
| 6 | 25 | 18 | 17 |
| 8 | 20 | 14 | 13 |
| 10 | 16 | 11 | 11 |
| 12 | 14 | 10 | 9 |

**TABLE 5.** Years before Break-even: Nondeductible IRA Contributions Taxable Percentage of Principal = 100%

| Interest rates | Marginal tax rates | | |
|:---:|:---:|:---:|:---:|
| | 15% | 28% | 33% |
| 4% | 50 | 45 | 44 |
| 6 | 34 | 30 | 30 |
| 8 | 26 | 23 | 23 |
| 10 | 21 | 19 | 19 |
| 12 | 18 | 16 | 16 |

**TABLE 6.** Years before Break-even: Deductible IRA Contributions Taxable Percentage of Principal = 50%

| Interest rates | Marginal tax rates | | |
|:---:|:---:|:---:|:---:|
| | 15% | 28% | 33% |
| 4% | 45 | 38 | 38 |
| 6 | 31 | 26 | 26 |
| 8 | 24 | 20 | 20 |
| 10 | 19 | 17 | 16 |
| 12 | 17 | 14 | 14 |

Remember that if a taxpayer and spouse have joint income in excess of $40,000 and if even one spouse is covered by a retirement plan, joint return deductions for payments to individual retirement accounts are phased out. In IRS Notice 87-16 the IRS held that if separate returns were filed, an IRA deduction could be taken by the spouse who was not in a retirement plan. For some couples that deduction might outweigh the tax cost of separate returns. However, the staff of Congress's Joint Tax Committee has reported that an IRA was not meant to be deductible on a separate return unless a couple "did not live together at any time during the taxable year." This contradicts the prior IRS holding and eliminates this avenue of tax deductibility.

Certain investments are off limits to IRA holders. They include investments in collectibles, such as rare books; rugs; artworks; metals, such as gold, silver, and platinum; antiques; stamps; coins; alcoholic beverages; and any other forms of tangible personal property. In addition, life insurance, as opposed to annuities offered by life insurance companies, is also off limits to IRA investors. Under the Tax Reform Act of 1986, however, you may invest in gold and silver coins issued by the United States. This provision is effective for coins acquired after 1986.

The deadline for making contributions to an IRA is April 15, the date for filing the taxpayer's return. Taxpayers who establish an individual retirement account or annuity are required to file Form 5239, Return for Individual Retirement Savings Arrangements, with their income tax return only if they owe IRA penalty taxes (for instance, excess contributions, premature distributions, or the failure to distribute at age 70½).

In private ruling 8527082 the IRS affirmed that you may deduct interest paid on money borrowed to put into an IRA. Note, however, that the Tax Reform Act of 1986 makes interest potentially nondeductible as "consumer interest" over a five-year phase-out period. Moreover, the IRS has ruled that the separate payment by an IRA beneficiary or trustee of administration fees for the IRA will not reduce the amount the beneficiary would otherwise be entitled to treat as a deductible contribution to the IRA, and is deductible as an expense incurred for the production or collection of income (Rev. Rul. 84-146). However, no separate deduction is allowed for brokers' commissions paid by IRAs or even qualified plans. Brokers' commissions are not recurring administrator for overhead expenses, such as trustee or actuary fees, incurred in connection with the maintenance of the trust or plan. Brokers' commissions rather are intrinsic to the value of a trust's assets—buying commissions are a part of the cost of the securities purchased and selling commissions are an offset against the sales price. Therefore, the Internal Revenue

Service has ruled that contributions to reimburse for brokers' commissions are not deductible (Rev. Rul. 86-142, 1986-48 IRB 4).

SIMPLIFIED PENSION PLANS

Under a normal IRA, your deduction is limited to the lesser of 100 percent of earned income or $2,000 ($2,250 in the case of spousal IRAs) for contributions made. Under the Simplified Pension Plan, the exclusion limitation for all contributions to this type of IRA is the lesser of $30,000 or 15 percent of compensation. In the case of a self-employed individual or owner-employee in a noncorporate plan, "compensation" is defined to mean net earnings from self-employment, less excludable contributions to the plan made on his or her own behalf. This effectively reduces the self-employed maximum contribution percentage from 15 to 13.04 percent. Moreover, if an employer maintains another qualified plan, the maximum amount that can be contributed to that plan for any employee is reduced by all amounts contributed to the SEP. There is a 25 percent limitation on deductible contributions to more than one qualified plan. [Internal Revenue Code Section 404(h)(3)]

The intent of this type of plan is to establish a simpler mechanism by which employers can make employer-deductible contributions to provide employees with retirement benefits. It offers the owner-employee the opportunity to increase the maximum contributions that may be made to a personal plan, but it does so at the cost of requiring contributions for certain other employees as well.

Contributions made to an SEP by the employer or by a self-employed individual are deposited into individual IRAs in the name of the plan member. Employer contributions to an SEP are not includable in an employee's gross income. The employer contribution must be a specified percentage of the employee's total compensation up to $208,940, and the same percentage rate must be used for all employees. That rate may be specified in the plan or set by the employer annually by a written resolution. Unlike profit-sharing plans, an SEP does not require employers to make recurring contributions to the plan to remain qualified.

Under prior law, an employee could contribute the lesser of $2,000 ($2,250 for an employee with a nonworking spouse) or his or her compensation. Any excess contribution by an employee or employer to the employee's account above the yearly deduction limitations may be withdrawn without penalty on or before the earlier of the employee's tax filing date or April 15. Excess contributions left beyond that time are subject to a 6 percent excise tax. Under the Tax Reform Act of 1986, employees may now make elective contributions to their Simplified Employee Pension up to $7,313 per year (indexed). These elective contributions are wages subject to FICA and FUTA taxes.

The five requirements for the establishment of a Simplified Pension Plan are as follows:

1. The IRA must be maintained solely by the individual employee. This means that all employees, including the owner as an employee, must maintain their own individual IRA accounts.

2. Employer contributions must be made pursuant to a written allocation formula.

3. The program must provide for contributions for each employee who has attained age 21, has performed services for the employer during any part of three of the immediately preceding five calendar years, and receives compensation of at least $313 during the current year (indexed). Employees under collective bargaining agreements and non-resident aliens may be excluded; part-time employees, however, must be covered.

4. Employer contributions must not discriminate in favor of officers, shareholders, or highly compensated employees. Generally, discrimination will not exist if the contributions bear a uniform relationship to the first $100,000 of each employee's total compensation. Employer contributions may be reduced by the amount of the employer's share of the social security tax.

5. No limitations may be imposed by the employer on the employee's right of withdrawal.

Unlike the Keogh plan, an SEP can be set up after the end of the calendar year so long as the contribution is made before April 16 of the year following. Moreover, there are no annual reporting requirements for SEPs, so long as each individual who participates in the plan receives a copy of the plan agreement and a written document from the employer each year informing that individual of the amount of contributions made on his or her behalf by the employer. An employer can create an SEP by using an unmodified Model Form (Form 5305-SEP), which is available from the Internal Revenue Service. If the employer follows the instructions on this two-page form, he will automatically satisfy IRS reporting and disclosure requirements.

Additional advantages of an SEP include the following:

- Low start-up costs compared to the cost of establishing regular pension or profit sharing plans

- No need to pay contributions to the SEP every year

- Portability of benefits—that is, participants who end their employment can take their benefits with them in the form of Individual Retirement Accounts

- Low administrative costs

- Reduced fiduciary responsibility, because participants choose their own vehicle when they establish an IRA

As noted, the deadline for making IRA contributions is April 15, but what if you don't have the necessary cash at the moment? One possible solution to this problem is to use a rollover IRA for the funds required for the current IRA contribution.

There are no immediate tax consequences when an individual withdraws part or all of his or her interest in an IRA and within 60 days rolls over the amount withdrawn into another IRA. The trustee of the original IRA must be notified that the withdrawal is for a rollover, and no more than one rollover is permitted within a one-year period. Therefore, if you have an IRA account established in an earlier year, you can withdraw $2,000 from it and use it for your subsequent year's contribution. So long as the rollover is completed within 60 days, there is no problem.

*Question:* Where do you get the money to roll over your original contribution? *Solution:* It is hoped that you get it with the refund you will get from your tax return as filed with the additional IRA deduction. *Worst case theory:* If you cannot find the $2,000 to roll over within the 60-day period, then you are still entitled to the deduction for the current contribution year, but you have to include the $2,000 withdrawn (with penalty) on your next year's tax return.

Rather than wait for the last minute, you should make your IRA contribution as early as possible. When you delay, you lose not only the tax-free interest for the year but the interest that would have been compounded on it in future years.

The following table shows how much you lose by making a contribution at the last minute. It assumes that $2,000 is placed annually into an IRA earning 10 percent interest, and it shows the interest forfeited after a given number of years when the contributions are regularly made as late as possible (April 15), as opposed to as early as possible (on January 1 of the year).

| Number of Years | Interest Lost |
|:---:|:---:|
| 5 | $ 1,500 |
| 10 | 4,000 |
| 15 | 8,000 |
| 20 | 14,000 |
| 30 | 41,000 |
| 40 | 112,000 |

In 1985, the Internal Revenue Service ruled that a jobless widow could add to her own IRA for the year her husband died. The decedent had created a spousal IRA for his unemployed wife in 1982 and 1983. He died on February 23, 1984, after earning over $2,250 but before adding to either IRA for that year. The taxpayer's spouse earned no wages in 1984 but wanted to make and deduct a $2,000 payment from the decedent's 1984 income to her spousal IRA for 1984. In Private Ruling 8527083, the Internal Revenue Service said that she could so long as she had no earned income of her own, filed a joint return, and showed that no 1984 payment was made to the decedent's IRA.

KEOGH PLAN

The alternative to an IRA or IRA/SEP is the Keogh plan. Since 1962, self-employed individuals and their employees have been eligible to receive qualified retirement benefits under what is known as an H.R. 10 or Keogh plan. These qualified pension, annuity, profit sharing, or bond purchase plans must meet the following qualifications:

1. They must be in writing.

2. They must be effective within the tax year for which a qualification is sought.

3. They must be established by an owner for the benefit of employees or their beneficiaries. Self-employed individuals will be treated as employees under these plans.

4. They must be funded plans (that is, a trust or custodial account, an insured plan, or a bond purchase plan).

5. They must benefit a stipulated percentage of employees, or alternatively, the owner may establish a classification of employees that is found by the Internal Revenue Service not to discriminate in favor of highly paid employees.

6. They may not discriminate in favor of highly paid employees for contributions or benefits.

7. In the case of a plan that provides contributions or benefits only for owner-employees, contributions made on behalf of any owner-employee may not exceed the amount deductible by the individual. This means that an owner cannot contribute into a personal plan, in an attempt to defer taxes, an amount in excess of what is deductible for employees.

   In 1983, if employer contributions were made in a tax year on behalf of an owner-employee *and* either a common law employee or a self-employed individual who is not an owner-employee, the plan could permit voluntary contributions by the owner-employee. However, these voluntary contributions had to be computed at the same rate (a percentage of income) permitted in the plan for other employees.

   Beginning in 1984, employers with Keogh plans are able to make nondeductible contributions each year *without* matching their contributions for their employees with a 10 percent maximum.

8. When an owner-employee covered under the plan, alone or in conjunction with another employee, controls the trade or business for which the plan is established, any transaction between that owner-employee and the trust forming part of the plan is prohibited. Transactions between the members of the owner-employee's family and the trust are deemed to be transactions between the owner-employee and the trust. Furthermore, even if the owner-employee does not control the trade or business, a transaction between the trust and that owner-employee is prohibited.

Generally, a disqualified person who engages in a prohibited transaction by contributing property to the trust is subject to a 5 percent excise tax on the amount involved in the transaction. An additional tax of 100 percent of the amount involved is imposed if the prohibited transaction is not corrected within 90 days from the mailing of a notice of deficiency.

9. A plan that covers an owner-employee also must cover all employees (whether or not U.S. citizens) of the trade or business who have completed three or more years of service. A year of service is a 12-month period, beginning on the date of hire, during which an employee has provided at least 1,000 hours of service. In addition, the employees' rights to contributions in their behalf must be 100 percent vested when the contributions are made.

   The following employees are not required to be covered under a self-employed retirement plan, even though they have completed one or more years of service:

   • Employees included in a unit covered by a collective bargaining agreement, if there is evidence that retirement benefits were subject to good faith bargaining between employee representatives and the employer.

   • Nonresident alien employees who do not have earned income from a U.S. source.

10. If the employer is a partnership, each partner is considered the employee of that partnership. The partners must mutually consent to the establishment of the plan, which means that one partner cannot establish a plan for individual services to that partnership. But each owner-employee can decide whether to be covered under the plan, so a partner who is an owner-employee can agree to the plan and still not participate in it.

Under a Keogh plan, both the maximum contribution permitted on behalf of owner-employees and the deduction allowed self-employed individuals are the lesser of:

a) $30,000; *or*

    b) 25 percent of the earned income from the trade or business for which the plan is established.

Note that a Keogh plan may be structured either as a "pension" plan or as a "profit-sharing" plan, or as a combination of both. An owner-employer must reduce his compensation base by the contribution made. This effectively translates into a limit for *profit-sharing* plan–based deductions of 13.043 percent and a limit for *pension* or combination *pension/profit-sharing* deductions of 20 percent of earned income.

The above contribution maximums were computed under what is known as a *defined contribution plan,* in which the limits are delineated on the basis of how much may be contributed. A self-employed individual may choose instead to establish what is known as a *defined benefit plan,* in which the limits are based on payable benefits. This type of plan permits a self-employed individual to state the retirement benefits desired and contribute amounts necessary to provide those benefits. In addition, a defined benefit plan permits yearly contributions to a plan without regard to profits.

Unlike an SEP or an IRA, lump-sum distributions from a Keogh plan qualify for what is known as the special 5-year forward averaging method. The theory behind the name is that the lump-sum payment is separated from the recipient's other taxable income and is taxed as if it had been received evenly over a 5-year period. This method ignores both the taxpayer's other income and the length of time in the plan. It is a significant benefit, which you should be aware of and take advantage of when appropriate.

BENEFITS OF RETIREMENT PLANS

It is almost always financially superior to adopt either an individual retirement account or a Keogh plan rather than have no plan at all. Both the IRA and the Keogh plan allow you to shelter current earnings and allow those earnings to appreciate without making that appreciation currently taxable. There may be an extraordinary situation in which having no plan would be superior. Such a situation would exist if the after-tax cash remaining from funds not invested in an IRA or Keogh plan could be invested in a project whose yield would exceed, after taxes, both the amount that could be earned on the qualified retirement investment and the amount initially lost in taxes.

For example, assume you could put $1,000 in an individual retirement account that would yield a 5 percent interest, or $50 a year. Your present tax bracket is 20 percent, so that if you do not adopt the individual retirement account, you would have only $800 to invest. But this $800 could be invested in a project yielding 25 percent, or $200 a year. After taxes (at 20 percent) the project would allow you to keep $160 a year. At the end of two years you would therefore have, after taxes, $800 + $160 + $160 = $1,120. (The example has been simplified by excluding compound interest on the investment yield.) Under the IRA, you would have only $1,000 + $50 + $50 = $1,100, and that $1,100 would be taxable at a later date, when withdrawn from the individual retirement account. In this case, the decision not to adopt any plan would clearly be superior.

In order to choose a Keogh plan in addition to an IRA, you must answer the following questions:

1. How much money can you afford to surrender the present use of? If not over $2,000 ($2,250 if you have an unemployed spouse), choose an IRA only.

2. What will be the tax savings on your contributions to each plan?

3. Must you make contributions for your employees?

4. What will be the after-tax cost of those contributions?

5. Compare the net after-tax savings from an individual retirement account alone and from the combination of a Keogh plan and an IRA.

For example, assume you are in the 33 percent bracket and are making $200,000 a year. You plan to retire in ten years. You can adopt a Keogh plan, yielding 5 percent. Under the Keogh plan, you would contribute $15,000 at the end of each year.

Under the Keogh plan, you would contribute $150,000 plus earnings on these contributions, for a total untaxed accumulation of $188,668. You would defer $62,260 in taxes.

But with a Keogh plan qualified employees must also be covered. If you have qualified employees, you would have to contribute 7.5 percent of their earnings (as you contribute 7.5 percent of your own earnings) each year. If you have one qualified employee earning $20,000, you would have to contribute an additional $1,500 per year ($20,000 × 7.5 percent), or $15,000 over the ten-year period. If you have four qualified employees, the contributions would rise to $60,000.

But you are in the 33 percent bracket. Therefore, this would involve an after-tax cost to you of only $40,200. But remember, Keogh savings is merely a tax *deferral*, not a savings. Therefore, the real question is whether the $40,200 after-tax outflow can be justified by a deferral on the taxes of $62,260!

Under the Keogh plan you would accumulate $188,668. If you expected to be in the 15 percent bracket after you retire, the difference between your marginal tax today and your postretirement marginal tax would be .18 (33 percent − 15 percent).[2] Therefore, your true net savings on the Keogh plan would be the difference in your tax bracket (.18) times the accumulations under the Keogh plan ($188,668), or a net savings of the present value of $33,960. Thus the determining question is whether the present value of $33,960 is greater than the present value of the after-tax outflow for the contributions you would have to make for your employees.

With a single employee, the cash outflow cost would be the present value of 33 percent of $15,000, or the present value of $4,950. Here the net savings of $33,960 would be greater than the incremental cost of $4,950, and therefore the Keogh adoption would be still superior. If there were four employees, the decision model would compare the present value of $33,960 with the present value of 67 percent of $15,000 × 4, or $40,200. Here the IRA would be financially superior.

Finally, you must consider whether the employee Keogh contributions would merely replace alternative additional compensation that would be paid to the employee in any case. If so, then the Keogh penalty for employee payments must be reduced by this amount.

### HEALTH INSURANCE DEDUCTION FOR SELF-EMPLOYEDS

Under the Tax Reform Act of 1986, self-employed individuals may deduct 25 percent of payments for health insurance for themselves, their spouse, and their dependents, but only on returns through the tax year 1989. This special deduction for health insurance is not subject to the floor of 7.5 percent of adjusted gross income for medical expense deductions.

Certain limitations apply to this new health insurance deduction. No deduction is allowed to the extent that health insurance payments exceed

---

2.    The numbers have been simplified for purposes of this example. You would not be in the 15 percent bracket with a lump-sum distribution of $188,668.

your earned income for the taxable year. Nor is any deduction allowed for any taxable year for which you are eligible to participate in a subsidized accident and health plan provided by an organization that employs (whether on a full- or part-time basis) either you or your spouse. Moreover, no deduction is allowed unless you provide coverage under one or more accident or health plans for all of your employees, should you have any. Those plans must also satisfy nondiscrimination rules.

This deduction is available even if you do not itemize your deductions. However, this deduction does not reduce your earnings for the computation of self-employment tax.

# CHAPTER 6

# "Below the Line" Deductions

*"I am proud to be paying taxes in the
United States. The only thing is—I could
be just as proud for half the money."*

ARTHUR GODFREY

Under the Tax Reform Act of 1986, you will not be required to reduce your itemized, or "below the line," deductions by the amount of the standard deduction (zero bracket amount). Instead, you will deduct 100 percent of your itemized deductions and not take the standard deduction. Therefore, you will itemize deductions only if they exceed the amount of your standard deduction.

For 1988, the standard deduction amounts are as follows:

| If your filing status is: | Your standard deduction is: |
|---|---|
| Single | $3,000 |
| Married, filing jointly, or a qualifying widow or widower | $5,000 |
| Married, filing separately | $2,500 |
| Head of household | $4,400 |

The minimum income levels for filing a tax return are:

| | |
|---|---|
| Single | $4,950 |
| Single, age 65 or older | $5,700 |
| Married, filing jointly | $8,900 |
| Married, filing jointly, one spouse, age 65 or older | $9,500 |
| Married, filing jointly, both spouses age 65 or older | $10,100 |
| Surviving spouse filing as "married, filing jointly" | $5,700 |
| Married, filing separately | $1,950 |
| Head of household | $4,950 |

In addition, the personal tax exemption is $1,950 in 1988.

## A  The Importance of Filing Status

Your filing status is determined on the last day of each year. This affords you another opportunity for sophisticated tax planning. The rates for married individuals, filing either jointly *or* separately, are much lower than those for single, unmarried taxpayers. For example, for 1988, on taxable income of $43,150, a single person pays a marginal tax rate of 33 percent and a total tax of $9,761.50. On the other hand, a married taxpayer with a spouse who has no income would pay a marginal rate of only 15 percent and a total tax of $8,214.50. If you are planning a New Year's wedding, advancing it only a few days to Christmas would therefore save you $1,547—enough to pay for your honeymoon.

Alternatively, if both married partners work, there is, in effect, a tax on the marriage. In 1988, two individuals each earning $17,850 in taxable income would each pay $2,677.50 in taxes for a total outlay of $5,355. If they got married before the year-end, their total income would be $35,700, and they would have filed either a joint return or a return as married, filing separately—either way mandating a total tax payment of $6,128.50, $773.50 more than what they would have paid had they remained unmarried!

This extraordinary penalty on marriage is the result of previous congressional actions that attempted to correct apparent inequities in the old tax structure. Prior to 1948, husbands and wives in community property states could each claim half of their household income for tax purposes even if only one of them actually earned all of the income. The law of the individual state attributed half of the income ("property") to the other spouse. For example, if only the husband worked, earning $30,000, both he and his wife would have reported $15,000 in income. Given our progressive tax rate, where each additional dollar earned is taxed at a higher rate, this was a substantial advantage. In 1948, the federal income tax code was amended to allow this benefit to all married taxpayers—including those in non-community property states. This was done by doubling the income brackets for married taxpayers associated with each rate. For example, if the first $500 of income was taxed at 11 percent for a single person, the first $1,000 of income for married couples would have also been taxed at 11 percent.

While those who were married rejoiced, single taxpayers making the same income as married couples were subject to much higher tax rates. In 1970, for example, single taxpayers could have been liable for as much as 42 percent more in taxes than a married couple earning an equivalent income. In response to this harsh inequity, Congress in 1971 changed the rates for single taxpayers to reduce this differential to a 20 percent maximum. The Tax Reform Act of 1986 reduced the differential even further.

The tax penalty on marriage where both husband and wife work is compounded by the standard deduction. A married couple is allowed a total of $5,000 of nontaxable income. Two single workers get $3,000 each for a total of $6,000. By getting married, an additional $1,000 becomes taxable—and at the highest rates!

Moreover, high-income earners who marry will also lose write-offs for personal exemptions faster than their single counterparts. Under the Tax Reform Act of 1986, the 1988 exemption of $1,950 is phased out for singles with taxable incomes above $89,560, but the phase-out for a married couple starts at $149,250, less than double the income amount for a single person.

Marriage may also wipe out potential IRA deductions. If two taxpayers with incomes of $25,000 each marry and either is covered by an employer plan, neither could write off an IRA contribution. They would lose $4,000 in deductions and, in 1988, pay as much as $1,320 more in total tax.

Because your marital status for the entire year is based upon your status as of December 31, many individuals have been advised to fly to a Caribbean divorce haven, such as the Dominican Republic, for a quickie divorce before the year ends and to remarry in January. The tax savings can often more than offset the cost of legal fees and the Caribbean "vacation."

The Internal Revenue Service has reacted to this situation, declaring: "If you obtain a foreign divorce for the sole purpose of enabling you and your spouse to qualify as unmarried individuals eligible to file separate returns, and if you then remarry each other early in the next tax year, you and your spouse must file as married individuals."

This response has been tested in the tax court with interesting results. The tax court has ruled that it will not recognize such "quickie divorces" solely on the basis of the fact that the state in which the taxpayers domiciled will not recognize such divorces. (The Fourth Circuit Court of Appeals ruled in 1981 that there may be a sham even if your state does recognize the divorce (668 F 2d. 1238). This ruling is not universally accepted—see *Wake Forest Law Review,* Volume 18, pages 881–901, 1982). But many states *do* recognize such divorces; by implication, therefore, if you reside in such a state, a "quickie" divorce and a remarriage could save you substantial tax dollars. Your divorce, though, must be real, with significant economic consequences—for example, loss of rights under a will—and not merely a sham. (See *Felt Estate v. Commissioner,* T.C. Memo 1987-465, September 16, 1987, in which a divorce decree obtained by a husband in the Dominican Republic was recognized for federal income tax purposes.)

In cases where divorces or legal separations would be either impractical or unwanted, you could at least make a substantial initial tax savings by postponing your original Christmas wedding until New Year's. This several days wait may be worth several thousand dollars in tax dollars.

Being single may also be an advantage in qualifying for excess itemized deductions. For example, assume your spouse has total below the line deductions of $5,000. As you are married and don't exceed the amount of the joint standard deduction, none of these deductions are allowable.

Filing separately may sometimes help, but a husband and wife filing separate returns must use the same method of claiming deductions; if one itemizes, the other must itemize as well. This could result in a situation in which one spouse who itemizes has an allowable itemized deduction in excess of the standard deduction by, say, $2,000, but the other spouse who has no itemized deductions would have to *add* $2,000 to the gross income (e.g., subtract $2,000 from $0 in deductions)!

This may be profitable if the spouse who has itemized deductions is in a higher tax bracket. For example, if one is in the 33 percent bracket and the other is in the 15 percent bracket, the first would save $660 ($2,000 $\times$ .33) at a cost to the second of only $300 ($2,000 $\times$ .15), or a net gain of $360.

However, this advantage may be dissipated by the greater advantage of the married tax schedule over the potentially more costly schedule for married filing separately. For example, filing jointly, a husband with a taxable income of $40,000 and a wife with $30,000 would pay $15,732.50 in taxes on a total income of $70,000. Filing separately, the husband would owe $9,468.75 and the wife $6,466.25, a total of $15,935 and a net *loss* of $202.50! Note that as the rates are condensed, the potential net loss is reduced.

The usual instance in which filing separately is advantageous is when substantial excess itemized deductions can be picked up. For example, as you will see later, medical expenses must be reduced by 7.5 percent of your adjusted gross income before they can be included in your itemized deduction computation. Assume one spouse has $3,000 in medical expenses and an adjusted gross income of $10,000, while the other spouse has no medical expenses and an adjusted gross income of $50,000. Filing separately would require a reduction of only $750 (7.5 percent of $10,000) rather than $4,500 (7.5 percent of $60,000)—a net additional itemized deduction of $2,250. In this case, depending upon the other itemized deductions and specific credits available to each spouse, it might pay to file separately. In any case, if you are married and both parties earn income, it is always to your advantage to prepare your return each way to see which provides the lower tax.

# B Tax Planning with Itemized Deductions

There are a number of general strategies that should be implemented when planning for your itemized deductions. The most important of these is the timing of your deductions. Many deductions can be shifted from one year to the next.

You might want to implement such shifting if your itemized deductions are close to the standard deduction amount. Your aim should be to bunch your deductions for expenses so that they exceed the full value of your standard deduction amount. For example, assume that you have itemized deductions of $4,000 each year, of which $3,000 can be accelerated or deferred. With a standard deduction amount of $5,000, none of these deductions would be allowed as excess. What you do, therefore, is to time the expenses you can control so as to itemize deductions of $7,000 in the alternate years ($4,000 + $3,000). This strategy allows you an extra deduction of $2,000 every second year ($7,000 − $5,000), and if you are in the 33 percent bracket, it saves you $660 in taxes each time.

In order for you to be able to claim all of your available itemized deductions and to time them appropriately, we must examine and dissect each one in turn.

# 41 Medical Expenses

You may deduct certain medical and dental expenses not only for yourself but for your spouse and your dependents as well. Medical expenses are payments that you make for the diagnosis, cure, relief, treatment, or prevention of disease. They also include payments for treatment affecting any part or function of the body. Expenses for transportation for needed medical care are included in medical expenses. Payments for insurance that provide medical care for you, your spouse, and your dependents are also included in medical expenses.

The following list shows those items that are generally deductible as medical expenses:

- Fees for doctors, surgeons, dentists, ophthalmologists, optometrists, chiropractors, osteopaths, chiropodists, podiatrists, psychiatrists, psychologists, and Christian Science practitioners.

- Fees for hospital services, therapy, nursing services (including nurses' meals while on duty), ambulance hire, and laboratory, surgical, obstetrics, diagnostic, dental, and X-ray services.

- Meals and lodging provided by a hospital during medical treatment, and meals and lodging provided by a center during treatment for alcoholism or drug addiction.

- Medical and hospital insurance premiums.

- Special equipment such as motorized wheelchairs, hand controls on a car, and special telephones for the deaf.

- Special items, including false teeth, artificial limbs, eyeglasses, hearing aids, crutches, and guide dogs for the blind or deaf.

- Transportation for needed medical care.

- Insulin and prescription medicines and drugs, including special foods and drinks your doctor prescribes specifically for the treatment of an illness, and pills, birth control items, and vitamins and iron your doctor prescribes.

- Under certain conditions, medical deductions may be allowed for boarding school expenses. In Letter Ruling 8447014, the IRS ruled that a psychiatrically oriented boarding school is a special school. Thus, the taxpayer was able to deduct, as a medical expense, tuition as well as transportation expenses to and from the school.

There are certain limitations on the amount you may deduct. You may deduct only that part of your medical and dental expenses that is more than 7.5 percent of your adjusted gross income. Drug expenses, which include *only* prescription drugs and insulin, are included in this 7.5 percent pool.

As of 1983, the separate deduction for one-half of medical insurance premiums up to $150 was eliminated. All medical insurance premiums are included in the 7.5 percent pool.

Medical care includes a wide array of services. It includes payments for a legal abortion as well as payments for an operation legally performed to make a person unable to have children. It includes payments for cosmetic surgery, such as a "face lift," as well as charges for medical care that are included in the tuition fee of a college or private school, as long as the breakdown of the charges is included in the bill given by the school.

Payments for acupuncture and payments to a treatment center for drug addicts or alcoholics, including meals and lodging provided by the center during the treatment, are also deductible. So too are payments for surgical, hospital, laboratory, and transportation expenses by an actual or possible donor of a kidney or other body organ.

Wages for an attendant who provides nursing services and any out-of-pocket amounts you pay for the attendant's meals are also deductible. Divide the food expense among the household members to find the cost of the attendant's food. If you had to pay additional out-of-pocket amounts for household upkeep because of the attendant, this extra amount you paid is deductible as well. This includes items such as extra rent you paid because you moved to a larger apartment to provide space for the attendant, or the extra cost of utilities for the attendant. If the attendant also provided personal and household services, costs for these must be separated from costs for the nursing, since only the amount spent for nursing services is allowable as a deduction. Remember, though, that even the part of the social security (FICA) tax you pay for a worker who provides medical care is deductible.

You may also deduct payments for psychiatric care mainly for relieving a mental illness or defect. You may include the cost of supporting a mentally ill dependent at a specially equipped medical center where the dependent receives medical care, as well as your transportation expenses for regular visits that are recommended as part of that dependent's treatment.

### MEDICAL INSURANCE PREMIUMS

Medical insurance premiums are deductible within the limits described earlier. The premiums you pay for medical insurance are for medical care, whether the insurance company pays the provider of the care (hospital, doctor, etc.) directly or reimburses you for payments you've made. Medical insurance premiums you pay may be included in your medical expenses if the premiums are for:

a) policies that pay for hospitalization, surgical fees, and other medical expenses;

b) policies that pay only for prescription drugs;

c) policies that replace lost or damaged contact lenses;

d) the medical part in policies that provide more than one type of payment, if the medical charge is reasonable and is stated separately in the insurance contract or is given to you in a separate statement;

e) membership in an association furnishing cooperative, "free choice" medical service, or group hospitalization clinical care;

f) Medicare B, supplementary medical insurance for the aged (check the information you receive from the Social Security Administration to find out your premium rate and the amount of your deduction);

g) Medicare A, the part of social security that covers basic Medicare (you may deduct premiums you voluntarily pay for Medicare A coverage if you are 65 or older and are not entitled to social security benefits; Medicare A premiums are not deductible if they are paid as part of your social security tax); *or*

h) prepaid insurance premiums you pay before you are 65 for medical care coverage—for yourself, your spouse, or dependents—after you are 65. These are deductible when paid if they are paid in equal installments yearly or more often. The payments must be made for ten years or more; if paid until you reach 65, the payments must be made for a minimum of five years.

You may not deduct premiums paid for life insurance policies or for policies providing repayment for loss of earnings or for the accidental loss of limb, life, sight, etc. Nor can you deduct premiums for a policy that guarantees a specified amount each week (for a specified number of weeks) if you are hospitalized for sickness or injury.

HOSPITAL MEALS AND LODGING

Meals and lodging are also deductible if they are furnished by a hospital or similar institution as a necessary part of medcial care and if the main reason for your being in the hospital is to receive that medical care. The cost of your meals or lodging while you are away from home for medical treatment, or for the relief of a specific condition, however, is not deductible if you are not at a hospital or similar institution, even if the trip is made on the advice of your doctor. Under the Tax Reform Act of 1984, a deduction of up to $50 per day per individual for lodging expenses, but not for meals, for the patient and certain accompanying individuals away from home to receive outpatient care at hospitals or certain outpatient clinics is allowed. For example, treatment in an outpatient clinic, such as the Mayo Clinic, that provides substantially similar services to those provided by a hospital would qualify. Moreover, although food costs are not deductible, presumably if they are included in the cost of the lodging, no allocation is necessary and the full cost will be deductible subject to the $50 per day per person limit. (See Letter Ruling 8516025.)

Alternatively, if an individual is in a nursing home or a home for the aged because of a physical condition, and the main reason for being there is to get medical care, the entire cost, including meals *and* lodging, may be included as a deductible medical expense.


TRANSPORTATION EXPENSES

Transportation payments necessary for medical care also qualify as a deductible medical expense. Assume that you have been ill with a bad heart condition and you live in an area that has extremely cold winters, which makes your condition worse. Your doctor advises you to spend the winter in a warmer place, and you and your family spend the winter in a rented house in Florida. The trip is made for a specific medical reason, and although none of your expenses for food and lodging while on your way to Florida or during your stay there are deductible, your share of the transportation expenses between your home and Florida *is* deductible.

Transportation expenses include the following:

- Amounts paid for bus, taxi, train, or plane fare, or for ambulance hire.

- Out-of-pocket expenses for your car, such as gas and oil. You may not deduct any part of general repair or maintenance expenses. If you do not wish to deduct your actual expenses, you may use the standard rate of 9¢ a mile for each mile you use your car for medical reasons, and add to that any parking fees and tolls that you pay.

- Transportation expenses of a parent who must accompany a child needing medical care.

- Transportation expenses of a nurse familiar with injections, medications, and other treatments required by a patient who is traveling to get medical care but cannot travel alone.

### CARE FOR THE HANDICAPPED

Special care may be needed for handicapped individuals. You may include the following payments for this care in your deductible medical expenses:

1. Payments to a special school for mentally or physically handicapped individuals, if the main reason for going is the school's means for relieving the handicap. The cost of sending a blind child to school to learn braille, or a deaf child to learn lip reading, is a medical expense. If you pay for remedial language training to correct a condition caused by a birth defect of the brain, you may deduct these payments as medical expenses.

   Tuition or tutoring expenses you pay on your doctor's advice for a child who has severe learning disabilities caused by a nervous system disorder are also medical expenses. So too are the costs of meals, lodging, and ordinary education supplied by the special school, but only if the main reason for the child's attendance is the availability of medical care.

2. The cost of keeping a mentally retarded individual, at the advice of a psychiatrist, in a specially chosen home that is not the home of a relative; for example, a "halfway" house to help in the adjustment from life in a mental hospital to community living.

3. Payments to a nonprofessional individual for giving "patterning" exercises (coordinated physical manipulation of the individual's limbs to imitate crawling and other normal movements) to a mentally retarded child.

4. Advance payments to a private institution for the lifetime care, treatment, and training of your physically and mentally handicapped dependent in the event that you die or become unable to care for your dependent. The payments must be required as a condition for the institution's future acceptance of your dependent and cannot be refundable.

5. Expenses paid for the care of your invalid spouse in your home. Only amounts spent for care to relieve your spouse's illness are deductible. The cost of household services, such as cooking and cleaning, is not deductible as a medical expense but may be eligible for the credit for household and dependent care expenses.

SPECIAL MEDICAL EQUIPMENT

Moreover, you may also deduct payments for special items and equipment. This includes payments for:

1. False teeth, artificial limbs, eyeglasses, hearing aids, and crutches, or the cost and care of guide dogs for the blind and deaf. Such expenses are medical, not business, even if you use the dog in carrying on your business.

2. The part of the cost of braille books and magazines that is more than the price for regular books and magazines.

3. The cost and repair of special telephone equipment that enables a deaf person to communicate over a regular telephone.

4. Amounts paid for oxygen equipment and oxygen to relieve problems in breathing due to a medical condition.

5. The cost of special attachments, such as a motorized wheelchair or autoette or special hand controls that are installed in a car for the use of a physically handicapped driver.

6. The amount you pay for a special design of a car to hold a wheelchair, as well as the cost of operating and keeping up an autoette or wheelchair used mainly for the relief of sickness or disability.

7. The cost of removing lead-based paints from walls, woodwork, etc., in your home to prevent a child who has lead poisoning (or who has had lead poisoning) from eating the paint. This must be on the advice of a doctor, and it must be determined that the paint contains lead. The areas covered with lead-based paint have to be in poor repair (peeling or cracking) or within the child's reach. The cost of painting the scraped area is not a deductible medical expense.

Payments for special equipment installed in a home, or similar improvements made for medical reasons, may be deductible even if they are capital improvements. If these expenses are for permanent improvements that increase the value of the property, only the amount in excess of the increase in value may be deducted as a medical expense. For example, assume you have a heart ailment, and on your doctor's advice you install an elevator in your home so that you will not need to climb stairs. The elevator costs $1,000. According to competent appraisals, the elevator increases the value of your home by $700. The $300 difference is a medical expense. If the elevator did not increase the value of your home, the whole cost would have been a medical expense.

If a capital expense qualifies as a medical expense, any amount paid for operation or upkeep also qualifies as a medical expense, as long as the medical reason for the capital expense still exists. These expenses are deductible even if none or only part of the original expense was deductible.

Amounts paid by a handicapped individual to buy and install special plumbing fixtures in a rented house are also deductible medical expenses. For example, assume you are handicapped with arthritis and a bad heart condition. You cannot climb stairs or get into a bathtub. On your doctor's advice, you install a bathroom with a shower stall on the first floor of your two-story rented house. The landlord does not pay any of the cost of buying or installing the special plumbing and does not lower your rent. The whole amount you pay for this bathroom is a deductible medical expense. A medical expense deduction is also available for the cost of special equipment used to display subtitles on the television set of a hearing impaired individual (Revenue Ruling 80-340).

In 1987, the IRS released a list of thirteen such deductible home improvements. If these improvements are made to accommodate yourself or a family member with a physical handicap, they count in full toward the 7.5 percent deduction floor (Revenue Ruling Section 7-106, IRB 1987-43).

The improvements on the IRS list are the following:

1.  Constructing entrance or exit ramps to the home

2.  Widening doorways and entrances or exits to the home

3.  Widening or otherwise modifying halls and interior doorways

4.  Installing railings, support bars, or other modifications to bathrooms

5.  Lowering or making other modifications to kitchen cabinets and equipment

6.  Altering the location of or otherwise modifying electrical outlets and fixtures

7.  Installing porch lifts or other forms of lifts (this does not include elevators, as they may increase the value of the home)

8.  Modifying fire alarms, smoke detectors, and other warning systems

9.  Modifying stairs

10.  Adding handrails and grab bars, whether or not in bathrooms

11.  Modifying hardware on doors

12.  Modifying areas in front of entrance and exit doorways

13.  Grading of ground to provide access to the home

Note that just because an improvement is not on the above list, this does not necessarily mean that such an improvement is not a fully deductible expense.

COMPUTING YOUR MEDICAL EXPENSES

Computing your medical expenses is a simple process. For 1987, your allowable drugs, your medical insurance premiums, plus all of your other medical expenses, are reduced by 7.5 percent of your adjusted gross income. Taxpayers and dependents 65 or older, as well as younger persons, are subject to 7.5 percent limitations.

If you and your spouse live in a community property state and file separate returns, any amount you paid for medical expenses out of community funds is divided equally. Each of you may deduct half of the expenses. If medical expenses are paid out of the separate funds of one spouse, only the spouse who paid the medical expenses may deduct them.

If you and your spouse do not live in a community property state and you file separate returns, each of you may deduct only the medical expenses you actually paid. Any medical expenses paid out of a joint checking account in which you and your spouse have the same interest are considered to have been paid equally by each of you, unless you can show otherwise. Furthermore, you must reduce your total medical expenses for the year by the total reimbursements (repayments) you receive from insurance or other sources for those expenses during the year. This includes payments you receive from Medicare A and Medicare B. The reimbursement may be paid directly to you or to the doctor or hospital.

The actual computation of your medical expense deduction can be demonstrated by the following example. Assume you and your spouse paid the following medical expenses during 1988:

a)  $595.60 for hospital insurance, $80.40 for medical and surgical insurance, $125 for allowable medicines and drugs, $237.86 for hospital bills, $39 for doctor bills, and $20 for transportation;

b) $200 for doctors and $75 for medicines and allowable drugs for your spouse's dependent mother;

c) $350 for doctors and $100 for medicines for your sister, whom you claim as your dependent.

The hospital and doctor expenses cited have already been reduced by repayment from your insurance company. Your adjusted gross income is $20,374.33. The deductible amount is computed as follows:

|  |  |  |
|---|---|---|
| Medicines and drugs | | |
| You and spouse | | 125.00 |
| Spouse's mother | | 75.00 |
| Sister | | +100.00 |
| Total medicines and drugs | | $300.00 |
| Insurance: | | |
| Hospitalization | $ | 595.60 |
| Medical and surgical | | + 80.40 |
| Total insurance | | 676.00 |
| Other medical expenses: | | |
| You and spouse (doctors) | | 39.00 |
| Spouse's mother (doctors) | | 200.00 |
| Sister (doctors) | | 350.00 |
| You and spouse (hosp.) | | 237.86 |
| Transportation | | + 20.00 |
| Total medical expenses [medicine plus insurance plus other expenses ($300.00 + 676.00 + 846.86)] | | 846.86 |
| | | 1822.86 |
| Minus 7.5 percent exclusion ($20,374.33 × .075) | | −1528.07 |
| Total deduction | | 294.79 |

Not only must you reduce your total medical expenses by the total reimbursements you have received from insurance and other sources for those expenses, but if you receive payment under an accident insurance contract, you must also reduce your medical expenses by that part of the payment set aside for hospitalization and medical care. However, you need not reduce medical expenses by any repayments you have received for loss of earnings or damages for personal injury. But you must also reduce medical expenses by that amount received in settlement of a damage suit for personal injuries that has been set aside for future medical expenses. Medical expenses paid this year and in future years because of these injuries must be reduced until the amount received in settlement has been completely used. Any amount you pay after that may be deductible.

Even if you fail to file a claim under an insurance policy that would have covered your medical expenses, those expenses that you pay are still deductible (*Weaver*, TCM 1984-634).

If you are reimbursed for medical expenses you deducted in an earlier year, you must report as income the amount of the reimbursement that is equal to or less than the amount you previously deducted as medical expenses. For example, assume you had an adjusted gross income in year A of $10,000, and during that year you paid medical insurance premiums of $200 and incurred medical expenses of $800. No amount was included for medicine and drugs. You deducted $250, figured as follows:

| | |
|---|---|
| Medical expenses | 800 |
| Plus insurance | +200 |
| Total medical expenses | 1000 |
| Minus 7.5 percent of adjusted gross income | −750 |
| Total deduction | $250 |

In year B you collected $200 under your insurance policy as reimbursement for part of your year A medical expenses. If you had collected in year A, your deduction for medical expenses would have been only $50, figured as follows:

| | |
|---|---|
| Medical expenses | 800 |
| Plus insurance | +200 |
| Total medical expenses | 1000 |
| Minus insurance reimbursements | −200 |
| Balance | 800 |
| Minus 7.5 percent of adjusted gross income | −750 |
| Total deduction | $50 |

Since the $200 reimbursement is less than the $250 deduction, you should include $200 in income in year B.

If you did not deduct a medical expense in the year you paid it, either because you did not itemize deductions or because your medical expenses were not more than the 7.5 percent limitation, you should not include in income the reimbursement for this expense that you received in a later year. For example, assume in year C you paid $150 for medical insurance premiums and $400 for medical expenses, but you could not deduct the $400 because it was under the 7.5 percent limitation. If in year D you were reimbursed for any of the $400 medical expenses, you would also not include the reimbursement in your gross income because you received no tax benefit for it in the earlier year.

There are a number of sophisticated tax planning strategies that you can utilize when claiming medical expense deductions. First, you must recognize that these expenses are deductible only in the year that they are paid. If you charge medical expenses to your credit card, these expenses are deducted in the year the charge is made—it does not matter when you paid the amount charged. But expenses for eyeglasses, dental work, hearing aids, elective surgery, and year-end doctor visits can often be juggled as to the year in which they are actually paid. Since these medical expenses must exceed 7.5 percent of your adjusted gross income before you can begin taking deductions, it may pay to bunch expenses in one year if that will get you over the hump. You currently cannot deduct a mere prepayment of a possible future bill, however. There must be an actual bill or at least an actual scheduling of services.

Medical expense shifting can be demonstrated by the following example. Assume your adjusted gross income is $30,000. Late this year your doctor bills you $2,000. Your other medical expenses amount to only $250. If you can, pay in January of next year. You will get no deduction in this year, anyway (7.5 percent of $30,000 is $2,250), so deferring the expense until next year will give you another chance of exceeding the 7.5 percent floor.

Alternatively, if you have already met your 7.5 percent floor, you should accelerate the payment of your medical expenses. Payments in December of this year will reduce your taxes and increase your cash balance, and the potential earnings on it, for all of next year. If you wait till January to make the payment, the deduction and its attendant tax benefit will be deferred for an additional year (even assuming that you meet the percent limit in the second year).

For example, assume you have exceeded the standard deduction amount and the 7.5 percent floor for deducting medical expenses. Further assume that in mid-December you have a $1,000 doctor bill due in 30 days. If you are in the 33 percent bracket and pay the bill in December, you save $330 in taxes, *and* you have an additional $330 on which you can earn interest throughout the next tax year. If you wait until January to make the payment, you will lose the interest on the saved $330 in taxes and may lose the deduction completely if you cannot both pass the percent floor test and exceed your standard deduction amount for excess itemized deductions. The solution in this case, clearly, is to make the payment on December 31.

TAX STRATEGIES

Sophisticated tax planning also involves knowing how to structure your personal deductions so that they qualify as allowable medical expenses. Many expenditures that do not readily appear to be deductible are allowable as medical expenses. For example, elastic stockings qualify as medical expenses if needed by an infirm or elderly woman. In one case, the cost of a sacroiliac belt prescribed by a doctor was deductible, as was the cost of high blood pressure medication and a blood sugar test. In another instance, a deduction was allowed for a device installed to add fluoride to a home water supply at a controlled rate; it was represented that fluoride is a chemical that strengthens the dental enamel as the teeth grow, making them more resistant to decay, and that the only purpose of the installation and use of the device was to prevent tooth decay. Travel to Alcoholics Anonymous meetings, based on medical advice, is a deductible medical expense (Revenue Ruling 63-273).

Deductions have been allowed for extraordinary forms of medical equipment. For example, the costs of oxygen equipment and oxygen to alleviate breathing difficulty *and* of a reclining chair recommended by a doctor for a person with a cardiac condition have qualified as medical deductions. So, too, have special mattresses and certain thicknesses of plywood boards prescribed for an individual who had arthritis of the spine. In one instance, a wig purchased to avoid mental upset to a patient who had lost her hair was deductible!

Super medical deductions can be obtained if your doctor can find an ailment in yourself, your spouse, or your dependents that would require you to have a whirlpool for baths, or central air conditioning to provide you or your dependents with pure, humid air. Even the expense of a swimming pool may be deducted if it is installed because of a physician's recommendation and if that facility in any way alleviates your physical condition (see *Cherry* TCM 1983-470 and Revenue Ruling 63-273, 1963-2 CB 112). If such a swimming pool is used for a specific medical purpose—for example, to provide hydrotherapy—then not only is a deduction allowed for the installation, but a deduction is also allowed for the cost of upkeep, including chemicals, cleaning, water, and utilities. Note, though, that the installation is a capital expenditure and therefore only the excess cost over the added value to your property is deductible. (See Revenue Ruling 83-33 and Letter Ruling 822-1128 and 832-6095.)

One of my own favorite medical deductions is the cost of an overseas trip for medical or dental work. For example, it has been established that the cost of extensive dental work is far less expensive in Europe than in the United States. Therefore, even adding the transportation costs to go to an overseas dentist, your total cash outlay is lower than having such work performed locally. On this basis, such transportation costs have been allowed as deductible medical expenses. One woman consulted three different dermatologists in the United States, but none was able to improve her skin condition. Finally, she was treated successfully as an outpatient in a foreign country. The IRS agreed that her expenses were deductible (Letter Ruling 812-6044).

Furthermore, amounts paid for "medical care" may be deductible even if they are for purposes that do not have the sanction of the medical profession or even if the payments are made to persons without medical qualifications. For example, amounts paid to such practitioners as psychotherapists are categorized for tax purposes as fees for medical care, even though those who perform the services may not be licensed, certified, or otherwise qualified to perform these services, and even if certification is required by law. In other words, payments to unlicensed practitioners are deductible if the type and quality of their services are not illegal and if such services may be deemed to fall within the parameters of "medical care." In fact, in IRS Letter Ruling 8442018, the Internal Revenue Service allowed as a deductible medical expense electrolysis performed by a nonlicensed technician as "medical care." Remember, medical care means any amounts paid for the diagnosis, cure, mitigation, treatment, or prevention of disease or for the purpose of affecting any structure or function of the body. (In Revenue Ruling 82-111, the IRS had ruled that hair removal through electrolysis performed by a state licensed technician was deductible as a medical expense.)

A second category of below the line deductions is the taxes that you pay during your tax year. Such taxes fall under three classifications, which will be discussed separately.

# 42

## Income Taxes

You may deduct some state and local income taxes, including taxes on interest income that is exempt from federal income tax. You may not deduct state and local taxes on any other exempt income. For example, the part of state income tax on a cost-of-living allowance that is exempt from federal income tax is not deductible.

State and local taxes are those imposed by the fifty states or any of their political subdivisions (such as a county or city) and by the District of Columbia. You may deduct state, local, or foreign income taxes withheld from your salary, as well as estimated payments made under a pay-as-you-go-plan of a state or local government. You also may deduct payments made on taxes due but not paid in an earlier year in the year they were actually withheld or paid. In sum, to be deductible the tax must be paid during your tax year. You may deduct only those taxes paid during the calendar year for which you file a return.

If you receive a refund of these taxes in a later year, you must include the return as income in the year you receive it. This would include refunds resulting from taxes that were overwithheld, not figured correctly, or figured again as a result of an amended return. If you did not itemize your deductions in a previous year, you do not have to include the refunds. Furthermore, the amount included in your income is limited to the tax benefit you received in the earlier years. For example, assume you deducted $500 in taxes and received a refund of $100; your total itemized deductions exceeded your standard deduction amount by only $50. The only tax benefit you received, therefore, was the $50 excess itemized deduction. On this basis you need only include $50 of the refund in your income for the subsequent year.

You also may deduct amounts required to be withheld from your wages for certain state disability benefit funds that provide against loss of wages. These payments to the disability fund are deductible as state income taxes. Furthermore, employee contributions to a state fund that provides indemnity coverage for the loss of wages caused by unemployment resulting from business contingencies are also deductible as taxes. Employee contributions to private disability plans, however, are not deductible.

Foreign taxes include those taxes imposed by a foreign country, a U.S. possession, or any of their political subdivisions.

Foreign income taxes that you pay may either be deducted as an itemized deduction or claimed as a credit against your U.S. tax.

## 43  Real Property Taxes

Real property (real estate) taxes are any state, local, or foreign taxes on real property levied for the general public welfare. Local benefit taxes are deductible if they are for maintenance or repair, or for interest charges related to these benefits. If only a part of the tax is for maintenance, repair, or interest, you must be able to show the amount of that part to claim the deduction. If you cannot determine what part is for maintenance or repair, none of it is deductible.

If you are a tenant shareholder in a cooperative housing corporation, you may deduct the amounts you pay to that corporation that represent your share of the real estate taxes the corporation pays or incurs on the property. If the corporation leases the land and buildings and is required to pay the real estate taxes under the terms of the lease agreement, however, your part of the taxes is not deductible. Moreover, if your landlord increases your rent in the form of a tax surcharge because of increased real estate taxes, you cannot deduct that increase as taxes either.

Real property taxes also do not include trash and garbage collection fees or homeowners association charges you may pay for the recreation, health, safety, and welfare of residents, and for maintaining common areas.

If real estate is sold during the tax year, the real estate taxes must be divided between the buyer and seller. These taxes must be divided according to the number of days in the real property tax year (the period to which the imposed tax relates) that each owns the property. The seller pays the taxes up to the date of the sale, and the buyer pays the taxes beginning with the date of the sale, regardless of the lien dates under local law. If you use the cash method and do not deduct taxes until they are paid, and the buyer of your property is personally liable for the tax, you are considered to have paid your portion of the imposed tax at the time of the sale. This permits you to deduct the portion of the tax to the date of sale even though you did not actually pay for it.

For example, assume that your real property tax year is the calendar year, with payment due on August 1. Your tax on your old home, sold May

5, was $300, and your tax on your new home, bought on May 3, was $200. You are considered to have paid a proportionate share of the real estate taxes on the old home even though you did not actually pay them to the taxing authority. On the other hand, you may claim only the proportionate share of the taxes you paid on your new property even though you paid the entire amount.

Because you held the old property for 125 days (January 1 to May 4, the day before the sale), you are entitled to a deduction of 125/365 of $300, or $102.73. You owned the new home for 243 days (May 3 to December 31, including the date of the purchase), so your taxes on the new home are 243/365 of $200, or $133.15. Your real estate tax deduction is therefore $102.73 + $133.15, or $235.88.

If you and your spouse held property jointly, and you file separate returns, each of you may deduct only the taxes each of you paid on the property.

# 44

## Personal Property Taxes

Some personal property taxes are also deductible, subject to certain requirements:

1. The tax must be based only on the value of the personal property. For example, assume your state charges a yearly motor vehicle registration tax of 1 percent of value plus 40¢ per hundredweight. You pay $28.60 based on the value ($1,500) and weight (3,400 pounds) of your car. You may deduct $15 as a personal property tax, since it is based on the value. The remaining $13.60, based on the weight, is not deductible.

2. The tax must be charged on a yearly basis, even if it is collected more or less often than once a year.

3. The tax must be charged on personal property. A tax is considered charged on personal property even if it is for the exercise of a privilege. A yearly tax based on value qualifies as a personal property tax although it is called a registration fee—that is, for the privilege of registering motor vehicles or using them on the highways.

# 45

## Interest

Some interest payments qualify as below the line deductions. The type of deduction you may take depends on whether the money was borrowed for personal use, for rental or royalty property, or for your business.

Interest payment on a loan for income-producing rental or royalty property, on a business loan, and on farm business loans are "above the line" deductions. Interest of a personal nature, such as home mortgage interest, is a "below the line" deduction; normally, so is interest paid on margin accounts held with your broker. Interest on these accounts is considered paid when the broker is paid, or when the interest becomes available to the broker through your account.

To deduct interest on a debt, you must be legally liable for that debt. No deduction will be allowed for payments you make for someone else if you are not legally liable to make them. Both the lender and the borrower must intend that the loan be repaid.

For example, assume you make a loan to your son, hoping to be repaid when he is able. If no true debtor-credit relationship is created, he is not legally liable to pay the debt and will not be able to deduct any interest paid. Here he should sign a note and make scheduled repayments to insure his interest deduction. Alternatively, if you cosign a note for a loan made by a bank to your son, even if your son is a student, and if both you and your son are jointly liable on the note, you may deduct any interest you pay on the loan in the year you pay it.

You must normally pay the interest before you may deduct it. But if you use the accrual method of accounting, you may deduct interest over the period it accrues regardless of when it is paid. To show how this works, suppose you borrow $1,000 in September, *payable in 90 days* at 12 percent interest. In December you make the payment with a new note for $1,030 due the following March. If you use the cash method of accounting, that $30 is not deductible in the year you give the new note, since you do not actually pay the interest. However, if you pay the $30 and give a new note for $1,000, the interest is deductible. If you are on the accrual method, the $30 is deductible in either case. If you pay interest in advance for a period that goes beyond the end of the tax year, you must spread the interest over the tax years to which it belongs. You may deduct in each year only the interest that belongs to that year.

The following items are generally deductible as interest:

Mortgage interest
"Points," if you are a buyer (see explanation that follows)
Mortgage prepayment penalties

Finance charges separately stated
Bank credit card plan interest
Note discount interest
Interest on a personal loan
Interest on a business loan
Installment plan interest

The following items normally are *not* deductible as interest:

"Points," if you are a seller
Service charges
Credit investigation fees
Loan fees
Interest relating to tax-exempt income
Interest paid to carry single-premium life insurance
Premium on a convertible bond
Interest owed to related taxpayers, unless there is an actual debtor-
   creditor relationship

One of the most usual types of personal interest expense is the interest on your mortgage. You may deduct only the interest part of your mortgage payment. If your records do not show the interest paid, get a statement showing that information from the lender who holds your mortgage. If you are a cash method taxpayer, you may deduct the full amount of interest paid during the year. If you are an accrual method taxpayer, you may deduct the amount accrued each year.

A point is equal to 1 percent of the loan amount, so on a $100,000 mortgage each point would cost you $1,000. If you pay off a mortgage over 30 years, each point on a 12 percent loan adds 0.13 percentage points to the interest rate. Thus on a 12 percent loan with 4 points charged, the effective interest rate is 12.52. On a 14 percent, 30-year loan, each point adds 0.15 percentage points. On a 16 percent loan, it is 0.17 percentage points. Keep in mind that these figures apply only if the mortgage is paid off over the full 30-year term. If you sell the property and pay off the loan sooner, the effective interest is higher, since those extra dollars paid up front are spread over fewer years of borrowing.

## Effective Interest Rates on Mortgages with Points

| Stated Rate (%) | Points (%) | | | | |
|---|---|---|---|---|---|
| | 1 | 2 | 3 | 4 | 5 |

*Assuming 30-year mortgage held to maturity*

| | | | | | |
|---|---|---|---|---|---|
| 5 | 5.09 | 5.18 | 5.27 | 5.36 | 5.46 |
| 6 | 6.09 | 6.19 | 6.29 | 6.29 | 6.48 |
| 7 | 7.01 | 7.20 | 7.30 | 7.41 | 7.52 |
| 8 | 8.11 | 8.21 | 8.32 | 8.44 | 8.55 |
| 9 | 9.22 | 9.23 | 9.34 | 9.46 | 9.58 |
| 10 | 10.12 | 10.24 | 10.37 | 10.49 | 10.62 |
| 11 | 11.13 | 11.26 | 11.39 | 11.52 | 11.66 |
| 12 | 12.13 | 12.27 | 12.41 | 12.55 | 12.70 |

*Assuming 30-year mortgage paid off in 15th year*

| | | | | | |
|---|---|---|---|---|---|
| 5 | 5.11 | 5.22 | 5.33 | 5.44 | 5.56 |
| 6 | 6.11 | 6.23 | 6.35 | 6.46 | 6.58 |
| 7 | 7.12 | 7.24 | 7.36 | 7.49 | 7.61 |
| 8 | 8.12 | 8.21 | 8.32 | 8.44 | 8.55 |
| 9 | 9.13 | 9.26 | 9.40 | 9.53 | 9.67 |
| 10 | 10.14 | 10.28 | 10.42 | 10.56 | 10.70 |
| 11 | 11.14 | 11.29 | 11.44 | 11.59 | 11.74 |
| 12 | 12.15 | 12.30 | 12.46 | 12.61 | 12.77 |

*Assuming 30-year mortgage paid off in 7th year*

| | | | | | |
|---|---|---|---|---|---|
| 5 | 5.18 | 5.36 | 5.55 | 5.73 | 5.92 |
| 6 | 6.18 | 6.37 | 6.56 | 6.75 | 6.95 |
| 7 | 7.19 | 7.38 | 7.57 | 7.77 | 7.97 |
| 8 | 8.19 | 8.39 | 8.59 | 8.79 | 8.99 |
| 9 | 9.20 | 9.40 | 9.61 | 9.81 | 10.02 |
| 10 | 10.20 | 10.41 | 10.62 | 10.83 | 11.05 |
| 11 | 11.21 | 11.42 | 11.64 | 11.86 | 12.08 |
| 12 | 12.22 | 12.44 | 12.66 | 12.88 | 13.11 |

*(continued on next page)*

*Assuming 30-year mortage paid off in 3rd year*

| | | | | |
|---|---|---|---|---|
| 5 | 5.37 | 5.74 | 6.12 | 6.50 | 6.89 |
| 6 | 6.37 | 6.75 | 7.13 | 7.52 | 7.91 |
| 7 | 7.38 | 7.76 | 8.15 | 8.54 | 8.93 |
| 8 | 8.38 | 8.77 | 9.16 | 9.56 | 9.96 |
| 9 | 9.39 | 9.78 | 10.18 | 10.58 | 10.98 |
| 10 | 10.39 | 10.79 | 11.19 | 11.60 | 12.01 |
| 11 | 11.40 | 11.80 | 12.21 | 12.62 | 13.04 |
| 12 | 12.40 | 12.81 | 13.22 | 13.64 | 14.06 |

The term "points" is sometimes used to describe the charges paid by a borrower. They are also called loan origination fees, maximum loan charges, or premium charges. If the payment of any of these charges is solely for the use of money, then it is considered interest.

In one case, the Tax Court allowed a taxpayer to deduct interest he paid on a mortgage on his residence, even though the title to the home was held in the name of his corporation. The Court reasoned that the taxpayer had always treated the home as his own and the mortgage indebtedness therefore was his (*Lang, Jr.*, TCM 1983-318).

The amount you pay in points is deductible in full in the year of payment only if it is paid to buy or improve your main home and if the loan is for that home. The charging of points has to be an established business practice in your area. The deduction may not be more than a number of points generally charged in your area. If these conditions are not met, points are treated as prepaid interest. They must be spread over the life of the mortgage, and are considered as paid and deductible over that period. Moreover, in IR Notice 86-68, May 13, 1986, the Internal Revenue Service ruled that points paid on refinancing a home mortgage are not *currently* deductible. Thus, they could only be deducted over the loan period. For example, assume that $2,400 of points is paid in connection with refinancing a mortgage that is to run for another 20 years (i.e., 240 monthly payments remain to be paid). These points are deductible over the term of the loan, $10 per monthly payment. The IRS reaffirmed this position in Rev. Rul. 87-22. However, several senators have introduced bills in Congress to overrule this decision.

Points charged for specific services by the lender for the borrower's account (such as a lender's appraisal fee, the cost of preparing the mortgage note or deed of trust, settlement fees, or notary fees) are not interest. Points charged for services in connection with getting a V.A. loan also are not interest. For example, assume you got a loan from a bank to buy your main home. The loan was insured by the Veterans Administration and you paid the bank a loan origination fee. This fee was 1 percent of the amount of the loan and was charged in addition to the maximum rate of interest permitted. The amount of the 1 percent loan origination fee (one "point") is not interest and may not be deducted.

Alternatively, assume you got a loan of $48,000 to buy a $60,000 home. In addition to interest at the rate of 9 percent, you paid the lender a loan processing fee of $1,440 (three "points"). None of the fee was for specific services. The charging of points was an established business practice in the area and the number of points was not more than that generally charged in the area. This loan processing fee to purchase a principal residence is interest and is deductible in full in the year of payment. [See Section 461(g)(2) and *Schubel,* 77 TC no. 701 (1981).] See also *Pacific First Federal Savings and Loan Association,* 79 TC No. 33 where points were found to be interest where the fee was for the use or forebearance of money and bore no relation to the actual cost to underwrite the loan.] Make sure you exchange checks with your bank rather than just reduce the amount received on your mortgage. Unless you formally exchange checks, the Internal Revenue Service will argue a lack of "payment."

The term "points" is also used to describe loan placement fees that the seller may have to pay to the lender to arrange financing for the buyer. You may *not* deduct these amounts as interest. However, these charges are a selling expense that reduces the amount realized by the seller. Furthermore, if you pay off your mortgage early, you may have to pay a penalty. This amount is deductible as interest, as is any amount you pay as a tenant stockholder in a housing cooperative for the interest on the cooperative's debt, or for points required in the year you became a tenant-stockholder.

In Revenue Procedure 87-15, IRB 1987-14, the Internal Revenue Service set forth the method for determining the amount of points allocable to each tax year during the term of an indebtedness in a situation where points charged to a taxpayer in respect of the indebtedness are required to be deducted over the period of indebtedness. Such points may be deductible on an internal rate of return basis—i.e., considering the time value of money with the bulk of the deduction being taken in the earlier years—or, alternatively, as a matter of administrative convenience, the Internal Revenue Service will allow a taxpayer consistently to allocate the points ratably over the indebtedness. For example, if $3,600 in qualified points were paid on a 30-year (360-month) loan, $10 per payment would be allowed as deductible point interest ($3,600 divided into 360 monthly payments).

Note that the points must be paid at the time the indebtedness is incurred. In *Schubel,* 77 T.C. 701 (1981), the Tax Court held that points withheld by a lender from loan proceeds may not be deducted by a borrower in the year the points are withheld, because the withholding did not constitute payment within that tax year.

Other payments also constitute interest. When you buy property on the installment plan, you may deduct your interest payments if they are separately stated, or if they can be determined and proved. Finance charges added to your monthly credit card statements also constitute deductible interest, as do one-time charges made on new cash advances and new check and overdraft advances added to your bank credit card account balance. No part of these one-time charges, though, can be a service charge, loan fee, credit investigation fee, or similar charge.

When you buy personal property such as clothing, jewelry, furniture, or appliances on the installment plan using a revolving charge account, there is usually a separately stated finance charge. The total amount of these finance charges is deductible as interest, subject to the consumer interest deduction phaseout discussed below. For example, if you buy a refrigerator for $300 from the American Department Store and charge it to your revolving charge account, there will be no extra charge if you pay the balance within 30 days after you are billed. But if you make installment payments, your account will be charged the finance charge of 1.5 percent on the unpaid balance each month. These finance charges are deductible as interest.

Sometimes when you borrow money the interest is subtracted from the face amount of the note and you receive the balance. If you use the cash method, you may deduct the interest only in the year you make payments. Alternatively, if you use the accrual method, you may deduct the interest as it accrues.

For example, assume you sign a note for $1,200 on March 27, agreeing to pay it in 12 equal installments beginning on April 28. The interest is $1,200 × 12 percent = $144 and is subtracted from the face value of the note so that you receive only $1,056. If you use the cash method, the interest is considered to be repaid in 12 installments of $12 each. Your deduction for the first year is $108 ($12 × nine payments). If you miss two payments in the first year and made only seven payments, your deduction is $84. If you use the accrual method, the deduction is determined by prorating interest over the period in which it accrues. You may therefore deduct $108 (9/12 × $144) in the first year and $36 (3/12 × $144) in the following year.

Interest often is "hidden" in other payments, such as in judgments and personal loans. If you make a late payment of taxes, or if you must pay additional taxes at a later date, part of the amount will usually be for interest. This interest is deductible. Penalties, however, are not deductible. Furthermore, you may not deduct interest on any money you borrow to buy tax-exempt securities or to buy a single-premium life insurance endowment or annuity contract. A single-premium contract includes policies on which you pay almost all the premiums within four years from the date you buy the contract; it also includes policies for which you deposit an amount with the insurer for the payment of future premiums. Also, you may not deduct interest on a loan that is used to buy stock if the collateral on the loan is a single-premium annuity contract.

However, according to Revenue Ruling 83-51, the Internal Revenue Service holds that the "contingent interest" portion of a shared appreciation mortgage (SAM) loan used by a cash-basis individual taxpayer to finance the purchase of a personal residence is deductible as interest when paid. The ruling deals with three situations. In each, the taxpayer purchases a home by securing a SAM from a financial institution. The SAM provides for a fixed interest annual rate and "contingent interest" equal to 40 percent of the appreciation in the value of the residence, payable when the SAM terminates. Termination is to occur at the earliest of (1) prepayment of the entire outstanding balance of the SAM, (2) sale of the residence, or (3) ten years from the SAM loan. The taxpayer also has the option to refinance the mortgage balance and contingent interest due at the prevailing interest rate. The SAM agreement provides that it creates no more than a debtor–creditor relationship.

In the first situation provided for under the ruling, the taxpayer sells the residence at a profit and uses a portion of the sales proceeds to pay the remaining SAM principal balance and the contingent interest. In the second situation, the taxpayer prepays the outstanding principal balance and contingent interest with funds not obtained from the SAM lender. In the third situation, the taxpayer refinances the principal balance and contingent interest due on maturity of the SAM by obtaining a conventional thirty-year mortgage from the SAM lender. The Internal Revenue Service holds that in the first and second situations, the taxpayer can deduct the contingent interest in the year the SAM is paid off, on the grounds that interest, to be deductible, need not be computed at a stated rate. All that is required is that a definitely ascertainable sum be paid for the use of borrowed money pursuant to a loan agreement. In the first and second situations, the contingent interest is ascertainable. In the third situation, however, the taxpayer cannot deduct contingent interest, because merely executing a new note does not constitute payment. But payments on the new note to the extent allocable to the contingent interest will be deductible in the year paid. In all three situations, the taxpayer can deduct the fixed interest when paid.

To insure that you have a debtor–creditor relationship and that the SAM does not in substance create an equity arrangement, the SAM agreement should provide, in addition to stating that only a debtor–creditor relationship is intended, that:

a) the mortgage secures only the indebtedness;

b) the mortgagor can sell, transfer, improve, and encumber the property without the mortgagee's consent;

c) the mortgagee is not liable for any decrease in the value of the property; *and*

d) the mortgagor is solely responsible to pay real estate taxes, insurance premiums, and other charges relating to ownership.

There are certain limitations on the amount of interest that you can deduct.

The deduction for investment interest incurred or continued is limited to net investment income to purchase or carry *property held for investment*. Disallowed investment interest can be carried forward indefinitely and allowed to the extent of future net investment income.

Investment income and investment expenses do not include any income or expenses taken into account when computing income or loss from a passive activity, including any interest paid or accrued on debt to acquire or carry an interest in a passive activity. However, it does include portfolio income from passive activities.

## DEFINITIONS

*Net investment income* means the excess of *investment income* over *investment expenses*. Investment income is defined as income from interest, dividends, rents, royalties, short-term capital gains arising from the disposition of investment assets, and certain recapture amounts (but only if the income is not derived from the conduct of a trade or business), except that all gain (not just short-term gain) attributable to the disposition of property held for investment is included. Investment expenses means deductible expenses (other than interest) directly connected with the production of investment income. Investment expenses should be considered as those allowed after application of the 2 percent floor for miscellaneous itemized deductions (see page 206). In computing the amount of expenses that exceed the 2 percent floor, expenses that are not investment expenses are disallowed before any investment expenses are disallowed.

*Property held for investment* includes property that produces interest, dividends, annuities, or royalties plus any interest held by a taxpayer in an activity involving the conduct of a trade or business that is not a passive activity and in which the taxpayer does not materially participate. A passive activity is defined as an activity that involves the conduct of a trade or business in which the taxpayer does not materially participate. The only activity excluded from this definition is a working interest in an oil and gas property that a taxpayer holds directly or through an entity that does not limit the liability of the taxpayer with respect to that activity. However, regulations may be issued that could broaden the class of activities that are excluded under the definition of a passive activity, and the class of activities so excluded would thereby be considered property held for investment.

### EXCEPTION FOR PASSIVE LOSSES DURING PHASE-IN OF THE PASSIVE LOSS RULES

Investment income of a taxpayer for any taxable year must be reduced by the amount of any passive activity loss that is allowed for the taxable year because of the phase-in of the passive loss rules. However, passive losses that are permitted under the $25,000 allowance for rental real estate activities in which the taxpayer actively participates do not reduce investment income when computing the investment interest expense limitation.

*Example 1:* In 1987 an investor had $20,000 of investment income, before taking into account passive losses that were allowable during the phase-in of passive losses. The investor also had $8,000 of passive losses that were allowable after application of the phase-in passive loss rules from passive activities other than rental real estate activities. The investment income for purposes of determining the limitation on investment interest was $12,000 ($20,000 − $8,000).

*Example 2:* In 1987 an investor had passive losses of $90,000, of which $40,000 was attributable to rental real estate activities in which the investor actively participated. Assuming the investor was entitled to deduct $25,000 of active rental losses under the special $25,000 allowance for rental real estate activities, then 65 percent (the applicable passive loss phase-in percentage for 1987) of the remaining $65,000 of passive activity losses, $42,250, would have been allowed as a deduction in 1987.

Of the deductible $42,250 of allowed passive losses, the portion not attributable to active rental activities reduced the investor's net income under the investment interest limitation for 1987. The portion of the allowable passive loss attributable to rental real estate activities was $9,750 (.65 × $15,000, where the $15,000 is determined by subtracting the $25,000 allowed under the special allowance from the $40,000 of total passive losses attributable to rental real estate activities). Therefore, when determining the amount of investment interest expense that could be deducted for the year, the taxpayer must have reduced investment income by $32,500 (the $42,250 of deductible passive losses minus the $9,750 of deductible passive losses attributable to rental real estate activities).

## PHASE-IN OF DISALLOWANCE

The limitation on investment interest will be phased in over four years. Taxpayers other than married individuals filing a separate return and trusts may deduct investment interest equal to net investment income plus investment interest paid or accrued in the taxable year in excess of net investment income in accordance with the following table:

| For taxable years beginning in: | The applicable amount is: |
| --- | --- |
| 1987 | $6,500 |
| 1988 | 4,000 |
| 1989 | 2,000 |
| 1990 | 1,000 |
| 1991 | 0 |

Any interest expense that is disallowed because of the investment interest expense limitation and is carried forward may not be deducted under the excess allowances for later taxable years.

In the case of married individuals filing separate returns the excess interest expense allowances given in the table above are cut in half. In the case of trusts no excess interest expense deductions are allowed in any year.

*Example 1:* In each of the four years after 1987 an investor has $20,000 of investment interest expense in excess of investment income. The investor's allowable deductions in excess of net investment income during the four-year period will be $6,500 in 1987, $4,000 in 1988, $2,000 in 1989, and $1,000 in 1990.

*Example 2:* In 1987 an investor has $20,000 of investment interest expense in excess of investment income. The investor is allowed to deduct $6,500 in 1987 and carries $13,500 over to 1988. In 1988 the investor has $10,000 more investment income than investment interest expense before taking into account the $13,500 carryover. The investor is allowed to deduct $10,000 of the investment interest expense carryover. The remaining $3,500 of investment interest expense carryover may not be deducted using the remaining $4,000 excess interest allowance for 1988 because that allowance only applies to investment interest expense paid or accrued in 1988, not carryovers from prior years.

## THE DISALLOWANCE OF DEDUCTION FOR PERSONAL INTEREST

Taxpayers other than corporations will no longer be allowed to deduct personal interest paid or accrued during the taxable year. Personal interest means any interest other than (1) interest paid or accrued on indebtedness incurred or continued in connection with the conduct of a trade or business, (2) any investment interest, (3) any interest taken into account when computing income or loss from a passive activity of the taxpayer, (4) any qualified residence interest, and (5) interest payable on extensions of time for payment of estate tax on the value of reversionary or remainder interests in property or where an estate consists largely of interests in a closely held business. In other words, virtually all personal or consumer interest (including interest on underpayment or late payment of taxes) that was allowable as a deduction without limit under prior law may no longer be deducted with the exception of qualified residence interest.

The term *qualified residence interest* means any interest that is paid or accrued during the taxable year on indebtedness secured by any property that (at the time such interest is paid or accrued) is a qualified residence of the taxpayer. The term *qualified residence* means the principal residence of the tax-payer and one vacation home.

## LIMITATION ON THE AMOUNT OF INTEREST DEDUCTIBLE AS QUALIFIED RESIDENCE INTEREST

The amount of interest that may be deducted on a debt secured by a qualified residence is limited in the following manner: interest is deductible only to the extent that the indebtedness does not exceed the lesser of (1) the fair market value of the qualified residence or (2) the taxpayer's basis in the qualified residence (adjusted only by the cost of any improvements to such residence). However, as of August 16, 1986, if the aggregate amount of outstanding in-debtedness secured by a qualified residence exceeded the taxpayer's basis in the property at that time, the amount of indebtedness at that time would sub-stitute for the taxpayer's basis in the qualified residence when determining qualified residence interest.

Taxpayers may deduct interest on debt secured by a qualified residence in excess of the limitation described above if the debt is secured to pay for *qualified medical expenses* or *qualified educational expenses* that are paid or incurred within a reasonable period of time before or after such indebtedness is incurred.

The term *qualified medical expenses* means amounts not compensated for by insurance or otherwise incurred for medical care for the taxpayer, his spouse, or a dependent. The term *qualified educational expenses* means qualified tuition and related expenses of the taxpayer, his spouse, or a dependent for attendance at a normal educational institution.

## PHASE-IN OF LIMITATION

The limitation on the deduction of personal interest is being phased in over the four years that began in calendar year 1987 and that will continue through 1990. The percentage of personal interest that may be deducted dur-ing the phase-in period is given in the following table:

| For taxable years beginning in: | The applicable percentage is: |
| --- | --- |
| 1987 | 65% |
| 1988 | 40% |
| 1989 | 20% |
| 1990 | 10% |
| 1991 | 0% |

The limitation on the deductibility of personal interest may encourage many taxpayers to seek other ways of financing consumer purchases. Two immediate methods of converting what would otherwise be nondeductible personal interest (except as allowed under the phase-in percentages) into deductible interest are (1) to borrow against marginable securities (or property held for investment) or (2) to borrow against a qualified residence. Each of these techniques presents potential problems.

## USING HOME EQUITY

First, interest paid on debt secured by a home may be deductible only to the extent that the debt does not exceed the lesser of (1) the fair market value of the home or (2) the taxpayer's adjusted basis in the home (or if the debt secured by the home exceeded the basis on August 16, 1986, that amount of debt).

Many homeowners who have owned their homes for many years or who have acquired new homes in recent years after rolling over gains from the sale of a previous home have relatively low bases in their homes. In addition, they may have debt secured by these homes that already exceeds their bases. Consequently, the opportunity to increase interest-deductible borrowing in many cases may be limited. Even in cases where the potential to tap home equity exists, in many cases it may be unwise to risk the loss of a home to finance consumer purchases since circumstances could evolve that preclude repayment of the debt.

However, taxpayers who have sufficient equity in their home and untapped borrowing capacity under the qualified residence interest rules may wish to finance new consumer purchases or consolidate consumer loans by increasing qualified residence borrowing.

Some homeowners over the age of 55 may wish to consider selling their homes, using the once-in-a-lifetime $125,000 gain exclusion, and purchasing a new home. The proceeds from the sale of the home could be used to purchase the new home. They would have potential interest-deductible borrowing capacity equal to the cost of their new homes.

The Revenue Act of 1987, signed in December 1987, modified the above rules on home equity indebtedness but introduced further—and more favorable—limitations for home acquisition indebtedness. Indebtedness that was incurred on or before October 13, 1987, and that was secured by a qualified residence on such date or on any date thereafter is classified as acquisition indebtedness. Such debt will not be subject to the new acquisition indebtedness limitation in 1988 or after. Therefore, interest that was associated with indebtedness incurred on or before October 13, 1987, and that exceeded the limitations under the 1986 Tax Reform Act will not exceed the limitations under the 1987 act. The related interest will be viewed as qualified residence interest for 1988 and thereafter.

Under the latest rules, the aggregate amount treated as acquisition indebtedness for any period cannot exceed $1,000,000 (or $500,000 in the case of a married individual filing a separate return). Also, refinancing of indebtedness after October 13, 1987, is considered acquisition indebtedness, but only to the extent of the refinanced indebtedness. If a qualified residence is refinanced for more than the existing indebtedness, the excess amount may qualify in total, in part, or not at all as acquisition indebtedness.

Home equity indebtedness is defined as any indebtedness (other than acquisition indebtedness) secured by a qualified residence to the extent that the aggregate amount for any period does not exceed the lesser of (1) $100,000 (or $50,000 for a married individual filing separately), or (2) the fair market value of such qualified residence less the amount of acquisition indebtedness with respect to the residence.

*Example 1:* Assume that you buy a house for $1,000,000 and borrow $800,000 to finance the purchase. You reduce your debt to $600,000 by making payments over several years. In 1988, you refinance and take out a new mortgage for $700,000. Your acquisition debt will still be $600,000. However, if you used $100,000 to substantially improve your home, the $100,000 would be added to acquisition debt.

*Example 2:* Assume that you bought your home 15 years ago for $50,000. You have completely paid off your mortgage, and the property is now worth $200,000. In 1988, you take out a $120,000 home loan. You use $110,000 to make additions to the home and $10,000 to buy a car. Interest on the entire loan is deductible: $110,000 of the loan is acquisition debt, and the balance qualifies as home equity debt.

*Example 3:* Assume that you have an unpaid balance of $90,000 on your home, which is valued at $300,000. You obtain a second mortgage of $110,000 and use the proceeds to help your parents buy a home and to buy personal assets. Interest on $100,000 of the new mortgage is deductible as qualified residence interest. Interest on the $10,000 balance is personal interest.

Note that the new limits on acquisition indebtedness make it very important not to overlook many elements of the cost of a house besides the amount paid to the seller. These would include appraisal fees, title search, transfer taxes, survey fees, bank or lender fees, legal fees, mortage taxes, brokers' commissions (if paid by the buyer), and other nondeductible closing costs. Note that the cost of the home and improvements does not include painting and routine maintenance and repairs. However, it does include additions to the home and improvement or replacement of equipment that is part of the home. Such improvements include landscaping; resurfacing the driveway; installing a swimming pool; constructing a new roof; finishing an attic or basement; replacing or making a major improvement to heating, air conditioning, or plumbing systems or to a water heater; or adding on a room or garage.

### USING DEBT SECURED BY INVESTMENT PROPERTY

The major advantage of borrowing against a home rather than against property held for investment is that qualified residence interest is not subject to the investment interest expense limitation. When borrowing against property held for investment, care must be taken not to generate investment interest expense in excess of net investment income (plus excess amounts allowed under the phase-in rules for investment interest), or the interest deductions will be disallowed in the year paid or incurred. However, any excess may be carried forward indefinitely and deducted in later years when investment income exceeds investment interest expense paid or incurred in that year. Therefore, carryovers of investment interest will still generally be preferable to personal interest, which is never deductible (except to the extent provided by the phase-in rules for personal interest).

Another disadvantage of using debt secured by investment property to finance consumer purchases is the margin limits set by the Federal Reserve. For example, debt secured by common stock may not exceed 50 percent of the value of the stock.

### PASSIVE ACTIVITIES WITH PASSIVE INCOME

Individuals who own passive activities that are earning passive income may wish to increase borrowing against that activity even if they do not wish to finance consumer purchases. The proceeds could be used to acquire investment assets with appreciation potential that could as well be leveraged up to their respective margin limits, thereby creating investment interest deductions to offset the current income from the portfolio.

The interest on debt used to acquire or carry an interest in a passive activity is not subject to the investment interest expense limitation. Such interest is fully deductible against passive income from the passive activity. However, if the interest expense exceeds the passive income from the passive activity, the excess interest will be treated as a passive loss. That loss may be deducted only against passive income from other passive activities or, on disposition of that passive activity, against gains on the disposition, passive income from other passive activities, and any active income or gain of the taxpayer, in that order. There are exceptions provided under the phase-in rules for passive losses.

## RENTAL REAL ESTATE ACTIVITIES WITH PASSIVE LOSSES

In general, passive losses that are allowable as a deduction under the phase-in of the passive loss rules reduce net investment income for purposes of determining the amount of investment interest expense that may be deducted under the investment interest limitation. However, this does not apply to passive losses that are allowable from rental real estate activities. Consequently, increasing debt secured by rental real estate, even when that activity is currently generating passive losses rather than passive income, may be advisable. During the phase-in period of the passive loss rules a certain percentage of the interest on that debt (65 percent in 1987, 40 percent in 1988, 20 percent in 1989, and 10 percent in 1990) will be allowable as a deduction with no corresponding reduction in the amount of investment interest expense otherwise deductible.

## PASSIVE ACTIVITIES WITH PASSIVE LOSSES

The same advice does not generally apply to debt secured by passive loss activities other than rental real estate. Any increase in passive losses due to the interest on the debt that is allowable as a deduction under the passive loss phase-in rules reduces the amount of investment interest expense otherwise deductible on a dollar-for-dollar basis (if investment interest expense already equals or exceeds the amount otherwise allowable for the year).

However, in some cases applying this strategy to passive activities other than rental real estate may still be beneficial.

Generally interest on debt to carry an interest in a passive activity is not deductible except against passive activity income. If an investor anticipates a large gain on the disposition of property held for investment in a subsequent year, the investor may create an "artificial" interest expense carryover. By increasing the allowable passive loss in a given year (by increasing debt and interest expense attributable to the passive activity), the investor may intentionally create an investment interest expense carryforward that may be used in the subsequent year to offset the anticipated gain on the disposition of the investment property. In effect the investor has circumvented the rule that disallows interest expense attributable to passive activities to offset income or gains from investment activities.

*Example:* In 1987 an investor had $20,000 of investment income and $26,500 of investment interest expense. He also owned an interest in a passive activity other than rental real estate that had $0 net passive income in 1987. In 1988 he has $15,000 of investment income and $19,000 of investment interest expense before taking into account the sale of common stock on which he has a $20,000 gain.

The investor was allowed to deduct all his investment interest expense in 1987 ($20,000 of net investment income plus $6,500 under the phase-in allowance). In 1988 the investor is allowed to deduct all his investment interest expense ($15,000 of net investment income plus $4,000 under the phase-in allowance) and has $20,000 of taxable gain.

If the investor secured additional debt on the passive activity in 1987 that generated $30,770 of interest each year, the passive loss from the activity would be $30,770. Under the phase-in of the passive loss rules, he could have deducted 65 percent of the $30,770, or $20,000, in 1987. In addition, the amount so allowed reduced his net investment income to $0 for purposes of determining the amount of investment interest he could deduct. Therefore, if he secured this debt, he would have created an investment interest expense carryover to 1988 of $20,000, which will exactly offset the gain in 1988.

What the investor does with the proceeds from the loan is important. If he uses it to purchase income-producing investment assets, the income earned on those assets will use up some or all of the carryover. However, if he purchases low-yielding investments such as growth stocks, the increase in investment income will be minimal and the artificial investment interest carryover will be preserved.

OTHER INTEREST PLANNING TIPS

To the extent that a loan finances an asset used partially for business and partially for personal purposes, it appears that interest would have to be prorated between the two uses.

*Example 1:* Ms. Agent, an insurance agent, finances a new automobile used 75 percent for business and 25 percent for personal purposes. She would treat 75 percent of the interest as deductible business interest and 25 percent as nondeductible consumer interest.

Under the 1986 law, debt incurred by an employee is treated as consumer debt. Apparently, interest on any amount borrowed to finance an employment-related expense is treated as nondeductible consumer interest rather than deductible business interest.

*Example 2:* In example 1, Ms. Agent was treated as a self-employed individual. If she was an outside salesperson and an employee, rather than a self-employed individual, apparently all the interest she would pay on her automobile loan would be treated as consumer interest and would not be deductible, even if she used the automobile 75 percent of the time in her employer's business.

Under the 1986 law, it is generally more advantageous to have a business-use vehicle owned by the employer rather than by the employee, even though the employee must include the value of any personal use as compensation income.

The term *residence* as used in the qualified residence interest exception includes, in addition to houses, condominium units and cooperative housing units and any other property that the taxpayer uses for personal purposes as a dwelling unit, which generally includes a mobile home, a motor home, or a boat with living accommodations. A taxpayer who owns a boat that is large enough to live aboard for short periods, a mobile home, or a motor home may be able to treat it as a second residence for purposes of the residential interest deduction.

The 1986 law completely reverses some of the tax-planning techniques used in seller-financed sales of property. Under prior law since gain on the sale was generally taxed at a favorable capital-gain rate, while interest income was taxed as ordinary income, sellers of property generally preferred to increase their sales price and lower the interest rate. Correspondingly purchasers frequently preferred lowering the price and increasing the interest rate because interest was fully deductible and gains on the ultimate sale of the property would be treated as capital gains. Since capital gains are now taxed at the same rates as ordinary income and with limitations on the deductibility of consumer and investment interest, these preferences may no longer apply. For business real estate the purchaser may wish to minimize the purchase price and to maximize the interest rate because of the longer depreciation periods for real estate. This may in fact be advantageous from the seller's tax standpoint as well.

Both purchasers and sellers in seller-financed residential real estate will generally obtain a tax advantage by minimizing the sales price and maximizing the interest rate. By so doing, the seller will increase investment income against which otherwise nondeductible investment interest expense can be deducted, and the purchaser will have fully deductible interest expense if the property qualifies as a principal or second residence.

Since both interest income and capital gains on the sale of investment property are treated as investment income for purposes of the investment interest deduction limitation, the seller will generally be neutral on the issue of price versus interest when selling investment property. In contrast, a purchaser who has substantial investment income would generally be better off with the lower purchase price and higher interest since the investment interest expense could be deducted against the investment income from other sources.

Taxpayers who owe interest to the IRS for underpayments of tax should consider paying the interest in 1988, or they will lose part or all of the interest deduction (subject to the phase-in rule).

Taxpayers should consider prepaying in 1988 one or more 1989 or later installments on nonresidential consumer loans. This will preserve and accelerate the maximum interest deduction.

Taxpayers who are planning to purchase a new home might consider having appliances and various options such as a deck, fencing, and landscaping installed by the builder and included in the sales price. The interest on these items would then qualify as fully deductible residential interest. Otherwise the interest will be treated as nondeductible consumer financing and will be deductible only to the extent permitted under the phase-in rule.

The use of interest-free and other below-market-rate loans is affected by the interest deduction limitation. An individual borrower's imputed interest deduction will no longer fully offset the imputed interest income. Both borrowers and lenders who are a party to employment-related or gift-type interest-free loans should reconsider whether these types of arrangements are still suitable.

Taxpayers with excess investment interest expense should consider recognizing capital gains by selling property held for investment.

There are a number of tax strategies that you should employ in planning your interest deductions. First, you must consider the timing of your actual interest payments in relation to both exceeding your standard deduction amount and determining your subsequent year's income. This technique has been discussed in detail under medical expenses and taxes. Second, you must recognize that unlike many other forms of expenditure, interest expenses need not be reasonable to be deducted. If you borrow money at an exorbitant rate, that interest is deductible regardless of what it has been labeled in order to circumvent a state law on maximum percentages.

Interest is also deductible if paid to a related party for a bona fide indebtedness. This means that if you actually have a legal debtor–creditor relationship with your spouse, for example, you may deduct interest paid to that spouse. In fact, parents may legitimately deduct interest paid on money borrowed from their minor children as long as there is an effective debtor–creditor relationship. This means that you sign a note, arrange for a repayment schedule, and meet that repayment schedule. Substantial savings can be accrued by paying legitimate interest to a child in a lower tax bracket. For example, assume that you paid $1,500 in interest to your 14-year-old child (who has no other income) and you are in the 33 percent bracket. The first $500 of that interest is not taxable to the child because of the standard deduction. Therefore, the child pays only $150 on the interest received ($1,000 $\times$ 15 percent). But if you are in the 33 percent bracket, you saved $495 in taxes—a net savings of $345!

Furthermore, any interest payments owed to the Internal Revenue Service for late payment of your taxes are also deductible, subject to the phaseout discussed above. The Internal Revenue Service currently charges an interest rate of about 10 percent on late tax payments. (This changes as of January 1, 1989.) Assuming that you are in the 33 percent bracket, this amounts to an after-tax cost of 8.68 percent (10% − [10% $\times$ 40% $\times$ 33%]). With the current availability of after-tax investment returns in excess of this 8.68 percent figure, it may be appropriate to consider having the Internal Revenue Service finance your investment opportunities at this minimal after-tax cost. (**Note:** See Appendix, page 575, for effective interest rates considering phaseout of deductibility.)

# 46 Charitable Contributions

A charitable contribution is a gift to a qualified charitable organization. (To be deemed as making a gift, the taxpayer must have "donative intent"—that is, a detached and disinterested generosity. There must be no *quid pro quo* expected or received.) The tax law allows charitable contributions to reduce taxable income, and therefore the actual cost of the donation will be reduced by your tax savings. As your income tax bracket increases, the real cost of your charitable gift will therefore decrease, making contributions more attractive for those in the higher brackets.

Regardless of the accounting method you use, contributions are usually deducted in the year in which they are paid. A contribution is paid when you unconditionally deliver or mail your gift to the recipient or to a designated agent or when you make a completed gift of property. A contribution made by a credit card is deductible immediately even if payment to the credit card company is made in a different year.

You can obtain an itemized deduction for your charitable contributions, but these deductions are limited to a maximum of 50 percent of your adjusted gross income for the year. These contributions may consist of gifts to public charities and certain private foundations.[1] If the 50 percent limit is not exhausted, you can deduct contributions to other entities subject to a more restrictive constraint of 20 percent of your adjusted gross income.[2] Appreciated capital gain property generally is further subjected to an additional 30 percent limit. These limits will be detailed in the analysis under planning considerations.

Charitable contributions can take numerous forms. Though cash and property are the main ones, there are others that must be considered. Unreimbursed costs incurred for charity contributions, dues, admission charges, and other payments may be deductible, but not if they are made in exchange for benefits or property you receive. The amount deductible is

---

1. The following types of organizations qualify: 1. private operating foundations; 2. all other private foundations that distribute all their contributions to public charities within two and one half months after the year end; and 3. pooled community foundations.
2. The Tax Reform Act of 1984 increased the limits on contributions to tax exempt private *nonoperating* foundations from 20 percent to 30 percent of adjusted gross income, for gifts of cash or ordinary income property. It also provided that excess post 1984 contributions can be carried forward for five years. The Act, in addition, provided a deduction at full fair market value for contributions of up to 10 percent of the stock of a corporation to a private *nonoperating* foundation, provided the stock is publicly traded and is long term capital gain property. These provisions are effective for contributions made after the enactment of the Act.

usually the property's fair market value, yet for gifts of appreciated property this value may be reduced under special rules. Cancelled checks and receipts offer the best proof to the contributor. When a charitable deduction is taken you must be able to state the name of each charity and the amount and date of each gift.

PLANNING CONSIDERATIONS

### Qualified Donees

You can deduct charitable contributions only if they are made to or for the use of a "qualified donee." No charitable contribution deduction is allowed for gifts to other kinds of organizations, even if those organizations are exempt from U.S. income tax.

The gift must be made directly to an organization to qualify for the deduction. However, in the case of *Rockefeller*, 76 T.C. 178 (1981), the court held that unreimbursed expenses incurred in rendering services to a qualified charitable organization constituted deductible contributions made "to" the charitable organization. The IRS has acquiesced to this decision (Revenue Ruling 84-61, I.R.B. 1984-17). No deduction to an individual or individuals is allowed by the IRS unless that individual or group is acting as an agent for a qualified organization. This rule is necessary because there is no guarantee that the money given to an individual will be forwarded to the charity. Payments to individual ministers have been disqualified as charitable contributions where there was no evidence that the money ever went to the minister's religious organization.

The Treasury Department publishes IRS Publication 78, which lists the organizations to which contributions are deductible, identifies each by type, and states their corresponding limit of deductibility. This list is updated annually. Three cumulative supplements listing only new additions are published every quarter. A list informing the public of organizations that no longer qualify as charitable organizations is published monthly.

Deductions are allowed for contributions given to or for the use of the following qualified organizations:

1. A state or possession of the United States, or the District of Columbia, if the contribution or gift is made for public purposes only.

2. A corporation, trust, or community chest, fund or foundation if created in the United States and organized and operated exclusively for

religious, charitable, scientific, literary, or educational purposes, or to foster national or international amateur sports competition (but not to help provide athletic equipment or facilities), or for the prevention of cruelty to children or animals. No part of the net earnings can benefit any private shareholder or individual. The organization can not be disqualified for tax exemption due to influencing legislation, and must not take part in any political campaign.

3.  A post or organization of war veterans, if organized in the United States and if no part of the net earnings benefits any private shareholders or individual. Any dues, fees, or assessments paid by members of these organizations do not qualify for deductions.

4.  A domestic or fraternal society, order, or association, operating under the lodge system, if the gift is to be used exclusively for religious, charitable, scientific, literary, or educational purposes, or to foster national or international amateur sports competition, or for the prevention of cruelty to children or animals. Dues to offset sickness or burial costs are deductible.

5.  A nonprofit cemetery company whose funds are totally devoted to the continuous upkeep of the cemetery.

A contribution must be to an organization that has been created domestically. To help resolve the vagueness of the domestic creation requirement, the IRS has come out with a number of Revenue Rulings. In summary, they say that the domestic creation requirement won't be satisfied unless the recipient organization controls the final disposition of the funds. Control means that the recipient has the right to decide if the funds will be used abroad. If the recipient organization is required to transfer the funds abroad, the deduction will be denied.

A charitable contribution is also allowed if you maintain a student in your house under a written agreement with a charity. The student must be a full-time pupil in an elementary, junior high, or high school in the United States. The student must not be your dependent or relative but must be a member of your household. A deduction of up to $50 per month for each full month of residence during which the student is attending school is permitted by law. A total of 15 or more days of the month constitute a full month. There is no deduction if you receive any compensation or reimbursement for maintaining the student.

In one case, the parents of a 19-year-old missionary serving the Church of Jesus Christ of Latter Day Saints (the Mormon church) made expenditures at the request of the Mormon Church to support their son's missionary work. Following the church's policy, the parents paid a travel agency $100 for part of their son's expenses in traveling to his mission post and paid $175 a month to their son to defray his living expenses. The Tenth Circuit Court of Appeals allowed a charitable deduction for the amounts that were paid to support the missionary work because "the primary purpose was to further the aims of a charitable organization or to benefit the person whose expenses were being paid." (*Don K. White, et al. v. United States*, No. 81-2033 [Tenth Circuit, January 20, 1984]; see also *Eldon D. Brinkley* [1984] No. 84-4722 [Feb. 20, 1986] in further support. For cases in conflict with these, however, see the Idaho District Court case of *Davis,* 87-2 U.S.T.C. Para. 9490.)

If an organization qualifies as a church for tax purposes, it need not be required to seek exemption and has no filing requirements. Since Congress did not define the term "church," the common meaning and usage of the term have been applied. In making this decision, the IRS utilizes the following thirteen characteristics of a church:

A distinct legal existence
A recognized creed and form of worship
A definite and distinct ecclesiastical government
A formal code of doctrine and discipline
A distinct religious history
A membership not associated with any other church or denomination
A complete organization of ordained ministers chosen after completing prescribed courses of study
Literature of its own
Established places of worship
Regular congregations
Regular religious services
Sunday schools for religious education of the young
Schools to prepare their ministers

Not all of the above characteristics must be satisfied, and no single factor is given controlling weight. By listing these characteristics as a rough outline, the IRS gives guidelines for its determination as to whether an organization may qualify as a "church."

Contributions cannot be deducted if they are:

a) gifts to certain private foundations and nonexempt trusts that must pay tax on termination of their exempt status;

b) gifts to certain taxable private foundations and nonexempt trusts organized after 1969 whose charter does not include prohibitions against conduct that would subject them to excise taxes; *or*

c) gifts to charitable organizations after October 9, 1969, that do not notify the Internal Revenue Service that they are claiming exempt status.

Contributions to foreign governments, charities and private foundations are disallowed. Gifts to communist-ruled organizations are also disallowed. The Treasury Department does not allow tax-exempt status for private schools that practice racial discrimination, and any donations to them will not qualify as charitable contributions.

No charity can take part in any political activity. Charity status is lost by an organization if any substantial segment of its activities is devoted to formulating propaganda or otherwise trying to influence legislation. However, an organization (other than a church) may qualify as a charity and still perform some of these activities by keeping its political expenditures within a sliding scale, which indicates how much a charity may expend on lobbying without incurring any penalty. The scale is arranged according to the charity's outlays for its exempt purpose as follows:

| Charitable Expenditures | Nontaxable Lobbying |
| --- | --- |
| up to $500,000 | 20% |
| $500,000–$1,000,000 | 15% |
| $1,000,000–$1,500,000 | 10% |
| over $1,500,000 | 5% |

The expenditures for lobbying may not exceed $1,000,000 for any year regardless of the scale. Furthermore, donations to needy individuals are not deductible under the law.

ADDITIONAL PLANNING CONSIDERATIONS

*Donation Limitations*

Only if you contribute more than 20 percent of your adjusted gross income to a qualified charity is it necessary to be knowledgeable about donation limitations. Contributions up to this limit are automatically deductible if you itemize. For those who give more than 20 percent, certain rules apply.

If the contributions are all made to maximum deduction organizations (see the list that follows), the deduction ceiling is 50 percent of the contribution base (except that contributions of appreciated capital gain property are subject to a 30 percent ceiling, unless a special election is made). The contribution base is defined as adjusted gross income computed without regard to any net operating loss carryback to the taxable year.

To qualify for the 50 percent ceiling, the contribution must be made "to" one of the maximum deduction organizations (as opposed to "for the use of" an organization). If the contributions are not "to" 50 percent charities but rather are "for the use of" any charities, the deduction limit is 30 percent. Contributions of appreciated capital gain property to non-operating foundations are limited to 20 percent. For contributions subject to the 20, 30, and 50 percent limits, the amount not deductible in the contribution year may be deductible in a future year as a carryover.

On a joint return, these limits apply to the aggregate contribution base.

You are allowed a 50 percent ceiling on contributions to any of the following maximum deduction organizations:

1. *Churches.*

2. *Tax-exempt educational organizations.* The educational organization should maintain a regular faculty and curriculum and have a regularly enrolled body of students in attendance at the place where its educational activities are regularly conducted.

   An organization set up for the benefit of certain state and municipal colleges and universities can also be included if it is organized and operated exclusively to receive, hold, invest, and administer property and to make expenditures to or for the benefit of an acceptable college or university.

The educational organization must be engaged entirely in educational activities (although noneducational activity incidental to the educational activities is allowable). Tuition payments are not deductible, and contributions made under circumstances where you or those related to you benefit may be examined to see if personal benefit is the purpose of the payment.

3. *Tax-exempt hospitals and certain medical research organizations.* Hospitals, in this case, do not include homes for children or the aged or institutes that provide vocational training for the handicapped. The medical research organization must be engaged primarily and directly in the continuous active conduct of medical research. In addition, it must be committed to spending each contribution received on such active conduct of medical research before January 1 of the fifth calendar year after the date the contribution is made.

4. *A government unit* as referred to in the Internal Revenue Code Section 170(c)(1) (such as a state or a political subdivision of a state).

5. *A "publicly supported" organization* (such as a community chest). This type of organization normally receives a substantial part of its support (exclusive of operating income) from a governmental unit or from direct or indirect contributions from the general public.

6. *Certain private nonoperating foundations.* These distribute all contributions they receive to public charities within two and one-half months after the foundations' fiscal year-end.

7. *A privately operating foundation.* This type of private foundation is one that pools all of its donations in a common fund. Any substantial contributor (or spouse) can annually direct the foundation as to which public charity shall receive the principal from his or her contribution and the interest from that principal.

8. *Certain membership organizations.* Only those in which more than one-third of their support comes from the general public are allowable.

*The Public Support Test*

To determine whether an organization is "publicly supported," you must apply the public support, or mechanical, test. An organization will be considered to be a "publicly supported" organization for its current taxable year and for the immediately succeeding taxable year if, for the four taxable years immediately preceding the current taxable year, the total amount of the support the organization received from governmental units, from donations made directly or indirectly by the public, or from a combination of the two equals 33.33 percent or more of the total support of the organization. In addition, contributions made by individuals, trusts, or corporations during the four taxable years may not exceed 2 percent of the organization's total support. The 2 percent limitation does not apply to support from governmental units or from other publicly supported organizations.

### The Facts and Circumstances Test

A corporation, trust, or community chest, fund, or foundation that does not qualify as a "publicly supported" organization under the mechanical test may qualify on the basis of the facts and circumstances test. There are several requirements, but only requirements 1 and 2 below must be met on an aggregate basis. However, a substantial number of the remaining ones must also be met in the four taxable years preceding the current taxable year.

1.  *10 percent of support limitations.* The percent of support "normally" received by an organization from governmental units, from the public, whether direct or indirect, or from a combination of these sources must be substantial. The amount of this support must equal at least 10 percent of the total support.

2.  *Attraction of public support.* An organization must be so organized and operated as to attract new and additional public or governmental support on a continuous basis. It must maintain a continuous program for canvassing funds from the general public, community, or membership groups involved, or it must carry on other activities to attract support.

3.  *Percent of financial support.* The percent of public support received will be considered. The higher the percent, the lesser will be the burden of establishing the publicly-supported nature of the organization.

4.  *Sources of support.* A large number of different contributors is preferred. In determining what a "representative number of persons" is,

consideration will be given to the type of organization involved, the length of time it has been in existence, and any restrictions it practices.

5. *Representative governing body.* The fact that the organization has a governing body that represents the broad interest of the public will also be considered in determining whether an organization is publicly supported.

6. *Availability of public facilities for the benefit of the public.* Public participation in programs or policies will also be reviewed.

7. *Additional factors.* Pertinent to membership organizations are answers to the following questions:

    a) Is the organization designed to enroll a substantial number of persons in a particular field?

    b) Are dues set at fixed rates to be affordable by a broad cross section of the interested public?

    c) Are the activities of the organization likely to appeal to persons with a broad range of interests, or do they focus on a particular purpose?

Those factors relevant to each case and the weight given to each factor may change depending upon the nature and function of the organization.

Contributions shall be considered as support from the *general public* only if the total amount of all contributions, direct and indirect, does not exceed 2 percent of the organization's total support for a set period, except as provided by the *exclusion of unusual grants.* The 2 percent limit does not apply to support received from governmental units. (The donation is included in full in the denominator but will only be included in the numerator of such a fraction to the extent that it does not exceed 2 percent of the denominator. Any unusual grants may be excluded entirely from the fraction.) The unusual grant exclusion is generally intended to apply to substantial contributions or bequests from disinterested parties whose contributions or bequests:

    a) are attracted by reason of the publicly supported nature of the organization;

    b) are in unusual or unexpected amounts; *or*

c) would, by reason of size, adversely affect the status of the organization as normally being publicly supported.

Support does *not* include the following:

- Any amounts received by an organization from the exercise or performance of its functional purpose, which comprises the basis for its exemptions.

- Contributions of services for which there is no deduction.

Both of the above must be excluded from the numerator and the denominator.

An organization dependent on gross receipts from related activities will not satisfy either the mechanical test or the facts and circumstances test. The condition for public support will also not be met if an insignificant amount of the organization's support comes through governmental units from contributions made directly or indirectly by the general public. Support from a governmental unit includes any amount received from a governmental unit, which covers donations, contributions, and amounts received in connection with an agreement with a governmental unit for either the execution of services or for a governmental research grant. However, such amounts will not count as support from a governmental unit if they are for the performance of the organization's exempt activity, and if the reason for the payment is to enable the organization to offer a facility for the direct benefit of the public, rather than to serve only its members.

To summarize the tests involved in determining whether organizations qualify as publicly supported: The organization must normally receive in excess of 33.33 percent of its support from a governmental unit and from direct and indirect donations from the general public to qualify under the mechanical test; or, alternatively, at least 10 percent of its support must come from governmental units and public donations, and most, if not all, of points 3 through 7 of the facts and circumstances test must apply.

## COMMUNITY TRUSTS

Community trusts have been established to invite large donations of a capital or endowment nature for the benefit of a certain community. Each has a governing body consisting of representatives of the community it serves. The contributions are often kept in the form of separate trusts or funds subject to changing degrees of control by the governing body.

A community trust must also meet the mechanical test or be able to attract sources on a continuous basis from the government and public in order to meet the facts and circumstances test. This test will usually be satisfied if the trust attracts a broad range of donors from the community served.

Another point concerning community trusts is the treatment of them as single entities. Any organization that meets the requirements described in points 2 through 5 below will be treated as a single entity; all funds linked with an organization that meets the requirements of point 1 will be considered as component parts of that organization.

1.  The organization must be established by a gift, bequest, legacy, devise, or other transfer to a community trust that is considered a single entity, and it may not be subjected by the transferrer to any restraints.

2.  The organization must be recognized as a community trust, fund, or foundation to support charitable events in the community it serves.

3.  All funds of the organization must be subject to common governing instruments.

4.  The organization must have a common governing body that administers the fund.

5.  Periodic financial reports must be prepared to show that all of the funds held by the community trust are funds of the organization.

A few final words on 50 percent limit contributions: Gifts made "for the use of" public charities or 50 percent limit private foundations do not qualify for the 50 percent limit. You must make the gift "to" a 50 percent charity to qualify for the donation. A charitable gift to a fraternal lodge that then contributes a gift to a 50 percent charity does not qualify for the 50 percent limit. A donation of an *income interest* is considered as made "for the use of" the recipient organization. Thus, you do not get the 50 percent limit. But a gift of a *remainder interest* is treated as made "to the donee charity," thus enabling you to reach the 50 percent ceiling.

LIMITS ON DEDUCTION

There is a 20 percent ceiling on deductions for any contributions of appreciated capital gain property to 30 percent charities—i.e., charitable organizations except those listed on pages 170–71 (e.g., a non-operating foundation). For years beginning with 1987, the amount of your deduction is limited to your basis. Any excess over the ceiling can be carried over to the five succeeding tax years.

For example, assume you have a painting with a basis of $15,000 and a $20,000 fair market value. You have an adjusted gross income of $100,000. You want to contribute the painting to a veterans organization (a non-public charity). Your 1987 charitable deduction will be $15,000, because your basis does not exceed your ceiling of $20,000 (20 percent of $100,000). There is, however, a special rule for gifts of stock. If you contribute qualified appreciated stock to a private non-operating foundation, you may take as a charitable deduction, subject to the above 20 percent ceiling limit, the full fair market value of the stock. Qualified appreciated stock is any stock of a corporation that (a) has price quotations readily available from an established securities market and (b) if sold would produce a long-term capital gain. This provision does not apply to the gift of any stock or portion of stock that exceeds 10 percent of the ownership interest in a corporation.

This special rule for stock will stay in effect through 1994.

If you give property that, if sold, would result in a long-term capital gain (appreciated capital assets or Section 1231 Property)[3], and the charity is a 50 percent donee, then you are subject to a 30 percent ceiling. If the contributions of capital gain property exceed 30 percent of your contribution base, the excess amount can qualify for a five-year carryover. Charitable contributions with 30 percent limitations paid during the taxable year are considered after all other charitable contributions.

Donation of a 30 percent capital gain property is defined as the charitable contribution of a capital asset that, if sold by the donor at its fair market value at the time of the contribution, would result in long-term gain; also, the amount of such a contribution must not be required to be reduced under Section 170(3)(1)(B) (this covers tangible personal property used by a donee in a function unrelated to the basis for its exemptions, and contributed "to" or "for the use of" certain private foundations).

You can make a special election to qualify for the 50 percent adjusted gross income limit on this property. In doing so, the deduction for the contribution is limited to your basis. If the election is made, it applies to all

---

3.   Section 1231 Property is real or personal property used in a trade or business that would normally produce ordinary gains or losses upon sale or exchange. Gains on such property are capital and losses are ordinary losses.

donations of capital gain property made during the year as well as to prior year carryovers of appreciated capital gain property. The election must be made by the due date of the return and cannot be made on an amended return.

For example, assume that you have some stock that you would like to give to a public charity. You have held the stock for a number of years and your adjusted gross income is $100,000. The stock has a basis of $45,000 and a fair market value at the time of the donation of $50,000. If you do not make the 50 percent election, your charitable contribution deduction is limited to $30,000 (30 percent of $100,000) with the remaining $20,000 carried over. If you do make the election, you would get a deduction of the full $45,000 basis. Note that in exchange for getting the full $45,000 in the current year, you lose $5,000 of your deduction.

When making this special election, you are actually exchanging a reduced deduction on each separate contribution of appreciated capital gain property for the more generous 50 percent limit. The election of the 50 percent deduction ceiling is made by attaching to the original return for the election year a statement that the election is being taken. The following guidelines should be used in deciding whether the election should be taken:

1. If your long-term capital gain property contributions to 50 percent charities will not total more than 30 percent of your contribution base, do not make the election.

2. If you give long-term capital gain property in excess of the 30 percent ceiling to 50 percent charities, consider the following factors:

   a) any excess over the 30 percent limit, which can be carried over;

   b) your income for the current year, which should be compared with what you expect to earn in the following years; *and*

   c) the amount of unrealized long-term capital gain included in the value of the property.

Where long-term appreciated property consists of tangible personal property, such as works of art, the amount of the deduction *depends upon its use* by the charitable organization. If its use by the charity is unrelated to the charity's exempt function, then the amount of the deduction is limited to your basis.

For example, you own a work of art that you have held for more than one year and then you donate that work to a museum. If the donation is used by the museum for display, it is deemed related to the museum's exempt purpose. Therefore, if the work of art has a fair market value of $24,000 on the date of donation, that donation gives you a deduction of $24,000.

If the donation is made to a hospital, however, the amount of the deduction is limited to your basis. If the basis of the property is $4,000, then the deduction is limited to $4,000.

## CARRYOVERS TO OTHER TAX YEARS

If the amount of contributions to 50 percent organizations made within a taxable year exceeds 50 percent of your contribution base for that year, the excess may be carried over for the next five succeeding taxable years. Current contributions must first be considered before any carryover is applied. Contributions that are carried over, plus the current year's contributions, must fall within the 50 percent limit. Five-year carryovers are also available for excess 20 percent and 30 percent contributions.

The amount of the carryover allowed is the lesser of:

a)  the excess of 50 percent of adjusted gross income minus the sum of any actual contributions to public charities in that year plus any deducted carryovers (except carryovers of appreciated capital gain property) from a year before the contribution year of this carryover; *or*

b)  the total carryovers available in the current year.

The charitable contribution deduction must be specially computed when taxpayers with carryovers change their filing status. Note that an unused carryover of a deceased spouse can be used on a return for the year the spouse dies; otherwise it is lost.

## ORDER OF DEDUCTIBILITY

The amount that you should deduct in any year is determined in the following order:

1.  gifts for the year to 50 percent charities

2.  carryover of gifts to 50 percent charities from the preceding five years, from the earliest year first

## Ordering of Deductions to Charity*

|  | **Deduct All:** | **Up to This % of Contribution Base** |
|---|---|---|
| First— | Cash contributions to public charities | 50% |
| Second— | Carryover of prior years' cash contributions to public charities | 50% |
| Third— | Cash contributions to private foundations | 30% |
| Fourth— | Carryover of prior years' cash contributions to private foundations | 30% |
| Fifth— | Capital gain property contributions to public charities | 30% |
| Sixth— | Carryover of prior years' capital gain property contributions to public charities | 30% |
| Seventh— | Qualified appreciated stock contributions to private foundations | 20% |
| Eighth— | Carryover of prior years' qualified appreciated stock contributions to private foundations | 20% |

*When contributions reach the indicated percentage, any excess must be carried over to the next year. If contributions in any tier are below the indicated percentage in any taxable year, contributions in the next lower tier may be deducted.

3.    gifts for the year to 30 percent charities

4.    carryover of gifts to 30 percent charities from the preceding five years, from the earliest year first

5.    gifts that are limited by the 20 percent ceiling

Your total deduction for any year cannot exceed 50 percent of your contribution base for that year and cannot exceed the amount actually contributed currently and in the past. Where 50 percent of your contribution base income exceeds the amount of your gifts, any carryovers from prior years are deductible, in order of time, to the extent of this excess. Any carryovers not used up may be carried forward to later years until exhausted or until the five-year period for each excess contribution runs out.

Contributions where the 20 percent limitation would apply should be avoided when gifts are made of 30 percent limit property to 50 percent limit organizations that surpass your 30 percent limit. In this situation, you should consider the special election to reduce the 30 percent limit items and receive the 50 percent ceiling on them. This especially applies if a carryover of such a contribution exists from a prior year. Prior years' deductions are not influenced by this special election.

FORM OF THE GIFT

The deduction for a contribution of property is normally equal to the fair market value of the property at the time the donation is made. No gain is normally realized on a charitable contribution of appreciated property. You have an advantage when you contribute appreciated property because you get a deduction for the full fair market value of the property contributed, including both your basis and your unrealized paper profit. You are not taxed on this profit, so in effect you receive a deduction for an amount that you need not report as income.

If the fair market value of the property donated is below its basis, no loss is recognized on this donation. In such a case it would be better to sell the property first, realize the loss for tax purposes, and then make a gift of the proceeds. Using this approach, a deduction is allowed for the entire basis of the property.

The deduction of certain contributions for appreciated property must be reduced in some cases, depending on the type of appreciated property or the character of the donee. The amount of deduction for appreciated property must be reduced below its fair market value by the sum of ordinary income or short-term capital gain that would result if the property were sold at the time of the gift. Both a capital asset held for not more than 6 months and property subject to recapture of depreciation would result in ordinary income. Any appreciation in excess of the recapture amount is handled as a contribution of capital gain property. The above rule applies regardless of the type of donee. Other examples of property that would result in ordinary income are letters, memoranda, and works of art created by the donor.

For example, if an artist contributed a personal piece to a charity, there would be no charitable deduction. This portrait would generate ordinary income if it were sold by the artist at fair market value. Therefore, the deduction would be reduced to zero by the subtraction of this ordinary income component.

If appreciated long-term capital gain property is donated to a private foundation that is not a 50 percent limit donee, then its value must be reduced by 100 percent of that long-term capital gain. Your deduction is limited to your basis. The deduction for contributed capital gain property that is tangible personal property is reduced in the same manner as when the use of the property is dissimilar to the donee's exempt status.

You will sometimes sell property to a charity for less than the property's fair market value, intending the "bargain" portion as a charitable contribution. Except in the case of ordinary income property sold for its adjusted basis, the seller may treat the amount of the bargain (fair market value minus purchase price) as a charitable donation for deduction reasons.

The donor usually also realizes taxable gain on the bargain sale; thus you must divide your basis (original cost) in the property between the part of the property sold and the part given. Your gain is determined only by that portion of your total cost that the bargain selling price (amount received) bears to the fair market value. The following formula can be used to calculate the adjusted basis of the property sold:

$$\frac{\text{Selling Price}}{\text{Fair Market Value}} \times \text{Property Basis} = \text{Adjusted Basis}$$

You must allocate this figure to the property sold and determine your taxable gain. For example, assume you have 100 shares of appreciated long-term capital gains stock with a tax basis of $4,000 and a fair market value of $10,000. You want to give $6,000 to The American College and you therefore sell this stock for your basis, or $4,000. Your realized gain is shown below:

| | | |
|---|---|---|
| Fair market value of stock | | $10,000 |
| Minus sale proceeds | | −4,000 |
| Charitable contribution | | $ 6,000 |
| Sale proceeds | | $ 4,000 |
| Tax basis in property sold: | | |
| Sale price | $ 4,000 | |
| | ────── × basis of | |
| Fair value | $10,000 | −1,600 |
| | $4,000 | |
| Gain realized | | $ 2,400 |

The rules for determining basis that apply to bargain sales also apply when mortgaged property is donated and the charity assumes the mortgage. The transfer is treated like a sale, with the purchase cost being the mortgage that the charity agrees to pay. In the case of both bargain sales and mortgaged property, the bargain sale rule does not apply unless the exchange produces a charitable deduction.

The courts have allowed owners of closely held corporations to withdraw funds from their firms tax-free by means of charitable contributions followed by a redemption: The owner gives stock to charity and at a later date the corporation redeems the stock. The donor is allowed a charitable contribution deduction, even though an understanding exists between the donor and donee that the stock will be redeemed shortly after contribution, where redemption is not required.

The valuation for the gift of stock is the average of the high and low sales price reported on the date of the gift.

CONTRIBUTION OF SERVICES

No deduction exists for the contribution of your services. However, unreimbursed expenses incurred during the rendering of free services for a qualified charity are deductible as charitable contributions.

Any cost incurred in traveling from your house to where you served is deductible. A standard mileage rate of 12¢ per mile is allowed if you use your car. Or you can choose to deduct your actual unreimbursed expenses for gas and oil. Parking fees and tolls are also deductible. No deduction is given for depreciation, insurance, or repairs on the car. Donating blood is considered the contribution of services and thus no deduction is allowed.

A deduction for reasonable outlays for meals and lodgings is also allowed if incurred while away from home. In addition, deductions have been allowed for the cost of baby-sitting services for children whose parents were performing services for charitable organizations.

LIFE INSURANCE POLICIES AND OTHER DONATIONS

If full rights of ownership are contributed, a gift of a life insurance policy is acceptable as a charitable gift. Any subsequent payments of premiums by the donor will also qualify as charitable contributions. The amount of the deduction for this type is its fair market value.

Dues, admission charges, etc., where you receive property or benefits can only be deducted if they exceed the value of the benefits received for them. Amounts paid for raffle tickets, bingo, or similar chance games and losses on games of chance are not deductible charitable contributions.

Where amounts are paid in connection with admission to fund-raising affairs for charity, you must show that a clearly identifiable segment of the payment is a gift, and only this amount will qualify. The same rule applies whether or not the tickets are actually used. If you have no intention of using the tickets, you should give them back and make a gift of the purchase price. Using this approach, you will get the full amount as a deduction.

Donations of less than your entire interest in property are not deductible, but there are certain exceptions to this rule. For example, the transfer of a remainder interest in a personal residence or a farm is deductible. Also, the contribution of an undivided portion of your entire interest in property will qualify for the deduction.

A charitable remainder gift made during your lifetime is also deductible, based upon the value of the remainder interest. The Internal Revenue Service tax code requires that a fixed percentage be paid to one or more persons for a specified term of years (not to exceed 20) or for the life or lives of the income beneficiaries, with an irrevocable remainder to be paid to the charitable organization. If the remainder interest to the charity is subject to a contingency, it is not deductible. In addition, the value of the gift must be readily determinable.

**PROOF**

You are required to provide information in support of all of your deductions; therefore, you should be able to prove all charitable contributions through receipts, canceled checks, etc. If a contribution is made in property other than money, you should state the kind of property contributed, the method used in ascertaining the fair market value of the property at the time the contribution is made, and whether the amount of the contribution is reduced because the property is either ordinary income or capital gain property.

If you contribute property other than money valued in excess of $500, you must attach Form 8283 to the income tax return with the following information:

a) the name and address of the donee organization;

b) the date of the actual contribution;

c) a description of the property;

d) the manner of acquisition;

e) the fair market value of the property at the contribution time and the method utilized in determining the fair market value; *and*

f) the cost or other basis of the property.

Expert witnesses are frequently brought in during tax court cases to evaluate contributed property. The burden is on the individual to establish the value of the contribution.

An appraisal may be your best method to avoid an audit, especially if the property is difficult to value and a substantial contribution is involved. An added attraction is that the appraiser's fees are also deductible.

For other gifts, have the charity value the gift and send you a receipt. This will establish the proof necessary for a gift, and may avoid valuation difficulties. Taking out an insurance policy reflecting the property's value might also be a useful technique to establish the true value of the property.

Furthermore, for tax years beginning after 1982, IRS Proposed Regulation Section 1.170 A-13 (a) would require an individual taxpayer (or a corporation) making a charitable contribution of money to maintain a cancelled check, a receipt, or other reliable written evidence showing the amount of the charitable contribution, the date contributed, and the name of the donee. In the absence of a cancelled check or receipt, the reliability of the other written evidence will depend on the facts and circumstances of the particular case but, in all events, the burden would be on the taxpayer to establish reliability. Factors indicating that such other written evidence is reliable include, but are not limited to, the contemporaneous nature of the writing evidencing the contribution, the regularity of the taxpayer's record-keeping procedures, and, in the case of the contribution of a small amount, any other written evidence from the donee charitable organization evidencing receipt of a donation that would not otherwise constitute a receipt.

For charitable contributions of property other than money for which the taxpayer claims a deduction in excess of $500, the taxpayer would be required to maintain additional records regarding the manner of acquisition of the property and the property's cost or other basis if it was held for less than one year prior to the date of contribution. For property held for one year or more preceding the date of contribution, cost or other basis information should be maintained by the taxpayer if it is available.

The Tax Reform Act of 1984 mandated the Internal Revenue Service to issue regulations, by December 31, 1984, which would impose appraisal and information reporting requirements on charitable contributions by individuals, closely held corporations, and personal service corporations. Appraisals will be required for each item with a claim value in excess of $5,000 ($10,000 for privately held stock). Similar items are to be added in determining the dollar threshold. This provision would not apply to publicly traded securities. When the rules apply, the donor must obtain a written appraisal of the property's fair market value from a qualified independent appraiser, and a summary of the appraisal must be attached to the donor's tax return.

If the donee charity sells, exchanges, or otherwise transfers donated property valued in excess of $5,000 within two years, the donee must furnish an information report to the IRS, with a copy to the donor. These provisions apply for contributions made after December 31, 1984.

Note that if a taxpayer contributes works of art with an aggregate value of at least $20,000, the taxpayer must attach a complete copy of the signed appraisal. In addition, an eight-by-eleven-inch color photograph, or a color transparency no smaller than four by five inches, must be submitted. For donations made after 1987, the submission of the appraisal is mandatory. It was optional for art donated before 1988.

For this purpose, the definition of art includes paintings, watercolors, prints, drawings, sculptures, ceramics, antique furniture, decorative arts, textiles, carpets, silver, rare manuscripts, historical memorabilia, and other similar objects. It does not include gems, jewelry, or books.

These requirements are intended to assist the IRS Art Advisory Panel, which is composed of art dealers, curators, museum directors, and other experts, in checking the valuation of artwork for tax purposes. An evaluation of $20,000 or more must be referred to the panel.

An interesting technique exists for obtaining a charitable deduction before a cash outlay. This can be done by establishing an irrevocable banker's letter of credit in favor of the charity. The full amount of the letter of credit will be deductible by you in the year in which it is established, even if the charity does not draw upon the credit until the next year. The charity, however, must have the absolute right to draw down the entire amount of the letter of credit immediately. This technique could present an important planning opportunity when you can reasonably expect that the charity would not draw down the funds immediately. For example, when the letter of credit will finance a construction project, it is reasonable to expect the charity to draw down those funds over the various phases of the construction, rather than immediately.

The tax saved from a charitable donation reduces the cost of donating. As the marginal tax rates increase, the actual cost of donating decreases. The actual cost to a person in the lowest tax bracket (15 percent) for a $1 charitable deduction is 85¢. For a person in the highest tax bracket (33 percent), the actual cost is only 67¢ on the dollar.

# 47 Casualty Losses

A *casualty* is the damage or destruction of property resulting from an identifiable event that is sudden, unexpected, or unusual in nature. Casualty losses can be used to lower your taxes.

Deductible casualty losses may result from a number of different causes, including but not limited to:

Automobile accidents
Civil disturbances
Drought
Earthquakes
Explosions
Fires
Flood
Freezing rain
Ice and snow
Hurricanes

Lightning
Mine cave-ins
Shipwrecks
Smog
Sonic booms
Storms
Vandalism
Winds and tornadoes

A reduction in your property's value because it is in or near an area that suffered a casualty or that might again suffer a casualty is usually not deductible. However, in *Finkbohner, Jr.,* 86-1 USTC para. 9393, 57 AFTRO 2d 86-1400 (CA-11, 1986), a permanent decline in market value due to buyer resistance was includable in the amount of a casualty loss deduction. There, the court refused to follow the prevailing view in two other circuits which limited the deduction to actual physical loss. In the *Finkbohner* case, the taxpayers' residence was unharmed, but seven of the twelve houses in the neighborhood had to be razed after a flood. The court ruled that the removal of most of the homes in the neighborhood was a permanent change. The diminished market value reflected more than a fear of future flooding, since the residence was above maximum flood levels. They concluded that the fair market value after the casualty would have to reflect such permanent loss of value. A loss is allowed only for the actual casualty damage to your property.

The partial or complete destruction of property must be the result of an identifiable event that is either sudden, unexpected, or unusual. For example, if your spouse, while washing the dishes, inadvertantly knocks a diamond ring that you put in a glass next to the sink down the drain and activates the garbage disposal unit, thus destroying the ring, this unusual event will qualify as a deductible casualty. So, too, will the loss of a diamond ring if your spouse slams the car door on your hand. Both of the events were sudden and unusual, therefore allowing the casualty deduction. However, a loss due to the accidental breakage of articles such as glassware or china under normal conditions is not a casualty loss. Neither is a loss due to damage done by a family pet.

The event must be one that is sudden—that is, swift, not gradual or progressive. If a steadily operating cause from a normal process damages your property, it is not considered a casualty. So, for example, the steady weakening of a building due to normal wind and weather conditions will not qualify as a casualty. On the other hand, the rust and water damage to rugs and drapes caused by the bursting of a water heater will qualify—but not the deterioration and damage to the water heater itself.

If trees, shrubs, or other plants are damaged or destroyed by a fungus, disease, insects, worms, or similar pests, the loss is not deductible as a casualty loss. However, a sudden, unexpected, or unusual infestation by beetles or other insects may result in a casualty loss. If trees and shrubs are damaged by a storm, flood, or fire, the loss also is a deductible casualty loss.

Normally a loss from an accident to your car is deductible. This is not true, though, if your willful negligence or willful act causes the accident, or if it is caused by the willful act or willful negligence of someone acting for you.

If you do have an accident, you must file a claim with your insurance company. If you do not file the claim, you will not be entitled to a casualty loss deduction for the damage done to your car. Casualty loss deductions are allowed only for losses not compensated for by insurance or otherwise. But "not compensated for" doesn't just mean actual payment. When a collectible insurance claim *can* be filed, a deliberate election not to file will not give rise to a casualty loss deduction. Your loss can be "compensated for."

Yet in a 1981 case the tax court allowed a theft loss deduction despite a refusal to make an insurance claim predicated on a fear of increased premiums.[4] The court concluded that "compensated" did not mean "covered" and that since no "compensation" was received, a deduction could be allowed. This ruling was confirmed in the case of *Dixon F. Miller v. Commissioner* on May 2, 1984; the Sixth Circuit joined the Eleventh Circuit and the Tax Court in taking the above position. The Tax Reform Act of 1986, however, imposed a new precondition on the allowance of casualty losses. Any loss that is covered by insurance is taken into account only if the taxpayer files a timely insurance claim. This new limitation applies only to the extent that the insurance policy would have provided reimbursement if a claim had been filed. [IRC §165(a)(4)(i)].

For example, if you sustain $800 worth of damage for an insured loss with a $500 deductible, if no claim is made $300 of your loss will not be allowable as a deduction. The $500 balance will count as a loss, subject to the $100 and 10 percent adjusted gross income floor.

---

4. *H.L. Hills.* 76 T.C. No. 42.

You should deduct your casualty loss in the year of occurrence. This timing rule is modified, though, when insurance enters the picture. In such a case, the loss deduction is limited to the part of the damage that is not reimbursed that year. If you deduct a casualty in the year of occurrence and receive insurance reimbursement in a later year, you should not amend the earlier return. Instead, the portion of the reimbursement that exceeds the original estimate of recovery should be taken back into income in the later year.

For example, you suffered a $6,000 deductible loss in 1988 and estimated an insurance recovery of $5,000, and you took a $1,000 casualty loss deduction in that year. In 1989, however, your insurance company pays the full $6,000. What you must do on your 1989 return is include the extra $1,000 as income. Note, though, that you must have received a tax benefit for the casualty loss in 1988. If you did not itemize your deductions in that year, you received no benefit and therefore have no additional taxable income when the insurance company repays the full $6,000 in 1989.

The amount of loss from a casualty that can be deducted is generally the lesser of the following two amounts:

a) the decrease in the fair market value of the property as a result of the casualty; *or*

b) your basis in the property before the casualty.

In the case of business property, if the fair market value of the property immediately before the casualty is less than the adjusted basis, the amount of the adjusted basis is deemed to be the amount of the loss. Alternatively, the loss may be measured by the cost of repairing the damage. In a case of nonbusiness (or personal use) property, the deduction is the amount by which the casualty loss exceeds 10 percent of your adjusted gross income and $100.

The fair market value must be based on a valid judgment of the selling price of the property at the time of the casualty. An appraisal is the best way to do this. The appraisal should be made by an experienced and reliable appraiser. Several factors are important in evaluating the accuracy of the appraisal:

- The appraiser's familiarity with your property before the casualty.

- Sales of comparable properties.

- Conditions in the area of the casualty.

- The method used in making the appraisal.

When available, photographs should be used in making the appraisal and in determining the extent of damage from a casualty. The costs of photographs obtained for this purpose are not a part of the loss but can be taken as a miscellaneous deduction. They are an expense of determining your tax liability. Furthermore, you may deduct as a miscellaneous deduction the amount you must pay for the appraisal itself, since it also is an expense of determining your tax liability.

The cost of cleaning up or making repairs after a casualty may be used as a measure of the decrease in fair market value if:

a) the repairs are necessary to restore the property to its condition before the casualty;

b) the amount spent for repairs is not excessive;

c) the repairs do no more than take care of the damage;

d) the value of the property after the repairs is not, as a result of the repairs, more than the value of the property before the casualty.

The cost of restoring landscaping to its original condition may also be taken as an indication of the decrease in fair market value. You may be able to measure your loss by what is spent on the following:

- Removing destroyed or damaged trees and shrubs, minus any salvage you receive.

- Pruning and other measures taken to preserve damaged trees and shrubs.

- Replanting that is necessary to restore the property to its approximate value before the casualty.

The incidental expenses you have due to a casualty, such as expenses for the treatment of personal injuries, for temporary housing, or for a rental car, are not deductible as casualty losses. Moreover, the cost of protecting your property against a potential casualty also is not deductible. For example, you cannot deduct what you spend on insurance or to board up your house against a storm. Expenses like these are only deductible by businesses as business expenses. If you make a permanent improvement to your property to protect it against a casualty, the cost should be added to your basis in the property. An example would be the cost of a dike to prevent flooding.

# 48

## Theft Losses

A *theft* is the unlawful and intentional removal of money or property from its rightful owner. It includes, but is not limited to, larceny, robbery, and embezzlement. If money or property is taken as the result of extortion, kidnapping for ransom, or blackmail, it may also be a theft. The simple disappearance of money or property does not constitute a theft. However, an accidental loss or disappearance of property may qualify as a casualty if it results from an identifiable event that is sudden, unexpected, or unusual in nature. The lost diamond ring in the example given in the previous section constitutes such a deductible casualty.

The amount of loss from a theft that can be deducted is generally the lesser of the following two amounts:

a) the decrease in the fair market value of the property as a result of the theft, *or*

b) your basis in the property before the theft.

The fair market value of property immediately after a theft is considered to be zero. That is, a theft loss deduction is either the full fair market value of the stolen property or its basis, whichever is less. If you get your stolen property back, however, your loss is measured like a casualty loss from vandalism. You must consider the actual fair market value of the property when you get it back in order to compute your loss.

The decrease in the fair market value must be based on a judgment of the actual price you could have asked if your property had been sold. Sentimental value is not a factor in determining the amount of the loss. Any loss from the theft of a family portrait, heirloom, or keepsake must be based on its actual market value apart from any sentiment. An appraisal is the best way to make this judgment. This appraisal must recognize the effect of any general market decline that may occur so that any deduction is limited to the actual loss resulting from deprivation of the property. See the preceding section on casualty losses for more information on appraisals.

The cost of any theft-preventive equipment, such as burglar alarm systems or theft insurance, is not deductible. If a protective device increases the value of your property, however, the cost may be added to your basis.

DEDUCTION LIMITS

The limits and computations for determining both casualty and theft loss deductions are very similar, so they are now grouped together for ease of discussion.

After you have figured the amount of your casualty or theft loss, you must figure how much of the loss you can deduct. There are three ways that you may adjust the casualty or theft loss before you can deduct it:

1.  If you receive insurance or another type of reimbursement for your loss, you must subtract the reimbursement from the amount of the loss before you figure your deduction. As noted above, if you expect to get a reimbursement but have not yet received payment, you must still subtract the expected reimbursement from the loss. In a business situation, though, the cost of repairs made for business purposes *is* deductible, even if insurance recovery later is likely. The amount of the final recovery that is attributable to previously deductible items will be taxable in the later year.[5]

2.  If the stolen, destroyed, or damaged property was for your own or your family's personal use, you must reduce each loss by an additional $100, because the first $100 of a casualty or theft loss on personal use property is not deductible. However, if you used the stolen, destroyed, or damaged property in your business or for investment purposes, this $100 limit does not apply.

3.  For nonbusiness losses, you must reduce the *total* amount of the losses by 10 percent of your adjusted gross income. This is done after the $100 reduction in adjustment 2 above and after any reimbursement from insurance. Note that under the Tax Reform Act of 1984, for purposes of computing the 10 percent floor, the casualty loss deduction (adjusted gross income) is determined without regard to the application of Section 1231 to gains or losses from involuntary conversions arising from a casualty or theft. Gain and losses from these personal casualties (without regard to the period the property was held) will be netted. If the recognized gains exceed the recognized losses from these transactions, then all such gains and losses will be treated as gains and losses from the sale or exchange of a capital asset,

---

5.  *R.R. Hensler, Inc. v. Commissioner* T.C. 317 (1979).

and the losses will not be subject to the 10 percent floor. (The amount of any recognized loss will be subject to the $100 floor before netting.) If the recognized losses exceed the recognized gains, all gains and losses will be ordinary. Losses to the extent of gains will be allowed in full. Losses in excess of gains will be subject to the 10% adjusted gross income floor.

For example, assume you have $100,000 of adjusted gross income without regard to casualty gains and losses, $50,000 of such casualty gains, and $40,000 of such casualty losses (after applying the $100 floor) for a taxable year. All your personal casualty gains and losses for that year will be treated as capital gains and losses. The 10 percent floor will not be applicable. Assume, however, that your losses for the year are $70,000 rather than $40,000. The gains and losses will all be treated as ordinary. $60,000 of losses will be allowed as a deduction ($50,000 plus the $10,000 excess of the remaining $20,000 over the $10,000 [10 percent of $100,000] adjusted gross income floor).

If an insurance company reimburses you for any of your living expenses after you lose the use of your home because of a casualty, the insurance payments are not considered a reimbursement reducing your casualty loss. Any part of these payments that covers normal living expenses that you and your family would have during this period anyway must be reported as income on your tax return, but any insurance payments that cover a temporary increase in your living expenses should *not* be reported as income. The same rule applies if you are denied access to your home by government authorities due to the threat of a casualty. Generally, the amount you do not have to report is the amount of your extra expenses for renting suitable housing and for transportation, food, utilities, and miscellaneous services during the period you are unable to use your home because of the casualty.

For example, assume that as a result of a fire you vacated your apartment and moved to a motel. You normally pay $200 a month rent, but none was charged for the month the apartment was vacated. Your motel rent for this month was $275, but you received only $240 in reimbursement for rental expenses from your insurance company. Part of that reimbursement, $75, covers the difference between your actual rent and your normal rent. You do not have to report this amount as income, but the balance of the reimbursement, $165, must be reported as income.

As mentioned, the first $100 of a casualty or theft loss of personal use property is not deductible. This limit applies *after* all reimbursements have been subtracted. Furthermore, a single $100 limit applies to each individual casualty or theft, no matter how many pieces of property are involved. Generally, events closely related in origin are considered a single casualty or theft, as when your summer home suffers wind damage and flood damage caused by a hurricane. A single casualty may also damage two or more widely separate pieces of property.

Remember, though, that the $100 exclusion does not apply if the loss is on business property, property that earns you rent or royalty income, or other investment property. Furthermore, if a husband and wife each sustain a loss from the same casualty or theft and they file a joint return, only one $100 limit applies. It does not matter whether the property involved is jointly or separately owned. If they file separate returns, however, each is subject to a separate $100 limit for the loss, regardless of whether the property is jointly or separately owned. A husband and wife who file separate returns and have a casualty loss on property they own together may deduct only one-half of the loss on each return. Either spouse may claim the entire deduction on a separate return.

COMPUTING THE DEDUCTION

The way to figure a deduction for a casualty or theft loss depends upon the kind of property involved. The rules for personal use property are different from those for business and investment property. The rules for real estate property, such as a house, differ from those for personal property, such as a car or furniture.

In figuring a loss to real estate property that you own for personal use, all improvements, such as buildings and ornamental trees, are considered together. A single loss is figured for the entire property. The amount of the loss is either the decrease in fair market value of the entire property or its adjusted basis, whichever is less. From this amount you must subtract any insurance or other reimbursement you receive or expect to receive. The amount remaining that is more than $100 is your personal casualty loss deduction.

As an example, assume that several years ago you bought a house that you then lived in as your home. You paid $5,000 for the land and $20,000 for the house itself; you also paid $1,000 for landscaping. In 1988, when your adjusted gross income was $10,000, your home was totally destroyed by fire. Competent appraisers said that before the fire the property as a whole had a fair market value of $36,000 but that its value after the fire was only $6,000. Shortly after the fire, the insurance company paid you $20,000 for the loss. Your casualty loss deduction is figured as follows:

| | |
|---|---:|
| Value of entire property before fire | $36,000 |
| Minus value of entire property after fire | − 6,000 |
| Decrease in value of entire property | $30,000 |
| Basis (cost for entire property) | $26,000 |
| Casualty loss (in this case, basis) | 26,000 |
| Minus insurance reimbursement | −20,000 |
| Casualty loss before the $100 limit | 6,000 |
| Minus: $100 nondeductible amount | − 100 |
| : 10% of adjusted gross income | − 1,000 |
| Casualty Loss Deduction | $ 4,900 |

Personal property is generally any property that is not real estate. If your personal property is stolen or is damaged or destroyed by a casualty, you must figure your loss separately for each individual item of property.

For example, assume a fire in your home damaged an upholstered chair and completely destroyed a rug and an antique table. You do not have fire insurance to cover your loss. The chair cost you $150, and you establish that it had a fair market value of $75 just before the fire and $10 just after the fire. The rug cost you $200 and had a value of $50 just before the fire. You bought the table at an auction for $15 before discovering it was a valuable antique. It was appraised at $350 before the fire.

The loss on the chair is limited to the difference in fair market value before and after the fire, or $65, since that decrease is less than its basis ($150). The loss on the rug is limited to its value of $50 just before the fire, because this amount is also less than its basis ($200). The table, on the other hand, had a value just before the fire that was greater than your basis in it. Your loss on the table, therefore, is its basis, $15. Your total loss from the fire is $130, and after subtracting the $100 limit, your deductible is $30 before the reduction for 10 percent of your adjusted gross income.

When a casualty involves both real and personal property, a single $100 limit applies to the total loss, but you must figure the amount of the loss separately for each type of property, as discussed above. Remember, a loss on business property, property that earns you rent or royalty income, or other investment property is *not* subject to the $100 limit. For business and investment property, you must figure your loss separately for each item that is stolen, damaged, or destroyed. If casualty damage occurs to a building and to trees on the same piece of property, the loss is measured separately for each.

If you have business or investment property that is completely lost because of a casualty or theft, your deductible is your basis in the property minus any salvage value and minus any insurance or other reimbursement that you receive or expect to receive. For example, suppose you owned a building that you rented out and your basis in it, not including land, was $20,000 before it was completely destroyed by fire. Its fair market value just before the fire was only $15,000.

Since this was investment property and since it was completely destroyed, the deductible is your basis in the building, $20,000, decreased by salvage value and by any insurance or other reimbursement. Fair market value is not considered when figuring your loss, even though it is less than your basis in the building.

If business or investment property is damaged but not completely destroyed in a casualty, the loss is the decrease in value because of the casualty, or your basis in the property, whichever is less. From this amount you must subtract any insurance or other reimbursements you receive or expect to receive.

After you take a casualty or theft loss deduction, you must subtract from your basis in the damaged, destroyed, or stolen property the amount of your deduction and the amount of any reimbursement you receive. The result is a new, lower total for your basis in the property. In some cases, this lower basis will carry over to any property you get to replace the property that is stolen or destroyed.

PROOF OF LOSS

To take a deduction for casualty or theft loss, you must be able to show that there was actually a casualty or theft, and you must be able to support the amount you take as a deduction. For a casualty loss, you should be able to show:

a) the nature of the casualty and when it occurred;

b) that the loss was a direct result of the casualty; *and*

c)  that you were the owner of the property; or, if you leased the property from someone else, that you were contractually liable to the owner for the damage.

For a theft, you should be able to show:

a)  the date on which you found that the property was missing;

b)  that your property *was* stolen; *and*

c)  that you were the owner of the property.

To qualify for a theft loss deduction, the taking of your property must be illegal under the laws of the state where it occurred. If a theft loss is not reported promptly to the police, you must offer as a substitute the testimony of anyone who witnessed the event or its aftermath. If records were burglarized, steps must be taken to reconstruct the records by gathering substitutes.

Proof of the amount of a theft loss is difficult in the case of cash, where there is little likelihood that there is any documentation of how much you had on your person or in your home. Deductions will be allowed in full when you have evidence of why you had such a large amount of money with you. One theft loss deduction was allowed because the records showed that the victim was on his way to complete the closing on the acquisition of a house.

You do not have to be virgin-pure to qualify for a theft loss deduction. Even if you were naive or greedy and that naïveté or greed resulted in your being the victim of a theft, you may still receive a deduction for that theft. "Indeed," according to one court, "gullibility or cupidity of the victim is often a crucial factor that enables the swindler to succeed in his fraud."[6]

For both casualty loss and theft losses you must be able to give evidence supporting the amount you deduct. You should have supporting evidence in the following three areas:

1.  *Basis.* The purchase contract or deed can show your original basis (its cost) in real estate. Improvements to the property that increase basis should be supported by checks, receipts, and similar items.

---

6.  *Perry A. Nichols, et al.,* T.C. 842 (1965).

2. *Decrease in fair market value.* Appraisals should be used where possible. Photographs of your property before it was damaged or stolen will be helpful in showing its condition and value before the casualty or theft. Photographs taken after a casualty will be helpful in establishing the condition and value of the property after it was damaged. Photographs showing the condition of the property after it was repaired, restored, or replaced may also be helpful.

3. *Insurance and other types of reimbursement.* Keep records of all you receive or expect to receive.

PLANNING CONSIDERATIONS

Ordinarily, a casualty loss is deductible in the year the event took place. However, the Internal Revenue Service tax code permits a special election to take "disaster area" loss deductions in the year prior to occurrence. To qualify, the president must declare the region a "disaster area" eligible for federal relief under the Disaster Relief Act of 1964. Once this is done you can make an irrevocable election to treat the entire disaster loss as having occurred in the prior tax year. This allows you to get an immediate tax benefit for the loss rather than forcing you to wait until the subsequent year to claim it.

For example, assume you suffered a casualty loss in 1988. In order to get the tax benefit for that loss, it would have to be claimed as a deduction from your 1988 taxes, payable in April of 1989. But if you elected and qualified for the optional disaster relief provision, you could take the disaster loss deduction on your 1987 return, either before the return has been filed or by filing an amended 1987 return. Alternatively, if your income increased in 1988 and put you in a higher bracket, you could decline to make the election and take the higher valued deduction on your 1988 return.

As explained above, expenses to prevent a casualty are not normally deductible as casualty losses. Such expenditures are likely to involve the acquisition of property with an estimated useful life of more than one year. But a tax deduction *can* be claimed if the preventive measures do not add to the value of the property. In one case a plant had sustained cave-ins under its flooring, and further trouble of the same sort was anticipated. The drilling and grouting undertaken to forestall this was a deductible business expense. In another case, an individual used temporary dikes to protect his personal residence as well as his business property from flooding. The dikes were constructed of earth and sand bags and were removed immediately after the floodwater receded. While the cost of constructing and removing the temporary dikes was not allowed as a casualty loss with respect to either the business or the nonbusiness property, the cost of constructing and removing the dikes to protect business property was deductible as an ordinary and necessary business expense. In a third case, an expense that had been incurred to prevent an accident—and *was* held to be a different kind of deduction—was the cost of a vasectomy! The moral here is simple: What you may think of only in terms of a casualty loss expense may qualify as a deduction under a noncasualty classification—for example, as an ordinary and necessary business expense or medical expense.

# 49

## Moving Expenses

Moving expenses incurred if you change job locations or if you start a new job are generally deductible if you meet certain requirements. Your new job location must be at least 35 miles from your former job location, you must make your move within one year from the date you start your new job, and you must work full-time for a specified period of time.

You may take a moving expense deduction, subject to dollar limits explained later, for the following expenses:

- Travel to your new job location.
- Moving your household goods and personal items.
- House-hunting trips before you move.
- Temporary living expenses at the new location.
- Expenses incurred in disposing of your former home and acquiring your new one.

You may qualify for such deductions whether you are self-employed or an employee. These expenses, though, must be in connection with starting work at a new job location. You will be able to deduct your moving expenses if you meet the requirements of certain tests.

THE DISTANCE TEST

You may deduct your moving expenses if your new principal job location is at least 35 miles further from your former home than was your former principal job location. In addition, the distance from your new home to your new job location must not be longer than the distance from your old home to the new job location. Your home is your primary residence; it may be a house, apartment, condominium, houseboat, housetrailer, or similar dwelling. It does not include other homes owned or kept up by you or members of your family, or a seasonal home (such as a beach cottage).

The distance between two points is measured by the shortest of the most commonly traveled routes between the points. If your old job was three miles from your former home, your new job must be at least 38 miles from that home. If you did not have an old job location, your new job location must be at least 35 miles from your former home. This does not apply to the location of your *new* home.

For example, assume your old job was three miles from your former home. Your new job is 40 miles from that home. You qualify because the difference (37 miles) is over the minimum of 35 miles. Your new home may be less than 35 miles from your former home, but it must be at least as close to your new job as your former home. If so, you have met the distance test.

|  | 40 miles | | |
|---|---|---|---|
| 3 miles | 34 miles | 6 miles |
| Old Job | Old Home | New Home | New Job |

New Job to Old Home = 40 miles    Old Home to New Job = 40 miles
Old Home to Old Job = −3 miles    New Home to Old Job =  6 miles
Qualifying distance    = 37 miles    New Home is at least as close to
                                     New Job as Old Home

Your principal job location is usually the place where you do most of your work and spend most of your time. A new principal job location is a new place where you will work on a permanent or indefinite basis rather than on a temporary basis. However, you may have a principal job location even if there is no one place where you spend a substantial part of your work and time. In this case, use the distance to the place where your work is centered—for example, where you report for work or otherwise have the "base" for your work.

If you work for a number of employers on a short-term basis, or get work under a union hall system (such as in construction and the building trades), use the distance between your home and the union hall.

TIME TEST

To deduct your moving expenses you also must meet one of the following time tests:

1.  If you are an employee, you must work full-time at least 39 weeks during the 12-month period following your arrival in the general area of your new job location. You do not have to work for one employer for the 39 weeks; you do not even have to work thirty-nine weeks in a row. But you must work full-time within the same general commuting area. Whether you are employed full-time depends upon the custom for your type of work. For example, a school teacher on a 12-month contract who teaches on a full-time basis for more than six months is considered a full-time employee for the entire 12 months. Any week that you work full-time is used to satisfy the 39 week full-time work test. If the work is seasonal, you are considered to be working full-time during the off-season weeks if your contract or agreement covers an off-season of less than six months. You are considered to be working during any week you are temporarily absent from work because of illness, strikes, natural disasters, or the like. You are also considered to be a full-time employee during any week you are absent from work for leave or for vacation that is provided for in your work contract or agreement.

2.  If you are self-employed, you must work full-time for at least 39 weeks during the first 12 months and a total of 78 weeks during the 24 months after your arrival in the area of your new job location. Whether you perform services full-time during any one week depends upon the custom of your type of work in your area.

Despite these restrictions, you may deduct your moving expenses even if you have not met the time test by the time your return is due. You may do this if you *expect* to work for 39 weeks by the end of the next year, or for 78 weeks by the end of the second year. Furthermore, you do not have to meet the time test at all if any one of the following situations applies:

- You are in the armed forces and your move is due to a permanent change of stations.

- You move to the United States because you retire or are the survivor of a person who dies while living and working outside the United States.

- Your job ends because of disability, transfer for the employer's benefit, or layoff other than for willful misconduct. The time test does not have to be met in case of your death. If you are transferred, you are expected to meet the test at the time you start the job.

THE START OF WORK TEST

In general you must have moving expenses within one year from the time you first report to your job or business at the new location, and the move must be in connection with the start of work at the new location. If you do not move within one year, the expenses are ordinarily not deductible unless you can show that certain circumstances prevent the move within that time period. For example, if your family moved more than a year after you started work at the new location in order to allow your child to complete junior high school in the same school, your allowable moving expenses are deductible.

A move is considered closely related to the start of work if:

a) you are required to live at the new location as a condition of employment; or

b) you will spend less time or money commuting from the new home to the new job.

It is important that you understand and recognize all of the possible expenses that are deductible under this category. You can deduct expenses of moving your possessions, traveling to your new home, looking for a new home, living temporarily in a new area, selling and buying a home, or settling and signing a lease.

If you use your car to take yourself, your family, or your things to your new home, or for house hunting, you figure your expenses in either of two ways:

1. You may deduct your actual expenses such as gas, oil, and repairs (but not depreciation) for the use of your car, if you keep an accurate record of each expense.

2. You may deduct 9¢ a mile instead of the actual costs if you can prove the mileage traveled. You may deduct parking fees and tolls you pay in moving no matter which way you figure your expenses.

Not only may you deduct the expenses of moving your own possessions, but you may also deduct the costs for transporting the possessions of the members of your household. This includes the actual cost of transportation or hauling from your former home to your new one. The cost of packing and crating, in-transit storage, and insurance is included. Expenses of storing and insuring household goods and personal effects are in-transit expenses if incurred within 30 consecutive days after your things are moved from your former home and before they are delivered at your new one.

Moving expenses also include the cost of transportation, lodging for yourself and members of your household while traveling to your new home, and 80 percent of the cost of meals while moving. This includes expenses for the day you arrive, and any meals and lodging expenses incurred in your old neighborhood within one day after your former home becomes uninhabitable because your furniture has been moved out. You may deduct expenses for only one trip to your new home for yourself and each member of your household. However, all members do not have to travel together.

Deductions are allowed as well for premove house-hunting expenses. House-hunting expenses include the cost of transportation, meals, and lodging for yourself and members of your household while traveling to and from the area of your new job and while you are there. You may deduct these expenses only if you begin your trip *after* you get the job in the new area and if you go primarily to look for a new place to live. Your house hunting does not have to be successful to qualify for this deduction. You and members of your household may travel separately. Furthermore, you are not limited in the number of trips you or members of your household may take.

You also may deduct the cost of temporary living expenses. These expenses include not only the cost of lodging in the area of your new job but the cost of meals as well.

HOME SALE, PURCHASE, OR LEASE EXPENSES

In addition, home sale, purchase, and lease expenses also are deductible. You therefore may deduct the costs of selling your home or settling your lease in the former area and buying or leasing a home in the new area.

When you sell or exchange a home, you may deduct real estate commissions, attorney's fees, title fees, escrow fees, points or loan placement charges you are required to pay, state transfer taxes, and similar expenses connected to the sale or exchange. You may not, however, deduct the cost of physical improvements intended to improve the condition or appearance of your former home. When you buy your new home, you may again deduct attorney's fees, escrow fees, appraisal fees, title fees, points and loan placement charges that do not represent payment or prepayment of interest, and similar expenses connected to the purchase. When you lease a new home, you cannot deduct payments or prepayments of rent.

There are certain dollar limits that you must remember. Deductions for the costs of moving household goods and traveling to your new home are not limited to any amount. For premove travel, meals, and lodging expenses, temporary living expenses, and home sale, purchase, or lease expenses, you may not deduct more than $3,000. Deductions for house-hunting trip costs and temporary living expenses together cannot be more than $1,500.

If you are a homeowner, you should claim the costs of premove house-hunting expenses and temporary living expenses before you claim the costs of selling and buying your home as moving expenses. However, within the dollar limits you may choose to deduct any combination of these expenses. If you have expenses from selling or buying a home that you cannot deduct as moving expenses because of the $3,000 limit, you should use these expenses to reduce the gain on the sale of your former home or to increase the basis of your new home.

The following items cannot be deducted as moving expenses:

Home improvements to help sell your home
Loss on the sale of your home
Mortgage penalties
Losses from the disposing of memberships and clubs
Any part of the purchase price of your new home
Real estate taxes
Car tax for the state you move to

Driver's license for the state you move to

Refitting carpets and draperies

New security deposits on a new lease

Security deposits on an old lease because the vacated space needs cleaning or redecorating when the lease ended

However, you may deduct a security deposit that you give up if the lease is broken as a result of the move.

TAX STRATEGIES

The availability of the moving expense deduction allows you several very sophisticated tax planning strategies. First, recognize that some expenses in connection with a change in employment involving moving your residence could be considered either as moving expenses or as expenses related to the sale of your old home or purchase of your new residence. Careful identification and documentation of such expenses can result in either a moving expense deduction or an adjustment of the gain from the sale of your former residence. You must carefully weigh the advantages of these alternative adjustments to your tax.

The second strategic tax move may come about if you are considering retirement and a move to a different—warmer—climate. If you make the move in connection with a change in employment and satisfy the 39-weeks work requirement, you get a deduction for your moving expenses. The tax effect of this deduction will, in effect, increase your compensation for the 39 weeks of work and perhaps make it worthwhile to postpone your actual retirement. Note that included in the definition of moving expenses are all of your "personal effects." See, for example, *John R. Fogg,* 89 T.C. No. 27 (decided in 1988), wherein a marine officer's moving expense deduction included the cost of moving his boat.

Finally, you should recognize that the deductibility of your moving expenses is in effect a tax subsidy of those expenses. So, for example, if you think it may be too expensive to hire a moving company, your decision to save money by moving your household goods yourself may be modified by considering the tax effect of the deduction for moving expenses. Moving company charges of $3,000 actually would represent a cash outflow of only $2,010 if you are single and have taxable income at the $43,150 level or above ($3,000 × .33 = $990 in tax savings).

# 50

## Miscellaneous Trade and Business Deductions of Employees

Prior to the Tax Reform Act of 1986, if you were an employee who had travel, entertainment, or gift expenses in connection with your employment, you would be entitled to deduct the amounts you spent in those areas as "above the line" deductions. *Note that under the Tax Reform Act of 1986, for years after December 31, 1986, all trade and business deductions of employees must be taken as miscellaneous itemized deductions. As of January 1, 1987, miscellaneous itemized deductions will be allowable only to the extent that they exceed 2 percent of your adjusted gross income.*

Under the Tax Reform Act of 1986, this 2 percent floor will not apply to moving expenses; impairment-related work expenses for handicapped employees; to gambling losses to the extent of gambling winnings; and to certain actors who would be allowed to report their income and expenses from acting as if they were independent contractors, if they had two or more employers in the acting profession during the tax year, and if the expenses relating to their acting profession exceeded 10 percent of their gross income and their adjusted gross income (before deducting expenses related to acting) did not exceed $16,000.

# 51

## Travel Expenses

If you are an employee, you may deduct as miscellaneous itemized deductions all the ordinary and necessary travel expenses, in excess of reimbursements, that you have in connection with your work.

"Ordinary and necessary" here again may be translated as "reasonable and customary." Travel expenses are those expenses incurred in traveling away from home for your business, profession, or job. Your tax home, for travel expense purposes, is your principal place of business or employment or your station or post of duty, regardless of where you maintain your family residence. The entire city or general area in which your business or work is located is your tax home.

For example, assume you live with your family in Chicago, but work in Milwaukee. You stay in a Milwaukee hotel and eat in a restaurant during the week and return to Chicago every weekend. You may not deduct any of your expenses for traveling back and forth, or for your meals and lodging in Milwaukee, because Milwaukee is your tax home and the travel over the weekends is not for a business reason.

If you regularly work in two or more separate areas, your principal tax home is the general area where your principal work or business is located. The main factors in determining your principal place of business or work are:

a) the total time ordinarily spent in performing your duties in each area;

b) the degree of your business activity in each area; *and*

c) the relative amount of your income from each area. (See *Bowles*, 85-1 USTC Para. 9244, 55 AFTR 2d, 85-1113 [DC Va. 1984], in which the place of the taxpayers' minor business in terms of income was held to be their tax home, since that was where they spent the majority of their time and effort.)

For example, assume you live in Miami where you have a seasonal job for eight months and earn $15,000, and you work the remaining four months in Cincinnati, also at a seasonal job, and earn $4,000. Miami is your principal place of work because you spend most of your time there and earn most of your income there.

You are considered "away from home" when you are on a *temporary* (rather than indefinite or permanent) job that takes you away from your regular or principal place of business. Temporary employment must be temporary in contemplation, and its termination must be foreseeable at the time of acceptance. (See Revenue Ruling 60-189, 1960-1 CB 60, Revenue Ruling 60-314, 1960-2 CB 48, and *Flowers,* 326 US 465 (S.Ct., 1946).)

In Revenue Ruling 83-82 the Internal Revenue Service stated that employment is temporary "only if its termination can be foreseen within a reasonably short period of time." Where a taxpayer anticipates employment to last for less than one year its status will be determined on the basis of the facts and circumstances. Where the taxpayer anticipates employment of one year or more, but less than two years, and it in fact falls within this range, there is a rebuttable presumption that the employment is "indefinite." An expected or actual stay of two years or longer is considered "indefinite" regardless of other facts and circumstances.

To rebut the one to two year presumption you must (1) clearly demonstrate by objective factors that you realistically expected that the employment in question would last less than two years and that you could then return to your claimed tax home, and (2) show that the claimed tax home is your regular place of abode in a real and substantial sense.

The following three factors may be used to determine if point (2) is met: (1) whether you have used the claimed abode as lodging while working in that vicinity immediately before the claimed temporary employment and you continue to maintain work contacts there; (2) whether your living expenses at the claimed abode are duplicated because of your work away from such abode; and (3) whether you (a) have a family member or members (marital or lineal only) currently residing at the claimed abode or (b) continue to currently use the claimed abode frequently for lodging.

If you satisfy the expectation test and all three of the abode tests the IRS will deem the work assignment "temporary." If only two of the three abode tests are met, then all the facts and circumstances will be subject to close scrutiny to determine if the assignment is temporary or indefinite. If only one of the abode tests is met the IRS will regard the assignment as indefinite.

You may also be considered as *traveling* away from home when your work in the same city in which you and your family live. Suppose your family residence is in Pittsburgh, where you work for 12 weeks a year. The remainder of the time you work for the same employer in Baltimore, where you eat in restaurants and sleep at a rooming house. Your salary is the same whether you are in Pittsburgh or Baltimore. Since you spend most of your working time and earn most of your salary in Baltimore, that city is your tax home and you may not deduct any expenses incurred for meals and lodging there. However, when you go to work in Pittsburgh, you are away from your tax home even though you stay at your family home. Therefore, you may deduct the cost of your round trip between Baltimore and Pittsburgh, and that part of your family living expenses for meals due to your living in Pittsburgh while working there.

Deductible travel expenses include the following:

Air, rail, and bus fares

Operation and maintenance of your automobile

Taxi fares or other costs of transportation between the airport or station and your hotel, from one customer to another, or from one place of business to another

Transportation from the place where you eat and sleep to your temporary work assignment

Baggage charges and transportation costs for sample and display material

Meals (limited to 80 percent of cost) and lodging when you are away from home on business

Cleaning and laundry expenses

Telephone and telegraph expenses

Public stenographer's fees

Operation and maintenance of house trailers

Tips that are incidental to any of these expenses

Similar expenses incident to qualifying travel

You are considered traveling away from home if your duties require you to be away from the general area of your tax home for a period substantially longer than an ordinary day's work. It is not necessary, however, to work the full time. It is reasonable for you to need and to get some sleep or rest to meet the demands of your work or business. This does *not* mean napping in your car to make sure you qualify for the full period. You need not be away from your tax home for an entire 24 hours or from dusk to dawn so long as your relief from duty (rest period) while you are traveling constitutes a sufficient period of time in which to get necessary sleep or rest.

For example, assume you are a railroad conductor and you leave your home terminal on a regularly scheduled round trip between two cities, returning home 16 hours later. During the run you are released for six hours at your turnaround point, where you eat two meals and rent a hotel room to get necessary rest before starting the return trip. You are considered to be away from home for tax travel purposes and may deduct the expenses you incur.

Alternatively, assume you are a truck driver. You leave your terminal and return later the same day. You are released at your turnaround point for one hour in order to eat. Since you are not released to obtain necessary sleep and the brief interval of release does not constitute an adequate rest period, you are not away from home.

Here again the opportunity for sophisticated tax planning presents itself. You may deduct all those travel expenses you incur in attending a convention if you can show that your attendance benefits or advances the interest of your own work or business, as distinguished from the business or work of another. If the convention is for political, social, or other purposes unrelated to your business or work, the expenses are not deductible. But the agenda of the convention need not deal specifically with your official duties. It is sufficient if the agenda is related to your duties and responsibilities in such a way that attendance for a business purpose is indicated.

Regardless of whether the primary purpose of your trip is business or pleasure, all expenses incurred at your destination that are properly attributable to your trade or business are deductible. So if you make a trip primarily for business and, while there, you extend your stay for non-business reasons, make a nonbusiness side trip, or engage in other nonbusiness activities, the travel expenses to and from your destination are still deductible. Furthermore, you may even deduct the expenses you paid or incurred in attending *foreign* conventions in a tax year. Here, however, the allowable expenses of attending the foreign convention must be extensively substantiated: You must make a schedule for the part of the total days of the trip devoted to business-related activities and even the number of hours of business activity you attend each day, which will limit the deduction.

No deductions are allowed for any travel expenses, including meals and lodging while away from home, for any expenses generally considered entertainment, amusement, or recreation expenses, including expenses for facilities used in connection with such activities, or for any gift expenses, unless you substantiate certain elements.

For *travel* you must prove *all* of the following elements:

- The amount of each separate expenditure for travel away from home, such as the cost of your transportation or lodging. The daily cost of your breakfast, lunch, and dinner and any incidental elements of such travel may be totaled if they are listed in reasonable categories, such as meals, gasoline and oil, and taxi fares.

- The dates of your departure and return for each trip, and the number of days spent on business away from home.

- The destination or locality of your travel, described by name of city, town, or similar designation.

- The business reason for your travel or the business benefit derived or expected from your travel.

On February 28, 1983, the IRS proposed regulations allowing standard per-day meal allowances of $14 for travel requiring a stay of less than thirty days in one general location and $9 for a stay of 30 days or more based on "secondary evidence, including oral testimony."

Furthermore, an employee who receives reimbursement from his employer for travel expenses is excused from the normal record keeping and substantiation requirements if the standard reimbursement and allowance rules are satisfied. Under these rules, reimbursement for actual subsistence or travel away from home (exclusive of transportation to and from the destination) is limited to the greater of $44 per day or the maximum per diem rate for US Government employees in the locality in which travel is performed. If you elect to use the optional allowance, it must be used in computing the deduction for *all* meal expenses for the year (Revenue Procedure 83-71, 1983-39 IRB 19).

The Tax Reform Act of 1986 further limited deductions for luxury water travel. (Luxury water travel consists of travel by ocean liner, cruise ship, or other form of luxury water transportation. This rule applies, for example, in the case of a taxpayer who has business reasons for traveling from New York City to London and who travels by ocean liner.) The deduction allowable in the case of luxury water travel cannot exceed twice the highest amount generally allowable with respect to a day of travel to employees of the executive branch of the federal government while away from home but serving in the United States, multiplied by the number of days the taxpayer was engaged in luxury water travel. For example, if during a particular taxable year the applicable federal per diem amount is $75, a taxpayer's deduction for a 6-day trip cannot exceed $900 ($150 per day times 6 days). The applicable per diem amount generally is the highest travel amount applying for an area in the conterminous United States.

Moreover, under the Reform Act, no deduction is allowed for travel as a form of education. This rule applies when a travel deduction would be allowable only on the ground that the travel itself serves an educational purpose. (For example, in the case of a teacher of French who travels to France in order to maintain general familiarity with the French language and culture.) This disallowance does not apply, however, when a deduction is claimed with respect to travel that is a necessary adjunct to engaging in an activity that gives rise to a business deduction relating to education. (For example, when a scholar of French literature travels to Paris to do specific library research that cannot be done elsewhere or to take courses that are offered only at the Sorbonne, in circumstances such that the nontravel research or course costs are deductible.)

The Tax Reform Act of 1986 also amended the rules on charitable travel. Under the Reform Act, as of January 1, 1987, no deduction will be allowed for transportation and other travel expenses incurred in performing services away from home for a charitable organization (whether paid directly by the individual or indirectly through a contribution to the organization) unless there is no significant element of personal pleasure, recreation, or vacation in the travel away from home.

Moreover, the Tax Reform Act of 1986 also provided that travel and other costs of attending a convention or seminar for investment purposes (i.e., not for trade or business purposes) are not deductible.

All of the foregoing provisions of the Tax Reform Act of 1986 are applicable for tax years beginning after December 31, 1986.

# 52

## Transportation Expenses

Transportation expenses, which must be differentiated from *travel* expenses, sometimes can be deducted. Transportation expenses include the cost of traveling by air, rail, bus, taxi, etc., and the cost of operating and maintaining your car, but *not* the cost of meals and lodging.

Commuting expenses, those expenses incurred between your principal or regular place of work and your home, are not part of deductible transportation expenses. This is true regardless of the distance between your home and your regular place of work or of whether you are employed at different locations on different days within the same city or general area. If you work at two places in a day, however, whether or not for the same employer, you may deduct the expense of getting from one to the other. These expenses are part of your allowable transportation deduction. Furthermore, if you have a temporary or minor assignment beyond the general area of your tax home and return home each evening, you can deduct the expenses of the daily round trip transportation.

If you use your car in your work, and you use it exclusively for that purpose, you may deduct the entire cost of its operation. Included among the deductible items are the cost of gas, oil, repairs, insurance, depreciation, interest to buy the car, taxes, licenses, garage rents, parking fees, tolls, etc.

If you use your car for both personal and business purposes, you must divide your expenses between business and personal use. For example, if you drive your car 20,000 miles during the year, 8,000 for business and 12,000 for personal use, only 40 percent (8,000 ÷ 20,000) of the cost of operating your car may be claimed as a work expense.

Furthermore, if you lease a car that you use in your business, you may deduct any lease payments that are for your business. You may not deduct any part of the lease payments for commuting or other personal use of the car, and any advance payments must be apportioned over the entire lease period. In addition, you may not deduct any payments you make toward the purchase of a car even if the payments are lease payments. They must be capitalized and recovered through a deduction for depreciation.

Instead of deducting your actual itemized automobile transportation costs, you may deduct a standard mileage rate. You must:

a)  own the car;

b)  not use the car for hire, for example, as a taxi;

c)  not operate a fleet of cars, using two or more at the same time;

d)  not have claimed depreciation using any method other than the straight-line method (equal depreciation over the life of the asset); *and*

e)  not have claimed additional first-year depreciation on the car.

The 1988 standard mileage rate is 22.5¢ a mile for the first 15,000 miles of business use each year and 11¢ a mile for each additional mile in the same year. In addition to the standard mileage rate, you can also deduct any tolls or parking fees paid. Of this 22.5¢ per mile, 10¢ a mile constitutes an allowance for depreciation, reducing your basis in the car (Revenue Procedure 87–49).

After a car has been fully depreciated, you can take only 11¢ a mile for all business travel. Under a recent Revenue Procedure, the Internal Revenue Service will consider a car fully depreciated after 60,000 miles of business use at the maximum standard mileage rate. This rule is effective for all expenses paid or incurred after December 31, 1979.[7] This rule has been modified, however, by Revenue Procedure 82-61, which states that for the purpose of expensing depreciation, a car will be considered as having been driven for a maximum of 15,000 business miles a year even if the actual mileage is higher. Thus, if a car is driven 20,000 miles per year for each of three years, the 22.5¢-per-mile rate can be used instead of the 11¢-per-mile rate for only the first 15,000 miles of the fourth year.

---

7.  Revenue Procedure 81-54, I.R.B. 1981-44.

In *Wicker* (TCM 1986-1), a nurse-anesthetist maintained an automobile for travel between her office in the cellar of her home and the hospital where she performed anesthesia services. Although she served as head of the Department of Anesthesiology, no office space was provided to her at the hospital. She practiced exclusively at the hospital. The court found that her home office was her principal place of business and that her travel between her home office and the hospital was, therefore, business travel, rather than commuting. The expenses incurred in such travel were deductible.

If you are reimbursed or receive an allowance for your car expenses, you may use the standard mileage rate to determine the cost of operating your car. However, only the cost so figured that is more than your reimbursement or allowance may be deducted.

If you and your spouse have separate cars, *each* one of you can compute the deduction by claiming 22.5¢ per mile for the first 15,000 miles and 11¢ per mile for the excess (Revenue Proclamation 80-32, 1980-2 C.B. 767).

Usually, you will be better off claiming actual costs rather than the mileage allowance. For example, according to the Federal Highway Administration, the cost per mile of operating 1984 cars of various sizes was as follows:

| | |
|---|---|
| Van | 38.3¢ |
| Large car | 29.7¢ |
| Intermediate | 26.9¢ |
| Compact | 22.4¢ |
| Subcompact | 21.8¢ |

These figures do not include parking and tolls, which are deductible separately even if the alternative mileage rate is used.

Moreover, the Internal Revenue Service has stated that depreciation will be considered to have been allowed for standard mileage property "at the rate of $.07 per mile for 1980 and 1981, $.075 per mile in 1982, and $.08 per mile in 1983, 1984, and 1985, $.09 for 1986, and $.10 for 1987" (Rev. Proc. 87-49) for the first 60,000 business miles at the maximum standard mileage rate. This per mile rate, according to the IRS, will be the "depreciation" used to adjust the basis of standard mileage property (see Revenue Ruling Procedure 85-49 and 87-49).

Most important, a car you acquire will qualify for the depreciation expense if it is used in your work or business. The deduction for transportation expenses may in effect reduce your net cash outlay for a new car to less than half its cost!

For example, assume you are in the 33 percent bracket and you bought a $6,000 car that you use 100 percent for business. You elect to expense the first $1,700 of the car's cost, reducing the basis for depreciation. You elect a five-year class recovery life for the car. If you run the car 30,000 miles in its first year, your net cost for the acquisition of the car can be reduced to less than half its cost as follows:

| | |
|---|---:|
| Cost of car | $6,000 |
| Minus: election to expense<br>$1,700 × .33 | − 561 |
| Minus depreciation<br>([$6,000 − $1,700] × .20) × .33 | 284 |
| Net cost of car | $5,155 |
| Minus expenses: | |
| 30,000 miles @ 10 mpg =<br>3,000 gallons @ $1.25/gal | $3,750 |
| repairs, oil, and upkeep | 900 |
| insurance | 1,210 |
| garage rent, license, &<br>registration | 750 |
| tolls, parking, interest on<br>auto loan, etc. ($6/day) | 2,190 |
| Total expense | $8,800 |
| Tax saving ($8,800 × .33) | −2,904 |
| Final Net Cost | $2,251 |

If you drive the car more than 30,000 miles you actually can *make* money on the car purchase!

Let's assume that you are in the 33 percent bracket. This means that if you are single all you need to earn in 1988 to be in this bracket is more than $43,150 in taxable income per year. Let's see what would happen if you run the car 60,000 miles over the first three years. Employing the appropriate tax-saving strategy above, not only would your net cost be zero, but you would have saved an *additional* $3,046 in taxes!

| | |
|---|---:|
| Cost of car | $6,000 |
| Minus: election to expense ($1,700 × .33)<br>and depreciation ($4,300 × .712 × .33) | −1,571 |
| Net cost of car (end of third year) | 4,429 |
| Minus expenses: | |
| 60,000 miles @ 10 mpg =<br>6,000 gallons @ $1.25/gal | $7,500 |

| | |
|---|---:|
| repairs, oil, and upkeep | 2,700 |
| insurance | 3,630 |
| garage rent, licenses, and registrations | 2,250 |
| tolls, parking, interest on auto loan, etc. ($6/day) | +6,570 |
| Total expenses | $22,650 |
| Tax savings ($22,650 × .33) | −7,475 |
| Final net cost | -0- |
| Incremental Tax Savings | $3,046 |

# 53

## Meals and Entertainment Expenses

Not only can you deduct the above travel and transportation expenses, but you can also take as additional miscellaneous deductions certain entertainment expenses. Entertainment expenses may be deducted if you can show that the entertainment of prospects has a direct effect on and can reasonably be expected to increase or maintain earnings or your commissions.

These entertainment expenses must be ordinary and necessary (reasonable and customary) and must be incurred in the course of your work. You may deduct entertainment expenses only if you can show that your employer required or expected you to have such entertainment expenses in connection with your work.

You must prove *all* the following elements for entertainment deductions:

- The amount of each separate expenditure for entertaining, except for incidental items such as taxi fares and telephone calls that may be totaled on a daily basis.

- The date the entertainment took place.

- The name, address or location, and type of entertainment, such as dinner or theatre, if the information is not apparent in the name or designation of the place.

- The reason for the entertainment or the business benefit derived or expected to be gained from entertaining and, except for certain business meals, any business discussion or activity that took place.

- The occupation or other information about the person or persons entertained, including the name, title, or other designation sufficient to establish the business relationship to you.

Under the Tax Reform Act of 1986, effective January 1, 1987, entertainment expenses are allowed only to the amount of 80 percent of what is spent. Exceptions allowing full deductibility include (a) expenses reimbursed by an employer (in which case the employer is subject to the 80 percent rule); (b) traditional employer-paid recreational expenses for employees (e.g., holiday parties); (c) items given as compensation to the recipient that are excludable from income as de minimis fringe benefits; (d) items made available to the general public (e.g., as promotional activities); and (e) tickets to certain charitable fund-raising sports events. Ticket costs in excess of face value are not deductible, except with regard to tickets for charitable fund-raising sports events. Moreover, deductions for the rental or other use of a sky box at a sports arena are disallowed, to the extent in excess of the cost of regular tickets, if the box is used by the taxpayer for more than one event. This sky box disallowal of deductibility is subject to a 3-year phaseout starting January 1, 1986.

In addition, the Tax Reform Act of 1986 also reduced to 80 percent the amount of deductions otherwise allowable for business meal expenses, including meals away from home and meals furnished on an employer's premises to its employees. Exceptions allowing full deductibility include (a) employee meal expenses reimbursed by the employer (in which case the employer is subject to the 80 percent rule); (b) employer-furnished meals that are excludable from the employee's income as de minimis fringes (including subsidized eating facilities); (c) meals taxed to employees as compensation; and (d) items sold to the public (such as the cost of food to restaurants) or furnished the public as samples or for promotion. Moreover, the meals, to be deductible at all, must be directly related to or associated with a business discussion—i.e., "quiet" business meals are no longer deductible.

# 54

## Gifts

You may deduct ordinary and necessary (reasonable and customary) expenses for business gifts made directly or indirectly to any individual. The total value of business gifts to any one individual during the tax year cannot be more than $25. If a gift is not intended for the eventual personal use or benefit of a particular individual or a limited class of individuals, the gift is not considered to be made to an individual.

A gift to the spouse or child of an individual with whom you are doing business is a gift to that individual. However, if one spouse has an independent bona fide business connection with you, such a gift generally will not be considered a gift to the other spouse unless it is intended for that spouse's eventual use or benefit.

An item costing $4 or less on which your name is clearly and permanently imprinted and which is one of a number of identical items distributed by you is not subject to the $25 rule. This includes such items as pens, desk sets, plastic bags, and cases. In addition, incidental costs, such as jewelry engraving or packaging, insuring, and mailing or other delivery costs, are not generally included in determining the cost of a gift for the $25 rule.

A related cost will be considered incidental only if it does not add substantial value to the gift. For example, although the cost of gift wrapping will be considered an incidental cost, the purchase of an ornamental basket for packaging fruit will not be considered an incidental cost of packaging if the basket has a value that is substantial in relation to the value of the fruit.

Furthermore, it must be remembered that we are dealing here with gift, entertainment, travel, and transportation expenses of *employees*. Any of these expenses incurred by employers may be deductible for adjusted gross income as trade or business deductions.

You must prove *all* the following to be allowed a deduction for business gifts:

- The cost.

- The date of the gift.

- A description of the gift.

- The reason for giving the gift or any business benefit derived or expected to be gained from giving it.

- The name, title, occupation, or other information about the person receiving the gift, or some other designation sufficient to establish the business relationship to you.

KEEP PROOF OF EXPENSES

Substantiation of travel, meals, entertainment, and business gift expenses should be kept in an account book, diary, statement of expense, or similar record, supported by adequate documentary evidence that together can support each element of an expenditure. For example, entries on a desk calendar, not supported by evidence, are not proper proof. The simple rule here, therefore, is to keep receipts and records. For example, if you take a business associate out to dinner, simply jot the associate's name and the general topic of discussion on the back of the receipt given to you by the restaurant.

In the area of such deductions there is no such thing as too much documentation. If these deductions are questioned by the Internal Revenue Service, the only thing an audit agent will look for are receipts. Therefore, *always* remember to get a receipt, note the cost of the expenditure, the person to whom it relates, and your business relationship. A total of 30 seconds of effort may guarantee you $100 of unquestioned deductions. If your 1988 taxable income is more than $43,150, that 30 seconds of effort would have saved you $33 in taxes—that's the equivalent of $3,960 an hour—even more than most tax attorneys make!

# 55 Reimbursable Employee Business Expenses

Normally, when reimbursement is available to an employee for a business expense he has incurred, if the employee does not obtain that reimbursement, no deduction is allowed [*Podems,* 24 T.C. 21 (1955)]. However, in *Kessler* (TCM 1985-254), the court ruled that if a taxpayer can establish that reimbursement, though nominally available, is unavailable as a practical matter, then out-of-pocket business expenses should be allowable as a deduction. (See also *Jetty,* TCM 1982-378.) The Tax Court's new position was recently reinforced and supported by the Internal Revenue Service in Action On Decision 1986-011, on January 8, 1986, wherein a recommendation was made that the IRS acquiesce in *Kessler.*

# 56 Educational Expenses

Educational expenses incurred to maintain or improve your skills in your current position are deductible as a miscellaneous itemized expense. In a recent private letter ruling (PLR 8706048), the IRS held that a financial consultant may deduct the cost of obtaining a Master of Science degree in financial planning. The taxpayer was a financial consultant and the degree was sought in order to maintain and improve the taxpayer's financial planning skills. If the eduction will qualify you for a new trade or business or is a minimum requirement for your current job, that education expense is not deductible. In the private letter ruling the Internal Revenue Service held that a master's degree in financial planning was not a minimum requirement for the taxpayer's job as a financial consultant and did not qualify the taxpayer for a new trade or business. Therefore, the taxpayer's expenses for tuition and books incurred in obtaining the degree in financial planning were deductible as ordinary and necessary expenses.

As a general rule, however, if you earn a degree that makes you eligible for a new trade or business, there is no deduction for tuition. The real key is your intent at the time you take the course. For example, in one case, after 23 years in the accounting field, a CPA attended law school at night. He took all the tax courses he could at law school, intending to improve himself as an accountant. He did not intend to go into the practice of law and in fact did not. His purpose was not to obtain a new position or advancement in position. His only intent was to improve his skills as an accountant. The expense of going to law school in this case was deductible (*Berry,* T.C. Memo 1971-110).

# C  Schedules of Deductions

# 57  Medical Deductions

Abortion
Acupuncture
Advances for lifetime care
Ambulance hire
Apartment rent
Artificial teeth or limbs
Autoette wheelchair
Automobile expenses

Birth control pills
Braille books and magazines
Capital expenditures in excess of
    property's increased value
Central air conditioning
Clarinet lessons
Commutation costs
Computer medical data bank

Contact lens insurance
Cosmetic surgery
Crutches
Dental care
Diagnostic services
Drug or alcohol therapy centers
Education aids
Elastic stockings
Employee medical plans
Eyeglasses
Guide dogs
Guide for blind individual
Handrails
Hearing aids and component parts
Hospital care
Invalid spouse
Iron lung
Kidney transplants
Laetrile
Last illness expenses
Lip reading
Massages
Mattresses and boards
Meals and lodging if part of hospital or treatment charge
Meat diet
Medical insurance premiums
Medical transportation
Medical travel
Medicare B
Medicinal liquors, if prescribed
Medicines and drugs
Nonlocal medical transportation costs
Nurse's transportation expenses
Nursing homes and homes for the aged
Nursing services
Operations affecting childbearing

Operations and treatments in general
Organic foods
Outdoor elevator
Oxygen and oxygen equipment
Paint removal
Patterning exercises
Physician's fees
Prepaid medical insurance
Prosthetic devices
Psychiatric or psychoanalytic care
Reclining chair
Remedial reading
Retirement homes
Salt-free diet
School for the physically or mentally handicapped
Sexual therapy
Smoke-ending program, if to cure specific disease
Special foods or beverages
Special home for mentally retarded
Special plumbing fixtures
Specially designed automobiles
Swimming pool
Telephone equipment
Throat treatment
Transporting patient's relative
Tutoring fees
Unlicensed practitioners
University medical plan, if charges separately stated
Vasectomy
Vitamins, if prescribed
Voluntary payments for Medicare A
Water fluoridation device
Wheelchair
X-ray treatment

# 58 Deductible Taxes

Taxes imposed by state, city, and possessions of the United States

Auto registration (to the extent that it is based on value)
Income (except where claimed as credit)
Personal property
Real property

Foreign taxes
Income, war profit, excess profit (unless claimed as credit)
Real estate

If paid or accrued in connection with business or for the production of income, you can also deduct these taxes:

Federal taxes

Excise
Import duties
Liquor

Railroad Retirement (employers)
Social security (employers)
Stamp
Tobacco
Unemployment (employers)

State and local taxes

Admission
Auto registration
Beverages
Cigarettes
Cosmetics
Driver's license fees
Excise
Liquors
Mortgage
Occupancy
Stock transfer
Tobacco
Transfer (except estate, inheritance, legacy, succession, and gift taxes)
Unemployment

# 59 Charitable Deductions

Aid to evacuees
Artwork contributed by owner
Automobile expenses
Bargain sales to charity
Benefit performances
Book samples
Charitable travel
Church bonds, if donated after purchase

Church building funds
Church dues
Church repairs
Civil Defense volunteer's out-of-pocket expenses
Community chests
Credit card contributions
Delegate's expenses
Domestic fraternal societies

Essays
Excess rent
Eyeglass donations
Films and tape recordings
Foster parent's expenses
Future interest in tangible personal
  property
Government contributions
Home for elderly
Hospital fees
Installment notes
Insurance policies
Inventory donated
Legal expenses donated
Maintaining student in home
Medical equipment
Membership in art or fine arts
  association

Music manuscripts
Ordinary income property
Out-of-pocket charitable expenses
Partial interest in property
Patents donated
Pension plan trust contributions
Promissory notes
Property donated
Rent in excess of fair rental value
Scenic easement
Tickets donated for resale
Uniforms
Unmarried pregnant women
  programs
Volunteer fire companies
Volunteer income tax assistance
War veterans' organizations

# 60 Casualty and Theft Loss Deductions

Accidents
Airplane, train, and other
  transport crashes
Appraisal fees
Automobile damage
Bomb damage
Casualty and theft losses of
  investment property
Cleanup and repair costs
Confiscation by foreign
  government
Disaster area losses
Driveway breakup
Earthquake or earth slide
Explosion
False representation or pretenses
Fire
Flood

Freeze
Hurricane
Insect and disease damage to trees
  and shrubs, if sudden
Lightning
Loss of property used partly for
  rental and partly for personal
  purposes
Mine cave-ins
Razing
Shipwrecks
Smog
Snow
Sonic boom
Storms
Swindles
Theft of business property
Theft of personal property

Thin ice
Tornado
Vandalism

Water damage (as from burst
water heater)

# 61 Miscellaneous Deductions

Attorney fees paid by spouse to
secure taxable alimony
Bad debts
Bar examination fee (amortizable)
Bond premium amortization
Gambling losses (to extent of
gambling gains)
Job-hunting expenses
Labor union dues and assessments
for noninsurance purposes
Loss on sublease of residential

apartment
Physician's hospital privilege fee
(amortizable)
Rent while attempting to sublease
residential house or apartment
Tax counseling costs
Tax litigation expenses
Tax return preparation
Uncollectible debts
Uncollectible loans

# 62 Employee Miscellaneous Deductions

Automobile expenses (allocatable
to business)
  Depreciation
  Garage rent
  Gasoline and oil
  Insurance
  Parking fees
  Repairs for business cars
  State inspection and
    registration fees
  Taxes
  Tolls
  Washing
Briefcase
Christmas gifts to customers
(limited)
Convention expenses
Dues
  Business association

Labor unions
Professional societies
Social or athletic clubs used
  primarily for business
  purposes
Educational expenses (limited)
Employment agency fees
Entertainment expenses
Fidelity bond costs
Gifts to customers and prospects
(limited)
Insurance premiums
  Automobile (to extent of
    business use)
  Bonds (fidelity, etc.)
  Malpractice
Job-hunting expenses
Labor unions, initiation fees, dues,
fines, assessments for pension

funds
Laundry and cleaning while
 traveling away from home
Meals or lodging while traveling
 away from home
Membership in social and athletic
 clubs if primarily for business
 purposes
Moving expenses (limited)
Office furnishings[8]
Outside sales business expenses
Passport fees for business travel
Reimbursed expenses (if
 reimbursement included in
 income)
Safety equipment
Subscriptions to professional
 journals and magazines
Tax return preparation
Technical periodicals
Telephone

Tips
Tools
Transportation expenses
Traveling expenses
 Baggage charges
 Fares
 Laundry and cleaning while
  away from home
 Meals and lodging while away
  from home
 Passport fees, if for business
 Sample rooms
 Taxis
 Telephone and telegraph
  messages
 Tips
Tuition fees
Uniforms not adaptable to general
 wear
Work clothes

# 63 Investor Deductions

Investors can deduct expenses incurred to produce or collect income and to conserve, manage, or maintain income-producing property. Anyone who owns securities, rents real estate, or owns other investments should not overlook the typical deductions listed below.

Accounting fees
Advertising expenses
Alterations and repairs
Attorneys' fees
Auditing expenses
Bad debts
Bookkeeping expenses

Collection of rent costs
Custodian fees
Damages paid for breach of
 contract or lease
Depreciation
 Buildings
 Furniture and fixtures

---

8.  For example, office furnishings bought by an executive with his own funds to maintain his image as a
    successful district sales manager (*Leroy Gillis,* T.C. Memo 1973–96).

Exchange of asset losses

Expenses of successfully resisting
  condemnation of property

Fire insurance premiums

Franchise taxes

Heat and light

Interest

Investment counseling costs

Leasehold improvements

Leases

  Amortization of improvements
    by lessee

  Amortization of lease
    acquisition costs

  Rentals paid

  Repairs made by lessee

  Taxes paid by lessee

Legal expenses

License taxes and fees (limited)

Losses (to extent not covered by
  insurance)

  Abandonment of worthless
    interest in real estate

  Bad debts

  Demolition of building

  Forced sales

  Foreclosure

  Forfeitures

  Property sales

  Property seized by
    government

Maintenance of property costs

Management expenses

Mortgage foreclosure losses

Moving expenses of machinery and
  equipment

Night protection services

Office rent

Porter and janitor services

Recordkeeping costs

Redecoration costs

Refuse and waste removal expenses

Repairs

Safe-deposit boxes

Salaries

Sales of assets losses

Stationery and supplies

Tax counseling costs

Tax return preparation

Taxes (state)

  General sales (add to basis)

  Gross income

  Income

  License fees (limited)

  Motor fuel

  Personal property

  Real estate

  Stamp

  Stock transfer (adjust basis)

  Transfer of property (except
    estate, inheritance, legacy,
    gift, etc.) (adjust basis)

Traveling expenses

Worthless bonds and stock

# CHAPTER 7

# Traditional Tax Shelters

*"As a citizen, you have an obligation to the country's tax system, but you also have an obligation to yourself to know your rights under the law and possible tax deductions. And to claim every one of them."*

DONALD ALEXANDER,
former commissioner of the Internal
Revenue Service under three presidents

*"The tax laws reflect a continuing struggle among contending interests for the privilege of paying the least."*

LOUIS EISENSTEIN,
*The Ideologies of Taxation*

The art of sophisticated tax planning requires you to understand the elements of tax-sheltered investments. These investments allow you to offset certain "artificial losses"—noneconomic losses, but losses that are available as deductions under the present tax laws, and not only against the income from those investments but also against your other income from your regular business or professional activity.

Often, tax shelters have been described by the unsophisticated as gimmicks or "loopholes." Nothing could be farther from the truth. These laws were adopted by Congress after careful deliberation, with the purpose of serving some major economic or social goal. Therefore, when you utilize these techniques you are not only improving your financial position, but you are also furthering a legitimate national economic goal. For example, the allowance of percentage depletion for oil and other tax provisions for mineral development have been effective incentives to investments in petroleum exploration and discovery. These attractive tax benefits have encouraged other taxpayers to provide the risk capital needed to bring into production many useful sources of oil that would otherwise go untapped. Special tax benefits for equipment leasing and life insurance also serve national economic and social goals.

The Internal Revenue Service, in a manner of speaking, sometimes finds itself involved in a shelter. For example, all of the staff at the regional IRS headquarters in New York are in a shelter. It seems the office building housing the Internal Revenue Service in New York has been sold to a syndicator.

Sales of publicly offered partnerships registered with the Securities and Exchange Commission and private limited partnerships exceeded $17.7 billion in 1984. Among those who have invested in tax shelters are former Attorney General William French Smith and former Internal Revenue Service Commissioner Rosco Egger, Jr. Clearly, tax shelters are investments that you should consider if appropriate.

### THE TAX REFORM ACT OF 1986

The Tax Reform Act of 1986 significantly affected the attractiveness of traditional tax shelters. As of January 1, 1987, the long-term capital gains deduction is repealed. Moreover, the 1986 Reform Act effectively limits losses from passive trade or business activities (limited partnership tax shelters, etc.), generally to offset passive income. What this means is that, effectively, tax shelter losses can be used only to offset tax shelter gains. Passive income does not include portfolio income—e.g., dividends on stocks and interest on bonds—nor gain from the sale of stocks and bonds. Although these limitations are going to be phased in over a 5-year period, they must be considered in any evaluation of a tax shelter offering. The following discussion explains the Tax Reform Act and details the remaining potential alternative tax shelter vehicles.

The new passive loss rules are sweeping provisions that in general deny any individual, estate, trust, closely held C corporation, or personal service corporation the use of losses or credits generated in "passive activities" to offset other income such as salary, interest, dividends, and active business income. Deductions from passive activities may offset income from passive activities. Credits from passive activities generally are limited to the tax attributable to income from passive activities.

Disallowed losses and credits are carried forward and treated as deductions and credits from passive activities in the next taxable year. Suspended losses from an activity are allowed in full when the taxpayer disposes of his entire interest in the activity in a fully taxable transaction. Suspended credits may not be claimed in full in the year in which the taxpayer disposes of the interest in the passive activity. Rather, they are carried forward until used to offset tax liability from passive income. However, upon a fully taxable disposition of a passive activity, taxpayers may elect to increase the basis of property immediately before the transfer by an amount equal to the portion of any suspended credit that reduced the basis of the property for the taxable year in which the credit arose.

If a closely held C corporation (other than a personal service or S corporation), has "net active income" for any taxable year, the passive activity loss for the taxable year will be allowable as a deduction against net active income. A similar rule applies in the case of any passive activity credit of the taxpayer. The term *net active income* means the taxable income of the taxpayer for the taxable year determined without regard for any income or loss from a passive activity and any *net portfolio income*.

## PASSIVE ACTIVITY DEFINED

In general, the term *passive activity* means any activity that involves the conduct of any trade or business and in which the taxpayer does not *materially participate*.

It also includes any rental activity of either real or tangible personal property regardless of whether the individual materially participates. With respect to equipment leasing, short-term rental to various users (where the lessor provides substantial services) is an active business rather than a passive activity.

In general, working interests in any oil or gas property that the taxpayer holds directly or through an entity that does not limit the taxpayer's liability with respect to such interests will be treated as an active trade or business and will not be subject to the passive loss rules.

## MATERIAL PARTICIPATION DEFINED

In general, a taxpayer will be treated as materially participating in an activity only if the taxpayer is involved in the operations of the activity on a regular, continuous, and substantial basis.

All limited partnership interests are treated as not materially participating.

Management decision making by an individual may constitute material participation if such services are substantial and bona fide. For example, when management services are rendered on a full-time basis, and the success of the activity depends on the exercise of an individual's business judgment, such services constitute material participation. The test applies regardless of whether an individual owns an interest in the activity directly or through a pass-through entity such as a general partnership or an S corporation.

Taxpayers who own working interests in oil and gas properties through a limited partnership will be subject to the passive loss rules with respect to that interest. That is notwithstanding the special exclusion for working interests in oil and gas properties.

In 1988, the IRS attempted to clarify the definition of "material participation" and provided special standards for limited partners. A taxpayer who is not a limited partner is a material participant in an activity during the tax year if one of the following tests is met:

1. The taxpayer participates for more than 500 hours.

2. The taxpayer's participation represents substantially all participation in the activity by individuals (including nonowners).

3. The taxpayer participates for more than 100 hours, and no other individual's participation in the activity exceeds that of the taxpayer.

4. The activity is a significant participation activity for the tax year, and the taxpayer's total participation in all significant participation activities for the year exceeds 500 hours.

5. The taxpayer has materially participated in the activity for five of the ten preceding years.

6. The activity is a personal service activity in which the taxpayer has materially participated for any three preceding years.

7. In light of the facts and circumstances, the taxpayer participates in the activity on a regular, continuous, and substantial basis. To satisfy this facts-and-circumstances test, the taxpayer must have at least 100 hours of participation.

Limited partners materially participate in an activity only if they meet one of tests 1, 5, or 6, above.

A significant participation activity is a new concept created by the Internal Revenue Service's temporary regulations. It is any trade or business activity in which the taxpayer has more than 100 hours of participation during the tax year but fails to satisfy all the material participation tests (other than test 4, above, relating to significant participation activities).

This concept is important for taxpayers involved in several trades or businesses, because it allows them to satisfy the material participation test by aggregating hours of participation in different businesses. However, if the taxpayer enjoys *net income* from significant participation activities during the year, that income is considered *nonpassive* and cannot be used to offset losses from other passive activities. If the significant participation activities produce a net loss, the loss is considered *passive* and must be suspended unless there is sufficient income from other passive activities to offset the loss.

## NET PORTFOLIO INCOME

In general, net portfolio income will not be included when determining the income or loss from any passive activity. Net portfolio income means gross income from interest, dividends, annuities, or royalties not derived in the ordinary course of a trade or business less expenses (other than interest) that are clearly and directly allocable to such gross income, less interest expense properly allocable to such gross income, plus gain or less loss attributable to the disposition of property held for investment or producing income such as interest, dividends, or royalties.

Any income, gain, or loss that is attributable to an investment of working capital will not be treated as income or loss from a passive activity.

This provision prevents taxpayers from placing property that would otherwise be producing active portfolio income into an entity that is subject to the passive loss rules, thereby using losses from passive activities to offset active portfolio income.

Income earned for personal services will not be taken into account in computing the income or loss from a passive activity for any taxable year. For example, if a limited partner is paid for performing services for the partnership (whether by way of salary, guaranteed payment, or allocation of partnership income), these payments cannot be sheltered by passive losses from the partnership or from any other passive activity.

## TREATMENT OF FORMER PASSIVE ACTIVITIES

If an activity is a former passive activity for any taxable year and has suspended losses or credits from prior years when the activity was passive, the suspended losses may be offset against the income from the activity for the taxable year. Suspended credits allocable to such activity may be offset against the regular tax liability allocable to that activity for the taxable year. Any remaining suspended losses or credits continue to be treated as arising from a passive activity.

It appears that suspended losses and credits from a passive activity may be used to offset active income from the activity in the year in which the activity changes from passive to active and in later years. Any remaining suspended losses or credits will also be allowed as a deduction to income or credit against tax attributable to other passive activities.

If a taxpayer ceases for any taxable year to be a closely held C corporation or personal service corporation, suspended losses and credits will continue to be treated in the same manner as if the taxpayer continued to be a closely held C corporation or personal service corporation, whichever is applicable.

## DISPOSITIONS OF ENTIRE INTERESTS IN PASSIVE ACTIVITY

If during the taxable year a taxpayer disposes of his entire interest in any passive activity (or former passive activity) and all gain or loss realized on such disposition is recognized, any suspended losses from the activity are no longer treated as passive activity losses and are allowable as a deduction against the taxpayer's income in the following order:

- income or gain from the passive activity for the taxable year (including any gain recognized on the disposition)

- net income or gain for the taxable year from all passive activities

- any other income or gain

However, if the person acquiring the interest is a related party to the taxpayer, then any suspended losses will not apply against the taxpayer's active income until the taxable year in which such interest is acquired by another person unrelated to the taxpayer. However, such suspended losses may be offset by income from other passive activities of the taxpayer.

To the extent that any loss recognized upon a disposition of an entire interest in a passive activity is a loss from the sale or exchange of a capital asset, the capital loss is limited to the amount of gains from the sale or exchange of capital assets plus $3,000 (in the case of individuals). The limitation on the deductibility of capital losses is applied before the determination of the amount of losses allowable upon the disposition under the passive loss rule.

For example, if a taxpayer has a capital loss of $10,000 upon the disposition of a passive activity that has $5,000 of suspended losses, the $5,000 of suspended losses are allowed, but the capital loss deduction is limited to $3,000 for the year (assuming the taxpayer has no other gains or losses from the sale of capital assets for the year). The remainder of the capital loss from the disposition is carried forward and allowed in accordance with the provisions determining the allowance of such capital losses.

### PARTIAL DISPOSITION OF AN INTEREST IN A PASSIVE ACTIVITY

The 1986 law makes no provision for the allowance of part or all of the suspended losses and credits attributable to a passive activity when an individual makes a partial or incomplete disposition of an interest in that passive activity. All losses and credits apparently remain suspended until offset by income from the individual's remaining interest in that passive activity or other passive activities, or until the individual completes the disposition of his entire interest in that passive activity.

### DISPOSITION AT DEATH

If an interest in an activity is transferred due to the taxpayer's death, suspended losses may be deducted against income to the extent such losses are greater than the excess (if any) of the basis of such property in the hands of the transferee, over the adjusted basis of such property immediately before the death of the taxpayer. Any unused suspended losses as a result of this limitation are not allowed as a deduction for any taxable year.

For example, assume Mother owns rental real estate with a market value of $70,000, an adjusted basis of $50,000, and $25,000 of suspended losses. Mother dies and leaves the property to Daughter. The basis is stepped up to $70,000 in the hands of Daughter. Only $5,000 of the suspended losses are deductible on the income tax return of the estate. The remaining $20,000 of suspended losses (equal to the step-up in basis) is lost forever.

### DISPOSITION BY INSTALLMENT SALE

If an individual disposes of an entire interest in an activity in an installment sale, suspended losses are allowed each year based on the ratio of gain recognized each year to the total gain on the sale.

### DISPOSITION BY GIFT

If an interest in a passive activity is disposed of by gift, the basis of the interest immediately before the transfer is increased by any suspended passive losses allocable to the interest. Suspended losses that are added to the basis because of the gift of an interest are not allowed as deductions for any taxable year.

Moreover, the specific language of the statute appears to imply that gain on the sale of an interest in a passive activity cannot be offset with passive losses and credits from other passive activities. Only suspended or current year losses and credits from the passive activity may be used to offset gains realized on the disposition of that activity.

For example, an individual has interests in two separate limited partnerships, A and B, which are separate passive activities. Assume the following facts apply in 1991:

|  | A | B |
| --- | --- | --- |
| Current year loss | ($30,000) | ($10,000) |
| Prior suspended losses | ($70,000) | ($25,000) |

Assume that the individual sells his interest in B for a gain of $40,000. The full amount of the losses from partnership B, $35,000, may offset this gain. However, it appears that none of the current or suspended losses from partnership A may offset the remaining $5,000 gain.

### SPECIAL RULE FOR RENTAL REAL ESTATE ACTIVITIES

In the case of rental real estate activities in which an individual *actively participates,* up to $25,000 of losses (and credits in a deduction-equivalent sense) from all such activities are allowed each year against nonpassive income of the taxpayer. The $25,000 amount that is allowed under this special provision is reduced by 50 percent of the amount by which the taxpayer's adjusted gross income for the taxable year exceeds $100,000. Any losses that this provision disallows in the year incurred and that carry over as suspended passive losses to later years may not be used under the $25,000 allowance in later years.

For example, an individual has $30,000 of net losses from rental real estate activities in which she actively participates. Her adjusted gross income, without regard to the net losses from the rental real estate activity, is $120,000. First, only $25,000 of her net losses are eligible for the special allowance. Second, the amount of the net loss she may deduct against active income (her adjusted gross income before deductions for net losses from rental activities) must be reduced by $.50 for each dollar of adjusted gross income over $100,000, or by $10,000. Therefore, she may deduct $15,000 of these net losses from her adjusted gross income when computing her taxable income. The remaining $15,000 of net losses are carried forward and may be used in future years only to offset passive income. The $15,000 of suspended losses may not be used in subsequent years under the $25,000 allowance.

The $25,000 allowance is applied by first netting income and loss from all of the taxpayer's rental real estate activities in which he actively participates. If there is net loss for the year from such activities, net passive income (if any) from other activities is then applied against it in determining the amount eligible for the $25,000 allowance.

For example, assume that a taxpayer has $45,000 of losses from a rental real estate activity in which he actively participates. If he also actively participates in another rental real estate activity from which he has $40,000 of passive income, resulting in a $5,000 net loss from rental real estate activities in which he actively participates, then only $5,000 is allowed under the $25,000 allowance for the year.

In the case of rehabilitation and low-income housing credits, the phase-out of the $25,000 allowance does not begin until the adjusted gross income of the taxpayer for the taxable year exceeds $200,000.

In the case of taxable years of an estate ending less than two years after the date of the decedent's death, the $25,000 allowance for rental real estate activities applies to all rental real estate activities with respect to which such decedent actively participated before his death.

Married individuals filing separate returns and living apart from their spouses at all times during the taxable year each qualify for half the $25,000 allowance. The phase-out begins for each at $50,000 rather than $100,000 for rental real estate activities other than low-income housing, and at $100,000 rather than $200,000 for low-income housing. If married taxpayers filing separate returns do not live apart from their spouses at *all* times during the taxable year, neither may use the $25,000 allowance for rental real estate activities.

### RENTAL ACTIVITY

A rental activity is any activity from which gross income is derived primarily from payments for the use of tangible property. In addition, an activity may qualify as a rental activity if the property is held out for rent, even though no rental income is received in a tax year.

There are six exceptions to the general rule. An activity involving the use of tangible property is not a rental activity in any tax year if *any one* of the following situations exists:

1. If the average rental period is seven days or less, the activity is not considered a rental activity. This exception would exclude many resort properties from the rental category. However, the activity may remain passive if the owner does not materially participate.

2. If the average rental period is 30 days or less and significant personal services are provided to the customers, the activity is not considered a rental activity.

3. The activity is not treated as a rental activity if extraordinary services are provided to the customers in connection with the use of the property. In order for the services to be "extraordinary," the use of the property by customers must be incidental to the receipt of such services. For example, providing a hospital room to patients would not be considered a rental activity, because the use of the room is incidental to the receipt of medical services.

4. The activity will not be treated as a rental activity if the rental is incidental to nonrental activity. For example:

   a) The property is held to realize gain for appreciation, and the gross rental income is less than 2 percent of the lesser of the unadjusted basis or fair market value of the property. This is the only situation in which rental property will be treated as property held for investment.

b) The property is generally used in a trade or business owned by the individual, and the gross rental income is insubstantial. This exception applies to property that was predominantly used in the trade or business either in the current year or in at least two of the five preceding tax years. The 2 percent test described above is used to test the substantiality of the rental income.

c) If the property is held for sale to customers in the ordinary course of business, the rental of the property will not be rental activity if the property is sold during the year.

d) Lodging rented to an employee for the convenience of the employee is not rental property.

5. If property is customarily made available for nonexclusive use by various customers during specific business hours, the activity is not a rental activity. For example, a golf course where customers either pay daily fees or purchase passes for a longer period is not considered a rental activity regardless of the average period of customer use.

6. If an owner of an interest in a partnership or S corporation provides property to be used in a nonrental activity of the entity, the partner or shareholder is not treated as being engaged in a rental activity if the property is provided in the owner's capacity as a partner or shareholder and no rent is charged.

### ACTIVE PARTICIPATION DEFINED

To qualify for the $25,000 allowance for rental real estate activities, an individual must actively participate in the rental activity. Individuals will not be treated as actively participating for any period if, at any time during such period, their ownership interest (including any interest of the individual's spouse) is less than 10 percent (by value) of all interests in such activity. The degree of participation that is required once this 10 percent or more ownership threshold is met is unclear. The Conference Report suggests that the degree of participation required to meet the active participation test is less than the material participation standard.

A limited partnership interest in rental real estate does not meet the active participation requirement (except as described below for rehabilitation and low-income housing credits).

What happens to the $25,000 deduction when you have several rental real estate properties? To the extent that the aggregate loss from several active participation rental real estate activities does not exceed $25,000, the entire loss is deductible. However, where the aggregate net loss exceeds $25,000, the loss must be allocated among activities on a pro rata basis with respect to the losses from each loss activity. For example, if a taxpayer who qualifies for the full $25,000 allowance has $10,000 of losses from one activity and $40,000 of losses from a second activity, then $5,000 is treated as allowed from the first activity and $20,000 is treated as allowed from the second activity.

This allocation is necessary in part because the suspended losses from a specific activity (those that are not deducted) are allowed in full when the taxpayer disposes of his or her interest in that activity.

Note that the IRS does not permit pro rata allocation between pre- and post-October 1986 investments. (See below for the phase-in of disallowance of losses and credits for interests held before October 23, 1986.) Where there were losses from both old (pre-October) activities and new (post-October) activities, the $25,000 allowance is applied to old activities first—that is, without proration. This generally results in a smaller amount of the loss being allowed.

For example, assume that you are an active participant in two rental real estate activities. In 1987, the loss from each was $50,000. One of the activities was acquired before October 23, 1986, and the other after. The following is a comparison of the Internal Revenue Service approach and the pro rata approach:

|  | IRS | | Pro Rata | |
| --- | --- | --- | --- | --- |
|  | *Pre-October 1986* | *Post-October 1986* | *Pre-October 1986* | *Post-October 1986* |
| Loss | $50,000 | $50,000 | $50,000 | $50,000 |
| Allowed under $25,000 rule | *$25,000* | *$0* | *$12,500* | *$12,500* |
| Balance subject to 65% phase-in rule | $25,000 | | $37,500 | |
| 65% phase-in | *$16,250* | | *$24,375* | |
| Total | $41,250 | | $49,375 | |

Note that the IRS method yielded an allowable loss for 1987 of $41,250 ($25,000 plus $16,250). The pro rata method would permit $49,375 of the loss to be deducted in 1987 ($12,500 plus $12,500 plus $24,375).

The following example shows you how losses are carried forward. Assume that you have invested in three separate passive activities. Activity A is an interest acquired in 1985; Activity B is an interest in a rental activity acquired in 1987; and Activity C is an interest in a rental realty acquired in 1987. Also assume that your gross income is under $100,000.

| *Activity A* | *Activity B* | *Activity C* |
|---|---|---|
| $10,000 | ($50,000) | ($100,000) |

1987 results:
Net passive activity loss ($140,000)
Net losses from B and C
  offset against A income:
  B = $10,000 × $50,000/$150,000 = ($3,333)
  C = $10,000 × $100,000/$150,000 = ($6,667)

Net loss from B offset
  against active and portfolio income: ($25,000)

Loss carryforward to 1988:
  B = $50,000 − $3,333 − $25,000 = ($21,667)
  C = $100,000 − $6,667 = ($93,333)
                                                                                  ($115,000)

Assume the following activity in 1988:

| *Activity A* | *Activity B* | *Activity C* |
|---|---|---|
| $110,000 | ($20,000) | ($40,000) |

1988 results:
Net passive activity loss:
  ($60,000 + $115,000 NOL carryover
  − $110,000 income) = ($65,000)
Net losses from B and C
  offset against A income:*
  B = $110,000 × $41,667/175,000 = $26,190
  C = $110,000 × $133,333**/175,000 = $83,810
                                                                         ($110,000)

Net loss from B offset
  against A income:
    ($21,670 + $20,000 − $26,190) =                              ($15,480)

Loss carryforward to 1989:

| *Activity A* | *Activity B* | *Activity C* |
| --- | --- | --- |
| -0- | -0- | ($49,520) |

*$21,667 + $20,000
**$93,333 + $40,000

## REHABILITATION AND LOW-INCOME HOUSING CREDITS

In the case of the rehabilitation and low-income housing credits (but not
losses), the $25,000 allowance applies on a credit-equivalent basis. This is so
regardless of whether the individual claiming the credit actively participates
in the rental real estate activity, including participation as a limited partner.
After December 31, 1989, investors in low-income housing projects must actively participate to claim the low-income housing credit against the $25,000
allowance. However, if the property is placed in service after December 31,
1989, but before January 1, 1991, an investor will still not have to meet the active participation standard with respect to the low-income housing credit if at
least 10 percent of the costs of such property are incurred before January
1, 1989.

The credit equivalent of the $25,000 allowance is $7,000 of passive
credits for an individual in the 28 percent tax bracket. However, where a taxpayer has more than $250,000 of adjusted gross income, the taxpayer will
generally receive no current benefit from the rehabilitation or low-income
housing credit.

## PHASE-IN OF DISALLOWANCE OF LOSSES AND CREDITS FOR INTERESTS HELD
## BEFORE OCTOBER 22, 1986

Interests in passive activities acquired by a taxpayer on or before October 22,
1986, are eligible for a phase-in under the passive loss rules. Interests in activities acquired after October 22, 1986, are not eligible for the phase-in but
instead are fully subject to the passive loss rules. However, a taxpayer who
had a binding contract to purchase an interest in a passive activity on October
22, 1986, would qualify under the phase-in rules.

Taxpayers who own interests in passive activities acquired both before and after October 22, 1986, will be permitted to apply the phase-in percentages (described below) only to the *lesser* of (1) their passive activity loss for the taxable year (including passive losses and passive income from *all* interests) or (2) the passive activity loss for the year attributable only to interests acquired before October 22, 1986.

Taxpayers who acquired interests after October 22, 1986, in passive activities that provide passive income for the year reduce the amount of passive losses that would otherwise be deductible under the phase-in rules for interests acquired before October 22, 1986. The passive losses from the pre-enactment interests must first be reduced by passive income from newly acquired interests before applying the phase-in percentages to determine the amount of losses that are deductible under the phase-in rule.

For example, in 1987 a taxpayer owns preenactment interests in passive activities that generate $25,000 of passive losses and acquires an interest in a passive activity that generates $10,000 of passive income. Only $15,000, the net passive loss from *all* passive activities, is eligible for deduction in 1987 (after applying the appropriate percentage as described below) and not the entire $25,000 of passive losses from preenactment interests only.

Passive activity losses or credits for any taxable year beginning in calendar years 1987 through 1990 that are attributable to interests in passive activities that qualify for the phase-in will be allowed as deductions against nonpassive income or credits against tax on nonpassive income to the extent of the percentages in the following table:

| Taxable years beginning in: | Applicable percentage is: |
| --- | --- |
| 1987 | 65% |
| 1988 | 40 |
| 1989 | 20 |
| 1990 | 10 |
| 1991 | 0 |

Any passive loss that is disallowed for a taxable year during the phase-in period and carried forward as a suspended loss is allowable in subsequent years only to the extent that there is net passive income in the subsequent years or when there is a taxable disposition of the activity.

For example, assume that a taxpayer has a passive loss of $100 in 1987 that qualifies for the phase-in, $65 of which is allowed under the applicable phase-in percentage for the year and $35 of which is carried forward. The $35 is not allowed in a subsequent year under the phase-in percentage applying for that year. If the taxpayer has a passive loss of $35 in 1988, including the amount carried over from 1987, then no relief under the phase-in is provided. If the taxpayer has a passive loss of $50 in 1988 (consisting of the $35 of suspended losses from 1987 and $15 from 1988, all of which is attributable to preenactment interests), then $6 of losses (40 percent of the $15 loss arising in 1988) is allowed against active income under the phase-in rule. The $35 loss carryover from 1987 is disallowed in 1988 and is carried forward (along with the disallowed $9 from 1988) and allowed in any subsequent year in which the taxpayer has net passive income or in which the taxpayer makes a fully taxable disposition of his entire interest in the passive activity.

The overall effect of the passive activity loss limitation is not to *disallow* the tax benefits of a loss but to *defer* the timing of those benefits until the taxpayer recognizes income from passive activities, or until the taxpayer disposes of the entire interest in a fully taxable transaction. Consequently, the current value of any investment in a passive loss activity, relative to the value of the same investment made under the prior law, is diminished by the time value of the deferred losses.

You will have to plan carefully when evaluating any new tax-sheltered investment opportunity. The economics of the investment will be critical, as it always should have been. "Investment" planning will now be composed of two separate packages of investments: portfolio investments and passive activities. Managing the passive activity package of investments will for the next few years be a highly complicated procedure. Investors must take into account the phase-in of the passive loss rules for their existing passive activities when determining which new passive activity investments would provide the most benefits in the passive activity portfolio.

Prospective investments in rental real estate should be evaluated primarily on their potential economic return, especially by taxpayers whose adjusted gross income exceeds $100,000 (the level at which the $25,000 allowance begins to phase out). However, rental property that qualifies for rehabilitation credits or low-income housing credits may still offer some tax benefits to taxpayers with adjusted gross incomes between $100,000 and $200,000. Income-producing limited partnerships, such as nonleveraged rental real estate, will become a popular vehicle to offset passive losses from other activities. Individuals with passive activity losses and no offsetting passive activity income may find it advantageous to convert income from an active business into passive activity income by reducing the level of involvement in the business. Conversely, individuals with passive activity losses and little or no passive activity income could attempt to convert the passive activity into an activity in which they materially participate. The potential for this would be greatest for passive S corporation shareholders who have invested in a business but who have only marginally participated in its operation.

An alternative avenue of attack would be to attempt to generate passive income from a Passive Income Generator (PIG). One suggestion for creating a controllable passive activity income with which to absorb passive losses is to lease real estate or equipment to a closely held corporation. That rental income will be passive and will offset passive tax-shelter losses. However, if you lease real estate or equipment to a partnership or an S corporation, such rental income, unless paid under a binding lease in effect before February 19, 1988, is recharacterized to active income, which is ineligible to offset tax-sheltered losses. The opportunity to create controllable passive activity income still exists, however, with a rental to a regular or C corporation.

Many taxpayers who actively participate in rental real estate activities may not realize that their effective marginal tax rate for income over $100,000 is considerably higher than 33 percent. The phase-out of the $25,000 allowance for income over $100,000 increases a taxpayer's effective marginal tax rate on income between $100,000 and $150,000 to 42.9 percent in 1988, 46.8 percent in 1989, 47.85 percent in 1990, and 49.5 percent in 1991 and later years.

The following example computes the effective marginal tax rate resulting from the passive loss limitation by comparing two situations that are identical except for an additional income of $20,000 in 1988.

*Example:* In 1988, Mr. and Mrs. Couple have adjusted gross income of $120,000, not counting $25,000 of losses from rental real estate activities in which Mrs. Couple actively participates. Under the passive loss limitation rules, $19,000 of the real estate losses can be used to offset their other income. (The $120,000 of income phases out $10,000 of the loss that would be allowed under the rental real estate allowance. However, the amount disallowed under the $25,000 allowance phase-out is then subject to the more general passive loss rule under which only 60 percent is disallowed in 1988. Therefore, they are allowed $15,000 of losses under the $25,000 allowance rule and $4,000 under the general passive loss rule.) Consequently, their adjusted gross income is $101,000. After itemized deductions and personal exemptions, their taxable income is $90,000. Their tax liability is $22,237.

Mr. and Mrs. Family have an identical income pattern except for the fact that they have an additional $20,000 of capital gains. Under the $25,000 allowance phase-out rule, only $5,000 of their real estate losses are deductible (the $140,000 of income causes $20,000 to be phased out). Of the remaining $20,000 of loss, the general passive loss rule permits $8,000 to be deducted ($20,000 reduced by 60 percent). This produces $127,000 of adjusted gross income. With the same itemized deductions and personal exemptions, their taxable income is $116,000, and their tax liability is $30,817.

*Summary:*    Mr. and Mrs. Family's tax        $30,817

Mr. and Mrs. Couple's Tax        $22,237
Tax on marginal income          $  8,580

Effective tax rate $= \dfrac{\$\ 8,580}{\$20,000} = 42.9\%$
on marginal income

# A  Deferral and Leverage

There normally are two elements that make up the typical tax shelter arrangement. One or both of these elements will be found in almost all tax shelters. The first is the *deferral concept,* in which deductions are accelerated in order to reduce the tax liability of an individual in the early years of the transaction instead of matching those deductions against the income that is eventually generated from the investment. This deferral of tax liability from the earlier years to the future years results, in effect, in an interest-free loan by the federal government, repayable when the investment either produces net taxable income, is sold, or is otherwise disposed of.

The other element of a typical tax shelter is *leverage,* in which borrowed funds are used in a taxpayer's investments to pay the expenses for which accelerated deductions are received. Your position is enhanced when the borrowing is on a nonrecourse basis, which means that you are not *personally* liable to repay loans and your personal investment risk is limited to your equity investment. Unfortunately, recent tax laws and Internal Revenue Service rulings have limited the availability of tax shelter investments with a nonrecourse loan basis.

Until the Tax Reform Act of 1986, a third tax shelter element for many investments was the *conversion* of ordinary income to capital gains at the time of the sale or other disposition of the investment. Conversion occured when the portion of the gain reflecting the accelerated deductions taken against ordinary income was taxed as a capital gain. If you were in a lower income tax bracket in the later years, you effectively converted the tax rate as well.

The rest of this chapter will discuss several of the traditional tax shelters and examine and analyze their elements, advantages, and disadvantages. I will focus on traditional tax shelter investments—real estate, oil and gas, equipment leasing, etc. In the next chapter, I will unveil those super-sophisticated, nontraditional tax shelters that can bring your effective tax liability down to zero.

# 64

## Real Estate

*"It'd take a genius to invest in real estate and pay taxes"*: House Ways and Means Committee member Fortney H. (Pete) Stark, D-Calif., on the committee's decisions regarding the taxation of real estate, 1986. Of the various forms of investments available to you that involve possible tax incentives, the most widely used is real estate. Historically, real estate has been sold as an investment for income and long-term gain, as well as a hedge against inflation. Real estate can be purchased in the form of shopping centers, warehouse net leases, apartment buildings, residential housing, and even raw land.

In the decade before reform, one of the major reasons for the high degree of tax shelter investment in real estate was that the "at risk" rules introduced by the Tax Reform Act of 1976 did not apply to any partnership in which the principal activity was investing in real estate. The "at risk" rules limited your tax deductions to the amount you invested plus the amount of borrowed funds for which you were personally liable. Real estate tax shelters were exempt from this requirement until January 1, 1987 (Tax Reform Act of 1986).

Prior to 1987, the law provided an at-risk limitation on losses from business and income-producing activities other than real estate and certain active corporate business activities applicable to individuals and to certain closely held corporations. Taxpayers could deduct losses from an activity only to the extent of the amount they had at risk in the activity. The amount at risk is generally the sum of (1) the taxpayer's cash contributions to the activity; (2) the adjusted basis of other property contributed to the activity;

and (3) recourse debt (amounts borrowed for use in the activity with respect to which the taxpayer has personal liability or has pledged property not used in the activity). Nonrecourse debt (amounts borrowed for use in the activity for which none of the participants assumes personal liability and which is secured only by the assets of the activity) is not considered an amount at risk in the activity. The amount at risk is generally increased (or decreased) each year by the taxpayer's share of income (or losses and withdrawals) from the activity.

The Tax Reform Act of 1986 applies the at-risk rules to the activity of holding real property, with an exception for *qualified nonrecourse financing*. In general, taxpayers will be considered at risk with respect to their share of any qualified nonrecourse financing that is secured by real property used in the activity. The term *qualified nonrecourse financing* means any financing that is borrowed by the taxpayer (1) with respect to the activity of holding real property; (2) from a *qualified person,* or represents a loan from a federal, state, or local government, or is guaranteed by any federal, state, or local government; (3) except to the extent provided in regulations, with respect to which no person is personally liable for repayment; and (4) which is not convertible debt.

In the case of a partnership, a partner's share of any qualified nonrecourse financing of the partnership will be determined on the basis of the partner's share of liabilities incurred in connection with the financing of the partnership.

Borrowing from a "qualified person" means (1) the loan is taken from an unrelated commercial lender, or is from or is guaranteed by certain government entities; (2) the property is acquired from an unrelated person; (3) the lender is unrelated to the seller; (4) the lender or a related person does not receive a fee with respect to the taxpayer's investment in the property; (5) debt is not convertible; and (6) the nonrecourse debt does not exceed 80 percent of the credit base of the property. However, nonrecourse debt acquired from related persons may still be qualified nonrecourse financing if the financing from the related person is "commercially reasonable and on substantially the same terms as loans involving unrelated persons."

An analysis of the nontax advantages of real estate investments follows.

LEVERAGE

Leverage is the use of borrowed funds with the anticipation that the property will increase in value at a rate greater than the cost of borrowing, so that a profit will be realized not only on the investor's own money but also on the use of someone else's money. For example, if you make an investment of $100, putting up $10 in cash and borrowing $90 at an interest rate of 10 percent, at the end of the first year you will have a net cash outflow of $19 (your $10 initial investment plus $9 interest on the $90 borrowed). Assume your property increases in value 20 percent during that same period and then you sell it, paying off your $90 debt. You receive a total of $120; subtract the $99 ($90 in principal plus $9 in interest), and you have a net gain of $21. On your initial cash investment of $10, this represents a 210 percent return. You can often use borrowed capital in a real estate purchase to finance as much as 80 percent of the total cost of the property.

### INFLATION HEDGE

The supply of real estate is clearly limited. For this reason, many people believe that investments in well-selected real estate can be expected to at least keep up with inflation, and perhaps even increase in value faster than inflation.

### CASH FLOW

In many cases, good income-producing real property will generate a favorable cash flow. This cash flow can be augmented by increased income tax savings due to the shelter aspects of real estate investments.

### EQUITY BUILDUP

Income-producing real estate may create increased liquidity. Debt reduction plus inflation may create equity that can be the source of new or additional financing.

### ABILITY TO POOL CAPITAL

Syndicates or partnerships enable investors to pool their capital in order to acquire large, select properties they would not be able to buy individually.

### DEDUCTIBLE EXPENSES

There are basically five different categories of expenses that are deductible on a real estate deal:

1. *Mortgage interest,* that portion of debt service payments represented by deductible interest costs.

2. *Depreciation,* an accounting adjustment that reflects the theoretical wear and tear and economic obsolescence of the property. Because of this, a portion of the income you receive is considered a return of your capital investment and not subject to tax.

3. *Operating expenses,* which include property management, maintenance, insurance, garbage removal, real estate taxes, common area utilities, etc.

4. *Construction period expenses,* deductible expenses incurred before the building is occupied, such as real estate taxes, interest on the construction loan, etc. These costs are not deductible when incurred, but must be amortized over a period of years as discussed earlier.

5. *Fees,* a portion of the purchase price that, frequently, the seller of the property agrees to take as payment for services, resulting in an immediate deduction—for instance, guarantees for "rent up," completion, financing, etc.

The tax advantage of real estate results from the possibility that your deductible expenses for tax purposes may exceed your cash outflow. Only operating expenses and mortgage interest are paid in cash from property operations. As a result, your taxable income—for instance, your rental income from the property minus the expenses listed above—does not reflect the cash flow from property operations. Your true cash flow, therefore, is your taxable income or loss *plus* construction period expenses and fees *and* depreciation *minus* mortgage principal payments. Construction period expenses and fees are those costs normally paid when incurred from the limited partner capital contribution or from the mortgage proceeds (but not from property operations). Depreciation is, of course, not a cash expense but rather a bookkeeping entry. Mortgage principal payments are not deductible for tax purposes because they have been included in your basis of the property and are reflected for tax purposes in your depreciation deductions.

The following computations show a hypothetical tax income statement loss and its conversion into a cash flow gain:

Tax Income Statement

| | | |
|---|---:|---:|
| Rental Income | | $500 |
| Less: | | |
| operating expenses | $150 | |
| mortgage interest | 250 | |
| construction period expenses | 80 | |
| fees | 25 | |
| depreciation | +175 | |
| | 680 | −680 |
| Tax Income (loss) | | ($180) |

Cash Flow

| | | |
|---|---:|---:|
| Tax Income (loss) | | ($180) |
| Add back: | | |
| construction period expenses | 80 | |
| fees | 25 | |
| depreciation | +175 | |
| | 280 | |
| | | 100 |
| Minus mortgage principal payments | | − 25 |
| Cash Flow from property operations | | $75 |

At a 33 percent marginal tax bracket you would save $59 in taxes and have a positive total cash flow of $134 ($59 + $75).

Moreover, the normal real estate tax shelter is usually structured so that any actual cash losses in the first years will be provided, or paid for, by the limited partners' capital contribution or the proceeds of the mortgage itself. This item is referred to as "rent-up loss"—the operating deficit during the period before the property is fully rented.

SUMMARY OF BENEFITS

As the preceding statements indicate, there are a number of benefits achieved from real estate tax shelter investing. The bottom line of the tax income statement shows your taxable loss. Multiply this figure by your tax bracket to determine your tax savings.

The cash flow statement represents the cash distributions you will be paid from the property's operations. Add to this the cash in pocket from the above tax savings and that yields your net cash increase in wealth.

An additional benefit that investing in real estate tax shelters will yield is your equity buildup. This is the amount of the mortgage principal that you are paying off each year. Even if the property value merely remains flat with no appreciation, your equity interest in that property will increase each year by the principal payoff.

The final benefit from such an investment is the potential appreciation in the property itself. Building costs are rising with inflation, so it is likely that in ten years the replacement cost of real estate will be much higher than construction costs today. If a property is well located and well maintained, its cash flow should expand over the years and its value should increase.

Before investing in a shelter you must recognize that real estate projects fall into three major categories:

Commercial
Residential
Government-supported housing

Each category of investment has its own rules and deduction limits for tax purposes. For example, rehabilitation costs on low-income housing and certified historic structures can still qualify for investment tax credits. For a building in service before 1936 (other than a certified historic structure), the credit is 10 percent; for a certified residential or commercial historic structure, the credit increases to 20 percent! This means that you get the equivalent of one-fifth off your rehabilitation expenses. If you use the rehabilitation credit, however, you must use straight-line depreciation, reduce the base by the full amount of its credit, and make a substantial rehabilitation of the building. This means that the qualifying expenditures of the tax year and the preceding tax year must exceed the adjusted basis of the property or $5,000, whichever is larger. For rehibilitations completed in phases, the 24-month measuring period is extended to 60 months. In addition, to qualify for the credit one of the following three tests must be met:

a) At least 50 percent of the external walls are retained as external walls;

b) at least 75 percent of the external walls are retained as either external or internal walls; *and*

c) at least 75 percent of the internal structural framework is retained in place.

Under government-sponsored housing, you can deduct construction loan interest and taxes immediately; with other real estate you must amortize them over four years. Furthermore, an owner of a subsidized housing project may defer any taxes due on the sale of the project if it is sold to a tenant cooperative and the proceeds reinvested in another subsidized housing project within one year.

The new rehabilitation credit may be used to offset tax on up to $25,000 of nonpassive income, regardless of whether the individual actively participates, subject to a phase-out between $200,000 and $250,000 of adjusted gross income.

Parties interested in obtaining further information on historic preservation opportunities and procedures should contact the various agencies and organizations listed below.

Copies of historic preservation standards and guidelines set forth by the government for certifying historic structures and a current list of state historic preservation offices are available by writing to the following address:

Tax Reform Act
Office of Archaeology and Historic Preservation
Department of the Interior
Washington, DC 20240

The following is the address of the historic preservation agency that administers the Department of the Interior's preservation tax incentive program:

Historic Preservation Tax Incentives
Archaeology and Historic Preservation
National Park Service
Washington, DC 20240

The following regional offices of the National Park Service review certification applications:

| Regional Office | States Administered for Tax Certification Purposes |
| --- | --- |
| Mid-Atlantic 143 South Third Street Philadelphia, PA 19106 (215)597-7013 | Connecticut, Delaware, District of Columbia, Maine, Maryland, Massachusetts, New Hampshire, New Jersey, New York, Pennsylvania, Rhode Island, Vermont, Virginia, West Virginia |
| Southeast 75 Spring Street, NW Atlanta, GA 30303 (404)242-2635 | Alabama, Florida, Georgia, Kentucky, Mississippi, North Carolina, Puerto Rico, South Carolina, Tennessee |
| Midwest Federal Building 200 East Liberty Street Ann Arbor, MI 48107 (313)378-2035 | Illinois, Indiana, Iowa, Kansas, Michigan, Minnesota, Missouri, Nebraska, Ohio, Wisconsin |
| Rocky Mountain P.O. Box 25287 Denver Federal Center Denver, CO 80225 (303)234-2915 | Colorado, Montana, North Dakota, South Dakota, Utah, Wyoming |
| Southwest 5000 Marble Street, NE Room 211 Albuquerque, NM 87110 (505)474-3514 | Arkansas, Louisiana, New Mexico, Oklahoma, Texas |
| West 450 Golden Gate Avenue P.O. Box 36063 San Francisco, CA 94102 (415)556-7741 or 556-7090 | Arizona, California, Hawaii, Nevada |
| Pacific Northwest Westin Building Room 1920 2110 Sixth Avenue Seattle, WA 98121 (206)399-0791 | Idaho, Oregon, Washington |

| Regional Office | States Administered for Tax Certification Purposes |
|---|---|
| Alaska 1011 East Tudor Street Suite 297 Anchorage, AK 99503 (907)277-1666 | Alaska |

The National Trust for Historic Preservation, a private, nonprofit membership organization, provides advice on preservation issues and techniques. For more information on membership, write:

National Trust for Historic Preservation
1785 Massachusetts Avenue, NW
Washington, DC 20036

The regional offices of the National Trust are as follows:

| Regional Office | States and Territories Administered |
|---|---|
| Northeast 100 Franklin Street 7th Floor Boston, MA 02110 (617)223-7754 | Connecticut, Maine, Massachusetts, New Hampshire, New York, Rhode Island, Vermont |
| Mid-Atlantic 1600 H Street, NW Washington, DC 20006 (202)673-4203 | Delaware, District of Columbia, Maryland, New Jersey, Pennsylvania, Puerto Rico, Virgin Islands, Virginia, West Virginia |
| South 456 King Street Charleston, SC 29403 (803)724-4711 | Alabama, Arkansas, Florida, Georgia, Kentucky, Louisiana, Mississippi, North Carolina, South Carolina, Tennessee |
| Midwest 407 South Dearborn Street Number 710 Chicago, IL 60605 (312)353-3419 or 353-3424 | Illinois, Indiana, Iowa, Michigan, Minnesota, Missouri, North Dakota, Ohio, South Dakota, Wisconsin |

Southwest/Plains
210 Colcord Building
Oklahoma City, OK 73102
(405)231-5126

Colorado, Kansas, Nebraska, New Mexico,
Oklahoma, Texas

West
681 Market Street
Number 859
San Francisco, CA 94105
(415)556-2707

Alaska, Arizona, California, Guam, Hawaii,
Idaho, Micronesia, Montana, Nevada,
Oregon, Utah, Washington, Wyoming

The combination of first-year accelerated depreciation and heavy start-up costs may produce tax deductions exceeding the size of your initial cash investment when 80 percent of the cost of that investment is financed with borrowings. What that means is that if you are in the 33 percent bracket, your net initial cash outlay may be reduced to zero! However, with any tax shelter, as with any investment, *never* invest just on the basis of tax deductions alone. You must always consider the total expected cash flow from the property. The advantages of a real estate tax shelter are that the risks are normally minimal and the total cash flow is normally augmented in the early years by substantial tax savings. Furthermore, a good shelter should be structured to give you substantial cash rental income that is either minimally taxed or not taxed at all due to offsetting depreciation expense deductions even in the middle years. These depreciation deductions are pencil transactions that do not involve any real cash outflow, and they arise out of basis created by borrowed money. In effect, with a properly structured transaction you get to eat your cake and keep it too.

Moreover, the Tax Reform Act of 1986 created a new low-income housing credit. This housing credit is claimed annually over a 10-year period with percentages set so that over that 10-year period, the credits will equal a present value of 70 percent of the basis of a new building which is not federally subsidized and 30 percent of the basis of an existing building or federally subsidized new building. The credit applies only to expenditures on the low-income units, and rehabilitation expenditures will qualify for the credit only if they exceed $2,000 per unit.

A building will qualify for the credit if either at least 20 percent of the units are occupied by individuals with incomes of 60 percent or less of area median income, or if at least 40 percent of the units are occupied by individuals with incomes of 50 percent or less of area median income. Furthermore, the rent charged to tenants may not exceed 30 percent of the applicable qualified income, which will vary depending on family size.

If a building is placed in service in 1987, the credit percentages are 9 percent annually over 10 years (that equates to the 70 percent present value credit), and/or 4 percent over 10 years (that equates to the 30 percent present value credit).

If a building is placed in service after 1987, the credit percentages will be adjusted monthly by the Treasury to reflect the present values of 70 percent and 30 percent at the time the building is placed in service. In a project consisting of two or more buildings placed in service in different months, a separate credit percentage may apply to each building.

One additional word on real estate tax shelters. The Senate Report on the Tax Reform Act of 1986 (S. Rep. at 742) states that hotel and motel properties are not considered to be rental activities, and thus are not per se designated as passive. Consequently, if a real estate investor holds hotel and motel property either through a general partnership interest or ownership in an S Corporation, and if that developer actively manages the property, it may be possible to have these properties designed as active businesses. In this case, the developer would be able to utilize losses from the property to offset other income.

Alternatively, if the hotel or motel is producing taxable income, holding such property through a limited partnership interest would characterize the income generated therefrom as passive. By eliminating hotel or motel properties from the rental income classification, the Tax Reform Act presents a unique planning opportunity with respect to such properties. Such ownership gives you, the investor, the opportunity to classify the activities as either active or passive, depending upon which planning approach you choose to undertake.

Watch out for fees in many limited partnership deals. A typical limited partnership will pay 7 to 10 percent of equity in sales commissions; 1 to 3 percent or more of the equity raised for legal, accounting, and paperwork expenses; and up to 15 percent of the equity for organization and mortgage finding fees. Later, sponsors may take 5 to 6 percent of the cash flow in property management fees. After the property is sold, 3 to 6 percent of the sales price may go for commissions, and an additional 10 to 33 percent of any profit on the sale may go to the sponsors. Clearly, the greater the front-end fee, the less money is left to invest in property. According to Arnold G.

Rudoff, who analyzes partnerships for the accounting firm of Price Waterhouse in San Francisco, real estate front-end fees should be under 20 percent.

According to a survey by the accounting firm of Coopers & Lybrand, privately offered real estate partnership transactions showed the following fees and structure:

|  | *Typical* | *Range* |
|---|---|---|
| Partnership participation |  |  |
| Cash flow | 10% | 1–10% |
| Tax benefits | 10% | 1–10% |
| Refinancing/disposition (subordinated) | 20% | 15–30% |
| Initial fees (as % of equity raised) |  |  |
| Sales commission | 8% | 6–10% |
| Acquisition and ancillary fees | 30% | 15–60% |
| Operating period (as % of revenues) |  |  |
| Property management | 4% | 3–6% |
| Partnership management | Modest | Modest |
| Reimbursable expenses | Modest | Modest |
| Disposition fees |  |  |
| Real estate commission | 3% | Competitive |
| Participation in residual value | 20% | 15–30% |

Reprinted with permission of Coopers & Lybrand © March 1985 Coopers & Lybrand (U.S.A.)

One measure of the fairness of offering terms is how the various fees relate to the North American Securities Administrators Association (NASAA) guidelines. These guidelines appear in the next section.

# 65

## Fees in Public Real Estate Partnerships

*Front-end fees* include sales commissions for the broker/dealer, offering and organization costs, and property acquisition fees paid to the general partner and unaffiliated third parties. The NASAA front-end fee standard is 20 percent of limited partner capital contributions for unleveraged properties, 28.1 percent for 50 percent leveraged properties, and 33 percent for 80 percent leveraged properties.

*Operational phase fees* are typically paid to the general partner from cash flow (earnings) of the real estate as compensation for management of the day-to-day operation of the partnership and the properties. NASAA approves "property management fees" equal to 6 percent of gross revenues for residential properties and 3 percent of gross revenues for commercial properties, plus a "promotional" interest of 10 percent of annual cash flow (if the liquidation phase fee from net proceeds, explained below, is limited to 15 percent).

*Liquidation phase fees* are payable to the general partner upon resale or refinancing of the properties. These fees consist of a real estate commission and a percentage of the net proceeds from the sale or refinancing of the property. Normally, these fees are subordinated (not paid to the general partner) until the return of the limited partners' investment, plus a minimum return. NASAA approves a real estate commission to all parties, not to exceed 3 percent. The promotional or incentive fee is limited to 15 percent if the sponsor also received 10 percent of annual cash flow, or 25 percent otherwise. The real estate commission and the appreciation percentage are "subordinated" to the return of limited partner capital, plus a minimum return of 6 percent per annum on initial capital reduced by periodic cash distributions.

# 66

## Oil and Gas

Petroleum and gas are important sources of energy throughout the world. Accordingly, Congress has determined that certain types of investments in oil and gas are deductible. Former Attorney General Smith invested in an oil and gas partnership. An investment in an oil and gas program is probably your most advantageous single-year tax-advantaged investment if the economics are viable.

The tax advantage in an oil and gas deal is the ability to deduct, as a current expense, the investments in capital expenditures known as intangible drilling and developing costs, or IDCs. The income tax regulations define *intangibles* as any cost incurred that has no salvage value and is "incident to and necessary for the drilling of wells and the preparation of wells for the production of oil and gas." This definition includes the hours worked by the drilling crew and the cost of the installation of tangible equipment placed *in the well*, although the cost of such equipment must be capitalized and recovered through depreciation. Expressly excluded from classification as *intangibles* are expenditures incurred in connection with equipment, facilities, or structures (including installation charges) that are not incident to or necessary for the drilling of oil or gas wells but are used in operations after the oil or gas is produced (for instance, structures for storing and treating oil or gas).

Essentially, then, nearly all costs of drilling and completing a well, except for the bare cost of the lease, the cost of tangible equipment and labor, and the geological and geophysical costs incurred prior to the selection of a drill site, are deductible in the year incurred. Without this special break accorded to intangible drilling and development costs, you would be unable to deduct them until drilling was either abandoned or the product was actually being extracted from the wells.

In the first year you are able immediately to deduct 70 percent to 80 percent of productive-well costs as intangible expenses, and 100 percent of dry well costs. In many public tax shelter programs, you pay for only intangible costs and can therefore immediately deduct up to 100 percent of the amount you invest.

There is a catch: with gas and oil deals the Internal Revenue Service will not permit deductions in excess of your personal cash investment, or "at risk" basis. In the past, however, it did permit the year-end deduction of all the intangible costs of wells even if those wells were not actually to be drilled until the following year. (Thus promoters of oil and gas shelters tried to "front load" deductions in the initial year of the shelter by prepayment of intangible costs.) In all other tax shelters, legislation has ruled out retroactive allocations of losses for year-end investments; it also no longer allows immediate deductions for many expenses that are incurred prior to actual operations—for example, cattle feeding programs—unless there is a clear business purpose. And on St. Patrick's Day, 1980, the Internal Revenue Service asserted that prepaid intangible drilling costs *also* must be disallowed as a deduction in the year paid—unless the taxpayer can demonstrate the existence of some commercial exigency making it advisable to prepay the costs.[1]

In an Eighth Circuit 1984 Court of Appeals Case (*Keller*, 84-1 USTC Par. 9194, 53 AFTR2d 84-663), the Court found that prepayments for intangible costs served no business purpose and materially distorted the taxpayer's income. The taxpayer's deduction, therefore, was deferred until the subsequent year.

---

1.  Revenue Ruling 80-71, I.R.B. 1980-11, 7.

The Keller case, however, did not involve a "turnkey" contract. In fact, the Court found that with a "turnkey" contract, where the amounts expended could not be refunded, a prepayment would be deductible in the year paid. This was a validation of the general rule that intangible drilling and development costs under a "turnkey" agreement were deductible in the year paid (*Ruth*, T.C. Memo 1983-586).

Furthermore, the Tax Reform Act of 1984 provided that "tax shelters" (other than forming syndicates), whether on the cash or accrual method, will not be able to deduct prepaid expenses until both economic performance occurs and the expenses actually paid are incurred. A deduction, however, will be allowed for prepaid expenses where economic performance occurs after the end of the year under the following conditions:

1.  economic performance occurs within 90 days after the end of the taxable year;
2.  the deduction is limited to the cash investment made by the person (i.e., not paid for with any recourse or nonrecourse liabilities); *and*
3.  the requirements of present laws are met.

For purposes of this exception in the case of intangible drilling expenses, economic performance occurs when the well is "spudded." If oil and gas prepayments do not meet the requirements of the 90-day exception, economic performance will occur as the drilling services are provided. If drilling is commenced in the year of prepayment (and the above exception is not met), only that portion of the intangible drilling cost attributable to drilling prior to the end of the year will be deductible in that year. This provision applies for prepayments made after March 31, 1984, and enhances the potential significance of a "turnkey" contract.

Note, in addition, that working interest in any oil or gas property that you hold directly or through an entity that does not limit your liability with respect to such interest will be treated as an active trade or business and will not be subject to the passive loss rules.

TAX SHELTER STRATEGIES

A sophisticated shelter will sustain the current deductibility of an intangible drilling cost prepayment by the following techniques:

*   The prepayment requirements should be set forth in the contract.

- The contract should set forth the particular well to be drilled and provide for a definite commencement date.

- If it is a co-owner situation, the same prepayment requirement should be imposed on other coowners.

- The contract should be with the actual driller, if possible, and not with an intermediary.

- There should be a business benefit to be derived from the prepayment requirement (that is, the price might be lower if the driller is paid in advance).

- The contract should be binding on the driller.

- Prepayment should not be more than a reasonable estimate of the amount to come due to the driller.

- The payments should actually be made prior to the end of the year, and the driller's access to the funds should not be restricted (that is, payment into an escrow account may not constitute a valid prepayment).

Additional tax shelter is still available through your ability to take 200 percent declining balance depreciation on the remaining 20 to 30 percent of the costs of the wells (capitalized costs). A statutory depletion deduction (one that is provided by law), which is 15 percent of your gross income from the well before expenses, also is available.

After the development of the property and the drilling are completed, the program will begin to receive cash from oil or gas sales, if any successful wells are drilled. If receipts exceed operating and overhead costs as well as depletion and depreciation, you will have taxable income.

The depletion allowance you are allowed to claim is the *greater* of cost depletion or percentage depletion.

COST DEPLETION

Cost depletion is computed by dividing the estimated total units (barrels of oil or thousand cubic feet of gas) recoverable from the property into its adjusted tax basis in order to obtain the per-unit depletion allowance, and then multiplying the per-unit depletion allowance by the number of units sold during the year. Cost depletion is then compared to percentage depletion on a property-by-property basis to determine the amount to be deducted.

PERCENTAGE DEPLETION

Percentage depletion for up to 1,000 barrels of average daily production of oil or 6 million cubic feet of domestic natural gas is allowed to "independent producers and royalty owners" at the rate of 15 percent of gross revenue. This depletion allowance is limited to 50 percent of the net income from the property. The allowance calculated is further limited to 65 percent of your taxable income (prior to taking the depletion allowance). The 65 percent limitation and average daily production limitation are calculated at the individual investor or partner level.

Both cost and percentage depletion are computed separately for *each* property in which you have an interest. Percentage depletion at the applicable statutory rate is computed on *gross* income from the property before deductions of any kind, including production or windfall profit taxes, operating expenses, or depreciation. Accordingly, the benefit obtained is significantly more than the statutory rate as a percentage of net (taxable) income.

The Supreme Court has ruled in *Commissioner v. Engle et ux*, S. Ct. Docket 82-599, that lessors of interests in mineral deposits are entitled to percentage depreciation allowances on any bonus or advanced royalties whether or not there is actual production of the underlying mineral in the year of payment. Production, therefore, has been found *not* to be a prerequisite for claiming percentage depletion deductions on lease bonus and advanced royalty income.

Percentage depletion is almost always larger than cost depletion. For example, if a well is drilled on a lease that cost $2,000 and yields an estimated 100,000 barrels of recoverable reserves, the rate of cost depletion for that property would be 2¢ per barrel of oil produced. This is far less than percentage depletion at the applicable rate. Fifteen percent of the gross income of oil selling at $16 per barrel is $2.40. The net impact of the depreciation and depletion deductions is that with normal operating expenses, from about a quarter to a third of your income from the well is tax-free.

Oil and gas drilling tax shelter programs break down into three types:

1. *Wildcatting,* also known as exploratory drilling, which involves drilling operations in search of a yet-undiscovered pool of oil or gas, or with the

hope of greatly extending the limits of a pool already developed. It is an attempt to find new fields where the probability of success for an individual well may be 10 percent and the chances of "proving," or discovering, a big field are about 1 percent to 2 percent.

2. *Development drilling,* which involves drilling an additional well to a reservoir that supports an already-producing well on a lease or on an offset lease that is usually close to or adjacent to the producing well. Development wells can have success rates of from 75 percent to 100 percent, but real fortunes are made only by "proving" a big field and selling or developing it.

3. *Balanced or combination programs,* which involve both exploratory and development drilling, therefore promising up-side potential with limited down-side risk. Unfortunately, most balanced programs combine wildcatting's delayed significant cash flow (three years can be common) with a development program's low multiple cash return (on average, 2.5 × the cash investment).

Unlike most investments, investments in oil and gas exploration may result in a complete loss. Industry statistics reflect that about 1 out of 10 wildcat wells is productive and that many of the productive wells do not have sufficient reserves to cover the drilling, equipping, and operating costs of the wildcat venture. Approximately 1 out of 200 wildcat wells discovers a medium-size field, and only 1 out of 1,000 discovers a large field. As indicated by the statistics, investments in oil and gas exploration should be spread over a sufficient number of prospects to provide you with a reasonable expectation of a return on your investment.

If you are interested in entering the oil business, there are several ways to participate, including the following:

- Participation with an oil operator on a selective basis for fractional interest in a number of oil and gas prospects.

- Participation with several different oil operators for a fractional interest in selected oil and gas prospects.

- Investments in a limited partnership with one or more oil and gas prospects.

- Various combinations of these.

NONTAX CONSIDERATIONS

In addition to the tax considerations discussed above, you must examine the following nontax considerations if you want to get involved with oil and gas.

### Management

Management in the oil business is of primary importance. The ability to operate an oil and gas investment program successfully consists basically of two skills: technical expertise and administrative competence. The organization must have the technical expertise to assemble prospects, select drilling sites, supervise the drilling and completion of wells, operate productive wells, and market the output. The competence of the technical staff is extremely difficult to evaluate on a short-run basis, since entirely new prospects are assembled and drilled each year.

### Program Size

There is no optimum program size. However, the size of the technical and administrative staffs will dictate certain minimum and maximum projects that can be undertaken. The program should have enough capital to drill a sufficient number of prospects for a reasonable spread of the risks; also, a minimum amount of capital must be raised to be used for administrative costs associated with offering the program and other administrative matters.

The area in which operations will be conducted is also important. A $5 million program that will explore an area where the average well costs $400,000 could offer a satisfactory spread of risk. A $5 million program exploring in areas where the average well costs $1.5 million may *not* offer an adequate spread. The geographic area in which the technical staff has expertise should also be considered. A technical staff with operating experience in Colorado and Wyoming may not be qualified to conduct operations in Texas and Louisiana.

### Past Performance

One of the most important nontax considerations that you must examine is the drilling company's past record of performance. You should measure and compare the net future revenues from proven oil and gas reserves in relation to limited partner capital contributions. Use only proven reserves, not what are called probable or possible reserves. Examine the price escalation figures and use only formulas provided by an independent reserve engineering firm.

Do not focus on past performance success ratios or cash distribution tables. The success ratio is the percent of all wells drilled that are completed as producing wells. A better success ratio does not necessarily mean a better economic result. For example, drilling in the Appalachian Basin (Ohio and West Virginia) should be successful 90 percent of the time, while drilling in Louisiana may be successful only perhaps 30 percent or 40 percent of the time. Why then should you invest in a project that drills in Louisiana? The answer is more abundant reserves and a potentially greater return on investment.

The cash distribution tables show the cash actually paid out to the investor. These can be deceiving in that some types of wells pay (or produce) over 50 percent of all that they will ever pay out in the first two years of their productive life; after the first four years, they do not produce any significant revenues. Other types of wells produce a lower percentage in their earlier life but continue to produce for as long as 20 to 30 years.

*Management Costs*

An additional nontax risk of oil and gas deals is the overpricing of the leases so that various parties in the promotional and marketing chain can realize this compensation from the initial capital invested. As compensation, the general partner and/or operator may receive up to 25 percent of the revenues earned by the limited partners after paying oil and gas royalties to the land owner and other promotional interests. In addition, there is usually a first-year management fee of about 5 percent of the amount of the investment.

Generally, you should expect to hold your interest in the well for its lifetime. Your investment is a capital asset and if sold should produce capital gains. But if the well is sold, then a portion of the intangible drilling costs deducted during the developmental phase of the shelter may be "recaptured" and treated as ordinary income, as may some of the depreciation taken. Many public programs offer buy-back provisions after two or three years of operation, but generally you will receive a better return if you wait five to seven years. With a successful shelter, you might well be advised to retain your interest in the shelter, collect the cash flow from the sale of the oil, and shelter this income with percentage depletion. It is not normally recommended that you buy the interest of an original investor as a tax shelter. This is because although percentage depletion is available to investors who are in a successful oil deal during the developmental phase, an investor who purchases the interest of the original investor in the deal is purchasing a "proven property" and therefore is not entitled to percentage depletion deductions.

### Compensation

If you are interested in involving yourself as an *active* developer of oil and gas properties, you should note that compensation paid in oil rights potentially can be tax free. In Letter Ruling 813-7006, the Internal Revenue Service held that a consultant who contributed only services to the pool of capital, acquiring in return an interest in the minerals (oil) in place, is not required to include that interest in his income. The same reasoning has been extended to accountants, lawyers, geologists, petroleum engineers, and lease brokers who receive an interest in an oil or gas drilling venture in return for services rendered. The contributors are not viewed as performing services for compensation but are viewed as acquiring capital interests through making a contribution to the pool of capital that is necessary for development (see Revenue Ruling 77-176, 1977-1 C.B. 78, and G.C.M. 22730, 1941-1 C.B. 214, but see Revenue Ruling 83-46, where overriding royalty interest to a corporate promotor, an attorney, and an employee were found to be includable in gross income at fair market value immediately).

### STRUCTURING A SUCCESSFUL OIL OR GAS TAX SHELTER

Assume that you are in the 43 percent bracket, including not only federal taxes but state and local income taxes as well. You invest $50,000 in an oil program in which 80 percent of your investment is deductible as intangible drilling costs. The remaining 20 percent is depreciated and deducted on a ten-year straight-line basis. Assume in addition that the well produces a lifetime total income of only $50,000.

*First Year*

| | |
|---|---:|
| IDC deduction (80% of $50,000) | $40,000 |
| Plus depreciation deduction (1/10 of 20% of $50,000) | + 1,000 |
| | 41,000 |
| First-year net cost [$50,000 − ($41,000 × .43) | $32,370 |

*Subsequent Years' Total*

| | | |
|---|---:|---:|
| Total income | | $50,000 |
| Depletion sheltered (15% × $50,000) | 7,500 | |
| Plus depreciation | | |
| (9/10 of 20% of $50,000) | + 9,000 | |
| Nontaxable cash income | 16,500 | |
| Plus after-tax cash from taxable income | | |
| − [$33,500 − (.43 × $33,500)] | +19,095 | |
| After-tax return | | 35,595 |
| Minus first-year net cost | | −32,370 |
| Net Cash Return | | $3,225 |

Note that while no allowance for discounting future income to present value is made in the above analysis, if your oil or gas investment returns a total income at least equal to your initial cash investment, it will be at least marginally successful. Any excess return over your initial investment will substantially multiply your yield on that investment, especially on an after-tax basis.

### SELF-EMPLOYMENT TAX TECHNIQUES

The Tax Reform Act of 1986 has made purchasing a working interest in oil and gas wells a popular technique by allowing a working interest owner to escape the passive loss rules and claim drilling costs against other income, such as salaries, interest, or dividends. An interesting opportunity has recently been created with respect to self-employment tax on oil and gas income. The IRS has taken the position that a working interest constitutes a trade or business for purposes of the self-employment (social security) tax. It is irrelevant whether operations were conducted by the working interest owner or by a third party. In that case, the IRS viewed the third-party operator as acting as the agent for the owner (Revenue Ruling 58-166). The position of the Internal Revenue Service, therefore, was that any income from a working interest in a gas or oil well constituted self-employment income. Such income or such losses were therefore added or subtracted if the taxpayer was not over the social security maximum with compensation from other employment and the like.

In *Howard W. Hendrickson,* T.C. Memo 1987-566, November 12, 1987, the Tax Court ruled that a salesman who had no experience in the oil and gas industry and who purchased a 21.875 percent interest in a gas well, as well as similar interest in two other wells, was not in the trade or business of producing oil and gas and therefore was not subject to self-employment tax.

These conflicting opinions allow you the following choice. If you are under the social security maximum and have losses from a working interest in a gas or oil well, the IRS position should be adopted to further reduce your potential self-employment taxes. However, if you have gains from a working interest and are not at the social security maximum, and if you fit within the perimeters of the *Hendrickson* case, you should adopt the position of the Tax Court and not increase your self-employment income for social security tax purposes.

# 67

## Equipment Leasing

Leasing, as a method of financing capital assets for industry, has grown tremendously in recent years and can be a good tax shelter. According to the National Association of Securities Dealers, equipment leasing deals have been the fastest growing category of direct placement programs (tax shelters). Capital assets frequently financed by leasing include computers, airplanes, railroad rolling stock, ships, pollution control equipment, and industrial machinery.

A lease contract allows the lessee to use the equipment for a specified length of time in return for periodic rental payments. While a variety of lease contracts have been developed, such contracts will normally be classified either as finance (full-payout) leases or as operating (nonfull-payout) leases.

*Finance leases* provide the lessor with recovery of the cost and a reasonable profit from rentals and tax benefits over the original noncancelable lease term. These leases may be leveraged or nonleveraged. A leveraged lease is one in which the lessor has financed a significant portion (typically up to 80 percent) of the equipment purchased from third-party lenders. In the case of a nonleveraged lease, the lessor provides 100 percent of the equipment cost, either entirely through equity or by a combination of equity and recourse debt (a debt on which you are personally liable). Finance leases are almost invariably net leases—that is, the lessee is obligated to pay for most of the expenses, such as maintenance and property taxes associated with the equipment and insurance.

*Operating leases* do not provide the lessor with a return of cost over the initial noncancelable lease term. In order to realize a profit, lessors rely on their ability to sell or re-lease the equipment profitably at the end of the initial lease term. An operating lease may or may not be a net lease. It is not unusual for lessors writing operating leases to provide other services, such as maintenance and repair, along with the equipment.

The typical format of an equipment leasing transaction includes the following:

- Purchase of the equipment by a limited partnership (or direct ownership by the investor) for a cash down payment plus financing (either recourse or nonrecourse) for the balance of the purchase price.

- The equipment is then typically leased as either a full-payout finance lease or an operating lease.

- The lease may grant an option to purchase the equipment at a specified price at its fair market value.

- The lease may contain renewal options.

NONTAX CONSIDERATIONS

As an investor-owner, you must be aware of several nontax considerations. First, with a normal financing lease, you are in effect making a loan to the lessee of the purchase price of the equipment. Under an equipment leasing deal, you normally will have a greater economic return than you could realize on a conventional loan transaction.

Alternatively, since you are the owner of the equipment, you must take the risk of technological improvements—for instance, the obsolescence of the equipment. This risk can be modified by leasing on what is known as a "hell and high water" basis. Under such an arrangement, the lessee is obligated to make lease payments whether or not continued use of the equipment is desired. In effect, you are shifting the risk of obsolescence to the lessee. But as a result of that shift, you will receive reduced lease payments.

In addition, you must face a credit risk. Will the lessee be financially able to meet the lease payments? If not, your cash flow will be terminated and you will have to find another lessee.

There is also an interest risk. You as a lessor are essentially extending credit throughout the lease term at a fixed rate, while at the same time you may obtain your funds at variable rates—usually from banks at the prime rate or higher. In addition, your total annual debt service cost can be quite a bit higher than the interest charge alone because of the repayment of principal. If the interest rates on your borrowing increase, they can completely eliminate your return. When the cost of debt service exceeds the cash flow from the property, you have what is known as "negative leverage." Under these circumstances, your only real alternative is to repay the debt.

Finally, the residual value risk must be considered. Will the property be worth the anticipated amount at the end of the lease term? If not, your return could be significantly reduced.

There are also some nontax considerations for the lessee. Normally, the lessee will be making lease rental payments in amounts less than the direct purchase price of the equipment, even if paid on an installment basis.

In many cases, the lessee is cash poor or has limited borrowing capacity, and an equipment leasing arrangement reduces short-term cash outlay. In some cases, equipment leasing tax shelters may be structured in a sale leaseback format: The lessee originally owns the equipment but sells it to meet an immediate cash need. Under the terms of sale, the lessee turns around and leases the equipment from the buyer-lessor. Such a transaction will immediately augment the lessee's short-term cash position.

TAX BENEFITS

The key tax benefit that results from equipment leasing is deferral, which is a means of postponing a tax liability until a later and more convenient time. In years when your tax liability is high, you can invest in an equipment leasing program. You deduct a large amount of depreciation in the first year, along with miscellaneous front-end expenses and interest on the borrowed capital. After the first three to five years, the lease will begin generating taxable income because depreciation and interest will have been reduced. Be aware, though, that there may not be any cash income paid to you because of the debt service payments due on the borrowed money. However, you should note that by the time you start receiving taxable income prior to sufficient tax-flow generation, you will have had the use and yield on the considerable tax savings for a significant period of time.

DEPRECIATION

The deferral advantage of equipment leasing discussed above comes mainly from depreciation. The accelerated depreciation rate is 200 percent of straight-line depreciation. Furthermore, what is known as "the half-year convention" is automatically imputed in the ACRS depreciation tables. The half-year convention allows a person who puts equipment into service anytime during the year to depreciate that equipment as though that person had had it for half the entire year. However, the Tax Reform Act of 1986 provides that a mid-quarter convention be applied to all property that is more than 40 percent of all property placed in service by a taxpayer during the last three months of the taxable year. This mid-quarter convention treats all property placed in service during any quarter of a taxable year as placed in service on the midpoint of such quarter. Moreover, if the leasing constitutes a trade or business, you now have the option of expensing up to $10,000 in personal property immediately rather than over time through depreciation deductions.

In addition, as an investor, you should recognize that you would normally need a long-term, full-recourse loan to help buy the equipment. Otherwise, the depreciation that you take will quickly exceed your cash basis, and you will not be able to take any further deductions. What this means is that you should be extremely careful in leasing the equipment. Your major risks are residual value and that the lessee will default, so a good equipment leasing program will involve major corporations with superior credit ratings. With such programs, your effective risk is minimal.

---

SUMMARY OF ADVANTAGES

By taking accelerated depreciation on the equipment over a life shorter than your loan repayment period, you can obtain substantial cash-flow benefits from federal income tax deferrals over the first few years of ownership. The total cash required to be put up is normally only about 20 percent of the cost of the equipment. These funds become available due to the tax deductions resulting from the purchase. Your tax deductions in each of the first few years of the transaction will be a significant multiple of the cash invested in that year. Substantial deductions will also normally be enjoyed for several more years.

You will enjoy an interest-free loan as a result of the transaction. If a reasonable value is attributed to the use of the funds produced by the interest-free loan, you will normally secure a return of your original investment in the equipment even if the equipment has less than the originally anticipated residual value at the end of the lease. An economic return over and above the profits earned on the interest-free loan is normally provided from re-lease revenues generated by the equipment at the end of the initial lease and by full payment of your bank debt.

# 68

## Single-Premium Life Insurance

Single-premium life insurance, after the Tax Reform Act of 1986, is one of the last remaining qualify tax shelters. With single-premium life insurance, for a single lump sum, which may range from $1,000 to $5 million, a policyholder gets a little insurance protection and a big tax-deferred investment account. Single-premium life insurance offers a tax-free buildup of cash along with life insurance. Unlike universal life, the policy carries just enough insurance to qualify for tax-free status under the Internal Revenue Code. Therefore, more of the premium goes toward earning tax-deferred interest rather than buying insurance.

In fact, some experts have said that the insurance is a "free" bonus, since most single-premium policies quote a net rate of return. There are no fees or up-front commissions. That means that all of your cash immediately starts growing at the full rate quoted.

In the case of single-premium whole life, there is usually a 4 percent minimum guaranteed return. With an investment in single-premium variable life, like other variable products, there are no guaranteed rates of return, but the policyholder can pick his investments and move between alternative investments.

One suggested technique to avoid the limitations on Clifford trusts and the new kiddie tax on children under 14 years of age is to purchase a single-premium policy on the life of the parent with a young child as owner and beneficiary. The income can accumulate inside the policy until the child reaches 14 or college age. At that point the child has two options: he can take out the income and be taxed at his own, lower bracket, or he can simply borrow it. If he borrows the money, there are no tax consequences. Policyholders can normally borrow against the amount of their initial deposit, in some cases at no interest, and in other cases with interest charges of 2 or 3 percent. They can borrow their accumulated interest typically at a rate equal to what the policy is then currently earning—e.g., at a net zero cost.

If the parent dies, the child receives the death benefit, and because the child is the owner of the policy, it does not go into the parent's estate. If the parent lives, the child is able to pay for his education with pre-tax dollars. The proceeds of the insurance policy are tax-free anyway, and the parent has leveraged his investment and the child's wealth has been magnified by compounding. If the loan is not repaid—it need never be—it is subtracted from the death benefit.

For example, a 35-year-old male pays $25,000 for a single-premium variable life insurance policy. He then can choose his own investment options and switch between different investments. For the $25,000, he would get a death benefit only of approximately $80,000 to $85,000 on a typical policy. While he could possibly buy the same protection for only $100 a year, the life insurance is not the real objective.

Assume the taxpayer is able, through a combination of stocks, bonds, and other investments, to achieve a return of 12 percent a year on the investment portion of his policy. At the end of 15 years, when he is 50 years old, the death benefit would be typically in excess of $230,000 and the policy would have a cash surrender value of $100,000.

If the taxpayer then cashes in the policy, he pays taxes at that time. Alternatively, he could borrow over $22,000 tax-free each year for four years to put his child through college. This would bring the death benefit down to between $160,000 and $170,000 with a cash surrender value of approximately $30,000.

If the taxpayer did not touch his policy until he retired at age 65, his 12 percent rate of return would give him a death benefit of approximately $650,-000 with a cash surrender value in excess of $400,000. At that time he could cash in his policy and pay tax on the money. Alternatively, he could annuitize part of the policy when he retires by rolling over part of the cash surrender value into an annuity that would pay him income for life, leaving enough money in the policy to keep it in force and provide a tax-free benefit to his spouse. There would be no taxes due on the money rolled over into the annuity. This would allow the taxpayer to buy a cheaper annuity on his own life only, while he is providing insurance benefits for his spouse.

There are innumerable creative ways of using single-premium life insurance policies. For example, assume you have $1 million in bank certificates of deposit paying 10 percent and you are in the 33 percent tax bracket. After tax you get $67,000 in earnings. If you were to put the $1 million into a single-premium whole-life policy, also earning 10 percent, it would throw off $100,000 in tax-free income through policy loans. Assume, to make the numbers simple, that you are also paying $100,000 in tax-deductible alimony. If you keep your $1 million in a taxable investment, remember you get to keep only $67,000 after tax. Alternatively, if you used your insurance policy $100,000 to pay the alimony, you would reduce your tax bill by $33,000 (33 percent of $100,000).

Single-premium life insurance policies are not without their disadvantages. If you cash in your policy, every penny earned inside the policy over however many years you have held it is taxed as ordinary income. In addition, most insurance companies impose a surrender charge in the first few years of the policy, although the charge usually shrinks year by year.

In shopping for single-premium life insurance, the following considerations should be evaluated:

1.  Does the life insurance company offering the policy have a rating of A or better from AM Best Corporation, the authoritative source on financial stability in the industry?

2.  What is the current net interest being paid on the policy? Does this take into consideration the mortality charge—i.e., has that charge been taken out of the rate that is quoted?

3.  Is the net rate guaranteed, and if so for what period of time?

4.  Is there any minimum interest rate guaranteed over the life of the policy?

5.  Is there a bailout provision under which you can get out of the policy if rates fall below a certain level?

6.  What is the surrender charge if you cash in the policy?

7.  Does the surrender charge decrease over a period of time?

8.  What is the rate at which you can borrow the accumulated interest?

9.  What is the rate at which you can borrow against your original premium?

10. Is there a minimum guaranteed death benefit?

11. Can you make additional payments, and if so what are the time and quantity limitations?

# 69

## Cattle Feeding Programs

A cattle feeding program can enable you to spread income earned in one year over a number of years so that it can be taxed at lower rates.

There are no capital gains or depreciation opportunities. You buy calves in the spring or early summer and deduct the cost of feeding them for the remainder of the year. When they reach commercial weight the following year, you will sell them and pay ordinary income taxes. You have, in effect, deferred income from one year to the next, unless beef prices have fallen in the interim.

Feeding programs seek to convert grain (or grass) into beef, at the same time offering a short-term tax deferral and an opportunity for substantial profit or loss. If the cost of converting feed to beef is less than the per-pound cost of the beef added, the cattle feeding program results in a profit to you. If the cost of feeding the cattle is more than the price of beef, you lose.

A 1979 IRS ruling made prepaid feed deductions difficult for tax shelter schemes.[2] Under the prior rule, a prepaid feed expense had to meet three criteria:

1.  It could not be on "deposit"—you had to own the feed and bear the economic risk of price fluctuations.

2.  The purchase of the feed had to be for a "valid" business purpose.

3.  The deduction could not result in a "material distortion of income."

Under the new rule, these three criteria are retained, but in addition the Internal Revenue Service looks at the substantive purpose behind the transaction. According to the latest ruling, a motive based on the income tax advantages of prepayment is *not* a valid business purpose, and if you lacked other motives, your deduction will be disallowed.

Moreover, the Tax Reform Act of 1984 included statutory language to include any arrangement with the principal purpose of tax avoidance within the definition of what constitutes a farm syndicate. According to the Conference Committee Report, "The prepaid expense provisions will apply to individual taxpayers engaged in farming activities with the principal purpose of tax avoidance. The conferees intend that marketed arrangements in which individuals carry on farming activities utilizing the assistance of a common managerial or administrative service may be presumed under certain circumstances to have the principal purpose of tax avoidance. If

---

2.  Revenue Ruling 79-229, 1979 CB 2.

under such arrangements, taxpayers prepay a substantial portion of their farming expenses with borrowed funds, they should generally be presumed to have a principal purpose of tax avoidance."

The Internal Revenue Service could argue that all feed lot customers are tax shelters because they use the high leverage customary to the industry and feed cattle through a custom feed yard. If so, then the 1984 provisions would effectively limit all deductions for commercial cattle feeders to consumed feed. There would be no allowance of prepayments for feed, seed, fertilizer, or other farm supplies unless the taxpayer were "actively participating in the management." In addition, if the above provisions were to apply, they would preempt and eliminate the 90-day allowance rule on prepayments as contained in Section 461(i). Therefore, if you want to receive the benefits of a cattle feeding program, you must be able to document "active participation," establish a substantial business purpose, and prove that your principal purpose is not tax avoidance, in order to still be eligible to deduct valid prepayments for your farm expenditures.

A typical cattle feeding tax shelter will provide for the purchase of very young calves (or feeders) in the summer or fall. The animals are generally raised in feed yards for which you will be charged a fee in addition to the cost of the feed. The cattle are usually sold the following year, when they reach their commercial weight. If you meet the "valid business purpose" test just described by proper timing of feeder-cattle purchases and sales, you should be able to deduct your expenses in the first year and pick up this amount, plus or minus the profit or loss, in the following year. You should be able to meet the "valid business purpose" test if you can establish a legitimate expectation of higher feed costs in the future—that is, it is cheaper to buy the feed now than to wait—and a legitimate expectation of profit on the ultimate sale of the cattle.

Moreover, under the Tax Reform Act of 1986, farmers using the cash method of accounting will not be allowed to deduct any amount paid for feed, seed, fertilizer, or other supplies prior to the year in which such items are used or consumed to the extent that they exceed 50 percent of expenses for which economic performance has occurred. This provision is effective for prepayments made on or after March 1, 1986. Since most investors in cattle feeding will not have other farm expenses, they will not be entitled to deduct prepaid feed costs. Except for investors in other farming ventures who may have such expenses and who will therefore be entitled to the deduction within the specified limits, cattle feeding as a tax deferral for non-full-time farmers is no longer an effective tax shelter.

# 70

## Cattle Breeding Programs

Cattle breeding programs seek to increase herd size. Prior to ultimate sale, the cattle breeding program offers substantial tax deductions of a long-range deferral nature.

In a cattle breeding program, you might purchase a herd of 50 to 100 cows, which should triple in three to four years. Over a five-year period your average annual outlay of cash on a 100-cow herd can be about $12,000. This outlay may be offset by tax deductions of $6,000 a year.

Expenses normally are deducted as incurred. This includes amounts paid for feed, seed, fertilizer, or other similar supplies. The provision that expenses are deducted as incurred normally prevents the allowance of current deductions for prepaid expenses. If use or consumption of the supplies during the taxable year is prevented on account of fire, storm, flood, or other casualty, however, the items may then be taken as an expense in the current period.

The cattle usually are bred in the summer or fall, so the calf crop will be born in warm weather. A calf crop of 75 percent to 95 percent can be expected. After the calves are weaned, the steers are sold and the heifers are retained to build up the breeding herd. The new crop of heifers is generally bred after two years. Each year, certain animals are culled from the breeding herd and sold.

After five to seven years, the entire herd is usually sold. You can take depreciation on your breeding cattle, but gain equal to the depreciation taken will be recaptured as ordinary income upon their sale. Depreciation can be taken over a five-year class using the 200 percent declining balance method.

Prior to 1986, you were also entitled to the investment tax credit in a breeding operation. That was a credit against your tax bill of 10 percent of the purchase price, not just your investment. For example, if you bought a herd for $20,000 in 1985, putting in $2,000 in cash and borrowing the additional $18,000, you got an investment tax credit of 10 percent of the total $20,000, or $2,000. In effect, therefore, your initial net cash investment was zero. The Tax Reform Act of 1986 eliminated the investment tax credit as of January 1, 1986.

You can get into the breeding business with as little as 10 percent equity. With feeders, you can get in with as little as 5 percent equity. Up to 90 percent or 95 percent of the purchase price can be borrowed from the feedlot operator, the rancher, or a bank. You can therefore heavily leverage your investment, but this leverage must be based upon full-recourse financing.

The economics of breeding and feeding cattle can be seriously affected by the cyclical market price of cattle. Conditions such as increased costs (feed grains and supplies), price controls, reduced consumption due to high beef prices, and large supplies of available fat cattle have, at times, forced many one-way ventures into economic losses.

Diversification into combined feeding and breeding provides for a longer-lasting investment. The yearly cycle of feeding is extended to a period that provides for the building of herds in hope of a rising demand. In both feeding and breeding programs, management compensation is normally 5 percent to 10 percent of the herd value in the first year, and 5 percent to 10 percent of the operating expenses in subsequent years. Both activities are subject to the "at risk" limitation, and you will be personally liable for any loans if you finance your investment to obtain added tax leverage in order to take the full deductions available.

One very real advantage of cattle breeding is the flexibility that it extends to tax planning. Just as you can defer the recognition of income in a cattle feeding program by continuing to reinvest the proceeds of the sale of cattle, you can also pick the date on which you wish to realize the majority of the income from the sale of your breeding herd. Similarly, depreciation of the purchased cattle, the cost of their maintenance, and interest on any debt create additional deductions until the herd is sold. Remember, though, this flexibility, while useful in tax planning, does not insure that when the herd is eventually sold, it will be sold at a profit. Furthermore, cattle breeding is a long-term investment. You can expect little, if any, cash flow from the breeding venture for a substantial period of time. But the potential gains are there. Prior to 1987, all gain on the raised portion of the herd that had been held for more than twenty-four months and any gain on purchased animals in excess of prior depreciation would receive long-term capital gain treatment. And throughout the breeding and raising period, you would have been taking ordinary income deductions for your expenses. By eliminating the long-term capital gains deduction, however, the 1986 Reform Act significantly impaired the tax advantage of cattle breeding programs. They do, however, still give you the advantage of tax deferral.

# 71

## Tax Straddles

A commodity tax straddle is designed to defer short-term capital gain into your next year or to convert it into long-term capital gain. Straddling involves a simultaneous purchase and *short sale* (the sale of a security you do not currently own) of two futures contracts—that is, agreements first to buy and then to sell stated amounts of the same commodity at set prices and times in the future.

To offset the short-term capital gain, you straddle a very volatile commodity (such as copper, silver, or pork bellies) near year-end, hoping for significant price movement—up *or* down—before December 31. If prices rise, you cover your short position at a loss; if prices fall, you liquidate the long position. Either way, the short-term capital loss from commodities offsets your short-term capital gain from other sources. After year-end you liquidate the profitable position. This moves your short-term gain into the next year or (depending on how you hold the contract) converts it to a long-term capital gain. According to former IRS Commissioner Jerome Kurtz, the worst that can happen is that you "receive the equivalent of an interest-free loan from the government for the period of deferral." But if the price does not move, or if it turns around before you can liquidate the profitable position, you will have a loss.

Straddles can be used not only with commodities but with government securities, such as treasury bills, bonds, or "Ginnie Maes," or with options on those securities as well. The objective is the same—to create a loss that will reduce your taxable income for one year while you also set the stage to cover that loss with a capital gain in the next year. If the year works out right, you get a current tax benefit and come close to breaking even on the transaction itself.

Prior to 1987 it was possible through straddling to reduce your tax rate by as much as 30 percent. Ordinary income, which was taxed up to 50 percent, was converted into long-term capital gains, which were taxed at a maximum of 20 percent. Moreover, unlike other investments, commodity investments could qualify for long-term capital gain treatment after only six (rather than 12) months.

Treasury bills were a favorite vehicle for straddles because, unlike most securities, they are not classified as capital assets. Under tax rules, any gain or loss from the sale of Treasury bills was treated as ordinary income. These bills are sold at a discount of face value and appreciate to *par* (face value) at maturity. Because the bills are such safe collateral, margin requirements on these straddles are low, as little as 3 percent of the bills' face value. The following example shows you how a Treasury bill straddle might have worked.

Assume that on December 17 you sell short $1 million in Treasury bills due December 26, and you buy $1 million in Treasury bills due the following March 26, which you intend to sell on January 2. The March maturity date allows for what is generally considered a reasonable period of market risk. But for purposes of this example, assume that between December 26 and January 2 interest rates are high. The result is that you don't receive the full $1 million face value because the bills due December 26 have nine days to go until maturity. Assuming a discount of 16.83 percent, the purchase price is $995,793. On the maturity date, you have to cover the sale of borrowed securities. This will cost $1 million, giving you a loss on the transaction of $4,027 for the year.

The $1 million in bills due March 26 that you buy after making the short sale have 99 days to maturity. Assuming a discount of 16.30 percent, the purchase price is $955,175. When you sell those bills on January 2, you collect $962,419, for a gain of $7,244.

After commission costs of approximately $1,200, the net economic gain on the two transactions is $1,837. This gain is reduced by any interest charges on a margin account. In terms of the tax deduction, the straddles save an investor in the 50 percent bracket $2,103.50 in taxes for the first year ($4,027 × .50).

Such commodity straddles appear to be no-lose situations. In fact, though, they may turn out to be no-win situations. The Internal Revenue Service views these transactions as "wholly tax motivated and without any real economic substance." Internal Revenue Service staff members who screen and classify returns are being trained to recognize "straddle" returns and are targeting them for an audit. According to the IRS, "taxpayers claiming tax benefits from these transactions will face a substantial likelihood of having their return selected for audit and their claims of artificial losses disallowed on examination."

The bottom line on commodity tax straddles is that until they have been court approved as legitimate tax strategies, they should be avoided. The Economic Recovery Tax Act has made this shelter a dead issue by requiring you to "mark to market"—i.e., close all your positions even if they are *not* sold at year-end. Moreover, the Tax Reform Act of 1986 eliminated the capital gains deduction. There is no reason, therefore, to use a tax straddle as a tax shelter. Stay away from straddles. There are too many *legal* tax shelters for you to buy into this kind of audit *dis*allowance.

# 72

## Art Reproduction

Art reproduction is another tax shelter that you should forget. Almost all lithograph shelters are going to be disallowed by the Internal Revenue Service. Under a lithograph shelter, you will be asked to purchase a lithograph plate that the artist uses to make a limited number of prints (50 to 500). An estimate of revenues available from sales is used to value the plates, from which investment tax credits and depreciation could be obtained.

In a typical shelter, you would give an artist $30,000 cash, say, plus a promissory note for $170,000 and assume the entire responsibility for marketing the prints. Prior to 1986, you would then seek a 10 percent investment tax credit and a first-year depreciation of 25 percent. At a 50 percent tax rate, you would reduce your tax payments by $43,750 [(200,000 − 10,000) × .25 = $47,500 in depreciation, or a tax savings of $23,750 at a 50 percent rate, plus an additional $20,000 from the 10 percent investment tax credit]. You would therefore be $13,750 ahead. However, the Internal Revenue Service would view the personal promissory note as a sham unless there was a real compulsion to pay it and would argue that the actual investment was only $30,000. In fact, most of these deals are marketed with the assumption that the full risk of the personal promissory note will be paid only out of the proceeds from the sale of the prints. In effect, they *are* really nothing but shams.

Out of the $30,000 cash paid, $7,500 might go for printing, advertising, and sales; $7,500 to accountants and lawyers; $6,000 to the promoter; and $9,000 to the artist. You must either market the prints yourself or hire the promoter's "marketing" firm to do so for you. In one case, an investor sought to claim depreciation deductions and investment tax credit as a result of the purchase of a lithographic plate "master" and prints made from the "master."[3] According to the Internal Revenue Service, no depreciation could be claimed because the master was a nondepreciable work of art with

---

3.   Revenue Ruling 70-432, I.R.B. 1979–53, 20.

a life of less than three years. The bottom line on this shelter is: Stay away.

# 73    Noncash Gift Shelters

This is another that you should avoid unless you are anxious to be part of an audit. The noncash gift shelter works as follows: You are asked to buy property such as books, Bibles, gemstones, etc., that are supposed to appreciate in value. You hold these objects for a period longer than twelve months and then contribute these "investments" to a charity. In return, you will get a charitable contribution deduction equal to the fair market value of the property.

For example, assume that you purchase rare Bibles at a cost of $5,000, and one year later they "appreciate" to a value of $30,000. You then contribute those Bibles to a church, claiming a deduction of their alleged fair market value of $30,000. If you are in the 33 percent bracket, this saves you $9,900 in tax—a $4,900 profit over your cost.

This is another shelter that the Internal Revenue Service considers nothing more than a sham. In one case a taxpayer-investor purchased limited-edition art books at a volume discount and then donated them to charity. The Internal Revenue Service ruled that the investor's activity was tantamount to that of an art dealer and that the investor's charitable deduction had to be reduced by the amount of gain that would not have been long-term capital gain had the investor sold the books.[4] In other words, the deduction was limited to only the cost basis.

Internal Revenue Service auditors have been instructed to look for noncash gift deductions exceeding $5,000, particularly for deductions of well over the property's cost or basis, and especially if the property was held for less than two years. They will consistently challenge any determination of fair market value and try to disallow all of these shelters that they catch.

I question the validity of the Internal Revenue Service's position where it applies to true investments (for instance, gemstones) that may appreciate substantially over a year's period. However, in *Anselmo* 80, T.C. No. 46, the Tax Court concluded that gems without settings would not be sold at retail, but rather sold to jewelers who would set the gems into rings or other jewelry. Since the jewelers are the consumers of gems, such stones should be

---

4.    Revenue Ruling 79-419, I.R.B. 1979–52, 9.

valued on the basis of what the jeweler would pay to a *wholesaler* to obtain comparable gems.

Nonetheless, even if your shelter were to be allowed as a matter of law, you would be buying an audit on the question of valuation. The courts have consistently ruled against the taxpayer in these situations. I therefore recommend avoiding these types of shelters where possible.

# 74

## Municipal Bond Swaps

A municipal bond swap is an intriguing tax idea that allows you to maintain your equivalent current investment and yet at the same time take a tax-deductible loss on it. The swap lets you write off current paper losses and keep the advantage of owning municipal bonds as a shelter from federal income taxes, and possibly from state and local taxes as well. When interest rates increase, municipal bonds will normally be traded at substantially less than their face value. To do a swap, you merely sell your devalued bonds. This gives you a tax deduction for the current year. Then you reinvest the proceeds in other municipals of comparable yield and quality.

If you are contemplating any kind of swap, you must be aware of—and *avoid*—the "wash sale": You can deduct the realized loss on your current federal income tax return by selling your devalued bonds any time right up through December 31. But the Internal Revenue Service will call it a wash sale—and disallow the loss deduction—if you turn around and buy the same bonds, or "substantially identical" ones, without waiting a full 30 days.

"Substantially identical" has never really been clearly defined. If the issuer is different, there should be absolutely no problem. But if the bonds you are selling and the bonds you are buying are from the same issuer, the farther apart they are in maturity or interest rate the safer you will be. At a minimum, you should look for a five-year difference in maturities, or a spread of at least 50 *basis points* (0.5 percent difference in yields to maturity).

If you hold the original bonds for a year or less, you have a short-term loss, which can be used to offset, dollar for dollar, gains from the sale of other assets. Likewise, long-term losses can be used to offset gains dollar for dollar.

Any loss up to $3,000 that isn't absorbed can be deducted from your ordinary income. Losses in excess of gains plus $3,000 can be carried over to future years.

# B  How to Analyze a Tax Shelter

The most important part of a tax shelter offering is the prospectus. It summarizes the deal, details the history of the participants, and gives you a lawyer's opinion as to the projected tax consequences. Read it carefully! The summary and introduction in the front of most prospectuses are a good starting point, but make sure that you go beyond them. Look at the section on sources and uses of the proceeds very carefully. This will indicate who gets what and how much of the proceeds are going to the promoters and their affiliates, as opposed to being invested in the main objective of the partnership. Read the tax risks and considerations section equally carefully, as this should explain in detail the various tax considerations that might affect you as an investor.

Choose carefully the lawyer or accountant who will evaluate the deal. An unfamiliar lawyer or accountant who brings a deal to your attention at a social gathering may simply be representing the promoters. Find out whether your lawyer or accountant will be receiving a commission from the promoters if the deal is sold. On the other hand, it could also be unwise to rely on your own lawyer or accountant in evaluating a deal. Lawyers and accountants are prejudiced in the other direction, since if the deal goes sour, they could lose you as a client. They therefore have very little incentive to recommend anything with any risk.

Make sure that the deal evidences an intent to make a profit. If a shelter is based on deductions of interest and depreciation, with only a remote possibility of the receipt of revenues, it stands a greater risk of being disallowed by the Internal Revenue Service. For example, a 1985 shelter that marked up a $10 product to $100, took a 10 percent investment tax credit to make the $10 initial contribution, and then took a depreciation on the whole $100 was a high risk and unlikely to be approved if questioned in an audit.

Always invest in a tax shelter on the basis of economic returns. For example, the phase-out rule with respect to actively managed real estate can also produce a devastatingly high marginal tax rate as you approach the phase-out point. For example, assume you and your spouse have $102,000 of adjusted gross income. You can claim up to $24,000 of losses from actively managed real estate. If you have $104,000 of adjusted gross income, then you claim $23,000 of deductions from such real estate activities. Assume instead that you had $1,000 of such losses from actively managed real estate activities and adjusted gross income of $148,000. Clearly the $1,000 is fully deductible. But, however, if you get a $2,000 raise, your adjusted gross income would rise to $150,000 and the $1,000 deduction would be disallowed. As a result, an extra $2,000 of gross income would be taxed at an effective rate of 49.5 percent, the reasons being that there would be a tax of $990 (33 percent of $3,000 increase in taxable income based on the extra $2,000 salary plus the $1,000 loss deduction), when your adjusted gross income rose only $2,000. This $990 increase in taxes on a $2,000 increase in your tax base produces a marginal rate of 49.5 percent.

Many shelters appear to give high write-offs on the basis of interest expense accrued according to the Rule of 78's. The Rule of 78's computes interest in a manner analagous to the sum of the year's digits methods for depreciation. The interest is ascertained by applying a fraction to the total interest due, the numerator of which is the number of payment periods remaining and the denominator of which is the sum of the periods. In Revenue Ruling 83-84, IRB 1983-23, 12, the IRS ruled that it would no longer recognize interest deductions computed under that rule which exceeded the "economic accrual of interest." An exception was made for short-term consumer loans in Rev. Proc. 83-40, IRB 1983-23, 22.

Determine the actual profit potential—that means measure the potential *after-tax return* against the *after-tax cost.* This allows a comparison of the cost of the tax shelter investment with other alternatives, such as stocks and bonds acquired with after-tax dollars. Make sure that you take into consideration how long it will take to get the yield from the after-tax dollars. For example, a three-to-one return ($3 of cash received for each $1 invested) looks better than a two-to-one return at first, but it will not be better if it takes several years longer to realize the full profit.

Examine the promoter's past history. What kind of track record does the person have? Have past deals been successful? Examine the financial statements of the general partner and evaluate them to ascertain that person's strength and staying power in the face of adversity. What are the sharing arrangements and front-end fees of the general partner? That person's share of revenues should be reasonably related to the services he or she renders to the program. Fees, commissions, and other front-end-loaded charges should be reasonable, too.

Does the program provide for additional assessments? You must be told (a) the maximum amount of additional capital that the general partner can assess for unexpected expenses, (b) when the assessment can be made, (c) the tax consequences of meeting the assessment, and (d) the penalty if you fail to comply.

CAREFULLY examine the forecast figures provided in the prospectus. Review even more carefully the footnotes accompanying the forecast, which explain the assumptions involved in putting that forecast together.

Review your state of mind. Probably the most important consideration that you must ponder before entering into a traditional tax shelter is your own personal tax-comfort level. Many people are not temperamentally suited to invest in projects that increase the possibility that they may be audited. It is important, therefore, for you to decide whether you can live comfortably with this added potential risk.

# 75

## Getting Out of the Tax Shelter

Tax shelters, by definition, are long-term investments. However, there may come a time when you need to get out of the shelter immediately because of pressing cash requirements. There are four major firms that purchase partnership units:

- Liquidity Fund (1900 Powell Street, Emeryville, California 94608; 415-652-1462) buys public and private real estate programs, with the exception of government-subsidized housing partnerships.

- MacKenzie Securities (650 California Street, San Francisco, California 94108; 800-854-8357; in California, 800-821-4252) buys only public and private real estate deals that are at least three years old and have current cash flow. The firm won't buy private programs if the investor still owes payments to the sponsors.

- Equity Resources Group (1776 Massachusetts Avenue, Cambridge, Massachusetts 02140; 617-876-4800) deals only in private real estate programs. It turns down programs with more than half the investment unpaid.

- Livon Oil (220 Bush Street, San Francisco, California 94104; 415-781-6427) buys units in public and private oil and gas drilling and income programs. It also won't purchase partnerships from investors who still owe payments to the sponsors.

Other such firms include the following:

- Raymond James Limited Partnership
Trading Desk
140 66th Street North
St. Petersburg, FL 33710
1-800-237-7591

- National Partnership Exchange
  P.O. Box 578
  Tampa, FL 33601
  (813)222-0555

- Investors Advantage Corp.
  The Fountains Financial Center
  US 19 North
  Suite 302
  Palm Harbor, FL 33563
  1-800-282-5865

- Partnership Securities Exchange
  1814 Franklin Street
  Suite 820
  Oakland, CA 94612
  (415)763-5555

- Realty Repurchase, Inc.
  50 California Street
  Suite 1300
  San Francisco, CA 94111
  1-800-233-7357

- Oppenheimer & Bigelow
  489 Fifth Avenue
  New York, NY 10017
  1-800-431-7811

In addition, the new Partnership Exchange (10051 Fifth Street, North, Box 21438, St. Petersburg, Florida 33742; 800-356-2739; in Florida, 800-336-2739) matches buyers and sellers of public real estate, oil and gas, equipment leasing, and cable TV partnerships.

# 76

## Master Limited Partnerships

A master limited partnership is not a tax shelter. It is merely a vehicle or form in which an investment can be made. A master limited partnership is a large publicly registered limited partnership that is the principal or sole owner of multiple assets or partnerships that themselves may have been structured as tax shelters.

Master limited partnerships can pass through income and losses like traditional limited partnerships but provide investors greater liquidity. Units in numerous master limited partnerships are listed for trading on national securities exchanges, and master limited partnerships generally have the ability to issue additional units in the future.

There are two basic forms of master limited partnerships. The first is the roll-up, in which multiple assets or small limited partnerships are consolidated into a large single master limited partnership. The second is the roll-out, in which the apparent entity, like a corporation, spins off some of its assets into a separate master limited partnership. A third form is known as a roll-in. In this form new assets are put into a master limited partnership with the promise to add additional assets in the future.

Master limited partnerships may be attractive as passive income generators to shelter passive losses from other activities. For example, dividends distributed by real estate investment trusts (REITs) are classified as portfolio income, which cannot be sheltered by passive losses. However, income distributed by real estate master limited partnerships will be treated as passive income.

Another advantage of the master limited partnership is that it can pass through to investors a greater portion of each dollar of operating income than a corporation since the master limited partnership itself is not subject to taxation. Moreover, unlike REITs, a master limited partnership can actively engage in real estate activities, and they are entitled to more favorable depreciation. The master limited partnership structure, however, increases the difficulty of complying with the new partnership allocation rules because of the large number of investors and constant trading of partnership interests.

The Revenue Act of 1987 had a substantial impact on master limited partnerships. Such partnerships, falling under the classification of publicly traded partnerships (PTPs), will be treated as corporations for tax years after 1987. An exception is made, however, for those partnerships whose gross income is predominantly (90 percent or more) "qualifying income." Qualifying income consists of the following:

1.  Interest: This category does not include interest derived in the conduct of a financial or insurance business, nor does it include amounts contingent on profits.

2.  Dividends.

3.  Real property rents: This category generally includes rents from interest in real property, charges for services customarily furnished in connection with the rental of real property, and rental income attributable to personal property in connection with the lease of real property. Amounts contingent on income or profits are not generally treated as rents from real property.

4.  Gain from the sale or other disposition of real property.

5.  Income or gains from the exploration, development, mining or production, refining, transportation, or marketing of any mineral or natural resource.

6.  Any gain from the sale or other disposition of a capital asset or Section 1231 asset held for the production of any type of income described in 1 through 5, above.

7.  Income and gains from commodities (other than those held for sale to customers in the ordinary course of business) and futures, options, or forward contracts with respect to other commodities.

Moreover, although the general corporate treatment applies for tax years beginning after 1987, in the case of an "existing partnership" it applies to tax years beginning only after 1997. An existing partnership is any one of the following:

1.  A partnership that was publicly traded on December 17, 1987.

2.  A partnership for which a registration statement was filed with the Securities and Exchange Commission on or before December 17, 1987.

3.  A partnership for which an application was filed with a state regulatory commission on or before December 17, 1987, seeking permission to restructure a portion of a corporation as a publicly traded partnership.

In the case of publicly traded partnerships that are not treated as corporations, the passive loss rules are to be applied separately for the items attributable to each PTP. The net losses of a partner from each PTP are to be suspended at the partner level and carried forward and netted against the partner's share of the nonportfolio income of that PTP in a later year or years. Generally, these losses may not be applied against passive income from other activities. Similarly, a partner's share of the credits are to be suspended, carried forward, and applied against the tax liability of a subsequent year or years attributable to that PTP. Generally, these credits may not be applied against tax liability attributable to other activities. Moreover, a partner's share in the net income of a PTP (both portfolio and business income) will generally not be treated as income from a passive activity; that is, it will generally be treated as portfolio income. However, a partner's share of the net business (nonportfolio) income of a PTP will be treated as passive income for carryover purposes. This means that a partner's share of a PTP's net business income may be offset by any suspended business losses of that PTP carried forward from an earlier year, but a partner's share of portfolio income may not be offset by any other current or carryover losses from other passive activities.

# CHAPTER 8

# Super Tax Shelters

*"When more of the people's sustenance is exacted through the form of taxation than is necessary to meet the just obligations of government . . . , such exaction becomes ruthless extortion and a violation of the fundamental principles of a free government."*

GROVER CLEVELAND
Second Annual Message
December 1886

This is the chapter that alone is worth more than a hundred times the cost of this book. Each of the following shelters is completely legal and has been sold to sophisticated taxpayers for thousands of dollars. These shelters have been worth the cost—they have saved those taxpayers many multiples of their acquisition price in taxes not paid. Each of these supershelters will be presented, explained, and structured in detail. Study them well. They will show you how legally and painlessly to reduce your own taxes to zero.

# A   Family Shifts

The first rule of income taxation is that a tax liability for personal service income may not be avoided by the earner of that income by assignment or other transfer before the income is realized. If you perform services that earn monetary reward, that income will be taxed to you. The second law of income taxation, however, is that income earned from *property* belongs to the owner of that property. Therefore, the first key to reducing your taxes is to transfer income-producing property to a family member in a lower bracket. If you make a bona fide transfer of income-producing property that you own, you have effectively shifted all future income from that property. After the transfer, the future income and all income tax due on that income will belong to the new owner in the lower tax bracket.

Part of your solution to the problem of reducing your tax, therefore, is to get your current income taxed to lower-bracketed family members. This strategy is based on the premise that a family is an economic and social unit and that it is immaterial to the welfare of the family as a whole which member derives income or owns property. From a tax perspective, however, it is extremely material.

For example, assume you are in the 33 percent bracket and transfer $500 of annual income to your son so that it is taxable to him instead of to you. Immediately you save $165 in taxes. Furthermore, the whole $500 will come tax-free to a child who has no other income, even if the $500 represents unearned income (for instance, interest, dividends, or rents). Moreover, not only can the savings be multiplied by the number of children involved, but if your son is under age 19 or is a full-time student, you can still claim the personal exemption for him on your tax return as long as you supply more than one-half of his total support.

The shift does not have to be made to a child. Suppose you are supporting a parent out of your current income. You might save an enormous amount of taxes if you could transfer some of that income so that the tax would be shifted from you directly to your lower-bracketed parent. For 1988, your parents, if over age 65, get personal exemptions of $1,950 × 2 and a standard deduction of $5,000 + $600 × 2. Thus, if you are paying $10,000 a year of your after-tax income to your parents, you could save $3,300 a year in taxes if you are in the 33 percent bracket. Such a shift of income can be accomplished through a direct gift of income-producing property or by using one of a number of trusts that will be examined later in this chapter.

The standard deduction now permits the tax-free transfer of $500 of investment income to a child or other member of your family who has no other income. Furthermore, if the child is of sufficient age to work, that child can earn an *additional* $2,500 a year in income and still pay zero taxes. Remember, however, that the objective is not necessarily that the family member pay zero taxes, but rather that the taxes paid be less than what you would pay if the income were taxed directly to you. For example, even if that family member is in the 15 percent bracket, a shift of $1,000 in income from you in the 33 percent would result in a net savings of $180.

There are a number of ways to effect an income shift within the family. Remember, when transactions among family members are genuine, they must be given full legal effect for tax purposes.

Note, however, that the Tax Reform Act of 1986 limits the availability of certain income-shifting techniques to children under age 14. Under the new law, all *net unearned income* (as defined in computation B below) of a child who has not attained age 14 before the close of the taxable year and who has at least one parent alive at the close of the taxable year will be taxed to the child at special rates. This applies to all net unearned income; the source of the assets creating the income or the date the income-producing property was transferred is irrelevant.

The tax payable by the child on net unearned income is essentially the additional amount of tax that the parent would have had to pay if the net unearned income of the child were included in the parent's taxable income.

If parents have two or more children with unearned income to be taxed at the parent's marginal tax rate, all of the children's applicable unearned income will be added together and the tax calculated. The tax is then allocated to each child based on the child's pro rata share of unearned income.

The intent of the law is to create three stages:

1.   There will be no tax on the first $500 of unearned income because of

the child's standard deduction. (The standard deduction offsets *un*earned income first, up to $500. Any remaining standard deduction is then available to offset earned income.)

2. The next $500 of unearned income will be taxed to the child at the child's bracket.

3. Unearned income in excess of the first $1,000 will be taxed to the child at the appropriate parent's rate.

*Computation A*

Technically the tax is computed by the following process:

(a) Compute the tax the child would have to pay on earned and unearned income at the child's rates.     $_____

(b) Compute the sum of
   (1) the tax payable if the child had no *net earned income,* plus     $_____
   (2) the child's share of the *allocable parental tax*     $_____

   Total     $_____

The tax on unearned income of children under age 14 is the greater of (a) or (b).

The term *unearned income* means income from sources *other* than wages, salaries, professional fees, and other amounts received as compensation for personal services actually rendered.

*Computation B*

Net unearned income can be determined by the following process:

(a) State total unearned income (or the child's taxable income if lower).     $_____

(b) Calculate the *protected amount,* the sum of     $_____
   (1) up to $500, plus
   (2) an *additional amount* which is either (a) allowable deductions directly related to the production of the child's unearned income

assuming the child itemizes or, if larger,
(b) $500   $ _____

Total   $ _____

(c)   Net unearned income is (a) minus (b).   $ _____

The $500 amounts allowable above are increased by inflation in taxable years beginning in calendar years after 1988.

## Computation C

To compute the allocable parental tax, use the following process:

(a)   State the tax that *would* have been imposed on the parent's taxable income if all the unearned income of *all* the parent's children under age 14 were added to the parent's taxable income.   $ _____

(b)   State the tax that *would* have been imposed on the parent's taxable income if *none* of the un-earned income of the parent's children under 14 were includable.   $ _____

(c)   Allocable parental tax is (a) minus (b).   $ _____

Note that in computing a deduction or credit of the parent for the (a) computation above, the net unearned income of all children cannot be taken into account.

## Computation D

To compute the child's share of the allocable parental tax, use the following process:

(a)   State the total allocable parental tax.   $ _____

(b)   State the child's net unearned income.   $ _____

(c)   State the aggregate net unearned income of all the parent's children under age 14.   $ _____

(d)   Divide (b) by (c).   $ _____

(e)    The child's share of allocable parental tax
       [multiply (d) by (a)].                                                    $_____

The parent whose taxable income will be taken into account is the cus-todial parent of the child in the case of unmarried parents. In the case of parents who are married but filing separately, the individual with the greater taxable income will be the parent whose taxable income is used in these calculations.

The parent of a child under 14 receiving unearned income is required to provide that child with the parent's taxpayer identification number (TIN). That number (typically the parent's social security number) must be included in the child's tax return.

Upon written request a parent's return must be disclosed to the child or the child's legal representative to the extent necessary for the child's return to be properly filed.

Two steps are necessary in the basic computational process. Step one determines how much, if any, of the child's unearned income is taxed to the child at the parent's bracket. Step two determines how much of the child's in-come is tax-free and how much is taxed at the child's own rates.

Here's how the law would work with respect to a child under age 14 in 1988:

*Example 1:* Assume the child has $400 of unearned income and no earned income. Step 1: Unearned income is $400. From that you would subtract the flat $500 (maximum) allowed under computation B above. It would not be necessary (or allowable) to use the second protective amount in computation B to arrive at net unearned income. Step 2: The child's standard deduction is limited to the greater of (a) $500 or (b) earned income. Here that amount would be $500. Therefore, there is no tax on this $500 amount. This eliminates any tax in this example.

*Example 2:* Assume the child has $900 of unearned income and no earned income. Step 1: Unearned income is $900. From that you sub-tract the flat $500 maximum from computation B. The protective amount allowed in addition to the $500 is the greater of (a) itemized deductions directly connected with the production of unearned income or (b) a maximum of $500. The two protective amounts exceed the $900 so there would be no net unearned income subject to tax at the parent's rates. Step 2: The child's standard deduction eliminates the tax on the first $500 of unearned income. The remaining $400 is subject to tax at the child's rates.

*Example 3:* Assume the child has $1,300 of unearned income and no earned income. Step 1: Unearned income is $1,300. From that you subtract the flat $500 maximum from computation B above. The additional protective amount that will be shielded against taxation at the parent's rates in addition to that is $500. The remaining $300 ($1,300 − $1,000) is the net unearned income. Three hundred dollars will be taxed at the appropriate parent's top rate. Step 2: The child's standard deduction eliminates the tax on the first $500 of unearned income. Three hundred dollars will be taxed to the child but at the parent's rate. The remaining $500 will be subject to tax at the child's rate.

*Example 4:* Assume the child has $300 of unearned income and $700 of earned income. Step 1: Unearned income is $300. From that you subtract the flat $500 amount from computation B above. This eliminates any threat of a parental tax on the $300 of unearned income. Step 2: The child's $700 (the greater of $500 or earned income) standard deduction eliminates the tax on the entire $300 of unearned income and $400 (out of $700) of earned income. Therefore $300 ($1,000 gross less $700 standard deduction) would be taxable to the child at the child's rate.

*Example 5:* Assume the child has $900 of unearned income and $800 of earned income. Step 1: Unearned income is $900. From that you subtract the flat $500 amount from computation B above. This leaves $400 exposed to the parental tax, but the threat is entirely eliminated by using the additional protective amount from computation B. So none of the unearned income would be subject to the parental tax rate. Step 2: The child's standard deduction would be $800 (the greater of $500 or earned income). This eliminates the tax on $800 of the $900 of unearned income. Therefore the child would have to pay tax on $100 ($900 − $800) at the child's rates. In addition, the child would pay tax on the entire $800 of earned income at the child's rates, a total of $900 exposed to tax at the child's rates.

*Example 6:* Assume the child has $1,200 of unearned income and $300 of earned income. Assume itemized deductions directly related to the production of the unearned income are $400 (in excess of the 2 percent floor). Assume additional deductions total $400. Step 1: Unearned income is $1,200. From that you would subtract the flat $500 and the additional protective amount which would be $500, the greater of the

$400 itemized deductions directly connected with the production of income or the $500 flat amount. Therefore the child's net unearned income would be $200 ($1,200 − $1,000). That amount of net unearned income would be subject to tax and payable by the child at the parent's bracket. Step 2: The child's standard deduction would be $500 (the greater of $500 or $300 of earned income). Itemized deductions eliminate the tax on $800 of income. Therefore you would use the larger of the two amounts, $800, to offset income. Four hundred dollars of the additional deductions would be applied against the $300 of earned income. This eliminates any tax on earned income and leaves $100 in additional deductions to be added to the $400 of directly related deductions which can be applied against the $1,200 of unearned income. This exposes $700 of unearned income to tax ($1,200 − $500). Two hundred dollars of the unearned income is already taxed to the child at the parent's rate. Therefore the child must pay tax at the child's rates on $500 ($700 − $200).

*Example 7:* Assume the child has $3,000 of unearned income and $700 of earned income. Assume $800 of itemized deductions (net of the 2 percent floor) are directly connected with the production of the unearned income. The child has $200 of other deductions. Step 1: Unearned income is $3,000. From that you would subtract the flat $500 amount and the additional protective amount of $800, the greater of (a) $500 or (b) $800 of itemized deductions directly related to the production of the unearned income. Therefore $1,700 would be considered net unearned income and taxed to the child at the parent's rate. Step 2: The child's standard deduction would be $700, the greater of (a) $700 earned income or (b) $500. But since deductions total $1,000, that higher amount would be used to offset income. Eight hundred dollars of itemized deductions directly related to unearned income would be applied against that income so that $2,200 of unearned income would remain subject to tax. Two hundred dollars of other deductions would reduce this $2,200 amount to $2,000. One thousand seven hundred dollars of this amount would be taxed to the child at the parent's bracket so that $1,000 would be taxed to the child at the child's bracket (including the $700 of earned income).

## PLANNING SUGGESTIONS

Note that the so-called *kiddie tax* rules discussed above apply regardless of who gave the children the income-producing property. They apply even if the cash or other property generating the income was transferred prior to 1987. So income from existing custodial accounts and income distributed from existing nongrantor trusts will be taxable to children under 14 at the parent's rates regardless of when the account or trust was created.

It may appear that the advantage of shifting income was eliminated by the reduction in bracket spreads (until 1987 the spread from the top bracket of 50 percent to the bottom bracket of 11 percent was 39 percentage points, but in 1988 the spread will be from 33 percent to 15 percent, an 18 percentage point difference). But this is an oversimplification. Once a child becomes 14, all earned and unearned income is taxed at the child's rate. So dropping $10,000 a year of income from the 33 percent bracket to the 15 percent bracket will save 18 percent per year of the amount of income shifted. In 10 years that amounts to $18,000 in tax savings!

If a child can be claimed as a dependent on a parent's return, the child may not take a personal exemption. Furthermore, the child's standard deduction is limited to the greater of (a) $500 or (b) the child's earned income (up to a maximum of that year's standard deduction). This will force more parents than ever to file tax returns for their children (children with more than $500 of unearned income will have to file income tax returns), those returns will be more complicated than ever (and therefore the cost of filing the returns will be increased), and the taxes payable by children will rise precipitously.

There are still many ways to shift both wealth and income and save taxes.

1.  Give a Series EE U.S. Savings Bond that will not mature until after the donee-child is age 14. No tax will be payable until the bond is redeemed. At that time the gain will be taxed at the child's relatively lower tax bracket. Remember that this strategy will not work if the child already owns Series EE bonds and is already reporting each year's interest accrual as income. Once the election to report income currently is made, it is irrevocable.

2.  Give growth stocks (or growth stock mutual funds) which pay little or no current dividends. The child will therefore pay no tax currently and can hold the stock until reaching age 14. Upon a sale the child will be taxed at the child's bracket.

3.  Give *deep discount* tax-free municipal bonds that mature on or after the child's 14th birthday. The bond interest will be tax-free to the child and the discount (face less cost basis) will be taxed to the child at the child's bracket when the bond is redeemed at maturity.

4.  Employ your children. Pay them a reasonable salary for work they actually perform. Remember that the new law standard deduction for children is the greater of (a) $500 or (b) earned income (up to a 1988 limit of $3,000). Regardless of how much is paid to the child, the business will have a deduction at its tax bracket, and the amount will be taxable to the child at the child's bracket. The child could establish an IRA to shelter income further.

5.  Sell all nonappreciated property (be sure to consider brokerage costs and time value of money) and purchase tax-free municipals for the child.

6.  Consider the multiple advantages of a *term of years* charitable remainder trust for children over age 14—so the income will be taxed to the child, but the grantor will receive an immediate income tax deduction.

7.  In making gifts to your children consider support obligation cases such as *Braun, Sutliff,* and *Miller.* Parents who can with ease meet the support needs of even an adult college-age child may be considered obligated to provide support. If UGMA (the Uniform Gifts to Minors Act) or 2503(c) trust funds are used to send a child to college, will the parent be taxed? Worse yet, do these cases mean the UGMA custodian (or 2503(c)) trustee violates a fiduciary duty by using such funds to pay for a college education when it's the parent's duty (thus making such funds unavailable for the very purpose for which they were intended)?

    Assuming the support problems addressed above are not applicable, judicious use of a 2503(c) trust (but not a UGMA account) will allow significant income shifting. The trust can accumulate income while the beneficiary is under age 14 and avoid the kiddie tax. Although only the first $5,000 of that income is taxed at a 15 percent rate, it may not be necessary to fund the trust with property generating more than $5,000 of income. This is so because the 2503(c) trust is designed to make distributions of principal and income to meet its funding objectives.

8.  Emphasis should now be placed on *convertible planning*—the use of a *value shift* followed at the appropriate time by an *income shift*. For example, a GRIT (Grantor Retained Income Trust) would retain for a

trust grantor the right to all trust income for a specified number of years. At the end of that time all income and principal will go to the grantor's child (who by then will be 14 or older). None of the principal or appreciation will be in the grantor's estate if the grantor survives the trust term. (Consider a savings clause that terminates the trust in favor of the grantor if tax law is changed to provide that a completed gift does not occur until the donor's interest is terminated.) Consider the joint purchase of an asset with the child. The parent buys and keeps an interest (either for life or a specified term of years), while the child buys and keeps the remainder. This can save estate taxes and generate deductions for the parent. The child's purchase money should come from the other parent, a grandparent, or some source other than the other owner-parent.

9.  Life insurance and annuity policies that stay within statutory guidelines (ask for a written guarantee from the home office) for life insurance should be particularly attractive, assuming *loading* costs are relatively low and/or backended. This includes universal, variable, and traditional whole life of the single-, annual-, and limited-payment types. In the case of the SPWL (Single-Premium Whole Life) the entire single premium paid at purchase starts earning the declared interest rate immediately. The cost of insurance and expenses is recovered by the insurer from the difference between the declared interest rate and the rate the insurer actually earns. If surrendered, any unrecovered expenses are deducted from the policy's cash values. The owner can obtain cash values at any time by (1) surrender (gain over cost is taxable) or (2) loan (loan interest is probably nondeductible). Interest is charged at about the same rate credited on borrowed sums and is free of current tax. Earnings compound free of current taxation. Unlike tax-free municipal bonds there is no market risk, and SPWL is highly liquid. A parent can purchase the product on his or her own life which makes college education for the children more likely, and the parent does not have to give up control or make a gift.

10. Concentrate on gift and estate tax savings devices such as the annual exclusion. Parents should consider gifting $10,000–$20,000 a year of non-income-producing assets to a minor's trust or custodial account, which could be converted into income-producing assets slowly after the child turns age 14. The fund can become self-liquidating and exhaust itself by the time the child finishes college/graduate school.

11. If the parent's return shows a loss, will the child's return be affected by it? The Code is silent.

12. The custodial parent is often the mother who may have less income (and therefore be in a lower tax bracket) than the father. But what about the logistics of tax-return disclosure where the father is filing returns and paying tax for the children? Suppose he doesn't want her to know how much he's put aside for the kids and she doesn't want to reveal her income or her new husband's income. Furthermore, the filing father cannot prepare the children's returns until the mother prepares her returns. What about multiple children from multiple marriages? Split custody?

13. The 1986 TRA still provides for limited shifting of income to children under the age of 14 with the $500 minimum standard deduction and the special rule taxing the first $500 of unearned income at the child's marginal tax rate. Assuming that the parent has the highest marginal tax rate in 1988 (33 percent during the phase-out of the fifteen percent bracket), the first $500 of income shifted to the child would result in $165 of tax savings ($500 × .33), and the next $500 of transferred income would result in $90 of tax savings [$500 × (.33 − .15)].

    Over a period of years, the tax savings generated by shifting $1,000 of income to the child can be significant. For example, if the annual tax savings were invested at 8 percent for a 14-year period, the total tax savings and interest would be $6,174. Furthermore, the gifts necessary to generate the $1,000 of unearned income would closely approximate the $10,000 annual gift tax exclusion for the parent, so that little, if any, of his or her unified credit is used. (Parents electing to make a split gift would have a $20,000 exclusion to offset such gifts.)

The above limitations apply only to the shifting of unearned income— e.g., interest, dividends, rents, etc. For those shifts discussed later in this chapter, assume that whenever there is a reference to shifting unearned income to children, those children are not under age 14. The following techniques can be used to shift income to lower-income members of your family.

# 77

## Outright Gifts

A gift of income-producing property to members of your family is perhaps the most common method of splitting income to gain a tax advantage. The simplest way to transfer money, tax-free, is by gifts in relatively small lumps. You can give an annual gift of $10,000 per person to any number of family members—$20,000 if the gift is made jointly with a spouse—without incurring any gift liability. In order to qualify for the $10,000 or the $20,000 exclusion in the year the gift is made, it must be a gift of a *present interest* (current value). A gift tax return is required for any gifts in excess of these amounts to any recipient in any year if the gift is one of a present interest. A gift tax return is required for a gift of *any amount* if it is of a future interest. A gift is a completed transfer of the entire legal and beneficial interest in the property given.

For a gift to your spouse, there is now an unlimited gift tax marital deduction. If the family members to whom you wish to give gifts are adults, then normally there are no problems. This is *not* true if the objects of your income shifting are minor children, who lack full legal capacity. In consequence, legal difficulties are often encountered in connection with their ability to manage and dispose of the property that they acquire. Furthermore, they normally lack full maturity and it is often less desirable from a practical standpoint to give them control over property.

Certain types of property are more suited than others to practical ownership by minors. Securities that require no management control can be put in the name of a minor when there is no desire to dispose of them before majority. If there is such a desire, the securities should be in bearer form or registered in the name of an adult nominee who may dispose of them at the direction of the minor. Under such circumstances you should file a Form 1087 putting the Internal Revenue Service on notice as to the true ownership of the stock. Alternatively, savings bonds may be purchased and registered in the sole name of a minor and may be redeemed at the option of the minor or a parent.

Cash is the simplest thing to give to a minor. It may be kept in a savings account by the parent in trust for the child. If you want to give cash to a family member but must sell appreciated stock to do so, it is normally cheaper to give your family member the securities and *then* have them sold. Any gain realized will be taxed at the lower marginal tax bracket rate of that person if he or she is 14 or older.

It is very important to note that under no circumstances should funds transferred to a minor be used to satisfy a parent's legal obligation of support (see *Sutliff v. Sutliff,* 489 A.2d 764 [Super. Ct. PA 1985], and *Braun v. Commissioner,* T.C. Memo 1984-285). If funds are so used, the income will be taxed to the parent!

### GUARDIANS

Many of the practical and legal difficulties inherent in dealing with minors can be alleviated either by having a guardian appointed for the minor or by creating a trust for the benefit of the minor. A guardian must be appointed by the state court having jurisdiction over such matters. There is normally little difficulty in securing the appointment on the petition, with the consent of both parents. Once appointed, the guardian usually becomes responsible to the appointing court for the proper and faithful performance of any duties. The judiciary standards governing a guardian's investment powers are those set by state law. A guardian is not allowed a choice or discretion beyond standards that are usually quite conservative. There are, however, a number of problems in using a guardian. The guardian is usually required by state law to furnish a bond for the faithful performance of duties. If sureties are required on the bond, the guardian is further restricted by the supervision exercised by the sureties. Furthermore, the guardian may be required to get court approval and certification that any actions—for instance, a sale of securities—are in the best interest of the ward.

Each state has its own standards and requirements detailing the duties and responsibilities of a guardian. For example, some statutes require that annual or periodic accounts be presented for approval by the courts. On the other hand, many of these provisions are often disregarded in a parent-guardian situation where harmony prevails within the family. This is because, as a practical matter, the courts usually do not take any action except on a complaint of a party in interest.

### TRUSTS

Many of the technical and legal difficulties of guardianship can be eliminated through the use of a trust for the benefit of the minor. The standards governing the investment and management powers of the trustee may be as broad or narrow as the creator of the trust desires. If the trust that is created comes into being during your lifetime (*inter vivos* trust), that trust usually is under no direct court supervision. Furthermore, if you should so provide, no bond will be required by the trustee for faithful performance of duties and no court approval will be necessary for the disposal of trust assets in the usual course of the trustee's administration of that trust. Furthermore, while it is usually preferable to have an independent trustee, it is legally permissible for you as a parent to act as trustee.

You should be aware, however, that there are certain limits and dangers in the use of the trust for income shifting:

1.  The income must not be "applied or distributed for the support or maintenance of a beneficiary (other than the grantor's spouse) whom the grantor is legally obligated to support or maintain." You have the legal obligation to support your minor children. If the income or principal of a trust you create is used to discharge this obligation, it is regarded as your income and taxable to you. The solution here is to use the funds for nonsupport purposes. For example, in most states a college education would not constitute a legal obligation that would fall under the umbrella of "support." In the case of *Frederick C. Braun, Jr, et al. vs. Commissioner* (T.C Memo 1984-285) however, the Tax Court found that under New Jersey law, financially able parents have the legal obligation to provide their children with a college education. The court therefore ruled that to the extent that income from two trusts was used to pay for tuition, room, and board for Braun's children, the income was taxable to Braun. The solution here would have been to distribute the income directly to the children and have them pay for their own college expenses. Structured that way, the income would not have been taxable to the parents. (See also the Pennsylvania case of *Sutliff v. Sutliff,* 489 A.2d 764, 1986, wherein the Appellate Court held that a parent may not use Uniform Gifts to Minors Act [UGMA] funds for a child's support. The import of this case, which arose out of a divorce situation, is that the court ruled that the parental duty of support may extend to providing a college education, even though the child has attained an age of majority under general state law but not under UGMA. See also *Stone,* T.C. Memo 1987-454, wherein the Tax Court again ruled that trust payments for private school tuition are within a parent's legal support obligation; thus, such payments are taxable to the grantor/

parent instead of the minor trust beneficiary. *Stone* involved only the payment of private school tuition to minor beneficiaries, thus avoiding the more difficult question of the support obligation in regard to payments of college expenses for adult children. These cases follow the analysis in *Braun* with reference to a college education constituting parental support, and its solution should be approached in the same manner—i.e., distributing the income directly to the children and having them pay for their own education expenses.)

2.  The trust must *not* be set up so that it could be considered to be carrying on a business or as having sufficient attributes of a corporation to make it taxable as a corporation by the federal government. An ordinary, valid, and legal trust is not an association taxed as a corporation.

3.  The property contributed to the trust by gift must not be deemed a gift of a future interest. If it is, the gift will not be entitled to the benefits of the annual exclusion for gift tax purposes. A gift to a minor, in trust or otherwise, will *not* be considered a gift of a future interest (and the annual exclusion will be available) if:

    a)  the property and income may be used for the benefit of the minor; *and*

    b)  any amount not so used will pass to the minor at age 21, or to that person's estate, or to any testamentary appointee in the event of an early death. A gift of an income interest that meets this test is considered a present interest.

4.  The trust must be irrevocable or, if the transfers to the trust were made prior to March 2, 1986, irrevocable for at least 10 years, and you as a grantor cannot retain powers that, in the eyes of the tax law, constitute a beneficial interest in the property.[1] I will examine these 10-year trusts in detail under the section on Clifford Trusts.

   To simplify the procedures for making gifts to minors of securities and other specified property, all states have enacted what is known as the Uniform Gift to Minors Act. The effect of this act is to permit such gifts to be made through a custodian, and to permit a subsequent transfer without the

---

1.  Internal Revenue Code, Section 676.

appointment of a guardian or the creation of a trust. Under the Act, securities can be transferred to minors by registering them in the donor's name, in the name of an adult member of the minor's family, or in the guardian's name, as *custodian* for the minor, and delivering the securities to the custodian. If the donor is the custodian, registration constitutes delivery. Securities in bearer form can be given by delivery to an adult member of the minor's family (other than the donor) or to the guardian as custodian for the minor, together with the deed in statutory form.

The custodian gets the managerial power a guardian would have, and the minor gets absolute legal title to the securities. The custodian can sell and reinvest, and can collect income and accumulate it or apply it for the minor's benefit. When the minor reaches the age of majority (21 or, in some states, 18), the custodian must turn over the securities and any accumulated income. If the minor dies before then, the securities and the income are part of the estate. Remember, however, that any income from the transfer that is used to discharge, in whole or in part, the legal obligation to support and maintain a minor is *pro tanto* taxable to the person who made the transfer. Furthermore, you should note that if you are the donor and name yourself as custodian of the securities or succeed to custodianship, your death before the minor reaches the age of majority will throw the securities into your estate.

# 78

## Clifford Trusts

Prior to March 2, 1986, as an alternative to a completed gift, you could have considered the creation of a temporary trust commonly known as a Clifford Trust. Clifford or temporary trusts to shift taxable income from a high-bracket taxpayer to a low-bracket taxpayer were extensively used in the past.

The Clifford Trust derived its name from a case in which a husband attempted to shift income to his wife by establishing a reversionary five-year trust. (A reversionary trust is one in which the principal returns to the grantor after a period of time.) He named himself as trustee and reserved broad administrative powers and sole discretion as to the amount distributed to his wife. The court held that Mr. Clifford had not parted with sufficient control of the corpus for enough time to avoid being considered the "owner" of the property for tax purposes, and thus was still taxable on the trust income.

In response to the uncertainty created by the Clifford decision in 1945, the Internal Revenue Service promulgated regulations defining the minimum time and control requirements necessary to avoid taxation of the trust income to the grantor. These regulations were later codified with modifications to require that the grantor be treated as the owner of any portion of a trust in which the grantor has reversionary interest in either the principal or the income if, as of the start of the trust, the reversionary interest will (or may reasonably be expected to) take effect in possession or enjoyment within ten years of the date of transfer of that trust.

The most common uses for the tax savings generated by such trusts were the financing of a child's college education or the support of a relative. These trusts could also be used to provide funds during the early earning years of adult children, either for their personal comfort or for initial business requirements. The common denominator of all of these trusts was that the overall income taxes to the family unit were reduced, and thus, the remaining spendable income of a family unit was increased.

For example, if you were in the 50 percent bracket and wanted to provide $5,000 for the support of an aged parent, you would have had to consume $10,000 of pretax income to do so. If assets earning $5,000 were transferred to a temporary trust for the benefit of the parent, your income was reduced by only $5,000, but—assuming the parent was in a lower tax bracket and paid little or no tax—about the same amount of support was provided to that beneficiary.

To create a Clifford Trust, a formal trust agreement must have been entered into. Prior to March 2, 1986, in order to shift the income to the beneficiary, the trust must have been effective for a term longer than ten years or for the life of the beneficiary. It is important to keep in mind that the transfer of the property, not merely the trust instrument itself, must have been for more than ten years. Therefore, if there might have been a few months' delay in transferring the property to the trust, it would have been wise to extend the trust instrument to ten years and six months to allow adequate time to complete the transfer of the property. Otherwise, the trust might have failed and the income might have been taxed to you as the grantor.

In Letter Ruling 8319022 the IRS ruled that a Clifford Trust could be funded with the installment obligations of the grantor without there being a taxable disposition. The grantor, however, would still pay tax on the capital gains, but not the income, portion of the notes, as the proceeds are received.

The income can be paid to the beneficiary currently, accumulated and paid at the end of the trust period, or distributed at the discretion of the trustee, with any unpaid amounts distributed at the end of the trust period. Where a temporary trust is required to distribute income currently, this income is taxed to the beneficiary each year at the beneficiary's lower tax bracket rate. This arrangement is called a *simple* trust and is generally the easiest to administer.

Where the trust accumulates part or all of its income for future distribution, it is known as a *complex* trust, and the income so accumulated each year is taxed to the trust as earned. When the accumulated income is later paid to the beneficiary, the tax on that income is computed under a complex averaging formula that assumes the income distributed was "thrown back" (earned equally over the number of years during which it was accumulated).

The annual tax on the average increase in the beneficiary's income is then computed by the use of a "with and without" calculation, which employs the middle three (in terms of taxable income) of the beneficiary's five prior taxable years. The increase in tax for these three years is then averaged and multiplied by the number of years of accumulation. Credit is allowed for the taxes paid by the trust, but it is limited to the amount of the increase in the beneficiary's tax, and no refund is available if the credit exceeds the recomputed tax.

Accumulations while the beneficiary is a minor are not "thrown back" to the years of accumulation unless the minor is the beneficiary of three or more trusts. For each beneficiary of three or more trusts in a taxable year, the accumulated income is "thrown back," but credit for taxes paid by the third and any additional trusts is not available except where the accumulated income distributed for a given year is less than that year's personal exemption. As you can see, the rules for complex trusts are detailed and complicated. Whether these trusts are best suited for you should be determined by your attorney or accountant.

Nevertheless, you as the grantor of a simple or complex trust must be careful to avoid retaining any power to control, directly or indirectly, the benefits of the trust within the ten-year period. If either the grantor or a nonadverse party (or both) exercises such a power without the approval of an "adverse" party, the income from the trust will be taxable to you as the grantor. There are certain powers that are excepted from this rule. These exceptions are:

- The power to use trust income for the support of a dependent whom the grantor is legally obligated to support. This is inadvisable, however, because the amount that is in fact used for that purpose will be taxed to you as the grantor.

- The power to change the income beneficiary after the ten-year period expires.

- The power to distribute income or principal to certain qualified charitable organizations.

- A testamentary power that is exercisable via your will, as long as the trust instrument does not allow the income to accumulate for distribution by the grantor's will.

- The power to withhold income *temporarily* from the beneficiary if the income is required to be distributed to that person or that person's estate or appointees.

- A power to distribute principal that is limited by a "reasonably defined standard" set forth in the trust instrument.

- The power to allocate receipts and disbursements between principal and income.

- The power to withhold income from any income beneficiary considered legally disabled or to withhold income while that person is under age 21.

Unlike the restrictions on the grantor's powers, an independent trustee may have the power to control the beneficial enjoyment of the trust. For the trustees to be "independent," no more than half of the trustees may be "related or subordinate" parties subservient to the grantor's wishes, and the grantor may not be a trustee. "Related or subordinate" parties include:

a) members of your family—that is, your spouse, father, mother, children, brothers, and sisters;

b) your employees;

c) a corporation or an employee of a corporation in which your shareholdings and those of the trust are significant from the standpoint of voting control;

d) a subordinate employee of a corporation in which you are an executive.

The superiority of a Clifford Trust over an outright gift lay in the amount of money that could be transferred without the imposition of a gift tax. When property was transferred to a Clifford Trust, you as a grantor were subject to a federal gift tax based upon the present value of the beneficiary's income interest. When the term of the trust is measured solely by a fixed period of time, the value of that interest is determined by actuarial tables, which recognize that the longer the term of the trust, the greater the potential income and the gift's value. For example, the value of a gift for a ten-year term would be equal to .61446 of the fair market value of the assets transferred, based upon an IRS assumed 10 percent annual rate of return. This assumed rate is to your benefit whenever it is possible to obtain a significantly higher return with reasonable safety.

In a trust with a fixed ten-year term, you and your spouse could have transferred free of gift tax a maximum of $32,548.90 in property per year for each child who is a beneficiary—$32,548.90 × .61446 = $20,000—which is equal to the sum of the $10,000 annual exclusion for each parent. This annual exclusion applied to each separate beneficiary. This was the major advantage of a Clifford Trust over a simple transfer of funds as a gift. A married taxpayer could transfer $32,548.90 per beneficiary per year with a Clifford Trust with a ten-year term without incurring any gift tax liability, whereas only $20,000 per beneficiary per year would be allowed if the Clifford Trust format were not used. Furthermore, as the principal of the trust would revert to you as the grantor, you would not be permanently parting with the funds transferred. Nevertheless, if a transfer of funds in excess of $32,548.90 per beneficiary was desired in order to shift greater income, a gift tax liability would be incurred. Furthermore, from an estate tax perspective, you would have a reversionary interest in the principal of the trust, which means that should you die during the trust term, the value of that interest would be included in your estate.

An exciting combination of a Clifford Trust and a traditional tax shelter was validated by the IRS in Letter Ruling 83-20012. This ruling covered a Clifford Trust that received from the trust grantor an interest in an income-producing oil and gas partnership. The trust agreement provided that in each year an amount equal to the depletion deduction would be set aside in a depletion reserve, rather than being distributed to the trust beneficiaries. At the end of the trust term the accumulated depletion reserve would be returned to the grantor, along with the rest of the trust principal.

The IRS ruled that the grantor of the trust would report taxable income each year equal to the amount placed in the depletion reserve. He would, however, have a deduction for depletion in the same amount and therefore would not incur any additional tax. By providing for the trust depletion reserve, the donor/grantor was able to retain the income sheltered by depletion and give away to his children, the beneficiaries, the unsheltered income from the partnership. Furthermore, in Revenue Ruling 84-14, the Internal Revenue Service ruled that neither the conveyance of an interest in oil and gas property to a Clifford Trust, nor the conveyance of the corpus of the trust to the grantor at the termination of the trust, will be a transfer of proven oil and gas properties that will cause the grantor to become ineligible for percentage depletion (see also IRS Letter Rulings 8128096 and 8320012).

The Tax Reform Act of 1986 effectively eliminated the use of Clifford Trusts. Except for transfers made prior to March 2, 1986—with another exception under which the 10-year rule of prior law would continue to apply to certain trusts created persuant to certain binding property settlements entered into before March 1, 1986—Clifford Trusts are taxed as grantor trusts as of January 1, 1987. That means that the income of the trust is taxed at *your* higher marginal tax bracket.

Irrevocable trusts, however, would be taxed as nongrantor trusts. Under the Tax Reform Act of 1986, undistributed income of both existing and newly created nongrantor trusts are taxed at the following rates: zero dollars to $5,000 at 15 percent, $5,000 or more at 28 percent. The benefit of the 15 percent bracket is phased out for trust taxable income between $13,000 and $25,000. These rate changes are effective on March 15, 1987. For 1987 returns, tax rate schedules blend the schedules of rates that would have been applied under prior law with the new rate schedules. Moreover, trusts other than charitable trusts would be required to use a calendar year as their taxable year for taxable years beginning after December 31, 1986. For more details on these amendments, please see Chapter 11, "The Tax Reform Act of 1986."

# 79    Interest-Free Loans

Because of the limits imposed on the transfer of funds to a Clifford Trust free of gift tax, an alternative planning strategy was devised. As an alternative or a supplement to transferring funds to a Clifford Trust, you could have made an unlimited interest-free loan to your lower-bracketed family member.

Unfortunately, the use of interest-free loans as a method to allocate income to lower bracketed taxpayers was effectively eliminated by the Tax Reform Act of 1984. Under that Act, foregone interest on a loan is treated as a gift from the lender to the borrower and is subject to the gift tax. Moreover, the lender (parent) is deemed to have an interest expense. For loans from a corporation to a shareholder, the interest element is treated as if a dividend includable in income was paid by the corporation to the shareholder. A loan to a person providing services results in the foregone interest being treated as compensation.

# 80

## The Schnepper Solution

Under prior law, loans between family members potentially resulted in taxable gifts in an amount equal to the value of the interest that was not charged.[2] No income tax consequences resulted, however, to either the

---

2. The Internal Revenue Service has determined that, for interest-free demand loan gifts made before January 1, 1984, you may not have to pay a gift tax. For a married couple electing the split gift provision, you may compute the value of gifts in any calendar period by multiplying the average outstanding loan balance for that period by the lesser of either the statutory interest rate for refunds and deficiencies or the annual average rate for three-month treasury bills.

    The applicable rates for years as far back as 1960 and the reporting exception amount are as follows:

|  | IRS Interest Rate Table | | | | |
|---|---|---|---|---|---|
| Year | Reporting Exception Amount* | IRS Interest Rate | Year | Reporting Exception Amount | IRS Interest Rate |
| 1983 | $232,558 | 8.6% | 1971 | $139,534 | 4.3% |
| 1982 | 188,679 | 10.6 | 1970 | 100,000 | 6.0 |
| 1981 | 100,000 | 12.0 | 1969 | 100,000 | 6.0 |
| 1980 | 100,000 | 11.5 | 1968 | 113,207 | 5.3 |
| 1979 | 100,000 | 6.0 | 1967 | 139,534 | 4.3 |
| 1978 | 100,000 | 6.1 | 1966 | 125,000 | 4.8 |
| 1977 | 115,384 | 5.2 | 1965 | 153,846 | 3.9 |
| 1976 | 122,448 | 4.9 | 1964 | 171,428 | 4.9 |
| 1975 | 103,448 | 5.8 | 1963 | 193,548 | 3.1 |
| 1974 | 100,000 | 6.0 | 1962 | 222,222 | 2.7 |
| 1973 | 100,000 | 6.0 | 1961 | 260,869 | 2.3 |
| 1972 | 150,000 | 4.0 | 1960 | 206,896 | 2.9 |

*The reporting exception amounts must be halved for single taxpayers.

lender or borrower. Furthermore, a number of cases held that demand loans by corporations to their shareholders, and by persons for whom services were performed to persons providing the services, generally did not have any federal tax consequences.[3] This led to the extensive use of interest free loans as a technique of income allocation and tax-free employee compensation.

Under the Tax Reform Act of 1984, low interest and interest free loans are generally recharacterized as:

**a)**  a loan to the borrower at a statutory interest rate, *and*

**b)**  either a gift (in the case of a gratuitous transaction), dividend (in a corporation-shareholder transaction), or compensation (in a transaction involving services), or some other payment in accordance with the substance of the transaction.[4]

The borrower is treated as paying interest on the loan at the statutory rate, resulting in income to the lender and a deduction to the borrower. An

---

2.  (continued) For years before 1960, the applicable interest rate will be the average three-month treasury bill rate for the year, since this rate was less than the statutory interest rate for all pre-1960 years.

    Furthermore, for administrative convenience, the IRS will not require gift tax reporting for interest-free demand loan gifts made before January 1, 1984 if the amount of the gift—valued by using the above rates—is less than the annual exclusion for the year, or if the annual outstanding balance of the interest-free demand loans did not total, in the aggregate, more than $50,000 per year per donee made by a single taxpayer ($100,000 made by a married couple). In addition, the IRS said no returns need to be filed for a period to January 1, 1984 if the only reason for filing is to elect the split-gift provisions for a gift arising from an interest-free demand loan.

    If a loan was made to a trust or other entity, the loan will be treated as separate loans made proportioantely to those individuals having beneficial interests in the trust or other entity. In the case of a loan to an entity, the administration exceptions for gift tax reporting are available only with respect to individuals who have a present interest in the loan proceeds or the income attributable to the loan proceeds. (Internal Revenue Service Information Release 84-60)

3.  See *Dean*, 35 T.C. 1083 (1961); *Saunders*, 294 F. Suppl, 1276 (DC Hawaii, 1968); *Joseph Lupowitz Sons, Inc.*, 497 F. 2d 862 (C.A.-3 1974), *Suttle*, T.C. Memo, 1978-393; *Johnson*, 254 F. Supp. 73 (D.C. Texas, 1966); *Greenspun*, 72 T.C. 78 (1979); *Goldsmith*, T.C. Memo, 1982-100 and *Hardee*, 84-79 (May 11, 1983) C.A.-Federal Circuit, even where the loan proceeds were used to purchase interest-free bonds! (Interest paid on a loan to purchase tax exempts is nondeductible under Section 265 (2)) but note that the non-interest-bearing note must be a demand note—see *Estate of Berkman*, T.C.M. 1979-46.

4.  See Tax Reform Act of 1984, Section 172 adding new Section 7872 to Subchapter C.

exception is provided for *de minimis* transactions that are not tax motivated. In addition, in the case of a loan in which the deemed payment by the lender to the borrower is a gift, the amount of deemed interest paid generally is limited to the amount of passive income of the borrower. This provision was made effective for below-market loans made on June 6, 1984 and to amounts outstanding on demand loans after that date. A demand loan outstanding on June 6, 1984, however, will not be subject to the above provisions if repaid prior to the 60th day after the date of enactment of the Act (July 18, 1984).

Specifically, under the Act, interest-free and below-market interest rate loans are recharacterized as arm's length transactions involving:

a) a gift, a dividend, a payment in the nature of compensation, or some other payment in accordance with the substance of the transaction to fund the payment of interest on the loan at a "statutory rate"; and

b) the payment of interest by the borrower at a "statutory rate" resulting in income to the lender and a deduction to the borrower.

With gift *term* loans, the Act treats the lender as making a gift, on the date the loan is made to the borrower, of the excess of the amount of the loan over the present value (using the "applicable federal rate" at the time that the loan is made) of the principal and interest payments required under the loan. The borrower then is treated as retransferring to the lender the amount of interest that would have accrued on an annual basis.

The "applicable federal rate" is determined by reference to the term of the loan, as set forth below:

| Term | Applicable Federal Rate |
|---|---|
| Less than three years | The Federal Short-term Rate |
| Over three years but not over nine years | The Federal Mid-term Rate |
| Over nine years | The Federal Long-term Rate |

The rates are to be determined within 15 days after the close of six-month periods ending on September 30 and March 31, respectively, and reflect the average market yield during such six-month period on outstanding marketable obligations of the United States with comparable maturities. The rates are compounded semiannually and are to be announced on or before September 30, 1984, and are to apply as of January 1, 1985. For periods prior to January 1, 1985, the applicable federal rate is deemed to be 10 percent compounded semiannually.

Furthermore, the Act provides that, where the interest on a gift term loan is forgiven on an annual basis, the transaction may be considered, in substance, as the economic equivalent of a below-market gift loan and will be treated as such.

The following example shows the new treatment of gift *term* loans:

On January 1, a father makes a $200,000 loan to his son for two years at 5 percent simple interest payable annually. If the applicable federal rate is 12 percent compounded semiannually, the amount treated as transferred by the lender to the borrower for *gift* tax purposes would be $24,760 (the excess of $200,000 over the present value of all payments due under the loan discounted at the 12 percent applicable federal rate).

The amount treated as retransferred by the borrower to the lender as *interest* on the last day of each of the two calendar years would be $14,720 (the excess of interest compounded semiannually over interest actually payable on the loan). This amount, which would be included in income by the lender and deductible by the borrower, would be in addition to the $10,000 interest actually due each year under the terms of the loan.

In the case of a below-market *demand* loan, the lender will be treated as transferring to the borrower, and the borrower will be treated as receiving from the lender, an amount equal to the "foregone interest" on an annual basis. An identical amount will be treated as being transferred from the borrower to the lender as a payment of interest at the same time. Thus, the lender will be treated as having made a gift or other type of transfer (such as compensation) to the borrower in an amount equal to the amount of foregone interest.

The amount that is deemed transferred will be included in income by the lender as interest and the borrower will be able to deduct such amounts, subject to the investment interest deduction limitations. Any amounts of foregone interest attributable to periods during any calendar year will be treated as transferred (and retransferred) on the last day of such calendar year.

Foregone interest is defined, with respect to any period during which a loan is outstanding, as the excess of the amount of interest that has accrued on the loan during the period, if interest accrued on the loan, at the applicable federal rate over any interest payable on the loan proper allocatable to such period.

If the below-market *term* loan is not a gift loan, the lender will be treated as transferring to the borrower, and the borrower as receiving from the lender, an amount equal to the excess of the amount of the loan over the present value of all principal and interest payments due under the loan. This transfer will be treated as a dividend, a payment in the nature of compensation, or some other payment in accordance with the substance of the transaction occurring on the date the loan is made. The present value of all principal and interest payments is to be determined under Regulations using a discount rate equal to the applicable federal rate compounded on a semiannual basis.

The excess of the present value of the loan over the present value of the payments due also will be treated as original issued discount (OID). Thus, the lender will be treated as receiving interest income at a constant interest *rate* over the life of the term loan. Likewise, the borrower will be treated as paying the same amount of interest. The interest that the borrower is treated as paying generally will be deductible by the borrower subject to the investment interest deduction limitations.

There is an exception to these rules for certain loans to employees. If the benefit received by the employee is nontransferrable and conditioned on the future performance of *substantial services* by the employee, the loan will be treated as a *demand* loan for purposes of determining the amount and timing of the transfers made. The loan, however, will be treated as a term loan for purposes of both determining the applicable federal rate and applying the effective date rules.

The Act provides for the following exceptions to the gift loan provisions:

1.  If the aggregate amount owed on a gift loan between an individual borrower and lender does not exceed $10,000, generally there are no income or gift tax consequences. This exception, however, will not apply where the gift loan is used to carry or purchase income-producing assets.

2.  If the aggregate amount owed by the borrower to the lender does not

exceed $100,000, there is no tax avoidance purpose, and the borrower's net investment income exceeds $1,000 in the taxable year involved, then the amount of interest income and expense imputed will be limited to such investment income.

3.  If the aggregate amount owed by the borrower to the lender does not exceed $100,000, there is no tax avoidance purpose, and the borrower's net investment income for the taxable year involved does *not* exceed $1,000, no interest income or expense will be imputed.

Thus loans to children, etc., to help them buy a house *may* escape the above tax burdens. In addition, specifically, under the committee minutes to the Act, a loan from a father to a son for educational purposes would *not* be treated as being made for tax avoidance purposes even though the son temporarily deposits the loan proceeds in a savings account. Furthermore, corporate-shareholder and employee loans totaling $10,000 or less generally will not be subject to tax under the new provisions, provided they are not made for tax avoidance purposes. Finally, the Conference Report on the Act anticipates that future regulations may provide that, if a loan is made requiring the payment of interest and the interest is cancelled, the recipient will have income if the cancellation is in the nature of a gift.

These interest-free and below-market loan provisions apply to *term* loans made after June 6, 1984 and to amounts outstanding on *demand* loans after that date. Any renegotiation, extension, revision, or modification of any of the terms of a loan after June 6, 1984 will be treated as a new loan.

In light of this, creative tax practitioners have sought an alternative to the prior use of interest-free demand notes. Whereas Clifford Trusts still are available, subject to the Tax Reform Act of 1986, the revision of the valuation tables in the Federal Register to assume a 10 percent rather than a 6 percent yield substantially reduced their attractiveness.[5] The gift tax value of an interest transfer to a Clifford Trust is the value of the income interest since the remainder reverts to the grantor. Under the old 6 percent assumption, a couple could have transferred approximately $45,000 to a Clifford Trust and have all of it qualify as an annual exclusion split gift. Currently, however, the revised tables reduce that amount to $32,549.

---

5.  48 Fed. Reg. 50087. These tables are found at Reg. Sec. 1.170A-12, 1.642(c)-6, 1.664, 20.2031-7(f), and 25.2512-5(f) of the Regulations. These tables are effective for transfers on or after December 1, 1983, and, in general, cause the values of income interests to increase and annuity interests to decrease relative to the respective remainder interests.

As an alternative to the Clifford Trust, the creation of a spousal remainder trust had been suggested. Similar to a Clifford Trust, the spousal remainder trust pays income to a beneficiary for a term of years, but at the conclusion of the term the principal passes to the grantor's spouse (or the spouse's estate). Because the trust principal does not revert to the grantor, the spousal remainder trust does not have the minimum ten-year-plus Clifford Trust requirement necessary to obtain the income shifting benefit.

Prior to the Tax Reform Act of 1986, with a spousal remainder trust, a grantor could have transferred assets for one year, two years, three years, or for any period that grantor so desired. With such a shorter trust term, the grantor had more flexibility in addressing the needs of the beneficiary. In addition, the shorter trust term also allowed the grantor to make substantially larger contributions to the trust than would have been possible with the Clifford Trust without exceeding the grantor's annual gift tax exclusion. Furthermore, unlike the Clifford Trust, contributions to a spousal remainder trust were excluded from the grantor's gross estate. The trust, therefore, not only shifted income to a potentially lower bracketed individual, but, in addition, potentially shifted assets to a spouse with a smaller estate for estate planning purposes.

For example, assuming a split gift election, a grantor could have transferred $220,000 to a spousal remainder trust for one year and have the income on that $220,000 principal taxed to the lower bracketed beneficiary. In contrast to the maximum $32,549 Clifford allocation, the spousal remainder trust with a two-year term would have allowed a transfer in excess of $115,000, with a three-year term in excess of $80,000.

The following chart demonstrates the maximum gift-tax-free contributions that could have been made to a spousal remainder trust.

| Trust Term (years) | Maximum Contribution per Donee without Subjection to Gift Tax |
|---|---|
| 1 | $220,000 |
| 2 | 115,238 |
| 3 | 80,423 |
| 4 | 63,094 |
| 5 | 52,759 |
| 6 | 45,921 |
| 7 | 41,081 |
| 8 | 37,489 |
| 9 | 34,729 |
| 10 | 32,549 |

The above chart assumes that no other gifts to the donee have been made during the taxable year, that the donor's spouse has consented to split the gifts for return purposes, and that the consenting spouse has made no other gifts to the donee during the taxable year. Note, however, the impact of the Tax Reform Act of 1986 on the use of spousal remainder trusts for income shifting, discussed below.

The spousal remainder trust worked because the value of the income interest to be paid to the beneficiary for a term of years qualified as a present interest for which the gift tax annual exclusion is available.[6] The remainder interest of the trust is a separate gift of a future interest which does not qualify for the annual exclusion.[7] The remainder interest passes to the spouse, however, and qualifies for the unlimited spousal marital deduction.[8]

For these reasons, the grantor of the spousal remainder trust will not consume any lifetime unified credit or incur any gift tax liability if the value of the income interest passing to the beneficiary does not exceed the unused annual exclusion.

The spousal remainder trust, however, was not without its drawbacks. First of all it is irrevocable—the grantor can retain no reversionary interest.[9] That reversionary interest must go to the grantor's spouse. The major limitation, therefore, of the spousal remainder trust is the grantor's ability and willingness to transfer ownership of substantial investment assets to his or her spouse.

Moreover, the trustee should have no discretion over the distribution of income or principal; all income must be distributed currently to the nonspouse beneficiary (or the beneficiary's estate), and the trust should prohibit the application of trust income to the payment of insurance premiums on the life of the grantor or the grantor's spouse.[10] Normally, without a trust provision to the contrary, capital gains are typically allocated to principal under state law. They therefore will be accumulated for the benefit of the grantor's spouse and taxable to the grantor.[11]

6. Treasury Regulation Section 25.2503-3(b).

7. Treasury Regulation Section 25.2503(a).

8. See Treasury Regulation Section 25.2523(a)-1(c) examples (5) and (6).

9. See Internal Revenue Code Section 673.

10. See Internal Revenue Code Section 676, 674, and Section 677(a)(3).

11. See Internal Revenue Code Section 677. The treatment here is not unlike the treatment of capital gains in a Clifford trust, which are similarly taxed to the grantor.

In addition, any contribution of separate property belonging to the grantor's spouse will cause the trust income attributable to that contribution to be taxable to the spouse as a reversionary interest unless the trust term remaining at the time of the contribution is at least ten years.[12] For this reason, it was important that the grantor transfer property that is exclusively his or hers.

Finally, the grantor and his/her spouse should not set up separate trusts for the same beneficiary with remainder interest passing to each other. The reciprocal trust doctrine will treat the remainder of each trust as a reversionary interest and all benefits will be lost. There is, however, no reason why a spouse cannot, at the termination of one spousal remainder trust, establish a new second trust with the original grantor as the remainder man. While this will return the original investment assets back to the original grantor, there must not be any obligation to create the second spousal remainder trust or any implication in any manner that it will be created; otherwise, the "step transaction" rule will eliminate all of the potential benefits.

Unfortunately, the Tax Reform Act of 1986 also effectively eliminated spousal remainder trusts as income shifting devices. Any income earned is taxed at the grantor's (your) higher marginal tax rate.

# 81 The Schnepper Shelter: Gift Leasebacks

An alternative technique used to increase income-shifting potential is the gift-leaseback transaction. In the typical situation, the taxpayer, usually a professional such as a doctor, attorney, accountant, or even a shareholder in a closely held corporation, establishes a trust for any children. Then business property, such as an office building, furniture, equipment, autos, trucks, or machinery, is transferred to the trust, which agrees to lease it back to the taxpayer. The lease payments are then deductible by the high-bracketed taxpayer and reported as income by the low-bracketed trust beneficiary.

In effect, the taxpayer has relinquished title in exchange for significant income shifting. There is no depreciation recapture on such transfers,[13] nor

---

12. See Internal Revenue Code Section 673.

13. See I.R.C. Section 1245(b)(1) and (3) and Section 1250(d)(1) and (3). Potential recapture is deferred until a subsequent disposition of the property—see *Rainier Companies, Inc.* v. *Comm.*, 61 T.C. 68 (1973), acq., 1974-1 C.B.2.

should there be any investment credit recapture.[14] In addition, not only is the first $500 of the shifted income to each child exempt from tax,[15] but the parent-taxpayer will also continue to be entitled to a personal exemption for each child until each is 19 or as long as each is a full-time student if more than half of each child's total support is received from the parent.[16]

The tax court has approved the gift-leaseback technique as a legitimate means of reducing your tax liability. It has developed four requirements that must be satisfied before it will permit a grantor to deduct the lease payments.[17] These requirements are as follows:

1. The grantor must not retain substantially the same control over the property that was held before making the gift. This requirement can be satisfied by appointing an independent trustee. The tax court has recognized both commercial banks[18] and personal attorneys[19] as independent trustees. In no case should the grantor-taxpayer become the trustee;[20] neither should the spouse.[21]

2. The leaseback should normally be in writing and must require payment of a reasonable lease rental. The trustee should have the trust property appraised[22] and find out the lease price of similar property to justify the reasonableness of the lease rental. A payment schedule should be established and adhered to.[23] Moreover, the trustee's powers detailed in the trust instrument should be broad enough to maintain

---

14. Reg. Section 1.47-3(g) provides that the recapture provisions will not apply where qualified property is disposed of and, as part of the same transaction, is leased back. The regulation is directed at sales but "disposed of" should incorporate and apply as well to gifts in trust situations.

15. I.R.C. Section 63(b)5.

16. See I.R.C. Section 152, Section 151(e)(1)(B) and Section 151 (e)(4).

17. See *Mathews* v. *Comm.,* 61 TC 12 (1973), rev'd, 520 F.2d 323, 75-2 USTC Par. 9734, 36 AFTR2d 75-5965 (CA-5, 1975) cert. den. See also *Rosenfeld v. Comm.*, (CA-2, 1983), 51 AFTR 2d 83-1251 (May 2, 1983), and *May v. Comm.* 76 TC 7 (1981) (CA-9, 1984), 53 AFTR 2d 84-626, where a gift leaseback was found valid despite an *oral lease!*

18. See *Serbousek,* TCM 1977-105.

19. See *Lerner,* 71 TC 290 (1978).

20. See *Penn,* 51 TC 144 (1968); *Van Zandt,* 40 TC 824 (1963), aff'd, 341 F.2d 440, 65-1 USTC Par. 9236, 15 AFTR2d 372 (CA-5, 1965) cert. den.

21. See *Larry Benson,* TC 86, for problems created with a spouse trustee. See also *Rosenfeld* TC Memo 1982-263 re: control.

22. Supra, note 13.

23. Supra, note 14.

independence. One suggested technique to assure the court's recognition of the trustee's independence is to make the initial term of the lease less than the term of the trust. In doing so the trustee is forced to exercise independent power to renegotiate renewal agreements.[24]

3. The leaseback (as distinguished from the gift) must have a bona fide business purpose. This requirement can be easily satisfied, since the trust property is business property intended to be used again in the taxpayer's business. Certain circuits of the U.S. district court, however, require a bona fide business purpose for *both* the leaseback *and the gift.* Merely to place trust property beyond the reach of creditors has been held to be insufficient as a business purpose for the gift.[25] One suggested business purpose would be to get managerial expertise in the control and operation of the property.[26] This would be especially effective, for example, if the taxpayer was a doctor, the property an office building, and the trustee an attorney expert in real estate.

4. The taxpayer must not possess a disqualifying "equity" in the property. Once the property is transferred, the taxpayer possesses only a reversionary interest in the trust property. The tax court holds that a reversionary interest is not a disqualifying equity, since its enjoyment is realized only after the trust expires.[27] Unfortunately, the Internal Revenue Service does not accept this position.[28] One way to avoid litigation on this matter would be to create a remainder interest that passes to the taxpayer's spouse or children, or to a corporation set up for the purpose, at the termination of the trust.[29]

Once the gift-leaseback trust is established, the benefits can be substantial. For example, assume a married taxpayer in the 33 percent tax bracket established a trust for three children by transferring business property valued at $60,000 into the trust. No gift taxes are payable on such a transfer.[30] Assume further that this is property that has been fully depreciated

---

24. See *Mathews,* supra, note 11, and *Quinlivan,* TCM 1978-70 aff'd 599 F.2d 269, 79-1 USTC Par. 9396, 44 AFTR2d 79-5059 (CA-8, 1979) cert. den.

25. See *Butler,* 65 TC 327 (1975).

26. See *Skemp,* 8 TC 415 (1947), rev'd, 168 F.2d 598, 48-1 USTC Par. 9300, 36 AFTR 1089 (CA-7, 1948).

27. See *Oaks,* 44 TC 524 (1965) and *Serbousek,* supra, note 12.

28. See Rev. Rul. 54-9, 1954-1 CB 20.

29. See supra, note 13 and supra, note 10.

30. Split gift ($10,000 × 2) × 3 = $60,000 exclusion.

and that therefore no further deductions are available to the taxpayer if the property is retained. The fair rental for such property, though, is $250 per month.

The higher-bracket taxpayer therefore pays lease rentals of $3,000 per year and takes that amount as a business deduction. This saves $990 in taxes.[31] The three children each include $1,000 in their income, less their share of the trustee's management fee. Ignoring that fee for illustrative purposes and assuming no other income, the three children may pay taxes as low as $75 × 3 and retain $2,775. As a result of a transfer of $3,000, total family wealth has increased by $3,765, for a net increase of $765.[32]

If the property were still subject to depreciation by the original taxpayer, the above benefits would be reduced by the tax savings from depreciation deductions foregone in the transfer. These deductions, though, would be available to the children-beneficiaries. Any maintenance or upkeep expenses incurred for the property can still be deducted by the lessee-taxpayer, if so provided in the lease agreement. Note that in this example the $925 retained by each child can be used to pay that child's college expenses.[33] If the trust were not used, to accumulate $2,775 for tuition would require the 33 percent taxpayer to earn an incremental $4,142 in pretax dollars.[34]

Furthermore, if the property that you're contemplating transferring into trusts for your children is subject to a mortgage, you should be aware that the Garn Act lists certain property transfers that should never trigger loan acceleration under a due on sale clause. These exceptions apply to all loans—to loans originated by state chartered institutions and by federal lending institutions, regardless of the date of their origination. Included in these safe harbor transfers is a transfer in which a spouse or *children* of the borrower receive ownership of the property.

Note that the Tax Reform Act of 1986 eliminated the viability of Clifford Trusts for tax savings. The above trust-leaseback technique, however, would still be viable using an irrevocable trust. All of the other provisions, as discussed above, would apply.

---

31. The lease payments would be deductible as ordinary and necessary business expenses under I.R.C. Section 162—$3,000 × .33 = $990 reduction in taxes at that bracket level.
32. $2,775 retained plus $990 saved in taxes.
33. Or any other nonsupport expenses. See supra, note 8.
34. $4,142 at a marginal 33 percent rate leaves $2,775 after taxes.

Trust leasebacks have been specifically validated in the following 23 states: Alaska, Arizona, Arkansas, California, Delaware, Hawaii, Idaho, Illinois, Indiana, Missouri, Montana, Nebraska, Nevada, New Jersey, New York, North Dakota, Oregon, Pennsylvania, Rhode Island, South Dakota, Vermont, Washington, and Wiconsin.

The IRS will no longer litigate gift leaseback cases where the leasee is a taxable entity separate from the grantor. This position was announced in an Action on Decision on April 23, 1984. By separate taxable entity, the IRS means a regular corporation, rather than a partnership or a Subchapter S corporation. Two-party gift leaseback arrangements have been upheld not only by the Tax Court but by the following circuits: the Second (*Rosenfeld*, 706 F. 2d 1277, 83-1 USTC para. 9341 [CA-2, 1983], see *Use of gift-leaseback to shift income given substantial boost by new decision*, 12 TL 128 [Sep/Oct 1983]); the Third (*Brown* 180 F. 2d 926, 50-1 USTC para. 9219; 39 AFTR 155 [CA-3, 1950]); the Seventh (*Skemp*, 168 F. 2d 598, 48-1 USTC para. 9300, 36 AFTR 1089 [CA-7, 1948]); the Eighth (*Quinlaven*, 599 F. 2d 269, 44-2 AFTR 2d 79-5059 [CA-7, 1979]), and the Ninth (*Brooke*, 468 F. 2d 1155, 72-2 USTC para. 9594, 30 AFTR 2d 72-5284 [CA-9, 1972]). However, they have been held invalid in the Fourth and Fifth Circuits (*Perry*, 520 F. 2d 235, 75-2 USTC para. 9629, 36 AFTR 2d 75-5500 [CA-4, 1975], and *Van Zandt*, 341 F. 2d 440, 65-1 USTC para. 9236, 15 AFTR 2d 372 [CA-5, 1965]). In the circuits where gift-leasebacks have been held invalid, however, the transactions only involved two parties; i.e., there was no corporation involved, but instead the lessee was the individual grantor.

An interesting twist on this technique has been developed by Schnepper Associates of Cherry Hill, New Jersey. Assume the children in the preceding example are too young for college and that the taxpayer has a current need for the funds being paid out in lease rentals. The Schnepper Shelter directs the taxpayer to make the lease payments and then to borrow back the money at a fair rate of interest.[35]

To use the above example, the taxpayer would make payments of $3,000 and borrow back $3,000, paying $600 in interest yearly (20 percent). Each child over age 14 would pay approximately an additional $30 in taxes on the interest payments, a total of an additional $90, but the taxpayer

---

35. Note that the interest expense need not be limited to the prime rate. In fact, "there is no requirement . . . that deductible interest be ordinary and necessary or even that it be reasonable." *Dorzback* v. *Collison,* 52-1 USTC Par. 9263, 195 F.2d 69, 72 (3d Cir. 1952). An interest payment as high as 60 percent to the taxpayer's *mother* has been upheld. *Raymond J. Barton* 38 TCM 934 (1979).

would save an additional $198 in taxes (33 percent of $600)—a difference of $108 per year or $540 over five years. Of course, as its lease rentals increase, so too do the tax savings. In 1988, up to $17,850 in taxable income can be taxed to a child over age 14 at the 15 percent rate.

When the children begin college and tuition is due, the taxpayer would then repay the borrowed money, in effect getting a current income tax deduction for future cash payments for the children's tuition. If the taxpayer dies before repayment is made, any remainder value in the trust is included in the estate,[36] but that estate (and therefore any tax due on it) is reduced by any debts owed to the trust—further magnifying the benefits of the Schnepper shelter.[37]

While the Schnepper shelter also appears to be contrary to congressional intent to eliminate assignment of income among family members, all of its components have been court tested and accepted. Here again, as long as the trustee is truly independent, the separate entity identity of the trust protects the legality and validity of a properly structured transaction. If such a shelter is to be eliminated, it too must be done through congressional action. Until such action, the Schnepper shelter is a viable technique that should be considered in your planning to reduce your taxes to zero.

Moreover, the leaseback technique can provide substantial advantages to a taxpayer whose passive losses have been reduced or eliminated by the Tax Reform Act of 1986. For example, assume a doctor who operates out of a professional corporation and who needs additional equipment, furniture, etc. Instead of buying that equipment through his corporation, the doctor will buy the equipment personally and lease it to the corporation. The lease rental payments made by the corporation would be extensively sheltered by the depreciation taken on this "leased business" equipment. Any net profits over and above the depreciation sheltered cash flow could be sheltered as passive income by the doctor's excess passive losses. By utilizing this technique, the doctor is able to take money out of his corporation at a zero tax cost. The cash flow is sheltered by his previously unused passive losses and by the depreciation on the new equipment. Moreover, his corporation is entitled to a tax deduction for the "nontaxable" lease rental payments made to him!

---

36.  See I.R.C. Section 2033. The value of that reversionary interest is determined by actuarial tables. See *Comm.* v. *Henry's Estate (Biddle)*, (3 Cir: 1947), 161 F2d 574, 35 AFTR 1252 aff'g 4TC 423.

37.  See I.R.C. Section 2051; Section 2053 (a)(3) and Section 2053 (a)(4).

Remember that the Tax Reform Act of 1986 effectively eliminates the use of Clifford Trusts as planning devices. Therefore, in order to effectively use the gift-leaseback technique, rather than a Clifford Trust, you should create an irrevocable trust. With an irrevocable trust, the property is transferred to the trust (beneficiaries) irrevocably. Unlike the Clifford Trust, you will not get it back after 10 years. However, if you are leasing back personal property—e.g., business furniture, equipment, etc.—that has been fully depreciated, that equipment would normally be over 15 years old when it would be returned using a Clifford Trust. The value of that equipment then would be minimal. Had you been gift-leasebacking an office building, however, the Tax Reform Act of 1986 forces you to relinquish present and future ownership of an asset with substantial value. If this is a strategy to be employed, the loss of that value is the price that must be paid.

# 82

## The Schnepper *Deep* Shelter

Another alternative for shifting income to a lower bracketed family member is to transfer rental property, excluding the building, to a trust for your children and rent the land back from the trust. The donor parent would still get all of the depreciation on the building, and the trust beneficiary children would be taxed on the lease rental income received. That lease rental income, however, would be a deductible investment expense by the father. In effect, the father would be paying lease rental income to his children, deducting that rent expense in his higher bracket, and having it taxed to his children at the lower bracket. Moreover, this transfer of family wealth could take place without any gift tax consequences. In *Stanley J. Wolfe*, T.C. Memo 1984-446, this arrangement was validated with a sale leaseback of land to an irrevocable 10-year trust. The leaseback had a bona fide business purpose, and the lease payments were determined to be reasonable rent. Here again, the Tax Reform Act of 1986 would require the use of an irrevocable trust if this technique were to be used effectively.

# 83

## Family Partnerships

If you are an individual business owner, the use of a family partnership can play an important role in your income tax planning. By giving or selling an interest in your business to members of your family (particularly to your children), you can decrease your personal income tax payments and thereby increase your family unit's spendable income and capital.

For this arrangement to work however, the establishment of the partnership must be genuine. This has been simplified by an IRS tax code section that specifically allows you to set up a family partnership by gift or purchase even though the family partners render no services.[38] Therefore, in those cases where capital is a material income-producing factor for the partnership, significant income shifting to lower-bracketed family members can be accomplished through the establishment of family partnerships.

A family partnership can be established in any of the following ways:

- Take into the partnership any child or relative who can contribute capital.

- Make a gift of a partnership interest to children or other relatives.

- Sell a partnership interest to children or other relatives. This sale can be substantially on credit, to be paid out of subsequent partnership income.

- Accept into partnership any child or other relative who can be expected to perform important work in the business on a regular basis.

# 84

## Family Trusts

A family trust should be very carefully differentiated from a family partnership. A family trust is a trust to which you transfer "the exclusive use of your lifetime services and all the currently earned remuneration therefrom."

The problem with family trusts is that they do not work. A basic rule of taxation is that income must be taxed to the person who earned it. The transfer of your lifetime services and the income earned through the performance of those services is simply an assignment of income, and therefore ineffective in shifting the tax burden from you to the trust. *You cannot shift income earned through personal service.* A family trust, therefore, is

---

38.   Section 704(e) of the Internal Revenue Code.

nothing more than a tax avoidance scheme.[39] Do not, however, confuse a family trust with a trust to which income-earning *property* is transferred. When property is transferred, the income from that property *can* be shifted.

# 85

## Employing Members of the Family

If you are an individual business owner, a simple and effective method of splitting your income with a family member is to employ that family member in your business and pay compensation. The employment must be bona fide and the salary paid must be reasonable in relation to the services rendered. Even a young child can be compensated for the reasonable value of such services as cleaning your office, mailing your letters, or opening your mail. A 1982 tax court decision allowed a $1,200 deduction for a 7-year-old child who performed a variety of services—maintenance and office work—for a mobile-home-park operator.[40] Be aware, however, that wages actually used by your children for their own support can affect your claim for their dependency exemptions. When in doubt, have your children bank their wages, thereby saving the exemption and teaching them the virtue of thrift as well.

If your business is not incorporated, services performed by your child under the age of 18 are excluded from social security coverage. (Prior to the Revenue Act of 1987, the exclusion was for a child under the age of 21, and payments to your spouse were also exempt.) This means that you can deduct the value of the services that you pay to your children from your income tax without the added expense of paying social security taxes on that compensation. Services performed in the employ of a corporation, however, are not within this exclusion. But all is not lost if you are in a corporate firm. If your spouse is a bona fide employee of your corporation, such tax breaks as social security, workmen's compensation, tax-free sick pay, pension or profit-sharing plan benefits, stock option plans, group life insurance, and many

---

39.   *Hailey, Jr.,* 73 TC No. 99 (1980).

40.   See *Eller,* 77 TC No. 66. See also *James A. Moriarty*, T.C. Memo 1984-249, where a doctor was allowed to deduct salaries he paid his teenage children for handling business correspondence, insurance forms, etc., and for keeping patient files in order.

others are open to you. According to IRS regulations, services performed in the employ of a partnership are also not within the exclusion *unless* the requisite family relationship exists between the employee and each of the partners comprising the partnership. Although wages paid to a child under age 18 by an unincorporated business are exempt from social security and federal unemployment taxes, wages paid to a parent are exempt from federal unemployment taxes but not from social security taxes.

Furthermore, if your spouse works for you, you may be able to deduct all your medical expenses. (If you hire your spouse, make sure that you can substantiate the payments that are made. Keep records or a journal of hours worked, and make payments with a check. No record-keeping means no substantiation. No substantiation means no deduction [L.T.R. 8753003].) Normally, the deduction for medical expenses is limited to expenses that exceed 7.5 percent of your adjusted gross income. If you have your own business, however, you can install a written medical reimbursement plan for your employees. As a sole proprietor, you would not be considered eligible because you do not qualify as a common-law employee. Your spouse, however, would qualify. *You* would qualify as well if the plan included all employees, the dependent children, and the employee's *spouse*! With such a plan, your cost for insurance coverage and for the medical reimbursement plan would be deductible in full as a business expense. Payments from the plan, of course, would be tax free to you and your spouse. To achieve the anticipated tax results, the plan must be a welfare plan for all employees (Revenue Ruling 71-588).

The work need not be full-time and can even be done during your children's summer vacations. Furthermore, provided that you continue to furnish more than one-half of your child's support and your child is younger than 19 or is a full-time student for part of each of five months during the year, you can continue to claim a personal exemption deduction for that child. Remember, a child with earned income in 1988 pays *zero* taxes on the first $3,000 worth of earned income. That means that if you are in the 33 percent bracket and pay each of your three children $3,000 for services rendered, their tax is zero, the money remains within the family group, and your tax savings is $2,970! Note that another $2,000 could be paid tax-free to each child if placed in an IRA. That could produce a total tax saving of $4,950 ([$3,000 + $2,000] × 3× .33).

# 86   Author's Delight

An interesting new income allocation technique has been made possible by a recent Internal Revenue Service ruling (Ltr. 8217037). A writer signed a contract with a publisher for royalties based on sales of a completed book. The contractual rights owned were then transferred to trusts for the benefit of minor children.

The IRS ruled that this was not a transfer of income, but rather of income-producing property. As long as the income was not used to meet the support obligations of the parents, such income would be taxed only to the trusts/children! In Letter Ruling 8444073, an author assigned to his child all royalties and interest in his publishing contract within 10 days after completing the book. The IRS again ruled that the author's child, not the author, would be taxed on the book royalties. Be careful, however; if an author assigns less than the entire contract, the IRS could assert the assignment of income doctrine to tax the income [see *Lewis,* 45-2 USTC Para. 9348, 34 AFTR 124 (CA-3, 1945)]. Both the contract and the royalties must be assigned; an assignment of the royalty income alone would not be a complete assignment of all of the author's property.

Note, however, that in IRS Letter Ruling 8444073, the IRS ruled that if the author was required in the contract to make revisions to the book, and no additional compensation was received for such revisions, the royalties would represent, in part, compensation for the author's services and would be taxable to that author. The measure of the compensation would presumably be what the publisher paid someone else to do the revisions. The solution to this problem is to have a separate contract or agreement specifying additional or different compensation for revisions. In addition, note that expenses incurred by an author in writing a book after 1986 must be capitalized and deducted over the life of the income stream of that book (Section 23[b] of the Tax Reform Act of 1986). However, the IRS has ruled that an author can deduct 50 percent of those expenses in the first year and 25 percent in each of the subsequent two years, in lieu of total income stream capitalization (Notice 88-62, 1988-22 IRB).

# B   Running Your Own Business

One of the important and effective techniques to reduce your taxes to zero is to convert your personal expenses to deductible *business* expenses. In order to do that you must own your own business. This is not complicated, expensive, or difficult to do, and incorporation is *not* needed. I will, however, detail the extensive tax benefits available if a corporate form of business is used.

To be in business, you merely declare yourself to be so. If you want to operate in a noncorporate form under a name different from your own, you can do that as well. In some states, however, if you are operating under an assumed name, you must file what is known as a "DBA" (Doing Business As) form with your local county clerk. Basically, this is merely a statement containing your name, address, and the assumed name under which you are doing business. For example, a form might merely say, "Jeff A. Schnepper is doing business under the name of 'Super Tax Savings Associates.'"

Moreover, your business need not make a profit in order for your expenses to be allowable deductions. All you need to do is establish a "profit motive." Under the Internal Revenue Service tax code, a "profit motive" is presumed if you earn any net income in any three out of five business years. In the early loss years you can insist that the Internal Revenue Service defer challenge until the five-year period is up (Form 5213). Furthermore, in fact, you need *never* have to actually show a profit if you can show a *profit motive*. (*Melvin Nickerson*, CA-7, No. 82-1323; see also *Paul Farrell*, T.C. Memo, 1983-542 where farming expenses were held deductible despite five straight years of losses. See also *Churchman*, 68 T.C. No. 59, where despite 20 years of losses, the court found a profit objective and allowed deductions of business losses in full, and *Frazier,* T.C. Memo 1985-61.)

The test for deductability is whether you have an actual and honest profit *objective*—you need not even have a reasonable expectation of profit (Treasury Regulation Section 1.183-2(a); *Dreicer v. Commissioner*, 78 T.C. 642, 1982). While the Tax Court requires a primary or dominant profit motive (*Lemmen,* 77 T.C. 1326 (1981)), in *Johnson,* 86-2 U.S.T.C. Par. 9705, 58 AFTR 2d 86-5894, the U.S. Claims Court held that having a reasonable chance to make a reasonable profit, apart from tax considerations, would suffice. Although the ultimate question is whether or not you have an intent to make a profit, the determination of your motive is made by reference to objective standards, taking into account all of the facts and circumstances. The facts that will be taken into consideration include the following:

1.    The manner in which you carry on the activity.

2.    The expertise of yourself and your advisors.

3.    The time and effort expended by you in carrying out this activity.

4.    The expectation that assets used in your business may appreciate in value.

5.    Your success in carrying on similar or dissimilar activities.

6.    Your history of income or losses with respect to the activity.

7.   The amount of occasional profits, if any, that are earned.

8.   Your financial status.

9.   The elements of personal pleasure or recreation.

The fact that you are employed full-time elsewhere will not bar a finding of your being in a separate trade or business. (See *Watson,* T.C. Memo 1988-29. See also *Riddle,* 205 F.2d 357, 62-2 USTC para. 9261, 10 AFTR 2d 5042 [DC Colo., 1962], wherein a full-time government employee was held to be in the trade or business of a consultant, despite the fact that he couldn't deal with anyone who had a government contract; and *Estes,* 69-1 USTC para. 9261, 23 AFTR 2d 69-903 [DC Ala., 1969], wherein another full-time government employee was held to be in the lapidary business, so that his expenses were deductible.)

One effective tax planning strategy, therefore, is to convert your personal hobby into a business. For example, one of my clients raced stock cars as a hobby. When he came to me, I converted that hobby into a business. He had cards and stationery printed. He ran ads looking for a sponsor. He gave his "hobby" the image and appearance of a "business," and he demonstrated a real profit motive. This client had a salary income of $40,000. When his new "business" expenses were deducted, not only did he pay zero taxes, but because he qualified for the earned income credit, the Internal Revenue Service paid him money!

Two years later he was audited on that year's return. The law requires that you prove your business expenses, with receipts, checks, or a log book that is updated daily. Unfortunately, he had not kept a log or any receipts for his expenses for the first year. His expenses, though, were legitimate, and he had receipts for the subsequent two years. On the basis of the receipts for the two subsequent years not in question, this taxpayer with $40,000 in other income and *no* receipts, after an IRS audit, paid less than $100 in taxes, including interest and penalties! Had he kept receipts for the first year, he would have paid zero.

To be allowable, your business expenses must be:

a)   ordinary and necessary;

b)   paid or incurred during the taxable year; *and*

c)   connected with the conduct of a trade or business.

"Ordinary and necessary" has been interpreted by the courts and the

Internal Revenue Service as "reasonable and customary" and this really depends upon your specific business and the business customs in your locale. In fact, an "ordinary" expense is one that is customary or usual. It need not be customary or usual for you, provided that it is customary or usual for your particular trade, industry, or community. The Supreme Court has held that even a one-time outlay falls within the definition (*Welch v. Helvering,* 290 US 111, 1933). Similarly, the Second Circuit Court of Appeals defined "necessary" as "appropriate" and "helpful," rather than necessarily essential to a taxpayer's business (*Blackmer v. Commissioner,* 70 F.2d 255).

For example, in one case a husband and wife produced, exhibited, and sold their sculptured works. The expenses incurred by them in doing so were held to be ordinary and necessary business expenses.[41] In another case, a breeder and raiser of bird dogs tried to develop an outstanding dog so that he could reap profits from sales and stud fees. Some years were profitable and some showed losses, yet all of the business expenses were found to be deductible.[42] In a third, a coal miner operated a kennel for bird dogs. Despite the fact that he sustained eleven years of losses, there was sufficient evidence of an ever-present profit motive for all of his expenses to be also allowed as deductible.[43] In fact, in *Donald C. Kimbrough,* T.C. Memo 1988–185, a high school teacher's golfing activity was engaged in "for profit," resulting in his losses being allowed as deductible expenses.

Owning your own business, therefore, affords you the opportunity to convert a great many of your personal expenses into allowable business deductions. The rest of the section will detail some of the most important reservoirs of deductible expenses.

# 87

## Your Home

Probably the most significant conversion of a personal expense into a business expense occurs when you use your home for your business. (This can apply to a primary *or* secondary business.) To be deductible, these home business expenses must be allowable under the Internal Revenue Service tax code.

The code states that no deduction for any business expenses attributable to an at-home office will be allowable unless these expenses are

---

41.  *Road,* 184 F. Supp. 791.
42.  *Sloan,* T.C. Memo 1956-36.
43.  *Sasso,* T.C. Memo 1961–216.

attributable to a portion of the home used "exclusively and on a regular basis" as:

a) the principal place of business; *or*

b) a place of business that is used by patients, clients, or customers in meeting or dealing with you in the normal course of your business.

While the code requires that any office at home constitutes your principal place of business, this does not mean that it must be your *single* principal place of business, where all of your businesses are considered together. The test according to the courts is "whether with respect to a particular business conducted by a taxpayer, the home office [is] his principal place for conducting that business." Your home office can therefore qualify if it is the principal place of your first *or* second business. In *Drucker, et al. v. Commissioner*, 52 AFTR 2d 83-5804, for example, the Second Circuit Court of Appeals allowed concert musicians home office deductions for the business use of their apartments because they spent most practice time at home and their employers did not provide the musicians with space for the essential task of private practice. In fact, in *Weissman v. Commissioner*, 84-4031, December 20, 1984, the U.S. Court of Appeals for the Second Circuit ruled that a college professor may deduct the expenses of maintaining a home office used exclusively to do most of the research and writing expected of him as a condition of retaining his teaching position. The Court found that the college professor's principal place of business was not necessarily the college at which he teaches any more than a musician's principal place of business is necessarily the concert hall at which he performs. However, the Tax Court, in *Neville Bardsley Dudley et ux.,* T.C. Memo 1987-607, ruled that a full-time business professor at the downtown campus of Wayne County Community College in Detroit was provided office space at the college, was not required to maintain an office in his home, and had no substantial out-of-classroom responsibilities such as research and publication. The Court concluded that Dudley's deduction for home office expenses was legitimate only if his home office was indeed his principal place of business. It was not, so Dudley was denied his deduction. (See also *John Meiers et ux. v. Commissioner,* No. 85-1209 [Seventh Cir., January 14, 1986] wherein the Seventh Circuit found that the "principal place of business" must be determined by looking at both hours worked and functions performed. The Court found that Meierses, who each day spent an hour in their laundromat and two hours at their home office devoted exclusively to administrative work on behalf of the laundry, were entitled to the claimed deductions for the home office. This was another reversal of the Tax Court's "focal point" test. Under that test, the principal place of business has been held to be that place where goods and services are provided to customers or clients or where income is produced.)

In another example, the taxpayer was a dermatologist, and the hospital was his principal place of business. But he also owned and managed six rental units, and he had set aside a room in his residence used exclusively for managing that activity. The court found that in this case the managing of rental property was a trade or business and that his home office expenses *were* deductible.[44] This decision was codified in PL 97–119 on December 28, 1981, when President Reagan signed into law an act specifically allowing a deduction for business use of a home for activities other than a taxpayer's primary occupation. (The Black Lung Benefits Revenue Act of 1981 [including other tax provisions adopted], Public Law No. 97-119, Section 113(c), 95 Stat. 1642 [1980].) Furthermore, these changes were made retroactive to years beginning after 1975. Moreover, on November 19, 1982, the Court of Claims ruled that investment activities can constitute a trade or business and therefore allowed home office deductions for taxpayers who managed large investment portfolios full time (*Moller*, 82-2 USTC Par. 9694, 51 AFTR 2d 83-369). Unfortunately, on November 18, 1983 the Claims Court was overruled by the Federal Circuit Court of Appeals. (721 F. 2d 810).

In *Anthony J. Ditunno* [80 T.C. No. 12 (February 7, 1983)], the Tax Court overruled prior precedent and provided a new definition and set of criteria for determining whether a taxpayer is engaged in a trade or business for tax purposes. The Court broadened the meaning of the phrase "trade or business" by replacing the previous "goods and services" test with a "facts and circumstances" test which requires a subjective determination to be made in each instance by "an examination of all the facts involved in each case." Despite a Second Circuit Court of Appeals decision to return to the "goods and services" test in *Gajewski*, 84-1 U.S.C. Par. 9116, 53, AFTR 2d 84-386 (CA-2, 1983), and the *Estate of Dan B. Cole*, No. 83-1601 (6th Circuit, October 23, 1984), where the Appeals Court ruled that one must hold oneself out to others as a provider of goods or services to be in a trade or business, the Tax Court has reaffirmed its "facts and circumstances" test in

---

44. *Edwin R. Curphey,* T.C. 61.

*Robert P. Groetzinger vs. Commissioner,* 82 T.C. No. 61 (May 24, 1983) where it ruled that Groetzinger's trade or business under the Code was gambling. However, on May 23, 1985, the Tax Court revised its decision and deferred to the Second Circuit when it ruled that Gajewski was not in a trade or business (*Gajewski,* 84 T.C. No. 63). *Groetzinger,* however, *was* affirmed by the 7th Circuit Court of Appeals on August 21, 1985 (No. 84-2507). These conflicting decisions were resolved when the Supreme Court, on February 24, 1987, again affirmed *Groetzinger,* ruling that the taxpayer, who made gambling his full-time livelihood "with continuity and regularity," was in a trade or business.

Furthermore, in *Morley v. Commissioner,* No. 40685-84, 87 T.C. No. 69, decided on November 19, 1986, the court ruled that a taxpayer's purchase, for the first time, of property that he intends to resell, followed promptly by bona fide efforts to resell the property, constituted a trade or business. Here, even the single purchase of a parcel of real estate, with the requisite intent, constituted a trade or business.

In 1982, the Tax Court ruled that an employee who was required by his employer to take frequent after-office-hours telephone calls from clients could deduct the cost of maintaining his at-home office used exclusively and regularly for that purpose. The Tax Court agreed with the Internal Revenue Service that the taxpayer had failed to prove it was "his principal place of business." But a majority of the Court, siding with the taxpayer, held that his office met the alternative test "as a place of business in which patients, clients, or customers meet or deal with the taxpayer in the normal course of the taxpayer's business." The significance of this decision is that the Court found no requirement "that such meetings or dealings are limited to physical encounters."[45] This decision, however, was reversed upon appeal to the Ninth Circuit on May 31, 1983, and the reversal was affirmed by the Tax Court in *Frankel,* 82 T.C. No. 26 on February 28, 1984. But in the case of *Feldman v. Commissioner,* 14126-82, 84 T.C. No. 1, on January 8, 1985, the Court allowed a taxpayer the costs of maintaining space in his home that he *leased* to his corporate employer for his use as a home office. Here Feldman maintained an office in his home that was rented to his employer for his own use. The employer, of which the taxpayer was a shareholder and director, paid $5,400 designated as rent to Feldman in 1979. The taxpayer reported the rental income and deducted his costs of maintaining the leased space,

---

45. *John W. Green,* 78 T.C. No. 30.

which he calculated as 15 percent of his home. The Court found, to the extent that the payments were reasonable, that they constituted rent and that the costs of producing that rental income may be deducted. By using the rental strategem, the taxpayer was able to create an allowable home office without "physical encounters." (But see below under depreciation for 1986 Tax Reform Act limits.) Moreover, in Rev. Rul. 86-148, the IRS allowed a deduction for a monthly fee to a security service for a home office used as a dental practice.

The following expenses for your home office will be allowable:

1. *Depreciation on your office furniture and equipment.* This would include any desks, chairs, couches, lamps, etc., that you put into your office. Unfortunately, however, the Tax Reform Act of 1986 provided that when an employee leases a portion of his home to his employer, no net losses would be allowable. It is possible, nevertheless, to avoid this provision if the house were owned exclusively by the employee-spouse who was the only party to the lease with the corporation. In that situation the prohibition between an *employee* and his employer would not be violated.

2. *Depreciation on your "office building."* If your home is owned, you can depreciate the portion of the acquisition cost and improvements allocatable to your home office. Note that in *Weightman,* TCM 1981-301, the Tax Court held that a taxpayer need not have an entire room as an office but could set aside an area for exclusive business use. Therefore, one part of a room could be used for personal reasons without affecting the deduction for the business use of another part of the room.

3. *Rent.* If your home is rented, you can depreciate an allocatable portion of that rent for your home office.

4. *Homeowner's insurance.* If you own your home, an allocatable portion of your homeowner's insurance is deductible.

5. *Electric utilities.* An allocatable portion of your electric bill for providing current and light to your home office is also deductible.

6. *Heating and air conditioning.* An allocatable portion for heating your home office in winter or air conditioning your home office in summer would also be an allowable, ordinary and necessary business expense.

In addition, if you put in an air conditioner that does not become a structural part of the building—a window or portable air conditioner—that air conditioner's cost can be recovered through depreciation.

7. *Phone.* The use of your home phone would also normally be an ordinary and necessary business expense. You can either deduct an allocatable portion of your regular phone bill or insert a separate line exclusively for the use of your "business." Even part of the basic charge for a home phone, when used for business, is deductible (*Robert H. Lee,* T.C. Memo 1960-58).

The following example demonstrates the available tax advantage of having a home office: Assume that you have a five-room home costing $150,000, with $50,000 allocatable to land and $100,000 allocatable to the building. The home has an 31½-year recovery life, because the "office space" is not *residential* rental space. You purchase $12,000 in furniture with a seven-year recovery life for your one-room home office and incur the following total costs over the year:

| | Allowable Deductions |
|---|---:|
| Heat and air conditioning ($2,400 × 1/5) = | $   480 |
| Electricity ($1,200 × 1/5) = | 240 |
| Phone (50 percent business) ($1,200 × 1/2) = | 600 |
| Depreciation on furniture: | |
|    Election to expense | 10,000 |
|    First year depreciation [($12,000 − $8,000) × .1428] | 286 |
| Depreciation on home [(100,000 ÷ 5) × .030423] | 608 |
| Total Deductions | $12,214 |
| Tax savings in the 33 percent bracket | $4,031 |

Under IRS regulations, these deductions are allowable only if they do not exceed the amount of gross income derived from the use of your home for your trade or business reduced by the deductions that are allowed without regard to their connection with your trade or business—that is, interest and taxes. Note that in addition to the expenses deducted above for your home office, you can also deduct an allocatable portion of the interest on your mortgage and your home taxes. These deductions are allowable as "above the line" business deductions even if you do not qualify to itemize your deductions.

The limitation on home office deductions can be shown by the following example. Assume the same deductions as in the previous case, but in addition, assume that you pay $3,000 in real estate taxes and $10,000 in mortgage interest. Furthermore assume that you have gross revenue of $5,000 from your "business." Your deductions are limited as follows:

| | |
|---|---:|
| Gross revenue (income) | $5,000 |
| Minus allocatable portion of interest in taxes | |
| [1/5 × ($10,000 + $3,000)] | −$2,600 |
| Limit on remaining expenses | $2,400 |
| Remaining expenses (from above) | $12,214 |
| Deductible Expenses (lesser of actual expenses or limit) | $2,400 |

Several additional factors should be noted. First, the Internal Revenue Service instructions talk about gross income, not gross revenue. They are equivalent. I am talking here about total inflow of dollars before *any* expenses. Second, with such high expenses in relation to income, you should elect straight-line depreciation over an extended life period. Third, note that even though your home office expenses are limited, there is no limitation on other expenses—for instance, travel, entertainment, supplies, etc.—for your business. Note that these examples do not contain *all* of the possible home office deductions. Anything that relates to your home office per se would be a potential deduction. For example, add any allocatable water charges, sewer charges, repairs, depreciation on such improvements as painting, aluminum siding, etc. In Revenue Ruling 86-148, the IRS allowed a deduction of a proportionate share of the monthly fee for a home security system, as well as depreciation deductions on that system, to a homeowner who used one-sixth of his house as office space. Your deductions are limited only by your imagination and your ability to relate your expenditures to your business.

Although the above limitations on home office deductions are contained in the Internal Revenue Service regulations, in the Tax Court case of *Scott v. Commissioner*, No. 18916-82, 84 T.C. No. 45, decided on April 15, 1985, Judge Simpson and the Court ruled that those regulations were invalid. According to the Judge, Section 280A(c) (5) limits the deductions allocable to the use of a home office to the gross income derived from such use. For purposes of this limitation, "gross income is not reduced by the other deductions attributable to the . . . businesses carried on in the . . . building." What this means is that in the above example, the deductions would be limited not to $2,400, but to the gross revenue of $5,000 (allowable, of course, to the actual remaining expenses incurred. While *Scott* was specifically overruled by the Tax Reform Act of 1986 for years after 1986, the Internal Revenue Service National Office has held that it will apply for open years prior to 1987 (TAM 8640001).

If you fear taxable recapture of depreciation upon sale of your house note that in Revenue Ruling 82-26 (February 8, 1982) the IRS ruled that the *prior* business use of a residence will not require the recognition of gain when the residence is sold. The IRS looks to the use of the residence at the time of the sale (Revenue Ruling 59-72). Thus, if the entire house is used as the principal residence in the year of sale, the entire gain on the sale may be eligible for tax-deferral, regardless of prior use. [See IRC Sections 1234 and 1250(d)(7)(A).]

To prove a home office, photograph it, have it on your business cards and stationery, and keep a log of whom you see, when you use the office, and what you work on.

In addition, travel expenses between your home office and job sites are deductible. For example, one taxpayer operated a home-repair business using his home as a business headquarters where he received inquiries for possible contracting services. He claimed a deduction for the expenses of traveling between his home and job sites. The deduction was allowable because his home was the sole fixed location of his business and was essential to his business operations (*Adams,* TCM 1982-223). In fact, in *Carl F. Worden*, T.C. Memo 1981-366, a home office had the effect of converting a personal residence into a job site. In that case, the Tax Court found that the insurance salesman's home was his place of business. Therefore, *all* his travel costs were allowable as business deductions. See also 76 T.C. No. 72, *Wisconsin Psychiatric Services, Limited*, where Wess R. Vogt, a psychiatrist, established that his home office was his principal office and therefore that trips to and from his home were business trips and not nondeductible commuting expenses; *Wicker,* TCM 1986-1, wherein the court ruled that a home office that was the principal place of business for a nurse-anesthesiologist enables her to deduct the costs of going from there to the hospital where she was associated and where she practiced exclusively, but without office space; and *Ronald Carey,* SD, OH, No. C-3-80-422, where a salesman who worked out of his home was able to deduct the cost of his daily sales trips because the salesman's home was his principal place of work.

Note that if you file a separate income tax from your spouse, an additional income-shifting opportunity is available. In Revenue Ruling 74-209, the Internal Revenue Service ruled that rent paid by a husband to his wife for the use of the jointly owned Wisconsin real estate that the husband used in his business is deductible as a business expense on the husband's separate income tax return. For this strategy to be successful, you should compare the net results on a joint return to those on separate returns. It is a technique that should be considered where appropriate.

Moreover, additional tax savings can be found if you have a home office that requires a secretary or a receptionist to be present at all times during business hours and the only person available is a member of your family. In the previous section we discussed the advantages of employing members of your family in your business as an income-shifting device. In this case, any member of your family, including your spouse, can reap enormous tax saving advantages. The Internal Revenue Service tax code excludes from gross income the value of any meals furnished to an employee by the employer for the convenience of the employer if the meals are furnished on the business premises of the employer.[46] If your spouse, for example, is required as your employee to be on your business premises—that is, your home office—as a receptionist, telephone operator, etc., then any meals (for instance, lunch) provided are not compensation that your spouse would include in gross income, but they are a *deductible* business expense to you! By structuring your first or second business in this manner, you can effectively and *legally* deduct the cost of your spouse's or children's lunches. Given the price of food today, this is an enormous benefit that can result in substantial tax savings. Moreover, no social security payments are due on such lunches. At $5 per lunch, five times a week for 50 weeks, your total deductible expense would be $1,250. In the 33 percent bracket, this saves you $413 in taxes!

---

46. Section 119 of the Internal Revenue Code.

# 88

## Your Car

Automobile expenses incurred in your business travel are deductible either as a travel expense (if away from home on business) or as a transportation expense (even if you are not away from home). Remember, transportation expenses are not normally deductible unless they are incurred in a business or investment situation. To get the deduction here, there must be a direct connection between the use of the car and your trade or business or some income-producing activity—for instance, to check on your investments. If you have one car that you use both for personal and for business use, only the portion of your car expenses directly attributable to business use is deductible.

In allocating your car expenses between business and personal use, there are a number of methods that you can use. One simple method is known as the mileage cost basis. Using this method, you multiply your business mileage by a standard mileage rate that the Internal Revenue Service allows in lieu of the operating and fixed costs of your car. This standard mileage rate is 22.5¢ per mile for the first 15,000 miles and 11¢ per mile thereafter, plus parking fees and tolls. So, for example, if you drive your car 20,000 business miles over the year, you will deduct $3,375 for the first 15,000 miles and $550 for the next 5,000. In addition to this $3,925 deduction, you will be allowed all of your expenses for parking fees and tolls.

As an alternative to the mileage cost basis, you can use either the mileage percentage basis or the weekly percentage basis. Under the mileage percentage method, you simply divide your business mileage by your total mileage and take that percentage of your total expenses as a deduction. Under the weekly percentage method, you take that percentage of the weekdays that you use your car for business use. So, for example, if you use your car two days a week on business, you will be able to deduct two-sevenths of your total auto expenses.

Included in such auto expenses, when using the mileage or weekly percentage method, are not only your parking fees and tolls but also depreciation on your car, registration and license fees, and gas, oil, and repair expenses. Given the cost of gasoline, it would probably be to your advantage to keep receipts and records of your actual expenditures. Whereas the Internal Revenue Service allows you a deduction of 22.5¢ per mile under the mileage cost basis, studies by auto-renting firms have established that actual mileage costs may be two to three times greater than that allowance.

There is a special tax planning strategy that you can use if you have two cars in your family. Assume that you have been using one car exclusively for business and the other exclusively for personal family use and that you put 36,000 miles each year on your business car and only 12,000 miles a year on your family car. Normally you can deduct only the costs of using the business car. Now, suppose you switched the use of each car every six months. The combined mileage of both cars in the original example is 48,000 miles per year. By rotating your cars equally between business and family use, each car will be driven 24,000 miles a year, 75 percent of which will be business miles (36 ÷ 48). Therefore, 75 percent of your depreciation and other costs on *each* car will be deductible. This can be a lot more than deducting all of the costs simply on one car and nothing on the other.

# 89   Meals and Entertainment

Wouldn't it be great to have the Internal Revenue Service pay part of the cost of your meals and entertainment? When you have your own business, you can have the Internal Revenue Service split the bills for these expenses with you.

Any expenses for food and drink furnished under circumstances of a type generally considered conducive to a business discussion, and when a business discussion is held, are deductible business expenses. Therefore, the custom of entertaining business clients or potential business clients with food and drink in restaurants and hotels will be deductible if they meet the requirements of an ordinary and necessary expense. When you go out with friends or relatives for a meal or drink, do you ever pick up their check? If they are or *could be* potential clients or customers for your business, and you discuss business, and if you discussed business with them, then that expense would be deductible. Alternatively, if they are in business and they pay your expenses for meals at a restaurant, those expenses would be deductible for them.

Note that under the Tax Reform Act of 1986, no deduction is allowed with respect to entertainment, amusement, or recreation unless the taxpayer establishes that the item was *directly related to* or, in the case of an item directly preceding or following a substantial and bona fide business discussion, that such item was *associated with* the active conduct of the taxpayer's trade or business and that meals are now included as entertainment expenses for this purpose. A meal expenditure is associated with the active conduct of a trade or business if the taxpayer establishes a clear business purpose in making the expenditure. The meal must directly follow or precede a substantial and bona fide business discussion. The directly follow or precede standard is satisfied if the meal occurs on the same day as the business discussion.

The directly related test is satisfied if any one of the following four tests is satisfied:

1.   The taxpayer had more than a general expectation of deriving some business benefit; the taxpayer actively engaged in a business meeting, negotiation, or other bona fide business transaction; the principal character or aspect of the meal was the active conduct of the taxpayer's business; and the expenditure was allocable to the taxpayer and persons with whom the taxpayer engaged in the active conduct of his business.

2.   The expenditure occurred in a clear business setting, directly in furtherance of the taxpayer's trade or business.

3.   The expenditure was made directly or indirectly for the benefit of an individual (other than an employee), and if such expenditure was in the nature of compensation for services rendered or paid as a prize or award, that is required to be included in gross income.

4.   The expenditure was made with respect to a facility used by the taxpayer for the furnishing of food or beverages in an atmosphere conducive to business discussion.

However, even if one of the four directly related tests is satisfied, expenditures will not be directly related to the active conduct of a trade or business if incurred under circumstances where there is little or no possibility of engaging in the active conduct of a trade or business.

You should have receipts specifying the name of the restaurant, the amount, and the date. The relationship of your guest to your business activity should also be noted. Recognize, however, that no actual business need come from the meeting so long as you discuss business at the restaurant. In this area be careful not to simply alternate days in which you and your friend pick up the check. Any "regular" exchange of meal checks, if caught by the

Internal Revenue Service, will be disallowed as a sham in an audit and subject you to fraud penalties.

Moreover, not only can you deduct meals, but you can also deduct business entertainment expenses. Amounts spent for business entertainment, amusement, or recreation will be allowable if you can show that the expense was:

a) for entertainment directly preceding or following a substantial bona fide business discussion (including business meetings at a convention that was associated with your trade or business); *or*

b) directly related to the active conduct of your trade or business.

Examples of entertainment, amusement, or recreation include entertaining guests at nightclubs, theatres, football games, prizefights, and on hunting, fishing, and vacation trips. In *Detko v. Commissioner,* No. 14790-81, T.C. Memo 1987-99, February 18, 1987, an anesthesiologist was found to be entitled to deductions for entertainment expenses and depreciation in connection with a *fishing boat* on which he entertained doctors who were his referral source!

In applying the "directly related" or "associated with" tests, remember these points:

1. The entertaining must be to further your trade or business. So, for example, if you entertain at a time when you already have more business than you can possibly handle, your deduction will be disallowed.

2. Expenses that violate public policy or local law—for instance, providing "call girls" for clients or serving liquor where it is against local law—will not be deductible.

3. Entertainment, amusement, or recreation expenses that are considered lavish or extravagant under the circumstances will be deductible *only* up to a reasonable amount. What a "reasonable amount" is depends upon all of the facts and circumstances; given today's business and entertainment climate, it would be very difficult to exceed a "reasonable amount."

Remember that the Tax Reform Act of 1986 limited deductions for most meals and entertainment to 80 percent of cost. Moreover, expenditures qualify as business meals or business entertainment only if business is actually discussed. Business transportation (airfare, taxis, etc.) remains fully deductible, but travel to *investment* seminars or *investment* conventions is not. The chart below summarizes these rules.

| Type of Expense | Deductible |
| --- | --- |
| Lunch with customer/client; business before, during, or after the meal | 80% |
| No business discussed | None |
| Cab fare to restaurant | 100% |
| Air fare to Philadelphia to call on customer/client | 100% |
| Lodging in Philadelphia | 100% |
| Meals in Philadelphia (alone) | 80% |
| Meals with customer/client; no business discussed: | |
| a. Your meal | 80% |
| b. Customer's/client's meal | None |
| Air fare to New York for dentist to attend dental convention | 100% |
| Meals in New York | 80% |
| Air fare to Dallas for investment seminar | None |
| Lodging in Dallas | None |
| Tickets to ball game for taxpayer and customer/client; business discussed | 80% |
| Taxi fare to game | 100% |
| Food and drink at game | 80% |
| Complimentary theater tickets for customer/client; taxpayer *not* present (note possible deduction as a gift) | None |
| Lunch at service organization as member | 80% |
| Tickets to charity golf tournament run by volunteers | 100% |
| Greens fees, carts, food and beverages consumed while hosting customer/client; business discussed | 80% |

Note that the 20 percent disallowance does not apply to pre-1989 expenses for food or beverages furnished as an integral part of a convention, seminar, annual meeting, or similar program if: (a) the meal charge is not separately stated, (b) more than 50 percent of the participants are away from home, (c) at least 40 individuals attend, and (d) the meal event includes a speaker.

With entertainment as well as with meals, your expenses must be substantiated. You should have a receipt detailing the amount paid, the client you entertained, the business relationship, the date, and the place. The deductions for meals and entertainment allow you substantial opportunities to convert your personal expenditures into allowable business deductions. Do not fail to claim them and do not fail to keep them because of lack of adequate substantiation. In the 33 percent tax bracket, $30 worth of football tickets costs you only $20. No matter how much money you are making, it would be worth $10 in tax savings to spend thirty seconds noting the name of your business client on the back of the ticket stub.

# 90

## Travel and Vacation

There is no law prohibiting you from combining a business trip and a vacation. The Internal Revenue Service concedes that you are entitled to a deduction for attending a business convention. While such attendance must benefit or advance your business to be a deductible expense, there is no reason why such a convention cannot coincide with your vacation. If a business purpose can be established, the expenses of your spouse may also be deductible (Revenue Ruling 56-168; see also *Bank of Stockton,* TCM 1977-24). Note, however, that such business conventions or seminars must relate to your specific business. For example, in IRS Letter Ruling 8451027 and Revenue Ruling 84-113, 1984-31 IRB 5, the Internal Revenue Service ruled that investment seminars in resort locations and a financial planning seminar dealing with general planning strategies were not deductible because they did not relate specifically to the taxpayer's activities.

### WITHIN THE UNITED STATES

If the business-vacation trip is within the United States, the transportation expenses will be deductible only if the trip is primarily for business. If the trip is primarily for pleasure, no transportation expenses can be taken as a deduction. This means that you have to establish a primary business motive for making the trip—for instance, a convention located in that city, or a client or potential client that you want to see at that location. It would be advisable under such a situation to write to this person and receive in return a letter requesting you to visit her or him to discuss business matters. The amount of time that you spend on business as opposed to pleasure will be a factor in answering the "primarily" question. For example, if you spend five days conducting business and three days sightseeing and seeing shows, the trip will be deemed primarily for business (five days vs. three days) and the transportation will be deductible. Alternatively, if you conducted business for two days and vacationed the remaining six, the trip will most likely be found primarily personal, and no transportation expenses will be allowed.

Even if the trip is found to be primarily personal, any expenses incurred at the destination that are properly allocatable to business—meals, lodging, and incidental expenses during your "business days"—will be deductible.

### OUTSIDE THE UNITED STATES

If the business-vacation trip is outside the United States, Canada, certain other Caribbean countries,[47] Mexico, and the Pacific Islands Trust Territories, special rules apply. If you were out of the country for seven days or less, or if less than 25 percent of the time was for personal purposes, no allocation of transportation expenses need be made. Furthermore, no allocation is required if you had no substantial control over the trip arrangements and if the desire for a vacation was not a major factor in taking the trip. Alternatively, if the trip was primarily for pleasure, none of the transportation expenses will be deductible. In all other cases, all travel expenses must be allocated between business and personal expenses, and days devoted to travel are considered business days.

---

47. The Caribbean Basin Initiative (CBI) was enacted on August 5, 1983, authorizing preferential tax measures for Caribbean Basin countries and territories. The Act allows deductions for business expenses incurred while attending conventions and meetings in a designated Caribbean Basin beneficiary country, if that country enters into an agreement with the United States to provide for the exchange of certain tax information. The provisions of the CBI expire September 30, 1995. Currently, the following countries are eligible and qualify for the benefits of the CBI: Antigua and Barbuda, the Bahamas, Barbados, Belize, Bermuda, the British Virgin Islands, Costa Rica, Dominica, the Dominican Republic, El Salvador, Grenada, Guatemala, Haiti, Honduras, Jamaica, Montserrat, the Netherlands Antilles, Panama, St. Christopher-Nevis, St. Lucia, St. Vincent, and Trinidad and Tobago. The countries that remain eligible but have not yet qualified for the benefits of the CBI are Anguilla, the Cayman Islands, Guyana, Nicaragua, Surinam, and the Turks and Caicos Islands (see Revenue Ruling 87-95). Updates to the list of qualifying countries can be obtained by calling (202)287-4851.

For example, assume that you took a trip from New York to London primarily for business purposes. You were away from home from July 20 through July 29 and spent three days vacationing and seven days conducting business (including two travel days). Your air fare was $500 and your meals and lodging amounted to $75 per day. You can deduct 70 percent of your transportation expenses (seven days out of ten) and $75 per day for seven business days, as you were away from home for more than seven days and more than 25 percent of your time was devoted to personal purposes.

If you find your trip is subject to the allocation rule, there is a planning strategy to maximize your tax deductions. When booking your flight, arrange for a stopover within the United States at the point closest to your destination. That way, the portion of the trip between your home and the stopover point will be fully deductible. You will have to allocate only the cost of the remainder of the trip.

For example, assume that you live in New York and will be attending a three-day business convention in the Bahamas that will be followed by a six-day vacation. If you fly directly to the Bahamas from New York, only one-third of the cost of your round-trip flight is deductible (three business days out of nine days total). However, if you fly from New York to Miami, conduct business in Miami, then take another flight to the Bahamas, the entire cost of the trip from New York to Miami would be deductible—as well as one-third of the cost of the trip from Miami to the Bahamas and back.

## FOREIGN CONVENTIONS

No deduction will be allowed for expenses attributable to a foreign convention/vacation unless it is "reasonable for the convention to be held outside North America." "North America" means the above countries including the Pacific Islands Trust Territories. In other words, there is no deduction if it is more reasonable to have the convention within rather than outside of North America. Three factors must be considered in determining the reasonableness of the convention location:

1. The purpose of the meeting and the activities taking place at the meeting.

2. The purpose and activities of the sponsoring organization or groups.

3. The residence of the active members of the sponsoring organization or groups and places where other meetings of the sponsors have been or will be held.

## CRUISE CONVENTIONS

In addition, there is no limit on the number of foreign conventions/ vacations that yield deductible expenses, but no deductions will be allowed for conventions, seminars, or other meetings held on cruise ships, except if:

a) the convention or meeting is directly related to your trade or business;

b) the cruise ship is U.S. registered; *and*

c) all ports of call are located in the U.S. or its possessions. Only the following ports qualify as possessions: The U.S. Virgin Islands (St. Thomas, St. John, St. Croix), American Samoa, Guam, the North Mariana Islands, and Puerto Rico.

Even under these circumstances, the maximum deduction is $2,000 for each taxpayer (Highway Revenue Act of 1982) and you must attach two written statements to your return. The first statement, signed by you, must include information as to the number of days that were devoted to scheduled business activities, a program of the scheduled business activities, and such other information as may be required by regulations. The other statement, signed by a representative of the sponsoring organization, must include a schedule of the business activities each day, the number of hours you attended such scheduled activities, and such other information as may be required by regulations. Business seminars on cruise ships that are U.S. registered are now being offered by American Hawaii Cruises (to Hawaii) and Delta Line Cruises (on the Ohio and Mississippi Rivers). In addition, American Cruise Lines and the new Clipper Cruise Line, which operates a variety of voyages in intercoastal waters from New England to Florida, are also operating under the seminar restrictions.

## WATER TRANSPORTATION

Note that the Tax Reform Act of 1986 limits the deduction for expenses incurred for transportation by water to twice the highest federal government per diem allowance (for employees traveling away from home but serving in the United States) times the number of days in transit. In addition, according to Notice 87-23, the 80 percent limitation on meals and entertainment is applied prior to the above maximum per diem limitations. If meal expenses are not separately stated, the amount deductible under the luxury water or travel limitation is not subject to the 80 percent rule.

Ship travel, however, can be an asset on a combined business-vacation trip. Days spent in transit count as business days in the allocation formula. For example, assume a two-day business meeting in London followed by a two-week British vacation. If you fly (one day each way), only 22 percent of your travel excluding transportation is deductible—two business days plus two days of travel out of a total of eighteen days away. But if you sail (five days each way), 46 percent is deductible—two business days plus ten days of travel out of a total 26 days away.

Remember, the key to being able to deduct your vacation as a business expense is prior planning. Make sure that you can substantiate your business purpose for the trip and your expenses. Properly planned and substantiated expenses will allow you to deduct the cost of your transportation, food, meals, lodging, entertainment, cleaning, etc. I have found that perhaps the easiest way to maintain a substantiation record is to keep a diary or account book of such expenses. Combined with appropriate receipts, such a diary will help reduce your taxes to zero.

# 91    Gifts

Ordinary and necessary expenses for business gifts you make directly or indirectly to any individual will be allowed as deductible expenses. However, the total value of business gifts during the tax year to any one individual cannot be more than $25, and in addition, gifts from a husband and wife are treated as coming from one donor in applying this limitation. Incidental costs, such as packaging, mailing or other delivery, and insuring the gifts, are not included in this limitation. The giving of business gifts is big business. According to *Incentive Marketing Magazine*, in 1983 approximately 50 million business gifts were purchased in the United States at a total cost of over 1 billion dollars.

The following items are not subject to the $25 limitation:

1. Items of a clear advertising nature that cost $4 or less,

    a)  on which your name is permanently printed; *or*

b) which are among a number of identical items generally distributed by you.

2. Signs, display racks, or other promotional material given by you as a producer or wholesaler to a retailer for use on the business premises of the retailer.

3. Employee awards (see page 41).

Here again you must provide substantiation for your expenses in order to make them allowable. While the price of allowance is increased recordkeeping, the benefit now is that gifts to friends, relatives, etc., who are or may become business clients or associates have been converted from nondeductible personal expenses to allowable income tax deductions. Every time you convert a personal expense to a deductible business expense you take one more step on the road to reducing your taxes to zero.

# 92

## Borrowing from Your Company

If your own business is in a corporate form, you have a special opportunity for tax savings. This opportunity is the supersophisticated technique of borrowing from your own corporation or from your corporate pension plan. This can be done as long as the loan bears a reasonable rate of interest—that is, the prime rate, give or take a percentage point.

This extraordinary technique allows you to borrow money, pay yourself interest, deduct the interest you pay (see Chapter 6 for limitations), and receive the same interest tax-free. It normally is done by having a qualified profit-sharing or pension plan make a loan to you as one of its participants. This technique was approved by the Internal Revenue Service for a qualified plan even with *single* participant.[48]

This technique will be approved by the Internal Revenue Service for a qualified plan that has a loan provision *if* the loan:

a) is available to all participants and beneficiaries on an equal basis;

b) is not made available to highly compensated office employees,

---

48. Letter Ruling 800-8059.

officers, or shareholders in a percentage amount greater than that available to other employees;

c)  is made in accordance with specific provisions regarding such loans set forth in the plan;

d)  bears a reasonable rate of interest; *and*

e)  is adequately secured.

The vested portion of your account (for a profit-sharing or money purchase plan) can be used as security for the loan. Moreover, loans from such plans can exceed the vested amount in your account without the plan's risking disqualification as long as:

- The loans are adequately secured by other than the nonvested portion of the plan.

- The loans bear a reasonable interest rate.

- The loans are repaid within a specified period of time.

Loan security for a defined benefit pension plan can be provided up to an amount equal to the actuarial equivalent, or present value, of your accrued benefit. Furthermore, the arrangement must be an actual loan. There must be evidence that a true debtor–creditor relationship exists; otherwise the "loan" will be labeled by the Internal Revenue Service as an "advance distribution," making such funds taxable income to you.

Note that the Tax Equity and Fiscal Responsibility Act of 1982 somewhat restricts borrowing against the vested benefits of your plan. Effective with respect to loans made after August 13, 1982, the law allows loans up to the lesser of $50,000 or 50 percent of the value of your vested employee benefit, but not less than $10,000. Additionally, the loan must be repaid within five years. But a loan used to acquire, construct, or rehabilitate your personal residence or the residence of a member of your family would not be subject to the five-year repayment rule.

The extraordinary savings from this technique can be demonstrated by the following example:

| | |
|---|---|
| Your vested share in a profit-sharing plan | $100,000 |
| Amount borrowed to purchase a home | $50,000 |

| | |
|---|---|
| Interest rate | 20% |
| Tax-free interest you pay into the plan | $10,000 |
| Amount deducted | $10,000 |
| Tax savings at 33% tax bracket | $ 3,300 |
| New value of your profit-sharing plan | $60,000 |

In effect, you pay yourself $10,000 and, by virtue of your tax deduction, come out ahead by $3,300!

Note that the Tax Reform Act of 1986 eliminated this benefit for key employee loans made after December 31, 1986. Effective for loans made after that date, the top loan is limited to $50,000 less the outstanding loan balance of plan loans on the date of the loan *and* less the excess of the highest outstanding loan balance from the plan during the one-year period ending on the day before the date of the loan over the outstanding loan balance of plan loans on the date of the loan. For example, assume you have a balance of $150,000 in your profit-sharing plan and have never made any loans from the plan. On January 1, 1988, you borrow $35,000. On May 1, 1988, the loan balance is $30,000. On November 1, 1988, the loan balance is $25,000. At that time you would like to borrow an additional amount without having to include it in income. The maximum amount you may borrow on that date is $15,000 ($50,000 − $25,000 − [$35,000 − $25,000]).

Moreover, the former five-year repayment period has been tightened. Effective for loans made after December 31, 1986, the five-year period may be extended only in the case of a loan made to purchase the principal residence of the plan participant. The extension of the five-year period is not permitted in the case of refinancing a principal residence. In addition, the repayment of loans made after December 31, 1986, must be made in level payments. The use of balloon payment arrangements is no longer permitted. Such payments must be made no less frequently than quarterly.

Finally, no interest is deductible for any post-1986 loan to a key employee. This means that even if you use the funds to purchase a principal residence, if you are a key employee, no interest will be deductible, even though all interest would have been fully deductible had you secured normal financing of the home.

A key employee is defined as a plan participant who at any time during the plan year or the preceding four plan years is (1) an officer of the company, (2) an employee owning one of the 10 largest interests in the company, (3) a 5 percent owner of the company, or (4) a 1 percent owner of the company earning more than $150,000 per year (IRC § 416)(i)(1)(A).

# 93

## Lending to Your Company

The previous technique demonstrated the tax saving opportunity in making loans *from* your corporation. But borrowing is a two-way street. You can make loans *to* your corporation and save taxes that way as well. If you have helped finance your corporation through loans over the years, there are some advantages in forgiving the principal and interest your corporation owes you. As far as the principal is concerned, the law provides that forgiveness of any principal due is a tax-free contribution to the capital of the corporation, and that you, as the stockholder, can increase the cost basis of your stock by the amount of the principal forgiven.

Interest unpaid to you by the corporation, however, is another matter. The Internal Revenue Service tax code allows your company to pay you interest, just as to any other lender, at a rate comparable to that charged by other lenders. If you are on the cash basis and wish to reduce your taxable income, simply do not collect the interest from your corporation. On the accrual basis, on the other hand, your company will accumulate the interest due on the loan and deduct it on its *own* tax return. Because of this tax benefit, the Internal Revenue Service has argued in the past that the unpaid interest should be treated as income to the company. This argument, however, was rejected by the tax court in 1976, when the court ruled that the unpaid interest was not income to the corporation, even though the company had accrued and deducted it in an earlier year.[49]

The net result of the case is that interest accrued and deducted by your corporation for a debt owed to you as one of its stockholders is not income either to the corporation or to you when you forgive that interest on that debt. This court-created tax loophole, however, will apply only if you do not own more than 50 percent of the corporate stock. Special rules in the Internal Revenue Code prohibit a corporation from deducting the interest in that case. But if you own 50 percent or less of the stock, and you are in a similar stockholder-lender position, you may want to forgive the interest that your company owes you. While this rule is an anomaly in the law, it is the law. So long as it is a completely legal technique, you should have no compunction about using it to reduce your taxes.

---

49. *Putoma,* 66 T.C. 652.

# 94

## Miscellaneous Corporate Advantages

There are a number of other miscellaneous tax saving strategies that owning your own company in a corporate form will allow you. They include the following:

1.  The corporation can purchase for you $50,000 of group term life insurance with tax-deductible dollars. Term life insurance in excess of $50,000 is also available at a negligible after-tax cost to you. For example, assume that you are 39 years old and the corporation purchases $100,000 in term life insurance for you. The premium would be 100 percent deductible to the corporation, and you would have to report only $66 per year of additional income. In the 33 percent bracket, this would cost only an additional $44.

2.  The corporation can pay health insurance premiums for you with tax-deductible dollars and no additional tax to you.

3.  Disability insurance premiums are also payable and deductible by the corporation with no tax to you.

4.  The corporation can accumulate dividend income or other income at the low rate of 15 percent on the first $50,000. Furthermore, the corporation can receive dividend income and exclude from taxation 80 percent of those dividends, reducing its effective tax rate to 3 percent (15% × 20% = 3%). Furthermore, such dividends can be placed tax-free into your retirement plan.

5.  The corporation can pay you and/or your estate a $5,000 death benefit free of income and estate taxes.

6.  The corporation can utilize retired life reserves or other similar life insurance plans with deductible dollars at the same time that it is building up cash reserves.

7.  Both Keogh and IRA plans absolutely prohibit owner-employees from borrowing money from the plan. But all plan participants *may* borrow their money from a corporate retirement plan. The advantages of such a provision have already been detailed.

    Remember, the interest earned on such loans will not be taxed to either the corporation or the plan and may be deductible by you on your personal income tax return. In the process, it will increase the amount of money accumulating tax-free in the plan, as well as your total financial wealth.

8. Prior to the Tax Reform Act of 1984, a current deduction for future college costs could have been allowed. The corporation could have set up an educational benefit plan in which a trust was established to which the corporation contributed funds to provide a given amount per year for each employee's child enrolled in an accredited college or university, without regard for financial need or academic achievement. In the case of *Greensboro Pathology Associates,* Federal Circuit, December 15, 1982, the Court ruled that the contributions to the trust were deductible when made by the corporation and only taxable income to the employees when the money was withdrawn. This can be a significant deferral tax advantage if the children are relatively young. In such a situation, the company can receive its deductions several years before the employees must pick up the income.

In determining that this was a welfare plan rather than a plan of deferred compensation wherein the corporate deduction would have been deferred until the employee recognized the income, the court looked at the following questions:

a)  Is the plan concerned with the employees' well-being?

b)  Are the benefits based on the earnings of the employees?

c)  Are benefits based on the length of service?

d)  Are benefits available to all employees?

e)  Are benefits really a substitute for salaries?

f)  Does the plan serve its stated purpose, or is it a sham?

g)  Does the employer lose control of the funds contributed?

h)  Can the funds revert to the company or its shareholders?

i)  Is the plan administered by someone independent of the company?

The court said that if items b and c were present, there was a strong presumption that the plan was a form of deferred compensation—no deduction allowed until funds were distributed. It also said that item d, availability to all employees, was essential if the plan was to qualify for current deductions.

The passage of the Tax Reform Act of 1984 appears, however, to effectively overrule the *Greensboro* case as to the immediate deductibility of plan contributions. The Tax Reform Act of 1984 provides that contributions to a funded welfare benefit plan will not be deductible under Section 162 but will now be governed by new Section 419. Section 419 provides that a contribution made to a funded welfare plan will be deductible in the year of contribution only to the extent that it would have been allowable as a deduction if the employer had paid the benefits directly and the employer used the cash-basis method of accounting. In essence, unless the plan is distributing benefits, no immediate deduction is allowable for fund contributions by the employer. Section 419, however, does provide for a carryover of contributions in excess of deductibility to the succeeding taxable year. Moreover, these new rules on plan contribution deductions apply not only to formal welfare benefit plans but to any method of employer contributions having the effect of a plan.

9. A final advantage of the corporate form of business is the elimination of the danger of vicarious liability that exists in a professional partnership. For example, assume that Dr. Smith and Dr. Jones operate as a partnership. Dr. Jones is on a vacation on the day that her partner, Dr. Smith, creates a potential malpractice problem in the operating room. Under the vicarious liability rules that apply to partnerships, Dr. Jones is just as responsible for the malpractice as is Dr. Smith, who is directly involved. In a corporate setting, Dr. Smith and the corporation are liable. Dr. Jones is personally off the hook.

# CHAPTER 9

# Investment Planning to Save Taxes

*"If Patrick Henry thought that taxation without representation was bad, he should see how bad it is with representation."*

OLD FARMERS ALMANAC

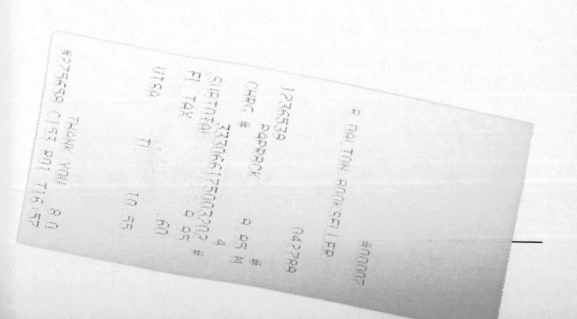

The first key to investment planning for 1988 tax purposes is recognition of the loss of the capital gains deduction on sales of capital assets. Capital assets include such things as stock, securities, real estate held as an investment, and most properties held for personal purposes. In fact, all property except the following is included under the umbrella of capital assets:

- Stock in trade, inventory, and other property held primarily for sale to customers in the ordinary course of business.

- Depreciable property used in a trade or business and real property used in a trade or business.

- Accounts and notes receivable acquired in the ordinary course of a trade or business for services rendered or from the sale of stock in trade, inventory, or other property held for sale to customers.

- A copyright or a literary, musical, or artistic composition held by a person whose personal efforts created it, or held by a taxpayer whose basis is determined by reference to the creator's basis (e.g., by gift).

- A letter or memorandum or similar property held by a person for whom the property was prepared or produced, or held by a taxpayer whose basis is determined by reference to the first person's basis (e.g., by gift).

- Obligations of the federal or a state government or one of its political subdivisions that are issued on a discount basis and payable without interest at a fixed maturity date not exceeding one year from the date of issue.

- Free U.S. Government publications.

Prior to 1987, an individual could deduct from gross income 60 percent of *net long-term capital gain* (the excess of net long-term capital gain over any net short-term capital loss), leaving only 40 percent taxable. Since the maximum regular income tax rate was 50 percent, the deduction meant that net capital gain was taxed at a maximum rate of 20 percent (50 percent $\times$ 40 percent).

Capital losses were allowed in full against capital gains. Capital losses were also allowed against up to $3,000 of ordinary income; however, only one-half of the excess of long-term capital loss over net short-term capital gain was allowed for this purpose. Unused capital losses could be carried forward indefinitely.

The Tax Reform Act of 1986 repealed the net long-term capital-gain deduction. However, the maximum rate on long-term capital gains of individuals was 28 percent in 1987. In 1988, it can go as high as 33 percent.

The 1986 law did not change the character of gain as ordinary or capital, or as long- or short-term capital gain. Capital losses are allowed in full against capital gain, as under prior law.

Capital-loss treatment also was changed by the 1986 law. Capital losses will continue to be fully offset by capital gains. The overall deduction limit of $3,000 per year (against ordinary income) still applies. Losses over that amount can be carried over to future years. Short-term capital losses will continue to be fully deductible against ordinary income, up to this $3,000 limit. Long-term capital losses also will be fully deductible against up to $3,000 of ordinary income. Beginning in 1987, both short-term and long-term capital-loss carry-forwards can be used to offset ordinary income on a dollar-for-dollar basis up to a $3,000 limit.

Note that the difference between long-term and short-term capital gains and losses still exists under current law. A gain from the sale or exchange of an asset acquired after December 31, 1987, will not be treated as long-term capital gain unless you held it for more than one year. The holding period was more than six months for assets acquired after June 22, 1984, and before January 1, 1988. Recognize that the longer holding period still has an impact, in that it affects charitable contributions of certain property. For example, a deduction normally cannot exceed 50 percent of your adjusted gross income. The equivalent limit for contributions to a private nonoperating foundation is 30 percent. For contributions of capital gain property, however, the limit is 30 percent of the contribution base, or 20 percent if the contribution is made to a private nonoperating foundation.

Capital-gain property includes only property that would have produced long-term capital gain if it had been sold at the time of the contribution. With the longer holding period, it would be that much longer before assets acquired after 1987 fall into that definition and within the lower percentage limits.

Moreover, the otherwise allowable deduction for a charitable contribution of property has to be reduced by the amount of gain that would not be long-term capital gain if the contributed property has been sold at the time of the contribution. That covers the amount of hypothetical gain that would have been recaptured in an actual sale (e.g., depreciation). However, it also covers all the hypothetical gain on an asset acquired after 1987 and not held for more than one year. Thus, the deduction for contributions of such post-1987 capital-gain property is limited to the property's adjusted basis.

Moreover, in post-1986 tax years, if the sale of the property would have produced long-term gain, the difference between the allowable deduction for the contributed property and its adjusted basis is a preference item for alternative minimum tax purposes.

Under current law it appears that if you've been in the highest tax bracket and will continue to be there in the future, the mathematics work out so that at most you'll pay only 13 percent extra on your long-term capital gain income in 1988 (33 percent rather than 20 percent). (The 33 percent rate is the maximum 28 percent rate plus the 5 percent added marginal tax from the phase-out of the 15 percent bracket.)

The last year in which a tax choice was available when publicly traded securities are sold during the last five trading days of the year was 1986. Starting in 1987, taxes must be paid the year the sale is made.

Under prior law it was important whether a stock redemption buy-sell agreement was characterized as a *sale* or *exchange,* typically resulting in long-term capital-gain treatment, or as a dividend, resulting in treatment of the entire distribution as ordinary income. The characterization made a significant difference.

*Example:*

### Sale or Exchange

| | |
|---|---:|
| Amount realized | $1,000,000 |
| Adjusted basis (cost) | 950,000 |
| Gain if sale or exchange | $    50,000 |
| 20% maximum tax (ignoring the alternative minimum tax) | $    10,000 |

### Dividend

| | |
|---|---:|
| Taxable if dividend | $1,000,000 |
| Maximum tax | $    50,000 |

### Tax Savings If Sale or Exchange

| | |
|---|---:|
| Tax if dividend | $  500,000 |
| Tax if sale or exchange | 10,000 |
| Tax savings | $  490,000 |

Under current law, the advantage of the lower marginal tax bracket on capital gains is lost. Sale or exchange treatment still retains the advantage of exposing only the gain (rather than the total distribution) to taxation. This advantage is particularly important if the selling shareholder's basis is high.

*Example:*

*Sale or Exchange*

| | |
|---|---:|
| Amount realized | $1,000,000 |
| Adjusted basis (cost) | 950,000 |
| Gain if sale or exchange | $    50,000 |
| 33% maximum tax (ignoring the alternative | |
|    minimum tax) | $    16,500 |

*Dividend*

| | |
|---|---:|
| Taxable if dividend | $1,000,000 |
| Maximum tax | $   280,000 |

*Tax Savings If Sale or Exchange*

| | |
|---|---:|
| Tax if dividend | $   280,000 |
| Tax if sale or exchange | 16,500 |
| Tax savings | $   263,500 |

Note that even under the new lower maximum tax rate, the total tax savings has decreased from $490,000 to $263,500 due to the loss of the capital gains deduction. Note also that even if the transaction is characterized as a sale or exchange, the tax is $6,500 higher ($16,500 − $10,000) than under prior law. This is due to the increase in the marginal capital gains rate from 20 percent to 33 percent for 1988.

These examples illustrate that if a shareholder has a *high* basis for his or her stock, the characterization of a sale of stock back to the corporation as a sale or exchange as opposed to a dividend is still very important. However, if the selling shareholder had a very *low* basis for the stock, the distinction between sale or exchange treatment and dividend characterization would make relatively little tax difference.

*Example:*

*Sale or Exchange*

| | |
|---|---:|
| Amount realized | $1,000,000 |
| Adjusted basis (cost) | 1,000 |
| Gain if sale or exchange | $ 999,000 |
| Gain at 33% (ignoring the alternative minimum tax) | $ 329,670 |

*Dividend*

| | |
|---|---:|
| Taxable if dividend | $1,000,000 |
| Maximum tax | $ 330,000 |
| Difference ($330,000 − $329,670) | $    330 |

The point is that the characterization of the transaction as a dividend rather than a sale or exchange makes relatively little difference. Therefore, is the reduction in control, share of profits, and share of assets necessary to achieve sale or exchange treatment worth that cost? If part of that cost included the steps necessary to waive family attribution (one of which is to give up all ties to the business), the total cost was and still is quite high. But if the shareholder's basis is low now, that cost may not be necessary.

# 95

## Municipal Bond Swaps

Muncipal bond swaps are transactions in which municipal bonds in a given portfolio are sold and the proceeds of the sale are then used to purchase other municipal bonds of like quality, coupon, par value, and yield.

Traditionally, this "tax swap" is the favorite method among individual investors to reduce their tax liabilities. Municipal bond market prices characteristically move up or down uniformly. Therefore, in most cases, if your bonds have depreciated in value, all other issues have as well, because interest rates have risen. The result is that by effectuating a swap, you merely establish paper losses for tax purposes. Your capital loss is the difference between your adjusted cost (or book value) and the current selling price of the bonds. The proceeds of a sale can be used to purchase other bonds, which should differ from those sold in coupon, maturity, or issuer. In most cases, tax swapping can be accomplished with a small adjustment (extension) of maturity to overcome market spreads.

Correctly done, a timely tax swap can provide you with the following benefits:

- Equal or greater income from your investments.

- Equivalent quality and/or maturity in bond portfolios.

- Continued participation in a favored security, or realizing tax losses that reduce your tax.

- Meaningful tax savings to offset both capital gains taken in your current year and up to $3,000 of other income, by using capital losses realized through the tax swap.

The mechanics of a tax swap are relatively simple. If you want to establish a capital loss for tax purposes, sell a bond for less than you paid for it. If at the same time you want to maintain your portfolio, buy a similar bond. There is no actual loss. At maturity the bond pays its face amount. If you buy one bond at $900 and sell it at $850, and then buy another at $850 and hold it to $1,000 maturity, you still make the $100 difference between your original purchase price and maturity; the intermediate sale and purchase do not matter. If you have a portfolio of bonds, therefore, you should contact your broker at year-end to arrange for an appropriate tax saving swap. If structured correctly, whether you do it with municipal bonds or with regular bonds, you should be a tax winner.

# 96

## Employee Options

Another investment tax saving strategy involves the handling of employee stock options. The grant of a nonqualified stock option results in no compensation to you as an employee. But exercising your option does result in compensation, measured by the difference between the option price and the fair market value at the time of the exercise.

For example, the *grant* of an option to buy 1,000 shares at $20 per share when the market value is $25 per share results in no income to you. If you *exercise* the option later when the market value is $40, you will recognize compensation income of $20,000 ($40,000 − $20,000). This taxable income plus the cash investment necessary to exercise the option are the major disadvantages of nonqualified stock options. In order to exercise the option in the above example, you must raise $26,600 in cash—$20,000 to buy the stock and as much as $6,600 to pay the tax in the 33 percent bracket.

The Internal Revenue Service has ruled that if full or partial payment for stock acquired upon exercise of a nonqualified stock option is made by transferring identical shares in the employer company, it will not result in any gain to you on the shares used to pay for the stock option.[1] The following example shows how you can take advantage of this ruling. Assume you own 1,000 shares of stock of your employer, acquired for $10 per share. You exercise a nonqualified option to acquire 2,000 shares of identical stock at an option price of $25 per share ($50,000 total). At the time of exercise, the market value of the stock is $50 per share ($100,000 total value).

If your employer agrees, you can pay for the 2,000 new shares by transferring to that employer the 1,000 shares of identical stock you already own. Since the value of the stock surrendered equals the option price, no cash is needed to buy the stock. In this way, you defer recognition of gain on the transfer of the 1,000 old shares, but you enjoy the full appreciated value by converting 1,000 shares of stock into 2,000 shares.

Using this technique, the cash required has been reduced to $16,500, the amount necessary to pay the tax on the $50,000 of compensation in the 33 percent bracket. Without this technique, you would also need $50,000 more to pay for the stock. Thus, the total cash outlay has been reduced from $66,500 to only $16,500. Of course, a proportionate reduction in the number of shares or the value of the shares would result in a proportionate reduction in the amount of cash that you actually would have to lay out.

# 97 Incentive Stock Options (Sec. 422A)

The Economic Recovery Tax Act of 1981 provides for a new type of stock option, called an "incentive stock option." No tax consequences result from the grant of an incentive stock option or from the exercise of an incentive stock option by an employee. You, the employee, will be taxed when you sell the stock. Furthermore, you must normally be an employee from the date of granting the option until three months before the date of exercise.

---

1. Revenue Ruling 80-244.

In its simplest form, a stock option is the right to buy a company's stock sometime in the future for a fixed priced. An option granted in 1987 to buy stock at $10 a share by 1996 yields a $5-a-share profit if the stock rises to $15 a share by then and the owner exercises the option and sells the stock.

Under pre-1987 law, an employee receiving an *incentive stock option* was not taxed on the exercise of the option and was entitled to capital gains treatment when the stock was sold. No deduction was taken by the employer when the option was granted or exercised. In order for options to qualify as incentive stock options, among other requirements, the options must have been exercisable in the order granted. Also the employer could not in any one year grant the employee such *options* to acquire stock with a value of (at the time the option was granted) more than $100,000 (increased by certain carry-over amounts).

The Tax Reform Act of 1986 repealed the requirement that the incentive stock options be exercisable in the order granted. It also modifies the $100,000 limitation. The 1986 law provides that an employer may not, in the aggregate, grant an employee incentive stock options that are first exercisable during any one calendar year to the extent the aggregate fair market *value of the stock* (determined at the time the options are granted) exceeds $100,000. For example, an employer cannot give an employee, in one year, qualifying incentive stock options to acquire 110 shares of stock currently selling at $1,000 per share. That would exceed the $100,000 value limitation.

The $100,000 limit was changed from the value of the *options* granted to the value of the *stock* covered by options that are exercisable. The availability of incentive stock options as an incentive is thereby reduced.

The repeal of the tax-favored treatment of capital gains will impact on the usefulness of incentive stock options for stock-based executive compensation. However, incentive stock options still retain an advantage for an employee over *nonstatutory options* (those options that do not qualify under Sec. 422A—for example, an option that is exercisable 11 years after the date it is granted). The recipient of an incentive stock option will continue to avoid regular income tax on the exercise of such an option. However, the *open* spread by which the fair market value of the incentive stock option, at time of option exercise, exceeds the stock's option price is a tax preference under the alternative minimum tax rules.

In contrast, upon *exercise* of a nonstatutory option, the excess of the nonstatutory option stock's fair market value over the option price is treated as additional compensation and taxed at regular income tax rates. Thus, an employee who exercises a nonstatutory option must find the funds to pay tax as well as to pay for the stock.

*Example:* Assume an executive in the 50 percent tax bracket exercised an incentive stock option in 1986 to acquire stock worth $150 for $100. His total *costs* for the stock ranged from $100 (if he is not subject to the alternative minimum tax) to a maximum of $110 ($100 option price plus 20 percent minimum tax on the $50 spread). In contrast, if the stock was acquired through the exercise of a nonstatutory option, the cost to the executive to buy the stock would be $125 ($100 option price plus 50 percent tax on the $50 spread). In 1988 the cost would be $116.50 ($100 option price plus 33 percent on the $50 spread).

The loss of the favorable capital gain treatment does not change the tax consequences of incentive stock options to the employer. The employer is not entitled to a deduction for the benefit realized by the executive on an incentive stock option exercise. Since a deduction continues to be available when a nonstatutory option is exercised, nonstatutory options retain the employer's tax advantage over incentive stock options after 1986. However, the reduction in corporate tax rates will reduce this advantage.

Therefore, incentive stock options continue to provide better tax advantages to employees than nonstatutory options, and since the current corporate tax rates reduce the employer's tax benefits from nonstatutory options, incentive stock options will continue to offer advantages for executive compensation packages.

An interesting twist on the incentive stock option concept is the junior stock plan, which works as follows. The employer corporation issues special "junior" non-voting common stock, paying dividends. These shares can be exchanged by holders for regular common stock, share for share, at a specified date if the holders meet certain conditions. The junior shares are sold to employee executives at a bargain price—for example, $20 while the regular common is trading at $30. Each executive pays taxes on the original price differential—the $10 price spread. At the end of the term, with the employer common stock trading at, for example, $80, the executives swap the junior stock for the common in a tax-free exchange. On sale of the common stock, the executive has a tax basis of $30—the $20 paid for the junior shares plus the $10 on which he was taxed. Thus he has a gain of $50 per share—$80 less $30—taxed at a maximum 20 percent rate prior to 1986, but at ordinary income rates for 1987 and after.

This technique adds several breaks not available under normal incentive stock option rules. For example, junior stock lets an executive effectively buy his company's shares at a price far below the market. This allows far easier financing of a purchase of a block of shares. Moreover, the plan escapes the $100,000-per-year limit on the value of incentive stock options shares bought by an executive.

# 98

## Year-End Stock Sales

The Internal Revenue Service had ruled that gains from stocks sold in a year's last week come under the installment sales law. That allowed you to choose—at leisure—to incur the tax in either the current year or the next. Prior to 1982, a gain on stocks sold through a broker in one year for payment in the next was considered taxable in the payment year; to make it taxable in the year of sale, you had to allow five business days for settlement. Under the installment sales law, however, an installment sale is one where any payment is made in a later year. That makes gain taxable in the later year *unless* you elect not to use the installment method; in that case, the gain is taxable in the sale year. You do not have to make an election to choose the year in which to incur the tax until the due date for your sale-year return, including the automatic four-month extension. This means that if you expect your income to increase, it may be advisable for you to recognize the gain earlier, in the lower-bracketed year.

Under the Tax Reform Act of 1986, effective January 1, 1987, taxpayers who sell stock or securities *on an established securities market* are *not* permitted to use the installment method to account for such sales. The trade date is considered the date of tax recognition.

# 99

## Tax-Exempt Income

A final word should be said about tax-exempt income. In the investment context, tax-exempt income results primarily from nontaxable interest from municipal securities. The table shown here indicates the equivalent rate of return that fully taxable income, such as rents or taxable interest, would have to yield in order to produce net income equivalent to that produced by various tax-exempt returns at the same tax rates.

### Equivalent Taxable and Tax-Exempt Returns on Investment, 1988

| % income tax bracket | Tax-exempt Yield | | | | | | |
|---|---|---|---|---|---|---|---|
| | 1% | 6½% | 7% | 7½% | 8% | 9% | 10% |
| 15% | 1.18 | 7.64 | 8.23 | 8.82 | 9.41 | 10.59 | 11.76 |
| 28% | 1.39 | 9.02 | 9.72 | 10.41 | 11.11 | 12.50 | 13.89 |
| 33%* | 1.49 | 9.70 | 10.45 | 11.19 | 11.94 | 13.43 | 14.93 |

*If 5% surcharge applies.

At a 33 percent marginal tax rate, you would need to earn 10.45 percent in taxable interest to have the same after-tax return as 7 percent tax-free.

To find the equivalent taxable income return for a tax-exempt return *not* given in the table, multiply the tax-exempt return rate by the figure in the 1 percent column next to the applicable tax rate. For example, at a 33 percent tax rate, a taxable investment would have to yield 14.90 percent to produce the same amount of after-tax income that is produced by a tax-exempt investment that yields a 10 percent return (10 percent × 1.49 = 14.90 percent).

To find the tax-free income equivalent to a given taxable income, divide that taxable income by the figure in the 1 percent column next to the given rate. For example, at a 33 percent tax rate, $2,000 in taxable income yields $1,342 ($2,000 ÷ 1.49).

Note, in addition, that state taxation of interest income should be taken into consideration in computing total yield. For example, most states do not tax interest on municipal bonds issued within their own state. Thus, a New Jersey tax-free municipal bond held by a New Jersey investor would be exempt both on the federal and on the New Jersey tax return. In many states there is no difference in the state tax treatment of in-state versus out-of-state bonds. For example, in 1987, in Illinois, Iowa, Kansas, Oklahoma, and Wisconsin, interest from state municipal bonds is subject to state tax. In 12 other states—Alaska, Florida, Indiana, Nebraska, Nevada, New Mexico, South Dakota, Texas, Utah, Vermont, Washington, and Wyoming—as well as in Washington, D.C., you do not have to pay state income taxes on interest from bonds issued by other states, either.

# 100

## Special Report

As a result of the magnitude of the American Telephone and Telegraph divestiture, taxpayers selling shares of the new AT&T or any of the seven regional telephone companies have had difficulty in allocating their cost with respect to the value of the package they received. On November 21, 1983, the first day of when-issued trading in such stock, the value of the package was:

|   |   |   |
|---|---|---|
| 1.0 share American Telephone | @ 18¼ = | $18.25 |
| 0.1 share Ameritech | @ 63⅜ = | 6.34 |
| 0.1 share Bell Atlantic | @ 67¾ = | 6.77 |
| 0.1 share BellSouth | @ 88⅝ = | 8.86 |
| 0.1 share NYNEX | @ 61⅛ = | 6.11 |
| 0.1 share Pacific Telesis | @ 54 = | 5.40 |
| 0.1 share Southwestern Bell | @ 61⅛ = | 6.11 |
| 0.1 share USWest | @ 57⅛ = | 5.71 |
| Total Value | = | $63.55 |

Note that because of a three-for-one subsequent split in BellSouth, the stock's value now must be calculated on the basis of 0.3 shares of BellSouth for each share of AT&T prior to divestiture.

# 101

## Alternative Minimum Tax for Individuals

Prior to 1987, individuals were subject to an alternative minimum tax (AMT), which was payable, in addition to all other tax liabilities, generally to the extent that it exceeded the individual's regular tax liability. The tax was imposed at a flat rate of 20 percent on alternative minimum taxable income (AMTI) in excess of an exemption amount.

In computing alternative minimum taxable income, adjusted gross income was reduced by AMT itemized deductions (which were a limited subset of the itemized deductions allowable for regular tax purposes).

The AMTI was computed by increasing the adjusted gross income (less allowable AMT itemized deductions) by the items of tax preference, which included the following:

- the dividend exclusion of $100 for a single return and $200 for a joint return

- for all real property and tangible personal property subject to a lease, the excess of accelerated depreciation over straight-line depreciation based upon the property's useful life

- an amount equal to the 60 percent net capital gain deduction for the year, other than gain from the sale of a personal residence

- for certified pollution-control facilities, the excess of 60-month amortization over the depreciation otherwise allowable

- for research and experimentation expenditures that were expensed rather than capitalized, the excess of the deduction claimed over the amount allowable if the expenditure were amortized over a 10-year period

- for mining exploration and development costs (other than intangible drilling costs [IDCs]), the excess of the amount expensed over that allowable if the expenses were amortized over a 10-year period

- for oil and gas IDCs, the amount by which the excess of the amount expensed exceeded the amount allowable if the IDCs were amortized over a 10-year period, and the amount of oil and gas income

- percentage depletion to the extent in excess of the adjusted basis of the property

- for circulation expenses relating to newspapers, magazines, and other periodicals, the excess of the amount expensed over the amount allowable if amortized ratably over a three-year period

- for incentive stock options, the excess of the fair market value received through the exercise of the option over the exercise price

For certain preferences, individuals could elect for regular tax purposes to take a deduction ratably over 10 years (three years in the case of circulation expenses) and thereby avoid an AMT preference.

In general, no refundable credits (such as investment tax credits) were allowed to offset the AMT except the foreign tax credit. Also, for years after 1982 net operating loss deductions were allowed in computing the AMT only to the extent not attributable to tax-preference items.

CURRENT LAW

The individual alternative minimum tax is retained under the current law, but with significant modifications. The AMT is computed starting with regular taxable income (rather than adjusted gross income, as under prior law), which is determined with certain adjustments. Preference items are then added back to regular taxable income in calculating the AMT. The minimum tax rate is increased from 20 to 21 percent. The exemption amount ($40,000 for married persons filing jointly, $30,000 for singles, and $20,000 for married persons filing separately) is reduced by 25 percent of the amount by which AMTI exceeds $150,000. For married taxpayers filing separately the phase-out will begin at $75,000 and for single taxpayers at $112,500. More important, the AMT becomes a separate tax computation with is own accelerated cost recovery system, basis, gain or loss computations, etc.

|  | Exemption | Phase-out begins at | Phase-out ends at |
|---|---|---|---|
| Married filing jointly and surviving spouse | $40,000 | $150,000 | $310,000 |
| Single and unmarried head of household | $30,000 | $112,500 | $232,500 |
| Married filing separately | $20,000 | $ 75,000 | $155,000 |

The phase-out of the exemption amount results in an effective marginal minimum tax rate of 26.25 percent for individuals in the phase-out income ranges.

*Preference Items and Adjustments*

The new law retains most of the prior law preferences, although it modifies the computation of certain items. The items of preference adjustments include the following:

- Accelerated depreciation on real property placed in service after 1986 will be considered a preference item to the extent that it exceeds depreciation computed on a 40-year straight-line basis. For personal property the preference item will be the excess of accelerated depreciation over the depreciation computed using the 150 percent declining-balance method (switching to straight line in the year necessary to maximize the deduction). However, the preference does not apply to property that is expensed under Sec. 179.

- Depreciation with respect to property placed in service prior to 1987 is treated as a preference only to the extent that it constituted a preference under prior law. Also, for property placed in service after 1986 with respect to which the alternative depreciation system is used, no AMT preferences will arise.

Under the revised AMT, the alternative depreciation system is substituted for the accelerated cost recovery system (ACRS). This system permits *netting*. If the AMT depreciation exceeds the ACRS with respect to real or personal property for that year, the amount of the preference is reduced. Since the AMT uses the alternative depreciation system, separate depreciation basis adjustments must be made for AMT purposes. Therefore, the amount of gain on disposition may differ for AMT and regular tax purposes.

- As under prior law, the rapid amortization for pollution-control facilities, the excess of allowable depletion over the adjusted basis of the property (determined without regard to the depletion deduction), mining exploration and development costs, circulation expenditures, research and development costs, the amount by which the fair market value of a share of stock at the time of exercise of an incentive stock option exceeds the option price, and intangible drilling costs (except that the net income offset is reduced from 100 percent to 65 percent) are all still tax preference items.

The 1986 law also adds the following new preference items and adjustments:

- Tax-exempt interest on nongovernmental purpose bonds issued after August 7, 1986. Exceptions are provided for bonds issued on behalf of certain tax-exempt organizations and certain bonds issued before September 1, 1986. However, no exceptions are provided for industrial development bonds.

- For any long-term contract entered into by the taxpayer after March 1, 1986, use of the completed contract is not permitted for AMT purposes. Instead, the taxpayer is required to use the percentage-of-completion method for AMT purposes.

- For dispositions after March 1, 1986, the use of the installment-sale method is not permitted for AMT purposes by dealers and others subject to proportionate disallowance of the installment method (sales of trade or business or rental property when the purchase price exceeds $150,000).

- Charitable contributions of appreciated property. A tax preference exists to the extent of the unrealized appreciation of contributed capital gain property. Therefore, for minimum tax purposes, the charitable-contribution deduction is limited to the property's adjusted basis. In calculating the amount of the preference, unrealized gains on appreciated property are offset by unrealized losses. The amount of preference is determined by disregarding any amount that is carried forward to another taxable year for regular tax purposes. Also the preference does not apply to carry-overs of the deduction with respect to contributions made before August 16, 1986.

- Passive activity losses that are allowed under the passive loss phase-in rules must be added back to taxable income in computing the AMT with the following revisions: (1) the amount of losses that otherwise would be added back for the current taxable year is reduced by the amount of the taxpayer's insolvency; (2) in calculating passive losses, minimum tax measurements of items of income and deduction will be used rather than regular tax measurements; and (3) the amount added back is reduced by other items of tax preference to prevent double counting.

  Because of these calculations the amount of suspended passive losses relating to a passive activity may differ for AMT and regular tax purposes. However, it appears that after the five-year phase-in of the regular tax passive loss rules, differences should be minimal.

- Passive farm losses from a tax-shelter farming activity are treated like passive activity losses with the revisions discussed immediately above (for passive activity losses) and with the following special provisions: (1) each farm is treated as a separate activity—no netting between farming activities is allowed; (2) the preference applies to personal service corporations; and (3) loss from a disposition of a tax-shelter farm activity shall be allowed for minimum tax purposes and not treated as a loss from a tax-shelter farm activity.

- The standard deduction must be added back to taxable income when computing the AMT.

- Non-AMT itemized deductions used in computing taxable income must be added back in computing the AMT.

- The $100 ($200 joint filing) exclusion for dividends and the net capital gain deduction have both been depleted as items of tax preference because they are no longer applicable for regular tax purposes.

*AMT Itemized Deductions*

In general, the AMT itemized deductions are the same as under prior law and include the following:

- theft, casualty, and wagering losses

- charitable contributions

- medical expenses, except the floor is 10 percent of adjusted gross income instead of 7.5 percent, as used for regular tax purposes

- qualified interest expenses (which include interest paid or incurred on debt to acquire, construct, or substantially rehabilitate the taxpayer's principal or qualified dwelling and other investment interest to the extent it does not exceed the taxpayer's qualified net investment income for the taxable year)

- the deduction for estate taxes for recipients of income in respect of decedents

The definition of investment interest is the same as under the new law for regular tax purposes. No AMT deduction is allowed for consumer interest. Disallowed investment interest deductions may be carried forward. Interest paid on a refinanced loan is treated as qualified residence interest if it qualified under the original loan and the amount of the loan was not increased. Also refunds of state and local taxes are not included in alternative minimum taxable income.

*Carry-over of Tax Credits*

As under prior law, nonrefundable credits are not allowed against minimum tax liability. Refundable credits that do not benefit the taxpayer because of the minimum tax can be carried back or forward to other taxable years. The foreign income tax credit is allowed against AMT.

*Minimum Tax Credit*

Under prior law minimum tax incurred by a taxpayer in one year had no effect on regular tax liability in other years.

The new law creates a minimum tax credit for prior-year minimum tax liability that may offset regular tax in later years. The AMT tax credit is equal to the excess of the AMT tax liability attributable to *deferral preferences* over the regular tax liability for the year. Deferral preferences are essentially all tax preferences except those relating to percentage depletion, tax-exempt interest, the appreciated-property charitable deduction, and regular tax itemized deductions that are not allowed for AMT purposes. The AMT credit can be carried forward (but not back) indefinitely.

> *Example:* In 1988 Ms. Fortunate has a regular tax liability of $35,000 after taking into account $15,000 of passive losses attributable to accelerated depreciation deductions on leased equipment that were deductible under the phase-in of the passive loss limitation. Her AMT is $39,000. She must pay tax of $39,000 in 1988 but has a minimum tax credit to the extent that her AMT was attributable to the accelerated depreciation deferral preferences. The minimum tax credit is $3,150 ($39,000 AMT − $35,850 adjusted net minimum tax).
>
> If Ms. Fortunate has a regular tax liability of $28,000 and an AMT of $26,000 in 1989, $2,000 of the minimum tax credit may be applied in 1989. The remaining $1,150 of credit carries forward to 1990 and, if necessary, later years.

*Net Operating Losses (NOLs)*

For AMT purposes a separate computation of NOLs and NOL carry-overs will be required. In general, the AMT NOL, which cannot offset more than 90 percent of AMT income, is computed in the same manner as the regular tax NOL, except for two special rules. The items of tax preference arising during the taxable year are added back to taxable income, and only AMT itemized deductions are taken into account.

*Example:* In year 1 a taxpayer has $10,000 of income and $35,000 of losses, of which $10,000 are preference items. The AMT NOL for year 1 is $10,000.

*Regular Tax Elections*

Under the new law taxpayers may still elect for regular tax purposes to deduct ratably over 10 years (three years for circulation expenditures) certain expenditures (IDCs and mining exploration and development expenditures) that are otherwise currently deductible and thus avoid treatment of the item as a minimum tax preference.

## PLANNING CONSIDERATIONS

In general, high-income individuals will have to pay even more attention to the alternative minimum tax. There are many changes. The AMT rate has been raised from 20 to 21 percent, and the exemption amounts of $40,000 for married couples filing jointly, $30,000 for singles, and $20,000 for married individuals filing separately are reduced by 25¢ for each dollar by which AMTI exceeds $150,000, $112,500, and $75,000 respectively. Net capital gains will be fully included in minimum taxable income, there will be a bigger effect for intangible drilling costs, private-activity bonds will be a preference, and there will be a preference for charitable contributions of appreciated property. The passive loss rules apply for AMT purposes, except that the preference is reduced by the amount, if any, of the taxpayer's insolvency. In addition, passive losses are reduced to the extent attributable to tax preference, since those preferences are added in elsewhere.

Tax planning for the AMT will involve many of the techniques applicable under prior law. In years when the AMT is inevitable, a taxpayer's objective should be to *accelerate* income and *defer* deductions. A taxpayer's marginal tax rate while subject to the AMT is 21 percent (26.25 percent for income in the range where the phase-out of the exemption applies) for all additional income realized until the AMT is used up. The taxpayer's tax rate jumps to the marginal rate for regular tax purposes as soon as the AMT is used. If a taxpayer is subject to the alternative minimum tax, non-AMT itemized deductions provide no tax benefit. Additional alternative minimum tax itemized deductions provide a tax deduction rate only equal to the AMT rate. Additional tax preferences, like non-AMT itemized deductions, provide no benefit when the taxpayer is subject to the AMT.

Methods taxpayers may wish to consider for accelerating income when subject to the AMT include:

- Take prepayments of salary and bonuses.

- Declare and pay corporate dividends from closely held corporations. This may also have a potentially positive effect on the corporation if it has a problem with the accumulated earnings tax.

- Consider redeeming Series EE U.S. savings bonds, or elect to report all the accrued interest on the bonds in the current year.

- Redeem certificates of deposit.

- Make early sales of U.S. T-bills.

- Make early sales of investment certificates.

- Recognize gains on portfolio securities.

- Elect out of the installment method for any installment sales (under Sec. 453(d)).

- Consider converting tax-free municipal investments into taxable investments.

- Sell stocks acquired by incentive stock options (ISOs) within a year after the ISOs are exercised. Under Sec. 422(a)(1) this is a disqualifying transaction that makes the gains taxable as ordinary income (even if the transaction takes place in a taxable year subsequent to the year the ISOs were exercised). In addition, this transaction eliminates the tax preference if the transaction takes place in the same taxable year as the exercise of the options. By so doing, you can possibly zero out the AMT (with no additional tax paid because the regular tax is increased while the AMT is reduced). You can immediately repurchase the stocks and effectively step up the basis in the stock and avoid the tax that would otherwise be realized sometime in the future.

- Withdraw funds from IRAs in some circumstances (if subsequent withdrawals are anticipated at tax rates greater than 31 percent—21 percent AMT plus 10 percent penalty).

Taxpayers may also benefit by deferring deductions, especially non-AMT itemized deductions.

Taxpayers subject to the AMT should also try to capitalize otherwise deductible expenses. For example, they should not expense any part of the cost of a depreciable business asset. They should consider electing 10-year write-offs on any portion of currently deductible expenses that constitute tax preferences (which also eliminates the preference). The items to which this applies are research and experimentation expenditures, mining exploration and development costs, and intangible drilling costs. In addition, magazine circulation expenses may be capitalized and written off over a three-year period. Taxpayers with research and experimentation expenditures for their own business should consider electing to amortize those expenditures over 60 months or longer. This will both shift deductions out of the current year and reduce AMTI. Taxpayers acquiring new depreciable property should consider electing depreciation under the alternative recovery system, which will defer deductions and reduce AMTI.

Note that you may be hit with the alternative minimum tax even if you don't have one single dollar of tax preferences. For example, assume that you had an adjusted gross income of $150,000. In 1987 you paid $25,000 in state and local income taxes (including your April 1987 payment for your 1986 taxes) and $22,000 in property taxes on raw land you own as an investment. You paid $6,000 in interest on home equity loans you took out to pay college expenses for your children and had $8,000 in other itemized deductions, including $2,000 for investment expenses in excess of 2 percent of your adjusted gross income. Assume further that you had absolutely no tax preferences.

Because your itemized deductions for purposes of the alternative minimum tax are not the same as your itemized deductions for your regular tax, your alternative minimum tax was $260 higher than your regular tax. Therefore, you paid an extra $260 in taxes for 1987. As the regular tax rates fall in 1988, however, the chance of being hit with the alternative minimum tax increases, and your potential alternative minimum tax bill gets bigger. For example, on these same facts, you would owe an alternative minimum tax of more than $2,400 in 1988!

### Individual AMT Work Sheet

Taxable Income (Form 1040)                                      _____
  Adjustments and Preferences:
    Non-AMT IDs/STD deduction                                 _____
    Excess depletion                                          _____
    Appreciated charitable property                           _____
    Tax-exempt interest on private-activity bonds             _____
    Excess depreciation                                       _____

| | | |
|---|---|---|
| Rapid amortization of pollution-control facilities | _____ | |
| Excess mining expenditures | _____ | |
| Circulation expenditures | _____ | |
| R & D costs | _____ | |
| Excess value on exercised ISOs | _____ | |
| IDCs | _____ | |
| Long-term contract adjustment | _____ | |
| Installment-sale adjustment | _____ | |
| Adjusted passive activity losses | _____ | |
| Adjusted passive farm losses | _____ | |

| | | | |
|---|---|---|---|
| Plus | Total adjustments and preferences | _____ | _____ |
| Minus | AMT NOL (limited to 90% of AMTI) | | _____ |
| Equals | AMTI | | _____ |
| Minus | Exemption Amount* | | _____ |
| Equals | AMT base | | _____ |
| Times | AMT rate | | $\times$ 21% |
| Equals | AMT (before foreign income tax credit, if any) | | _____ |
| Minus | Foreign income tax credit (limited to 90% of AMT) | | _____ |
| Equals | AMT (after foreign income tax credit) | | _____ |

*Calculation of Exemption Amount

| Filing Status | Exemption Amount | AMTI Range |
|---|---|---|
| Married, filing jointly | $40,000<br>$77,500 − .25 $\times$ AMTI<br>$     0 | For AMTI less than $150,000<br>For AMTI between $150,000 and $310,000<br>For AMTI greater than $310,000 |
| Single | $30,000<br>$58,125 − .25 $\times$ AMTI<br>$     0 | For AMTI less than $112,500<br>For AMTI between $112,500 and $232,500<br>For AMTI greater than $232,500 |
| Married, filing separately | $20,000<br>$38,750 − .25 $\times$ AMTI<br>$     0 | For AMTI less than $75,000<br>For AMTI between $75,000 and $155,000<br>For AMTI greater than $155,000 |

Alternative Minimum Tax Preference Items under Present Law and New Law

| Tax Preferences | Individual | | Description of Tax Preference |
| | Prior Law | Current Law | |
| --- | --- | --- | --- |
| Long-term contracts | No | Yes | Income must be calculated on the percentage-of-completion method for new contracts |
| Certain tax-exempt interest | No | Yes | Interest income on certain private-activity tax-exempt bonds issued after August 7, 1986 |
| Appreciated property charitable deduction | No | Yes | Unrealized appreciation on long-term capital gain property |
| Passive activity losses | N/A | Yes | Net losses from passive activities |
| Accelerated depreciation on new property | N/A | Yes | Depreciation for AMT is calculated using the Alternative Depreciation System except that the preference for personal property is based on the 150 percent DB method |
| Premodified ACRS and pre-ACRS depreciable leased personal property | Yes | Yes | Excess of accelerated over straight-line deductions |
| Mining exploration and development costs | Yes | Yes | Excess over amount allowable if amortized ratably over 10 years |
| Circulation expenditures | Yes | Yes | Excess over amount allowable if amortized ratably over three years |
| Research and experimental costs | Yes | Yes | Excess over amount allowable if amortized ratably over 10 years |

| Tax Preferences | Individual | | Description of Tax Preference |
|---|---|---|---|
| | Prior Law | Current Law | |
| Depletion | Yes | Yes | Excess of depletion over adjusted basis in property |
| Incentive stock options | Yes | Yes | Excess of fair market value over option price at date of exercise (basis of stock adjustment for AMT) |
| Dividend exclusion from income | Yes | N/A | Amount of dividends excluded |
| Capital gains | Yes | N/A | Under present law full LTCG deduction is a preference |
| Intangible drilling costs | Yes | Yes | Excess over amount allowable if amortized ratably over 120 months over 65% of net income from oil and gas |
| Pollution-control facilities | Yes | Yes | Excess of amortization over allowable depreciation |
| Individual itemized deductions | Yes | Yes | Certain itemized deductions not allowed |
| Alternative tax net operating loss | Yes | Yes | NOLs with certain adjustments |
| Installment method accounting | No | Yes | Installment method generally not allowed for AMT purposes |

# 102 The Schnepper-Leimberg "SPLIT" (Joint) Purchase

As to the astuteness of taxpayers in ordering their affairs so as to minimize taxes, it has been said that "the very meaning of a line in the law is that you intentionally may go as close to it as you can if you do not pass it." *Superior Oil Co. v. Mississippi,* 280 U.S. 390, 395–96. This is so because "nobody owes any public duty to pay more than the law demands: taxes are enforced exactions, not voluntary contributions." Frankfurter, J., *Atlantic Coast Line v. Phillips,* 322 U.S. 168, 172–73 (1947).

Here is a technique whereby a financial planner may accomplish presumably the best of all worlds:

- reduce your current income tax

- reduce your potential estate tax

- transfer substantial wealth without the imposition of a gift tax

- potentially take as much as almost $2 in deductions for every dollar that you invest

- potentially convert nondepreciable assets—e.g., stocks and bonds—into depreciable/amortizable assets on which you may recover your basis.

This technique consists of a SPLIT purchase of a life estate and a remainder interest in income-producing property. Ownership of property can be broken down into two elements. The first is a "life estate"—the right to use, possess, or enjoy the property and the income it produces for as long as the holder of that life estate lives. The second part is "remainder interest"—the balance of the property interest not owned by the life tenant. When the life tenant dies, the holder of the remainder interest receives by operation of law all of the interest in that property. This is how a split works.

### SPLIT DEFINED

A "SPLIT" is an arrangement under which two parties purchase an asset from a third party. One party (generally a parent or grandparent) purchases a life estate (the right to receive the income from the property or the right to use, possess, and enjoy the property itself for as long as the life tenant lives). The second party (usually a son or daughter or grandchild of the life tenant) purchases a remainder interest (the right to the property—whatever it is worth—when the first party's interest terminates. If the first party purchased a life interest, by definition his interest terminates when he dies). Each party to the SPLIT pays the actuarial value of the interest purchased.

## WHY A SPLIT PURCHASE?

There are many financial and estate-planning advantages to a SPLIT. Two major tax advantages are that: (1) upon the life tenant's death, none of the property should be in his estate for estate, inheritance, or generation-skipping tax purposes, since he never owned the right to transfer an interest at his death, and (2) the life tenant's estate is depleted at no gift, estate, or generation-skipping transfer tax cost by the amount of his contribution to the SPLIT.

## WHEN A SPLIT SHOULD BE CONSIDERED

A SPLIT is indicated as a potential solution when it is desirable to reduce estate tax or avoid a generation-skipping transfer tax. A split gift could save hundreds of thousands or even millions of dollars of transfer costs. There can be no federal estate or generation-skipping transfer tax because, at the death of the life tenant, there is no transfer.

A SPLIT has utility when you would like to improve current income but lower or stabilize current income taxes. If a SPLIT is used to purchase income-producing investment property, your income is enhanced by the remainderman's investment (see the NUMBERCRUNCHER illustrations on pages 372–73 under the "Return on Investment" discussion). Yet it may be possible to amortize your investment and therefore shield a significant portion of investment income (from the SPLIT or *other* investment) from income tax.

Consider the mathematics of a SPLIT when you want to transfer substantial wealth without the imposition of a gift tax. The SPLIT is in all respects a bona fide arm's-length transaction between the two parties (life tenant and remainderman) and between the third party from whom the property is purchased. Assuming no fraud, the property is purchased for its fair market value, and each of the buyers is paying his actuarially fair share of the purchase price. There is, therefore, no gift involved since the purchase price is presumptively the fair market value.

A SPLIT is a particularly useful tool when it is important to keep property within a family, but you want to enjoy it or need to use it or receive its income for life. A SPLIT may be strong protection against a will contest or an election against the will. SPLIT property passes by contract and should not be part of the probate estate. So a disgruntled heir would have no rights to property purchased through a SPLIT.

SPLITs can be used to avoid ancillary administration. The SPLIT accomplishes this objective since at the termination of the first party's interest, the remainderman automatically—by contract—becomes full and complete owner of the property. This means the cost of multiple probates is avoided.

A SPLIT should be considered in every case where a low-risk, highly reliable, and relatively simple wealth-shifting tool is desired for assets to be purchased in the future. The SPLIT is both a "freezing" and an "eliminating" device that has not been adversely affected by recent tax law changes and is unlikely to be challenged by the IRS if arranged properly. (Compare the SPLIT with the RIT, the remainder interest transaction, a much more aggressive technique in which a slight understatement of value could result in estate tax inclusion.)

## ESSENTIAL ELEMENTS OF A SPLIT

Property is purchased by two parties, a life tenant and a remainderman, from a third party in an arm's-length transaction for the property's fair market value.

Ownership of the property is bifurcated into two parts: the first part, a "life estate," is the right to use, possess, or enjoy the property and the income it produces for as long as the holder of that life estate lives. The second part is the "remainder interest," the balance of the interest in the property not owned by the life tenant. When the life tenant dies, the holder of the remainder interest receives by contract all of the interest in the property.

Each party must pay his proportionate share of the cost based on table A in Treasury Regulation 25.2512-2, single life unisex 10 percent tables, illustrating the actuarial value of life (column 3) and remainder (column 4) interests. As explained below, the use of these government-issued tables is essential so that the life tenant does not inadvertently make a gift to the remainderman. (Note that all tables presented in this section are reproduced from Leimberg, *Tools and Techniques of Estate Planning,* sixth edition, The National Underwriter Company, Cincinnati, Ohio 45202.)

The life tenant should be entitled to the exclusive use and benefit of any income from the property from the date of its purchase until the date he dies. Correspondingly, the life tenant should pay all expenses and charges (according to state law) that are properly chargeable to a life tenant. The life tenant cannot use the actual property itself (as opposed to the interest in the property) as collateral or otherwise encumber it without the express written permission of the remainderman. The life tenant must not abuse his interest or in any way endanger the remainderman's interest.

The asset subject to the SPLIT arrangement cannot be sold by the life tenant without the written consent of the remainderman. If it is sold, as explained below, the parties must share the proceeds according to the actuarial interests they had on the date of sale or exchange (presumably using whatever actuarial tables are in effect at that time).

## MATHEMATICS OF THE SPLIT

The subject is a divorced 50-year-old real estate developer who is about to purchase a $1,000,000 office building. He is already in a 50 percent estate tax bracket and in the top income tax bracket. He has a daughter to whom he wants to shift wealth, but he has already fully utilized his annual exclusion and his unified credit. He would like to increase his spendable income but at the same time begin to shift wealth to his daughter, who is a successful women's clothing designer. If he purchases the building in his own name, he knows that half its value would be lost in federal estate taxes alone when he dies. He expects the building to appreciate at least 13 percent per year.

The 50-year-old father purchases a life estate in the building. He must pay, according to the government's actuarial tables (table A), 84.743 percent of the $1,000,000 fair market value, $847,430. His daughter must pay the balance, 15.257 percent of the $1,000,000 fair market value, $152,570. (Note that *her* age is not relevant.)

If the father lives his full life expectancy (33.1 years according to the most recent IRS life expectancy table), the property will have grown to a value of $57,134,243 if his 13 percent growth rate projections are realized. If the property had been included in his estate, at a 50 percent estate tax bracket, the federal estate tax (assuming a 50 percent marginal rate) would have been $28,567,122. But because none of it will be included in the client's estate, it will all escape federal estate tax with a resulting savings of $28,567,122 (less state death tax and other estate settlement expenses). The daughter will receive property worth $57,134,243 at a cost of $152,570.

### SPLIT Interest Purchase

| | | |
|---|---|---:|
| Input: | Value of property purchased ........................ | $ 1,000,000 |
| Input: | After-tax growth rate on property ................... | 0.130 |
| Input: | Life tenant's age ................................... | 50 |
| | Value of life interest ............................. | $   847,430 |

SPLIT Interest Purchase (*Continued*)

|  |  |  |
|---|---|---|
| Value of remainder interest ........................ | $ | 152,570 |
| Life tenant's annual amortization deduction ......... | $ | 25,602 |
| Life tenant's pre-tax return on investment ........... |  | 0.184 |
| Input: Number of years until sale (or death) ............... |  | 33.1 |
| Input: Assumed value in that year ........................ |  | $57,134,243 |
| Remainderman's return on investment ............. |  | 0.196 |
| Assumed value of investment at death .............. |  | $57,134,243 |
| Input: Combined federal and state death tax bracket ........ |  | 0.500 |
| Potential death tax savings ........................ |  | $28,567,122 |

## TAX IMPLICATIONS

Assuming that (a) the asset in question is purchased from a third-party seller and the purchase price is therefore presumably the fair market value, and (b) both purchasers' contributions to the purchase price were computed using the appropriate IRS tables, there is no gift and so there should be no gift tax. Both the father and the daughter in the example above have paid the full value of what they own.

Since the father owns no property interest at death, he has no property interest that falls within the ambit of the federal estate tax. There has been no transfer at death from father to daughter so there can be no argument by the Service that there was a transfer with a retained life estate.

A tax trap to avoid in this area is a gift from the father to the daughter to enable her to purchase the property. If the parent makes the gift that enables the child to purchase the remainder interest, the IRS will probably collapse the transaction and argue that the real substance of the situation is a gift with a retained life estate. Aside from potential gift tax liability, this would mean the entire date-of-death value of the property would be in the father's estate.

This problem could be avoided in a number of ways: (1) the gift could come from a relative other than the "splitting" parent; (2) an irrevocable trust that already holds assets for the child (for instance, a 2503(c) trust) could split-purchase the property with the parent (assuming the trust contains powers or could be amended to add powers authorizing the trustee to enter into a

SPLIT); (3) the adult child could borrow money from a relative or a bank to contribute to the SPLIT. As a last (and most aggressive) resort, the child could borrow money from a bank and the parent could sign as a guarantor of the child's note.

If the child lacks sufficient funds to pay his or her share, it is clear that the parent cannot safely make a gift of the child's share. But can the parent safely lend an adult child the money if the loan is fully secured and bears interest at a fair market rate and under "third-party" type terms? This seems to pass the "smell test" if in fact the loan is at arm's length and the parties honor the loan. Could a parent cosign a loan for a child? This may be too close to the edge and at the least invites IRS scrutiny.

To avoid any unintentional gift, you must be sure that neither party pays more than his share of the initial purchase price. A gift is made from parent to child if the parent pays too much. A gift is made from child to parent if the child pays too much.

If either party makes improvements to the property that enhance its value or extend its useful life and the contribution is more than the contributing party's actuarially proper share, the IRS will claim a gift has been made. Financing used to purchase the property must be arranged in an actuarily correct manner. Debt should be allocated proportionately between the life tenant and the remainderman.

The remainderman's basis will be the amount he or she pays. There will be no step-up or down in basis at death since the SPLIT property will not be in the estate of the life tenant. Is this a major flaw in the utility of a SPLIT? Consider that (a) if nothing is done the estate tax rates start at 37 percent while the maximum income tax rates when fully phased in are 33 percent; (b) many assets are not depreciable by the remainderman in any event (such as land or a vacation home), and so basis is not an issue unless or until the asset is sold; and (c) no income tax gain is reportable in any event until the remainderman chooses to sell his interest. In other words, by using a SPLIT any gain can be deferred indefinitely or recognized (reported) at the discretion of the remainderman who at the life tenant's death can choose to sell it at any time. If there is no SPLIT, federal and state taxes (plus administrative costs) will be due within nine months of the parent's death. There would be no choice and little potential for "timing" the tax.

If the SPLIT asset is depreciable, tax law requires the life tenant to depreciate the property using the *entire* basis. In other words, in spite of the SPLIT, the deduction is computed just as if the life tenant were the absolute owner of the property. At the life tenant's death, any depreciation deductions remaining are allowed to the remainderman.

If the SPLIT asset is an income-producing investment, the life tenant can amortize the cost of the life estate. In the example above the father has purchased an asset that diminishes in value to zero by the date of his death. Tax law allows a recovery of capital in the form of an amortization deduction as long as the property purchased is held for the production of income.

This amortization deduction is available even if the property itself is not depreciable. A purchaser of a life estate may amortize the purchaser's capital investment over his or her life expectancy. The point is that even if the father and the daughter had purchased intangible assets such as stocks or bonds, the father could amortize the cost of the $847,430 life estate he purchased in our example and deduct, on a straight-line basis, that amount over his actuarial life expectancy according to IRS life expectancy Table V. Since Table V projects a 33.1-year life expectancy for a 50-year-old, he could deduct $25,602 a year ($847,430 ÷ 33.1). This amortization deduction could be used to offset income produced by the SPLIT property itself or other investment income.

Taking this concept one step further may prove most advantageous. Consider a SPLIT involving the purchase of tax-free municipal bonds. Even though the actual income generated would be tax-free, since the life tenant's interest is diminishing, he is still allowed to recover his cost through a yearly amortization deduction.

It is clear that no amortization deduction will be allowed where the client, without an additional investment, attempts to partition nondepreciable property into two parts. So a wealthy parent can't split up an asset and then sell the remainder interest to his son. SPLITs work only if a purchase of an asset is made from a third party; one cannot bifurcate property already owned and achieve the tax benefits of a SPLIT.

If the parties to the SPLIT sell the property during their lifetimes, the parent (in our example the father) will have to report gain equal to the difference between the amount he realizes on the sale (the portion of the sales proceeds allocable to the life estate at the time of the sale according to IRS actuarial tables then in effect) and his adjusted basis. Note that the older the parent at the time of the sale, the smaller the value of the life estate. This translates into a lower amount received, which in turn means the gain reportable by the parent is lower. This lower amount payable to the parent is consistent with the major objective of the SPLIT: a low-risk, low-cost method of "intentionally defunding" the parent's estate and shifting future wealth to a younger generation.

## "LAST SPOUSE TO DIE" SPLIT

If you are married, it is possible to significantly increase the value of the life estate merely by providing that the remainder would not vest until the second spouse dies. The advantage of increasing the value of the life estate is that the value of the remainder interest (the amount the child or grandchild or other individual must pay) is significantly reduced. For instance, if both a husband and wife are 60 years old, under table A(2) of Regulation 20.2031-7(f), the remainder interest would have a value of 13.843 percent of the purchase price if the "last spouse to die" SPLIT concept was used. Under a typical first-to-die SPLIT, the remainderman would have to pay about 25 percent of the purchase price.

### Present Worth of $1 Due at Death of Survivor
### Assuming Interest at 10 Percent

| Couple Both Age | Present Value of |
|:---:|:---:|
| 30 | .01258 |
| 35 | .01946 |
| 40 | .02985 |
| 45 | .05417 |
| 50 | .06710 |
| 55 | .09759 |
| 60 | .13843 |
| 65 | .19181 |
| 70 | .25907 |
| 75 | .34068 |
| 80 | .43104 |

There are two other advantages to this "last-spouse-to-die" SPLIT: (1) the larger the amount paid by the spouses, the more they "intentionally defund" (at no gift tax cost) their estates, and (2) the more the spouses pay for their joint life interest, the larger their amortization deduction.

## "TERM OF YEARS" SPLIT

A SPLIT can last for a term of years rather than a life estate. The result of a SPLIT for a term of years may be advantageous. The table below shows the purchase of a $1,000,000 property in which a 50-year-old parent bought the right to the property for 15 years (assume, for instance, that he wanted income only until his company pension began at age 65). His child purchased a remainder interest. The value of the 15-year term interest is $760,608. The child's portion was $239,392.

SPLIT Interest Purchase: Term of Years

| | | |
|---|---|---|
| Input: | Value of property purchased ......................... | $1,000,000 |
| Input: | Years term interest runs .............................. | 15 |
| Input: | Rate of return on property ......................... | 0.090 |
| | Value of term interest ............................... | $  760,608 |
| | Value of remainder interest ......................... | $  239,392 |
| | Annual income from property ...................... | $   90,000 |
| | Annual amortization deduction ...................... | $   50,707 |
| | Annually taxable amount .......................... | $   39,293 |
| | Term owner's pre-tax return on investment ........... | 0.185 |

The table shows that the father's investment of $760,608 could be amortized over the 15-year period. This would provide the father with an annual deduction of $50,707 ($760,608 ÷ 15). Assuming the investment generated 9 percent on $1,000,000, it would produce $90,000 of income a year. But because of the amortization deduction of $50,707, the annually taxable amount to the father would be only $39,293. In effect, by creating a SPLIT for a 15-year term, the father has created a super tax shelter.

As with any transaction that provides tax advantages, there are costs, risks, and other disadvantages. The SPLIT term of years has two major potential disadvantages: (1) at the end of the term, the parent loses the property and any income it produces (not a problem at all if shifting wealth and income was the major objective and the parent can afford both financially and psychologically to do without both the capital and the income it produces), and (2) if the parent dies before the term expires, the actuarial value of his interest (the present value of the right to the income from the property for the balance of the term) will be included in his estate.

This potential problem could be (a) negated to the extent that the $600,000 unified credit equivalent sheltered the tax, or (b) eliminated if the right to the income for the term of years remaining at the parent's death was left in a qualifying manner to a surviving spouse (the marital deduction would eliminate any federal estate tax), or (c) eliminated if the right to income was left to a charity in a qualifying manner (the charitable deduction would eliminate any estate tax).

## RETURN ON INVESTMENT

As the NUMBERCRUNCHER below (courtesy of Financial Data Corporation, 1-800-392-6900) illustrates, the return on investment is extremely critical to the wealth-shifting success of the split purchase. Note that both the life tenant and the remainderman do well given normal life expectancy of the life tenant.

### SPLIT Interest Purchase

| | | |
|---|---|---:|
| Input: | Value of property purchased ...................... | $ 1,000,000 |
| Input: | After-tax growth rate on property ................... | 0.090 |
| Input: | Life tenant's age ................................. | 50 |
| | Value of life interest .............................. | 847,430 |
| | Value of remainder interest ....................... | 152,570 |
| | Life tenant's annual amortization deduction .......... | 25,602 |
| | Life tenant's pre-tax return on investment ........... | 0.136 |
| Input: | Number of years until sale (or death of life tenant) .... | 33.1 |
| Input: | Assumed value in that year ........................ | $17,330,739 |
| | Remainderman's return on investment ............. | 0.154 |
| | Assumed value of investment at death ............... | $17,330,739 |
| Input: | Combined federal and state death tax bracket ........ | 0.500 |
| | Potential death tax savings ........................ | $ 8,665,369 |

It is true that when a father and son split-purchase an asset from a third party, the son does not receive a step-up in basis at the father's death.

As the table below illustrates, the premature death of the parent within a few years of the transaction significantly enhances the "return" on the remainderman's investment. For instance, assume a million-dollar property is purchased from a third party by a man, age 50, and his daughter. Assume a 9 percent return on the property. The value of the life interest would be $847,430. The remainder interest would be valued at $152,570. The life tenant's pre-tax return on investment would be 13.6 percent. The remainder-man's return on the investment—assuming the life tenant lived to life expectancy according to IRS Table No. V (33.1 years)—would be 15.4 percent. (See the illustration above.)

But if the life tenant died after only five years, when the property was worth $1,538,624 at a 9 percent after-tax growth rate, the remainderman's return on investment would skyrocket to 58.8 percent. The point is that if the remainderman's interest "matures" sooner than expected because of the premature death of the life tenant, the remainderman's return is greatly increased. If the SPLIT was contracted based on a joint life estate for both client and spouse, both age 50, the daughter would have to pay only $67,100 for her remainder interest. This would further magnify the daughter's return on investment.

## SPLIT Interest Purchase

| | | |
|---|---|---:|
| Input: | Value of property purchased ......................... | $1,000,000 |
| Input: | After-tax growth rate on property .................... | 0.090 |
| Input: | Life tenant's age ..................................... | 50 |
| | Value of life interest ................................. | 847,430 |
| | Value of remainder interest .......................... | 152,570 |
| | Life tenant's annual amortization deduction ........... | 25,602 |
| | Life tenant's pre-tax return on investment ............. | 0.136 |
| Input: | Number of years until sale (or death of life tenant) ..... | 5.0 |
| Input: | Assumed value in that year ......................... | $1,538,624 |
| | Remainderman's return on investment ................ | 0.588 |
| | Assumed value of investment at death ................ | $1,538,624 |
| Input: | Combined federal and state death tax bracket ......... | 0.500 |
| | Potential death tax savings .......................... | $ 769,312 |

**CREATIVE SPLITS**

Parties other than a parent (or grandparent) and a child (or grandchild) can successfully employ the SPLIT technique. For instance, the "post-death shift" proves there is life to estate planning in the hereafter. Consider, for example, the purchase of split interests between a marital trust (which buys a life interest) and a CEBT (credit equivalent bypass trust) which purchases a remainder interest. Assume the husband's will established a Q.T.I.P. (Qualified Terminal Interest Property) marital trust with several million dollars. Assume the CEBT was funded with $600,000 and allows the trustee discretion to "spray" both principal and income to the spouse or other heirs of the decedent.

If the trustee of the Q.T.I.P. trust does nothing, the entire value of the assets in the trust will be in the wife's estate at her death. Instead, the trustee purchases a life interest in property based on the age of the surviving spouse. The balance of the cash to buy the asset is obtained from the CEBT which purchases a remainder interest.

There are several advantages to this "marital-bypass SPLIT" technique. First, the surviving spouse's income is increased by the return on the investment made by the trustee of the bypass trust. Second, there would be an intentional defunding of the Q.T.I.P. trust. So at the surviving spouse's death the cash used to purchase the SPLIT property would be removed from her gross estate. Third, none of the SPLIT property itself would be in the surviving spouse's estate. It is important that the trustee be given a general investment power authorizing investments in both terminable interests and other property. It is even more important that the power be stated in such a manner that it is permissive rather than mandatory. If the trustee was required to invest in a terminable interest (which the life estate clearly is), the IRS would disallow the marital deduction. But as long as the husband's will does not require that the trustee of the marital trust purchase a life estate (or term of years), the result should be no different than if the surviving spouse (or the trustee on her behalf) decides to purchase an annuity.

This marital-bypass SPLIT technique could be turbocharged by a split purchase of tax-free municipal bonds. The surviving spouse's net income is enhanced because even though the income from the municipal bonds is tax-free (beware of 1986-TRA AMT implications of certain otherwise tax-free bonds), the trust would be allowed an amortization deduction (in spite of the general disallowance of the deduction for expenses incurred in connection with the purchase or carrying of tax-free municipal bonds under Code Sec. 265 since the amortization *deduction* is neither an expense nor interest).

### SELECTING PROPERTY TO SPLIT

Most authorities feel that the best property to use in a SPLIT is an income-producing, appreciating asset that does not have a limited useful life. A good example is land or other rental real estate. In the case of land the SPLIT in essence makes what is otherwise nondepreciable into a depreciable asset. The amortization deduction shelters a portion of the income from the land if it is purchased for investment use and creates a tax shelter for both income and estate tax purposes.

Tax-free municipal bonds that throw off high amounts of nontaxable income are good assets to purchase in a SPLIT because of the life (or term) tenant's amortization deduction (resulting in a net shelter).

Closely held stock is typically difficult to value accurately and usually does not pay a steady income. The IRS could claim that a true life estate has not been purchased because the interest purcahsed pays no income. But consider the purchase of closely held stock that has recently been valued for income, gift, or estate tax purposes. If the IRS has recently agreed that the price claimed by the taxpayer is correct (or the price has been agreed upon by both the IRS and the taxpayer either in or out of court), such stock would be ideal for a SPLIT.

Real property with a mortgage is contraindicated because of practical difficulties; the payment of the mortgage by the life tenant may constitute a series of gifts (with the retention of a life estate) to the remainderman.

### THE BUY-SELL SPLIT

There would be significant estate planning utility to the concept of a "buy-sell SPLIT": instead of buying a decedent's stock in the normal outright manner, a surviving shareholder would purchase a life estate (or term of years). Children working with him in the business would purchase a remainder interest.

First, this would give the surviving shareholder an amortization deduction for his payment (in effect making the buyout at least partially tax-deductible). Second, there would be no estate tax payable upon the surviving shareholder's death with respect to the stock. It would belong to the children working in the business without generating any federal estate tax. Third, there would be no possibility of an election against the will or a will contest enabling a nonworking child, spouse, or other relative to obtain the stock. Because this is a more aggressive use of the SPLIT, it is recommended that the stock at least pay some dividends after the SPLIT.

## UNSPLITTING THE SPLIT

A SPLIT can be unwound if the parties want to get out of it. One of the major advantages of a SPLIT as opposed to other estate-freezing devices is that it can be severed at any time. For instance, assume a 60-year-old father buys a life interest in $1,342,444 of securities for $1,000,000. His son would pay $342,444, the actuarial value of the right to the securities at the projected death of a 60-year-old. Now assume that five years later the father and son decide to sell the securities. They would split the proceeds according to the actuarial values of their respective interests. The father, now age 65, would have a life interest which has reduced down to about 68 percent of the proceeds. The son's interest would have increased to 32 percent.

## SENIOR CITIZEN SPLITS

The older the person, the less effective the SPLIT in most cases. This is because a very old person has a relatively short life expectancy and therefore the value of his life interest is low relative to the purchase price. This makes the child's interest more valuable (some spell this "EXPENSIVE"). For instance, if the father were 90 years old, his portion of the purchase price is about 28 percent. That makes the child's (or grandchild's) portion of the purchase price about 72 percent.

Because of the confiscatory nature of the generation-skipping transfer tax and its impact upon ultra-wealthy individuals, it might still pay to arrange a SPLIT with an adult grandchild even under these conditions. If necessary, the grandchild's father could give or loan cash to the grandchild who could split-purchase assets with his or her grandfather. Not incidentally, the poorer the health of the life tenant, the more mathematically feasible and attractive the SPLIT is. (The government's actuarial tables *must* be used unless the life tenant's death is imminent. Death from a current illness within three months would normally be consdiered imminent; death after 12 months should clearly not be imminent. Any period in between would be decided on all of its facts and circumstances.)

One solution to the problem of affordability on the part of the child or grandchild is to structure the life income interest as a "last-to-die" SPLIT. In other words, income would be retained until the last of two individuals died. For example, assume a 65-year-old whose life interest is worth $679,700, about 68 percent of the full value of a $1,000,000 property to be purchased. This means his child would have to pay about 32 percent, $320,300. (This is about twice as much as the son would have had to pay if the SPLIT was done just 10 years earlier.)

Now assume the father and mother—both age 65—purchase a "last-to-die" SPLIT, which means they retain an interest in the property until the second of them dies. The value of the income interest is obviously larger, which makes the remainder interest much smaller. In fact, according to IRS table A(2), the value of the son's remainder interest drops from 32.03 percent to 19.181 percent. So to purchase his share of a $1,000,000 property, the son would have to pay only $191,810. If the father were age 52 and the mother were age 50, the value of the remainder interest would drop to only 7.233 percent of the fair market value of the property. So the son would pay only $72,330 to purchase his actuarial share of a $1,000,000 property.

### DOWNSIDE RISKS AND DISADVANTAGES

There are downside risks and disadvantages to a SPLIT as there are with every planning tool or technique. A SPLIT is a relatively new concept that has not been judicially tested. Obviously (as is the case with any tool or technique), it is not appropriate in every situation or in the case of every asset. Assumptions and expectations of the parties entering into the SPLIT may not be realized. For example, will the asset yield, appreciation rate, income and estate tax rates of the parties be as expected? What alternative investment opportunities exist for the remainderman (could the child do better investing elsewhere)? Will amortization or depreciation deductions be available—and if so to what extent can they be utilized under existing tax laws? Will the actuarial tables or life expectancy tables be changed and, if so, will those changes be retroactive or will there be grandfathering of existing law?

Obviously, there are trade-offs. All actions must be compared with (a) doing nothing and (b) appropriate alternatives. You must examine not only the federal but also state estate, income, and gift tax consequences, as well as the cash flow and psychological implications and risk-reward economic cost-benefit parameters. Although "tax savings are not for the timid, when you have to litigate, it's not whether you win or lose that counts; it's how much it costs to play their [the IRS's] game." (It's the IRS's game because they have an unlimited amount of your dollars to use against you.)

Excellent articles on SPLITs (as well as GRITs and RITs) have been written by Stanley Johanson, Howard Zaritsky, Richard Covey, Richard Oshins, Rox Adams, Malcolm Moore, and Bertil Westlin.

The following chart, adapted with permission from the sixth edition of *The Tools and Techniques of Estate Planning,* compares split interest (SPLITs) with (1) gifts, (2) GRITs (grantor retained income trusts), and (3) RITs (remainder interest transactions):

## Relative Odds of Avoiding Estate Tax Inclusion

| | | |
|---|---|---|
| SPLITs | High | This assumes the remainderman does *not* acquire his contribution from the life or term tenant. Net after-tax income received by life or term tenant will be includable to the extent not consumed or given away. |
| GIFT | High | Only adjusted taxable gifts enter the estate tax computation. The future income stream produced by the gift is removed from the donor's estate. |
| GRITs | Low/High | If the gift occurs within the term for which the grantor has retained the right to income, inclusion is certain. But if death occurs beyond that point, it is likely there will be no inclusion. Net after-tax income received by the life or term tenant will be includable to the extent not consumed or given away. |
| RITs | Low | Sales of remainder interests are likely to succeed only if the price paid by the remainderman was fair at the time the agreement was executed. Net after-tax income received by the life or term tenant will be includable to the extent not consumed or given away. |

## Relative Ability to "Defund" Client's Estate

| | | |
|---|---|---|
| SPLITs | Very high | Neither the value of the appreciated property nor the value of the amount of the life or term tenant's contribution to the purchase will be in his estate. Since there is no gift, the life tenant's annual exclusions and unified credit remain intact and can be used to offset otherwise taxable gifts and are therefore available to further defund the estate. |
| GIFT | High | A gift removes from the gross estate (a) the property itself, (b) future appreciation on the property, and (c) income from the property. But depending on the size of the gift, some or all of |

## Relative Ability to "Defund" Client's Estate (*Continued*)

| | | |
|---|---|---|
| | | the client's annual exclusion and unified credit must be used to offset otherwise taxable gifts and are therefore not available to further defund the estate. |
| GRITs | High | Assuming the grantor outlives the specified term, the following are removed from his estate: (a) the property itself and (b) all appreciation. Net after-tax income received and not consumed or given away by the grantor will be in his estate. Since, by definition, the GRIT involves a future interest gift to the remainderman, to the extent used to offset the taxable gift, the unified credit will not be available to further defund the estate. |
| RITs | Moderate | The asset itself and all appreciation are removed from the client's estate. But to the extent not consumed or given away, the after-tax sales proceeds are includable in the client's estate. Because there is no gift, neither the gift tax annual exclusion nor the unified credit have been used. Therefore, both are available to further defund the client's estate. |

## Relative Cost of Technique in Terms of Unified Credit

| | | |
|---|---|---|
| SPLITs | Very low | Since there is no gift, there is no gift tax to offset. Therefore, the use of this device does not use up any of the unified credit. |
| GIFT | High | To the extent the value of the gift exceeds the annual exclusion or for any reason does not qualify as a present interest gift, the unified credit must be used to offset what would otherwise be a gift tax. |
| GRITs | Moderate | Since the gift to the remainderman is a future interest gift and therefore is taxable, the unified credit is used. But because the gift is not the entire value of the property but merely the value |

### Relative Cost of Technique in Terms of Unified Credit (*Continued*)

|  |  |  |
|---|---|---|
|  |  | of the remainder interest, the use of the unified credit can be leveraged. This leverage can be multiplied if the grantor retains an income interest lasting for the lesser of (a) the specified term or (b) the grantor's lifetime. But if death occurs prior to the end of the specified period of time, assets in the trust revert to the grantor's estate. This contingency significantly reduces the value of the remainderman's interest (and therefore the taxable gift is reduced). |
| RITs | Very low | By design, there is no gift. Therefore, no utilization has been made of the unified credit. |

### Relative Importance of Proper Valuation to Estate Tax Success

|  |  |  |
|---|---|---|
| SPLITs | Low | It is assumed that a split interest transaction involves a purchase at arm's length from a third party for the property's fair market value and that the appropriate government tables have been used to determine the respective payments. If these guidelines have been met, a later valuation challenge should not raise any significant estate tax problems. |
| GIFT | Low | If the Service determines that the gift was undervalued, the result will be an increase in adjusted taxable gifts—typically resulting in a greater use of the unified credit. |
| GRITs | Low | If the Service determines that the gift was undervalued, the result will be an increase in adjusted taxable gifts—typically resulting in a greater use of the unified credit. |
| RITs | Very high | The remainderman must be able to prove that—at the time of the sale—the price paid was an adequate and full consideration for the property interest purchased. The IRS would argue that a transfer for less would fall within the ambit of |

Relative Importance of Proper Valuation to Estate Tax Success *(Continued)*

---

Code Section 2036. Therefore, the federal estate tax value (less consideration actually paid) would be included in the decedent's gross estate.

## Relative Probability of Estate Tax Saving Success Based on Current Law and Cases

---

| | | |
|---|---|---|
| SPLITs | High | The life tenant does not own an interest at death. Since there has been no gratuitous transfer with a retained life estate, there should be no section 2036 inclusion. |
| GIFT | Very high | Once the gift is made (with the exception of certain gifts made within three years of death), it is highly likely that it will escape the ambit of the federal estate tax. |
| GRITs | High | Assuming the grantor outlives the specified term, there is a high likelihood that there will be no federal estate tax inclusion. |
| RITs | Moderately high | Assuming the remainderman paid consideration that is adequate and full at the time of purchase. |

## Advantageous Basis to Ultimate Recipient of Property

---

| | | |
|---|---|---|
| SPLITs | Very low | The remainderman's basis is price paid for the remainder interest. |
| GIFT | Low | The donee takes the donor's basis plus a step-up for gift taxes paid on the appreciated portion of the gift. |
| GRITs | Very low | The remainderman receives a fractionalized portion of the grantor's basis. |
| RITs | Very low | The remainderman's basis is the price paid for the remainder interest. |

Relative Amount of Money Ultimate Recipient of Property Must Have to Make Transaction Work

| | | |
|---|---|---|
| SPLITs | Moderate | Must have or obtain enough cash to purchase remainder interest. |
| GIFT | None | Unless "net gift" requires donee to pay gift tax. |
| GRITs | None | Remainderman has no outlay. |
| RITs | Moderate | Remainderman must have sufficient funds to purchase remainder interest. Installment sale, self-canceling installment note, or private annuity may make it possible to "annualize" what would otherwise be a lump-sum payment requirement. A gift from the life tenant to finance the remainder interest would likely cause the remainder interest transaction to be categorized as a gift with a retained life estate. |

Probability That the Device Will Shift Income

| | | |
|---|---|---|
| SPLITs | None | In fact, the life or term tenant may be receiving more after-tax income after the transaction than before. But the remainderman receives no income (and therefore no income shift is possible) until after the life (or term) tenant's interest expires. |
| GIFT | High | Subject to expanded grantor trust and under age 14 "kiddie tax" rules, a gift will shift income from donor to donee, but at the cost of both the property and its income. |
| GRITs | None | By definition, the grantor retains income and therefore no shift occurs until the specified term ends and the property itself belongs to the remainderman. |
| RITs | None | Again by definition, all income (or all rights to possess or enjoy the property) is retained. In the case of a RIT, this continues until the life tenant's death, so no lifetime income shifting is possible. |

Probability That the Client Will Receive a Depreciation or Amortization Deduction

| | | |
|---|---|---|
| SPLITs | High | Even if the property itself is a nondepreciable asset such as land, if it is held for investment purposes, an amortization deduction is allowed based on the life tenant's basis since the life tenant's interest has (like the life tenant himself) a limited life (amortization is subject to the 2 percent floor on the deductibility of miscellaneous itemized expenses). Although there appears to be no Code provision barring both amortization of a life estate and a depreciation deduction if the property is depreciable, the double write-off is an aggressive position. |
| GIFT | None | If the property is depreciable, that deduction can be taken by the property's new owner, the donee. |
| GRITs | None | Since the trust is, by definition, a grantor trust, the grantor will, however, be entitled to any depreciation deductions inherent in the property. |
| RITs | None | Although the transaction itself does not produce or result in any new depreciation deductions, any depreciation inherent in the property can still be taken by the life tenant (up to the basis retained and not sold by the life tenant). |

Impact of Life Expectancy on Success Potential of Device

| | | |
|---|---|---|
| SPLITs | High | A split interest purchase is particularly attractive where the client's life expectancy is short. Where the client's life expectancy is longer than what could be predicted from the government's tables, the remainderman may have paid too much. But if the property appreciates at a rate in excess of the government's presumed rate of 10 percent, or if certainty of obtaining the property is important to the remainderman, a split may still be indicated. |

Impact of Life Expectancy on Success Potential of Device *(Continued)*

| | | |
|---|---|---|
| GIFT | High | An outright gift is particularly attractive when the client's actual life expectancy is substantially greater than the expectancy projected in government tables. This is because after the gift, none of the appreciation enters into the estate tax computation. If the client's life expectancy is short, a gift is often contraindicated since the loss of a stepped-up basis must be weighed against a small possibility of substantial post-gift appreciation. Little leveraging of the annual exclusion and unified credit is likely when the client has a less than normal life expectancy. |
| GRITs | High | A GRIT is particularly attractive where a client has an actual life expectancy in excess of the life expectancy projected under government tables. Conversely, if the client is likely to die within the specified term, the odds of estate tax inclusion and therefore failure to accomplish a major planning objective are high. |
| RITs | High | A remainder interest transaction is particularly attractive when a client has a life expectancy lower than the life expectancy projected under government tables. Conversely, if the client lives significantly longer than the projected life expectancy, the remainderman will mathematically have paid too much. But if property appreciates at a rate in excess of 10 percent per year, or if certainty of receiving the property is important to the remainderman, these factors may outweigh the mathematics. |

## THE SCHNEPPER-IVERS-LEIMBERG ULTIMATE SPLIT

Besides suggesting a strategy for the elimination of the estate tax, the spousal SPLIT purchase techniques may also present an opportunity for significant lifetime income tax planning. In a lifetime situation, property is often purchased jointly by husband and wife. Rather than using this form of ownership, I suggest that property be purchased on a SPLIT basis—that is, with one spouse owning the life estate and the other spouse the remainder interest. Property owned in this manner will accomplish (1) the advantages of joint ownership—potential transfer without the imposition of state inheritance tax; (2) avoidance of the federal estate tax; and (3) the elimination of probate costs. It also should create an income tax deduction in the nature of an amortization of the life estate.

If a SPLIT purchase between husband and wife of $3 million of marketable securities were made with the life interest being held by a 55-year-old spouse who contributes $2.4 million, an annual amortization deduction of almost $84,000 would be created for the husband and wife. By using this technique, both spouses will realize a tax benefit upon the filing of a joint return.

To have both the life tenant and owner of the remainder interest receive an income tax benefit from a SPLIT purchase is a very desirable result. It should be noted that even though this result may appear to be too good to be true, the filing of a joint return is a tax privilege that is independent of the separate requirements that must be met to properly structure the spousal SPLIT purchase. Therefore, the mere fact that the parties of the transaction file a joint return should not affect the legitimacy of the technique.

Planners should be careful to avoid the potential application of the step transaction doctrine. The IRS should not be given a factual pattern that would enable it to argue that the transaction was only a SPLIT of currently owned property. Any funds transferred between spouses for this purpose should be held and invested independently by the receiving spouse for a period of time prior to the joint purchase (long enough so that the interspousal transfer is "old and cold"). I suggest that, at a minimum, any such gift and the SPLIT purchase should fall in two separate tax years.

If Congress were to pass a law eliminating the spousal SPLIT and make that law retroactive—despite any constitutional issues—taxpayers should be in no worse shape taxwise than if they had purchased the investment on a nonSPLIT basis—for example, as joint tenants. The SPLIT purchase concept presents significant tax planning opportunities that should be explored by every eligible taxpayer.

# CHAPTER 10

# Last-Minute Tax Planning

*"Potius sero quam num quam."*
*(Better late than never.)*

TITUS LIVIUS, 59 B.C.–A.D. 17

While effective tax planning is basically a year-round proposition, certain techniques are still available even if you buy this book during the last week in December. This chapter will explain those last-minute tax strategies that can help you reduce your overall tax burden.

# 103   Defer Taxes

Certain kinds of investments allow you to postpone paying taxes from the year in which the income is earned to a later year. At that point, you may be in a lower tax bracket, or you will at least have had the use and yield on the tax savings in the interim.

Series EE savings bonds, which pay interest at a rate that is adjusted periodically to keep it equal to 85 percent of the average yield on 5-year Treasury securities, offer this feature, as do deferred annuity contracts. Interest on savings bonds is normally not taxed until the bonds are cashed. With an annuity, you postpone taxes on the interest until the income is actually paid out. Note also that Series EE savings bonds have a *minimum* guaranteed yield of 6 percent (7.5 percent if purchased between November 1, 1982, and October 31, 1986) if the bonds are held for at least 5 years. When alternative investments are yielding amounts equal to or less than the 6 percent rate, the investment attractiveness of Series EE bonds is magnified even more.

The interest on Series EE bonds does not accrue daily, but only on two days every year. The interest accrual dates are:

1. the anniversary of the bond's issue date;

2. the midpoint between anniversary dates.

Thus, an owner who is considering an exchange or a cashing out of his bond would do well to do so on or shortly after an interest accrual date.

Taxes are also deferred on income that builds up in individual retirement account, corporate pension, and Keogh plans. Furthermore, as discussed earlier, if you qualify for these plans, you also can deduct from your current taxable income the amount you contribute to your plan each year.

A tax planning strategy for taxpayers close to retirement is to buy Series EE savings bonds today and, when they retire, exchange those bonds for HH bonds, which are available only through such an exchange. This would allow you to defer tax on the interest the EE bonds earned before the exchange until you redeem the HH bonds. In the meantime, you will get a check for interest on the HH bonds every six months. That interest rate is fixed, however, and is taxable.

If you buy certain six-month bank certificates of deposit (CDs) now, you can defer paying part of the tax on the interest until you file your return in the subsequent year. The CD must be the type on which the interest is neither credited to your account nor made available to you without substantial penalty before the maturity date. In addition, an investment in U.S. Treasury bills provides a similar tax benefit. This is because interest on them is not recognized until the bills are redeemed. Note, furthermore, that Treasury bill (also called T-bill) interest is not subject to state or local tax; however, taxable short-term CDs may yield a higher rate of interest.

You also can defer your taxes on fees and compensation. For example, a binding agreement to delay until January the grant of a bonus otherwise payable in December defers taxation on that bonus until the subsequent year. But this agreement must be entered into before the bonus is "constructively received." Deferring fees or service compensation is easy. All you need to do is delay billing until late December. You will not receive payment—therefore, no taxable income either—until the next year.

A final alternative strategy for delaying your tax payments is to delay your receipt of income with an installment sale. You should consider postponing part or all of the profit from a big gain to next year or later. Not only could an installment sale keep this year's tax cost down (you pay tax only on the share of the profit you receive during the year), but it could also allow you to avoid a big bulge in income that could force you into a higher bracket.

# 104 Accelerate Expenses

You may have a great deal of flexibility in the timing of a number of your expenses. For example, any of your medical expenses not reimbursed are deductible in the year they are paid. An effective tax reducing strategy, therefore, would be to concentrate as many expenses as possible in a year when it appears that the percent medical expense deduction limit will be exceeded. If, at year-end, it is apparent that no deduction will be available, defer payment of medical bills until the following year when the situation may be otherwise. In a year when the deduction is probable, make sure that all medical needs are satisfied and paid for in that year.

For example, eye examinations, new glasses, and dental work may be accelerated by a month or two to permit a deduction; the remaining balance on your children's orthodonture work may be paid immediately in full. Note, however, that a deduction *is* available in the current year for medical needs charged to your credit card before the year-end, even if payment is not actually made until the subsequent year.

Tax payments can also be accelerated. The principal categories here are real estate taxes, personal property taxes, and state and local income taxes. Amounts withheld for income taxes are deductible in the year withheld. If your state or city income tax exceeds your withholding, estimated tax payments are probably required. The last installments of these taxes should be paid before the end of the current year even though they may not be due until the next year. This will accelerate your deduction into the current year. Moreover, prepayments of real estate taxes are deductible in the year paid— if they are not merely advance deposits paid before the tax becomes a liability. Each of these accelerated payments represents a current deduction from your income tax liability.

Charitable contributions are also susceptible to acceleration. Sometimes it is feasible to make a large contribution in a high-income year in order to satisfy a charitable commitment extending over a number of years. Never make a contribution on January 1 that you could have made on December 31. Remember, however, that contributions are deductible subject to certain limitations based upon your adjusted gross income. Contributions that exceed these limitations should *not* be made.

Moreover, contributions of appreciated capital gain property, such as securities held over six months, will allow you a tax deduction equal to their full market value. Therefore, a gift of appreciated securities has the advantage of a market value deduction without the payment of a tax. Conversely, you should never make charitable donations of securities that have depreciated in value below cost, since you would forfeit the tax loss. In those situations, it is better to sell the securities, take the tax loss, and contribute the cash proceeds.

# 105   Accelerate Special Deductions

The election to expense allowance is available for depreciable personal property used in your business and acquired after 1981. This is a deduction against your income. This accelerated expense is *in addition* to your regular depreciation (on the reduced basis) and is $10,000.

And, again, it does not matter how late in the year the property is put into service.

# 106  Dependents and Personal Exemptions

A dependent is someone related to you or a member of your household for whom you provide more than half the support. You may claim a 1988 dependency exemption of $1,950 for each person who meets *all* five dependency tests, with certain exceptions. For example, the gross income test does not apply if your child is a full-time student or under age 19. Also, special support rules apply to children of divorced parents and to those dependents being claimed under multiple support agreements. Furthermore, whether the dependent is born or dies during the year is irrelevant. If you pass the five tests for the portion of the year during which the dependent was alive, you will receive the full $1,950 exemption.

The following five tests must be met with respect to the person in question in order to qualify you for a dependency exemption:

1.  *Support*

    You must furnish over one-half of the total support of the person in the calendar year in which your tax year begins. Support includes amounts spent for food, shelter, clothing, medical and dental care, education, church contributions, child care expenses, wedding apparel and receptions, capital items (a car or a TV set), and the like. It does *not* include the value of services performed for a dependent, or scholarships received by a dependent student. Also, support is what is spent, not what is available. This means that even if your child earns $10,000 and banks $5,000 of it, as long as you contribute $5,001 in support, you have contributed more than one-half.

    Several tax-saving strategies present themselves in this area. A year-end budgeting of support expenditures can produce substantial tax benefits and thus reduce the out-of-pocket cost of supporting a dependent. For example, assume that you are unmarried and live with your mother. By December 1, your mother has spent $4,000 of her nontaxable social security payments for her own support and you have contributed $2,000 for her support. During the rest of the year, you provide for all of your mother's support at a cost of $800 and give her a $1,400 television set for her exclusive use in her room. Consequently, you provide more than 50 percent of your mother's total support (that is, $4,200 of a total of $8,200) for this year. Thus, you can claim the $1,950 dependency deduction for your mother.

When two or more persons furnish the support of a dependent, one of the contributing group is entitled to take the deduction for the dependent if:

a)  no one person contributes more than half of the dependent's support; *and*

b)  each member of the group, were it not for the support test, would be entitled to claim the individual as a dependent; *and*

c)  the one claiming the deduction gives more than 10 percent of the dependent's support; *and*

d)  every other person who gives more than 10 percent of the dependent's support files a written relinquishment of the claim to the exemption in the same calendar year.

2.  *Relationship of dependent*

The person supported must be your relative or a member of your household. Your relatives include your children, grandchildren, great-grandchildren, and step-children; brothers, sisters, half-brothers, half-sisters, step-brothers, and step-sisters; parents, grandparents, great-grandparents, step-mother, and step-father; nephews, nieces, uncles, and aunts; and sons-in-law, daughters-in-law, fathers-in-law, mothers-in-law, brothers-in-law, and sisters-in-law. A legally adopted child or one placed with you for adoption is considered a child by blood. Furthermore, on a joint return, this condition is satisfied if the qualifying relationship exists between the person claimed as a dependent and either you *or* your spouse.

If a person is not one of your relatives, that person may qualify as a dependent if he or she is a member of your household. A member of your household is one who, during your entire tax year, or during part of it, uses your home as the principal dwelling.

3. *Dependent's gross income*

Your dependent's gross income for the calendar year in which your tax year begins must be less than $1,950. This does not apply to children who are students or under age 19. A child is a student if, during each of any five months of the calendar year in which your tax year begins, he or she (a) is in full-time attendance at an educational institution or (b) is taking a full-time course of institutional or farm training.

In figuring your dependent's gross income, you exclude any type of exempt income. This includes social security benefits, tax-exempt interest, etc. Remember, though, that if your dependent has used these tax-exempt benefits for support, generally the benefits *will be* considered in determining whether the support test has been met.

4. *Joint return*

Generally, you will lose an exemption for a married dependent who files a joint return. This rule does not apply, however, if neither the dependent nor his or her spouse is required to file a return but they file a joint return solely to claim a refund of tax withheld. Here you should examine the advantage to your dependent in terms of tax savings from filing a joint return as opposed to the tax cost to you from losing the $1,950 exemption. In many cases it would pay for you to compensate your dependent for a tax loss and claim the deduction for the exemption. For example, assume that you are in the 33 percent bracket and that the tax loss to your married dependent from filing a separate as opposed to a joint return is $200. The $1,950 personal exemption would save you $643.50 in taxes in your tax bracket. In this case, it would pay for you to give $200 to your dependent for this "loss." After taxes, you would still be ahead $443.50.

5. *Citizenship or residency*

A dependent, to qualify you for an exemption, must be a U.S. citizen or a resident of the United States, Canada, or Mexico at some time during the calendar year in which your tax year begins.

The above rules and tests are used to determine whether your dependent qualifies you for the $1,950 dependency deduction. If you fail the gross income test—that is, your dependent has a taxable income of $1,950 or more—but you pass the other four tests, you have what is known as a *nondeductible* dependent. This still affords several significant advantages. For example, a nondeductible dependent could qualify an unmarried taxpayer to use the more advantageous head of household rate schedule; likewise, a married but separated taxpayer with a nondeductible dependent child could also use the more advantageous single taxpayer or head of household rate schedule. Moreover, any payments made by you for a nondeductible dependent's medical expenses can qualify as a medical expense deduction on your return.

For example, assume that your mother and father, who have no tax liability, reside in a nursing home, primarily to obtain medical care. Therefore, the entire cost of their maintenance (including meals and lodging) at the home qualifies as a medical expense. You pay your parents' nursing home bills, totaling $12,400 yearly, and thereby provide over half of their support. Furthermore, assume that you are single, that you have an adjusted gross income of $80,000, and that, after all deductions except those relating to your parents, you are in the 33 percent bracket.

You can now claim a medical expense deduction of $6,400 ($12,400 − 7.5% of $80,000) and (if they pass the gross income test) a dependency deduction of $1,950 each for your mother and father. In the 33 percent bracket, this will save you $3,399 in taxes ($10,300 × .33). Moreover, you can probably reduce your taxes even further because you are now entitled to compute your tax as head of household instead of single taxpayer.

Note, however, that an individual who is eligible to be claimed as a dependent by another is not eligible for his or her own personal exemption. For that reason it becomes very important to examine the potential tax consequences to your parents. The loss of the dependency exemption may cause them to pay taxes in excess of your own tax savings. In all situations, therefore, a comparative analysis should be made to maximize the tax savings to all parties.

# 107 Timing Strategies

We have already discussed timing strategies in terms of accelerating expenses and deferring income. Remember, you can take deductions on items paid for by check in the current year, even if you mail the check on New Year's Eve, as long as there is no impediment to cashing the check in the ordinary course of business in early January. If you mail a check covering a large deductible item in late December, use certified mail so that you will receive a date-stamped receipt as proof that you actually mailed the payment in the earlier year.

Furthermore, wherever possible you should charge deductible items on credit cards. Deductible items charged in the current year on credit cards can be deducted in that year, even if you do not actually pay (or receive) the credit card bill until next year. Credit card charges also provide excellent proof as to the amount and nature of expenses—especially travel and entertainment expenses. (In addition, credit card charges have been known to get lost. Lost credit card charges do not reduce your taxes but do provide you with free goods and services.)

# 108 Retirement Plans

If you participate in a qualified retirement plan of your employer, you receive a number of tax advantages—especially if you are your own employer. The employer is entitled to deduct payments to the plan immediately. As an employee, you do not have to recognize current income from the contributions; rather, you will be taxed only when you receive distributions from the plan. Since distributions are normally made after you retire and have less taxable income, these distributions may be taxed at lower rates. Moreover, the retirement plan itself is exempt from tax. This means that your earnings will accumulate tax-free at a faster rate.

If you are self-employed, you have the option of two basic forms of noncorporate qualified retirement plans, discussed in the next two sections.

# 109 Individual Retirement Plans (IRAs)

Even if you are covered by an employer retirement plan, and if you do not exceed the appropriate income limits, you may establish an IRA for your own retirement. You are eligible for an IRA deduction even if you have a Keogh. The maximum allowable deduction is the lesser of $2,000 or earned income. In order to generate a deduction, the contribution must be made (and the plan established) by the due date (not including extensions) for filing your return. According to the IRS national office, you should make the contribution prior to filing the return—i.e., you cannot take the deduction and file on March 1 and make the contribution on April 15.

For married persons, the maximum deduction is computed separately for each individual who has compensation. An eligible individual with a nonemployed spouse may make a deductible contribution to a special joint IRA account in an amount up to $2,250 (but limited to earned income).

Furthermore, in a 1983 Private Letter Ruling 832-9049 the IRS has held that a separate payment to an IRA for custodian fees does not constitute an excess contribution and such a payment is deductible as an itemized expense under Section 212. Moreover, according to IRS Letter Ruling 8432109, the amount that you can contribute to an IRA is not diminished by the *separate payment* of brokerage commissions or other fees. Accordingly, the payment of brokerage commissions and other fees, such as administrative and service fees that are separately billed and paid, will not be considered additional contributions to your IRA.

# 110   H.R. 10 or Keogh Plans

In general, the maximum annual deduction for self-employed retirement plans is the lesser of 20 percent of earned income before the deduction or $30,000. (This equates to 25 percent of net earned income after the deduction.) Under certain circumstances, a defined benefit type of self-employed retirement plan may allow a contribution in excess of the usual limits.

Individuals who have part-time self-employment income, such as directors and consultants, are allowed to establish such a plan. Thus, even if you are covered by your employer's qualified retirement plan, you might also establish a Keogh plan with any outside fees or other income that you receive. If your self-employment income is from a business that has employees, they must also be included under the plan.

With a Keogh plan you may deduct contributions made *after* the end of the taxable year, if paid by the due date for filing your return. The plan must be established before the end of the tax year.

There are substantial tax advantages to either of these plans. You obtain an immediate tax deduction for the contribution; earnings accumulate on the contributions free of current taxes; and when distributed, the plan benefits may be taxed at a lower rate.

A number of considerations are involved in deciding whether to establish a retirement plan and selecting between IRAs and Keogh plans. For example, the amount that may be contributed under a Keogh plan is greater than the amount allowable under an IRA. Alternatively, using an IRA rather than a Keogh plan will allow you to restrict the retirement plan to cover only yourself, which can mean a substantial tax savings if you have a lot of employees. All of these factors must be considered and discussed with your tax advisor.

# 111  Marital Status

Whether you are single or married can have a substantial impact on your tax bill. Speeding or delaying the ceremony can yield you an enormous one-time tax savings.

In general, marriage will cut taxes only if one spouse works or earns almost all of the income. Alternatively, if both spouses work and earn relatively good salaries, marriage will substantially boost your taxes. This is because holy wedlock will push your combined income into a higher tax bracket.

If you are planning an end of the year/New Year's day wedding, it would be well worth your while to compute your taxes both singly and jointly. You may find that the savings from deferring (or accelerating) your wedding date could be enough to pay for your honeymoon vacation.

In conclusion, recognize that the focus of this chapter has been to reduce your current year's income tax. Due to inflation, any tax liability deferred to a later year will be paid with cheaper dollars. Moreover, a deferral of income to a later year is the equivalent of an interest-free loan because it enables you to use the funds that you would otherwise have to pay toward your tax liability. Be aware, however, that this might not always be the correct planning strategy. If you expect your income to go up substantially in later years, you do not want to bunch more income into those years, because the graduated rates could bring about a greater total aggregate tax liability over the years involved. Furthermore, you should *always* take into consideration the political climate for tax changes. If tax rates are expected to go down in the future, then income deferral and expense acceleration is the right strategy. Alternatively, if rates go in the other direction, you will want to recognize your income now and defer your expenses until later.

# 112    The Goldinger Deferral

An interesting tax deferral technique has been developed by Jay Goldinger in Beverly Hills. He suggests the acquisition of a one- or two-month bank certificate of deposit by putting up 1.5 percent of the purchase price and borrowing the rest from your broker. The deal is close to a wash. Assume the certificates would pay about 9.25 percent, and the loan would cost 9 percent, including the broker's markup. But by paying the interest on or before December 31, you could deduct the expense from your current year's income. If the certificate of deposit is from a sound bank, your risk is low.

To swing such a deal on a one-month $1 million certificate of deposit, the smallest negotiable denomination, you would need $24,000—a $15,000 down payment and about $9,000 for interest on the loan. In January of the next year, when the certificate matures, you would repay the loan and collect the income on the certificate of deposit. That income would be taxable in the new year, but you would have a $9,000 deduction allowable in the earlier year.

# CHAPTER 11

# The Tax Reform Act of 1986

*"There's nothing more dangerous than the U.S. Congress with an idea."*

E. PATRICK MCGUIRE of the Conference Board
opening a conference examining tax incentives

*"If our current tax structure were a TV show, it would either be 'Foul-ups, Bleeps and Blunders,' or 'Gimme a Break.' If it were a record album, it would be 'Gimme Shelter.' If it were a movie, it would be 'Revenge of the Nerds' or maybe 'Take the Money and Run.' And if the IRS ever wants a theme song, maybe they'll get Sting to do 'Every breath you take, every move you make, I'll be watching you.'"*

PRESIDENT REAGAN, in remarks to students at Northside
High School, Atlanta, Georgia, June 6, 1985

The Tax Reform Act of 1986 marked the 20th major legislative change in the tax laws affecting individuals in the past 24 years. The Revenue Act of 1987 makes it 21 out of 25.

*"When Congress talks of tax reform, grab your wallet and run for cover."*

SENATOR STEVE SYMMS of Idaho

On October 22, 1986, President Reagan signed into law the Tax Reform Act of 1986. This Act constitutes the most sweeping revision of the tax code since 1954 and touches the lives of all American taxpayers.

The Tax Reform Act of 1986 dramatically cuts tax rates and pays for this decline by eliminating or reducing a vast array of tax breaks. The law drops the top tax rate on individuals to 28 percent from 50 percent. This new rate is less than half of the 70 percent rate that was in effect when President Reagan took office in 1981.

The 28 percent top statutory rate may be misleading, however. Certain high-income families could face a "marginal" or incremental tax rate of 33 percent because of provisions phasing out the benefits of the 15 percent rate and the personal exemption. Nevertheless, the total average tax paid by individuals under the new law will never exceed 28 percent on total income.

The Tax Reform Act of 1986 was supposed to bring simplification to our tax system. The following are among the new forms to be filled out:

- Form 8582—to be completed if you have passive losses from tax shelters, so that you can figure how much of these losses you can write off (one side, four pages of instructions, 72 minutes to complete).

- Form 8598—to be filled out if you refinanced your mortgage, took out a second mortgage, or opened a home equity line of credit after August 16, 1986, to determine how much of your interest is deductible (two sides, four pages of instructions, 64 minutes).

- Form 8606—to be filed if you make nondeductible contributions to your IRA (one side, one page of instructions, 19 minutes).

- Form 8615—to be filed for children under age 14 with more than $1,000 investment income. The excess over $1,000 is taxed at the parents' rate if that rate is higher than the child's rate (one side, one page of instructions, 47 minutes).

The above-mentioned times represent the number of minutes it would take an attorney or certified public accountant to complete each form. Double them if you think an asset is a small donkey.

So much for simplification.

The Tax Reform Act of 1986 provides significant opportunities to increase your financial wealth. But similar to previous tax acts, it also creates dangerous tax traps for the unwary. This chapter will discuss and summarize the highlights and pertinent provisions of the new tax law. Because of its sweep and potential complexity, the Tax Reform Act of 1986 has been dubbed the "Attorneys' and Accountants' Full Employment Act of 1986."

## A   Changes Affecting Individuals

# 113

## Tax Rates and Schedules

Under prior law, individual tax rates ranged from 11 to 50 percent. Under the 1986 Act, tax rates are set at 15 and 28 percent. There is a 5 percent adjustment rate based on taxable income, rather than adjusted gross income. This adjustment rate can bring the highest marginal tax up to the aforementioned 33 percent.

For 1987, there was no phase-out of the lower rates or the personal exemptions. Rates for 1987 returns were as follows:

|  | Taxable Income | Rate |
|---|---|---|
| Single taxpayers, no dependents | $ 0–$ 1,800 | 11% |
|  | $ 1,801–$16,800 | 15% |
|  | $16,801–$27,000 | 28% |
|  | $27,001–$54,000 | 35% |
|  | Over $54,000 | 38.5% |
| Married individuals filing joint returns and surviving spouses | $ 0–$ 3,000 | 11% |
|  | $ 3,001–$28,000 | 15% |
|  | $28,001–$45,000 | 28% |
|  | $45,001–$90,000 | 35% |
|  | Over $90,000 | 38.5% |

| | Taxable Income | Rate |
|---|---|---|
| **Married individuals filing separate returns** | $    0–$ 1,500 | 11% |
| | $ 1,501–$14,000 | 15% |
| | $14,001–$22,500 | 28% |
| | $22,501–$45,000 | 35% |
| | Over $45,000 | 38.5% |
| **Heads of households** | $    0–$ 2,500 | 11% |
| | $ 2,501–$23,000 | 15% |
| | $23,001–$38,000 | 28% |
| | $38,001–$80,000 | 35% |
| | Over $80,000 | 38.5% |

For 1988 and beyond, the rates are as follows:

### 1988 Schedule X: Single Taxpayers, No Dependents

| Taxable Income | | | | | Of the |
|---|---|---|---|---|---|
| Over | But Not Over | Pay | + | % on Excess | Amount Over |
| $    0–$ 17,850 | | $    0 | | 15% | $    0 |
| 71,850– 43,150 | | 2,677.50 | | 28 | 17,850 |
| 43,150– 100,480 | | 9,761.50 | | 33 | 43,150 |
| 100,480– ... | | 28,680.40 | | 28 | 100,480 |

*Note:* The 33 percent taxable income bracket in the schedule above reflects the phaseout of the 15 percent tax rate that begins at the $43,150 taxable income level and ends at $89,560 and the further phaseout of the taxpayer's one exemption, beginning at the $89,560 taxable income level and ending at $100,480, at which point the 28 percent rate again applies. For each additional exemption (see the schedule below), the upper end of the 33 percent taxable income bracket is increased by $10,920 (as reflected in the $111,400 figure below).

| *Phaseout Ranges, Two Exemptions* | | | |
|---|---|---|---|
| $ 43,150–$111,400 | $ 9,761.50 | 33% | $ 43,150 |
| 111,400– ... | 32,284.00 | 28 | 111,400 |

### 1988 Schedule Y: Married Individuals Filing Joint Returns and Surviving Spouses

| Taxable Income | | | | | |
|---|---|---|---|---|---|
| Over | But Not Over | Pay | + | % on Excess | Of the Amount Over |
| $ 0–$ 29,750 | | $ 0 | | 15% | $ 0 |
| 29,750– 71,900 | | 4,462.50 | | 28 | 29,750 |
| 71,900– 171,090 | | 16,264.50 | | 33 | 71,900 |
| 171,090– ... | | 48,997.20 | | 28 | 171,090 |

*Note:* The 33 percent taxable income bracket in the schedule above reflects the phaseout of the 15 percent tax rate that begins at the $71,900 taxable income level and ends at $149,250 and the further phaseout of two exemptions, beginning at the $149,250 taxable income level and ending at $171,090, at which point the 28 percent rate again becomes effective. For each additional exemption (see the schedules below), the upper end of the 33 percent taxable income bracket is increased by $10,920 (as reflected in the $182,010 figure for three exemptions, the $192,930 figure for four exemptions, the $203,850 figure for five exemptions, and the $214,770 figure for six exemptions).

*Phaseout Ranges, Three Exemptions*

| | | | |
|---|---|---|---|
| $ 71,150–$182,010 | $16,264.50 | 33% | $ 71,900 |
| 182,010– ... | 52,600.80 | 28 | 182,010 |

*Four Exemptions*

| | | | |
|---|---|---|---|
| $ 71,900–$192,930 | $16,264.50 | 33% | $ 71,900 |
| 192,930– ... | 56,204.40 | 28 | 192,930 |

*Five Exemptions*

| | | | |
|---|---|---|---|
| $ 71,900–$203,850 | $16,264.50 | 33% | $ 71,900 |
| 203,850– ... | 59,808.00 | 28 | 203,850 |

*Six Exemptions*

| | | | |
|---|---|---|---|
| $ 71,900–$214,770 | $16,264.50 | 33% | $ 71,900 |
| 214,770– ... | 63,411.60 | 28 | 214,770 |

### 1988 Schedule Y: Married Individuals Filing Separate Returns

| Taxable Income | | | | | |
|---|---|---|---|---|---|
| Over | But Not Over | Pay | + | % on Excess | Of the Amount Over |
| $      0–$  14,875 | | $      0 | | 15% | $      0 |
| 14,875–  35,950 | | 2,231.23 | | 28 | 14,875 |
| 35,950–  124,220 | | 8,132.25 | | 33 | 35,950 |
| 124,220–   . . . | | 37,261.35 | | 28 | 124,220 |

*Note:* The 33 percent taxable income bracket in the schedule above reflects the phaseout of the 15 percent tax rate that begins at the $35,950 taxable income level and ends at $113,300 and the further phaseout of one exemption, beginning at the $113,300 taxable income level and ending at $124,220, at which point the 28 percent rate again applies. For each additional exemption (see the schedules below), the upper end of the 33 percent taxable income bracket is increased by $10,920 (as reflected in the $135,140 figure for two exemptions and the $146,060 figure for three exemptions).

*Phaseout Ranges, Two Exemptions*

| | | | |
|---|---|---|---|
| $ 35,950–$135,140 | $ 8,132.25 | 33% | $ 35,950 |
| 135,140–   . . . | 40,864.95 | 28 | 135,140 |

*Three Exemptions*

| | | | |
|---|---|---|---|
| $ 35,950–$146,060 | $ 8,312.25 | 33% | $ 35,950 |
| 146,060–   . . . | 44,468.55 | 28 | 146,060 |

### 1988 Schedule Z: Heads of Households

| Taxable Income | | | | | |
|---|---|---|---|---|---|
| Over | But Not Over | Pay | + | % on Excess | Of the Amount Over |
| $      0–$  23,900 | | $      0 | | 15% | $      0 |
| 23,900–  61,650 | | 3,585.00 | | 28 | 23,900 |
| 61,650–  145,630 | | 14,155.00 | | 33 | 61,650 |
| 145,630–   . . . | | 41,868.40 | | 28 | 145,630 |

*Note:* The 33 percent taxable income bracket in the schedule above reflects the phaseout of the 15 percent tax rate that begins at the $61,650 taxable income level and ends at $123,790 and the further phaseout of two exemptions, beginning at the $123,790 taxable income level and ending at $145,630, at which point the 28 percent rate again applies. For each additional exemption (see the schedules below), the upper end of the 33 percent taxable income bracket is increased by $10,920 (as reflected in the $156,550 figure for three exemptions and the $167,470 figure for four exemptions).

*Phaseout Ranges, Three Exemptions*

| | | | |
|---|---|---|---|
| $ 61,650–$156,550 | $14,155.00 | 33% | $ 61,650 |
| 156,550–  ... | 45,472.00 | 28 | 156,550 |

*Four Exemptions*

| | | | |
|---|---|---|---|
| $ 61,650–$167,470 | $14,155.00 | 33% | $ 61,650 |
| 167,470–  ... | 49,075.60 | 28 | 167,470 |

**1988 Income Tax Rate Schedule for Use By Estates and Nongrantor Trusts**

| Taxable Income | | Pay | + | % on Excess | Of the Amount Over |
|---|---|---|---|---|---|
| Over | But Not Over | | | | |
| $ 0–$ 5,000 | | $ 0 | | 15% | $ 0 |
| 5,000– 13,000 | | 750 | | 28 | 5,000 |
| 13,000– 26,000 | | 2,990 | | 33 | 13,000 |
| 26,000–  ... | | 7,280 | | 28 | 26,000 |

*Note:* The 33 percent rate in the above schedule is due to the fact that the benefit of the 15 percent rate is phased out between $13,000 and $26,000.

## CAVEAT

While most proponents of the 1986 Tax Reform Act talked about a top maximum rate of 28 percent, in actuality, when taxable income reaches a certain critical point, the *marginal* rate goes up to 33 percent. This is because as taxable income exceeds this critical point, the tax code phases out the 15 percent rate. Moreover, savings due to personal exemptions of taxpayers and dependents are also recouped by raising the marginal rate again to 33 percent. By phasing out the 15 percent rate and the personal exemptions, in effect at a certain range you will be paying a flat tax of 28 percent on the first taxable dollar earned. The extent of the 33 percent *marginal* rate on additional dollars earned is shown below.

| Individuals | 33% rate starts at: | 33% rate ends at: |
|---|---|---|
| Number of dependents | | |
| None | $43,150 | $100,480 |
| One | 43,150 | 111,400 |
| Two | 43,150 | 122,320 |
| Three | 43,150 | 133,240 |
| Four | 43,150 | 144,160 |

| Joint filers | | |
|---|---|---|
| Number of dependents | | |
| None | $71,900 | $171,090 |
| One | 71,900 | 182,010 |
| Two | 71,900 | 192,930 |
| Three | 71,900 | 203,850 |
| Four | 71,900 | 214,770 |

| Heads of household | | |
|---|---|---|
| Number of dependents | | |
| One | $61,650 | $145,630 |
| Two | 61,650 | 156,550 |
| Three | 61,650 | 167,470 |
| Four | 61,650 | 178,390 |

In addition, the marginal rate for certain taxpayers with rental real estate could be as high as 49.5 percent. This is because families with adjusted gross income of less than $100,000 can take up to $25,000 of rental real estate losses where they actively participate in the rental activities. Once their income exceeds $100,000, however, that deduction is phased out with $.50 of the loss being denied for every extra dollar earned. These losses are deferred until there is income from the property to offset them, or until the property is disposed of. This results in a surtax of 16.5 percent (50 percent of 33 percent) in oncome between $100,000 and $150,000. This creates a top rate for certain taxpayers of 33 percent plus 16.5 percent, or 49.5 percent.

# 114   Standard Deduction

The standard deduction was raised for everyone effective January 1, 1988, as follows:

| Filing Status | Standard Deduction |
|---|---|
| Joint returns and surviving spouses | $5,000 |
| Heads of households | 4,400 |
| Single individuals | 3,000 |
| Married individuals filing separately | 2,500 |

These deductions will be indexed for inflation beginning in 1989.

An additional standard deduction amount of $600 is allowed for an elderly or blind individual who is married ($1,200 for a married individual who is both elderly and blind). An additional standard deduction amount of $750 is allowed for an unmarried individual who is elderly or blind ($1,500 if both). For elderly or blind taxpayers only, the new standard deduction amounts and the additional $600 or $750 standard deduction amounts were effective beginning in 1987. Beginning in 1989, the $600 and $750 additional standard deduction amounts will be adjusted for inflation.

For 1987, for all taxpayers other than elderly or blind individuals, the standard deduction amounts were $3,760 for married individuals filing jointly and surviving spouses; $2,540 for heads of households and single individuals; and $1,880 for married individuals filing separately.

# 115   Personal Exemptions

Personal exemptions are increased from $1,080 in 1986 to $1,900 in 1987, $1,950 in 1988, and $2,000 in 1989. In the future, the exemption amount will be adjusted for inflation. The additional exemption for elderly or blind individuals was repealed in 1987.

# 116   Rules for Dependents

Under the Tax Reform Act of 1986, the personal exemption is not allowed to an individual who is eligible to be claimed as a dependent on another taxpayer's return (for example, when a child is eligible to be claimed as a dependent on his or her parents' return). This rule is intended to preclude the doubling of tax benefits allowed under prior law, whereby the personal exemption for a child could be claimed by the parents on their return and also by the child on his or her return. However, unlike prior law, which allowed such dependent to use the standard deduction (zero bracket amount) only to offset earned income, the Tax Reform Act of 1986 provides that the dependent may still use up to $500 of his or her standard deduction to offset unearned income. These rules for dependents were effective beginning in 1987.

# 117 The Two-Earner Deduction

The deduction for two-earner families was repealed effective January 1, 1987.

# 118 Income Averaging

Income averaging was repealed effective January 1, 1987.

# 119 Earned Income Credit

The earned income credit is increased to 14 percent of the first $5,000 of earned income (maximum credit of $800). The income level at which the phase-out begins is raised to $9,000, with a total phase-out at $17,000. The maximum amount of the credit, as well as the phase-out income levels, will be adjusted for inflation. The changes in the earned income credit are effective as of January 1, 1988.

# 120 Unemployment Compensation

All unemployment compensation benefits received after December 31, 1986, are now includable in gross income.

# 121 Scholarships and Fellowships

The exclusion for degree candidates is now limited to scholarship or fellowship grants up to the amount spent on tuition and course-related equipment. Amounts spent for room, board, or incidental expenses are not excludable. Moreover, the exception allowing the exclusion for payments for services required of all candidates for a particular degree is repealed, as is the exception relating to certain federal grants. These new rules are effective for scholarships and fellowships granted after September 25, 1985.

# 122 Prizes and Awards

The prior exclusion for awards for charitable achievement and the like is repealed, except where the recipient assigns the prize or award to a tax-exempt organization. Employee awards during the year for length of service or safety achievement are excludable by an employee and deductible by an employer to the extent not in excess of $1,600 for all awards and $400 for all awards that are not qualified plan awards. All other awards by employers to employees are not excludable from income. These provisions are effective for years beginning after 1986.

# 123 Itemized Deductions for State and Local Sales Taxes

The itemized deduction for state and local sales taxes is now repealed. State, local, and foreign taxes for which an itemized deduction is not allowed but that are allocable to a purchase of property are now added to the basis of such property. This rule is effective as of January 1, 1987.

# 124 Charitable Deductions for Nonitemizers

For 1986, nonitemizers were allowed to deduct the full amount of their charitable contributions in addition to taking the standard deduction (zero bracket amount). No deduction (beyond the standard deduction) is now provided for charitable contributions by nonitemizers made after 1986.

# 125 Medical Expense Deduction

The floor under the itemized medical expense deduction was increased from 5 percent to 7.5 percent of adjusted gross income, effective January 1, 1987.

# 126 Moving Expenses

Moving expenses, formerly an above-the-line deduction, are an itemized deduction as of January 1, 1987.

# 127 Adoption Expenses

The itemized adoption expense deduction is repealed effective for adoption expenses paid after 1986. Prior law, however, applied for adoptions in 1987 for which deductible expenses were incurred in 1986.

# 128 Employee Business Expenses, Investment Expenses, and Other Miscellaneous Itemized Deductions

Employee business expenses, other than reimbursements, are now allowable only as itemized deductions and are now subject to a new floor of 2 percent of adjusted gross income. Exceptions to this floor are available for impairment-related work expenses for handicapped employees, certain adjustments when a taxpayer restores amounts held under a claim of right, estate taxes in the case of income in respect of a decedent, amortizable bond premiums, certain costs of cooperative housing corporations, expenses of short sales in the nature of interest, certain terminated annuity payments, and gambling losses to the extent of gambling winnings. Moreover, certain actors are allowed to report their income and expenses from acting as if they were independent contractors if the taxpayer has two or more employers in the acting profession during the tax year, if the expenses relating to the acting profession exceed 10 percent of gross income, and if adjusted gross income before deducting expenses relating to acting does not exceed $16,000.

# 129 Travel Expenses for Attending Conventions

Travel and other costs of attending of a convention or seminar for investment purposes (i.e., not for trade or business purposes) are not deductible. Bermuda is now treated as part of North America for purposes of the convention deductibility rules if the president certifies that such treatment is in the U.S. national security interest and that Bermuda's information exchange programs do not materially impede U.S. tax laws. These provisions were effective after December 31, 1986.

# 130 Political Contributions Tax Credit

The political contributions credit was repealed effective January 1, 1987.

# 131 Dividend Exclusion

The $100/$200 dividend exclusion was repealed for taxable years after December 31, 1986.

# 132 Health Insurance

Under prior law, health insurance as a benefit was not taxed. Under the Tax Reform Act of 1986, health insurance benefits provided by an employer would still not be taxed. Self-employed individuals, however, are now allowed a 25 percent business deduction for health insurance premiums paid after December 31, 1986 and before January 1, 1990.

This deduction is taken "above the line" in calculating adjusted income, rather than as an itemized deduction. It would therefore be available even to taxpayers who claim the standard deduction. However, the deduction cannot exceed the self-employed taxpayer's net earnings from self-employment. Moreover, no deduction is allowed for any year in which the taxpayer or his spouse is eligible to participate (on a subsidized basis) in an employer-sponsored health plan.

If you are not covered under an employer plan and pay your own health insurance premiums, you may want to consider moonlighting to generate self-employment income against which you can deduct part of your health insurance costs.

Note, also, that any amount deductible under this provision will not be taken into account in computing net earnings from self-employment for social security tax purposes. What this means is that the deduction will not reduce your income base on which your self-employment tax is computed.

# 133 Casualty Loss Reimbursement

Under prior law, a casualty loss deduction was allowed to the extent that losses not compensated by insurance (or otherwise) exceeded 10 percent of a taxpayer's adjusted gross income. The deduction was allowable even if the taxpayer elected not to file a claim. Under the Tax Reform Act of 1986, a casualty loss deduction is denied to the extent that a taxpayer has insurance coverage on nonbusiness property and elects not to file a claim. This provision is effective for taxable years beginning after December 31, 1986.

# 134 Exclusions

Under prior law, employer-provided group term life insurance, legal services, dependent care, education assistance, and van pooling were excluded from income. Under the Tax Reform Act of 1986, the $50,000 exclusion for employer-provided group term life insurance is continued, the exclusion for legal services and education assistance is extended through 1987, and a $5,000 cap is placed on dependent care. The economic benefit from employer-provided van pooling, however, is now taxed.

# 135 Consumer (Personal) Interest

Under prior law, all consumer interest was deductible, and the deduction for investment interest was limited to $10,000 plus net investment income. Under the Reform Act, *no deduction* is allowed for consumer interest, and the deduction allowable for investment interest is limited to an amount equal to net investment income. This repeal of the consumer interest expense deduction is phased in over 5 years; 35 percent of consumer interest is disallowed in 1987, 60 percent in 1988, 80 percent in 1989, 90 percent in 1990, and then such interest will be totally disallowed in 1991 and later years. Interest on underpayments—other than Section 6161 and Section 6166 deferred estate taxes—will be considered "consumer interest" and therefore nondeductible.

# 136

## Mortgage Interest

Under the Tax Reform Act of 1986, interest on mortgages for both principal residences and second homes will be deductible but will be coupled with antiabuse provisions limiting the amount deductible. These provisions limit the amount of interest deductible to amounts incurred on loans only up to the sum of (a) the purchase price of the real estate plus (b) the cost of any improvements (unless the loan was incurred for educational or medical expenses).

Note that you can borrow up to the cost of your house (purchase price) plus improvements, not merely the basis of that house. For example, if you bought a $200,000 house after rolling over a $100,000 gain from the sale of a prior principal residence, the basis on that new house would be reduced by the deferred gain on the original residence—i.e., the basis on the new house would be only $100,000. Nevertheless, you would still be able to borrow and deduct interest on the cost of the new residence—$200,000—under the new law. Note, in addition, that the new law allows unlimited mortgage interest—e.g., second mortages—if the new loan was incurred for educational or medical expenses. (Note that additional restrictions, discussed on page 157, were added by the Revenue Act of 1987.)

The above provisions provide substantial planning opportunities for the knowledgeable taxpayer. Consumer interest will not be deductible, whereas mortgage interest may be. You should therefore try to immediately convert all consumer interests into mortgage interest. A technique for doing so is to apply for, and use when necessary, home equity credit lines. Home equity credit lines are attractive to borrowers for many reasons. Once established, your credit line will remain in place for years and can be tapped at any time by check and sometimes by credit card. Moreover, the interest rates on a home equity credit line are normally substantially less than those paid on credit card borrowings. Home equity credit lines cost nothing until they are used, provide instant availability of funds, and normally have lower rates than alternative sources of money. Especially in view of the Tax Reform Act's disallowance of consumer interest, there is no reason why such a home equity credit line should not immediately be made part of your investment arsenal.

# 137   Individual Retirement Accounts (IRAs)

Under prior law, all taxpayers were eligible to deduct IRA contributions. Under the Tax Reform Act of 1986, as of January 1, 1987, the $2,000 IRA deduction continues only for taxpayers *without* employer-sponsored retirement plans. In addition, deductions will be allowed for joint filers covered under retirement plans, but such deductions will be phased out beginning at adjusted gross income of $40,000 and eliminated completely at adjusted gross income over $50,000. Single taxpayers who are covered by employer-sponsored retirement plans can also take deductions for IRA contributions, with such deductions phased out between $25,000 and $35,000. For spouses with no compensation, a $250 spousal IRA is allowed. For married taxpayers, the phase-out and loss of deduction applies where either spouse is covered by an employer-provided retirement plan. Moreover, taxpayers who do not qualify to make deductible contributions may make *non*deductible contributions, with the earnings in those accounts building up on a tax-free basis.

Under the Tax Reform Act of 1986, IRAs are now permitted to invest in gold and silver coins issued by the United States. This provision is effective for coins acquired after 1986.

# 138   Investment Term: IRA Versus Taxable Account

Note that although the Tax Reform Act of 1986 allows earnings on an IRA to avoid immediate tax, the advantage of tax-free compounding is not substantial until the account has grown for a number of years. For example, assume that you are in the 28 percent tax bracket and that you put $2,000 a year into a nondeductible IRA earning 8 percent interest. In 20 years, you will have $6,538 more aftertax than if the $2,000 had been invested outside an IRA. In the case of an IRA, the tax is paid only on the earnings when they are withdrawn. Since deposits were not tax deductible, they would not be taxed at withdrawal. In the non-IRA investment, taxes are paid on the interest yearly. The advantage of the IRA narrows to $2,284 over 15 years and only $562 over 10 years. A lower tax bracket at withdrawal, perhaps when you are retired, could boost this difference. However, in 20 years when you retire the tax bracket may then be even higher than the current 28 percent.

$2,000 Investment per Year in an IRA
Compounding at 8 Percent, with the Interest
Taxed at 28 Percent on Withdrawal, Compared
to a Taxable Account at 8 Percent per Annum,
Paying 28 Percent in Taxes Each Year

| Term | IRA | Taxable Account |
|---|---|---|
| 5 years | $11,924 | $11,867 |
| 10 years | $28,130 | $27,568 |
| 15 years | $50,627 | $48,343 |
| 20 years | $82,369 | $75,831 |

# 139 401(k) Deductions

For 1986, contributions to 401(k) plans were limited to $30,000 annually. Effective January 1, 1988, the maximum annual elected deferral for an employee under all qualified cash or deferred arrangements [i.e., 401(k) plans] is limited to $7,313. This amount is indexed in the same manner as the dollar limit on contributions to a defined contribution plan.

# 140 Trusts Other Than Grantor Trusts

Undistributed income of both existing and newly created nongrantor trusts is now taxed at the following rates:

| 0–$5,000 | 15 percent |
| $5,000 or more | 28 percent |

The benefit of the 15 percent bracket is phased out for trust taxable income between $13,000 and $25,000. Moreover, trusts other than charitable trusts are required to use a calendar year as their taxable year. The rate changes were effective March 15, 1987. For returns made after that date, tax rate schedules blend the schedules of rates that would have been applied under prior law with the new rate schedules.

The change in taxable year rules is effective for taxable years beginning after December 31, 1986.

This provision eliminates many of the prior super tax-saving strategies that involved income shifting through the use of trusts. Moreover, the Tax Reform Act of 1986 does not grandfather any prior trusts created in earlier years. This provision, therefore, significantly reduces the advantages of family income shifting through the use of trust vehicles. For example, the standard Clifford Trust technique for shifting income to a lower-bracket family member is no longer viable after the Tax Reform Act of 1986.

# 141  Grantor Trusts

The Tax Reform Act of 1986 modified the grantor trust rules to delete the 10-year exception under prior law (e.g., Clifford Trusts) and the exception for spousal remainder trusts. These changes are effective for transfers made after March 1, 1986, with an exception under which the 10-year rule of present law could continue to apply to certain trusts created pursuant to certain binding property settlements entered into before March 1, 1986. Again, these provisions substantially eliminate the use of trusts as income-shifting vehicles. Income earned by such trusts will now be taxed at the grantor's marginal tax bracket unless distributed to beneficiaries. Such distributions will be taken as per the provisions below.

# 142  Unearned Income of a Minor Child

Unearned income of a child under 14 years of age will be taxed to the child at the top marginal rate of the parents. The intent of the law is to create three stages:

1.  There will be no tax on the first $500 of unearned income because of the child's standard deduction. (The standard deduction offsets *unearned* income first, up to $500. Any remaining standard deduction is then available to offset earned income.)

2.  The next $500 of unearned income will be taxed to the child at the child's bracket.

3.  Unearned income in excess of the first $1,000 will be taxed to the child at the appropriate parent's rate.

This provision is effective for taxable years beginning after December 31, 1986.

The effect of this provision is to further limit the income-shifting techniques discussed under super tax planning strategies. Those strategies and techniques *ARE* available for children 14 years of age and older. If your child is under 14, other techniques become more advantageous.

For example, one major strategy should be to defer the recognition of income in excess of $1,000 until a child reaches 14 years of age. An excellent vehicle for doing so would be an investment in U.S. savings bonds. Such bonds, held at least 5 years, have a minimum guaranteed 6 percent rate of return, and no income need be recognized until they are cashed in. An alternative vehicle for deferring income would be investments in interest sensitive insurance products. Such investments can earn tax deferred income and, in fact, such income can be withdrawn on a "loan" basis without *ever* incurring a tax liability.

# 143 $1,000 Exclusion for Interest on Installment Payments of Insurance Proceeds

Under prior law, the beneficiary of a life insurance policy could receive installment payments of the proceeds of the policy. Amounts in the nature of interest, up to $1,000 annually, on the unpaid proceeds paid to the insured's surviving spouse were not included in that spouse's income. The 1986 law repeals that $1,000 exclusion.

# 144 Interest Paid on Policyholder Loans

Under prior law, personal or business interest paid on insurance policyholder loans was potentially deductible—subject to the rule that no deduction was allowed for amounts paid or accrued on indebtedness incurred or continued to carry a single premium life insurance contract. Under the 1986 law, however, a deduction for interest on policyholder loans is not allowed in the case of loans aggregating more than $50,000 per officer, employee, or owner of an interest in a trade or business carried on by the taxpayer. Interest attributable to loans in excess of $50,000, therefore, would be nondeductible. Note that this limited deductibility of interest paid on policyholder loans applies only to business loans. Interest paid on loans that would constitute consumer debt—i.e., loans for nonbusiness purposes—would not be deductible at all under the repeal of the consumer interest deduction.

# B Changes Affecting Businesses and Investments

# 145 Business Meal Expenses

The allowable deduction for business meals (including business meals away from home and meals furnished on an employer's premises to its employees) was reduced to 80 percent effective January 1, 1987. Moreover, no deduction is allowed unless business is discussed during or directly before or after the meal (except for an individual eating alone while away on business). Prior law regarding substantiation of meal expenses under $25 and other entertainment expenses continues to apply.

Note that the Tax Reform Act requires that the meal have a clear business purpose presently related to the active conduct of a trade or business. This clear business requirement is not satisfied in the case of a meal where the business discussion does not concern a specific business transaction or arrangement. In addition, the cost of the meal is not deductible if it serves a nontrade or nonbusiness purpose of the taxpayer (e.g., investment purposes) rather than a trade or business purpose. For example, if you pick up the tab for lunch with a stockbroker or an insurance salesman, no part of that lunch will be deductible.

In addition, if you negligently or fraudulently claim business meal deductions to which you are not entitled, a special penalty will apply. The otherwise applicable negligence penalty will not be less than 40 percent of the underpayment resulting from the improperly claimed deduction. If the error is due to fraud, the penalty is equal to 100 percent of the additional tax due.

# 146 Business Entertainment Expenses Other Than for Meals

The allowable deduction for business entertainment expenses was also reduced to 80 percent. Moreover, ticket costs in excess of face value are not deductible, except with regard to tickets for charitable fund-raising

5384345

4333 0661 7500 3202

ALEXANDER J SAPIANO
08/90 CV

B DALTON #153
5174400101101534    042789
DATTONA BEACH    FL
4094302189

X _____
CUSTOMER SIGNATURE

SAFEPERF® U.S. Pat. 4,403,793

| QTY. | CLASS | DESCRIPTION | PRICE | AMOUNT |
|------|-------|-------------|-------|--------|
| 1 | | | B DALTON | #153 |
| | | | 37466175002702A | |
| | | | TOTAL | 10.55 |
| | | | VISA | 10.55 |
| | | | 27465153010427GA | |
| | | | | 9.95 |
| | | | SUB TOTAL | |
| | | | TAX | .60 |

DATE  4/27/89

AUTHORIZATION | CLERK | REG./DEPT. | TOTAL  10.55
153

THIS FORM TO BE USED WITH

AMERICAN EXPRESS    MasterCard    VISA
DISCOVER

SALES SLIP

CUSTOMER COPY    IMPORTANT: RETAIN FOR YOUR RECORDS

sporting events. Deductions for the rental or other use of a luxury sky box at sports arenas will be disallowed to the extent that they exceed the cost of regular tickets if the box is used by the taxpayer for more than one event. The nondeductibility of sky boxes will be phased in over 3 years.

# 147 Business Travel Expenses (Other Than Conventions)

Deductions for cruise ship or other luxury water transportation are limited (subject to certain exceptions) to twice the highest federal per diem in the United States times the number of days in transit. This limitation does not apply to deductions for cruise ship conventions, which remain subject to prior law limitations, or where an exception to the 80 percent deduction rule (above) applies. No deduction is allowed for costs of travel that would be deductible only on the ground that the travel constitutes a form of education. For example, a French teacher who goes to France merely to improve her ability to speak French will no longer be able to deduct the travel expenses as a form of education. Transportation and other travel expenses incurred in performing services away from home for a charitable organization will be deductible. However, no deduction is allowed for such expenses unless there is no significant element of personal pleasure, recreation, or vacation in such travel away from home.

# 148 Home Office Expenses

New limits apply when an employee leases a portion of his home to his employer. The deduction is limited to the taxpayer's net income from the business (i.e., gross income minus deductions attributable to the business). These provisions reverse the Tax Court decisions in both *Feldman* and *Scott*. Disallowed home office deductions may be carried forward to later years.

# 149 Hobby Losses

An activity (other than horse breeding or racing) is presumed not to be a hobby if it is profitable in three out of five consecutive years. Prior law presumption rules are retained for horse-breeding activities. This provision was effective January 1, 1987, and changed the prior law's two out of five years profit presumption.

# 150 Capital Gains

Prior law provided for a 60 percent exclusion for net long-term capital gains in excess of net short-term capital losses. This created a maximum capital gains rate, at the 50 percent bracket, of 20 percent. Under the Tax Reform Act of 1986, this capital gains deduction is repealed. The maximum rate on long-term capital gains will not exceed the maximum individual rates. For 1987, the highest capital gains rate was 28 percent. Capital losses are allowed in full against capital gains plus $3,000 of other income.

# 151 Tax Shelter At-Risk Rules

The Reform Act extends the at-risk rules to real estate activities. This means that for you to have basis for depreciation or losses based upon money borrowed, you must be personally liable for those loans. An exception is provided for real estate losses, in that third-party nonrecourse debt is still considered "at risk." Such loans could be made by related parties provided that the terms of the loan are commercially reasonable and substantially similar to loans made by unrelated parties.

# 152 Tax Shelters: Limitations on Losses from Passive Activities

Prior to the Tax Reform Act of 1986, losses from passive trade or business activities (limited partnership tax shelters) could be used to offset earned income. Under the Tax Reform Act of 1986, losses from passive trade or business activities as well as credits from those activities can be used only to offset passive income. Moreover, passive income does not include portfolio income (dividends, interest, and capital gains). Disallowed losses and credits can be carried forward and used in the next taxable year. Disallowed losses are allowed in full when the taxpayer disposes of his entire interest in the activity in a taxable transaction. However, disallowed credits would not be allowed upon such disposition.

These requirements apply to individuals, estates, trusts, and personal service corporations. Closely held corporations can use passive losses and credits to offset active business income, but not portfolio income.

In the case of *rental real estate activities* in which an individual actively participates, up to $25,000 of losses and credits from all such activities is allowed each year against nonpassive income. This $25,000 amount is phased out between $100,000 and $150,000 of adjusted gross income determined without regard to passive losses. The phase-out range is increased to between $200,000 and $250,000 for rehabilitation and low-income housing credits. This exception for low-income housing credits applies (for the original credit compliance period) only to property placed in service before 1990, except if the property is placed in service before 1992 and 10 percent or more of the total project costs are incurred before 1990. Carryforward and property disposal rules apply. In addition, low-income housing credits can be taken against nonpassive income without regard to a taxpayer's participation.

These limitations on passive income and credits are effective for taxable years beginning after 1986, with a phase-in rule. Investments made before the date of enactment are subject to disallowance—35 percent in taxable years beginning in 1987, 60 percent in taxable years beginning in 1988, 80 percent in taxable years beginning in 1989, 90 percent in taxable years beginning in 1990, and 100 percent in taxable years beginning after 1990. There is no phase-in for investments made on or after the date of enactment (October 22, 1986).

Note that passive activities are defined to include trade or business activities in which a taxpayer does not materially participate (e.g., a limited partnership interest in an activity) and rental activities. Passive activities do *not* include working interests in gas or oil property in which a taxpayer's form of ownership does not limit liability.

# 153 Investment Interest Limitations

*Nonbusiness interest* means all interest not incurred in a taxpayer's trade or business as well as other interest attributable to an activity in which a taxpayer does not materially participate or, in the case of rental real estate, does not actively participate. *Consumer interest* means interest not attributable to a trade or business or an activity engaged in for profit.

As discussed above, consumer interest is not deductible, except, with limits, interest on debts secured by your principal residence or a second home. Under the Tax Reform Act of 1986, the deduction for investment interest of noncorporate taxpayers is limited to net investment income plus certain deductible expenditures in excess of rental income from net leased property. Interest (and income) from activities subject to the passive rules is not treated as investment interest (or investment income). In calculating net investment income, passive losses that are allowed under the passive loss phase-in provisions are subtracted from investment income.

Like the limitations on consumer interest, these provisions were effective for taxable years beginning after December 31, 1986, but are phased in. During the phase-in period, the amount of interest disallowed under these provisions is limited to 35 percent in taxable years beginning in 1987, 60 percent in taxable years beginning in 1988, 80 percent in taxable years beginning in 1989, 90 percent in taxable years beginning in 1990, and 100 percent in taxable years beginning in 1991 and thereafter. Interest that is disallowed for a taxable year during the phase-in period and carried forward may be allowed in subsequent years only to the extent that there is investment income in excess of net investment interest paid or incurred in such subsequent years.

# 154 Investment Tax Credits

The Tax Reform Act of 1986 eliminated the investment tax credit as of January 1, 1986. You are allowed a 3-year carryback and a 15-year carryforward of unused investment tax credit. The Act provides, however, that investment tax credit carryovers (and investment tax credits earned on transition property) be reduced by 35 percent. The amount of reduction for 1987 was 17.5 percent.

# 155 Section 179 Expensing

Prior law allowed a taxpayer to expense as much as $5,000 per year in furniture and equipment purchased for a trade or business. This expensing was in lieu of depreciation. The new law increases this amount to $10,000 annually but is unavailable for taxpayers with more than $200,000 in equipment purchases per year. For every dollar of qualifying investment in excess of $200,000, the $10,000 limit is reduced by $1. Moreover, this expensed amount is limited to the taxable income derived from any active trade or business, and the difference between expensing and accelerated depreciation deductions is recaptured if the property is converted to nonbusiness use at any time before the end of the property's recovery period.

# 156 Cost Recovery/Depreciation

The new law creates a new accelerated depreciation system, which groups property in the following classes:

- 3-year class—asset depreciation range (ADR) midpoints of 4 years and less, except that automobiles and light trucks are excluded and present law for horses that are in the 3-year class is retained. The method is 200 percent declining balance, switching to straight line.

- 5-year class—ADR midpoints of more than 4 years and less than 10 years, adding automobiles, light trucks, qualified technological equipment, computer-based central office switching equipment, renewable energy and biomass properties that are small power production facilities, and research and experimentation property. The method is 200 percent declining balance.

- 7-year class—ADR midpoints of 10 years and more but less than 16 years, adding single-purpose agricultural and horticulture structures and property with no ADR midpoint that is not classified elsewhere. The method is 200 percent declining balance.

- 10-year class—ADR midpoints of 16 years and more but less than 20 years. The method is 200 percent declining balance.

- 15-year class—ADR midpoints of 20 years and more but less than 25 years, including sewerage treatment plants and telephone distribution plants and related equipment used for the two-way exchange of voice and data communications. The method is 150 percent declining balance.

- 20-year class—ADR midpoints of 25 years and more, other than real property with an ADR midpoint of 27.5 years and more, and including sewer pipes. The method is 150 percent declining balance.

- 27.5 years—residential real property. The method is straight line.

- 31.5 years—nonresidential real property (real property that is not residential rental property and does not have an ADR midpoint of less than 27.5 years). The method is straight line.

For personal property, both the first and last depreciation allowances for an asset reflect the one-half-year convention. The prior law midmonth convention applies to real property, and a midquarter convention applies to taxpayers who place more than 40 percent of their property in service during the last quarter of the taxable year.

Moreover, there is no recapture of previously allowed depreciation deductions in the case of residential rental property and nonresidential real property. Because of the elimination of capital gains, all gains will now be ordinary income.

Generally, the effective date for all depreciation provisions is for property placed in service on or after January 1, 1987. However, the Act allows taxpayers to start using the new system for property placed in service after July 31, 1986. In other words, buyers of 3- and 5-year property did not have to wait until January 1987 to get the benefit of the more rapid write-offs if property was placed in service between July 31, 1986, and December 31, 1986. The benefits here could be substantial. For example, the first-year deduction for a $100,000 tractor under the new law is $33,333, versus $25,000 under prior law. These benefits continued through 1987 as well. A tractor placed in service in the last five months of 1986 receives a $44,444 deduction under the new system, versus $38,000 under prior law. Therefore, the combined write-off in 1986 and 1987 would be $14,777 greater under the new option than under prior regulations.

The following tables list percentages for property in the 3-, 5-, 7-, 10-, 15-, and 20-year classes.

Table 1. General Depreciation System
Applicable Depreciation Method: 200 or 150 Percent
Declining Balance Switching to Straight Line
Applicable Recovery Periods: 3, 5, 7, 10, 15, 20 Years
Applicable Convention: Half-Year

| If the Recovery Year Is: | and the Recovery Period is: | | | | | |
|---|---|---|---|---|---|---|
| | 3-Year | 5-Year | 7-Year | 10-Year | 15-Year | 20-Year |
| | | | the Depreciation Rate Is: | | | |
| 1 | 33.33 | 20.00 | 14.29 | 10.00 | 5.00 | 3.750 |
| 2 | 44.45 | 32.00 | 24.49 | 18.00 | 9.50 | 7.219 |
| 3 | 14.81 | 19.20 | 17.49 | 14.40 | 8.55 | 6.677 |
| 4 | 7.41 | 11.52 | 12.49 | 11.52 | 7.70 | 6.177 |
| 5 | | 11.52 | 8.93 | 9.22 | 6.93 | 5.713 |
| 6 | | 5.76 | 8.92 | 7.37 | 6.23 | 5.285 |
| 7 | | | 8.93 | 6.55 | 5.90 | 4.888 |
| 8 | | | 4.46 | 6.55 | 5.90 | 4.522 |
| 9 | | | | 6.56 | 5.91 | 4.462 |
| 10 | | | | 6.55 | 5.90 | 4.461 |
| 11 | | | | 3.28 | 5.91 | 4.462 |
| 12 | | | | | 5.90 | 4.461 |
| 13 | | | | | 5.91 | 4.462 |
| 14 | | | | | 5.90 | 4.461 |
| 15 | | | | | 5.91 | 4.462 |
| 16 | | | | | 2.95 | 4.461 |
| 17 | | | | | | 4.462 |
| 18 | | | | | | 4.461 |
| 19 | | | | | | 4.462 |
| 20 | | | | | | 4.461 |
| 21 | | | | | | 2.231 |

Table 2. General Depreciation System
Applicable Depreciation Method: 200 or 150 Percent
Declining Balance Switching to Straight Line
Applicable Recovery Periods: 3, 5, 7, 10, 15, 20 Years
Applicable Convention: Mid-Quarter (Property Placed in
Service in First Quarter)

| If the Recovery Year Is: | and the Recovery Period is: | | | | | |
|---|---|---|---|---|---|---|
| | 3-Year | 5-Year | 7-Year | 10-Year | 15-Year | 20-Year |
| | the Depreciation Rate Is: | | | | | |
| 1 | 58.33 | 35.00 | 25.00 | 17.50 | 8.75 | 6.563 |
| 2 | 27.78 | 26.00 | 21.43 | 16.50 | 9.13 | 7.000 |
| 3 | 12.35 | 15.60 | 15.31 | 13.20 | 8.21 | 6.482 |
| 4 | 1.54 | 11.01 | 10.93 | 10.56 | 7.39 | 5.996 |
| 5 | | 11.01 | 8.75 | 8.45 | 6.65 | 5.546 |
| 6 | | 1.38 | 8.74 | 6.76 | 5.99 | 5.130 |
| 7 | | | 8.75 | 6.55 | 5.90 | 4.746 |
| 8 | | | 1.09 | 6.55 | 5.91 | 4.459 |
| 9 | | | | 6.56 | 5.90 | 4.459 |
| 10 | | | | 6.55 | 5.91 | 4.459 |
| 11 | | | | 0.82 | 5.90 | 4.459 |
| 12 | | | | | 5.91 | 4.460 |
| 13 | | | | | 5.90 | 4.459 |
| 14 | | | | | 5.91 | 4.460 |
| 15 | | | | | 5.90 | 4.459 |
| 16 | | | | | 0.74 | 4.460 |
| 17 | | | | | | 4.459 |
| 18 | | | | | | 4.460 |
| 19 | | | | | | 4.459 |
| 20 | | | | | | 4.460 |
| 21 | | | | | | 0.557 |

Table 3. General Depreciation System
Applicable Depreciation Method: 200 or 150 Percent
Declining Balance Switching to Straight Line
Applicable Recovery Periods: 3, 5, 7, 10, 15, 20 Years
Applicable Convention: Mid-Quarter (Property Placed in
Service in Second Quarter)

| If the Recovery Year Is: | and the Recovery Period is: | | | | | |
|---|---|---|---|---|---|---|
| | 3-Year | 5-Year | 7-Year | 10-Year | 15-Year | 20-Year |
| | the Depreciation Rate Is: | | | | | |
| 1 | 41.67 | 25.00 | 17.85 | 12.50 | 6.25 | 4.688 |
| 2 | 38.89 | 30.00 | 23.47 | 17.50 | 9.38 | 7.148 |
| 3 | 14.14 | 18.00 | 16.76 | 14.00 | 8.44 | 6.612 |
| 4 | 5.30 | 11.37 | 11.97 | 11.20 | 7.59 | 6.116 |
| 5 | | 11.37 | 8.87 | 8.96 | 6.83 | 5.658 |
| 6 | | 4.26 | 8.87 | 7.17 | 6.15 | 5.233 |
| 7 | | | 8.87 | 6.55 | 5.91 | 4.841 |
| 8 | | | 3.33 | 6.55 | 5.90 | 4.478 |
| 9 | | | | 6.56 | 5.91 | 4.463 |
| 10 | | | | 6.55 | 5.90 | 4.463 |
| 11 | | | | 2.46 | 5.91 | 4.463 |
| 12 | | | | | 5.90 | 4.463 |
| 13 | | | | | 5.91 | 4.463 |
| 14 | | | | | 5.90 | 4.463 |
| 15 | | | | | 5.91 | 4.462 |
| 16 | | | | | 2.21 | 4.463 |
| 17 | | | | | | 4.462 |
| 18 | | | | | | 4.463 |
| 19 | | | | | | 4.462 |
| 20 | | | | | | 4.463 |
| 21 | | | | | | 1.673 |

Table 4. General Depreciation System
Applicable Depreciation Method: 200 or 150 Percent
Declining Balance Switching to Straight Line
Applicable Recovery Periods: 3, 5, 7, 10, 15, 20 Years
Applicable Convention: Mid-Quarter (Property Placed in
Service in Third Quarter)

| If the Recovery Year Is: | and the Recovery Period is: | | | | | |
|---|---|---|---|---|---|---|
| | 3-Year | 5-Year | 7-Year | 10-Year | 15-Year | 20-Year |
| | | | the Depreciation Rate Is: | | | |
| 1 | 25.00 | 15.00 | 10.71 | 7.50 | 3.75 | 2.813 |
| 2 | 50.00 | 34.00 | 25.51 | 18.50 | 9.63 | 7.289 |
| 3 | 16.67 | 20.40 | 18.22 | 14.80 | 8.66 | 6.742 |
| 4 | 8.33 | 12.24 | 13.02 | 11.84 | 7.80 | 6.237 |
| 5 | | 11.30 | 9.30 | 9.47 | 7.02 | 5.769 |
| 6 | | 7.06 | 8.85 | 7.58 | 6.31 | 5.336 |
| 7 | | | 8.86 | 6.55 | 5.90 | 4.936 |
| 8 | | | 5.53 | 6.55 | 5.90 | 4.566 |
| 9 | | | | 6.56 | 5.91 | 4.460 |
| 10 | | | | 6.55 | 5.90 | 4.460 |
| 11 | | | | 4.10 | 5.91 | 4.460 |
| 12 | | | | | 5.90 | 4.460 |
| 13 | | | | | 5.91 | 4.461 |
| 14 | | | | | 5.90 | 4.460 |
| 15 | | | | | 5.91 | 4.461 |
| 16 | | | | | 3.69 | 4.460 |
| 17 | | | | | | 4.461 |
| 18 | | | | | | 4.460 |
| 19 | | | | | | 4.461 |
| 20 | | | | | | 4.460 |
| 21 | | | | | | 2.788 |

Table 5. General Depreciation System
Applicable Depreciation Method: 200 or 150 Percent
Declining Balance Switching to Straight Line
Applicable Recovery Periods: 3, 5, 7, 10, 15, 20 Years
Applicable Convention: Mid-Quarter (Property Placed in
Service in Fourth Quarter)

| If the Recovery Year Is: | and the Recovery Period is: | | | | | |
|---|---|---|---|---|---|---|
| | 3-Year | 5-Year | 7-Year | 10-Year | 15-Year | 20-Year |
| | | | the Depreciation Rate Is: | | | |
| 1 | 8.33 | 5.00 | 3.57 | 2.50 | 1.25 | 0.938 |
| 2 | 61.11 | 38.00 | 27.55 | 19.50 | 9.88 | 7.430 |
| 3 | 20.37 | 22.80 | 19.68 | 15.60 | 8.89 | 6.872 |
| 4 | 10.19 | 13.68 | 14.06 | 12.48 | 8.00 | 6.357 |
| 5 | | 10.94 | 10.04 | 9.98 | 7.20 | 5.880 |
| 6 | | 9.58 | 8.73 | 7.99 | 6.48 | 5.439 |
| 7 | | | 8.73 | 6.55 | 5.90 | 5.031 |
| 8 | | | 7.64 | 6.55 | 5.90 | 4.654 |
| 9 | | | | 6.56 | 5.90 | 4.458 |
| 10 | | | | 6.55 | 5.91 | 4.458 |
| 11 | | | | 5.74 | 5.90 | 4.458 |
| 12 | | | | | 5.91 | 4.458 |
| 13 | | | | | 5.90 | 4.458 |
| 14 | | | | | 5.91 | 4.458 |
| 15 | | | | | 5.90 | 4.458 |
| 16 | | | | | 5.17 | 4.458 |
| 17 | | | | | | 4.458 |
| 18 | | | | | | 4.459 |
| 19 | | | | | | 4.458 |
| 20 | | | | | | 4.459 |
| 21 | | | | | | 3.901 |

The following tables show recovery percentages for residential and non-residential real property. They are based on a mathematical application of the prescribed depreciation methods. Note that there are no official tables at this time.

## Table 6. General Depreciation System
### Applicable Depreciation Method: Straight Line
### Applicable Recovery Period: 27.5 Years
### Applicable Convention: Mid-Month

| If the Recovery Year Is: | and the Month in the First Recovery Year the Property Is Placed in Service Is: the Depreciation Rate Is: | | | | | | | | | | | |
|---|---|---|---|---|---|---|---|---|---|---|---|---|
| | 1 | 2 | 3 | 4 | 5 | 6 | 7 | 8 | 9 | 10 | 11 | 12 |
| 1 | 3.485 | 3.182 | 2.879 | 2.576 | 2.273 | 1.970 | 1.667 | 1.364 | 1.061 | 0.758 | 0.455 | 0.152 |
| 2 | 3.636 | 3.636 | 3.636 | 3.636 | 3.636 | 3.636 | 3.636 | 3.636 | 3.636 | 3.636 | 3.636 | 3.636 |
| 3 | 3.636 | 3.636 | 3.636 | 3.636 | 3.636 | 3.636 | 3.636 | 3.636 | 3.636 | 3.636 | 3.636 | 3.636 |
| 4 | 3.636 | 3.636 | 3.636 | 3.636 | 3.636 | 3.636 | 3.636 | 3.636 | 3.636 | 3.636 | 3.636 | 3.636 |
| 5 | 3.636 | 3.636 | 3.636 | 3.636 | 3.636 | 3.636 | 3.636 | 3.636 | 3.636 | 3.636 | 3.636 | 3.636 |
| 6 | 3.636 | 3.636 | 3.636 | 3.636 | 3.636 | 3.636 | 3.636 | 3.636 | 3.636 | 3.636 | 3.636 | 3.636 |
| 7 | 3.636 | 3.636 | 3.636 | 3.636 | 3.636 | 3.636 | 3.636 | 3.636 | 3.636 | 3.636 | 3.636 | 3.636 |
| 8 | 3.636 | 3.636 | 3.636 | 3.636 | 3.636 | 3.636 | 3.636 | 3.636 | 3.636 | 3.636 | 3.636 | 3.636 |
| 9 | 3.636 | 3.636 | 3.636 | 3.636 | 3.636 | 3.637 | 3.636 | 3.636 | 3.636 | 3.636 | 3.636 | 3.636 |
| 10 | 3.637 | 3.637 | 3.637 | 3.637 | 3.637 | 3.636 | 3.636 | 3.636 | 3.636 | 3.636 | 3.636 | 3.637 |
| 11 | 3.636 | 3.636 | 3.636 | 3.636 | 3.636 | 3.637 | 3.637 | 3.637 | 3.637 | 3.637 | 3.637 | 3.637 |
| 12 | 3.637 | 3.637 | 3.637 | 3.637 | 3.637 | 3.637 | 3.636 | 3.636 | 3.636 | 3.636 | 3.636 | 3.636 |

| | | | | | | | | | | | | |
|---|---|---|---|---|---|---|---|---|---|---|---|---|
| 13 | 3.636 | 3.636 | 3.636 | 3.636 | 3.636 | 3.636 | 3.637 | 3.637 | 3.637 | 3.637 | 3.637 | 3.637 |
| 14 | 3.637 | 3.637 | 3.637 | 3.637 | 3.637 | 3.637 | 3.636 | 3.636 | 3.636 | 3.636 | 3.636 | 3.636 |
| 15 | 3.636 | 3.636 | 3.636 | 3.636 | 3.636 | 3.636 | 3.637 | 3.637 | 3.637 | 3.637 | 3.637 | 3.637 |
| 16 | 3.637 | 3.637 | 3.637 | 3.637 | 3.637 | 3.637 | 3.636 | 3.636 | 3.636 | 3.636 | 3.636 | 3.636 |
| 17 | 3.636 | 3.636 | 3.636 | 3.636 | 3.636 | 3.636 | 3.637 | 3.637 | 3.637 | 3.637 | 3.637 | 3.637 |
| 18 | 3.637 | 3.637 | 3.637 | 3.637 | 3.637 | 3.637 | 3.636 | 3.636 | 3.636 | 3.636 | 3.636 | 3.636 |
| 19 | 3.636 | 3.636 | 3.636 | 3.636 | 3.636 | 3.636 | 3.637 | 3.637 | 3.637 | 3.637 | 3.637 | 3.637 |
| 20 | 3.637 | 3.637 | 3.637 | 3.637 | 3.637 | 3.637 | 3.636 | 3.636 | 3.636 | 3.636 | 3.636 | 3.636 |
| 21 | 3.636 | 3.636 | 3.636 | 3.636 | 3.636 | 3.636 | 3.637 | 3.637 | 3.637 | 3.637 | 3.637 | 3.637 |
| 22 | 3.637 | 3.637 | 3.637 | 3.637 | 3.637 | 3.637 | 3.636 | 3.636 | 3.636 | 3.636 | 3.636 | 3.636 |
| 23 | 3.636 | 3.636 | 3.636 | 3.636 | 3.636 | 3.636 | 3.637 | 3.637 | 3.637 | 3.637 | 3.637 | 3.637 |
| 24 | 3.637 | 3.637 | 3.637 | 3.637 | 3.637 | 3.637 | 3.636 | 3.636 | 3.636 | 3.636 | 3.636 | 3.636 |
| 25 | 3.636 | 3.636 | 3.636 | 3.636 | 3.636 | 3.636 | 3.637 | 3.637 | 3.637 | 3.637 | 3.637 | 3.637 |
| 26 | 3.637 | 3.637 | 3.637 | 3.637 | 3.637 | 3.637 | 3.636 | 3.636 | 3.636 | 3.636 | 3.636 | 3.636 |
| 27 | 3.636 | 3.636 | 3.636 | 3.636 | 3.636 | 3.636 | 3.637 | 3.637 | 3.637 | 3.637 | 3.637 | 3.637 |
| 28 | 1.970 | 2.273 | 2.576 | 2.879 | 3.182 | 3.485 | 3.636 | 3.636 | 3.636 | 3.636 | 3.636 | 3.636 |
| 29 | 0.000 | 0.000 | 0.000 | 0.000 | 0.000 | 0.000 | 0.152 | 0.455 | 0.758 | 1.061 | 1.364 | 1.667 |

## Table 7. General Depreciation System
### Applicable Depreciation Method: Straight Line
### Applicable Recovery Period: 31.5 Years
### Applicable Convention: Mid-Month

| If the Recovery Year Is: | And the Month in the First Recovery Year the Property Is Placed in Service Is: | | | | | | | | | | | |
|---|---|---|---|---|---|---|---|---|---|---|---|---|
| | the Depreciation Rate Is: | | | | | | | | | | | |
| | 1 | 2 | 3 | 4 | 5 | 6 | 7 | 8 | 9 | 10 | 11 | 12 |
| 1 | 3.042 | 2.778 | 2.513 | 2.249 | 1.984 | 1.720 | 1.455 | 1.190 | 0.926 | 0.661 | 0.397 | 0.132 |
| 2 | 3.175 | 3.175 | 3.175 | 3.175 | 3.175 | 3.175 | 3.175 | 3.175 | 3.175 | 3.175 | 3.175 | 3.175 |
| 3 | 3.175 | 3.175 | 3.175 | 3.175 | 3.175 | 3.175 | 3.175 | 3.175 | 3.175 | 3.175 | 3.175 | 3.175 |
| 4 | 3.175 | 3.175 | 3.175 | 3.175 | 3.175 | 3.175 | 3.175 | 3.175 | 3.175 | 3.175 | 3.175 | 3.175 |
| 5 | 3.175 | 3.175 | 3.175 | 3.175 | 3.175 | 3.175 | 3.175 | 3.175 | 3.175 | 3.175 | 3.175 | 3.175 |
| 6 | 3.175 | 3.175 | 3.175 | 3.175 | 3.175 | 3.175 | 3.175 | 3.175 | 3.175 | 3.175 | 3.175 | 3.175 |
| 7 | 3.175 | 3.175 | 3.175 | 3.175 | 3.175 | 3.175 | 3.175 | 3.175 | 3.175 | 3.175 | 3.175 | 3.175 |
| 8 | 3.175 | 3.174 | 3.175 | 3.174 | 3.175 | 3.174 | 3.175 | 3.175 | 3.175 | 3.175 | 3.175 | 3.175 |
| 9 | 3.174 | 3.175 | 3.174 | 3.175 | 3.174 | 3.175 | 3.174 | 3.175 | 3.174 | 3.174 | 3.174 | 3.175 |
| 10 | 3.175 | 3.174 | 3.175 | 3.174 | 3.175 | 3.174 | 3.175 | 3.174 | 3.175 | 3.174 | 3.175 | 3.174 |
| 11 | 3.174 | 3.175 | 3.174 | 3.175 | 3.174 | 3.175 | 3.175 | 3.174 | 3.174 | 3.175 | 3.174 | 3.175 |
| 12 | 3.175 | 3.174 | 3.175 | 3.174 | 3.175 | 3.174 | 3.175 | 3.175 | 3.175 | 3.174 | 3.175 | 3.174 |
| 13 | 3.174 | 3.175 | 3.174 | 3.175 | 3.174 | 3.175 | 3.174 | 3.175 | 3.174 | 3.175 | 3.174 | 3.175 |

| | | | | | | | | | | | | | | |
|---|---|---|---|---|---|---|---|---|---|---|---|---|---|---|
| 14 | 3.175 | 3.174 | 3.175 | 3.174 | 3.175 | 3.174 | 3.175 | 3.174 | 3.175 | 3.174 | 3.175 | 3.174 | 3.175 | 3.174 |
| 15 | 3.174 | 3.175 | 3.174 | 3.175 | 3.174 | 3.175 | 3.174 | 3.175 | 3.174 | 3.175 | 3.174 | 3.175 | 3.174 | 3.175 |
| 16 | 3.175 | 3.174 | 3.175 | 3.174 | 3.175 | 3.174 | 3.175 | 3.174 | 3.175 | 3.174 | 3.175 | 3.174 | 3.175 | 3.174 |
| 17 | 3.174 | 3.175 | 3.174 | 3.175 | 3.174 | 3.175 | 3.174 | 3.175 | 3.174 | 3.175 | 3.174 | 3.175 | 3.174 | 3.175 |
| 18 | 3.175 | 3.174 | 3.175 | 3.174 | 3.175 | 3.174 | 3.175 | 3.174 | 3.175 | 3.174 | 3.175 | 3.174 | 3.175 | 3.174 |
| 19 | 3.174 | 3.175 | 3.174 | 3.175 | 3.174 | 3.175 | 3.174 | 3.175 | 3.174 | 3.175 | 3.174 | 3.175 | 3.174 | 3.175 |
| 20 | 3.175 | 3.174 | 3.175 | 3.174 | 3.175 | 3.174 | 3.175 | 3.174 | 3.175 | 3.174 | 3.175 | 3.174 | 3.175 | 3.174 |
| 21 | 3.174 | 3.175 | 3.174 | 3.175 | 3.174 | 3.175 | 3.174 | 3.175 | 3.174 | 3.175 | 3.174 | 3.175 | 3.174 | 3.175 |
| 22 | 3.175 | 3.174 | 3.175 | 3.174 | 3.175 | 3.174 | 3.175 | 3.174 | 3.175 | 3.174 | 3.175 | 3.174 | 3.175 | 3.174 |
| 23 | 3.174 | 3.175 | 3.174 | 3.175 | 3.174 | 3.175 | 3.174 | 3.175 | 3.174 | 3.175 | 3.174 | 3.175 | 3.174 | 3.175 |
| 24 | 3.175 | 3.174 | 3.175 | 3.174 | 3.175 | 3.174 | 3.175 | 3.174 | 3.175 | 3.174 | 3.175 | 3.174 | 3.175 | 3.174 |
| 25 | 3.174 | 3.175 | 3.174 | 3.175 | 3.174 | 3.175 | 3.174 | 3.175 | 3.174 | 3.175 | 3.174 | 3.175 | 3.174 | 3.175 |
| 26 | 3.175 | 3.174 | 3.175 | 3.174 | 3.175 | 3.174 | 3.175 | 3.174 | 3.175 | 3.174 | 3.175 | 3.174 | 3.175 | 3.174 |
| 27 | 3.174 | 3.175 | 3.174 | 3.175 | 3.174 | 3.175 | 3.174 | 3.175 | 3.174 | 3.175 | 3.174 | 3.175 | 3.174 | 3.175 |
| 28 | 3.175 | 3.174 | 3.175 | 3.174 | 3.175 | 3.174 | 3.175 | 3.174 | 3.175 | 3.174 | 3.175 | 3.174 | 3.175 | 3.174 |
| 29 | 3.174 | 3.175 | 3.174 | 3.175 | 3.174 | 3.175 | 3.174 | 3.175 | 3.174 | 3.175 | 3.174 | 3.175 | 3.174 | 3.175 |
| 30 | 3.175 | 3.174 | 3.175 | 3.174 | 3.175 | 3.174 | 3.175 | 3.174 | 3.175 | 3.174 | 3.175 | 3.174 | 3.175 | 3.174 |
| 31 | 3.174 | 3.175 | 3.174 | 3.175 | 3.174 | 3.175 | 3.174 | 3.175 | 3.174 | 3.175 | 3.174 | 3.175 | 3.174 | 3.175 |
| 32 | 1.720 | 1.984 | 2.249 | 2.513 | 2.778 | 3.042 | 3.175 | 3.174 | 3.175 | 3.174 | 3.175 | 3.174 | 3.175 | 3.174 |
| 33 | 0.000 | 0.000 | 0.000 | 0.000 | 0.000 | 0.000 | 0.000 | 0.000 | 0.132 | 0.397 | 0.661 | 0.926 | 1.190 | 1.455 |

*Example:* Assume American Corporation bought a residential apartment building in January 1986 and a second residential apartment building in January 1987. Both buildings cost $100,000 (exclusive of land).

The 1986 apartment building has a 19-year ACRS recovery period. The depreciation deduction for the first year is $8,800 and for the second year, $8,400—a total of $17,200.

The 1987 apartment building has a 27.5-year recovery period and must be depreciated on a straight-line basis. Based on percentages under the new law, the first-year depreciation deduction is $3,485 and the second-year deduction is $3,636—a total of $7,121.

Placing property in service in 1987 rather than 1986 caused a reduction in depreciation deductions over the first two years of $10,079, a 58.6 percent decrease. If the building were a department store, the first two years' depreciation deductions would be $3,042 and $3,175 under the new law. This $6,217 total is $10,983 less than under prior law—a 63.9 percent reduction.

# Revenue Procedure 83-35
## I.R.B. 1983-20, 54

Asset Guideline Classes and Periods, Asset Depreciation Ranges, and Annual Asset Guideline Repair Allowance Percentages

The asset guideline classes, asset guideline periods, asset depreciation ranges, and annual asset guideline repair allowance percentages are prescribed as set forth below:

| Asset guide-line class | Description of assets included | Asset depreciation range (in years) | | | Annual asset guide-line repair allowance percentage |
|---|---|---|---|---|---|
| | | Lower limit | Asset guideline period | Upper limit | |

**SPECIFIC DEPRECIABLE ASSETS USED IN ALL BUSINESS ACTIVITIES, EXCEPT AS NOTED:**

| | | | | | |
|---|---|---|---|---|---|
| 00.11 | **Office Furniture, Fixtures, and Equipment:** Includes furniture and fixtures that are not a structural component of a building. Includes such assets as desks, files, safes, and communications equipment. Does not include communications equipment that is included in other CLADR classes …………………… | 8 | 10 | 12 | 2 |
| 00.12 | **Information Systems:** Includes computers and their peripheral equipment used in administering normal business transactions and the maintenance of business records, their retrieval and analysis. Information systems are defined as: | | | | |

*(continued on next page)*

| Asset guideline class | Description of assets included | Asset depreciation range (in years) | | | Annual asset guideline repair allowance percentage |
|---|---|---|---|---|---|
| | | Lower limit | Asset guideline period | Upper limit | |
| | 1) Computers: A computer is an electronically activated device capable of accepting information, applying prescribed processes to the information, and supplying the results of these processes with or without human intervention. It usually consists of a central processing unit containing extensive storage, logic, arithmetic, and control capabilities. Excluded from this category are adding machines, electronic desk calculators, etc. | | | | |
| | 2) Peripheral equipment consists of the auxiliary machines that may be placed under control of the central processing unit. Nonlimiting examples are: Card readers, card punches, magnetic tape feeds, high speed printers, optical character readers, tape cassettes, mass storage units, paper tape equipment, keypunches, data entry devices, teleprinters, terminals, tape drives, card sorters, plotters, and collators. Peripheral image projector tubes, card sorters, plotters, and collators. Peripheral equipment may be used on-line or off-line. | | | | |
| | Does not include equipment that is an integral part of other capital equipment that is included in other CLADR classes of economic activity, i.e., computers used primarily for process or production control, switching, channeling, and automating distributive trades and services such as point of sale (POS) computer systems ............ | 5 | 6 | 7 | 7.5 |
| 00.13 | Data Handling Equipment, except Computers: Includes only typewriters, calculators, adding and accounting machines, copiers, and duplicating equipment .................. | 5 | 6 | 7 | 15 |

| Account | Description | | | | |
|---|---|---|---|---|---|
| 00.21 | Airplanes (airframes and engines), except those used in commercial or contract carrying of passengers or freight, and all helicopters (airframes and engines) | 5 | 6 | 7 | 14 |
| 00.22 | Automobiles, Taxis | 2.5 | 3 | 3.5 | 16.5 |
| 00.23 | Buses | 7 | 9 | 11 | 11.5 |
| 00.241 | Light General Purpose Trucks: Includes trucks for use over the road (actual unloaded weight less than 13,000 pounds) | 3 | 4 | 5 | 16.5 |
| 00.242 | Heavy General Purpose Trucks: Includes heavy general purpose trucks, concrete ready-mix trucks, and ore trucks, for use over the road (actual unloaded weight 13,000 pounds or more) | 5 | 6 | 7 | 10 |
| 00.25 | Railroad Cars and Locomotives except those owned by railroad transportation companies | 12 | 15 | 18 | 8 |
| 00.26 | Tractor Units For Use Over-The-Road | 3 | 4 | 5 | 16.5 |
| 00.27 | Trailers and Trailer-Mounted Containers | 5 | 6 | 7 | 10 |
| 00.28 | Vessels, Barges, Tugs, and Similar Water Transportation Equipment, except those used in marine construction | 14.5 | 18 | 21.5 | 6 |
| 00.3 | Land Improvements: Includes improvements directly to or added to land, whether such improvements are section 1245 property or section 1250 property, provided such improvements are depreciable. Examples of such assets might include sidewalks, roads, canals, waterways, drainage facilities, sewers, wharves and docks, bridges, fences, landscaping, shrubbery, or | | | | |

(Continued on next page)

| Asset guideline class | Description of assets included | Asset depreciation range (in years) | | | Annual asset guideline repair allowance percentage |
| --- | --- | --- | --- | --- | --- |
| | | Lower limit | Asset guideline period | Upper limit | |
| 102 | radio and television transmitting towers. Does not include land improvements that are explicitly included in any other class, and buildings and structural components as defined in section 1.48-1(e) of the regulations. Excludes public utility initial clearing and grading land improvements as specified in Rev. Rul. 72-403, 1972-2 C.B. 102 . . . . . . . . . . . . . . . | — | 20 | — | — |
| 00.4 | **Industrial Steam and Electric Generation and/or Distribution Systems:** Includes assets, whether such assets are section 1245 property or 1250 property, providing such assets are depreciable, used in the production and/or distribution of electricity with rated total capacity in excess of 500 Kilowatts and/or assets used in the production and/or distribution of steam with rated total capacity in excess of 12,500 pounds per hour for use by the taxpayer in its industrial manufacturing process or plant activity and not ordinarily available for sale to others. Does not include buildings and structural components as defined in section 1.48-1(e) of the regulations. Assets used to generate and/or distribute electricity or steam of the type described above but of lesser rated capacity are not included, but are included in the appropriate manufacturing equipment classes elsewhere specified. Also includes electric generating and steam distribution assets, which may utilize steam produced by a waste reduction and resource | | | | |

recovery plant, used by the taxpayer in its industrial manufacturing process or plant activity. Steam and chemical recovery boiler systems used for the recovery and regeneration of chemicals used in manufacturing, with rated capacity in excess of that described above, with specifically related distribution and return systems are not included but are included in appropriate manufacturing equipment classes elsewhere specified. An example of an excluded steam and chemical recovery boiler system is that used in the pulp and paper manufacturing industry ................................. 17.5  22  26.5  2.5

## DEPRECIABLE ASSETS USED IN THE FOLLOWING ACTIVITIES:

**01.1  Agriculture:**
Includes machinery and equipment, grain bins, and fences but no other land improvements, that are used in the production of crops or plants, vines, and trees; livestock; the operation of farm dairies, nurseries, greenhouses, sod farms, mushroom cellars, cranberry bogs, apiaries, and fur farms; the performance of agriculture, animal husbandry, and horticultural services ................................. 8  10  12  11

| Class | Description | | | | |
|---|---|---|---|---|---|
| 01.11 | Cotton Ginning Assets | 9.5 | 12 | 14.5 | 5.5 |
| 01.21 | Cattle, Breeding or Dairy | 5.5 | 7 | 8.5 | — |
| 01.22 | Horses, Breeding or Work | 8 | 10 | 12 | — |
| 01.23 | Hogs, Breeding | 2.5 | 3 | 3.5 | — |
| 01.24 | Sheep and Goats, Breeding | 4 | 5 | 6 | — |
| 01.3 | Farm Buildings | 20 | 25 | 30 | 5 |

*(Continued on next page)*

| Asset guideline class | Description of assets included | Asset depreciation range (in years) | | | Annual asset guideline repair allowance percentage |
|---|---|---|---|---|---|
| | | Lower limit | Asset guideline period | Upper limit | |
| 10.0 | **Mining:** Includes assets used in the mining and quarrying of metallic and nonmetallic minerals (including sand, gravel, stone, and clay) and the milling, beneficiation and other primary preparation of such materials ............ | 8 | 10 | 12 | 6.5 |
| 13.0 | **Offshore Drilling:** Includes assets used in offshore drilling for oil and gas such as floating, self-propelled and other drilling vessels, barges, platforms, and drilling equipment and support vessels such as tenders, barges, towboats and crew boats. Excludes oil and gas production assets ... | 6 | 7.5 | 9 | 3 |
| 13.1 | **Drilling of Oil and Gas Wells:** Includes assets used in the drilling of onshore oil and gas wells and the provision of geophysical and other exploration services; and the provision of such oil and gas field services as chemical treatment, plugging and abandoning of wells and cementing or perforating well casings. Does not include assets used in the performance of any of these activities and services by integrated petroleum and natural gas producers for their own account ............ | 5 | 6 | 7 | 10 |
| 13.2 | **Exploration for and Production of Petroleum and Natural Gas Deposits** | | | | |

| Asset class | Description of assets included | | | | |
|---|---|---|---|---|---|
| | Includes assets used by petroleum and natural gas producers for drilling of wells and production of petroleum and natural gas, including gathering pipelines and related storage facilities. Also includes petroleum and natural gas offshore transportation facilities used by producers and others consisting of platforms (other than drilling platforms classified in Class 13.0), compression or pumping equipment, and gathering and transmission lines to the first onshore transshipment facility. The assets used in the first onshore transshipment facility are also included and consist of separation of natural gas, liquids, and solids; compression or pumping equipment (other than equipment classified in Class 49.23); and liquid holding or storage facilities (other than those classified in Class 49.25). Does not include support vessels .................. | 11 | 14 | 17 | 4.5 |
| 13.3 | **Petroleum Refining:** Includes assets used for the distillation, fractionation, and catalytic cracking of crude petroleum into gasoline and its other components .................. | 13 | 16 | 19 | 7 |
| 15.0 | **Construction:** Includes assets used in construction by general building, special trade, heavy and marine construction contractors, operative and investment builders, real estate subdividers and developers, and others except railroads .................. | 5 | 6 | 7 | 9 |
| 20.1 | **Manufacture of Grain and Grain Mill Products:** Includes assets used in the production of flours, cereals, livestock feeds, and other grain and grain mill products .................. | 13.5 | 17 | 20.5 | 6 |

*(Continued on next page)*

| Asset guideline class | Description of assets included | Asset depreciation range (in years) | | | Annual asset guideline repair allowance percentage |
|---|---|---|---|---|---|
| | | Lower limit | Asset guideline period | Upper limit | |
| 20.2 | **Manufacture of Sugar and Sugar Products:** Includes assets used in the production of raw sugar, syrup, or finished sugar from sugar cane or sugar beets .............. | 14.5 | 18 | 21.5 | 4.5 |
| 20.3 | **Manufacture of Vegetable Oils and Vegetable Oil Products:** Includes assets used in the production of oil from vegetable materials and the manufacture of related vegetable oil products .............. | 14.5 | 18 | 21.5 | 3.5 |
| 20.4 | **Manufacture of Other Food and Kindred Products:** Includes assets used in the production of foods and beverages not included in classes 20.1, 20.2 and 20.3 .............. | 9.5 | 12 | 14.5 | 5.5 |
| 20.5 | **Manufacture of Food and Beverages—Special Handling Devices:** Includes assets defined as specialized materials handling devices such as returnable pallets, palletized containers, and fish processing equipment including boxes, baskets, carts, and flaking trays used in activities as defined in classes 20.1, 20.2, 20.3 and 20.4. Does not include general purpose small tools such as wrenches and drills, both hand and power-driven, and other general purpose equipment such as conveyors, transfer equipment, and materials handling devices ..... | 3 | 4 | 5 | 20 |
| 21.0 | **Manufacture of Tobacco and Tobacco Products:** Includes assets used in the production of cigarettes, cigars, smoking and chewing tobacco, snuff, and other tobacco products .......... | 12 | 15 | 18 | 5 |

**22.1 Manufacture of Knitted Goods:**
Includes assets used in the production of knitted and netted fabrics and lace. Assets used in yarn preparation, bleaching, dyeing, printing, and other similar finishing processes, texturing, and packaging are elsewhere classified .......................... 6 7.5 9 7

**22.2 Manufacture of Yarn, Thread, and Woven Fabric:**
Includes assets used in the production of spun yarns including the preparing, blending, spinning, and twisting of fibers into yarns and threads, the preparation of yarns such as twisting, warping, and winding, the production of covered elastic yarn and thread, cordage, woven fabric, tire fabric, braided fabric, twisted jute for packing, mattresses, pads, sheets, and industrial belts, and the processing of textile mill waste to recover fibers, flocks, and shoddies. Assets used to manufacture carpets, man-made fibers, and nonwovens, and assets used in texturing, bleaching, dyeing, printing, and other similar finishing processes, are elsewhere classified ......................

**22.3 Manufacture of Carpets, and Dyeing, Finishing, and Packaging of Textile Products and Manufacture of Medical and Dental Supplies:**
Includes assets used in the production of carpets, rugs, mats, woven carpet backing, chenille, and other tufted products, and assets used in the joining together of backing with carpet yarn or fabric. Includes assets used in washing, scouring, bleaching, dyeing, printing, drying, and similar finishing processes applied to textile fabrics, yarns, threads, and other textile goods. Includes assets used in the production and packaging of textile products, other than apparel, by creasing, forming, trimming, cutting, and sewing, such as the preparation of 9 11 13 16

(Continued on next page)

| Asset guideline class | Description of assets included | Asset depreciation range (in years) | | | Annual asset guideline repair allowance percentage |
|---|---|---|---|---|---|
| | | Lower limit | Asset guideline period | Upper limit | |
| | carpet and fabric samples, or similar joining together processes (other than the production of scrim reinforced paper products and laminated paper products) such as the sewing and folding of hosiery and panty hose, and the creasing, folding, trimming, and cutting of fabrics to produce nonwoven products, such as disposable diapers and sanitary products. Also includes assets used in the production of medical and dental supplies other than drugs and medicines. Assets used in the manufacture of nonwoven carpet backing and hard surface floor covering such as tile, rubber, and cork are elsewhere classified .... | 7 | 9 | 11 | 15 |
| 22.4 | **Manufacture of Textured Yarns:** Includes assets used in the processing of yarns to impart bulk and/or stretch properties to the yarn. The principal machines involved are falsetwist, draw, beam-to-beam, and stuffer box texturing equipment and related high-speed twisters and winders. Assets, as described above, which are used to further process man-made fibers are elsewhere classified when located in the same plant in an integrated operation with man-made fiber producing assets. Assets used to manufacture man-made fibers and assets used in bleaching, dyeing, printing, and other similar finishing processes are elsewhere classified ................. | 6.5 | 8 | 9.5 | 7 |

| | | | | |
|---|---|---|---|---|
| **22.5 Manufacture of Nonwoven Fabrics:** Includes assets used in the production of nonwoven fabrics, felt goods including felt hats, padding, batting, wadding, oakum, and fillings, from new materials and from textile mill waste. Nonwoven fabrics are defined as fabrics (other than reinforced and laminated composites consisting of nonwovens and other products) manufactured by bonding natural and/or synthetic fibers and/or filaments by means of induced mechanical interlocking, fluid entanglement, chemical adhesion, thermal or solvent reaction, or by combination thereof other than natural hydration bonding as occurs with natural cellulose fibers. Such means include resin bonding, web bonding, and melt bonding. Specifically includes assets used to make flocked and needle punched products other than carpets and rugs. Assets, as described above, which are used to manufacture nonwovens are elsewhere classified when located in the same plant in an integrated operation with man-made fiber producing assets. Assets used to manufacture man-made fibers and assets used in bleaching, dyeing, printing, and other similar finishing processes are elsewhere classified .................. | 8 | 10 | 12 | 15 |
| **23.0 Manufacture of Apparel and Other Finished Products:** Includes assets used in the production of clothing and fabricated textile products by the cutting and sewing of woven fabrics, other textile products, and furs; but does not include assets used in the manufacture of apparel from rubber and leather ................. | 7 | 9 | 11 | 7 |
| **24.1 Cutting of Timber:** Includes logging machinery and equipment and roadbuilding equipment used by logging and sawmill operators and pulp manufacturers for their own account ................. | 5 | 6 | 7 | 10 |
| **24.2 Sawing of Dimensional Stock from Logs:** Includes machinery and equipment installed in permanent or well-established sawmills ................. | 8 | 10 | 12 | 6.5 |

*(Continued on next page)*

| Asset guideline class | Description of assets included | Asset depreciation range (in years) | | | Annual asset guideline repair allowance percentage |
|---|---|---|---|---|---|
| | | Lower limit | Asset guideline period | Upper limit | |
| 24.3 | **Sawing of Dimensional Stock from Logs:** Includes machinery and equipment installed in sawmills characterized by temporary foundations and a lack, or minimum amount, of lumberhandling, drying, and residue disposal equipment and facilities .......... | 5 | 6 | 7 | 10 |
| 24.4 | **Manufacture of Wood Products and Furniture:** Includes assets used in the production of plywood, hardboard, flooring, veneers, furniture, and other wood products, including the treatment of pulp and timber ............ | 8 | 10 | 12 | 6.5 |
| 26.1 | **Manufacture of Pulp and Paper:** Includes assets for pulp materials handling and storage, pulp mill processing, bleach processing, paper and paperboard manufacturing, and on-line finishing. Includes pollution control assets and all land improvements associated with the factory site or production process such as effluent ponds and canals, provided such improvements are depreciable, but does not include buildings and structural components as defined in section 1.48-1(e)(1) of the regulations. Includes steam and chemical recovery boiler systems, with any rated capacity, used for the recovery and regeneration of chemicals used in manufacturing. Does not include assets used either in pulpwood logging or in the manufacture of hardboard ............ | 10.5 | 13 | 15.5 | 10 |

| | | | | | |
|---|---|---|---|---|---|

26.2 **Manufacture of Converted Paper, Paperboard, and Pulp Products:**
Includes assets used for modification or remanufacture of paper and pulp into converted products, such as paper coated off the paper machine, paper bags, paper boxes, cartons and envelopes. Does not include assets used for manufacture of non-wovens that are elsewhere classified .................. 8  10  12  15

27.0 **Printing, Publishing, and Allied Industries:**
Includes assets used in printing by one or more processes, such as letterpress, lithography, gravure, or screen; the performance of services for the printing trade, such as bookbinding, typesetting, engraving, photo-engraving, and electrotyping; and the publication of newspapers, books, and periodicals .................. 9  11  13  5.5

28.0 **Manufacture of Chemicals and Allied Products:**
Includes assets used to manufacture basic organic and inorganic chemicals; chemical products to be used in further manufacture, such as synthetic fibers and plastic materials; and finished chemical products. Includes assets used to further process man-made fibers, to manufacture plastic film, and to manufacture non-woven fabrics, when such assets are located in the same plant in an integrated operation with chemical products producing assets. Also includes assets used to manufacture photographic supplies, such as film, photographic paper, sensitized photographic paper, and developing chemicals. Includes all land improvements associated with plant site or production processes, such as effluent ponds and canals, provided such land improvements are depreciable, but does not include buildings and structural components as defined in section 1.48-1(e) of

*(Continued on next page)*

| Asset guideline class | Description of assets included | Asset depreciation range (in years) | | | Annual asset guideline repair allowance percentage |
|---|---|---|---|---|---|
| | | Lower limit | Asset guideline period | Upper limit | |
| | the regulations. Does not include assets used in the manufacture of finished rubber and plastic products or in the production of natural gas products, butane, propane, and by-products of natural gas production plants .......... | 7.5 | 9.5 | 11.5 | 12.5 |
| 30.1 | **Manufacture of Rubber Products:** Includes assets used for the production of products from natural, synthetic, or reclaimed rubber, gutta percha, balata, or gutta siak, such as tires, tubes, rubber footwear, mechanical rubber goods, heels and soles, flooring, and rubber sundries; and in the recapping, retreading, and rebuilding of tires .......... | 11 | 14 | 17 | 5 |
| 30.11 | **Manufacture of Rubber Products—Special Tools and Devices:** Includes assets defined as special tools, such as jigs, dies, mandrels, molds, lasts, patterns, specialty containers, pallets, shells; and tire molds and accessory parts such as rings and insert plates used in activities as defined in class 30.1. Does not include tire building drums and accessory parts and general purpose small tools such as wrenches and drills, both power and hand-driven, and other general purpose equipment such as conveyors and transfer equipment .......... | 3 | 4 | 5 | — |
| 30.2 | **Manufacture of Finished Plastic Products:** Includes assets used in the manufacture of plastic products and the molding of primary plastics for the trade. Does not include assets used | | | | |

in the manufacture of basic plastic materials nor the manufacture of phonograph records .................................

**Manufacture of Finished Plastic Products—Special Tools:**
Includes assets defined as special tools, such as jigs, dies, fixtures, molds, patterns, gauges, and specialty transfer and shipping devices, used in activities as defined in class 30.2. Special tools are specifically designed for the production or processing of particular parts and have no significant utilitarian value and cannot be adapted to further or different use after changes or improvements are made in the model design of the particular part produced by the special tools. Does not include general purpose small tools such as wrenches and drills, both hand and power-driven, and other general purpose equipment such as conveyors, transfer equipment, and materials handling devices .....

**Manufacture of Leather and Leather Products:**
Includes assets used in the tanning, currying, and finishing of hides and skins; the processing of fur pelts; and the manufacture of finished leather products, such as footwear, belting, apparel, and luggage ...

**Manufacture of Glass Products:**
Includes assets used in the production of flat, blown, or pressed products of glass, such as float and window glass, glass containers, glassware and fiberglass. Does not include assets used in the manufacture of lenses .............................

**Manufacture of Glass Products—Special Tools:**
Includes assets defined as special tools such as molds, patterns, pallets, and specialty transfer and shipping devices such as steel racks to transport automotive glass, used in activities as defined in class 32.1. Special tools are specifically designed for the production or processing

| Class | | | | |
|---|---|---|---|---|
| | 9 | 11 | 13 | 5.5 |
| 30.21 | | | | |
| 31.0 | 3 | 3.5 | 4 | 5.5 |
| 32.1 | 9 | 11 | 13 | 5.5 |
| 32.11 | 11 | 14 | 17 | 12 |

(Continued on next page)

| Asset guide-line class | Description of assets included | Asset depreciation range (in years) | | | Annual asset guideline repair allowance percentage |
| --- | --- | --- | --- | --- | --- |
| | | Lower limit | Asset guideline period | Upper limit | |
| | of particular parts and have no significant utilitarian value and cannot be adapted to further or different use after changes or improvements are made in the model design of the particular part produced by the special tools. Does not include general purpose small tools such as wrenches and drills, both hand and power-driven, and other general purpose equipment such as conveyors, transfer equipment, and materials handling devices .................. | 2 | 2.5 | 3 | 10 |
| 32.2 | **Manufacture of Cement:** Includes assets used in the production of cement, but does not include any assets used in the manufacture of concrete and concrete products nor in any mining or extraction process .................. | 16 | 20 | 24 | 3 |
| 32.3 | **Manufacture of Other Stone and Clay Products:** Includes assets used in the manufacture of products from materials in the form of clay and stone, such as brick, tile, and pipe; pottery and related products, such as vitreous-china, plumbing fixtures, earthen-ware and ceramic insulating materials; and also includes assets used in the manufacture of concrete and concrete products. Does not include assets used in any mining or extraction processes ............ | 12 | 15 | 18 | 4.5 |
| 33.2 | **Manufacture of Primary Nonferrous Metals:** Includes assets used in the smelting, refining, and electrolysis of nonferrous metals from ore, pig, or scrap; the rolling, drawing, and | | | | |

alloying of nonferrous metals; the manufacture of castings, forgings, and other basic products of nonferrous metals; and the manufacture of nails, spikes, structural shapes, tubing, wire, and cable ......... 11 14 17 4.5

**33.21 Manufacture of Primary Nonferrous Metals—Special Tools:**
Includes assets defined as special tools such as dies, jigs, molds, patterns, fixtures, gauges, and drawings concerning such special tools used in the activities as defined in class 33.2, Manufacture of Primary Nonferrous Metals. Special tools are specifically designed for the production or processing of particular products or parts and have no significant utilitarian value and cannot be adapted to further or different use after changes or improvements are made in the model design of the particular part produced by the special tools. Does not include general purpose small tools such as wrenches and drills, both hand and power-driven, and other general purpose equipment such as conveyors, transfer equipment, and materials handling devices. Rolls, mandrels and refractories are not included in class 33.21 but are included in class 33.2 ..................................

**33.3 Manufacture of Foundry Products:**
Includes assets used in the casting of iron and steel, including related operations such as molding and coremaking. Also includes assets used in the finishing of castings and patternmaking when performed at the foundry, all special tools and related land improvements ............ 5 6.5 8 4

**33.4 Manufacture of Primary Steel Mill Products:**
Includes assets used in the smelting, reduction, and refining of iron and steel from ore, pig, or scrap; the rolling, drawing and alloying of steel; the manufacture of nails, spikes, structural shapes, tubing, wire, and cable. Includes assets used by steel service centers, ferrous metal 11 14 17 18

(Continued on next page)

| Asset guideline class | Description of assets included | Asset depreciation range (in years) | | | Annual asset guideline repair allowance percentage |
|---|---|---|---|---|---|
| | | Lower limit | Asset guideline period | Upper limit | |
| | forges, and assets used in coke production, regardless of ownership. Also includes related land improvements and all special tools used in the above activities .................. | 12 | 15 | 18 | 18 |
| 34.0 | **Manufacture of Fabricated Metal Products:** Includes assets used in the production of metal cans, tinware, fabricated structural metal products, metal stampings, and other ferrous and nonferrous metal and wire products not elsewhere classified. Does not include assets used to manufacture non-electric heating apparatus .................. | 9.5 | 12 | 14.5 | 6 |
| 34.01 | **Manufacture of Fabricated Metal Products—Special Tools:** Includes assets defined as special tools such as dies, jigs, molds, patterns, fixtures, gauges, and returnable containers and drawings concerning such special tools used in the activities as defined in class 34.0. Special tools are specifically designed for the production or processing of particular machine components, products, or parts, and have no significant utilitarian value and cannot be adapted to further or different use after changes or improvements are made in the model design of the particular part produced by the special tools. Does not include general purpose small tools such as wrenches and drills, both hand and power-driven, and other general purpose equipment such as conveyors, transfer equipment, and materials handling devices ..... | 2.5 | 3 | 3.5 | 3.5 |

**35.0 Manufacture of Electrical and Non-Electrical Machinery and Other Mechanical Products:**

Includes assets used to manufacture or rebuild finished machinery and equipment and replacement parts thereof such as machine tools, general industrial and special industry machinery, electrical power generation, transmission, and distribution systems, space heating, cooling, and refrigeration systems, commercial and home appliances, farm and garden machinery, construction machinery, mining and oil field machinery, internal combustion engines (except those that power airborne vehicles), turbines (except those elsewhere classified), batteries, lamps and lighting fixtures, carbon and graphite products, and electromechanical and mechanical products including business machines, instruments, watches and clocks, vending and amusement machines, photographic equipment, medical and dental equipment and appliances, and ophthalmic goods. Includes assets used by manufacturers or rebuilders of such finished machinery and equipment in activities elsewhere classified such as the manufacture of castings, forgings, rubber and plastic products, electronic subassemblies or other manufacturing activities if the interim products are used by the same manufacturer primarily in the manufacture, assembly, or rebuilding of such finished machinery and equipment. Does not include assets used in mining, assets used in the manufacture of primary ferrous and nonferrous metals, assets included in guideline classes 00.11 through 00.4 and assets elsewhere classified . . . . . . . . . 8    10    12    11

**36.0 Manufacture of Electronic Components, Products, and Systems:**

Includes assets used in the manufacture of electronic communication, computation, instrumentation and control systems, including airborne applications; also includes assets used in the manufacture of electronic products such as frequency and amplitude modulated

*(Continued on next page)*

| Asset guideline class | Description of assets included | Asset depreciation range (in years) | | | Annual asset guideline repair allowance percentage |
|---|---|---|---|---|---|
| | | Lower limit | Asset guideline period | Upper limit | |
| | transmitters and receivers, electronic switching stations, television cameras, video recorders, record players and tape recorders, computers and computer peripheral machines, and electronic instruments, watches, and clocks; also includes assets used in the manufacture of components, provided their primary use is in products and systems defined above such as semiconductors, electron tubes, capacitors, coils, resistors, printed circuit substrates, switches, harness cables, lasers, fiber optic devices, and magnetic media devices. Specifically excludes assets used to manufacture electronic products and components, photocopiers, typewriters, postage meters and other electromechanical and mechanical business machines and instruments that are elsewhere classified ................... | 5 | 6 | 7 | 8 |
| 37.11 | **Manufacture of Motor Vehicles:** Includes assets used in the manufacture and assembly of finished automobiles, trucks, trailers, motor homes, and buses. Does not include assets used in mining, printing and publishing, production of primary metals, electricity, or steam, or the manufacture of glass, industrial chemicals, batteries, or rubber products, which are classified elsewhere. Includes assets used in manufacturing activities elsewhere classified other than those excluded above, where such activities are incidental to and an integral part of the manufacture and assembly of finished motor vehicles such as the manufacture of parts and | | | | |

subassemblies of fabricated metal products, electrical equipment, textiles, plastics, leather, and foundry and forging operations. Does not include any assets not classified in manufacturing activity classes, e.g., does not include assets classified in asset guideline classes 00.11 through 00.4. Activities will be considered incidental to the manufacture and assembly of finished motor vehicles only if 75 percent or more of the value of the products produced under one roof are used for the manufacture and assembly of finished motor vehicles. Parts that are produced as a normal replacement stock complement in connection with the manufacture and assembly of finished motor vehicles are considered used for the manufacture and assembly of finished motor vehicles. Does not include assets used in the manufacture of component parts if these assets are used by taxpayers not engaged in the assembly of finished motor vehicles .................. 9.5 12 14.5

37.12 **Manufacture of Motor Vehicles—Special Tools:**
Includes assets defined as special tools, such as jigs, dies, fixtures, molds, patterns, gauges, and specialty transfer and shipping devices, owned by manufacturers of finished motor vehicles and used in qualified activities as defined in class 37.11. Special tools are specifically designed for the production or processing of particular motor vehicle components and have no significant utilitarian value, and cannot be adapted to further or different use, after changes or improvements are made in the model design of the particular part produced by the special tools. Does not include general purpose small tools such as wrenches and drills, both hand and power-driven, and other general purpose equipment such as conveyors, transfer equipment, and materials handling devices ................. 2.5 3 3.5 12.5

(Continued on next page)

| Asset guideline class | Description of assets included | Asset depreciation range (in years) | | | Annual asset guideline repair allowance percentage |
|---|---|---|---|---|---|
| | | Lower limit | Asset guideline period | Upper limit | |
| 37.2 | **Manufacture of Aerospace Products:** Includes assets used in the manufacture and assembly of airborne vehicles and their component parts including hydraulic, pneumatic, electrical, and mechanical systems. Does not include assets used in the production of electronic airborne detection, guidance, control, radiation, computation, test, navigation, and communication equipment or the components thereof .............. | 8 | 10 | 12 | 7.5 |
| 37.31 | **Ship and Boat Building—Machinery and Equipment:** Includes assets used in the manufacture and repair of ships, boats, caissons, marine drilling rigs, and special fabrications not included in asset guideline classes 37.32 and 37.33. Specifically includes all manufacturing and repairing machinery and equipment, including machinery and equipment used in the operation of assets included in asset guideline class 37.32. Excludes buildings and their structural components .............. | 9.5 | 12 | 14.5 | 8.5 |
| 37.32 | **Ship and Boat Building—Dry Docks and Land Improvements:** Includes assets used in the manufacture and repair of ships, boats, caissons, marine drilling rigs, and special fabrications not included in asset guideline classes 37.31 and 37.33. Specifically includes floating and fixed dry docks, ship basins, graving docks, shipways, piers, and all other land improvements such as water, sewer, and electric systems. Excludes buildings and their structural components .............. | 13 | 16 | 19 | 2.5 |

| Account number | Description of assets included | Lower limit | Asset guideline period | Upper limit | Annual asset guideline repair allowance percentage |
|---|---|---|---|---|---|
| 37.33 | **Ship and Boat Building—Special Tools:** Includes assets defined as special tools such as dies, jigs, molds, patterns, fixtures, gauges, and drawings concerning such special tools used in the activities defined in classes 37.31 and 37.32. Special tools are specifically designed for the production or processing of particular machine components, products, or parts, and have no significant utilitarian value and cannot be adapted to further or different use after changes or improvements are made in the model design of the particular part produced by the special tools. Does not include general purpose small tools such as wrenches and drills, both hand and power-driven, and other general purpose equipment such as conveyors, transfer equipment, and materials handling devices ......... | 5 | 6.5 | 8 | 0.5 |
| 37.41 | **Manufacture of Locomotives:** Includes assets used in building or rebuilding railroad locomotives (including mining and industrial locomotives). Does not include assets of railroad transportation companies or assets of companies which manufacture components of locomotives but do not manufacture finished locomotives ................... | 9 | 11.5 | 14 | 7.5 |
| 37.42 | **Manufacture of Railroad Cars:** Includes assets used in building or rebuilding railroad freight or passenger cars (including rail transit cars). Does not include assets of railroad transportation companies or assets of companies which manufacture components of railroad cars but do not manufacture finished railroad cars ................. | 9.5 | 12 | 14.5 | 5.5 |
| 39.0 | **Manufacture of Athletic, Jewelry and Other Goods:** Includes assets used in the production of jewelry; musical instruments; | | | | |

*(Continued on next page)*

| Asset guideline class | Description of assets included | Asset depreciation range (in years) | | | Annual asset guideline repair allowance percentage |
|---|---|---|---|---|---|
| | | Lower limit | Asset guideline period | Upper limit | |
| | toys and sporting goods; motion picture and television films and tapes; and pens, pencils, office and art supplies, brooms, brushes, caskets, etc. .......................... | 9.5 | 12 | 14.5 | 5.5 |
| | **Railroad Transportation:**<br>Classes with the prefix 40 include the assets identified below that are used in the commercial and contract carrying of passengers and freight by rail. Assets of electrified railroads will be classified in a manner corresponding to that set forth below for railroads not independently operated as electric lines. Excludes the assets included in classes with the prefixes beginning 00.1 and 00.2 above, and also excludes any nondepreciable assets included in Interstate Commerce Commission accounts enumerated for this class. | | | | |
| 40.1 | **Railroad Machinery and Equipment:**<br>Includes assets classified in the following Interstate Commerce Commission accounts:<br>Roadway Accounts:<br>(16) Station and office buildings (freight handling machinery and equipment only)<br>(25) TOFC/COFC terminals (freight handling machinery and equipment only)<br>(26) Communication systems<br>(27) Signals and interlockers<br>(37) Roadway machines<br>(44) Shop machinery<br>Equipment Accounts:<br>(52) Locomotives<br>(53) Freight train cars<br>(54) Passenger train cars<br>(57) Work equipment .......................... | 11 | 14 | 17 | 16.5 |

**40.2  Railroad Structures and Similar Improvements:**
Includes assets classified in the following Interstate Commerce Commission accounts:

(6) Bridges, trestles, and culverts
(7) Elevated structures
(13) Fences, snowsheds, and signs
(16) Station and office buildings (stations and other operating structures only)
(17) Roadway buildings
(18) Water stations
(19) Fuel stations
(20) Shops and enginehouses
(25) TOFC/COFC terminals (operating structures only)
(31) Power transmission systems
(35) Miscellaneous structures
(39) Public improvements construction .......... 24   30   36   5

**40.3  Railroad Wharves and Docks**
Includes assets classified in the following Interstate Commerce Commission accounts:

(23) Wharves and docks
(24) Coal and ore wharves ........... 16   20   24   5.5

**40.51  Railroad Hydraulic Electric Generating Equipment** ........... 40   50   60   1.5

**40.52  Railroad Nuclear Electric Generating Equipment** ........... 16   20   24   3

**40.53  Railroad Steam Electric Generating Equipment** ........... 22.5   28   33.5   2.5

**40.54  Railroad Steam, Compressed Air, and Other Power Plant Equipment** ........... 22.5   28   33.5   7.5

| Account | | | | |
|---|---|---|---|---|
| 40.2 (39) | 24 | 30 | 36 | 5 |
| 40.3 (24) | 16 | 20 | 24 | 5.5 |
| 40.51 | 40 | 50 | 60 | 1.5 |
| 40.52 | 16 | 20 | 24 | 3 |
| 40.53 | 22.5 | 28 | 33.5 | 2.5 |
| 40.54 | 22.5 | 28 | 33.5 | 7.5 |

(Continued on next page)

| Asset guideline class | Description of assets included | Asset depreciation range (in years) | | | Annual asset guideline repair allowance percentage |
|---|---|---|---|---|---|
| | | Lower limit | Asset guideline period | Upper limit | |
| 41.0 | **Motor Transport—Passengers:** Includes assets used in the urban and interurban commercial and contract carrying of passengers by road, except the transportation assets included in classes with the prefix 00.2 .......... | 6.5 | 8 | 9.5 | 11.5 |
| 42.0 | **Motor Transport—Freight:** Includes assets used in the commercial and contract carrying of freight by road, except the transportation assets included in classes with the prefix 00.2 .......... | 6.5 | 8 | 9.5 | 11 |
| 44.0 | **Water Transportation:** Includes assets used in the commercial and contract carrying of freight and passengers by water except the transportation assets included in classes with the prefix 00.2. Includes all related land improvements .......... | 16 | 20 | 24 | 8 |
| 45.0 | **Air Transport:** Includes assets (except helicopters) used in commercial and contract carrying of passengers and freight by air. For purposes of section 1.167(a)-11(d)(2)(iv)(a) of the regulations, expenditures for "repair, maintenance, rehabilitation, or improvement" shall consist of direct maintenance expenses (irrespective of airworthiness provisions or charges) as defined by Civil Aeronautics Board uniform account | | | | |

5200, maintenance burden (exclusive of expenses pertaining to maintenance of buildings and improvements) as defined by Civil Aeronautics Board uniform account 5300, and expenditures which are not "excluded additions" as defined by section 1.167(a)-11(d)(2)(vi) of the regulations and which would be charged to property and equipment accounts in the Civil Aeronautics Board uniform system of accounts ......................................

| | Lower | Period | Upper | Repair allowance |
|---|---|---|---|---|
| | 9.5 | 12 | 14.5 | 15 |

**45.1 Air Transport (restricted):**
Includes each asset described in the description of class 45.0 which was held by the taxpayer on April 15, 1976, or is acquired by the taxpayer pursuant to a contract which was, on April 15, 1976, and at all times thereafter, binding on the taxpayer. This criterion of classification based on binding contract concept is to be applied in the same manner as under the general rules expressed in section 49(b)(1), (4), (5) and (8) of the Code ......................................

**46.0 Pipeline Transportation:**
Includes assets used in the private, commercial, and contract carrying of petroleum, gas and other products by means of pipes and conveyors. The trunk lines and related storage facilities of integrated petroleum and natural gas producers are included in this class. Excludes initial clearing and grading land improvements as specified in Rev. Rul. 72-403, 1972-2 C.B. 102, but inclues all other related land improvements ......................................

| | Lower | Period | Upper | Repair allowance |
|---|---|---|---|---|
| | 5 | 6 | 7 | 15 |

**Telephone Communications:**
Includes the assets identified below and that are used in the provision of commercial and contract telephonic services such as:

| | Lower | Period | Upper | Repair allowance |
|---|---|---|---|---|
| | 17.5 | 22 | 26.5 | 3 |

(Continued on next page)

| Asset guideline class | Description of assets included | Asset depreciation range (in years) | | | Annual asset guideline repair allowance percentage |
|---|---|---|---|---|---|
| | | Lower limit | Asset guideline period | Upper limit | |
| 48.11 | **Telephone Central Office Buildings:** Includes assets intended to house central office equipment, as defined in Federal Communications Commission Part 31 Account No. 212 whether section 1245 or section 1250 property ............... | 36 | 45 | 54 | 1.5 |
| 48.12 | **Telephone Central Office Equipment:** Includes central office switching and related equipment as defined in Federal Communications Commission Part 31 Account No. 221 .... | — | 18 | — | — |
| 48.13 | **Telephone Station Equipment:** Includes such station apparatus and connections as teletypewriters, telephones, booths, private exchanges, and comparable equipment as defined in Federal Communications Commission Part 31 Account Nos. 231, 232, and 234 .................... | 8 | 10 | 12 | 10 |
| 48.14 | **Telephone Distribution Plant:** Includes such assets as pole lines, cable, aerial wire, underground conduits, and comparable equipment, and related land improvements as defined in Federal Communications Commission Part 31 Account Nos. 241, 242.1, 242.2, 242.3, 242.4, 243, and 244 ........... | 28 | 35 | 42 | 2 |
| 48.2 | **Radio and Television Broadcasting:** Includes assets used in radio and television broadcasting, except transmitting towers ................ | 5 | 6 | 7 | 10 |

Telegraph, Ocean Cable, and Satellite Communications (TOCSC): Includes communications-related assets used to provide domestic and international radio-telegraph, wire-telegraph, ocean-cable, and satellite communications services; also includes related land improvements.

| Asset class | | | | |
|---|---|---|---|---|
| 48.31 | TOCSC—Electric Power Generating and Distribution Systems: Includes assets used in the provision of electric power by generation, modulation, rectification, channelization, control, and distribution. Does not include these assets when they are installed on customer's premises .................. | 15 | 19 | 23 |
| 48.32 | TOCSC—High Frequency Radio and Microwave Systems: Includes assets such as transmitters and receivers, antenna supporting structures, antennas, transmission lines from equipment to antenna, transmitter cooling systems, and control and amplification equipment. Does not include cable and long-line systems ............. | 10 | 13 | 15.5 |
| 48.33 | TOCSC—Cable and Long-line Systems: Includes assets such as transmission lines, pole lines, ocean cables, buried cable and conduit, repeaters, repeater stations, and other related assets. Does not include high frequency radio or microwave systems ............. | 21 | 26.5 | 32 |
| 48.34 | TOCSC—Central Office Control Equipment: Includes assets for general control, switching, and monitoring of communications signals including electromechanical switching and channeling apparatus, multiplexing equipment, patching and monitoring facilities, inhouse cabling, teleprinter equipment, and associated site improvements ............. | 13 | 16.5 | 20 |

(Continued on next page)

| Asset guideline class | Description of assets included | Asset depreciation range (in years) | | | Annual asset guideline repair allowance percentage |
|---|---|---|---|---|---|
| | | Lower limit | Asset guideline period | Upper limit | |
| 48.35 | **TOCSC—Computerized Switching, Channeling, and Associated Control Equipment:** Includes central office switching computers, interfacing computers, other associated specialized control equipment, and site improvements .......... | 8.5 | 10.5 | 12.5 | — |
| 48.36 | **TOCSC—Satellite Ground Segment Property:** Includes assets such as fixed earth station equipment, antennas, satellite communications equipment, and interface equipment used in satellite communications. Does not include general purpose equipment or equipment used in satellite space segment property ...... | 8 | 10 | 12 | — |
| 48.37 | **TOCSC—Satellite Space Segment Property:** Includes satellites and equipment used for telemetry, tracking, control, and monitoring when used in satellite communications ............ | 6.5 | 8 | 9.5 | — |
| 48.38 | **TOCSC—Equipment Installed on Customer's Premises:** Includes assets installed on customer's premises, such as computers, terminal equipment, power generation and distribution systems, private switching center, teleprinters, facsimile equipment, and other associated and related equipment ........... | 8 | 10 | 12 | — |

| Asset class | Description of assets included | | | | |
|---|---|---|---|---|---|
| 48.39 | TOCSC—Support and Service Equipment: Includes assets used to support but not engage in communications. Includes store, warehouse and shop tools, and test and laboratory assets ...... | 11 | 13.5 | 16 | — |
| | **Cable Television (CATV):** Includes communications-related assets used to provide cable television (communications antenna television services). Does not include assets used to provide subscribers with two-way communications services. | | | | |
| 48.41 | CATV—Headend: Includes assets such as towers, antennas, preamplifiers, converters, modulation equipment, and program non-duplication systems. Does not include headend buildings and program origination assets ...... | 9 | 11 | 13 | 5 |
| 48.42 | CATV—Subscriber Connection and Distribution Systems: Includes assets such as trunk and feeder cable, connecting hardware, amplifiers, power equipment, passive devices, directional taps, pedestals, pressure taps, drop cables, matching transformers, multiple set connector equipment, and converters ...... | 8 | 10 | 12 | 5 |
| 48.43 | CATV—Program Origination: Includes assets such as cameras, film chains, video tape recorders, lighting, and remote location equipment excluding vehicles. Does not include buildings and their structural components ...... | 7 | 9 | 11 | 9 |
| 48.44 | CATV—Service and Test: Includes assets such as oscilloscopes, field strength meters, spectrum analyzers, and cable testing equipment, but does not include vehicles ...... | 7 | 8.5 | 10 | 2.5 |

*(Continued on next page)*

| Asset guideline class | Description of assets included | Asset depreciation range (in years) | | | Annual asset guideline repair allowance percentage |
|---|---|---|---|---|---|
| | | Lower limit | Asset guideline period | Upper limit | |
| 48.45 | **CATV—Microwave Systems:** Includes assets such as towers, antennas, transmitting and receiving equipment, and broad band microwave assets if used in the provision of cable television services. Does not include assets used in the provision of common carrier services ................... | 7.5 | 9.5 | 11.5 | 2 |
| | **Electric, Gas, Water and Steam Utility Services:** Includes assets used in the production, transmission and distribution of electricity, gas, steam, or water for sale including related land improvements. | | | | |
| 49.11 | **Electric Utility Hydraulic Production Plant:** Includes assets used in the hydraulic power production of electricity for sale, including related land improvements, such as dams, flumes, canals, and waterways ................... | 40 | 50 | 60 | 1.5 |
| 49.12 | **Electric Utility Nuclear Production Plant:** Includes assets used in the nuclear power production of electricity for sale and related land improvements. Does not include nuclear fuel assemblies ................... | 16 | 20 | 24 | 3 |
| 49.121 | **Electric Utility Nuclear Fuel Assemblies:** Includes initial core and replacement core nuclear fuel assemblies (i.e., the composite of fabricated nuclear fuel and container) when used in a | | | | |

boiling water, pressurized water, or high temperature gas reactor used in the production of electricity. Does not include nuclear fuel assemblies used in breeder reactors ..............

| | | | |
|---|---|---|---|
| 4 | 5 | 6 | — |

49.13   **Electric Utility Steam Production Plant:**
Includes assets used in the steam power production of electricity for sale, combustion turbines operated in a combined cycle with a conventional steam unit and related land improvements. Also includes package boilers, electric generators and related assets such as electricity and steam distribution systems as used by a waste reduction and resource recovery plant if the steam or electricity is normally for sale to others ..............

| | | | |
|---|---|---|---|
| 22.5 | 28 | 33.5 | 5 |

49.14   **Electric Utility Transmission and Distribution Plant:**
Includes assets used in the transmission and distribution of electricity for sale and related land improvements. Excludes initial clearing and grading land improvements as specified in Rev. Rul. 72-403, 1972-2 C.B. 102 ..............

| | | | |
|---|---|---|---|
| 24 | 30 | 36 | 4.5 |

49.15   **Electric Utility Combustion Turbine Production Plant:**
Includes assets used in the production of electricity for sale by the use of such prime movers as jet engines, combustion turbines, diesel engines, gasoline engines, and other internal combustion engines, their associated power turbines and/or generators, and related land improvements. Does not include combustion turbines operated in a combined cycle with a conventional steam unit ..............

| | | | |
|---|---|---|---|
| 16 | 20 | 24 | 4 |

49.21   **Gas Utility Distribution Facilities:**
Includes gas water heaters and gas conversion equipment installed by a utility on customer's premises on a rental basis ..............

| | | | |
|---|---|---|---|
| 28 | 35 | 42 | 2 |

*(Continued on next page)*

| Asset guideline class | Description of assets included | Asset depreciation range (in years) | | | Annual asset guideline repair allowance percentage |
| --- | --- | --- | --- | --- | --- |
| | | Lower limit | Asset guideline period | Upper limit | |
| 49.221 | **Gas Utility Manufactured Gas Production Plant:** Includes assets used in the manufacture of gas having chemical and/or physical properties which do not permit complete interchangeability with domestic natural gas. Does not include gas producing systems and related systems used in waste reduction and resource recovery plants which are elsewhere classified .................. | 24 | 30 | 36 | 2 |
| 49.222 | **Gas Utility Substitute Natural Gas (SNG) Production Plant (naphtha or lighter hydrocarbon feedstocks):** Includes assets used in the catalytic conversion of feedstocks or naphtha or lighter hydrocarbons to a gaseous fuel which is completely interchangeable with domestic natural gas .................. | 11 | 14 | 17 | 4.5 |
| 49.223 | **Substitute Natural Gas—Coal Gasification:** Includes assets used in the manufacture and production of pipeline quality gas from coal using the basic Lurgi process with advanced methanation. Includes all process plant equipment and structures used in this coal gasification process and all utility assets such as cooling systems, water supply and treatment facilities, and assets used in the production and distribution of electricity and steam for use by the taxpayer in a gasification plant and attendant coal mining site processes but not for assets used in the production and distribution of electricity and steam for sale to others. Also includes all other related | | | | |

| | | Lower limit | Asset guideline period | Upper limit | Repair allowance % |
|---|---|---|---|---|---|
| | land improvements. Does not include assets used in the direct mining and treatment of coal prior to the gasification process itself .......... | 14.5 | 18 | 21.5 | 15 |
| 49.23 | Natural Gas Production Plant ............. | 11 | 14 | 17 | 4.5 |
| 49.24 | **Gas Utility Trunk Pipelines and Related Storage Facilities:** Excluding initial clearing and grading land improvements as specified in Rev. Rul. 72-403 .................................. | 17.5 | 22 | 26.5 | 3 |
| 49.25 | **Liquefied Natural Gas Plant:** Includes assets used in the liquefaction, storage, and regasification of natural gas including loading and unloading connections, instrumentation equipment and controls, pumps, vaporizers and odorizers, tanks, and related land improvements. Also includes pipeline interconnections with gas transmission lines and distribution systems and marine terminal facilities ................... | 17.5 | 22 | 26.5 | 4.5 |
| 49.3 | **Water Utilities:** Includes assets used in the gathering, treatment, and commercial distribution of water ............................. | 40 | 50 | 60 | 1.5 |
| 49.4 | **Central Steam Utility Production and Distribution:** Includes assets used in the production and distribution of steam for sale. Does not include assets used in waste reduction and resource recovery plants which are elsewhere classified ........... | 22.5 | 28 | 33.5 | 2.5 |

LAW PRIOR TO THE TAX REFORM ACT OF 1986

The following table is provided for tangible personal property depreciation. It uses the 150 percent declining balance method changing to straight-line with the half-year convention.

Property Placed in Service after December 31, 1980

| Ownership Year | Class of Investment | | | |
|---|---|---|---|---|
| | 3-Year | 5-Year | 10-Year | 15-Year Utility Property |
| | % | % | % | % |
| 1 | 25 | 15 | 8 | 5 |
| 2 | 38 | 22 | 14 | 10 |
| 3 | 37 | 21 | 12 | 9 |
| 4 | | 21 | 10 | 8 |
| 5 | | 21 | 10 | 7 |
| 6 | | | 10 | 7 |
| 7 | | | 9 | 6 |
| 8 | | | 9 | 6 |
| 9 | | | 9 | 6 |
| 10 | | | 9 | 6 |
| 11 | | | | 6 |
| 12 | | | | 6 |
| 13 | | | | 6 |
| 14 | | | | 6 |
| 15 | | | | 6 |
| | 100 | 100 | 100 | 100 |

Property Placed in Service after May 8, 1985: ACRS Cost Recovery Tables for 19-Year Real Property (19-Year 175% Declining Balance) (Assuming Mid-Month Convention)

The applicable percentage is:

If the Recovery Year Is:

(Use the column for the month in the first recovery year the property is placed in service)

| Recovery Year | 1 | 2 | 3 | 4 | 5 | 6 | 7 | 8 | 9 | 10 | 11 | 12 |
|---|---|---|---|---|---|---|---|---|---|---|---|---|
| 1 | 8.8 | 8.1 | 7.3 | 6.5 | 5.8 | 5.0 | 4.2 | 3.5 | 2.7 | 1.9 | 1.1 | .4 |
| 2 | 8.4 | 8.5 | 8.5 | 8.6 | 8.7 | 8.8 | 8.8 | 8.9 | 9.0 | 9.0 | 9.1 | 9.2 |
| 3 | 7.6 | 7.7 | 7.7 | 7.8 | 7.9 | 7.9 | 8.0 | 8.1 | 8.1 | 8.2 | 8.3 | 8.3 |
| 4 | 6.9 | 7.0 | 7.0 | 7.1 | 7.1 | 7.2 | 7.3 | 7.3 | 7.4 | 7.4 | 7.5 | 7.6 |
| 5 | 6.3 | 6.3 | 6.4 | 6.4 | 6.5 | 6.5 | 6.6 | 6.6 | 6.7 | 6.8 | 6.8 | 6.9 |
| 6 | 5.7 | 5.7 | 5.8 | 5.9 | 5.9 | 5.9 | 6.0 | 6.0 | 6.1 | 6.1 | 6.2 | 6.2 |
| 7 | 5.2 | 5.2 | 5.3 | 5.3 | 5.3 | 5.4 | 5.4 | 5.5 | 5.5 | 5.6 | 5.6 | 5.6 |
| 8 | 4.7 | 4.7 | 4.8 | 4.8 | 4.8 | 4.9 | 4.9 | 5.0 | 5.0 | 5.1 | 5.1 | 5.1 |
| 9 | 4.2 | 4.3 | 4.3 | 4.4 | 4.4 | 4.5 | 4.5 | 4.5 | 4.5 | 4.6 | 4.6 | 4.7 |
| 10 | 4.2 | 4.2 | 4.2 | 4.2 | 4.2 | 4.2 | 4.2 | 4.2 | 4.2 | 4.2 | 4.2 | 4.2 |
| 11 | 4.2 | 4.2 | 4.2 | 4.2 | 4.2 | 4.2 | 4.2 | 4.2 | 4.2 | 4.2 | 4.2 | 4.2 |
| 12 | 4.2 | 4.2 | 4.2 | 4.2 | 4.2 | 4.2 | 4.2 | 4.2 | 4.2 | 4.2 | 4.2 | 4.2 |
| 13 | 4.2 | 4.2 | 4.2 | 4.2 | 4.2 | 4.2 | 4.2 | 4.2 | 4.2 | 4.2 | 4.2 | 4.2 |
| 14 | 4.2 | 4.2 | 4.2 | 4.2 | 4.2 | 4.2 | 4.2 | 4.2 | 4.2 | 4.2 | 4.2 | 4.2 |
| 15 | 4.2 | 4.2 | 4.2 | 4.2 | 4.2 | 4.2 | 4.2 | 4.2 | 4.2 | 4.2 | 4.2 | 4.2 |
| 16 | 4.2 | 4.2 | 4.2 | 4.2 | 4.2 | 4.2 | 4.2 | 4.2 | 4.2 | 4.2 | 4.2 | 4.2 |
| 17 | 4.2 | 4.2 | 4.2 | 4.2 | 4.2 | 4.2 | 4.2 | 4.2 | 4.2 | 4.2 | 4.2 | 4.2 |
| 18 | 4.2 | 4.2 | 4.2 | 4.2 | 4.2 | 4.2 | 4.2 | 4.2 | 4.2 | 4.2 | 4.2 | 4.2 |
| 19 | 4.2 | 4.2 | 4.2 | 4.2 | 4.2 | 4.2 | 4.2 | 4.2 | 4.2 | 4.2 | 4.2 | 4.2 |
| 20 | 0.2 | 0.5 | 0.9 | 1.2 | 1.6 | 1.9 | 2.3 | 2.6 | 3.0 | 3.3 | 3.7 | 4.0 |

## Optional ACRS Straight-Line Method

The applicable percentage is:

If the Recovery Year Is:

(Use the column for the month in the first recovery year the property is placed in service)

| Recovery Year | 1 | 2 | 3 | 4 | 5 | 6 | 7 | 8 | 9 | 10 | 11 | 12 |
|---|---|---|---|---|---|---|---|---|---|---|---|---|
| 1 | 5.0 | 4.6 | 4.2 | 3.7 | 3.3 | 2.9 | 2.4 | 2.0 | 1.5 | 1.1 | 0.7 | 0.2 |
| 2–13 | 5.3 | | | | | | | | | | | |
| 14–19 | 5.2 | | | | | | | | | | | |

The following are the cost recovery tables for real estate created by the Tax Reform Act of 1984.

1.  **18-Year Property (Mid-Month Convention)**—For property placed in service 6/23/84 until 5/8/85

The applicable percentage is:

If the Recovery Year Is:

(Use the column for the month in the first recovery year the property is placed in service)

| | 1 | 2 | 3 | 4 | 5 | 6 | 7 | 8 | 9 | 10 | 11 | 12 |
|---|---|---|---|---|---|---|---|---|---|---|---|---|
| 1 | 9 | 9 | 8 | 7 | 6 | 5 | 4 | 4 | 3 | 2 | 1 | 0.4 |
| 2 | 9 | 9 | 9 | 9 | 9 | 9 | 9 | 9 | 9 | 10 | 10 | 10.0 |
| 3 | 8 | 8 | 8 | 8 | 8 | 8 | 8 | 8 | 9 | 9 | 9 | 9.0 |
| 4 | 7 | 7 | 7 | 7 | 7 | 8 | 8 | 8 | 8 | 8 | 8 | 8.0 |
| 5 | 7 | 7 | 7 | 7 | 7 | 7 | 7 | 7 | 7 | 7 | 7 | 7.0 |
| 6 | 6 | 6 | 6 | 6 | 6 | 6 | 6 | 6 | 6 | 6 | 6 | 6.0 |
| 7 | 5 | 5 | 5 | 5 | 6 | 6 | 6 | 6 | 6 | 6 | 6 | 6.0 |
| 8 | 5 | 5 | 5 | 5 | 5 | 5 | 5 | 5 | 5 | 5 | 5 | 5.0 |
| 9 | 5 | 5 | 5 | 5 | 5 | 5 | 5 | 5 | 5 | 5 | 5 | 5.0 |
| 10 | 5 | 5 | 5 | 5 | 5 | 5 | 5 | 5 | 5 | 5 | 5 | 5.0 |
| 11 | 5 | 5 | 5 | 5 | 5 | 5 | 5 | 5 | 5 | 5 | 5 | 5.0 |
| 12 | 5 | 5 | 5 | 5 | 5 | 5 | 5 | 5 | 5 | 5 | 5 | 5.0 |
| 13 | 4 | 4 | 4 | 5 | 4 | 4 | 5 | 4 | 4 | 4 | 5 | 5.0 |
| 14 | 4 | 4 | 4 | 4 | 4 | 4 | 4 | 4 | 4 | 4 | 4 | 4.0 |
| 15 | 4 | 4 | 4 | 4 | 4 | 4 | 4 | 4 | 4 | 4 | 4 | 4.0 |
| 16 | 4 | 4 | 4 | 4 | 4 | 4 | 4 | 4 | 4 | 4 | 4 | 4.0 |
| 17 | 4 | 4 | 4 | 4 | 4 | 4 | 4 | 4 | 4 | 4 | 4 | 4.0 |
| 18 | 4 | 3 | 4 | 4 | 4 | 4 | 4 | 4 | 4 | 4 | 4 | 4.0 |
| 19 | | 1 | 1 | 1 | 2 | 2 | 2 | 3 | 3 | 3 | 3 | 3.6 |

2. **18-Year Real Property (No Mid-Month Convention)**—For property placed in service after 3/15/84 and before 6/23/84

The applicable percentage is:

| If the Recovery Year Is: | (Use the column for the month in the first recovery year the property is placed in service) | | | | | | | | | | |
|---|---|---|---|---|---|---|---|---|---|---|---|
| | 1 | 2 | 3 | 4 | 5 | 6 | 7 | 8 | 9 | 10–11 | 12 |
| 1 | 10 | 9 | 8 | 7 | 6 | 6 | 5 | 4 | 3 | 2 | 1 |
| 2 | 9 | 9 | 9 | 9 | 9 | 9 | 9 | 9 | 9 | 10 | 10 |
| 3 | 8 | 8 | 8 | 8 | 8 | 8 | 8 | 8 | 9 | 9 | 9 |
| 4 | 7 | 7 | 7 | 7 | 7 | 7 | 8 | 8 | 8 | 8 | 8 |
| 5 | 6 | 7 | 7 | 7 | 7 | 7 | 7 | 7 | 7 | 7 | 7 |
| 6 | 6 | 6 | 6 | 6 | 6 | 6 | 6 | 6 | 6 | 6 | 6 |
| 7 | 5 | 5 | 5 | 5 | 6 | 6 | 6 | 6 | 6 | 6 | 6 |
| 8 | 5 | 5 | 5 | 5 | 5 | 5 | 5 | 5 | 5 | 5 | 5 |
| 9 | 5 | 5 | 5 | 5 | 5 | 5 | 5 | 5 | 5 | 5 | 5 |
| 10 | 5 | 5 | 5 | 5 | 5 | 5 | 5 | 5 | 5 | 5 | 5 |
| 11 | 5 | 5 | 5 | 5 | 5 | 5 | 5 | 5 | 5 | 5 | 5 |
| 12 | 5 | 5 | 5 | 5 | 5 | 5 | 5 | 5 | 5 | 5 | 5 |
| 13 | 4 | 4 | 4 | 5 | 5 | 4 | 4 | 5 | 4 | 4 | 4 |
| 14 | 4 | 4 | 4 | 4 | 4 | 4 | 4 | 4 | 4 | 4 | 4 |
| 15 | 4 | 4 | 4 | 4 | 4 | 4 | 4 | 4 | 4 | 4 | 4 |
| 16 | 4 | 4 | 4 | 4 | 4 | 4 | 4 | 4 | 4 | 4 | 4 |
| 17 | 4 | 4 | 4 | 4 | 4 | 4 | 4 | 4 | 4 | 4 | 4 |
| 18 | 4 | 4 | 4 | 4 | 4 | 4 | 4 | 4 | 4 | 4 | 4 |
| 19 | | | 1 | 1 | 1 | 2 | 2 | 2 | 3 | 3 | 4 |

3.  **Optional Straight-Line Method for 18-Year Property (Mid-Month Convention)**—For property placed in service 6/23/84 until 5/8/85

The applicable percentage is:

| If the Recovery Year Is: | (Use the column for the month in the first recovery year the property is placed in service) | | | | | |
|:---:|:---:|:---:|:---:|:---:|:---:|:---:|
| | 1-2 | 3-4 | 5-7 | 8-9 | 10-11 | 12 |
| 1 | 5 | 4 | 3 | 2 | 1 | 0.2 |
| 2 | 6 | 6 | 6 | 6 | 6 | 6.0 |
| 3 | 6 | 6 | 6 | 6 | 6 | 6.0 |
| 4 | 6 | 6 | 6 | 6 | 6 | 6.0 |
| 5 | 6 | 6 | 6 | 6 | 6 | 6.0 |
| 6 | 6 | 6 | 6 | 6 | 6 | 6.0 |
| 7 | 6 | 6 | 6 | 6 | 6 | 6.0 |
| 8 | 6 | 6 | 6 | 6 | 6 | 6.0 |
| 9 | 6 | 6 | 6 | 6 | 6 | 6.0 |
| 10 | 6 | 6 | 6 | 6 | 6 | 6.0 |
| 11 | 5 | 5 | 5 | 5 | 5 | 5.8 |
| 12 | 5 | 5 | 5 | 5 | 5 | 5.0 |
| 13 | 5 | 5 | 5 | 5 | 5 | 5.0 |
| 14 | 5 | 5 | 5 | 5 | 5 | 5.0 |
| 15 | 5 | 5 | 5 | 5 | 5 | 5.0 |
| 16 | 5 | 5 | 5 | 5 | 5 | 5.0 |
| 17 | 5 | 5 | 5 | 5 | 5 | 5.0 |
| 18 | 5 | 5 | 5 | 5 | 5 | 5.0 |
| 19 | 1 | 2 | 3 | 4 | 5 | 5.0 |

4. **Optional Straight-Line Method for 18-Year Property (No Mid-Month Convention)**— For property placed in service after 3/15/84 and before 6/23/84

The applicable percentage is:

| If the Recovery Year Is: | 1 | 2–3 | 4–5 | 6–7 | 8–9 | 10–11 | 12 |
|---|---|---|---|---|---|---|---|
| | (Use the column for the month in the first recovery year the property is placed in service) | | | | | | |
| 1 | 6 | 5 | 4 | 3 | 2 | 1 | 0.5 |
| 2 | 6 | 6 | 6 | 6 | 6 | 6 | 6.0 |
| 3 | 6 | 6 | 6 | 6 | 6 | 6 | 6.0 |
| 4 | 6 | 6 | 6 | 6 | 6 | 6 | 6.0 |
| 5 | 6 | 6 | 6 | 6 | 6 | 6 | 6.0 |
| 6 | 6 | 6 | 6 | 6 | 6 | 6 | 6.0 |
| 7 | 6 | 6 | 6 | 6 | 6 | 6 | 6.0 |
| 8 | 6 | 6 | 6 | 6 | 6 | 6 | 6.0 |
| 9 | 6 | 6 | 6 | 6 | 6 | 6 | 6.0 |
| 10 | 6 | 6 | 6 | 6 | 6 | 6 | 6.0 |
| 11 | 5 | 5 | 5 | 5 | 5 | 5 | 5.5 |
| 12 | 5 | 5 | 5 | 5 | 5 | 5 | 5.0 |
| 13 | 5 | 5 | 5 | 5 | 5 | 5 | 5.0 |
| 14 | 5 | 5 | 5 | 5 | 5 | 5 | 5.0 |
| 15 | 5 | 5 | 5 | 5 | 5 | 5 | 5.0 |
| 16 | 5 | 5 | 5 | 5 | 5 | 5 | 5.0 |
| 17 | 5 | 5 | 5 | 5 | 5 | 5 | 5.0 |
| 18 | 5 | 5 | 5 | 5 | 5 | 5 | 5.0 |
| 19 | | 1 | 2 | 3 | 4 | 5 | 5.0 |

5. **Optional 35-Year Straight-Line Method for 18-Year Real Property (Mid-Month Convention)**—For property placed in service 6/23/84 until 5/8/85

The applicable percentage is:

| If the Recovery Year Is: | (Use the column for the month in the first recovery year the property is placed in service) | | | | |
|---|---|---|---|---|---|
|  | 1–2 | 3–6 | 7–10 | 11 | 12 |
| 1 | 3 | 2 | 1 | 0.4 | 0.1 |
| 2 | 3 | 3 | 3 | 3.0 | 3.0 |
| 3 | 3 | 3 | 3 | 3.0 | 3.0 |
| 4 | 3 | 3 | 3 | 3.0 | 3.0 |
| 5 | 3 | 3 | 3 | 3.0 | 3.0 |
| 6 | 3 | 3 | 3 | 3.0 | 3.0 |
| 7 | 3 | 3 | 3 | 3.0 | 3.0 |
| 8 | 3 | 3 | 3 | 3.0 | 3.0 |
| 9 | 3 | 3 | 3 | 3.0 | 3.0 |
| 10 | 3 | 3 | 3 | 3.0 | 3.0 |
| 11 | 3 | 3 | 3 | 3.0 | 3.0 |
| 12 | 3 | 3 | 3 | 3.0 | 3.0 |
| 13 | 3 | 3 | 3 | 3.0 | 3.0 |
| 14 | 3 | 3 | 3 | 3.0 | 3.0 |
| 15 | 3 | 3 | 3 | 3.0 | 3.0 |
| 16 | 3 | 3 | 3 | 3.0 | 3.0 |
| 17 | 3 | 3 | 3 | 3.0 | 3.0 |
| 18 | 3 | 3 | 3 | 3.0 | 3.0 |
| 19 | 3 | 3 | 3 | 3.0 | 3.0 |
| 20 | 3 | 3 | 3 | 3.0 | 3.0 |
| 21 | 3 | 3 | 3 | 3.0 | 3.0 |
| 22 | 3 | 3 | 3 | 3.0 | 3.0 |
| 23 | 3 | 3 | 3 | 3.0 | 3.0 |
| 24 | 3 | 3 | 3 | 3.0 | 3.0 |
| 25 | 3 | 3 | 3 | 3.0 | 3.0 |
| 26 | 3 | 3 | 3 | 3.0 | 3.0 |
| 27 | 3 | 3 | 3 | 3.0 | 3.0 |
| 28 | 3 | 3 | 3 | 3.0 | 3.0 |
| 29 | 3 | 3 | 3 | 3.0 | 3.0 |

The applicable percentage is:

| If the Recovery Year Is: | (Use the column for the month in the first recovery year the property is placed in service) | | | | |
|---|---|---|---|---|---|
| | 1–2 | 3–6 | 7–10 | 11 | 12 |
| 30 | 3 | 3 | 3 | 3.0 | 3.0 |
| 31 | 2 | 2 | 2 | 2.6 | 2.9 |
| 32 | 2 | 2 | 2 | 2.0 | 2.0 |
| 33 | 2 | 2 | 2 | 2.0 | 2.0 |
| 34 | 2 | 2 | 2 | 2.0 | 2.0 |
| 35 | 2 | 2 | 2 | 2.0 | 2.0 |
| 36 | | 1 | 2 | 2.0 | 2.0 |

6. **Optional 45-Year Straight-Line Method for 18-Year Real Property (Mid-Month Convention)**—For property placed in service 6/23/84 until 5/8/85

The applicable percentage is:

| If the Recovery Year Is: | (Use the column for the month in the first recovery year the property is placed in service) | | | | | | | | | | | |
|---|---|---|---|---|---|---|---|---|---|---|---|---|
| | 1 | 2 | 3 | 4 | 5 | 6 | 7 | 8 | 9 | 10 | 11 | 12 |
| 1 | 2.1 | 1.9 | 1.8 | 1.6 | 1.4 | 1.2 | 1.0 | 0.8 | 0.6 | 0.5 | 0.3 | 0.1 |
| 2 | 2.3 | 2.3 | 2.3 | 2.3 | 2.3 | 2.3 | 2.3 | 2.3 | 2.3 | 2.3 | 2.3 | 2.3 |
| 3 | 2.3 | 2.3 | 2.3 | 2.3 | 2.3 | 2.3 | 2.3 | 2.3 | 2.3 | 2.3 | 2.3 | 2.3 |
| 4 | 2.3 | 2.3 | 2.3 | 2.3 | 2.3 | 2.3 | 2.3 | 2.3 | 2.3 | 2.3 | 2.3 | 2.3 |
| 5 | 2.3 | 2.3 | 2.3 | 2.3 | 2.3 | 2.3 | 2.3 | 2.3 | 2.3 | 2.3 | 2.3 | 2.3 |
| 6 | 2.3 | 2.3 | 2.3 | 2.3 | 2.3 | 2.3 | 2.3 | 2.3 | 2.3 | 2.3 | 2.3 | 2.3 |
| 7 | 2.3 | 2.3 | 2.3 | 2.3 | 2.3 | 2.3 | 2.3 | 2.3 | 2.3 | 2.3 | 2.3 | 2.3 |
| 8 | 2.3 | 2.3 | 2.3 | 2.3 | 2.3 | 2.3 | 2.3 | 2.3 | 2.3 | 2.3 | 2.3 | 2.3 |
| 9 | 2.3 | 2.3 | 2.3 | 2.3 | 2.3 | 2.3 | 2.3 | 2.3 | 2.3 | 2.3 | 2.3 | 2.3 |
| 10 | 2.3 | 2.3 | 2.3 | 2.3 | 2.3 | 2.3 | 2.3 | 2.3 | 2.3 | 2.3 | 2.3 | 2.3 |
| 11 | 2.3 | 2.3 | 2.3 | 2.3 | 2.3 | 2.3 | 2.3 | 2.3 | 2.3 | 2.3 | 2.3 | 2.3 |
| 12 | 2.2 | 2.2 | 2.2 | 2.2 | 2.2 | 2.2 | 2.2 | 2.2 | 2.2 | 2.2 | 2.2 | 2.2 |
| 13 | 2.2 | 2.2 | 2.2 | 2.2 | 2.2 | 2.2 | 2.2 | 2.2 | 2.2 | 2.2 | 2.2 | 2.2 |

*(continued on next page)*

The applicable percentage is:

If the
Recovery
Year Is:

(Use the column for the month in the first recovery year
the property is placed in service)

| | 1 | 2 | 3 | 4 | 5 | 6 | 7 | 8 | 9 | 10 | 11 | 12 |
|---|---|---|---|---|---|---|---|---|---|---|---|---|
| 14 | 2.2 | 2.2 | 2.2 | 2.2 | 2.2 | 2.2 | 2.2 | 2.2 | 2.2 | 2.2 | 2.2 | 2.2 |
| 15 | 2.2 | 2.2 | 2.2 | 2.2 | 2.2 | 2.2 | 2.2 | 2.2 | 2.2 | 2.2 | 2.2 | 2.2 |
| 16 | 2.2 | 2.2 | 2.2 | 2.2 | 2.2 | 2.2 | 2.2 | 2.2 | 2.2 | 2.2 | 2.2 | 2.2 |
| 17 | 2.2 | 2.2 | 2.2 | 2.2 | 2.2 | 2.2 | 2.2 | 2.2 | 2.2 | 2.2 | 2.2 | 2.2 |
| 18 | 2.2 | 2.2 | 2.2 | 2.2 | 2.2 | 2.2 | 2.2 | 2.2 | 2.2 | 2.2 | 2.2 | 2.2 |
| 19 | 2.2 | 2.2 | 2.2 | 2.2 | 2.2 | 2.2 | 2.2 | 2.2 | 2.2 | 2.2 | 2.2 | 2.2 |
| 20 | 2.2 | 2.2 | 2.2 | 2.2 | 2.2 | 2.2 | 2.2 | 2.2 | 2.2 | 2.2 | 2.2 | 2.2 |
| 21 | 2.2 | 2.2 | 2.2 | 2.2 | 2.2 | 2.2 | 2.2 | 2.2 | 2.2 | 2.2 | 2.2 | 2.2 |
| 22 | 2.2 | 2.2 | 2.2 | 2.2 | 2.2 | 2.2 | 2.2 | 2.2 | 2.2 | 2.2 | 2.2 | 2.2 |
| 23 | 2.2 | 2.2 | 2.2 | 2.2 | 2.2 | 2.2 | 2.2 | 2.2 | 2.2 | 2.2 | 2.2 | 2.2 |
| 24 | 2.2 | 2.2 | 2.2 | 2.2 | 2.2 | 2.2 | 2.2 | 2.2 | 2.2 | 2.2 | 2.2 | 2.2 |
| 25 | 2.2 | 2.2 | 2.2 | 2.2 | 2.2 | 2.2 | 2.2 | 2.2 | 2.2 | 2.2 | 2.2 | 2.2 |
| 26 | 2.2 | 2.2 | 2.2 | 2.2 | 2.2 | 2.2 | 2.2 | 2.2 | 2.2 | 2.2 | 2.2 | 2.2 |
| 27 | 2.2 | 2.2 | 2.2 | 2.2 | 2.2 | 2.2 | 2.2 | 2.2 | 2.2 | 2.2 | 2.2 | 2.2 |
| 28 | 2.2 | 2.2 | 2.2 | 2.2 | 2.2 | 2.2 | 2.2 | 2.2 | 2.2 | 2.2 | 2.2 | 2.2 |
| 29 | 2.2 | 2.2 | 2.2 | 2.2 | 2.2 | 2.2 | 2.2 | 2.2 | 2.2 | 2.2 | 2.2 | 2.2 |
| 30 | 2.2 | 2.2 | 2.2 | 2.2 | 2.2 | 2.2 | 2.2 | 2.2 | 2.2 | 2.2 | 2.2 | 2.2 |
| 31 | 2.2 | 2.2 | 2.2 | 2.2 | 2.2 | 2.2 | 2.2 | 2.2 | 2.2 | 2.2 | 2.2 | 2.2 |
| 32 | 2.2 | 2.2 | 2.2 | 2.2 | 2.2 | 2.2 | 2.2 | 2.2 | 2.2 | 2.2 | 2.2 | 2.2 |
| 33 | 2.2 | 2.2 | 2.2 | 2.2 | 2.2 | 2.2 | 2.2 | 2.2 | 2.2 | 2.2 | 2.2 | 2.2 |
| 34 | 2.2 | 2.2 | 2.2 | 2.2 | 2.2 | 2.2 | 2.2 | 2.2 | 2.2 | 2.2 | 2.2 | 2.2 |
| 35 | 2.2 | 2.2 | 2.2 | 2.2 | 2.2 | 2.2 | 2.2 | 2.2 | 2.2 | 2.2 | 2.2 | 2.2 |
| 36 | 2.2 | 2.2 | 2.2 | 2.2 | 2.2 | 2.2 | 2.2 | 2.2 | 2.2 | 2.2 | 2.2 | 2.2 |
| 37 | 2.2 | 2.2 | 2.2 | 2.2 | 2.2 | 2.2 | 2.2 | 2.2 | 2.2 | 2.2 | 2.2 | 2.2 |
| 38 | 2.2 | 2.2 | 2.2 | 2.2 | 2.2 | 2.2 | 2.2 | 2.2 | 2.2 | 2.2 | 2.2 | 2.2 |
| 39 | 2.2 | 2.2 | 2.2 | 2.2 | 2.2 | 2.2 | 2.2 | 2.2 | 2.2 | 2.2 | 2.2 | 2.2 |
| 40 | 2.2 | 2.2 | 2.2 | 2.2 | 2.2 | 2.2 | 2.2 | 2.2 | 2.2 | 2.2 | 2.2 | 2.2 |
| 41 | 2.2 | 2.2 | 2.2 | 2.2 | 2.2 | 2.2 | 2.2 | 2.2 | 2.2 | 2.2 | 2.2 | 2.2 |
| 42 | 2.2 | 2.2 | 2.2 | 2.2 | 2.2 | 2.2 | 2.2 | 2.2 | 2.2 | 2.2 | 2.2 | 2.2 |
| 43 | 2.2 | 2.2 | 2.2 | 2.2 | 2.2 | 2.2 | 2.2 | 2.2 | 2.2 | 2.2 | 2.2 | 2.2 |
| 44 | 2.2 | 2.2 | 2.2 | 2.2 | 2.2 | 2.2 | 2.2 | 2.2 | 2.2 | 2.2 | 2.2 | 2.2 |
| 45 | 2.2 | 2.2 | 2.2 | 2.2 | 2.2 | 2.2 | 2.2 | 2.2 | 2.2 | 2.2 | 2.2 | 2.2 |
| 46 | 0.1 | 0.3 | 0.4 | 0.6 | 0.8 | 1.0 | 1.2 | 1.4 | 1.6 | 1.7 | 1.9 | 2.1 |

7. **Optional 35-Year Straight-Line for 18-Year Real Property Used Predominantly Outside the U.S. (Mid-Month Convention)**— For property placed in service 6/23/84 until 5/8/85

The applicable percentage is:

| If the Recovery Year Is: | (Use the column for the month in the first recovery year the property is placed in service) | | | | | | |
|---|---|---|---|---|---|---|---|
| | 1 | 2 | 3 | 4–5 | 6–8 | 9–11 | 12 |
| 1 | 4 | 4 | 3 | 3 | 2 | 1 | 0.2 |
| 2 | 4 | 4 | 4 | 4 | 4 | 4 | 4.0 |
| 3 | 4 | 4 | 4 | 4 | 4 | 4 | 4.0 |
| 4 | 4 | 4 | 4 | 4 | 4 | 4 | 4.0 |
| 5 | 4 | 4 | 4 | 4 | 4 | 4 | 4.0 |
| 6 | 3 | 3 | 3 | 3 | 4 | 4 | 4.0 |
| 7 | 3 | 3 | 3 | 3 | 3 | 3 | 3.8 |
| 8 | 3 | 3 | 3 | 3 | 3 | 3 | 3.0 |
| 9 | 3 | 3 | 3 | 3 | 3 | 3 | 3.0 |
| 10 | 3 | 3 | 3 | 3 | 3 | 3 | 3.0 |
| 11 | 3 | 3 | 3 | 3 | 3 | 3 | 3.0 |
| 12 | 3 | 3 | 3 | 3 | 3 | 3 | 3.0 |
| 13 | 3 | 3 | 3 | 3 | 3 | 3 | 3.0 |
| 14 | 3 | 3 | 3 | 3 | 3 | 3 | 3.0 |
| 15 | 3 | 3 | 3 | 3 | 3 | 3 | 3.0 |
| 16 | 3 | 3 | 3 | 3 | 3 | 3 | 3.0 |
| 17 | 3 | 3 | 3 | 3 | 3 | 3 | 3.0 |
| 18 | 3 | 3 | 3 | 3 | 3 | 3 | 3.0 |
| 19 | 3 | 3 | 3 | 3 | 3 | 3 | 3.0 |
| 20 | 3 | 3 | 3 | 3 | 3 | 3 | 3.0 |
| 21 | 3 | 3 | 3 | 3 | 3 | 3 | 3.0 |
| 22 | 3 | 3 | 3 | 3 | 3 | 3 | 3.0 |
| 23 | 3 | 3 | 3 | 3 | 3 | 3 | 3.0 |
| 24 | 3 | 3 | 3 | 3 | 3 | 3 | 3.0 |
| 25 | 3 | 2 | 3 | 2 | 2 | 3 | 3.0 |
| 26 | 2 | 2 | 2 | 2 | 2 | 2 | 2.0 |
| 27 | 2 | 2 | 2 | 2 | 2 | 2 | 2.0 |
| 28 | 2 | 2 | 2 | 2 | 2 | 2 | 2.0 |

*(continued on next page)*

The applicable percentage is:

| If the Recovery Year Is: | (Use the column for the month in the first recovery year the property is placed in service) | | | | | | |
|---|---|---|---|---|---|---|---|
| | 1 | 2 | 3 | 4–5 | 6–8 | 9–11 | 12 |
| 29 | 2 | 2 | 2 | 2 | 2 | 2 | 2.0 |
| 30 | 2 | 2 | 2 | 2 | 2 | 2 | 2.0 |
| 31 | 2 | 2 | 2 | 2 | 2 | 2 | 2.0 |
| 32 | 2 | 2 | 2 | 2 | 2 | 2 | 2.0 |
| 33 | 2 | 2 | 2 | 2 | 2 | 2 | 2.0 |
| 34 | 2 | 2 | 2 | 2 | 2 | 2 | 2.0 |
| 35 | 2 | 2 | 2 | 2 | 2 | 2 | 2.0 |
| 36 | | 1 | 1 | 2 | 2 | 2 | 2.0 |

The following tables were issued by the Treasury Department on September 10, 1981, for depreciating real estate under the ACRS system from 1/1/81 until 3/15/84.

## 1. All Real Estate (Except Low-Income Housing)

The applicable percentage is:

| If the Recovery Year Is: | (Use the column for the month in the first year the property is placed in service) | | | | | | | | | | | |
|---|---|---|---|---|---|---|---|---|---|---|---|---|
| | 1 | 2 | 3 | 4 | 5 | 6 | 7 | 8 | 9 | 10 | 11 | 12 |
| 1 | 12 | 11 | 10 | 9 | 8 | 7 | 6 | 5 | 4 | 3 | 2 | 1 |
| 2 | 10 | 10 | 11 | 11 | 11 | 11 | 11 | 11 | 11 | 11 | 11 | 12 |
| 3 | 9 | 9 | 9 | 9 | 10 | 10 | 10 | 10 | 10 | 10 | 10 | 10 |
| 4 | 8 | 8 | 8 | 8 | 8 | 8 | 9 | 9 | 9 | 9 | 9 | 9 |
| 5 | 7 | 7 | 7 | 7 | 7 | 7 | 8 | 8 | 8 | 8 | 8 | 8 |
| 6 | 6 | 6 | 6 | 6 | 7 | 7 | 7 | 7 | 7 | 7 | 7 | 7 |
| 7 | 6 | 6 | 6 | 6 | 6 | 6 | 6 | 6 | 6 | 6 | 6 | 6 |
| 8 | 6 | 6 | 6 | 6 | 6 | 6 | 5 | 6 | 6 | 6 | 6 | 6 |
| 9 | 6 | 6 | 6 | 6 | 5 | 6 | 5 | 5 | 5 | 6 | 6 | 6 |

The applicable percentage is:

If the
Recovery
Year Is:

(Use the column for the month in the first year
the property is placed in service)

| | 1 | 2 | 3 | 4 | 5 | 6 | 7 | 8 | 9 | 10 | 11 | 12 |
|---|---|---|---|---|---|---|---|---|---|---|---|---|
| 10 | 5 | 6 | 5 | 5 | 5 | 5 | 5 | 5 | 5 | 5 | 6 | 5 |
| 11 | 5 | 5 | 5 | 5 | 5 | 5 | 5 | 5 | 5 | 5 | 5 | 5 |
| 12 | 5 | 5 | 5 | 5 | 5 | 5 | 5 | 5 | 5 | 5 | 5 | 5 |
| 13 | 5 | 5 | 5 | 5 | 5 | 5 | 5 | 5 | 5 | 5 | 5 | 5 |
| 14 | 5 | 5 | 5 | 5 | 5 | 5 | 5 | 5 | 5 | 5 | 5 | 5 |
| 15 | 5 | 5 | 5 | 5 | 5 | 5 | 5 | 5 | 5 | 5 | 5 | 5 |
| 16 | — | — | 1 | 1 | 2 | 2 | 3 | 3 | 4 | 4 | 4 | 5 |

## 2. Low-Income Housing

The applicable percentage is:

If the
Recovery
Year Is:

(Use the column for the month in the first year
the property is placed in service)

| | 1 | 2 | 3 | 4 | 5 | 6 | 7 | 8 | 9 | 10 | 11 | 12 |
|---|---|---|---|---|---|---|---|---|---|---|---|---|
| 1 | 13 | 12 | 11 | 10 | 9 | 8 | 7 | 6 | 4 | 3 | 2 | 1 |
| 2 | 12 | 12 | 12 | 12 | 12 | 12 | 12 | 13 | 13 | 13 | 13 | 13 |
| 3 | 10 | 10 | 10 | 10 | 11 | 11 | 11 | 11 | 11 | 11 | 11 | 11 |
| 4 | 9 | 9 | 9 | 9 | 9 | 9 | 9 | 9 | 10 | 10 | 10 | 10 |
| 5 | 8 | 8 | 8 | 8 | 8 | 8 | 8 | 8 | 8 | 8 | 8 | 9 |
| 6 | 7 | 7 | 7 | 7 | 7 | 7 | 7 | 7 | 7 | 7 | 7 | 7 |
| 7 | 6 | 6 | 6 | 6 | 6 | 6 | 6 | 6 | 6 | 6 | 6 | 6 |
| 8 | 5 | 5 | 5 | 5 | 5 | 5 | 5 | 5 | 5 | 5 | 6 | 6 |
| 9 | 5 | 5 | 5 | 5 | 5 | 5 | 5 | 5 | 5 | 5 | 5 | 5 |
| 10 | 5 | 5 | 5 | 5 | 5 | 5 | 5 | 5 | 5 | 5 | 5 | 5 |
| 11 | 4 | 5 | 5 | 5 | 5 | 5 | 5 | 5 | 5 | 5 | 5 | 5 |
| 12 | 4 | 4 | 4 | 5 | 4 | 5 | 5 | 5 | 5 | 5 | 5 | 5 |
| 13 | 4 | 4 | 4 | 4 | 4 | 4 | 5 | 4 | 5 | 5 | 5 | 5 |
| 14 | 4 | 4 | 4 | 4 | 4 | 4 | 4 | 4 | 4 | 5 | 4 | 4 |
| 15 | 4 | 4 | 4 | 4 | 4 | 4 | 4 | 4 | 4 | 4 | 4 | 4 |
| 16 | — | — | 1 | 1 | 2 | 2 | 2 | 3 | 3 | 3 | 4 | 4 |

# 157

## Business Use of "Listed Property"

Prior to 1984, computers, automobiles, and other types of personal property were eligible for annual depreciation deductions with accelerated rates and recovery periods. Where such property was partly used for business purposes and partly used for personal purposes, the allowable amount of the otherwise available depreciation deduction was determined on the basis of the proportion of business use.

In 1984, Congress drew a sharp distinction between property used more than 50 percent for business purposes as compared to property having business use of 50 percent or less. Furthermore, for automobiles, additional restrictions have been imposed upon the maximum amount of yearly depreciation deductions.

The property covered by the stricter rules is referred to as "listed property" and includes the following:

1. passenger automobiles,

2. other transportation property,

3. entertainment, recreation, or amusement facilities,

4. computers and peripheral equipment, *and*

5. "other" property to be specified by regulations.

For *all* categories of the above listed property used 50 percent or less for business purposes, depreciation is to be determined on the straight-line method over a period of years that is longer than the minimum period otherwise provided.

In addition, satisfaction of the 50 percent test will be determined solely with reference to the use of the property in a *trade or business*. Use of the property in connection with the production of investment income is not taken into account for this purpose. Once it is determined, however, on the basis of business use, as to whether the property is to be treated under the more than 50 percent or the 50 percent or less rule, the use of the property in investment activities will be taken into account in determining the proportion of the tax benefits that are allowable.

For example, assume a computer is used 40 percent in the conduct of a trade or business and 30 percent for investment activities. Therefore, the more than 50 percent business use test is *not* satisfied. Depreciation will be determined on the straight-line method. However, *70* percent of that depreciation so determined will be allowable.

Except for *automobiles*, the depreciation deductions for listed property used *more* than 50 percent in a trade or business will be determined under prior law. The accelerated rates and periods under 1987 modified ACRS may be used to determine depreciation and then the percentage of business use will be combined with the percentage of use in investment activities to determine the portion of the total amount of depreciation that will be allowable.

With automobiles, however, including those with more than 50 percent business use, there are additional restrictions and limitations. Depreciation deductions are limited to $2,560 for the first year in the recovery period, $4,100 for the second, $2,450 for the third, and $1,475 for each succeeding year. These fixed limitations apply to all depreciation deductions, not just depreciation under the accelerated method.

If business use is less than 100 percent, you are entitled to claim the portion of the depreciation deductions allowable which corresponds to your business use percentage.

Moreover, leasing an automobile will not avoid the limitations. Leasees of property will be subject to restrictions on lease payments. These restrictions are comparable to the limitations on depreciation that would apply if the automobile were owned instead of leased. The percentage of lease payments allowable will be calculated pursuant to tables by the Treasury. These restrictions, however, do not apply to the tax benefits available under prior law to the leasors of property regularly engaged in the business of leasing property.

# 158 Employees

If you are an employee, the rules are even more stringent. *No* depreciation will be allowable for listed property owned by employees unless the property is:

1. required for the convenience of the employer, *and*

2. required as a condition of employment.

These requirements will *not* be satisfied merely by an employer's statement that the property is required as a condition of employment. It is intended that the property must be required in order for an employee to properly perform the duties of his/her employment.

Furthermore, if in years subsequent to the year of purchase, there is a reduction of the percentage of business use, that reduction can trigger an investment credit recapture. If the business use declines to 50 percent or less of the use of the property in the subsequent year, the *entire* amount of the investment credit will be recaptured. However, the Treasury can provide a rule that a *de minimus* reduction in the business use of the property will not trigger any recapture.

In addition to the existing rules governing the recapture of depreciation, the law requires recapture in the event property used more than 50 percent for business in the year it is placed in service declines to 50 percent or less of business use in a subsequent year. The amount of the recapture will be based upon the difference between the depreciation allowed in prior years and the amount that would have been allowed if the applicable accelerated rate and period of ACRS had not been available in such years. The Treasury has been instructed to provide for comparable recapture requirements applicable to leasees whose business use declines in subsequent years.

In IRS Letter Ruling 8615024, the IRS ruled that an employee's use of a personal computer did *not* meet the convenience of the employer and condition of employment tests. In denying any deduction or credit, the Internal Revenue Service said that to meet the convenience of the employer test, the employee must be *required* to purchase the computer to properly perform the duties of her employment. In that case, the taxpayer was not "required" to purchase the computer to properly perform her duties. Although the benefits of the taxpayer's use of the computer may inure to her employer, the purchase of a computer was clearly not required as a condition of employment. The facts of the case suggested that computer use, although work-related, was not inextricably related to proper performance of the taxpayer's job. Moreover, there appeared no evidence in the facts that those employees who did not purchase a computer were professionally disadvantaged.

In IRS Letter Ruling 8710009, this position was reiterated. Here the Internal Revenue Service held that an insurance agent's use of a portable computer as an aid in selling financial products did not meet the convenience of the employer test. They concluded that the taxpayer, who used the computer exclusively for business purposes, must be required to purchase the computer to properly perform the duties of his employment in order to take the deduction. The computer purchase was optional rather than mandatory. "The facts indicate that computer use, although work related, is not inextricably related to the proper performance of 'the taxpayer's' job. Further, there appears no evidence that those employees who do not purchase computers are professionally disadvantaged." (See also Rev. Rul. 86-129, 1986-45 IRB 4 and Letter Rul. 8725067.)

# 159 Luxury Cars

The Tax Reform Act of 1986 defined a passenger automobile as any four-wheeled vehicle that is manufactured primarily for use on public streets, roads, and highways and is rated at 6,000 pounds unloaded gross vehicle weight or less. The Act requires that fixed limitations on automobile deductions be conformed to the new recovery period, so that the price range of affected cars is unaffected. Depreciation deductions are limited to $2,560 for the first year in the recovery period, $4,100 for the second, $2,450 for the third, and $1,475 for each succeeding year. These fixed limitations apply to all depreciation deductions, not just depreciation under the accelerated method.

Limitations on Luxury Auto Depreciation Deductions

| | Yearly Maximum | | | |
|---|---|---|---|---|
| Date of purchase | 1 | 2 | 3 | 4 and after |
| 6/19/84 to 4/2/85 | $4,000 (25%) | $6,000[a] (38%) | $6,000[a] (37%) | $6,000[a] |
| 4/3/85 to 12/31/86 | 3,200 (25%) | 4,800 (38%) | 4,800 (37%) | 4,800 |
| 1987 and after | 2,560 (20%) | 4,100 (32%) | 2,450 (19.2%) | 1,475 (11.52%) |

[a]The limit is $6,200 if placed in service after 12/31/84 and before 4/3/85.

The following is a worksheet to determine the expense deduction for a $10,000 automobile placed in service in 1988 and used 100 percent for business:

**Determination of the Sec. 179 Expense Deduction to Achieve a Targeted Total ACRS Deduction for an Asset (or Total Assets)**

(1) Enter targeted total ACRS deduction (include the Sec. 179 expense deduction in line 1)  $ 2,560

(2) Percentage of business use: 100% or 1.000                                    100%
(3) Basis of asset                                                            10,000
(4) Business percentage of basis (multiply the amount on
    line 3 by the percentage on line 2)                                       10,000
(5) Enter the first-year ACRS percentage: 20% or 0.20                             .20
(6) Multiply the amount on line 4 by the percentage on
    line 5                                                                     2,000
(7) Subtract line 6 from line 1                                                  560
(8) Total asset value as a percent: 100.0% or 1.000                             1.00
(9) Enter first-year ACRS percentage: 20% or 0.20                                .20
(10) Subtract line 9 from line 8                                                 .80
(11) Divide line 7 by line 10. This is the exact Sec. 179
    expense deduction to achieve the targeted total ACRS
    deduction for the year                                                      700

Total deduction:
(a) ($10,000 − $700) × .20 =                                               $1,860
(b) Sec. 179 expense                                                          700
                                                                          $2,560

Note that the 1986 law put automobiles in the 5-year class. However, if the amount limitation prevents full use of the percentage depreciation in any year, the recovery period will be extended. Any unrecovered cost will be treated as an automobile expense subject to the annual limitation in taxable years after the end of the ordinary recovery period. The annual depreciation deduction, assuming the 200 percent declining-balance method, therefore, will be the lesser of the expense deduction or the percentage depreciation, as follows:

| Year | Depreciation Deduction | Percentage of Basis |
|---|---|---|
| 1 | $2,560 | 20 |
| 2 | 4,100 | 32 |
| 3 | 2,540 | 19.2 |
| 4 | 1,475 | 11.52 |
| 5 | 1,475 | 11.52 |
| 6 | 1,475 | 5.76 |

*Example:* Assume two cars were purchased in January 1987 to be used 100 percent for business at a cost of $12,900 and $15,000, respectively. The depreciation deductions allowed would be as follows:

| Year | $12,900 Car | $15,000 Car |
|------|-------------|-------------|
| 1987 | $ 2,560 | $ 2,560 |
| 1988 | 4,100 | 4,100 |
| 1989 | 2,450 | 2,450 |
| 1990 | 1,475 | 1,475 |
| 1991 | 1,475 | 1,475 |
| 1992 | 743 | 864 |
| 1993 | 97 | 1,475 |
| 1994 | 0 | 601 |
| | $12,900 | $15,000 |

Note that in 1992, the percentage limitation prevents expensing up to the amount of the annual limitation.

The dollar caps must be proportionately reduced if the business or investment use is less than 100 percent.

*Example:* A taxpayer bought a $20,000 car in 1987 to be used 60 percent for business and 40 percent for personal driving. His depreciation deduction for 1987 was $1,536 [the lesser of $2,560 × 60 percent business use ($1,536), or 20 percent of $20,000 × 60 percent ($2,400)].

If qualified business use in the year the automobile is placed in service does not exceed 50 percent, then the basis must be recovered over 5 years using the straight-line method and the half-year convention. If qualified business use falls to 50 percent or less of total use during any part of the recovery period, part of the depreciation claimed in prior years must be included in the taxpayer's income, and a switch must be made to straight-line depreciation.

Appropriate limitations with respect to comparable dollar caps will be applicable to leased automobiles. Lessees of luxury automobiles used in business will be required to have income included to reflect the reduction in their deduction for lease payments. This income inclusion will be based on special tables provided by the Treasury after netting out the repeal of the investment tax credit. See below for inclusions required for 1986 and after.

# 160    Auto Leases

Lessors of automobiles having a cost of more than $11,250 had to include in their 1986 income an amount based on tables in Announcement 85-127 that was equal to the value of the limitations imposed by the 1985 law change. For example, a lessee(s) (including an employer or self-employed individual) who leased a car worth $14,300 that was first used on September 1, 1985, and was used 90 percent for business, included approximately $61 in income ($204 times 122/365 of a year times 90 percent business use).

For any passenger automobile leased after April 2, 1985, but before January 1, 1987, the inclusion amount for each of the first three taxable years during which the automobile was leased was based on the fair market value of the automobile, the leasee's amount of business use, and the quarter of the taxable year during which the automobile was first used under the lease.

The inclusion amount is based upon the following tables and is computed as follows:

1.  For the appropriate range of fair market values, find the dollar amount from the column for the quarter of the taxable year in which the automobile is first used under the lease.

2.  Prorate the dollar amount for the number of days of the lease term included in the taxable year.

3.  Multiply the prorated dollar amount by the percentage of business use for the taxable year.

Price-Based Inclusion Table for Cars Leased After April 2, 1985, but Before 1987

| Fair Market Value | | Taxable Year Quarter | | | |
| --- | --- | --- | --- | --- | --- |
| | | Fourth | Third | Second | First |
| Greater than | But not greater than | | | | |
| $11,250 | $11,500 | $8 | $7 | $6 | $6 |
| 11,500 | 11,750 | 24 | 21 | 19 | 17 |
| 11,750 | 12,000 | 40 | 35 | 32 | 29 |
| 12,000 | 12,250 | 56 | 49 | 44 | 40 |
| 12,250 | 12,500 | 72 | 64 | 57 | 52 |

Price-Based Inclusion Table (*Continued*)

| Fair Market Value | | Taxable Year Quarter | | | |
|---|---|---|---|---|---|
| | | Fourth | Third | Second | First |
| 12,500 | 12,750 | 88 | 78 | 70 | 63 |
| 12,750 | 13,000 | 104 | 92 | 83 | 75 |
| 13,000 | 13,250 | 120 | 106 | 95 | 86 |
| 13,250 | 13,500 | 144 | 128 | 115 | 104 |
| 13,500 | 13,750 | 172 | 153 | 137 | 124 |
| 13,750 | 14,000 | 200 | 177 | 159 | 145 |
| 14,000 | 14,250 | 228 | 202 | 182 | 165 |
| 14,250 | 14,500 | 256 | 227 | 204 | 185 |
| 14,500 | 14,750 | 284 | 252 | 226 | 206 |
| 14,750 | 15,000 | 312 | 277 | 249 | 226 |
| 15,000 | 15,250 | 340 | 302 | 271 | 246 |
| 15,250 | 15,500 | 369 | 327 | 293 | 266 |
| 15,500 | 15,750 | 397 | 352 | 316 | 287 |
| 15,750 | 16,000 | 425 | 377 | 338 | 307 |
| 16,000 | 16,250 | 453 | 402 | 360 | 327 |
| 16,250 | 16,500 | 481 | 426 | 383 | 348 |
| 16,500 | 16,750 | 509 | 451 | 405 | 368 |
| 16,750 | 17,000 | 537 | 476 | 428 | 388 |
| 17,000 | 17,500 | 579 | 514 | 461 | 419 |
| 17,500 | 18,000 | 635 | 563 | 506 | 459 |
| 18,000 | 18,500 | 691 | 613 | 550 | 500 |
| 18,500 | 19,000 | 748 | 663 | 595 | 541 |
| 19,000 | 19,500 | 804 | 713 | 640 | 581 |
| 19,500 | 20,000 | 860 | 763 | 685 | 622 |
| 20,000 | 20,500 | 916 | 812 | 729 | 662 |
| 20,500 | 21,000 | 972 | 862 | 774 | 703 |
| 21,000 | 21,500 | 1028 | 912 | 819 | 744 |
| 21,500 | 22,000 | 1084 | 962 | 863 | 784 |
| 22,000 | 23,000 | 1169 | 1036 | 930 | 845 |
| 23,000 | 24,000 | 1281 | 1136 | 1020 | 926 |
| 24,000 | 25,000 | 1393 | 1236 | 1109 | 1007 |
| 25,000 | 26,000 | 1506 | 1335 | 1199 | 1089 |
| 26,000 | 27,000 | 1618 | 1435 | 1288 | 1170 |
| 27,000 | 28,000 | 1730 | 1534 | 1377 | 1251 |
| 28,000 | 29,000 | 1842 | 1634 | 1467 | 1332 |
| 29,000 | 30,000 | 1955 | 1734 | 1556 | 1413 |
| 30,000 | 31,000 | 2067 | 1833 | 1646 | 1495 |
| 31,000 | 32,000 | 2179 | 1933 | 1735 | 1576 |
| 32,000 | 33,000 | 2292 | 2032 | 1824 | 1657 |
| 33,000 | 34,000 | 2404 | 2132 | 1914 | 1738 |

(*Continued on next page*)

Price-Based Inclusion Table (*Continued*)

| Fair Market Value | | Taxable Year Quarter | | | |
|---|---|---|---|---|---|
| | | Fourth | Third | Second | First |
| 34,000 | 35,000 | 2516 | 2232 | 2003 | 1819 |
| 35,000 | 36,000 | 2629 | 2331 | 2093 | 1901 |
| 36,000 | 37,000 | 2741 | 2431 | 2182 | 1982 |
| 37,000 | 38,000 | 2853 | 2530 | 2271 | 2063 |
| 38,000 | 39,000 | 2965 | 2630 | 2361 | 2144 |
| 39,000 | 40,000 | 3078 | 2730 | 2450 | 2225 |
| 40,000 | 41,000 | 3190 | 2829 | 2540 | 2307 |
| 41,000 | 42,000 | 3302 | 2929 | 2629 | 2388 |
| 42,000 | 43,000 | 3415 | 3028 | 2718 | 2469 |
| 43,000 | 44,000 | 3527 | 3128 | 2808 | 2550 |
| 44,000 | 45,000 | 3639 | 3228 | 2897 | 2631 |
| 45,000 | 46,000 | 3752 | 3327 | 2987 | 2713 |
| 46,000 | 47,000 | 3864 | 3427 | 3076 | 2794 |
| 47,000 | 48,000 | 3876 | 3526 | 3165 | 2875 |
| 48,000 | 49,000 | 4088 | 3626 | 3255 | 2956 |
| 49,000 | 50,000 | 4201 | 3726 | 3344 | 3037 |

For any passenger automobile that has a fair market value greater than $18,000, but not greater than $50,000, the inclusion amount for the fourth, fifth, and sixth taxable years during which the automobile is leased is determined by using the table below instead of the formulas provided in Section 1.280F-5T(d)(1)(i) through (iv) of the temporary regulations. The inclusion amount is computed as follows: (1) For the appropriate range of fair market values, select the dollar amount from the column for the taxable year in which the automobile is used under the lease; (2) prorate the dollar amount for the number of days of the lease term included in the taxable year; and (3) multiply this dollar amount by the percentage of business use for the taxable year.

## Inclusion Amounts: Years 4–6

| Fair Market Value | | Year 4 | Year 5 | Year 6 |
|---|---|---|---|---|
| Greater than | But not greater than | | | |
| $18,000 | $18,500 | $ 15 | — | — |
| 18,500 | 19,000 | 45 | — | — |
| 19,000 | 19,500 | 75 | — | — |
| 19,500 | 20,000 | 105 | — | — |
| 20,000 | 20,500 | 135 | — | — |
| 20,500 | 21,000 | 165 | — | — |
| 21,000 | 21,500 | 195 | — | — |
| 21,500 | 22,000 | 225 | — | — |
| 22,000 | 23,000 | 270 | — | — |
| 23,000 | 24,000 | 330 | $ 42 | — |
| 24,000 | 25,000 | 390 | 102 | — |
| 25,000 | 26,000 | 450 | 162 | — |
| 26,000 | 27,000 | 510 | 222 | — |
| 27,000 | 28,000 | 570 | 282 | — |
| 28,000 | 29,000 | 630 | 342 | $54 |
| 29,000 | 30,000 | 690 | 402 | 114 |
| 30,000 | 31,000 | 750 | 462 | 174 |
| 31,000 | 32,000 | 810 | 522 | 234 |
| 32,000 | 33,000 | 870 | 582 | 294 |
| 33,000 | 34,000 | 930 | 642 | 354 |
| 34,000 | 35,000 | 990 | 702 | 414 |
| 35,000 | 36,000 | 1050 | 762 | 474 |
| 36,000 | 37,000 | 1110 | 822 | 534 |
| 37,000 | 38,000 | 1170 | 882 | 594 |
| 38,000 | 39,000 | 1230 | 942 | 654 |
| 39,000 | 40,000 | 1290 | 1002 | 714 |
| 40,000 | 41,000 | 1350 | 1062 | 774 |
| 41,000 | 42,000 | 1410 | 1122 | 834 |
| 42,000 | 43,000 | 1470 | 1182 | 894 |
| 43,000 | 44,000 | 1530 | 1242 | 954 |
| 44,000 | 45,000 | 1590 | 1302 | 1014 |
| 45,000 | 46,000 | 1650 | 1362 | 1074 |
| 46,000 | 47,000 | 1710 | 1422 | 1134 |
| 47,000 | 48,000 | 1770 | 1482 | 1194 |
| 48,000 | 49,000 | 1830 | 1542 | 1254 |
| 49,000 | 50,000 | 1890 | 1602 | 1314 |

For any passenger automobile that has a fair market value greater than $50,000, the inclusion amount for the first six taxable years during which the automobile is leased is determined according to special rules. (*Source:* See Internal Revenue Service Announcement 85-127.) For cars leased after 1986, see the table below.

### Price-Based Inclusion Table for Cars Leased after 1986

| Fair Market Value | | Year of Lease* | | | | |
|---|---|---|---|---|---|---|
| Greater than | But not greater than | First | Second | Third | Fourth | Fifth and later |
| $12,800 | $13,100 | $ 2 | $ 5 | $ 7 | $ 8 | $ 9 |
| 13,100 | 13,400 | 6 | 14 | 20 | 24 | 28 |
| 13,400 | 13,700 | 10 | 23 | 34 | 41 | 47 |
| 13,700 | 14,000 | 15 | 32 | 47 | 57 | 65 |
| 14,000 | 14,300 | 19 | 41 | 61 | 73 | 84 |
| 14,300 | 14,600 | 23 | 50 | 74 | 89 | 103 |
| 14,600 | 14,900 | 27 | 59 | 88 | 105 | 122 |
| 14,900 | 15,200 | 31 | 68 | 101 | 122 | 140 |
| 15,200 | 15,500 | 35 | 77 | 115 | 138 | 159 |
| 15,500 | 15,800 | 40 | 87 | 128 | 154 | 178 |
| 15,800 | 16,100 | 44 | 96 | 142 | 170 | 196 |
| 16,100 | 16,400 | 48 | 105 | 155 | 186 | 215 |
| 16,400 | 16,700 | 52 | 114 | 169 | 203 | 234 |
| 16,700 | 17,000 | 56 | 123 | 182 | 219 | 253 |
| 17,000 | 17,500 | 62 | 135 | 200 | 240 | 277 |
| 17,500 | 18,000 | 69 | 150 | 223 | 267 | 309 |
| 18,000 | 18,500 | 76 | 166 | 246 | 294 | 340 |
| 18,500 | 19,000 | 83 | 181 | 268 | 321 | 371 |
| 19,000 | 19,500 | 90 | 196 | 291 | 348 | 402 |
| 19,500 | 20,000 | 97 | 211 | 313 | 375 | 433 |
| 20,000 | 20,500 | 104 | 226 | 336 | 402 | 465 |
| 20,500 | 21,000 | 111 | 242 | 358 | 429 | 496 |
| 21,000 | 21,500 | 117 | 257 | 381 | 456 | 527 |
| 21,500 | 22,000 | 124 | 272 | 403 | 483 | 558 |
| 22,000 | 23,000 | 135 | 295 | 437 | 524 | 605 |
| 23,000 | 24,000 | 149 | 325 | 482 | 578 | 667 |
| 24,000 | 25,000 | 163 | 356 | 527 | 632 | 729 |

| Fair Market Value | | Year of Lease* | | | | |
| --- | --- | --- | --- | --- | --- | --- |
| Greater than | But not greater than | First | Second | Third | Fourth | Fifth and later |
| 25,000 | 26,000 | 177 | 386 | 572 | 686 | 792 |
| 26,000 | 27,000 | 190 | 416 | 617 | 740 | 854 |
| 27,000 | 28,000 | 204 | 447 | 662 | 794 | 917 |
| 28,000 | 29,000 | 218 | 477 | 707 | 848 | 979 |
| 29,000 | 30,000 | 232 | 507 | 752 | 902 | 1,041 |
| 30,000 | 31,000 | 246 | 538 | 797 | 956 | 1,104 |
| 31,000 | 32,000 | 260 | 568 | 842 | 1,010 | 1,166 |
| 32,000 | 33,000 | 274 | 599 | 887 | 1,064 | 1,228 |
| 33,000 | 34,000 | 288 | 629 | 933 | 1,118 | 1,291 |
| 34,000 | 35,000 | 302 | 659 | 978 | 1,172 | 1,353 |
| 35,000 | 36,000 | 316 | 690 | 1,023 | 1,226 | 1,415 |
| 36,000 | 37,000 | 329 | 720 | 1,068 | 1,280 | 1,478 |
| 37,000 | 38,000 | 343 | 751 | 1,113 | 1,334 | 1,540 |
| 38,000 | 39,000 | 357 | 781 | 1,158 | 1,388 | 1,602 |
| 39,000 | 40,000 | 371 | 811 | 1,203 | 1,442 | 1,665 |
| 40,000 | 41,000 | 385 | 842 | 1,248 | 1,496 | 1,727 |
| 41,000 | 42,000 | 399 | 872 | 1,293 | 1,550 | 1,789 |
| 42,000 | 43,000 | 413 | 902 | 1,338 | 1,604 | 1,852 |
| 43,000 | 44,000 | 427 | 933 | 1,383 | 1,658 | 1,914 |
| 44,000 | 45,000 | 441 | 963 | 1,428 | 1,712 | 1,976 |
| 45,000 | 46,000 | 455 | 994 | 1,473 | 1,766 | 2,039 |
| 46,000 | 47,000 | 468 | 1,024 | 1,518 | 1,820 | 2,101 |
| 47,000 | 48,000 | 482 | 1,054 | 1,563 | 1,874 | 2,164 |
| 48,000 | 49,000 | 496 | 1,085 | 1,608 | 1,928 | 2,226 |
| 49,000 | 50,000 | 510 | 1,115 | 1,653 | 1,982 | 2,288 |
| 50,000 | 51,000 | 524 | 1,146 | 1,698 | 2,036 | 2,351 |
| 51,000 | 52,000 | 538 | 1,176 | 1,743 | 2,090 | 2,413 |
| 52,000 | 53,000 | 552 | 1,206 | 1,788 | 2,144 | 2,475 |
| 53,000 | 54,000 | 566 | 1,237 | 1,834 | 2,198 | 2,538 |
| 54,000 | 55,000 | 580 | 1,267 | 1,879 | 2,252 | 2,600 |
| 55,000 | 56,000 | 594 | 1,297 | 1,924 | 2,306 | 2,662 |
| 56,000 | 57,000 | 607 | 1,328 | 1,969 | 2,360 | 2,725 |
| 57,000 | 58,000 | 621 | 1,358 | 2,014 | 2,414 | 2,787 |
| 58,000 | 59,000 | 635 | 1,389 | 2,059 | 2,468 | 2,849 |
| 59,000 | 60,000 | 649 | 1,419 | 2,104 | 2,522 | 2,912 |

*For the last tax year of the lease, use the dollar amount for the preceding year.

HOW TO FIGURE FRINGE BENEFITS WHEN YOUR CORPORATION LEASES

If your corporation leases a car for your professional use, you must pay taxes on what the IRS deems a fringe benefit—the mileage you put on the car for your personal use. To determine the value that must be shown on your W-2 Form, multiply the amount this table shows as a fringe benefit by your percentage of personal use.

| Car's Market Value at Purchase | IRS-Attributed Value of Full Use |
|---|---|
| $ 5,000– 5,999 | $ 1,850 |
| 6,000– 6,999 | 2,100 |
| 7,000– 7,999 | 2,350 |
| 8,000– 8,999 | 2,600 |
| 9,000– 9,999 | 2,850 |
| 10,000–10,999 | 3,100 |
| 11,000–11,999 | 3,350 |
| 12,000–12,999 | 3,600 |
| 13,000–13,999 | 3,850 |
| 14,000–14,999 | 4,100 |
| 15,000–15,999 | 4,350 |
| 16,000–16,999 | 4,600 |
| 17,000–17,999 | 4,850 |
| 18,000–18,999 | 5,100 |
| 19,000–19,999 | 5,350 |
| 20,000–20,999 | 5,600 |
| 21,000–21,999 | 5,850 |
| 22,000–22,999 | 6,100 |
| 23,000–23,999 | 6,350 |
| 24,000–24,999 | 6,600 |
| 25,000–25,999 | 6,850 |
| 26,000–27,999 | 7,250 |
| 28,000–29,999 | 7,750 |
| 30,000–31,999 | 8,250 |
| 32,000–33,999 | 8,750 |
| 34,000–35,999 | 9,250 |
| 36,000–37,999 | 9,750 |

(continued on next page)

| Car's Market Value at Purchase | IRS-Attributed Value of Full Use |
|---|---|
| 38,000–39,999 | 10,250 |
| 40,000–41,999 | 10,750 |
| 42,000–43,999 | 11,250 |
| 44,000–45,999 | 11,750 |
| 46,000–47,999 | 12,250 |
| 48,000–49,999 | 12,750 |
| 50,000–51,999 | 13,250 |
| 52,000–53,999 | 13,750 |
| 54,000–55,999 | 14,250 |
| 56,000–57,999 | 14,750 |
| 58,000–59,999 | 15,250 |

For vehicles that have a fair market value in excess of $59,999, the annual lease value is equal to (.25 × the fair market value of the car) + $500. Fuel cost must be added at the rate of 5.5 cents per personal mile.

For example, assume that an employee is provided with an auto with a fair market value of $15,000. He drives a total of 16,000 miles during the year, 4,000 of which are personal miles. The personal use percentage is 25 percent (4,000 divided by 16,000). The lease value for an auto worth $15,000 is $4,350; 25 percent of $4,350 is $1,088. To this, add 5.5 cents times the 4,000 personal miles, or $220. Thus, the employee must include in his annual income $1,208 ($1,088 plus $220). If the employee had access to the auto for only part of the year, the lease value would be reduced proportionately.

# 161 Depreciation Planning

Under the Tax Reform Act of 1986, if the cost of your business purchases (including cars) in the last quarter of the year exceeds 40 percent of your business purchases for the entire year (other than land or real estate), a special depreciation rule comes into play. For these personal property purchases, a mid-quarter convention applies. For automobiles, in effect your first-year depreciation is reduced from 20 percent (or $2,560) down to 5 percent.

For example, assume you bought a new car in 1988 for $13,000. The car is used 100 percent for business and you made no other purchases of business property or equipment during the year. If you bought the car and placed it in service prior to October 1, 1988, you can claim the maximum depreciation—$2,560. If you put the car into service on or after October 1, 1988, your depreciation deduction for 1988 is limited to 5 percent of your purchase price, or $650. A one-day delay can cost you an extra $1,910 in deductions.

There is an answer to this dilemma, however. Instead of claiming a depreciation deduction for your car, claim a Section 179 expensing deduction. Similar to depreciation, your expensing deduction on a car cannot exceed $2,560 (the remaining cost being recovered in future years through depreciation). But this special expensing is not subject to the restrictive special rule on last quarter purchases. With expensing, you are able to get the same $2,560 deduction whether you buy the car in January or in December.

# 162    Loans Under Qualified Plans

Under the 1986 law, a plan loan must be amortized in level payments, made not less frequently than quarterly, over the term of the loan. Moreover, the exception to the treatment of a loan from a qualified plan to a participant as a taxable distribution is modified. The $50,000 maximum limitation on such exempt loans would have to be reduced by the highest outstanding loan balance during the prior 12 months. The exception to the rule requiring payment of an exempt loan within 5 years is limited to loans applied to the purchase of the participant's principal residence.

Furthermore, the Reform Act provides a deferral of the deduction (to the extent otherwise allowable under the provisions of the conference agreement) for interest paid by key employees on loans from any qualified plan. The deferral would be accomplished by denying the deduction for interest and increasing the participant's basis under the plan by the amount of nondeductible interest paid. These provisions are generally effective for amounts received as a loan after December 31, 1986.

# 163    Tax Credits

The Tax Reform Act of 1986 affects various tax credits, as follows:

1.  Investment tax credit—eliminated as of January 1, 1986.

2. Rehabilitation credits—reduced to 10 percent for nonhistoric structures and 20 percent for historic structures.

3. Energy credits—The residential energy credit has been allowed to expire, but business credits for solar, geothermal, and oceanthermal property are extended through 1988. The business energy tax credit for renewable solar products is extended through 1988 at a 15 percent rate in 1986, a 12 percent rate in 1987, and a 10 percent rate in 1988. The business credit for geothermal projects is extended through 1988 at a 15 percent rate in 1986, a 10 percent rate in 1987, and a 10 percent rate in 1988. The business credit for oceanthermal projects is extended at a 15 percent rate through 1988.

4. Research and development tax credits—The prior 25 percent credit is reduced to 20 percent and expires after 1988. The definition of eligible expenditures is tightened, and a new 20 percent credit is created for corporate deductions to fund university basic research. The provision extending the research credit is effective for taxable years ending after December 31, 1985, with respect to expenditures prior to January 1, 1989. The provisions modifying the credit are effective for taxable years beginning after December 31, 1985, except that the modifications to the university basic research credit are effective for taxable years beginning after December 31, 1986.

5. Orphan drug clinical testing credit—The tax credit for clinical testing of orphan drugs is extended for an additional 3 years—i.e., through December 31, 1990.

6. Low-income housing credits—The new law adds three new credits for investments in new multifamily low-income housing and for expenses incurred in rehabilitating older housing units. These credits are allowed at a rate of 9 percent annually for 10 years for new construction and 4 percent for the acquisition of existing housing.

7. Targeted jobs tax credit—The new law extends the targeted jobs credit for 3 additional years—i.e., for first-year wages paid to individuals who begin work for the employer before 1989. Under the new law, the credit for first-year wages is reduced from 50 percent to 40 percent of the first $6,000 of qualified wages; wages paid in the second year of a targeted individual's employment are not eligible for the credit; and the credit is not available if the employee works less than 90 days (14 days in the case of qualified summer youth employees) or 120 hours

(20 hours in the case of qualified summer youth employees). These modifications to the credit apply with respect to individuals who begin to work for the employer after 1985.

## C  Changes Affecting Corporations

# 164  Corporate Tax Rates

The 1986 law provides a new three-bracket graduated corporate tax structure, as follows:

| Taxable Income | Tax Rate |
| --- | --- |
| Not over $50,000 | 15 percent |
| Over $50,000 but not over $75,000 | 25 percent |
| Over $75,000 | 34 percent |

This structure reduces the number of corporate income tax brackets, from five to three and lowers the tax rate applicable to large corporations from 46 to 34 percent. The benefit of graduated rates is fully phased out for corporations with more than $335,000 of taxable income (compared to $1,405,000 under prior law).

The graduated income tax rates are effective for taxable years beginning after July 1, 1987. For taxable years including July 1, 1987, blended rates apply.

# 165  Corporate Dividends Received Deduction

The 85 percent dividends received deduction under prior law is reduced to 80 percent for dividends received after December 31, 1986.

# 166  Gain or Loss on Liquidating Sales and Distributions

Under prior law, no gain was recognized at the corporate level on sales made in liquidation of a corporation and the distributions of appreciated property. This favorable treatment (known as the "General

Utilities Doctrine") is repealed for distribution and sales completed after January 1, 1987, subject to certain technical exceptions.

## D  Miscellaneous Provisions

# 167  Penalties

The prior law $50 penalty for failure to file an information return with the IRS and the prior law $50 penalty for failure to supply a copy of the information return to the taxpayer is now subject to a new maximum of $100,000 for each category. The Reform Act also provides a new $50 penalty for failure to include correct information on an information return. These changes apply to information returns with due dates after December 31, 1986.

The 1986 law also increases the penalty for failure to pay taxes from one-half of one percent under prior law to one percent after the IRS notifies the taxpayer that the IRS will levy upon the assets of the taxpayer. This applies to amounts assessed after December 31, 1986.

The scope of the negligence penalty is also expanded by making it applicable to all taxes under the Internal Revenue Code. Failure to report on a tax return any amount reported on an information return is considered negligence in the absence of clear and convincing evidence to the contrary. The new law modifies the fraud penalty by increasing the rate to 75 percent of the underpayment (from 50 percent) but applying the penalty only to the amount of the underpayment attributable to fraud. These provisions are effective for returns with due dates after December 31, 1986.

The Reform Act provides that failure of a taxpayer to use reasonable efforts to resolve his case administratively before going to the Tax Court constitutes an additional basis for imposition of the discretionary penalty for delay under Code Section 6673. This section authorizes damages in an amount not in excess of $5,000 to be awarded to the United States by the Tax Court if it finds that proceedings before it have been instituted or maintained by a taxpayer primarily for delay or that the taxpayer's position in such proceedings is frivolous or groundless.

Moreover, the Reform Act increases the penalty for substantial understatement of tax liability from 10 to 20 percent [increased to 25 percent by the Budget Reconciliation Act (H.R. 5300)] of the amount of the underpayment of tax attributable to the understatement. This provision is also effective for returns with due dates after December 31, 1986.

# 168 Interest Provisions

The Tax Reform Act of 1986 provides that the government pay interest to taxpayers at the federal short-term rate plus two percentage points and that taxpayers pay interest to the government at the federal short-term rate plus three percentage points. These rates will be adjusted quarterly and will apply to interest for periods after December 31, 1986. Note that this interest will be nondeductible "consumer interest."

# 169 Real Estate Information Reporting

The 1986 law provides that the person responsible for closing a real estate transaction must provide an information report on the transaction. This provision is effective beginning January 1, 1987.

# 170 Taxpayer Identification Numbers of Dependents

The 1986 law requires that any taxpayer claiming a deduction for a dependent who is at least 5 years old must report the taxpayer identification number of that dependent on that tax return; this is effective for returns required to be filed after December 31, 1987.

# 171 Estimated Tax Payment

The 1986 law increases from 80 to 90 percent the proportion of the current year's tax liability that individual taxpayers must make as estimated tax payments in order to avoid the estimated tax penalty. This change is effective for taxable years beginning after December 31, 1986.

# 172 Award of Attorneys' Fees in Tax Cases

The 1986 law extends permanently the authorization of awards for attorneys' fees and other court costs and expands prior law to include awards for proceedings in the U.S. Tax Court. The standard that the government's position must be "substantially justified" is also to be applied to administrative action or inaction on which the proceeding is based. No award is allowed to a prevailing party who unreasonably protracted the proceedings. The prior law $25,000 award cap is eliminated, but a $75 per hour limitation on attorneys' fees is imposed, unless the court determines that a higher rate is justified. These changes are effective for actions commenced after December 31, 1985, but no payment may be made under the provisions before October 1, 1986.

# 173 Tax Court Provisions

The 1986 law permits the Tax Court to impose a practice fee of not more than $30 per year, clarifies that the Tax Court has jurisdiction over the penalty for failure to pay tax, clarifies that the Tax Court may obtain the assistance of U.S. Marshals, clarifies the pay and travel rules pertaining to special trial judges, permits a judge to elect to practice law after retirement and receive retirement pay, allows interlocutory appeals to be certified to the Court of Appeals, and conforms the survivor's annuity provisions to those applicable to the District Court.

# 174 Authority to Rescind Notice of Deficiency/ Update Interest

The 1986 law gives the Internal Revenue Service authority, after taxpayer consent, to rescind the statutory notice of deficiency. It also gives the IRS the authority to abate interest attributable to error or delay by an IRS employee in performing a ministerial act.

# CHAPTER 12

# How to Avoid/Survive an IRS Audit

The objective of the Internal Revenue Service is to "encourage and achieve the highest degree of voluntary compliance with the tax laws and regulations and to maintain the highest degree of public confidence in the integrity and efficiency of the IRS" (IRS statement of organization and functions, 39 Fed. Reg. 11,572, 1974).

*"A taxpaying public that does not understand the law is a taxpaying public that cannot comply with the law."*

IRS Commissioner Lawrence B. Gibbs, March 2, 1987

*Some agents "need more training in how to be courteous."*

IRS Commissioner Lawrence B. Gibbs, April 14, 1987.

*Dear Taxpayer:*
*This is to inform you that we, at the Internal Revenue Service, have lost your file. Unless we find it within thirty (30) days, you will face a $10,000 fine and a jail sentence of not less than five (5) years. Please advise.*

The letter on the preceding page is, of course, a phony. But the paranoia it suggests is very real. To most American taxpayers, receiving correspondence from the Internal Revenue Service is on a par with spending three weeks in a dentist's chair or two hours in a locked room with an encyclopedia salesperson. Greetings from the IRS means one thing: the ultimate curse of a civilized society—a tax audit.

The Internal Revenue Service defines an audit as "an impartial review of the taxpayer's return to determine its completeness and accuracy." Senator Edward V. Long of Missouri doesn't agree. He has compared the Internal Revenue Service to a "Gestapo preying upon defenseless citizens." His Senate committee found the audit and investigative techniques of the IRS to include defying court orders, picking locks, stealing records, illegally tapping telephones, intercepting and reading personal mail, using hidden microphones to eavesdrop on the private conversations of taxpayers with their lawyers, employing undercover agents with assumed identities, and using sexual entrapment.

In an April 26, 1982, hearing before the House Ways and Means Subcommittee on Oversight, Representative George Hansen of Idaho alleged the existence of "IRS Hit Lists, Snooping and Spying Operations, political retaliatory audits . . . and arbitrary assessments and seizures for punitive rather than tax collection purposes . . . ." The case against the Internal Revenue Service, however, was presented more strikingly by the alleged victims of Internal Revenue Service brutality, who methodically testified to individual confrontations with the service in great detail, including descriptions of forced detention, physical force, and the use of weapons for intimidation.

One taxpayer's wife, stricken with polio, needed an iron lung to keep her alive. An IRS agent threatened to seize the iron lung unless taxes claimed to be due were immediately forthcoming. The panicked taxpayer paid the claimed deficiency immediately.

IRS terrorists show no fear. In Kansas City, police officer Paul Campbell stopped a speeder and started to write a ticket. The offending driver, after making the usual objections, identified himself as an agent for the Internal Revenue Service. When Officer Campbell continued to write, the agent sneered, "We'll just have to check out your taxes." Soon after Campbell filed his next tax return, he was ordered to report to the Internal Revenue Service for an audit. It took four months of agency interrogations, repeated phone calls, and constant letter writing before the IRS finally admitted that Campbell owed it nothing.

In *Richman*, 78-1 U.S.T.C. Par. 9331, 41 AFTR 2d 78-1072 (DC Ill., 1978), the court was outraged at the lengths to which the IRS went to collect and keep some $5,000 to which, it turned out, it was not entitled. The IRS agents had padlocked the door to the taxpayer's place of business and discussed with the taxpayer the various sources from which he might beg or borrow the money in a conversation "distressingly like those between 'juice loan' debtors and creditors." The court found that the "conduct of the IRS agents was almost beyond belief."

In a more recent case, Senator Nancy Kassebaum (R-Kansas) remarked, "They should not be hit with outlandish penalties for failing to memorize the Federal Tax Code." She was talking about a $50 penalty against an 84-year-old Kansas City woman who underpaid her income tax by $0.60! According to the *Washington Post*, on July 11, 1984, one couple was assessed $205 when they were found to be one cent shy after paying taxes of nearly $9,000!

In a 1977 incident, several IRS collection agents bashed in the side window of a Volkswagen owned by a woman in Alaska who owed some taxes, then dragged her from the car and seized it as a payment for the money she owed. A photographer caught the incident on film; otherwise, it would have gotten little national notice.

According to Beryl Abbin, Director of Federal Tax Services for Arthur Andersen and Company, "On the local IRS level, you have some very bad apples out there—agents who try to push their way and intimidate."

In a recent study of the Internal Revenue Service, almost half the agents surveyed said they are hesitant to reveal their occupation to people they meet. Their general attitude is, "People don't trust us." Understandably so. As Internal Revenue Service agent Thomas Mennitt so succinctly put it in public testimony, "I violate laws at all times; it's part of my duties."[1] On June 28, 1987, the *Washington Post* reported three instances of the IRS intercepting first class mail and altering checks that were made out to third parties. These allegations followed an earlier report about a San Francisco man whose $1,300 mortgage check to a bank was intercepted by the IRS in July 1986. The words "Internal Revenue Service" were stamped over the bank's name, and the check was then cashed. According to Ronald Noll of the Pennsylvania Society of Public Accountants, testifying before a House subcommittee in Congress, "The IRS has sunk so low in public opinion that

---

1. Jeff A. Schnepper, *Inside IRS* (New York: Stein and Day, 1978), p. 187.

a responsible accountant honestly believes he needs a hood to protect himself from IRS retaliation." IRS agents have been authorized to pose as doctors, lawyers, journalists, and clergy to conduct undercover investigations.

Moreover, despite Internal Revenue Service National Office policy against collection quotas, IRS regional managers continue to instruct their revenue agents to make collections at almost any cost. According to a June 22, 1987, hearing before the Senate Finance Subcommittee on IRS Oversight, there is considerable competition among revenue officers and almost a daily comparison of what they have collected. Management challenges employees to "go out and make seizures . . . " and " . . . intimidation, and [the] abusiveness and harshness . . . is passed down to [the] taxpayers."

Apparently, no one is immune from foul-ups by the Internal Revenue Service. In the summer of 1987, the Internal Revenue Service acknowledged that it had accidentally placed an erroneous $338.85 lien against President and Mrs. Reagan. Although the lien was discovered and rescinded, it will remain a permanent entry in the County Court record system where it had been filed.

Fear of the Internal Revenue Service *is* justified. All too often IRS agents are arbitrary, antagonistic, and capricious. According to a study commissioned by the Federal Administrative Conference, the Internal Revenue Service has been found to be "whimsical, inconsistent, unpredictable, and highly personal" in dealing with those caught in its machinery. The study concluded, among other things, that different IRS districts follow different rules and that the same district can be either easy or tough depending upon whether it is ahead or behind its acknowledged "quota" for recoveries.

For example, according to the conference, a New Yorker's chances of being audited averaged 1:39, compared to 1:78 in New Mexico. IRS audit negotiators in Brooklyn averaged 32¢ on the dollar in settling disputes, while those in Baltimore extracted 74¢. In Albany, New York, six of every ten delinquent accounts led to tax seizures, but only three of ten did in New Mexico. The Federal Administrative Conference also found that the higher the deficiency the Internal Revenue Service claimed, the lower the percentage it finally accepted in settlement. The conference suggested that this was due to the ability of rich taxpayers to hire lawyers to argue their cases while poorer taxpayers had no choice but to pay up.

## Probability of an IRS Audit for Individuals

| | Audit Rate (%) |
|---|---|
| United States | 1.09 |
| | |
| **IRS Region** | |
| West (W) | 1.68 |
| Southwest (SW) | 1.55 |
| North Atlantic (NA) | 1.00 |
| Midwest (MW) | 0.90 |
| Central (C) | 0.86 |
| Southeast (SE) | 0.86 |
| Mid-Atlantic (MA) | 0.60 |
| | |
| **States and IRS Districts** | |
| 1. Alaska (W) | 2.46 |
| 2. Nevada (W) | 1.89 |
| 3. Wyoming (SW) | 1.68 |
| 4. Utah (SW) | 1.61 |
| 5. Oklahoma (SW) | 1.45 |
| 6. North Dakota (MW) | 1.40 |
| 7. Texas (all) (SW) | 1.36 |
| Austin District | 1.23 |
| Dallas District | 1.21 |
| Houston District | 1.81 |
| 8. California (all) | 1.31 |
| Laguna Niguel District | 1.46 |
| Los Angeles District | 1.18 |
| Sacramento District | 1.00 |
| San Francisco District | 1.77 |
| San Jose District | 1.22 |
| 9. Washington (W) | 1.20 |
| 10. Montana (MW) | 1.11 |
| 11. Colorado (SW) | 1.07 |
| 12. Arizona (SW) | 1.03 |
| International[a] | 0.99 |
| 13. Kansas (SW) | 0.95 |
| 14. Idaho (W) | 0.94 |
| 15. Hawaii (W) | 0.93 |
| 16. Georgia (SE) | 0.93 |

*(continued)*

| | |
|---|---:|
| 17. Illinois (all) (MW) | 0.93 |
|     Chicago District | 1.01 |
|     Springfield District | 0.71 |
| 18. Louisiana (SE) | 0.71 |
| 19. New Mexico (SW) | 0.93 |
| 20. Ohio (all) (C) | 0.90 |
|     Cincinnati District | 0.69 |
|     Cleveland District | 1.06 |
| 21. Minnesota (MW) | 0.89 |
| 22. New York (all) (NA) | 0.89 |
|     Albany District | 0.68 |
|     Brooklyn District | 0.82 |
|     Buffalo District | 0.72 |
|     Manhattan District | 1.30 |
| 23. Delaware (MA) | 0.86 |
| 24. Nebraska (MW) | 0.85 |
| 25. Maryland[b] (MA) | 0.81 |
| 26. Missouri (MW) | 0.81 |
| 27. Alabama (SE) | 0.80 |
| 28. Indiana (C) | 0.77 |
| 29. Mississippi (SE) | 0.77 |
| 30. Oregon (W) | 0.77 |
| 31. Vermont (NA) | 0.77 |
| 32. Tennessee (SE) | 0.76 |
| 33. Florida (SE) | 0.74 |
| 34. South Dakota (MW) | 0.72 |
| 35. Connecticut (NA) | 0.70 |
| 36. West Virginia (C) | 0.70 |
| 37. Pennsylvania (all) (MA) | 0.69 |
|     Philadelphia District | 0.71 |
|     Pittsburgh District | 0.64 |
| 38. Michigan (C) | 0.67 |
| 39. Virginia (MA) | 0.64 |
| 40. South Carolina (SE) | 0.63 |
| 41. Arkansas (SE) | 0.62 |
| 42. Kentucky (C) | 0.62 |
| 43. New Jersey (MA) | 0.62 |
| 44. Iowa (MW) | 0.59 |
| 45. North Carolina (SE) | 0.59 |
| 46. New Hampshire (NA) | 0.58 |
| 47. Wisconsin (MW) | 0.57 |
| 48. Massachusetts (NA) | 0.57 |
| 49. Rhode Island (NA) | 0.56 |
| 50. Maine (NA) | 0.54 |

*Source:* Derived from statistics in the 1987 Commissioner's Annual Report.

[a]Returns filed in Puerto Rico and from abroad.

[b]Includes the District of Columbia.

### Average Yield of an IRS Audit

| | |
|---|---|
| **United States** | $5,330 |
| | |
| **IRS Region** | |
| Southwest (SW) | $7,883 |
| North Atlantic (NA) | $7,606 |
| Mid-Atlantic (MA) | $5,013 |
| West (W) | $4,441 |
| Southeast (SE) | $4,401 |
| Midwest (MW) | $3,665 |
| Central (C) | $3,424 |
| | |
| **States and IRS Districts** | |
| 1. Colorado (SW) | $17,614 |
| 2. Texas (all) (SW) | $9,780 |
|    Austin District | $4,002 |
|    Dallas District | $1,665 |
|    Houston District | $6,789 |
| 3. Alaska (W) | $8,973 |
| 4. Maryland[a] (MA) | $7,532 |
| 5. Oklahoma (SW) | $7,382 |
| 6. Arkansas (SE) | $7,218 |
| 7. Florida (all) SE | $7,136 |
|    Fort Lauderdale District | $8,980 |
|    Jacksonville District | $5,826 |
| 8. Nevada (W) | $6,566 |
| 9. New Jersey (MA) | $6,341 |
| 10. Idaho (W) | $6,295 |
| 11. New York (all) NA | $6,216 |
|    Albany District | $3,846 |
|    Brooklyn District | $6,216 |
|    Buffalo District | $3,846 |
|    Manhattan District | $8,414 |
| 12. Massachusetts (NA) | $5,642 |
| 13. California (all) (W) | $5,608 |
|    Laguna Niguel District | $4,735 |
|    Los Angeles District | $9,538 |
|    Sacramento District | $4,138 |
|    San Francisco District | $3,884 |
|    San Jose District | $3,884 |

*(continued)*

| | |
|---|---|
| 14. Oregon (NW) | $5,561 |
| International[b] | $5,391 |
| 15. Illinois (all) (MW) | $5,176 |
| Chicago District | $5,590 |
| Springfield District | $3,422 |
| 16. Kansas (SW) | $4,825 |
| 17. Pennsylvania (all) (MA) | $4,572 |
| Philadelphia District | $5,089 |
| Pittsburgh District | $3,550 |
| 18. Utah (SW) | $4,372 |
| 19. Michigan (C) | $4,315 |
| 20. Arizona (SW) | $4,290 |
| 21. Tennessee (SE) | $4,178 |
| 22. Wyoming (SW) | $4,154 |
| 23. Louisiana (SE) | $4,140 |
| 24. New Hampshire (NA) | $3,957 |
| 25. Connecticut (MA) | $3,889 |
| 26. Hawaii (W) | $3,882 |
| 27. Delaware (MA) | $3,756 |
| 28. Georgia (SE) | $3,727 |
| 29. Kentucky (C) | $3,713 |
| 30. Virginia (MA) | $3,640 |
| 31. New Mexico (SW) | $3,590 |
| 32. Ohio (all) (C) | $3,534 |
| Cincinnati District | $3,057 |
| Cleveland District | $3,765 |
| 33. Wisconsin (MW) | $3,382 |
| 34. North Carolina (SE) | $3,286 |
| 35. South Carolina (SE) | $3,209 |
| 36. Washington (NW) | $3,188 |
| 37. Indiana (C) | $3,180 |
| 38. Maine (NE) | $3,069 |
| 39. Iowa (MW) | $3,049 |
| 40. Rhode Island (NE) | $2,965 |
| 41. Minnesota (MW) | $2,949 |
| 42. Missouri (MW) | $2,922 |
| 43. Nebraska (MW) | $2,728 |
| 44. South Dakota (MW) | $2,629 |
| 45. Mississippi (SE) | $2,529 |
| 46. Alabama (SE) | $2,513 |
| 47. West Virginia (SE) | $2,375 |
| 48. Montana (MW) | $2,181 |
| 49. Vermont (NE) | $2,095 |
| 50. North Dakota (MW) | $1,825 |

*Source:* Derived from statistics in the 1987 Commissioner's Annual Report.
[a]Includes the District of Columbia.
[b]Returns filed in Puerto Rico and from abroad.

### Percentage of Returns Examined Based on Geographical Location in 1986

|  | Individual | Corporation | Partnership |
|---|---|---|---|
| Manhattan, N.Y. | 1.49% | 1.64% | 1.61% |
| San Francisco, Calif. | 2.11 | 3.91 | 1.35 |
| Chicago, Ill. | 0.91 | 1.67 | 1.18 |
| New Orleans, La. | 1.21 | 1.54 | 0.99 |
| Dallas, Tex. | 1.50 | 1.91 | 1.24 |
| Boston, Mass. | 0.58 | 1.60 | 0.58 |
| Atlanta, Ga. | 0.97 | 1.70 | 1.25 |
| Los Angeles, Calif. | 1.73 | 1.73 | 1.50 |
| Newark, N.J. | 0.89 | 1.30 | 1.09 |
| Detroit, Mich. | 0.72 | 1.61 | 0.83 |
| Jacksonville, Fla. | 0.87 | 0.82 | 1.14 |
| Philadelphia, Pa. | 0.69 | 1.33 | 0.83 |

### Percentage of Returns Examined Based on Geographical Location in 1984

|  | Individual | Corporation | Partnership |
|---|---|---|---|
| Manhattan, N.Y. | 1.98% | 2.83% | 3.42% |
| San Francisco, Calif. | 1.38 | 2.08 | 1.71 |
| Chicago, Ill. | 0.99 | 2.65 | 1.28 |
| New Orleans, La. | 1.31 | 2.01 | 1.37 |
| Dallas, Tex. | 1.21 | 2.79 | 1.54 |
| Boston, Mass. | 0.69 | 2.68 | 2.25 |
| Atlanta, Ga. | 1.21 | 2.37 | 2.27 |
| Los Angeles, Calif. | 1.89 | 1.41 | 2.57 |
| Jacksonville, Fla. | 1.37 | 1.41 | 2.02 |
| Newark, N.J. | 1.34 | 1.86 | 1.17 |

The last two charts show the variation in the percentage of returns examined in 1986 and 1984 in various IRS districts.

The variations between these districts may be, at least in part, due to differences in income categories—i.e., a greater or lesser proportion of "high-income" returns.

Currently, Congress is considering a Taxpayer's Bill of Rights. The creation of Senator David Pryor of Arkansas, it consists of procedural safeguards and penalties to help clarify and ensure the rights and obligations of a taxpayer and the IRS during an audit or appeal, as well as during the refund and collection processes. As Finance Committee Chairman Lloyd Bentsen put it, the bill's provisions counter the "bully mentality" that many taxpayers perceive behind IRS tax law enforcement. The focus of the bill is to create a more balanced relationship between the tax agency and the citizenry. Although the bill has strong support within Congress, as of this writing it has not yet been signed into law.

Short of adopting a vow of poverty and hiding in a monastery or joining the ever-growing army of tax evaders, what can you do? The best defense is a good offense. If you know how the service works internally and where it is vulnerable, you can at least better your odds of winning when the tax man calleth.

Making your return indistinguishable from the "average" individual return can lessen your chances of facing an audit. Once you have prepared and signed your return, you mail it to the IRS Regional Service Center for your geographical area. The center checks some of the figures and transfers all information to magnetic tape, which then goes to the IRS computer center in Martinsburg, West Virginia. Here it becomes part of a master file for the Internal Revenue Service's complex automatic data processing system, which computerized tax data from 86 million individual tax returns plus corporate, fiduciary, gift and estate, excise tax, and employee plan returns, totaling over 193 million returns for fiscal 1987. With the master file, the Internal Revenue Service can locate people who fail to file returns and taxpayers who do not report such income as dividends or bank interest. Each tax return is assigned a document locator number (DLN) by the local Service Center. To better understand the document locator system, let us "decode" a hypothetical DLN: 3414133300134. Working from left to right, the digits indicate the following:

    34 = the IRS district (viz., the Cleveland District)
     1 = the tax class (viz., withholding tax)
    41 = the document code (viz., Form 941)
   333 = the control date (the numeric day of the year remittance was
          made)
   001 = the block number
    34 = the serial number of the specific DLN

An understanding of the document locator number system can help you better understand the communication process of the Internal Revenue Service.

In addition to printing out notices and letters to advise you of a tax refund due, to request information, or to report actions taken on returns already filed and the status of your account, the system is programmed to check returns for three basic mistakes.

First, all returns are examined for mathematical errors. Mistakes in arithmetic or in transferring figures from one schedule to another—for example, the total of excess itemized deductions to the Form 1040—result in an immediate correction notice. If the error leads to a tax deficiency, you automatically receive a bill for that amount. If you overpaid, the excess is applied to future taxes, credited, or refunded at your request. You cannot appeal such corrections, but you can ask in writing that they be reviewed. Errors in arithmetic alone rarely lead to a full audit.

The Internal Revenue Service's second computer check also provides for automatic adjustments to your return before any audit is made. This Unallowable Items Program is designed to catch clearly illegal deductions, such as claiming an exemption for a spouse who is filing separately. Under this program, the computer cross-checks reported income against the W-2 forms received from your employer. The dividends and interest reported by banks, brokerage houses, and other financial institutions are cross-checked in about 90 percent of the cases. The Internal Revenue Service attempts to match almost 100 percent of the information returns that they receive on computer tape and about 50 percent of those that are on paper. As a result of this cross-checking, the Internal Revenue Service sends out notices for taxes and interest on overdue taxes or for income or other payments that were not reported. Unfortunately, however, according to IRS statistics, about one notice in four is in error even though IRS workers personally check each return that the computers question. If you get an incorrect notice, follow the appropriate procedures to contest it, or contact your local Problem Resolution Office.

Another common mistake picked up by this program is a claim for a deduction that exceeds limits set by the Internal Revenue Service tax code. For example, not all medical expenses may be claimed. You may itemize and write off only those medical expenses that exceed 7.5 percent of adjusted gross income. The Unallowable Items Program is also likely to catch excessive deductions for charitable contributions or failure to reduce a "casualty loss" by $100, as required by the tax code. When an adjustment is made, you receive a letter allowing you to explain or protest. If you accept the change, you are asked to sign the "correction notice."

Unless the mistakes are extensive, these automatic adjustments do not usually lead to a full audit. However, basic errors like these should be avoided: Anytime your return is made to stand out, *for any reason,* it increases your chances for a full audit, with all the corresponding consequences.

Another IRS program for checking tax returns is the Questionable Items Program. Here, your whole return or a part of it is subjected to a detailed investigation. You are, in effect, being challenged rather than corrected. You must justify each deduction to the last penny, and to the satisfaction of the examining agent.

IRS computer programs use three techniques to decide which returns to review under this program: random selection, "discriminate function" selection, and special target selection.

Your income, claimed deductions, and profession are irrelevant when returns are selected at random. A student earning only $3,000 a year at part-time jobs may be invited to the local IRS office for a tax audit only to find a business executive making $300,000 in the same situation.

Once the return is in the computer, you are at the mercy of the second selection criterion—"discriminant function" analysis. Based on previous experience, the Internal Revenue Service has created a number of composite hypothetical "taxpayers." These composite "norms" are determined by interviewing a random selection of taxpayers. Unfortunately, this can be a horror for the taxpayer selected as a "norm": The IRS agent asks questions about every single item on the return; the taxpayer has to produce a birth certificate, marriage certificate—the works. Each item is checked, and the results are fed into the computer. In a "discriminant function" analysis, the characteristics of these "average" taxpayers are given different weights and compared to a return selected for audit.

First, the deductions on the selected returns are added up and weighed for what is called the "discriminant function" score. The computer then recommends audits for significantly differing returns. The computer is also programmed to notice special deviations. For example, it may recommend an audit if all your deductions turn out to be nicely rounded even numbers. It will also compare your deductions to your job. A person who works as a construction laborer will rarely have a need for a home office deduction. The computer model-match takes into account income level, profession, number of dependents claimed, whether your spouse works, and even your address: A Beverly Hills zip code with a ghetto-level reported income will immediately signal for an audit. According to former IRS Commissioner

Roscoe L. Egger, Jr., two-thirds of the audited returns are selected on the basis of the IRS discriminate function formula. The rest are chosen on the basis of tax-avoiding trends, such as abusive tax shelters.

You should also understand the bar-coded envelopes and peel-off labels that come with your returns. Some taxpayers believe that the coding somehow triggers an audit. In fact, the coding simply allows the IRS to process the mail on their automatic sorting machine, which reads the bar codes and separates the mail by type of return (i.e., 1040A, 1040EZ, 1040), thus expediting processing. Uncoded mail must be sorted by hand, which is much more time-consuming and slows up processing, which slows up refunds.

The coded numbers on the preprinted address label affixed to your tax package also speed up processing of returns and expedite refunds. Again, the label coding has no relationship to audits. It assures the IRS that the name and social security number are valid and it includes, for each taxpayer, an assigned "check digit"—two characters based on the taypayer's name. Data transcribers pick up the two-stroke check digit and the social security number from the label to input tax information to a taxpayer's account. If the label is not used, your full name, social security number, and complete address must be input—significantly extending processing time and adding the potential for common errors that delay the issuance of refunds. The illustration on this page shows the preprinted label and explains the meaning of the various coded symbols.

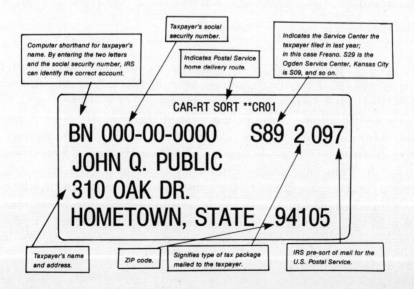

Computer shorthand for taxpayer's name. By entering the two letters and the social security number, IRS can identify the correct account.

Taxpayer's social security number.

Indicates Postal Service home delivery route.

Indicates the Service Center the taxpayer filed in last year; in this case Fresno. S29 is the Ogden Service Center, Kansas City is S09, and so on.

CAR-RT SORT **CR01

BN 000-00-0000     S89 2 097
JOHN Q. PUBLIC
310 OAK DR.
HOMETOWN, STATE  94105

Taxpayer's name and address.

ZIP code.

Signifies type of tax package mailed to the taxpayer.

IRS pre-sort of mail for the U.S. Postal Service.

Actually, a single oversized deduction will probably not trigger an immediate audit. For you the name of the game is to match the computer's norm as closely as possible. The accompanying table reveals average deductions claimed on returns filed in 1987 for 1986.

#### Average Itemized Deductions for 1986 by Adjusted Gross Income

| Adjusted Gross Income Ranges | Average Deductions for | | | |
|---|---|---|---|---|
| | Medical Expenses | Taxes | Contributions | Interest |
| Under $5,000 | $ 3,469 | $ 839 | $ 428 | $ 2,834 |
| $5,000–$10,000 | 3,269 | 1,113 | 583 | 2,583 |
| $10,000–$15,000 | 2,611 | 1,391 | 663 | 2,979 |
| $15,000–$20,000 | 2,012 | 1,629 | 720 | 3,137 |
| $20,000–$25,000 | 1,795 | 1,855 | 767 | 3,298 |
| $25,000–$30,000 | 1,548 | 2,331 | 815 | 3,636 |
| $30,000–$40,000 | 1,817 | 2,817 | 885 | 4,369 |
| $40,000–$50,000 | 2,201 | 3,590 | 1,077 | 5,305 |
| $50,000–$75,000 | 3,330 | 4,869 | 1,499 | 6,910 |
| $75,000–$100,000 | 4,887 | 7,241 | 2,468 | 10,151 |
| $100,000–$200,000 | 12,603 | 11,603 | 4,308 | 13,939 |
| $200,000–$500,000 | 28,636 | 23,737 | 16,393 | 22,761 |
| $500,000–$1 million | 31,738 | 48,283 | 31,983 | 41,593 |
| $1 million and over | 62,000 | 151,897 | 199,875 | 97,161 |

*Source:* 1986 Statistics of Income, Internal Revenue Service.

A dual expansion of IRS computer operations was substantially completed in 1985. First, the major equipment replacement program, with a new UNIVAC 1100 System, was made operational in all 10 Service Centers. This new system triples current capacity and speed of the old equipment. Second, administration of office examinations is now computerized and operates from the 10 Service Centers. As District appointments become available, the computer selects cases by priority and generates both appointments and taxpayer notification letters. These letters detail the time and place of the examination, the issues to be resolved, what to bring, etc. The new system also identifies whether the taxpayer has other years under examination and automatically routes the new examination to the same agent.

After the computers have "graded" income tax returns to determine their "audit worthiness," the returns with the highest scores are screened by humans. The following characteristics are what these human screeners look for:

- Insufficient income to support claimed deductions.

- Refunds out of line with gross income and exemptions.

- Possibility of unreported income.

- Profit from business or profession below the "norm."

- Investment yield or profits below the interest income that would have been earned if the funds had been deposited in savings accounts.

Other Internal Revenue Service guidelines used in choosing returns to be audited include:

- Comparative size of the item—a questionable expense item of $5,000 when expenses total $25,000 would be significant; however, if total expenses were $250,000, the item ordinarily would not be significant.

- Absolute size of the item—despite the comparability factor, size itself may be significant. For example, a $60,000 item may be significant even though it represents a small percentage of taxable income.

- Inherent character of the item—although the amount of an item may be insignificant, the *nature* of the item may be significant. For example, airplane expenses claimed by a carpenter may be significant.

- Evidence of intent to mislead—this may include missing, misleading, or incomplete schedules, or showing an item incorrectly on the return.

- Beneficial effect of the manner in which an item is reported—expenses claimed on a business schedule rather than claimed as itemized deductions may be significant.

- Relationship to other items—the absence of a deduction for interest expense when real estate taxes are claimed may be significant. Similarly, the lack of dividends reported when the return shows sales of stock may also be significant.

According to a recently declassified handbook, the IRS looks for the following in selecting returns for an audit: exemptions claimed by non-custodial parents; losses claimed on rental property recently converted from a residence; and high receipt, low net profit business schedules for nonitemizers. The above deductions are listed as higher priority items than large medical expenses of large families or older taxpayers, home mortgage interest, auto expenses of users of the standard mileage rate, or transportation expenses of construction workers who work at more than one job site for more than one employer (*The Classification Handbook*, IRMO 41 (12) 0).

The Internal Revenue Service expects its management to use employee time productively. Therefore, each year, top administrators will "target" taxpayers in specific professions or with incomes from unusual sources where the highest potential monetary recovery may be found. For example, dentists, doctors, lawyers, and even accountants may receive much of their income in cash payments. The Internal Revenue Service believes that this permits them to "forget" to report all of their receipts. The Service also believes that the incentive to underreport would be greatly dulled if these professionals knew that, as a class, they were more likely to be audited. Therefore, as a class, they *are* more likely to be audited.

The IRS audit manual, *The Policies of the Internal Revenue Service Handbook*, sets as the "primary objective" in selection of tax returns "*the highest possible revenue yield from the examination man hours expended,* and the examination of as many returns as is feasible for the maintenance of a high degree of voluntary taxpayer compliance." (author's italics)

Our federal income tax rates are imposed on a graduated progressive schedule. When you earn $1 more than the top of the previous bracket, a higher percentage of that *additional* dollar will be taken as taxes. Therefore, the more money you earn, the higher the potential return is likely to be on the time invested by the Internal Revenue Service in the case. If an agent denies a $100 deduction to a taxpayer in the 33 percent bracket, the United States Treasury receives $33, as opposed to only $15 from a taxpayer in the 15 percent bracket.

The Internal Revenue Service has also found that returns filed by people who make over $50,000 provide fertile grounds for audit reviews. Other groups watched closely include taxpayers with a second or sideline business, those who report hefty capital gain income, and all who might be involved in a partnership tax shelter.

The IRS has lately adopted a new, more efficient system for classifying individual taxpayers of similar economic circumstances in order to select returns for an audit. In the past, returns were selected on the basis of adjusted gross income. Under that old system, individuals were selected for audit by separating business and nonbusiness returns, grouping them into examination classes according to adjusted gross income, and running each class through the mathematical "discriminant function" formula to identify returns with high audit potential.

This system had definite drawbacks from the Internal Revenue Service's perspective, because adjusted gross income is determined *after* deductions and adjustments, which are of primary interest to auditors. A return showing a high gross income but large offsetting deductions (as from tax shelters) would present a relatively low adjusted gross income. Therefore, it would be assigned to a low adjusted gross income examination class, would generally receive light audit coverage, and would be scored under a "discriminant function" formula not geared to test its true audit potential.

The IRS's new classification system is based upon total positive income, relying on the total income of a taxpayer *before* adjustments or deductions. This is the sum of all positive items on your return. Any negative items—for instance, losses from tax shelters—are treated as zero. As a result of this reclassification, suspicious deductions and adjustments will not escape notice in, or distort the voluntary compliance level of, an examination class designed for lower-income taxpayers.

There is an additional reason why your return might be chosen for an audit. While the Internal Revenue Service does not publicly encourage tax informers, its representatives admit that many investigations could not be successfully conducted without the use of paid informants or the direct purchase of evidence. Most informers are former employees of a business that has been underreporting its income. A disgruntled employee who does not "rat" on the business itself may "rat" on its owner, or on a disliked manager.

But a neighbor who objects to your loud stereo at midnight or becomes jealous of your new car each year may just as quickly turn informer. These unofficial "agents" are used extensively in cases where the taxpayer under investigation is allegedly engaged in illegal activity. Tax informers are normally rewarded with up to 10 percent of the additional tax collected up to a $100,000 maximum. The Internal Revenue Service paid $853,698 in the year ending September 30, 1984, to informants who provided it with information that enabled it to collect extra taxes from cheats. That figure was up 36 percent from the year before and up 56 percent from 1982. The IRS does not divulge the identity of its informants, but such rewards are fully taxable.

Over the last nine years, only about one out of every eleven claims from tipsters has been judged worthy of a reward. In 1986, the IRS paid a reward on 820 claims. However, tipsters helped the IRS recover $258 million in additional taxes, more than five times the $48 million recovered in 1985. Informers normally receive 10 percent of the first $75,000 recovered, 5 percent of the next $25,000, and 1 percent of everything over that. To them, though, the money is often secondary to revenge. You should, therefore, keep two rules in mind:

1. Never cheat on your income taxes.

2. If you do, never anger anyone who might know about it.

Despite its image as a bureaucracy of terror, in all fairness another side of the IRS story must be told. Even before the so-called Tax Simplification Act of 1978, the service was responsible for interpreting and administrating codes, regulations, and revenue manuals that filled over 32 shelf-feet with an incredible 40,000 pages of the most arcane, unintelligible gobbledygook ever written. There have been several "tax reform" bills since 1978.

The law is so complex, so convoluted, that it is incomprehensible. As former Citicorp Chairman Walter B. Wriston pointed out: "All the Congress, all the accountants and tax lawyers, all the judges and a convention of wizards cannot tell for sure what the income tax law says." Asked to perform an impossible function, it's not surprising that the IRS agent often fails.

Such failure was documented by Ralph Nader's Tax Reform Research Group. They prepared 22 identical tax reports based on the fictional economic plight of a married couple with one child, and these twenty-two identical copies were submitted to 22 different IRS offices around the country.

Each office came up with an entirely different tax figure. The results varied from a refund of $811.96 recommended in Flushing, New York, to a tax-due figure of $52.14 derived by the tax office in Portland, Oregon. The General Accounting Office revealed in 1981 that Internal Revenue advisers were providing the wrong answer to one out of every ten questions asked by taxpayers.

In 1983, *USA Today* took an informal telephone survey of IRS tax-assistance offices in 15 major cities across the United States. Seven questions were picked that private tax consultants agreed were common and difficult but fair. For each question, interviewers called ten IRS telephone tax assistants—70 phone calls in all. In 20 cases—28.6 percent of the time—the Internal Revenue Service's answers were wrong. In five more cases, the Internal Revenue Service's answers were only partly correct, bringing the total of incorrect or incomplete answers to 35.7 percent.

Furthermore, getting through to the Internal Revenue Service by phone was close to impossible. In the *USA Today* study, it was found that the IRS telephone line was busy nine times out of ten in New York City. When it did ring, the phone often went unanswered. On one try it rang 48 times before being picked up, and twice it rang 25 times to no avail.

On February 12, 1985, the *Wall Street Journal* asked the same four tax law questions to 17 IRS offices. Two questions, involving the casualty loss deduction and one-time diesel credit, were answered correctly most of the time. The other two, involving the medical expense deduction and the wash sale rules, resulted in totally or partially wrong answers most of the time. Walter M. Alt, Director of the IRS Taxpayers' Services Division, told the *Journal* that he was "dismayed and unhappy" about the errors. IRS advice is not binding—whether oral or in print. In fact, the IRS is not bound by statements contained in its own publications, including *Your Federal Income Tax*, the IRS's free instruction booklet (*Thomas R. Underwood*, T.C. Memo 1983–99; *Harvey Richard Bennett*, T.C. Memo 1983–183; see also *Sundermeier,* T.C. Memo 1987–50, wherein taxpayers were not permitted to rely on an IRS publication, even though their local IRS office advised them that there was no other information available).

According to U.S. District Court Judge Michael M. Mihm, in his opinion in *Sinn Oil Company, et al. v. United States*: "The case law has girded the Internal Revenue Service with a nearly impregnable shield against the people it serves. Beginning with a Code which in its complexity is well nigh unfathomable to the average citizen . . . the judicial coup de grace is executed with the insistence that, if the taxpayer could find the relevant section and if he could be assured that there is not some supervening or nullifying regulation elsewhere and if he could then read and understand it, his reliance on the verbal representations of an agent [is] unreasonable."

The General Accounting Office did a study of its own: It checked out a sample of 2,543 tax returns in which the Internal Revenue Service had found 3,720 errors in arithmetic. Unfortunately, the General Accounting Office noted that the Internal Revenue Service itself had made nearly two-thirds of the errors. The General Accounting Office said that 33 million errors were found on the 94 million individual income tax returns processed in the fiscal year 1981, of which 37 percent were made by taxpayers and *63 percent* were made by employees of the IRS!

Another General Accounting Office survey in February and March of 1987 also faulted the accuracy of the IRS taxpayer telephone assistance program. The GAO found that taxpayers who called the Internal Revenue Service with tax law questions got inaccurate or incomplete answers more than one-third of the time. The survey showed that the IRS assisters provided correct answers to basic questions posed by callers from the General Accounting Office 63 percent of the time, correct but incomplete answers 15 percent of the time, and incorrect answers 22 percent of the time. (Things are no better when the IRS takes the time to write. A GAO review dated May 24, 1988, found that IRS centers issued incorrect, incomplete, unresponsive, or unclear correspondence only half the time. The GAO considered IRS errors in 30 percent of this correspondence critical; these letters each contained at least one instance in which the Adjustment/ Correspondence Branch either provided incorrect information, failed to address all the taxpayer's questions, or acted incorrectly in adjusting or failing to adjust the taxpayer's account.)

Thankfully, IRS Commissioner Lawrence Gibbs, in a hearing of the Senate Finance Committee on Private Retirement Plans and IRS Oversight, stated that the IRS would not impose penalties on taxpayers who relied on incorrect information supplied by IRS telephone taxpayer assistance personnel. Nevertheless, the tax itself would not be forgiven, and the taxpayer would have the burden of maintaining a record of the name of the IRS employee who supplied the incorrect information as well as the date of the conversation.

Internal Revenue Code Section 7605(a) gives the IRS the authority to fix the time and place of an audit as is reasonable under the circumstances. The Internal Revenue Manual states that IRS examiners should endeavor to make appointments at a time and place convenient for the taxpayer (IRM 4261.2).

Generally, the office that handles your audit will be determined by your domicile—where you live. However, the Internal Revenue Service will approve a request for a transfer of an audit if your domicile has changed before or during the examination or if you have died and your legal representative is in another district. The following rules for audit location generally apply:

1. A request for a transfer to a district closer to your residence will normally be approved.

2.  If you live in one district, work in another, and are not represented by a Power of Attorney, you will be examined in the district where you reside.

3.  If you are called for an audit in one district but live in another district that is within commuting distance (not defined) of the first, and are represented by a Power of Attorney within that distance, the audit will normally take place in the district where you reside.

4.  If you live in one district and are represented by a Power of Attorney doing business in another district that is within commuting distance of the first, you will be audited in the district where you live.

5.  If you live in another district outside commuting distance of the district where your return is scheduled for audit and are represented by a Power of Attorney in the other district, you will have a transfer request approved.

6.  If you reside in the district where the audit is scheduled and are represented by a Power of Attorney in a district outside commuting distance of the first, you may obtain a transfer if the receiving district agrees.

Each IRS district office is made up of four divisions. Each division is subdivided into branches, the titles of which describe what is done in each branch. The four divisions are Administration, Collection, Audit, and Intelligence.

The Administration Division handles such matters as personnel, training, and facilities management of all types—from selection of the site of the office to ordering pens and paper.

The Collection Division is the bill-collecting arm of the Internal Revenue Service. It is represented in the field by Revenue Officers and in the Office Branch. The Collection Division also has a section known as the Taxpayer Service Section, which is a year-round information center manned by Taxpayer Service Representatives.

The Intelligence Division is the branch of the Internal Revenue Service that handles criminal investigations. It is staffed with Special Agents, who are enforcement officers and whose work is primarily technical. The main objective of an investigation by a Special Agent is to determine whether or not there should be criminal prosecution—as contrasted with an Internal Revenue Agent's objective, which is to determine the proper tax to be paid.

The Audit Division is charged with verifying the accuracy of tax returns filed, regarding both the substance of the law and the validity of the amounts reported. The major branches of the Audit Division are Field Audit, Office Audit, Review, and Audit Service. They have been renamed Examinations Branch. Field Audit employs Internal Revenue Agents and Estate Tax Examiners, and they are charged with auditing the more complex tax returns filed. Office Audit is staffed with Tax Auditors, who primarily audit individual returns. The Review staff is composed of former Field Agents and Tax Auditors, who check the accuracy of the audits made by the examining officers. Audit Service maintains the files on prior reports by examining officers and is a control center for cases under audit or cases that have been audited.

Victims of IRS errors now have a form on which to claim reimbursement. Such a claim is allowable under 31 U.S.C. Section 3732 but is limited to $1,000 and must be submitted within one year of its accrual. Filers of new Form 8489, Claim for Reimbursement for Expenses Incurred Due to Service Error, are instructed to submit substantiating documentation and are cautioned not to claim expenses for telephone calls, mileage or parking, lost wages, postage, or other nonreimbursable costs of the kind that are common to any disputed bill.

The scope of an audit will depend on various factors, but according to a recent addition to the IRS Manual, there are four items that *must* be reviewed by an agent:

1. Income probes, including bank statement analysis, bartering schemes, sale of assets, prizes, alimony, pensions, income tax refunds, etc.

2. Determination of the results of previous audits, including when the last took place, the results, and any recent correspondence the taxpayer may have had with the IRS.

3. Examination of subsequent and prior years' returns to make sure whether they were filed on time, where similar adjustments to the year under examination are necessary, and whether there are other issues that should be probed.

4. Determination of whether penalties have been previously assessed and whether they should be assessed as a result of the current examination.

The IRS Manual instructs the agents to comment on these items in their workpapers or to document the reasons why they were not examined.

According to IRS guidelines, unless specific recordkeeping requirements must be met, statements by the taxpayer, or others, may serve as adequate evidence in an audit. The IRS Manual notes that adequate evidence does not require complete documentation (IRM 4231, Audit Guidelines for Examiners, 330[2]).

Because the law is so vague in spots and so complicated, an intensive review and appeals procedure is available to you. Once your audit has been completed, the agent will present a Revenue Agent's Report stating recommendations and advising of any additional tax you owe. You will then be asked to sign a waiver indicating that you agree with the assessment. At this point you have three choices:

1. You can accept the adjustments, sign the waiver, and pay the tax.

2. You can pay the tax and file for a refund of the disputed amount.

3. You can request a conference with the IRS Appellate Division.

Prior to October 2, 1978, you could have taken a dispute with a revenue agent to a district conference. If an agreement was not reached there, a second hearing was available at the appellate division level. Alternatively, you could have elected to go directly to the appellate division. Under the present system the Internal Revenue Service maintains appeals offices at all locations where full-time district conferees and regional appellate offices were formerly located. The theory of eliminating the district conference is that, according to the Internal Revenue Service, the two-level system of administrative review was a costly duplication, for both the taxpayer and the service.

The Internal Revenue Service believes that settlement results under the new single level of appeal are comparable to those under the old two-level appeal system. About 85 percent of the cases were agreed or defaulted in fiscal 1979. Of the remainder, about 5 percent claimed refunds and 10 percent filed tax court petitions.

It is almost universally agreed that it is best to settle at the agent level, if possible. If the tax deficiency involved is small, it may not justify the cost in time and dollars of pursuing your case to a higher level. Moreover, if the agent has missed items that you don't want questioned, your best approach may be to pay the deficiency and run. But *never* settle or concede any issue until the audit is completed. When the agent's cards are on the table, you have more leeway in planning your negotiation strategy.

For a psychological advantage, where appropriate, you may wish to tape record the audit proceedings. The Internal Revenue Service has revised the table of contents for, and added new text to, IRM 7600, Processing Determination Letter Applications. The new text, IRM 7610, Verbatim Recording of Conversations During Determination Proceedings, provides that verbatim recordings of Determination Proceedings will be permitted ordinarily with group manager approval (Manual Transmittal 7600-50 (11-18-83); *Mott*, 214 F. Supp. 20 (N.D. Cal. 1963); 1 Audit, CCH Internal Revenue Manual 4245; but see *Huehne*, 83-2345 (October 23), wherein the Court ruled that the taxpayer did not have a right to videotape the audit).

If you disagree with the agent's assessment, you will receive a copy of the revenue agent's report with a preliminary note advising you that you have 30 days to appeal. If you ignore this letter, you will then receive a "90-day" letter advising you to pay or to petition the tax court for redetermination.

After receiving the 30-day letter, but before receiving the 90-day letter, you may request a hearing by notifying your IRS regional appeals office. If the original audit was conducted by a tax auditor at an IRS office or by correspondence, you do not have to file a written protest to begin the appeal process. Until recently, if the disputed amount was $2,500 or less, the same was true of a field examination conducted at your place of business; and if your field audit resulted in a disputed amount over $2,500, a written protest was necessary. On October 16, 1987, these rules were changed by the IRS. Now, a written protest is required for field examinations only if the amount at issue for any tax year exceeds $10,000. (If the amount at issue does not exceed $10,000 but exceeds $2,500, a brief written statement of disputed issues is required. As under prior law, no brief written statement or written protest is required to obtain an appeals office conference, in-office interview, or correspondence examination. An oral request will still suffice.) The protest should be filed in duplicate and should contain the following:

a) your name and address;

b) the date and case reference symbols on the letter from the Internal Revenue Service transmitting the findings that you are protesting;

c) the tax years or periods involved;

d) an itemized schedule of adjustments or findings with which you do not agree;

e) a statement that you want to appeal the findings of the revenue agent;

f) a statement of factual evidence supporting your position in the contested issues, which should be sworn to as true, under penalties of perjury;

g) a statement outlining the law or other authority upon which you are relying.

In response to your protest, an appellate conferee will meet with you at the regional office to discuss the disputed issues. While such a hearing is an informal procedure, you must remember that the burden of proof is still on you to provide clear and convincing evidence that the revenue agent's report should be amended. While oral statements and evidence will be considered, the best evidence is documentary—books, records, worksheets, journals, and so forth.

The informality of the conference hearing is designed to save time and trouble for all parties. You may represent yourself, or you may be represented by an attorney, CPA, or individual licensed to practice before the Internal Revenue Service. The aim of this stage of the appeals process is to resolve the issues with as little difficulty as possible. The objective here is to *settle*! In fiscal 1979 IRS agents at this level proposed to assess $1,900,124,000 in added tax and penalties. They *closed* these cases for $1,161,977,000—about 61 percent of the proposed assessments. In 1982, appeals officers heard more than 50,000 cases covering an estimated 150,000 separate tax returns in over 500 locations. According to Howard T. Martin, director of the Appeals Division, "Appeal officers have more flexibility, and we never give up the idea of resolving a case." A 1982 survey by the General Accounting Office found that extra taxes and penalties were reduced or eliminated in 84 percent of the cases in appeals. Unlike agents at the audit level, Appeals Officers can settle cases based on "hazards of litigation." Thus, in Appeals, it is possible to split or trade issues.

The Internal Revenue Service tells its Appellate personnel to negotiate settlements "on a basis which is fair to both the Government and the taxpayer. Strive to close on an agreed basis the highest possible number of cases." They are to maintain an overall agreement rate of at least 85 percent in cases not yet docketed for trial in the Tax Court except for certain tax shelter, protestor, and similar cases. In docketed cases, the Internal Revenue Service wants to "maximize" settlements, with the aim to maintain or improve the agreement rate achieved in the previous year.

If you want to stop the running of interest on any potential deficiency, you are entitled to make what is known as a "deficiency deposit." Such a deposit should be made before the mailing of a deficiency notice and designated in writing as a "deposit in the nature of a cash bond." If you request a part or all of your deficiency deposit to be returned before the assessment of any tax, the request will be granted—unless the Internal Revenue Service determines that the deposit should be applied against a jeopardy assessment or another tax liability. No interest will be paid or allowed with respect to an amount returned to you.

There's one additional avenue of administrative redress for taxpayer problems. In 1977, the IRS instituted "problem resolution offices" (PROs) to handle problems that have not been resolved through normal channels. Such problems include not only complaints by disgruntled taxpayers but lost, stolen, or delayed refund checks, billing errors, and hardship situations. The following table lists the addresses and telephone numbers of all 59 problem resolution offices. For each district, address correspondence to the Problem Resolution Officer, Internal Revenue Service.

**Alabama**
2121 Eighth Ave. N.
Room 1205
Birmingham, AL 35203
205/254-1177

**Alaska**
P.O. Box 101500
Anchorage, AK 99510
907/261-4230

**Arizona**
2120 N. Central Ave.
Stop 504
Phoenix, AZ 85004
602/261-3604

**Arkansas**
P.O. Box 3778
Stop 3
Little Rock, AR 72203
501/378-6260

**California**
P.O. Box 36136
Stop 13-0-04
450 Golden Gate Ave.
San Francisco, CA 94102
415/556-5046

P.O. Box 1791
Los Angeles, CA 90053
213/688-6111

**Colorado**
P.O. Box 1302
Denver, CO 80201
303/844-2305

**Connecticut**
P.O. Box 959
Hartford, CT 06101
203/722-3473

**Delaware**
P.O. Box 2415
Wilmington, DE 19899
302/573-6052

**Florida**
P.O. Box 35045
Stop 800
Jacksonville, FL 32202
904/791-3440

**Georgia**
4800 Buford Hwy.
Room 513A
Chamblee, GA 30341
404/455-5232

**Hawaii**
P.O. Box 50089
Honolulu, HI 96850
808/546-8932

**Idaho**
550 W. Fort St.
Box 041
Boise, ID 83724
204/334-1324

**Illinois**
230 S. Dearborn St.
Room 2869
Chicago, IL 60604
312/886-4394

P.O. Box 398
Springfield, IL 62705
217/492-4517

**Indiana**
P.O. Box 44687
Indianapolis, IN 46244
317/269-6332

**Iowa**
P.O. Box 1337
Room 345
Des Moines, IA 50305
515/284-6223

**Kansas**
P.O. Box 2907
Wichita, KS 67201
316/269-6223

**Kentucky**
P.O. Box 1735
Louisville, KY 40201
502/582-6030

**Louisiana**
P.O. Box 30806
New Orleans, LA 70190
504/589-3001

**Maine**
P.O. Box 787
Augusta, ME 04330
207/780-3310

**Maryland**
P.O. Box 1553
Baltimore, MD 21203
301/962-2082

**Massachusetts**
310 Lowell St.
Andover, MA 05501
617/681-5549

**Michigan**
P.O. Box 32514
Detroit, MI 48232
313/226-7899

**Minnesota**
P.O. Box 43599
St. Paul, MN 55164
612/725-7077

**Mississippi**
100 W. Capital St.
Stop 31A
Suite 504, Room 101A
Jackson, MS 39201
601/960-4800

**Missouri**
P.O. Box 1548
St. Louis, MO 63188
314/425-6770

**Montana**
Federal Bldg. Drawer 10016
Helena, MT 59626
406/449-5244

**Nebraska**
106 S. 15th St.
Stop 2
Omaha, NE 68102
402/221-4181

**Nevada**
P.O. Box 16045
Las Vegas, NV 89101
702/388-6281

**New Hampshire**
P.O. Box 720
Portsmouth, NH 03801
603/433-0571

**New Jersey**
P.O. Box 476
Newark, NJ 07101
201/645-6263

**New Mexico**
P.O. Box 1040
Albuquerque, NM 87103
505/766-1197

**New York**
Leo O'Brien Federal Bldg.
Clinton Ave. & N. Pearl St.
Albany, NY 12207
518/472-4482

G.P.O. Box 380
Brooklyn, NY 11202
718/780-6511

P.O. Box 500
Niagara Square Station
Buffalo, NY 14201
716/846-4574

P.O. Box 408
Church Street Station
New York, NY 10008
212/264-2850

**North Carolina**
320 Federal Pl.
Room 214-B
Greensboro, NC 27401
914/378-5497

**North Dakota**
P.O. Box 8
Fargo, ND 58107
701/237-5771 Ext. 141

**Ohio**
P.O. Box 1818
Cincinnati, OH 45201
513/684-3094

P.O. Box 99709
Cleveland, OH 44199
800/424-1040

**Oklahoma**
P.O. Box 1040
Oklahoma City, OK 73101
405/272-9531

**Oregon**
P.O. Box 3341
Portland, OR 97208
503/221-2333

**Pennsylvania**
P.O. Box 12010
Philadelphia, PA 19106
215/597-3377

P.O. Box 705
Pittsburgh, PA 15230
412/644-5987

**Rhode Island**
P.O. Box 6528
Providence, RI 02940
401/528-4288

**South Carolina**
P.O. Box 386
Room 466
Columbia, SC 29202
803/253-3029

**South Dakota**
P.O. Box 370
Aberdeen, SD 57401
605/225-0250 Ext. 215

**Tennessee**
P.O. Box 1107
Stop 22
Nashville, TN 37202
615/251-5219

**Texas**
P.O. Box 1863
Stop 105
Austin, TX 78767
512/397-5875

P.O. Box 1040
Mail Code 171
Dallas, TX 75221
214/767-1289

3223 Briar Park Ave.
Stop 1005-BP
Houston, TX 77042
713/953-6436

**Utah**
P.O. Box 2069
Salt Lake City, UT 84110
801/524-6287

**Vermont**
11 Elmwood Ave.
Burlington, VT 05401
802/951-6354

**Virginia**
P.O. Box 10113
Richmond, VA 23240
804/771-2643

**Washington**
P.O. Box 2207
Mail Stop 405
Seattle, WA 98111
206/442-7393

**West Virginia**
P.O. Box 1388
Parkersburg, WV 26102
304/422-6616

**Wisconsin**
P.O. Box M-383
Room 118
Milwaukee, WI 53201
414/291-3046

**Wyoming**
308 W. 21st St.
Cheyenne, WY 82001
301/778-2162

When the Internal Revenue Service determines that a deficiency exists, it must first send you a notice of the deficiency determination. You are then allowed a specific period—normally 90 days, beginning with the mailing of the notice—in which to file a petition for redetermination with the Tax Court. At that point the Internal Revenue Service is prohibited, with certain exceptions, from undertaking any assessment or collection activity until the deficiency notice has been mailed, the specified period has expired, and, if a Tax Court petition has been timely filed, the decision has become final [Section 6213(a)]. During the time this prohibition is in force, it is expressly provided that any assessment or collection activity by the IRS is subject to injunctive relief, notwithstanding the Anti-Injunction Act.

An *assessment* is, in essence, a bookkeeping notation that occurs when the IRS establishes an account against a taxpayer on the tax rolls. Technically, the assessment is made by an assessment officer for the district or regional service center by signing the summary record of assessment, which, through supporting records, provides the taxpayer's identification, the type of tax and taxable period, and the amount of the assessment. The date of the assessment is the date of the signing.

As soon as practical, and within 60 days after making the assessment, the IRS must give you notice of the unpaid amount and demand its payment by leaving the notice at your dwelling or usual place of business or by mailing it to your last known address. If you neglect or refuse to pay within ten days after notice and demand, the IRS can proceed to collect the amount owed by levy. A *levy* includes the power of distraint and seizure by any means [IRC Section 6331(b)]. Ordinarily, a levy requires written notice of intent to levy at least ten days prior to the day of levy, either in person or by leaving it at the dwelling or usual place of business or by certified or registered mailing to the last known address of the taxpayer [IRC Section 6331(d)(1), (2)]. In circumstances where you neglect or refuse to pay the tax after demand, a lien is created in favor of the United States on all property owned by you. The lien arises from the date of the assessment and is effective as against certain persons upon proper filing of a notice of lien. The Internal Revenue Service possesses additional power, subject to certain limitations, to sell property that it has seized (see IRC Sections 6335 and 6336). Remember, however, that a petition to the Tax Court, timely filed, will prevent the Internal Revenue Service from proceeding with any of these potential administrative actions.

If you are not satisfied at the administrative level, you must go to court. Even if the law is probably in favor of the Internal Revenue Service, it may pay for you to move a case into the judiciary if the dollar amount is large enough. This is because it provides an additional opportunity for you to compromise the case. When you go to court, the case is removed from the jurisdiction of the Internal Revenue Service district office, which started the investigation, and placed in the hands of the regional counsel. While agents in the district office are primarily concerned with the letter of the law, the regional counsel's staff is more concerned with disposing of cases. Remember, it costs the Internal Revenue Service time and money to litigate a case, just as it costs you. If there is no special reason, such as emphasizing an IRS stand on a particular issue for contesting a case, the regional counsel may offer a settlement just to save the trouble of going to court. Even if the offer is only 10 percent of an amount that the district office disallowed completely, you may still come out ahead.

The general rule is that a taxpayer will lose if he attempts to sue an IRS agent for harrassment. In *Pope v. Organ*, 82-2 USTC Par. 9613, 50 AFTR 2d

82-5273 (DC Texas, 1982), the court held that an agent would be immune from prosecution if both of the following conditions were met: (1) the action was taken with the belief that it was lawful and without malicious intent to cause deprivation of constitutional rights, and (2) given the discretion of the official and the circumstances, it was reasonable to believe that there was a right to take the action.

However, on April 11, 1983, the U.S. Court of Appeals for the Fifth Circuit ruled that a taxpayer *could sue* an IRS agent as a federal official, acting under color of federal law when he allegedly violated taxpayers' constitutional rights to due process by willfully and maliciously assessing them for taxes they did not owe and harrassing them into paying those taxes. (*Rutherford* 83-1 USTC Par. 9289, 51 AFTR 2d 83-1084.) The Court allowed suit for compensatory damages for mental anguish and for the legal fees incurred in resisting the government's claim as well as *punitive damages* in retribution for the agent's abuses of authority.

Moreover, before you go to court, you have one more alternative option. An offer and compromise is a contract (Form 656) with the Internal Revenue Service whereby you recognize your liability but offer to satisfy it for less than its full amount. Some indication of when an offer and compromise will be accepted was provided in the July 1984 issue of the Salt Lake City District Tax Practitioner Newsletter. Such offers are entertained only when there is doubt regarding either the taxpayer's liability or the collectibility of the amount assessed.

According to the IRS District Director's letter, before the IRS will accept an offer and compromise, it will almost always require the taxpayer to enter into a collateral agreement to make payments from future income. Where liability has been established by a valid court judgment, the IRS will not compromise the liability. An offer and compromise is made on Form 656 and must be accepted in writing by the Internal Revenue Service.

The advantages of an offer and compromise are:

1. You may be able to satisfy the liability by paying less than the full amount.

2. You can defer payment over a number of years, thus reducing the immediate tax burden.

3. Making an offer will delay collection action, even if the offer is not accepted.

4. The compromise offer fixes your liability for the period once it is accepted.

5. If the offer is accepted, and you live up to it, there will be no surprise collection action by the IRS.

6. If you enter into a collateral agreement to make payments from future income, the IRS normally will release any tax liens that have been filed on your property.

Alternatively, the rejection of an offer can result in immediate collection action by the IRS. In addition, the offer requires the submission of detailed financial statements, which will aid the IRS Collection Division should the offer not be accepted; the offer requires a waiver of the statute of limitations; and when an offer is made, you will usually be required to make a cash deposit. This deposit will not draw interest, and it is subject to collection in case the offer is rejected.

It is important to recognize that *oral* compromise agreements and unsigned settlements will not bind the Internal Revenue Service (see *Boulez*, 87-1 USTC Par. 9177, 59 AFTR 2d 87-608 (CA-D.C., 1987) and *Estate of Oman*, TCM 1987-71).

However, a negotiated agreement to pay in monthly installments over a lengthy period of time is now within the recognized policy guidelines of the IRS. IRS Policy Statement P-5-14 (approved on March 3, 1976) states: "Although there is no specific authority for allowing a taxpayer to liquidate a delinquent account by installment payments, installment agreements are to be considered, and may be entered into, when appropriate." IRM 5223: (4)(g) states that "the amount to be paid monthly on an installment agreement payment will be the difference between the taxpayer's net income and allowable expenses rounded down to the nearest $5.00 increment."

In entering the judiciary, you have three basic options:

1. The U.S. Tax Court

The U.S. Tax Court was first established in 1923. It is made up of nineteen judges who travel around the country and hear cases in major cities on a regular basis. It handles only tax litigation and consists exclusively of tax experts. The major advantage of choosing this court is that it will decide the case BEFORE you have to pay the tax. When you receive the 90-day letter, if you file a petition with the U.S. Tax Court within ninety days of the date of the letter, the Internal Revenue Service may not initiate any further tax collection mechanics until after the case is decided. Be careful: Your letter must be postmarked within 90 days after the *date* of the IRS letter, not after you receive it.

To get complete instructions on how to file a petition, write to the Clerk, United States Tax Court, 400 2nd Street, N.W., Washington, D.C. 20217, or call (202)376-2754. Although you may represent yourself at the tax court, it is best to have an attorney specializing in taxation to handle the case.

If the disputed tax is $10,000 or less for any taxable year, a simplified alternative procedure is available. Here you may want to represent yourself. Upon your request and with approval of the tax court, your case can be handled by the small claims division, under the small tax case rules, at little cost to you in time or dollars. Cases in the small claims division are heard by "special trial judges." If you want to use this procedure, write to the previously given address and ask that the clerk send you the small tax case division filing form, Petition, Form 2. You must file two copies of the petition, a copy of the 90-day letter, and a fee of $60, along with your pick of one of the more than 100 cities in which the small claims division of the tax court sits. The fee for cases that are not small claims cases is also $60. The case is heard informally by a trial judge and the formal rules of evidence do not apply. One special caveat, however: If you lose your case before the small claims division you cannot appeal. Their decision is final and binding.

Several final comments must be made about the tax court. First, while the disputed tax is not paid until after the trial, or until the case is settled, any tax found due will be paid with interest. This interest, however, is tax-deductible (to be phased out between 1987 and 1991, after which it will no longer be deductible). Second, remember that the tax court consists exclusively of expert judges. There are no jury trials before the tax court. Therefore, if you have a case where the equities are strongly on your side, but the law itself is against you, you might be better advised to stay out of the tax court. Finally, don't expect quick action if you file a case in the tax court. The court is struggling to cope with a massive and ever-growing backlog of pending cases at a time when it also faces financial woes. Taxpayers in some large cities must now wait as long as a year and a half for their cases to come to trial. Furthermore, experts have predicted the problem will intensify, reflecting the complexity of new laws and confusing tax shelter controversies.

In Revenue Procedure 82-42, the Internal Revenue Service announced new procedures for processing tax court cases in an attempt to facilitate earlier disposition through trial or settlement. Docketed cases will be referred by district counsel to the appeals division for settlement unless counsel determines it unlikely that even a partial settlement will be reached there. Cases involving deficiencies of more than $10,000 (including tax and penalties for a period) will then be promptly returned to counsel when it appears that no progress towards a settlement has been made, unless counsel agrees to extend the period for the appeals division's consideration. Cases involving deficiencies of $10,000 or less (including small claims cases) will stay in the appeals division for six months or until receipt of notice of trial in regular cases, or 15 days before the trial calendar call in small claims tax cases if that is earlier. Again, counsel may extend the period in appeals division if it appears that a settlement may be reached.

2.    The U.S. District Court

The U.S. District Court, which is part of the federal judiciary system, is the only place where a jury trial is available. These courts hear all kinds of litigation involving federal laws and any kind of law, state or federal, if the litigants are citizens of different states. You can represent yourself in a district court, but the judges frown upon it. The advantages of going to the district court include the availability of a sympathetic jury and the fact that the judge may be more sympathetic to the equities of your case than to the letter of the tax law. To get into a U.S. District Court, however, you must first pay your tax deficiency and then file a claim for a refund with the Internal Revenue Service. Though the Internal Revenue Service has six months to act on your claim, chances are it will reject the claim promptly and you can then file suit for a refund in your district court. You can obtain information about the procedures for filing suit in a U.S. District Court by calling or writing the Clerk of the Court in the district in which you reside. See below for the address of your area's office.

**ALABAMA**
Northern District
104 Federal Courthouse
Birmingham, AL 35203

Middle District
P.O. Box 711
Montgomery, AL 36101

Southern District
P.O. Box 2625
Mobile, AL 36652

**ALASKA**
Federal Building
701 C Street
Anchorage, AK 99513

**ARIZONA**
Room 1400, U.S. Courthouse
& Federal Building
230 N. 1st Avenue
Phoenix, AZ 85025

**ARKANSAS**
Eastern District
P.O. Box 869
Little Rock, AR 72203

Western District
P.O. Box 1523
Fort Smith, AR 72902

**CALIFORNIA**
Northern District
U.S. Courthouse
P.O. Box 36060
San Francisco, CA 94102

Eastern District
2546 U.S. Courthouse
650 Capitol Mall
Sacramento, CA 95814

Central District
U.S. Courthouse
312 N. Spring Street
Los Angeles, CA 90012

Southern District
940 Front Street
San Diego, CA 92189

**COLORADO**
Room C-145, U.S.
Courthouse
1929 Stout Street
Denver, CO 80294

**CONNECTICUT**
141 Church Street
New Haven, CT 06510

**DELAWARE**
Lockbox 18
Federal Building
844 King Street
Wilmington, DE 19801

**DISTRICT OF
COLUMBIA**
U.S. Courthouse
3rd & Constitution Ave.,
N.W.
Washington, DC 20001

**FLORIDA**
Northern District
110 East Park Avenue
Tallahassee, FL 32301

Middle District
P.O. Box 53558
Jacksonville, FL 32201-3558

Southern District
301 N. Miami Avenue
Miami, FL 33128-7788

**GEORGIA**
Northern District
75 Spring Street, S.W.
2211 U.S. Courthouse
Atlanta, GA 30335

Middle District
P.O. Box 128
Macon, GA 31202

Southern District
P.O. Box 8286
Savannah, GA 31412

**GUAM**
6th Floor
Pacific News Building
238 O'Hara Street
Agana, Guam 96910

**HAWAII**
P.O. Box 50129
Honolulu, HI 96850

**IDAHO**
U.S. Courthouse
P.O. Box 039
550 West Fort Street
Boise, ID 83724

**ILLINOIS**
Northern District
U.S. Courthouse
219 South Dearborn Street
Chicago, IL 60604

Central District
P.O. Box 315
Springfield, IL 62705

Southern District
U.S. Courthouse & P.O.
Building
P.O. Box 677
Benton, IL 62812

**INDIANA**
Northern District
Federal Building
Room 305
204 S. Main Street
South Bend, IN 46601

Southern District
U.S. Courthouse, Room 105
46 East Ohio Street
Indianapolis, IN 46204

**IOWA**
Northern District
Federal Building
P.O. Box 4411
Cedar Rapids, IA 52407

**Southern District**
U.S. Courthouse, Room 200
E. 1st & Walnut Streets
Des Moines, IA 50309

**KANSAS**
204 U.S. Courthouse
401 N. Market
Wichita, KS 67202

**KENTUCKY**
**Eastern District**
P.O. Box 741
Lexington, KY 40586

**Western District**
230 U.S. Courthouse
601 West Broadway
Louisville, KY 40202

**LOUISIANA**
**Eastern District**
U.S. Courthouse
500 Camp Street
Chambers C-151
New Orleans, LA 70130

**Middle District**
Room 139, 707 Florida
  Avenue
Federal Building & U.S.
  Courthouse
Baton Rouge, LA 70801

**Western District**
106 Joe D. Waggonner
  Federal Building
500 Fannin Street
Shreveport, LA 71101

**MAINE**
P.O. Box 7505 DTS
Portland, ME 04112

**MARYLAND**
U.S. Courthouse
101 W. Lombard Street
Baltimore, MD 21201

**MASSACHUSETTS**
1525 Post Office &
  Courthouse Building
Boston, MA 02109

**MICHIGAN**
**Eastern District**
U.S. Courthouse
Room 133
Detroit, MI 48226

**Western District**
458 Federal Building
110 Michigan Street, N.W.
Grand Rapids, MI 49503

**MINNESOTA**
708 Federal Building
316 N. Robert Street
St. Paul, MN 55101

**MISSISSIPPI**
**Northern District**
P.O. Box 727
Oxford, MS 38655

**Southern District**
P.O. Box 769
Jackson, MS 39205

**MISSOURI**
**Eastern District**
U.S. Court & Custom House
1114 Market Street
St. Louis, MO 63101

**Western District**
U.S. Courthouse
811 Grand Avenue
Room 201
Kansas City, MO 64106

**MONTANA**
Room 5405, Federal
  Building
316 N. 26th Street
Billings, MT 59101

**NEBRASKA**
P.O. Box 129
Downtown Station
Omaha, NE 68101

**NEVADA**
300 Las Vegas Blvd., S.
Las Vegas, NV 89101

**NEW HAMPSHIRE**
P.O. Box 1498
Concord, NH 03301

**NEW JERSEY**
U.S. Post Office &
  Courthouse
P.O. Box 419
Newark, NJ 07102

**NEW MEXICO**
P.O. Box 689
Albuquerque, NM 87103

**NEW YORK**
**Northern District**
Box 950
Albany, NY 12201

**Southern District**
U.S. Courthouse
Foley Square
New York, NY 10007

**Eastern District**
U.S. Courthouse
225 Cadman Plaza East
Brooklyn, NY 11201

**Western District**
604 U.S. Courthouse
Buffalo, NY 14202

**NORTH CAROLINA**
**Eastern District**
P.O. Box 25670
Raleigh, NC 27611

**Middle District**
P.O. Box V-1
Greensboro, NC 27402

**Western District**
P.O. Box 92
Asheville, NC 28802

**NORTH DAKOTA**
P.O. Box 1193
Bismarck, ND 58501

**NORTHERN MARIANA ISLANDS**
P.O. Box 687
Saipan, 96950

**OHIO**
Northern District
102 U.S. Courthouse
201 Superior Avenue, NE
Cleveland, OH 44114

Southern District
328 U.S. Courthouse
85 Marconi Blvd
Columbus, OH 43215

**OKLAHOMA**
Northern District
411 U.S. Courthouse
333 W. 4th Street
Tulsa, OK 74120

Eastern District
P.O. Box 607
U.S. Courthouse
Muskogee, OK 74401

Western District
Room 3210
U.S. Courthouse
Oklahoma City, OK 73102

**OREGON**
516 U.S. Courthouse
620 S.W. Main Street
Portland, OR 97205

**PENNSYLVANIA**
Eastern District
2609 U.S. Courthouse
Independent Mall West
601 Market Street
Philadelphia, PA 19106

Middle District
P.O. Box 1148
Scranton, PA 18501

Western District
P.O. Box 1805
Pittsburgh, PA 15230

**PUERTO RICO**
P.O. Box 3671
San Juan, PR 00904

**RHODE ISLAND**
119 Federal Building &
U.S. Courthouse
Providence, RI 02903

**SOUTH CAROLINA**
P.O. Box 867
Columbia, SC 29202

**SOUTH DAKOTA**
Federal Building & U.S.
Courthouse
Room 220
400 South Phillips Avenue
Sioux Falls, SD 57102

**TENNESSEE**
Eastern District
P.O. Box 2348
Knoxville, TN 37901

Middle District
800 U.S. Courthouse
801 Broadway
Nashville, TN 37203

Western District
950 Federal Building
167 North Main Street
Memphis, TN 38103

**TEXAS**
Northern District
U.S. Courthouse
1100 Commerce Street
Room 15C22
Dallas, TX 75242

Southern District
P.O. Box 61010
Houston, TX 77208

Eastern District
309 Federal Building &
U.S. Courthouse
211 W. Ferguson Street
Tyler, TX 75702

Western District
Hemisfair Plaza
655 E. Durango Boulevard
San Antonio, TX 78206

**UTAH**
P.O. Box 45390
Salt Lake City, UT 84145

**VERMONT**
P.O. Box 945
Burlington, VT 05402

**VIRGINIA**
Eastern District
307 U.S. Courthouse
600 Granby St.
Norfolk, VA 23510

Western District
P.O. Box 1234
Roanoke, VA 24006

**VIRGIN ISLANDS**
P.O. Box 720
Charlotte Amalie
St. Thomas, VI 00801

**WASHINGTON**
Eastern District
P.O. Box 1493
Spokane, WA 99210

Western District
308 U.S. Courthouse
Seattle, WA 98104

**WEST VIRGINIA**
Northern District
P.O. Box 1518
Elkins, WV 26241

Southern District
P.O. Box 2546
Charleston, WV 25329

| WISCONSIN | Western District | WYOMING |
|---|---|---|
| **Eastern District** | P.O. Box 432 | P.O. Box 727 |
| Room 362, U.S. Courthouse | Madison, WI 53701 | Cheyenne, WY 82001 |
| 517 East Wisconsin Avenue | | |
| Milwaukee, WI 53202 | | |

3.  The U.S. Claims Court

The U.S. Claims Court is a special court that hears all sorts of claims against the United States, including the claim of overpaying taxes and wanting the money back with interest. Here, too, the tax has to be paid in advance. The major advantage of the claims court is that it does not have to follow the same precedents as do the tax court and district courts. If the other courts appear unfavorable, this may be your best avenue of appeal.

Currently, judges of the claims court usually hear case argument only in Washington, D.C. However, before the argument, there is a fact-finding hearing before a trial judge of the claims court. This hearing will be conducted by the trial judge in a city near where you live. The trial judge will file the findings and the recommended decision. If either you or the Internal Revenue Service disagree, the case will come on for arguments before the full court in Washington. Legal briefs, which must be printed, are also required of both parties. Here the major disadvantage is the substantial expense of litigation. For information on filing suit here, contact the Clerk of the Court of Claims, 1717 Madison Place, N.W., Washington, D.C. 20005.

Appeals from both the tax court and the U.S. district courts go to the U.S. courts of appeals. The United States is divided geographically into twelve judicial circuits, each with its own court of appeals. District and tax court decisions in each circuit must follow the precedents of that circuit's court of appeals. Note, however, that decisions of the claims court do not have to follow such precedents. Furthermore, the courts of appeals in different circuits do not have to agree with each other. And if one circuit's court of appeals has not ruled on an issue, the lower courts may disagree among themselves. This means that a supereffective tax planning strategy for tax appeals is to file your case, whenever possible, in a judicial circuit whose precedents support your position.

Appeals from U.S. courts of appeals go directly to the Supreme Court. In addition, if you lose in the claims court, your appeal is directed first to the Federal Circuit Court of Appeals, then the Supreme Court, which may or may not accept such an appeal. As a practical matter, it accepts very few tax appeals from the claims court, or from appeals courts. Usually, it will only agree to do so where two U.S. courts of appeals have reached opposite results on a similar issue of fact and law.

One final note about going to court: Under Internal Revenue Code Section 7430, enacted by Section 292(a) of the Tax Equity and Fiscal Responsibility Act of 1982, Public Law 97-248 (September 3, 1982), the tax court is enabled to award reasonable litigation costs to a prevailing party who establishes that the position of the IRS commissioner was unreasonable. That means if you exhaust administrative remedies, go to court, and win, and the position of the Internal Revenue Service was not "reasonable," your costs, including what you have to pay to your attorney, will be reimbursed by the Treasury. The Tax Reform Act of 1986 changed the "not reasonable" requirement to one where the taxpayer must establish that the government's position was "not substantially justified." These awards are now being given— see *Ashburn*, D.C. Alabama, June 15, 1983. In the case of *David Kaufman v. Roscoe Egger*, on March 19, 1985, the First Circuit Court of Appeals ruled that "unreasonable" IRS conduct, even prior to a suit, can be considered. Examining the underlying congressional committee reports, the Court concluded "that Congress intended IRS' liability to be triggered by unreasonable IRS conduct regardless of which stage in the proceedings such conduct occurs." Moreover, the purpose of the provision would be frustrated if the Internal Revenue Service, "after causing the taxpayer all kinds of bureaucratic grief at the administrative level, could escape attorney's fee liability by merely changing its tune after the initiation of a suit by the taxpayer." These litigation costs can be awarded without limit at a rate of $75 per hour (unless the court finds justification for a higher rate)! Moreover, this provision applies to suits not only in the District Court but also in the Tax Court (suits in the U.S. Claims Courts are covered only between February 28, 1983, and December 31, 1985—see the Tax Reform Act of 1984, Section 714(c)).

To survive an audit you must be able to document all deductions and you should demand the audit agent to document any claims of fact or law alleged. Alternatively, some tax practitioners have advised, "When in doubt, deduct." The rationale behind this perspective is that even if your deductions are disallowed, your maximum exposure is to pay the tax you would have paid originally plus 10 percent interest which is deductible subject to phaseout (this rate will change every six months; the next change is scheduled for January 1, 1988). Remember, however, that your focus must be on tax avoidance rather than tax evasion. The focus of this book, as well, has been on avoidance—the completely legal objective of minimizing your taxes. You should *never* intentionally attempt to defraud the government with reference to your taxes. Such actions can bring about *criminal* penalties. However, the Internal Revenue Service has told its agents not to pursue criminal prosecution of most tax cheaters unless the underpayments average at least $2,500 a year for three straight years. Under these guidelines, a married person earning $20,000 a year and not itemizing deductions could file no return at all and not risk a felony prosecution, although civil penalties would probably be sought.

Further IRS internal guidelines with reference to criminal penalties include the following:

- Do not recommend felony prosecution in complex tax evasion schemes requiring difficult methods of proof unless the total amount of unpaid taxes is at least $10,000, including at least $3,000 for any single year.

- Do not recommend felony prosecution for willful failure to file or for filing a false return unless the average yearly unpaid tax involved is at least $2,500 over a three-year period.

- Do not recommend misdemeanor prosecution for delivery or disclosure of false returns or documents unless the unpaid tax involved is more than $500.

The above guidelines contain exceptions for "flagrant or repetitious conduct," which would allow IRS agents to ignore the minimum dollar amounts. These exceptions are more likely to be used against celebrities whose prosecution would be covered by the news media and therefore serve as a deterrent to others. If a doctor were to be prosecuted, for example, they would probably select one who had just written a popular diet book. Alternatively, if they were to look at an attorney, they would want someone well known, particularly a tax lawyer.

If you are due a refund and if you file by April 15, that refund must be paid by June 1 or else the IRS must pay you interest. Interest on your refund starts accruing 45 days after the return's due date or the date on which you actually filed, whichever is later, and ends accruing 30 days before the date on which the IRS makes out a check to you. The status of a refund may be checked by calling the IRS during regular business hours on a special number available in 27 cities. Under this system, 10 weeks after the return is filed, you may dial the special automated service, then dial your social security number and the amount of the expected refund. You will then be advised when to expect a check. The numbers to call are listed below:

| | | | |
|---|---|---|---|
| New Jersey | 1-800-554-4477 | St. Louis, MO | 314-241-4700 |
| Phoenix, AZ | 602-261-3560 | Newark, NJ | 201-624-1223 |
| Los Angeles, CA | 213-617-3177 | Brooklyn, NY | 212-858-4461 |
| Oakland, CA | 415-839-4245 | Buffalo, NY | 716-856-9320 |
| Denver, CO | 303-592-1118 | Manhattan, NY | 212-406-4080 |
| Washington, DC | 202-628-2929 | Cincinnati, OH | 513-684-3531 |
| Jacksonville, FL | 904-353-9579 | Cleveland, OH | 216-522-3037 |
| Atlanta, GA | 404-221-6572 | Portland, OR | 503-294-5363 |
| Chicago, IL | 312-886-9614 | Philadelphia, PA | 215-592-8946 |
| Indianapolis, IN | 317-634-1550 | Nashville, TE | 615-242-1541 |
| Baltimore, MD | 301-244-7306 | Dallas, TX | 214-767-1792 |
| Boston, MA | 617-523-8602 | Houston, TX | 713-850-8801 |
| Detroit, MI | 313-961-4282 | Seattle, WA | 206-343-7221 |
| St. Paul, MN | 612-224-4288 | Milwaukee, WI | 414-886-1615 |

In conclusion, it is important to reiterate that this book has not taught you how to evade taxes but rather how legally, within the full ambit of our tax code, to reduce your taxes to zero. According to a 1987 report issued by the American Bar Association's Commission on Taxpayer Compliance, one-third of all taxpayers deliberately fail to claim tax deductions to which they believe they are entitled. (Reasons for not taking these deductions include concern that they might not be correct, ignorance or forgetfulness, insufficient records, perceptions that the deduction was too trivial or too complicated, and fear of audits.) If you want to pay more in taxes than the law requires, you may. In 1983, 3,500 taxpayers voluntarily coughed up a total of $300,000 in voluntary donations to the Internal Revenue Service in an attempt to reduce the national debt. In fiscal 1984, the government received 2,513 gifts, totaling $405,007. Through July 27, 1985, the Internal Revenue Service counted an additional 2,205 voluntary—and deductible—gifts, totaling $350,394, to help Uncle Sam reduce the public debt.

Americans donated $1,697,366 to the Bureau of the Public Debt in fiscal 1986 for the Debt Reduction Fund. Of this amount, $1.1 million came via the Internal Revenue Service, thanks to a note in tax return instructions. An additional $719,516 arrived in the six months ending March 31, 1987, bringing the then-to-date total since 1961 to $13,138,462. If you want to pay more taxes, you therefore have the opportunity to do so. A great deal has been written and said on the question of the morality of tax saving in general, and on those who save taxes in particular. Perhaps the best statement on tax avoidance—the legal minimization of your tax liability— was written by Judge Learned Hand:

> If I understand the Commissioner, he wishes us to consider that these deeds may have been a preliminary step in a reprehensible scheme to lessen . . . income taxes. There is not the faintest ground for imputing any such purpose to the parties at bar; and if there were, it ought not to count. Over and over again courts have said that there is nothing sinister in so arranging one's affairs as to keep taxes as low as possible. Everybody does so, rich or poor; and all do right, for nobody owes any public duty to pay more than the law demands; taxes are enforced exactions, not voluntary contributions. To demand more in the name of morals is mere Cant. (*Comissioner v. Neuman,* 159 F. 2d 848.)

According to IRS figures, the 1.1 million taxpayers audited in 1987 were assessed over $6 billion in additional tax and penalties. The percentage of individual income tax returns audited in 1987 was 1.09 percent. This is lower than the 1.12 percent audited in 1986, which itself was down from 1.31 percent in 1985. It was 1.27 percent in 1984, 1.49 percent in 1983, 1.55 percent in 1982, 1.77 percent in 1981, and 2.02 percent in 1980.

|  | Percentage of Returns Audited | | | | |
|---|---|---|---|---|---|
|  | 1987 | 1986 | 1985 | 1984 | 1983 |
| Individuals—Nonbusiness (based on total positive income) |  |  |  |  |  |
| Under $10,000 (1040A) | .53 | .30 | .35 | .29 | .32 |
| Under $10,000 (non-1040A) | .42 | .37 | .44 | .46 | .78 |
| $10,000 under $25,000 (with itemized deductions) | 1.30 | 1.26 | 1.67 | 1.49 | 2.15 |

*(continued on next page)*

|  | Percentage of Returns Audited | | | | |
|---|---|---|---|---|---|
|  | 1987 | 1986 | 1985 | 1984 | 1983 |
| $10,000 under $25,000 (without itemized deductions) | .64 | .48 | .64 | .63 | .64 |
| $25,000 under $50,000 | 1.40 | 1.64 | 2.02 | 2.05 | 2.61 |
| $50,000 and over | 2.24 | 2.81 | 3.53 | 4.00 | 4.93 |
| **Individuals filing Schedule C, showing gross receipts as indicated** | | | | | |
| Under $25,000 | 1.41 | 1.33 | 1.45 | 1.43 | 1.63 |
| $25,000 under $100,000 | 2.01 | 2.44 | 2.55 | 2.56 | 3.28 |
| $100,000 and over | 3.86 | 4.68 | 5.40 | 5.30 | 6.12 |
| **Individuals filing Schedule F, showing gross receipts as indicated** | | | | | |
| Under $25,000 | .91 | .94 | 1.53 | 1.69 | 1.52 |
| $25,000 under $100,000 | 1.13 | 1.14 | 1.78 | 1.85 | 2.02 |
| $100,000 and over | 2.34 | 2.91 | 4.36 | 4.09 | 4.14 |
| Fiduciary | .22 | .35 | .39 | .48 | .42 |
| **Corporations (based on assets)** | | | | | |
| $1,000,000 under $10,000,000 | 4.10 | 5.72 | 6.89 | 9.30 | 9.90 |
| $10,000,000 under $100,000,000 | 22.92 | 10.80 | 29.76 | 25.27 | 22.47 |
| $100,000,000 and over | 69.08 | 74.51 | 86.26 | 70.95 | 57.83 |
| Small business corporations | 1.12 | 1.08 | .97 | 1.02 | 1.31 |
| Partnerships | 1.15 | 1.00 | 1.42 | 1.57 | 2.41 |
| **Estate tax (based on gross estate)** | | | | | |
| Under $1,000,000 | 16.93 | 15.91 | 15.91 | 13.49 | 13.36 |
| $1,000,000 under $5,000,000 | 38.01 | 46.02 | 73.09 | 49.87 | 66.87 |
| $5,000,000 and over | 62.85 | 76.44 | 108.60 | 73.77 | 90.81 |
| Gift tax | 1.65 | 1.90 | 2.11 | 2.23 | 3.59 |

For examined returns, the "no change" rate for individual returns averaged 12 percent for field audits and 14 percent for both office audits and service center examinations.

In 1987, 77.6 percent of the cases taken to the Appellate level of the Internal Revenue Service were settled by agreement where a petition had been filed with the Tax Court, and 80.3 percent where no petition had yet been filed. The corresponding figures for 1986 were 67.5 percent and 66.1 percent; for 1985, 89.6 percent and 84.9 percent; and for 1984, 83 percent and 84 percent.

In disputes carried beyond the IRS to a court, here is how taxpayers made out in fiscal 1986:

| Trial<br>Court | Taxpayer<br>Won | IRS<br>Won | Decision<br>Split |
|---|---|---|---|
| Tax Court | | | |
|    Small cases | 4.6% | 50.3% | 45.1% |
|    Regular cases | 5.5 | 31.6 | 62.9 |
| District Court | 16.8 | 80.4 | 2.7 |
| Claims Court | 11.1 | 85.2 | 3.7 |

SOURCE: The 1987 Annual Report, Commissioner and Chief Counsel, Internal Revenue Service (Publication 55).

Of the 489 tax cases that were appealed to and decided by the Court of Appeals in fiscal 1986, 87.5 percent were decided against the taxpayer, 9.6 percent were decided for the taxpayer, and 2.9 percent were split decisions—i.e., partially for and partially against the taxpayer.

### PENALTIES AND INTEREST

*Late Filing of a Return:* There is a penalty of 5 percent of the unpaid tax for each month or fraction thereof that the return is late, up to a maximum of 25 percent. For example, assume you owe $2,000 on your Form 1040, which you file on April 20 (five days late). The late filing penalty is $100. There is a minimum late *filing* penalty of the lesser of $100 or the tax due if the return is not filed within 60 days of the prescribed due date.

*Understatement of Taxes:* In IRS ruling 8802003, the Internal Revenue Service ruled that a taxpayer was liable for a 25 percent substantial understatement penalty even though his tax liability had been satisfied through withholding or estimated payments. In this case, the tax returns for more than three years were filed only after numerous contacts and inquiries by IRS personnel. The IRS ruled that the substantial underpayment penalty is imposed if an underpayment of taxes is attributable to an understatement that

**Original Income Tax Return, 1913**

TO BE FILLED IN BY INTERNAL REVENUE BUREAU.

File No. ......................

Assessment List

Page .......   Line .......

Form 1040.

# INCOME TAX.

**THE PENALTY**

FOR FAILURE TO HAVE THIS RETURN IN THE HANDS OF THE COLLECTOR OF INTERNAL REVENUE ON OR BEFORE MARCH 1 IS $20 TO $1000.

(SEE INSTRUCTIONS ON PAGE 4.)

TO BE FILLED IN BY COLLECTOR.

List No. ..................

......... District of .........

Date received ................

UNITED STATES INTERNAL REVENUE.

## RETURN OF ANNUAL NET INCOME OF INDIVIDUALS.

(As provided by Act of Congress, approved October 3, 1913.)

RETURN OF NET INCOME RECEIVED OR ACCRUED DURING THE YEAR ENDED DECEMBER 31, 191___

(FOR THE YEAR 1913, FROM MARCH 1 TO DECEMBER 31.)

Filed by (or for) ...................... of ......................

(Full name of individual.)

(Street and No.)

in the City, Town, or Post Office of ...................... State of ......................

(Fill in pages 2 and 3 before making entries below.)

| | | | |
|---|---|---|---|
| 1. GROSS INCOME (see page 2, line 12) | | $ | |
| 2. GENERAL DEDUCTIONS (see page 3, line 7) | | $ | |
| 3. NET INCOME | | $ | |

Deductions and exemptions allowed in computing income subject to the normal tax of 1 per cent.

4. Dividends and net earnings received or accrued, of corporations, etc., subject to like tax. (See page 2, line 11) .......... $

5. Amount of income on which the normal tax has been deducted and withheld at the source. (See page 2, line 9, column A) ..........

6. Specific exemption of $3,000 or $4,000, as the case may be. (See Instructions 3 and 19) ..........

Total deductions and exemptions. (Items 4, 5, and 6) .......... $

7. TAXABLE INCOME on which the normal tax of 1 per cent is to be calculated. (See Instruction 3). .......... $

8. When the net income shown above on line 3 exceeds $20,000, the additional tax thereon must be calculated as per schedule below:

| | INCOME | | | TAX | | |
|---|---|---|---|---|---|---|
| 1 per cent on amount over $20,000 and not exceeding $50,000 | $ | | | $ | | |
| 2 " 50,000 " 75,000 | | | | | | |
| 3 " 75,000 " 100,000 | | | | | | |
| 4 " 100,000 " 250,000 | | | | | | |
| 5 " 250,000 " 500,000 | | | | | | |
| 6 " 500,000 | | | | | | |

Total additional or super tax .......... $

Total normal tax (1 per cent of amount entered on line 7) .......... $

Total tax liability .......... $

exceeds the greater of 10 percent of the tax required to be shown on the return or $5,000. An understatement is generally the excess of the amount of tax required to be shown on a tax return over the actual amount of tax shown on the return. The IRS concluded that for this purpose, the amount of tax shown on the return did not include any additional tax shown on a return filed *after* the Internal Revenue Service had contacted the taxpayer about his liability for the year. Moreover, the amount of tax required to be shown on the return is the tax *without* regard to any payments of tax or estimated tax by the taxpayer.

However, the Tax Court has held that the 25 percent penalty on a tax underpayment attributable to a substantial understatement of tax applies to the unpaid amount of tax after reduction by the amount of federal taxes withheld from a taxpayer's wages. (See *W. A. Woods II,* C.C.H. Dec. 44903 91 T.C.-, No. 11.)

*Negligence:* There is a negligence penalty of 5 percent of the underpaid tax, plus 50 percent of the interest due on the portion of the underpayment attributable to negligence or intentional disregard. This 50 percent of the interest charge is a penalty and cannot be deducted from federal taxes.

Moreover, in Technical Advice Memorandum 8527012, the Internal Revenue Service ruled that a 5 percent negligence penalty may be imposed in the case of a taxpayer who was entitled to a refund on a late-filed return where the late filing was due to negligence or intentional disregard of the rules and regulations. According to the TAM, "the failure to file a timely tax return in itself can constitute the negligence or intentional disregard of rules and regulations." Whether this Technical Advice Memorandum can withstand the test of judicial scrutiny, however, is arguable.

*Late Payment of Tax:* There is a penalty of .5 percent (increasing to 1 percent the day 10 days after the date of which a notice of levy is given) of the tax due for each month or fraction thereof that the payment is late, up to a maximum of 25 percent. For example, assume you owe $2,000 on your Form 1040, which you filed timely, but did not pay the tax due until April 30. The late *payment* penalty is $10. In the event that the return is neither timely *filed* nor timely *paid,* both penalties will apply for the first five months, but the combined monthly penalty cannot exceed 5/(5.5) percent. After the five-month period, the late payment penalty continues at .5 percent per month until the maximum 25 percent is reached. Obviously, if you are short of cash and cannot pay the tax due at the filing date, you should still file the return. Remember that an extension of time avoids a penalty for failure to file but does not extend the time to pay the tax. These penalties apply to most types of returns, such as income, payroll, and fiduciary tax returns.

They will be waived only if the failure to file or failure to pay is due to "reasonable cause," such as illness or incapacity.

*Interest:* In addition to the penalties, interest will compound daily on any taxes and penalties due until they are paid. The current interest rate, about 10 percent, will change on January 1, 1989. The rate is adjusted quarterly and calculated on the basis of the short-term federal rate plus 3 percent as of the first month of each quarter, effective as of the following calendar quarter.

For example, the short-term federal rate during January 1987 was 6 percent. Therefore, an underpayment rate of 9 percent was established for the calendar quarter beginning April 1, 1987. Note that rates of interest paid by the IRS to taxpayers for underpayments are always 1 percent lower than the rates paid to the Internal Revenue Service for overpayments. The interest paid is deductible (to be phased out), but the penalties are not.

*Failure to File Information Returns:* There is a $50 penalty for failure to file required information returns and statements with the IRS. There is an additional $50 penalty for failure to provide a copy to the payee. Thus, a failure *both* to file the information return with the IRS and to provide a copy to the payee results in a penalty of $100 per failure, with a total aggregate maximum penalty of $200,000. Every person engaged in a trade or business (including nonprofit organizations) must file an information return for payments of employees' salaries, rent and royalties, nonemployee compensation (independent contractors), interest, and dividends. Information returns are required if payments to a single individual total $600 or more, except for interest and dividends, where the limit is $10. Of course, all employee wages and salaries are reported on Form W-2 regardless of amount paid.

*Stopping Interest:* Interest on taxes owed is compounded daily, and charging interest on interest is allowed. In Revenue Proclamation 84-58, IRB 1984-33, 9, the IRS detailed the steps that should be taken to stop the running of interest on a contested IRS determination. You may stop the running of interest by prepaying the amount contested, without jeopardizing your right to contest the issue, or by posting a cash bond. The prepayment would draw interest and the bond would not. However, the bond could be withdrawn at any time before assessment. Note, however, that a payment response to a proposed liability—e.g., as a result of a revenue agent's report—will be treated as a payment of tax, rather than a cash bond, unless you specifically designate the remittance as a "deposit in the nature of a cash bond." A remittance that is made before liability is proposed, however, will be treated as a cash bond. If the cash bond exceeds the amount of tax ultimately determined, you may have it applied against other liabilities, either assessed or unassessed. Furthermore, you may make a partial payment, but you must designate the part of the liability that is proposed to be satisfied. If the IRS cannot tell whether the payment is a partial payment of tax or a cash bond, it will treat it as being in the latter category. Moreover, the bond must include interest to date in order to stop the further running of interest on any interest accrued.

*Partial Payments:* If you do not pay the entire amount owed to the Internal Revenue Service, a partial payment generally will be applied first to tax, then to penalty, and finally to the interest that is owed.

*Frivolous Tax Penalty:* A frivolous tax penalty of up to $5,000 can be assessed on a taxpayer who institutes a Tax Court proceeding primarily to delay payment or for frivolous reasons. Moreover, a $5,000 penalty can be imposed upon any taxpayer who, in furtherance of a frivolous position or with a prima facie intent to delay or impede administration of the tax law, files a purported return that fails to contain information from which the correctness of a reported tax liability can be determined, or that clearly indicates that the tax liability shown must be substantially incorrect.

In fact, the IRS can assess a penalty against a taxpayer who files a return that it deems frivolous even when no taxes are owed and a return is not required to be filed. For example, in *Bradley v. U.S.* (No. 85-2445, May 22, 1987, CA9), the taxpayer wrote a statement to the IRS saying that he refused to pay taxes because of the government's intervention in Central America and filed that statement with his Form 1040. The taxpayer owed no tax and was not required to file a return. However, a notice was sent to Bradley informing him that he had filed a frivolous return and that a penalty was being assessed. The court upheld the penalty because the Form 1040 that Bradley returned purported to be a tax return but lacked the information on which the substantial correctness of the self-assessment could be judged and took a frivolous position.

## STATE TAXES

To aid in the filing of state tax returns, the Alabama Society of CPAs has published the following list of telephone numbers and addresses for obtaining out-of-state income tax forms:

**Alabama** (205) 261-3355
Department of Revenue
Income Tax Division
Room 106
Montgomery, Alabama 36130

**Alaska** (907) 465-2333
Department of Revenue
State Office Bldg., Pouch SA
Juneau, Alaska 99811

**Arizona** (602) 255-3381
Department of Revenue
1700 W. Washington
State Capitol Building
Phoenix, Arizona 85007

**Arkansas** (501) 371-1476
Dept. of Finance and
    Administration
P.O. Box 3628
Little Rock, Arkansas 72203

**California** (916) 369-0500
Forms Request Unit
Franchise Tax Board
Forms Warehouse
11345 Folsom Boulevard
Rancho Cordova, California
    95670

**Colorado** (303) 839-5600
Taxpayer's Service
Department of Revenue
1375 Sherman Street
Denver, Colorado 80261

**Connecticut** (203) 566-8520
State Tax Department
92 Farmington Avenue
Hartford, Connecticut 06105

**Delaware** (302) 571-3300
Division of Revenue
Public Service Forms Dept.
P.O. Box 2044
Wilmington, Delaware 19899

**Florida** (904) 488-2574
Department of Revenue
Taxpayer Assistance Section
Carlton Building
Tallahassee, Florida 32301

**Georgia** (404) 656-4293
Income Tax Unit
Department of Revenue
Trinity-Washington Bldg.
Atlanta, Georgia 30334

**Hawaii** (808) 548-4013
First Taxation District
P.O. Box 259
Honolulu, Hawaii 96809

**Idaho** (208) 334-3560
Dept. of Revenue and Taxation
State Tax Commission
P.O. Box 36
Boise, Idaho 83722

**Illinois** (217) 782-3336
Department of Revenue
P.O. Box 3545
Springfield, Illinois 62708

**Indiana** (317) 232-2215
Department of Revenue
100 North Senate Ave.
Room 113
Indianapolis, Indiana 46204

**Iowa** (515) 281-5370
Department of Revenue
Hoover State Office Building
Des Moines, Iowa 50319

**Kansas** (913) 296-3051
Dept. of Revenue
Division of Taxation
Box 12001
Topeka, Kansas 66612

**Kentucky** (502) 564-4580
Department of Revenue
New Capitol Annex
Frankfort, Kentucky 40601

**Louisiana** (504) 925-7532
Dept. of Revenue & Taxation
P.O. Box 201
Baton Rouge, Louisiana 70821

**Maine** (207) 289-3695
Bureau of Taxation
Income Tax Division
State Office Building
Augusta, Maine 04333

**Maryland** (301) 383-3131
Comptroller of the Treasury
Income Tax Division
State Office Building
Room 310
Annapolis, Maryland 21401

**Massachusetts** (617) 727-4545
Commonwealth of
    Massachusetts
Department of Revenue
Leverett Saltonstall Bldg.
100 Cambridge Street
Boston, Mass. 02204

**Michigan** (517) 373-3200
Department of Treasury
Treasury Building, 2nd Fl.
Walnut & Allegan Street
Lansing, Michigan 48922

**Minnesota** (612) 296-3781
Minnesota Dept. of Revenue
Income Tax Division
B-20 Centennial Office Bldg.
St. Paul, Minnesota 55145

**Mississippi** (601) 359-1141
State Tax Commission
P.O. Box 1033
Jackson, Mississippi 39205

**Missouri** (314) 751-4388
Department of Revenue
P.O. Box 2200
Jefferson City, Missouri 65105

**Montana** (406) 444-2837
Income Tax Division
Department of Revenue
Mitchell Building
Helena, Montana 59620

**Nebraska** (402) 471-2971
Department of Revenue
Box 94818
Lincoln, Nebraska 68509

**Nevada** (702) 885-4820
Dept. of Taxation
Capitol Complex
Carson City, Nevada 89710

**New Hampshire**
   (603) 271-2186
State of New Hampshire
P.O. Box 637
Concord, New Hampshire
   03301

**New Jersey** (609) 292-6400
Division of Taxation
South Barrack St.
Trenton, New Jersey 08646

**New Mexico** (505) 798-2290
Taxation and Revenue Dept.
P.O. Box 630
Santa Fe, New Mexico 87502

**New York** (518) 457-2231
Department of Taxation and
   Finance
Forms Control Section
State Campus Building No. 8
Albany, New York 12227

**North Carolina**
   (919) 733-4682
Department of Revenue
Box 25000
Raleigh, North Carolina 27640

**North Dakota** (701) 224-2770
State Tax Department
State Capitol
Bismarck, North Dakota 58505

**Ohio** (614) 466-7910
Department of Taxation
P.O. Box 2476
Columbus, Ohio 43216

**Oklahoma** (405) 521-3108
Tax Commission
2501 Lincoln Blvd.
Oklahoma City, Oklahoma
   73194

**Oregon** (503) 371-2244
Department of Revenue
Administration Service Div.
Revenue Building
Salem, Oregon 97310

**Pennsylvania** (717) 233-3443
Department of Revenue
Bureau of Administrative
   Services
2850 Turnpike Industrial Park
Middletown, Pennsylvania
   17057

**Rhode Island** (401) 277-2934
Division of Taxation
ATTN: Forms Unit
289 Promenage Street
Providence, Rhode Island
   02908

**South Carolina** (803) 758-2217
Tax Commission
Individual Income Tax Div.
P.O. Box 125
Columbia, South Carolina
   29214

**South Dakota** (605) 773-3311
Department of Revenue
700 North Illinois Street
Kneip Building
Pierre, South Dakota 57501

**Tennessee** (615) 741-3311
Department of Revenue
505 Andrew Jackson
State Office Bldg.
500 Deadrick Street
Nashville, Tennessee 37242

**Texas** (512) 475-1914
Comptroller of Public Accounts
LBJ State Office Building
Austin, Texas 78774

**Utah** (801) 533-5947
State Tax Commission
P.O. Box 4000
Salt Lake City, Utah 84134

**Vermont** (802) 828-2725
Department of Taxes
Montpelier, Vermont 05602

**Virginia** (804) 257-8205
Department of Taxation
Forms Request Unit
P.O. Box 1317
Richmond, Virginia 23210

**Washington** (206) 753-5540
Department of Revenue
General Administration Bldg.
Olympia, Washington 98504

**Washington, D.C.**
   (202) 727-6104
District of Columbia
Finance Office
Revenue Division
300 Indiana Ave. N.W.
Washington, D.C. 20001

**West Virginia** (304) 348-2071
State Tax Department
Income Tax Division
Charleston, West Virginia
   25305

**Wisconsin** (608) 266-1961
Department of Revenue
P.O. Box 8903
Madison, Wisconsin 53708

**Wyoming** (307) 777-7311
State of Wyoming
Secretary of State
Capitol Building
Cheyenne, Wyoming 82002

# Appendix

## How Much Are You Really Paying in Interest?

The true cost of borrowing money is what is paid in interest after taxes are taken into account. For example:

In 1988, you can deduct only 40 percent of your interest payments on a personal loan (e.g., credit card charges, education loan, car financing). The deductible portion will be reduced each year until, by 1991, no personal interest payments will be deductible. Interest on a loan used for business purposes, however, will continue to be fully deductible. Interest on an investment-connected loan will also be fully deductible up to the amount of your investment income.

The table below shows the net aftertax interest rate for individuals in two tax brackets.

| Year | Stated Interest Rate | | | | | | |
|------|------|------|------|------|------|------|------|
|      | 6%   | 7%   | 8%   | 9%   | 10%  | 11%  | 12%  |
| *28 Percent Tax Rate Personal Loan* | | | | | | | |
| 1987 | 4.91 | 5.73 | 6.54 | 7.36 | 8.18 | 9.00 | 9.82 |
| 1988 | 5.33 | 6.22 | 7.10 | 7.99 | 8.88 | 9.77 | 10.66 |
| 1989 | 5.66 | 6.61 | 7.55 | 8.50 | 9.44 | 10.38 | 11.33 |
| 1990 | 5.83 | 6.80 | 7.78 | 8.75 | 9.72 | 10.69 | 11.66 |
| 1991 | 6.00 | 7.00 | 8.00 | 9.00 | 10.00 | 11.00 | 12.00 |
| *Business/Investment Loan* | | | | | | | |
| 1987 | 4.32 | 5.04 | 5.76 | 6.48 | 7.20 | 7.92 | 8.64 |
| *33 Percent Tax Rate Personal Loan* | | | | | | | |
| 1987 | 4.71 | 5.50 | 6.28 | 7.07 | 7.86 | 8.64 | 9.43 |
| 1988 | 5.21 | 6.08 | 6.94 | 7.81 | 8.68 | 9.55 | 10.42 |
| 1989 | 5.60 | 6.54 | 7.47 | 8.41 | 9.34 | 10.27 | 11.21 |
| 1990 | 5.80 | 6.77 | 7.74 | 8.70 | 9.67 | 10.64 | 11.60 |
| 1991 | 6.00 | 7.00 | 8.00 | 9.00 | 10.00 | 11.00 | 12.00 |
| *Business/Investment Loan* | | | | | | | |
| 1987 | 4.02 | 4.69 | 5.36 | 6.03 | 6.70 | 9.37 | 8.04 |

# Index